Communications in Computer and Information Science   1033

Commenced Publication in 2007
Founding and Former Series Editors:
Phoebe Chen, Alfredo Cuzzocrea, Xiaoyong Du, Orhun Kara, Ting Liu,
Krishna M. Sivalingam, Dominik Ślęzak, Takashi Washio, and Xiaokang Yang

More information about this series at http://www.springer.com/series/7899

Constantine Stephanidis (Ed.)

HCI International 2019 - Posters

21st International Conference, HCII 2019
Orlando, FL, USA, July 26–31, 2019
Proceedings, Part II

Editor
Constantine Stephanidis
University of Crete
and Foundation for Research
and Technology – Hellas (FORTH)
Heraklion, Crete, Greece

ISSN 1865-0929   ISSN 1865-0937 (electronic)
Communications in Computer and Information Science
ISBN 978-3-030-23527-7   ISBN 978-3-030-23528-4 (eBook)
https://doi.org/10.1007/978-3-030-23528-4

This Springer imprint is published by the registered company Springer Nature Switzerland AG
The registered company address is: Gewerbestrasse 11, 6330 Cham, Switzerland

Foreword

The 21st International Conference on Human-Computer Interaction, HCI International 2019, was held in Orlando, FL, USA, during July 26–31, 2019. The event incorporated the 18 thematic areas and affiliated conferences listed on the following page.

A total of 5,029 individuals from academia, research institutes, industry, and governmental agencies from 73 countries submitted contributions, and 1,274 papers and 209 posters were included in the pre-conference proceedings. These contributions address the latest research and development efforts and highlight the human aspects of design and use of computing systems. The contributions thoroughly cover the entire field of human-computer interaction, addressing major advances in knowledge and effective use of computers in a variety of application areas. The volumes constituting the full set of the pre-conference proceedings are listed in the following pages.

This year the HCI International (HCII) conference introduced the new option of "late-breaking work." This applies both for papers and posters and the corresponding volume(s) of the proceedings will be published just after the conference. Full papers will be included in the *HCII 2019 Late-Breaking Work Papers Proceedings* volume of the proceedings to be published in the Springer LNCS series, while poster extended abstracts will be included as short papers in the HCII 2019 *Late-Breaking Work Poster Extended Abstracts* volume to be published in the Springer CCIS series.

I would like to thank the program board chairs and the members of the program boards of all thematic areas and affiliated conferences for their contribution to the highest scientific quality and the overall success of the HCI International 2019 conference.

This conference would not have been possible without the continuous and unwavering support and advice of the founder, Conference General Chair Emeritus and Conference Scientific Advisor Prof. Gavriel Salvendy. For his outstanding efforts, I would like to express my appreciation to the communications chair and editor of *HCI International News,* Dr. Abbas Moallem.

July 2019   Constantine Stephanidis

HCI International 2019 Thematic Areas
and Affiliated Conferences

Thematic areas:

- HCI 2019: Human-Computer Interaction
- HIMI 2019: Human Interface and the Management of Information

Affiliated conferences:

- EPCE 2019: 16th International Conference on Engineering Psychology and Cognitive Ergonomics
- UAHCI 2019: 13th International Conference on Universal Access in Human-Computer Interaction
- VAMR 2019: 11th International Conference on Virtual, Augmented and Mixed Reality
- CCD 2019: 11th International Conference on Cross-Cultural Design
- SCSM 2019: 11th International Conference on Social Computing and Social Media
- AC 2019: 13th International Conference on Augmented Cognition
- DHM 2019: 10th International Conference on Digital Human Modeling and Applications in Health, Safety, Ergonomics and Risk Management
- DUXU 2019: 8th International Conference on Design, User Experience, and Usability
- DAPI 2019: 7th International Conference on Distributed, Ambient and Pervasive Interactions
- HCIBGO 2019: 6th International Conference on HCI in Business, Government and Organizations
- LCT 2019: 6th International Conference on Learning and Collaboration Technologies
- ITAP 2019: 5th International Conference on Human Aspects of IT for the Aged Population
- HCI-CPT 2019: First International Conference on HCI for Cybersecurity, Privacy and Trust
- HCI-Games 2019: First International Conference on HCI in Games
- MobiTAS 2019: First International Conference on HCI in Mobility, Transport, and Automotive Systems
- AIS 2019: First International Conference on Adaptive Instructional Systems

Pre-conference Proceedings Volumes Full List

1. LNCS 11566, Human-Computer Interaction: Perspectives on Design (Part I), edited by Masaaki Kurosu
2. LNCS 11567, Human-Computer Interaction: Recognition and Interaction Technologies (Part II), edited by Masaaki Kurosu
3. LNCS 11568, Human-Computer Interaction: Design Practice in Contemporary Societies (Part III), edited by Masaaki Kurosu
4. LNCS 11569, Human Interface and the Management of Information: Visual Information and Knowledge Management (Part I), edited by Sakae Yamamoto and Hirohiko Mori
5. LNCS 11570, Human Interface and the Management of Information: Information in Intelligent Systems (Part II), edited by Sakae Yamamoto and Hirohiko Mori
6. LNAI 11571, Engineering Psychology and Cognitive Ergonomics, edited by Don Harris
7. LNCS 11572, Universal Access in Human-Computer Interaction: Theory, Methods and Tools (Part I), edited by Margherita Antona and Constantine Stephanidis
8. LNCS 11573, Universal Access in Human-Computer Interaction: Multimodality and Assistive Environments (Part II), edited by Margherita Antona and Constantine Stephanidis
9. LNCS 11574, Virtual, Augmented and Mixed Reality: Multimodal Interaction (Part I), edited by Jessie Y. C. Chen and Gino Fragomeni
10. LNCS 11575, Virtual, Augmented and Mixed Reality: Applications and Case Studies (Part II), edited by Jessie Y. C. Chen and Gino Fragomeni
11. LNCS 11576, Cross-Cultural Design: Methods, Tools and User Experience (Part I), edited by P. L. Patrick Rau
12. LNCS 11577, Cross-Cultural Design: Culture and Society (Part II), edited by P. L. Patrick Rau
13. LNCS 11578, Social Computing and Social Media: Design, Human Behavior and Analytics (Part I), edited by Gabriele Meiselwitz
14. LNCS 11579, Social Computing and Social Media: Communication and Social Communities (Part II), edited by Gabriele Meiselwitz
15. LNAI 11580, Augmented Cognition, edited by Dylan D. Schmorrow and Cali M. Fidopiastis
16. LNCS 11581, Digital Human Modeling and Applications in Health, Safety, Ergonomics and Risk Management: Human Body and Motion (Part I), edited by Vincent G. Duffy

17. LNCS 11582, Digital Human Modeling and Applications in Health, Safety, Ergonomics and Risk Management: Healthcare Applications (Part II), edited by Vincent G. Duffy
18. LNCS 11583, Design, User Experience, and Usability: Design Philosophy and Theory (Part I), edited by Aaron Marcus and Wentao Wang
19. LNCS 11584, Design, User Experience, and Usability: User Experience in Advanced Technological Environments (Part II), edited by Aaron Marcus and Wentao Wang
20. LNCS 11585, Design, User Experience, and Usability: Application Domains (Part III), edited by Aaron Marcus and Wentao Wang
21. LNCS 11586, Design, User Experience, and Usability: Practice and Case Studies (Part IV), edited by Aaron Marcus and Wentao Wang
22. LNCS 11587, Distributed, Ambient and Pervasive Interactions, edited by Norbert Streitz and Shin'ichi Konomi
23. LNCS 11588, HCI in Business, Government and Organizations: eCommerce and Consumer Behavior (Part I), edited by Fiona Fui-Hoon Nah and Keng Siau
24. LNCS 11589, HCI in Business, Government and Organizations: Information Systems and Analytics (Part II), edited by Fiona Fui-Hoon Nah and Keng Siau
25. LNCS 11590, Learning and Collaboration Technologies: Designing Learning Experiences (Part I), edited by Panayiotis Zaphiris and Andri Ioannou
26. LNCS 11591, Learning and Collaboration Technologies: Ubiquitous and Virtual Environments for Learning and Collaboration (Part II), edited by Panayiotis Zaphiris and Andri Ioannou
27. LNCS 11592, Human Aspects of IT for the Aged Population: Design for the Elderly and Technology Acceptance (Part I), edited by Jia Zhou and Gavriel Salvendy
28. LNCS 11593, Human Aspects of IT for the Aged Population: Social Media, Games and Assistive Environments (Part II), edited by Jia Zhou and Gavriel Salvendy
29. LNCS 11594, HCI for Cybersecurity, Privacy and Trust, edited by Abbas Moallem
30. LNCS 11595, HCI in Games, edited by Xiaowen Fang
31. LNCS 11596, HCI in Mobility, Transport, and Automotive Systems, edited by Heidi Krömker
32. LNCS 11597, Adaptive Instructional Systems, edited by Robert Sottilare and Jessica Schwarz
33. CCIS 1032, HCI International 2019 - Posters (Part I), edited by Constantine Stephanidis

http://2019.hci.international/proceedings

HCI International 2019 (HCII 2019)

The full list with the Program Board Chairs and the members of the Program Boards of all thematic areas and affiliated conferences is available online at:

http://www.hci.international/board-members-2019.php

HCI International 2020

The 22nd International Conference on Human-Computer Interaction, HCI International 2020, will be held jointly with the affiliated conferences in Copenhagen, Denmark, at the Bella Center Copenhagen, July 19–24, 2020. It will cover a broad spectrum of themes related to HCI, including theoretical issues, methods, tools, processes, and case studies in HCI design, as well as novel interaction techniques, interfaces, and applications. The proceedings will be published by Springer. More information will be available on the conference website: http://2020.hci.international/.

General Chair
Prof. Constantine Stephanidis
University of Crete and ICS-FORTH
Heraklion, Crete, Greece
E-mail: general_chair@hcii2020.org

http://2020.hci.international/

Contents – Part II

Human Robot Interaction

AI and Machine Learning in HCI

Physiological Measuring

Object, Motion and Activity Recognition

Virtual and Augmented Reality

Intelligent Interactive Environments

Interacting with Games

Do Self-reported Playing Preferences Correlate with Emotional Reactions During Playing? Evidence from Psychophysiological Recordings

Suvi K. Holm[1]([⊠]), Santtu Forsström[1], Johanna K. Kaakinen[1], and Veikko Surakka[2]

[1] Department of Psychology, University of Turku, 20014 Turku, Finland
suvi.holm@utu.fi
[2] TAUCHI Research Center, University of Tampere, 33014 Tampere, Finland

Abstract. According to certain player typologies, players report preferring some game dynamics more than others [1]. However, it is unclear whether these self-reported preferences show carryover effects during actual playing. For instance, do players who report liking dynamics of killing and shooting show positive emotions during playing games that incorporate such elements? We recruited active gamers (N = 24) and divided them into two groups: those who preferred and those who disliked aggressive game dynamics. In the experiment, both groups played a first person shooter game as well as watched a video of someone else playing the game. We recorded psychophysiological responses for facial muscle activation, electrodermal activity and heartbeat to explore the participants' emotional valence and arousal states during playing and watching. The results indicate that the groups did not differ in their emotional responses, suggesting that self-reported playing preferences may not be an accurate way to measure actual emotional responses during playing. The results also illustrate that gaming seems to affect players in a similar way regardless of their self-reported likes and preferences. Furthermore, the results showed that actual playing induces more positive and negative emotions (as indexed by smiling and frowning) than watching someone else play, and is emotionally more arousing.

Keywords: Player types · Emotions · Games

1 Introduction

Previous research has identified player types [2] based on in-game behavior [3–5], demographic segmentations such as age and gender [6, 7], players' internal motivations and personality differences [8–12], types of games played (such as casual or hardcore games, see [13] for a discussion), and recently through game dynamics preferences [1, 14]. However, little effort has been made to validate these player types by experimental means. Our study aims to ameliorate the situation by exploring whether self-reported game dynamics preferences can be detected during the process of playing through emotional responses. Comparisons of emotional responses were made between watching a gameplay video and actual gaming.

© Springer Nature Switzerland AG 2019
C. Stephanidis (Ed.): HCII 2019, CCIS 1033, pp. 3–11, 2019.
https://doi.org/10.1007/978-3-030-23528-4_1

2   Method

2.1   Participants

Participants were recruited from an internet survey that focused on their preferred game dynamics, i.e. player-game interaction modes. We set out to recruit active gamers and the survey was thus distributed in different gaming communities as well as posted to gaming-related forums, social media and web pages. 513 participants answered the survey. After cleaning the dataset from underage respondents and answers that were obviously misleading, a dataset of 481 participants was left. Some respondents left their contact information in order to participate in further research on digital gaming. Of these volunteers, 30 participants eventually took part in the laboratory experiment. Six participants had to be dropped from the final dataset because of poor quality of elec-trophysiological data. The final dataset thus consisted of 24 participants (20 men, 4 women, Mage = 28.67, SDage = 6.18).

We invited the participants of the final dataset to the laboratory experiment based on their preference for aggressive action gaming dynamics. Namely, we created pairs of players with similar experience of playing but opposite preferences for aggressive action dynamics: those who particularly preferred them and those who disliked them. For this division, we used an updated 50-item version [1] of the Core Game Dynamics scale [personal communication]. More specifically, we used only responses pertaining to dynamics associated with what could be termed as "aggressive action". The items included, for example: *"Firing enemies and avoiding enemy fire in a high speed"* and *"Close-combat by using fighting techniques and by performing combo attacks"*. This selection was done because it was the dynamics group that divided participants the most and games that incorporate such characteristics are easily found among the first-person shooter game genre. Participants were to rate how much their level of satis-faction depended on these game dynamics either based on their earlier experiences or on their experiences in trying a new game. Ratings were given on a 5-point Likert scale (1 = Very Dissatisfying, 2 = Dissatisfying, 3 = Neither, 4 = Satisfying, 5 = Very Satisfying).

The participants were thus divided into two groups: those who had a high pref-erence for aggressive action (n = 12, 3 women, Mage = 28.58 years, SDage = 9.22 years) and those who had a low preference for aggressive action (n = 12, 1 woman, Mage = 28.75 years, SDage = 10.1 years). Both groups consisted of active gamers. Those with a preference for aggressive action played on average 15.67 h weekly (SD = 9.2), and those with a low preference for aggressive action played an average of 18.75 h weekly (SD = 10.1).

2.2   Apparatus

Biopac® MP150 (Biopac Systems, Inc., Santa Barbara, CA) with added EMG100C, GSR100C and PPG100C modules were used for data collection. The data was recorded using AcqKnowledge 4.4.0 software (Biopac Systems, Inc., Santa Barbara, CA). The PlayStation 3 gaming console (Sony Computer Entertainment) attached to a 24" and

144 Hz screen (Benq XL2420Z) was used for gaming. The participants sat at a distance of 90 cm from the screen and the volume was kept on the same comfortable level for all the participants.

Two different sets of electrodes were used for measuring electrodermal activity (EDA). For the first 14 participants, we used two 8 mm Ag/Ag-Cl electrodes that were attached to the participants' right foot's index and middle toe using wrap-around bands (Biopac TSD203). For the rest of the participants, recordings were made using two 4 mm electrodes that were attached to the participants' right foot's sole using tape. The electrodes were filled with isotonic gel (Biopac GEL 101). They were attached to the participants' feet in order to keep their hands free for using a gaming pad and to decrease artefacts that might have resulted from pressure to the electrodes if they were attached to fingers. During the experiment, the participants' feet were resting on a footstool and they were instructed not to move them. The EDA signal was relayed to the Biopac GSR100C module. The raw signal was amplified (gain = 5 $\mu\Omega$/V) and bandwidth filtering was set between 0.5 to 1 Hz.

For recording heart rate, we used a photoplethysmogram (PPG) transducer (Biopac TSD200C) that was attached to the earlobe using a clip. The signal from the transducer was relayed to the PPG100C module and amplified (gain = 100). A bandwith filter was set between 0.5 and 10 Hz.

For recording facial muscle activation (electromyography, EMG), we placed two sets of 4 mm Ag/Ag-Cl electrodes on the zygomaticus major and the corrugator supercilii muscles, representing smiling and frowning activity, respectively. To improve electrode impedance, the skin was cleansed with mild soap, slightly abraded, and then wiped with an antiseptic solution of alcohol before attaching the electrodes. The electrodes were attached using adhesive tape and filled with isotonic gel (Biopac GEL 100). The signal from the electrodes was amplified (gain = 500) using the EMG100C module, with bandwith filtering of 10–500 Hz. The notch filter was turned off.

2.3 Materials

Game Description. Call of Duty: Modern Warfare 2 (Activision, 2009) was chosen to represent an aggressive action game. As a first person shooter (FPS) game it contains all of the game dynamics included in the participant selection criteria. Therefore we had reason to assume that the participants would react differently to the game based on their self-reported preferences for such game dynamics. In the levels used in this experiment, the player must always follow the leader of the troop and act according to his missions, ensuring relative similarity of exposure to events in the game.

For this experiment, we used two different levels for both the video watching and the playing condition. For the video condition, we recorded two videos (levels A and B) of a player playing the same levels with the same frame rates and volume as in the playing condition. Both videos were 6 min long. The playing and watching conditions were counterbalanced so that every other participant played level A and every other played level B. Likewise, every other participant watched a gameplay video of level A, and every other watched a video of level B. This was done to ensure that everyone was exposed to the same levels, either by playing or by watching. Every other player started by playing the level A and every other started by watching the video of level A. The same screen was used for both watching and playing conditions.

Practice Level. Because we assumed that there would be differences in the players' skill levels, and that not all players would be familiar with playing with PlayStation 3, every participant completed a practice level before moving onto the playing condition. The practice level did not end before it was successfully completed, ensuring that the participant had enough practice of using the controls. After completing the practice level, the game automatically set a difficulty level appropriate for the participant. This difficulty level was used during the playing condition.

Procedure. The experiment commenced by giving the participants instructions and having them sign an informed consent form, after which electrodes were attached. After this, electrode attachments were checked by insuring that appropriate responses were seen during online data surveillance.

There were two conditions in the actual experiment: playing an aggressive action videogame or watching a gameplay video. Every participant took part in both conditions, but the order of the conditions was counterbalanced so that half of the participants first played and then watched the video, whereas the other half first watched the video and then played.

The participants had a chance to play for 15 min, or less if they completed the level before that. However, data was only collected from the first six minutes of the playing condition, which was in accordance with the length of the video condition.

Data Preparation and Processing. The recorded data was processed using the AcqKnowledge 4.4.0 software (Biopac Systems, Inc., Santa Barbara, CA).

For the EMG signal, we used average rectifying and multiplied the signal by 10,000. In the case of one participant, the data for the EMG had to be dropped entirely because of poor quality, resulting in a total of 23 participants in the analysis of EMG results. The same participant's data for EDA and heart rate were deemed of good quality and retained in the analyses, resulting in 24 participants for the EDA and heart rate analyses.

For EDA, we resampled the signal to 62.5 samples per second and then used median smoothing, with a median of 50 samples per second. A low pass filter of 1 Hz was utilized.

For the PPG signal, we removed the comb band stop frequency of 50 Hz and used the waveforms created by the PPG signal to measure heartbeat. For this, we used the "find rate" option of the software and inspected the data manually for artefacts. We then converted the signal to the "beats per minute" form provided by the software.

Creating Epochs and Time Windows. After processing the raw data, it was divided into one second epochs, each containing the mean values for the signals. We then created time windows of 60 s and calculated the averages for each of those time windows. Every participant therefore had six one-minute long averages of each measurement in the playing and the watching condition.

3   Results

The data was analyzed using repeated measures ANOVAs in which the player group (non-aggressive vs. aggressive preference) was a between-subjects factor and condition (video vs. playing) and time window (1 min to 6 min) were repeated measures. It was thus a 2 (group) × 2 (condition) × 6 (time) repeated measures setting.

3.1   Electrodermal Activity

Means and 95% confidence intervals for electrodermal activity in different conditions across time are presented in Table 1. There was no interaction effect between group, condition and time ($F_{1,32} = 1.92$, $p = .172$). Furthermore, none of the two-way inter-actions were statistically significant ($F < 1$). However, the difference between the video and playing conditions did approach significance ($F_{1,22} = 4.01$, $p = .058$), indicating that electrodermal activity might be higher in the playing condition, although this result was not robust enough to reach significance. Overall, there was fluctuation in partic-ipants' electrodermal activity during the experiment ($F_{2,43} = 6.13$, $p = .005$). There was no main effect of participant group, i.e. aggression preference ($F_{1,22} = .178$, $p = .677$).

Table 1. Means and 95% Confidence Intervals for electrodermal activity measured in microsiemens (μS) for each player group in different time windows.

Player preference group		Condition			
		Playing		Watching	
		M	95% CI	M	95% CI
Non-aggressive	1 min	12.49	[8.00, 16.98]	11.96	[7.54, 16.39]
	2 min	11.99	[7.62, 16.36]	11.60	[7.29, 15.91]
	3 min	11.69	[7.39, 16.00]	11.34	[7.05, 15.63]
	4 min	11.59	[7.31, 15.88]	11.06	[6.86, 15.26]
	5 min	11.71	[7.51, 15.92]	11.46	[7.09, 15.82]
	6 min	11.53	[7.32, 15.74]	11.51	[7.16, 15.86]
Aggressive	1 min	10.62	[6.14, 15.11]	10.95	[6.52, 15.38]
	2 min	10.50	[6.12, 14.87]	10.45	[6.15, 14.76]
	3 min	10.66	[6.35, 14.97]	10.19	[5.90, 14.48]
	4 min	10.72	[6.43, 15.01]	9.89	[5.69, 14.09]
	5 min	10.74	[6.54, 14.95]	9.90	[5.54, 14.26]
	6 min	10.69	[6.48, 14.90]	9.80	[5.45, 14.15]

3.2   Heart Rate

Means and 95% confidence intervals for heart rate in different conditions across time can be found in Table 2. There was no interaction effect between group, condition and time ($F_{2,55} = 1.564$, $p = 214$.) Furthermore, none of the two-way interactions were statistically significant ($F < 2$). As for main effects, condition approached significance ($F_{1,22} = 3.254$, $p = .085$), but remained non-significant. This trend seemed to stem from participants having a higher heart rate when playing as opposed to watching a video in both player groups. Overall, there was fluctuation in heart rate over the course of playing ($F_{2,52} = 5.019$, $p = .007$). There was no main effect of player group ($F_{1,22} = .247$, $p = .624$).

Table 2. Means and 95% confidence intervals for heart rate (beats per minute) for each player group in different time windows

Player preference group		Condition			
		Playing		Watching	
		M	95% CI	M	95% CI
Non-aggressive	1 min	80.61	[71.83, 89.39]	78.42	[70.44, 86.41]
	2 min	81.74	[73.03, 90.44]	78.24	[70.07, 86.40]
	3 min	79.87	[70.95, 88.79]	79.20	[71.22, 87.17]
	4 min	80.86	[71.88, 89.83]	78.64	[70.60, 86.67]
	5 min	82.29	[73.45, 91.13]	81.84	[73.88, 89.80]
	6 min	82.02	[72.96, 91.08]	81.06	[73.25, 88.87]
Aggressive	1 min	83.54	[74.76, 92.32]	81.99	[74.00, 89.98]
	2 min	84.11	[75.41, 92.81]	83.30	[75.14, 91.46]
	3 min	83.62	[74.70, 92.53]	82.19	[74.22, 90.17]
	4 min	82.81	[73.83, 91.79]	82.28	[74.24, 90.31]
	5 min	84.71	[75.87, 93.55]	82.65	[74.69, 90.61]
	6 min	84.36	[75.30, 93.42]	82.83	[75.02, 90.63]

3.3   EMG: Zygomaticus Major

Means and 95% confidence intervals for activity of the zygomaticus major muscle (i.e. smiling) in different conditions across time can be found in Table 3. There was no interaction effect between group, condition and time ($F_{1,29} = .116$, $p = .817$). Furthermore, none of the two-way interactions were statistically significant ($F < 2$). There was no main effect of condition ($F_{1,21} = 3.245$, $p = .086$), although there was a trend towards more smiling activity in the playing condition as opposed to the watching condition. The main effects of time ($F_{1,30} = 1.226$, $p = .295$) and group ($F_{1,21} = .598$, $p = .448$) were not significant.

3.4   EMG: Corrugator Supercilii

Means and 95% confidence intervals for activity of the corrugator supercilii muscle (i.e. frowning) in different conditions across time can be found in Table 4. There was no interaction effect between group, condition and time ($F_{2,37} = 1.191$, $p = .310$). Furthermore, none of the two-way interactions were significant ($F < 1$). There was a

Table 3. Means and 95% confidence intervals for activity of the zygomaticus major muscle (10^{-4} microvolts), i.e. smiling activity for each player group in different time windows

Player preference group		Condition			
		Playing		Watching	
		M	95% CI	M	95% CI
Non-aggressive	1 min	5.67	[4.66, 6.68]	5.43	[5.12, 7.23]
	2 min	5.47	[5.05, 5.90]	5.46	[5.43, 6.32]
	3 min	5.45	[5.10, 5.80]	5.42	[5.42, 6.16]
	4 min	5.46	[5.13, 5.80]	5.38	[5.38, 6.08]
	5 min	5.63	[4.80, 6.47]	5.45	[5.15, 6.89]
	6 min	5.55	[5.08, 6.02]	5.41	[5.33, 6.30]
Aggressive	1 min	6.18	[5.24, 5.62]	5.41	[5.21, 5.61]
	2 min	5.87	[5.26, 5.65]	5.42	[5.22, 5.63]
	3 min	5.79	[5.16, 5.68]	5.39	[5.12, 5.65]
	4 min	5.73	[5.19, 5.57]	5.38	[5.18, 5.58]
	5 min	6.02	[5.21, 5.70]	5.43	[5.18, 5.69]
	6 min	5.81	[5.19, 5.63]	5.37	[5.14, 5.59]

Table 4. Means and 95% confidence intervals for activity of the corrugator supercilii muscle (10^{-4} microvolts), i.e. frowning activity for each player group in different time windows

Player preference group		Condition			
		Playing		Watching	
		M	95% CI	M	95% CI
Non-aggressive	1 min	2.86	[1.16, 4.58]	1.67	[1.12, 2.22]
	2 min	3.22	[1.35, 5.09]	1.85	[1.18, 2.52]
	3 min	3.00	[1.48, 4.52]	1.89	[1.05, 2.73]
	4 min	3.26	[1.59, 4.94]	2.20	[.66, 3.74]
	5 min	3.52	[1.46, 5.58]	2.25	[.80, 3.71]
	6 min	3.33	[1.28, 5.38]	2.42	[.85, 3.98]
Aggressive	1 min	3.53	[1.75, 5.32]	2.15	[1.58, 2.72]
	2 min	3.97	[2.01, 5.93]	2.34	[1.64, 3.04]
	3 min	3.38	[1.79, 4.97]	2.61	[1.74, 3.49]
	4 min	3.55	[1.80, 5.30]	3.40	[1.80, 5.00]
	5 min	3.98	[1.83, 6.13]	3.39	[1.87, 4.91]
	6 min	4.31	[2.17, 6.45]	3.47	[1.84, 5.11]

main effect of condition ($F_{1,21} = 9.992$, $p = .005$), indicating that there was more frowning activity in the playing as opposed to watching condition. There was fluctuation in frowning activity over the course of the experiment ($F_{2,32} = 5.820$, $p = .012$). There was no main effect for participant group ($F_{1,21} = .550$, $p = .467$).

4 Conclusion

Our aim was to investigate whether emotional reactions to aggressive action games are universal or whether these types of games affect players differently based on their playing preferences. We recorded psychophysiological responses for playing vs. watching a video of a game that contained high amounts of aggressive action dynamics. There were two groups of participants: those who liked and those who disliked such dynamics. Overall, the results indicate that the groups did not differ in their emotional responses, indicating that these kinds of games induce universal emotional reactions. Furthermore, the results suggested that actual playing is emotionally more arousing than watching someone else play. Playing also seems to induce more smiling and frowning activity than watching a video.

References

1. Vahlo, J., Kaakinen, J.K., Holm, S.K., Koponen, A.: Digital game dynamics preferences and player types. J. Comput. Mediat. Commun. **22**(2), 88–103 (2017)
2. Hamari, J., Tuunanen, J.: Player types: A meta-synthesis. Trans. Digit. Games Res. Assoc. **1** (2), 29–53 (2014)
3. Bartle, R.: Hearts, clubs, diamonds, spades: players who suit MUDs. J. MUD Res. **1**, 19 (1996)
4. Drachen, A., Canossa, A., Yannakakis, G.N.: Player modeling using self-organization in Tomb Raider: underworld. In: 2009 IEEE Symposium on Computational Intelligence and Games (CIG 2009), pp. 1–8 (2009)
5. Ahmed, I., Mahapatra, A., Poole, M.S., Srivastava, J., Brown, C.: Identifying a typology of players based on longitudinal game data. In: Ahmad, M.A., Shen, C., Srivastava, J., Contractor, N. (eds.) Predicting Real World Behaviors from Virtual World Data, pp. 103–115. Springer, Cham (2014). https://doi.org/10.1007/978-3-319-07142-8_7
6. Griffiths, M.D., Davies, M.N.O., Chappell, D.: Online computer gaming: a comparison of adolescent and adult gamers. J. Adolesc. **27**(1), 87–96 (2004)
7. Terlecki, M., et al.: Sex differences and similarities in video game experience, preferences, and self-efficacy: implications for the gaming industry. Curr. Psychol. **30**(1), 22–33 (2011)
8. Bateman, C., Lowenhaupt, R., Nacke, L.E.: Player typology in theory and practice. In: Proceedings of the 2011 DiGRA International Conference: Think Design Play (DiGRA 2011) (2011)
9. Tseng, F.-C.: Segmenting online gamers by motivation. Expert Syst. Appl. **38**(6), 7693–7697 (2011)
10. Whang, L.S.-M., Chang, G.: Lifestyles of virtual world residents: Living in the on-line game "Lineage". CyberPsychol. Behav. **7**(5), 592–600 (2004)
11. Yee, N.: Motivations for Play in online games. J. CyberPsychol. Behav. **9**(6), 772–775 (2006)
12. Yee, N., Ducheneaut, N., Nelson, L.: Online gaming motivations scale: development and validation. In: Proceedings of the SIGCHI Conference on Human Factors in Computing Systems (CHI 2012), pp. 2803–2806 (2012)

13. Kuittinen, J., Kultima, A., Niemelä, J., Paavilainen, J.: Casual games discussion. In: Proceedings of the 2007 Conference on Future Play (Future Play 2007), pp. 105–112 (2007)
14. Tondello, G., Wehbe, R., Orji, R., Ribeiro, G., Nacke, L.: A framework and taxonomy of videogame playing preferences. In: Proceedings of the Annual Symposium on Computer-Human Interaction in Play, pp. 329–340 (2017)

Design Strategies of Corporate Gamification Systems that Evokes Employee Motivation – Creative Process of Gathering Game Design Elements into Working System

Michal Jakubowski[✉]

Kozminski University, Warsaw, Poland
mjakubowski@kozminski.edu.pl

Abstract. In the paper Author will describe outcomes of his interviews with focus on how certain game elements are chosen and compiled into working gamification systems. Most popular elements which can be found in current gamified platforms and literature reviews are leaderboards, points, badges and levels. It seems that designers are using it over and over again as it would be the only possibility when one thinks about boosting engagement. What is the reason that designers won't take advantage of other combinations of game design elements? How they are guiding the creative process of game design construction in gamification design process? Following poster will try to deliver answers basing on data gathered during the research.

Keywords: Gamification design · Game design

1 Introduction

Following article will summarize research project about the strategical perspective of gamification system design in the area of employee engagement. The target group of the research was 15 experienced gamification designers with at least 2 finished and implemented projects in the past. Basing on cross-analysis of multiple case study that will gather the design perspective of corporate gamification systems the expected result will be a set of best working design guidelines in corporate area. Guidelines will be corrected by the end-user perspective and will state open perspectives for future development.

Hamari positions gamification in the field of hedonistic-utilitarian information systems (Hamari and Koivisto 2015). Within such systems, each interaction that takes place is by definition seen as an awakening pleasant feelings. Birth of that systems can be connected to the mutual interest of software developers (software like office application) and video games developers. Software developers appreciated the effectiveness of modeling engaging user experience in games. Game developers on the other hand use knowledge about building the correct architecture of information and deliver features according to recipients expectations (Ferrara 2012).

One of the reasons why gamification is treated as a negative phenomenon is too shallow design perspective that uses constantly the same game mechanics

© Springer Nature Switzerland AG 2019
C. Stephanidis (Ed.): HCII 2019, CCIS 1033, pp. 12–16, 2019.
https://doi.org/10.1007/978-3-030-23528-4_2

(Bogost 2014). Current state of art of gamification research in enterprise area is confirming that revelations (Cardador et al. 2016; Hamari et al. 2014; Rapp et al. 2016; Robson et al. 2016). Unfortunately, none of the reviewed research papers takes account designer perspective nor knowledge or skill of their gamification designs. The way of how next iterations of gamification systems will be created have crucial meaning not only for that area but also for the quality of its influence inside organizations.

2 Project Description

Scientific problem of that project is the design strategies of gamification systems. Basing on cross-analysis of multiple case study that will gather the design perspective of gamification systems the expected result will be a set of best working design guidelines. Guidelines will be corrected by the end-user perspective and will state open perspectives for future development. The initial study will involve a thorough examination of circumstances for building well-functioning gamification system for employee engagement improvement and management. Results will come from the literature review of research domains and gamification design guidelines described by respondents.

Main findings from the literature review were positioned around two works. Raftopoulos (2014) analyzed what are the effective approaches to enterprise gamification and what can be potential tools that assist such gamification. Having scope on the corporate environment doesn't mean it can't be related to learning. One of the enterprise activities where employees are gamified is in-house learning (about the company, product, skills). An outcome of her study presented a framework based on more than 300 gamification artifacts and their design.

Second work by Morschheuser et al. (2017) again tries to set a framework for proper gamification design. With the use of design science authors conceptualized and then build artifact of the gamification design process. Based on literature review, desk research and most important – in-depth interviews with gamification designers, they prepared a comprehensive method of gamification.

Both sources have a rather limited view of what are the game elements that should be used in gamification systems. Raftopoulus mentions key mechanics and core gameplay groups as design elements, but there are no guidelines on how to connect elements of those groups into working and engaging system that will answer the problem. Second work brings ideation toolbox which is a guide of best practices about combining game elements in gamification design.

3 Methodology

Research methodology in the following project is positioned in interpretative-symbolic paradigm (Konecki 2000). Qualitative methods can be sufficient to explain a phenomenon that appears in reality. The research will be constructed upon a grounded theory which assumes that research area can be understood best by engaged in actors (Glaser 1992). Research hypothesis will emerge during the collection of research evidence. There is also an assumption that some elements or areas, that were not stated at first, will appear somewhere during the research and will have important meaning for research problem.

That methodology results from a relatively fresh area which is gamification. Because of its characteristic of long-term influence on implementing subjects (Herger 2014) and a small number of long-enough implementations, state of art of gamification in employee engagement management is still open for new findings. Qualitative methods that explore research area have better application in the following project than explanative ones. As for now - broadest knowledge of the research area still lies in the hands of practitioners and using their experience this research project will deliver new and structured information.

Research method will be an exploratory case study (Yin 2017) in the form of group case analysis. A juxtaposition of a couple of cases will help with a deeper understanding of the research problem. To strengthen qualitative results I will use questionnaire method with employees who took part in gamification activities. That group perspective will help with the supplement of knowledge and experience of the designer by adding conclusions which they could overlook.

The research was structured as design science research. Gasparski (1988) distinguish design science subdisciplines like design phenomenology (background, taxonomy, technology); design praxeology (analysis of design activities and organization) and design philosophy (axiology, epistemology, and pedagogy of design). Here Author will analyze how the design is processed, so the praxeology of that action is in the main focus of the research. When it comes to design methodology then it will be covered different types of design activities and its analysis, description of design tasks and procedures which Gasparski titles as a pragmatic design methodology.

Research group:

- 15 gamification designers

Research tools:

- IDI script,
- Observation diary,
- Data from designers (design documents, guidelines, frameworks)

IDI script was divided into three parts: questions about gamification, questions about design, and questions about game design. Then each chapter of the interview was covered with a couple of question starting from general topics and finishing with specific ones. Each of the interviews has followed the same script, but the characteristics of IDI allowed Author to sometimes ask additional questions if something emerged during the talk.

4 Results

The outcome of this research project was to present multiple case study of gamification design strategies and gather best practices in one framework that can be a guide for other designers. The following poster will cover the latter with a focus on the creative process of gathering game design elements. It was the first idea of the Author to research what are the real purposes of combining such elements and why is that so popular to use often similar elements (i.e. points, badges, leaderboards) when there is the much broader choice.

General analysis of the interviews was conducted with use of Johnny Saldana method that uses two cycles of coding (Saldaña 2015). Figure 1 covers categories and codes that emerged after the first cycle of analysis. The second cycle will be shown on the poster.

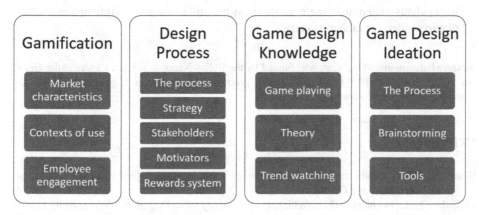

Fig. 1. Categories and codes

Although some insights about design strategies should be presented as well. To make it more clear for the purpose of this paper it will be presented as list with short description of each element.

1. Project vs product approach. There are those two styles of thinking and working on gamification solutions. Project work assumes that each solution will be build up from scratch, with ground research of the problem and tailor-made mechanisms. It is more costly and time-consuming but the results are generally better. Product means that the company has some already existing gamification 'engine' which is prepared and modified accordingly to clients requirements.
2. Generic vs mature gamification. Generic gamification is the easiest way of using points, badges, and leaderboards as a layer on existing activities that gain new instruments to measure the performance of its peers. Mature gamification states to be more immersing, uses other – often experimental – elements for engaging user behavior.
3. The user is less important than some stakeholders. That is something that was observed in some interviews, designers were not interested in the user perspective on the first place. It was dictated by the business objectives of the project and end users were involved in the project only at the testing phase or in one case – not at all!

4. Rewards should fit user characteristics and needs. Different levels of employees in the organization have different needs and expectations about the prizes. Managers were more into using their gamification capital (like virtual currencies) for charity or knowledge enhancers (books, training). However, lower level employees love physical goods and rewards that can improve their status.
5. Heavy use of tools known in human-computer interactions design (user journey map, user stories, storyboards, personas). It can also lead to other connections with user experience design and the general image of how gamification blends with UX.
6. Brainstorming while playing games can deliver innovative mechanics. Most of the respondents stated that there is the positive influence on design process when playing video (or tabletop) games.

Acknowledgements. This work was funded by the Polish National Science Center under Grant No. 2016/23/N/HS4/03839 titled "Factors that promote specific design of gamified systems for managing employee motivation.".

References

Bogost, I.: "Why gamification is bullshit". Gameful World: Approaches, Issues, Applications. MIT Press, Cambridge (2014)

Cardador, M.T., Northcraft, G.B., Whicker, J.: A theory of work gamification: something old, something new, something borrowed, something cool? Hum. Resour. Manag. Rev. **27**, 353–365 (2016)

Ferrara, J.: Playful Design: Creating Game Experiences in Everyday Interfaces. Rosenfeld Media, Brooklyn (2012)

Gasparski, W.: Science of Designing. Elements of the Study of Designing (1988)

Glaser, B.G.: Basics of Grounded Theory Analysis: Emergence vs Forcing. Sociology Press, Mill Valle (1992)

Hamari, J., Koivisto, J.: Why do people use gamification services? Int. J. Inf. Manag. **35**(4), 419–431 (2015)

Herger, M.: Gamification in human resources. Enterprise Gamification, vol. 3 (2014)

Konecki, K.: A study of the qualitative research methodology. Grounded theory (2000)

Morschheuser, B., Werder, K., Hamari, J., Abe, J.: How to gamify? Development of a method for gamification. In: Proceedings of the 50th Annual Hawaii International Conference on System Sciences (HICSS), Hawaii, USA, 4–7 January 2017 (2017)

Raftopoulos, M.: Towards gamification transparency: a conceptual framework for the development of responsible gamified enterprise systems. J. Gaming Virtual Worlds **6**(2), 159–178 (2014)

Saldaña, J.: The Coding Manual for Qualitative Researchers. Sage, Upper Saddle River (2015)

Yin, R.K.: Case Study Research and Applications: Design and Methods. Sage Publications, Upper Saddle River (2017)

Computational and Network Utilization in the Application of Thin Clients in Cloud-Based Virtual Applications

Chandler Lattin, Glenn A. Martin[✉], Shehan Sirigampola,
and Steven Zielinski

University of Central Florida, Orlando, FL 32826, USA
martin@ist.ucf.edu

Abstract. Typically, training using virtual environments uses a client-server or a fully distributed approach. In either arrangement, the clients used are full computers (PCs) with an adequate processor, memory, and graphics capability. These are reasonably costly, require maintenance, and have security concerns. In the office desktop environment, the use of thin clients is well known; however, the ‘application of thin clients with cloud-based servers to virtual training is relatively new. Thin clients require less initial cost, require less setup and maintenance, and centralize the virtual environment configuration, maintenance, and security to virtual cloud servers. Rather than housing an expensive computer (a so-called thick client) at each station, functionality is replaced using a streaming protocol, a remote server, and a thin client to allow the user to interact. This paper reviews two game-focused streaming protocols running across a set of four thin clients (of various capability and cost) from both local and remote cloud-based data centers. Data were gathered to measure latency and network and computational utilization across each client using two scenarios in both local and remote conditions. Results of these experiments indicate that thin clients for use in virtual training is viable regardless of local or remote server location.

Keywords: Thin clients · Virtual training · Cloud computing

1 Introduction

Virtual training refers to the use of an interactive, computer-generated world where a user learns and practices a task (or tasks). Current virtual training systems use one of two methods: a server-client arrangement (most game-based systems) or a fully-distributed approach (where no single computer maintains the main copy of data, but rather a copy of data exists on each node). In either approach, the client stations run applications that are fairly intensive in terms of computational and graphical load. Of course, this requires that computers be used that can adequately support those applications. Virtual Battlespace 3 (VBS3), a game-based training application used by the U.S. military, recommends a computer with an Intel Core i5-2300 or AMD Phenom II 940 CPU, 8 GB RAM, and an Nvidia GeForce GTX 560 or AMD Radeon HD 7750 (with 1024 MB VRAM) [1]. Such a system may be reasonable for a home user or a single training station; however, the cost of these systems multiply quickly when

© Springer Nature Switzerland AG 2019
C. Stephanidis (Ed.): HCII 2019, CCIS 1033, pp. 17–24, 2019.
https://doi.org/10.1007/978-3-030-23528-4_3

installing multiple stations within a training center. These high-fidelity computers may also be supported in multiple (geographically-separated) training centers, making security and maintenance an additional cost and challenge.

Many training centers are already investigating reducing overall hardware footprints by developing a new cloud-based infrastructure [2]. This approach can provide the simulations to less-capable clients (so-called "thin clients"), thereby addressing weaknesses in cost, security, maintenance, and deployment. The use of a cloud-based approach begins to provide the infrastructure needed to reduce client hardware footprint. In addition to providing the server side (in client-server game-based simulation), cloud servers could also provide the client side (host the user's game itself). In this case, the trainee receives the view through some mechanism, and input from the trainee transmitted back. Doing so centralizes the significant computational resources and allow for easier deployment and maintenance, reducing cost and enhancing security.

With client applications provided from the cloud, one open question is the presentation of the application to the user. Various "remote desktop" technologies already exist. Virtual Network Computing (VNC) [3] and Microsoft's Remote Desktop [4] are two well-known examples. In addition, companies such as Citrix and VMware have developed their own proprietary approaches.

1.1   Game-Based Streaming

"Remote desktop" approaches provide a generic capability for display of any kind of content (whether game-based simulations or office applications such as word processing or spreadsheets). Other companies and groups have developed approaches focused on the remote display of *interactive, 3-D graphical* content, and others continue to do so. As a comparison to the typical desktop approaches, how might these graphical streaming protocols perform to achieve the needs for streaming content for virtual training? We initially investigated multiple protocols in a functional sense ("do they install and work?"). While developers continue to develop and leverage technologies such as HTML5 (through a system such as Guacamole) [5] and GamingAnywhere [6], these are not yet capable enough for game-based virtual training. However, Nvidia's GameStream [7] and Steam's In-Home Streaming [9] do appear promising and they quickly became the focus of this work.

GameStream uses H.264 encoding to send video from server to client. Nvidia has optimized the encoding in terms of both speed and size. As a part of this process, the server leverages the GPU; in fact, both Nvidia's GeForce GTX and GRID cards include special hardware for H.264 encoding/decoding. While not required, if the clients have an Nvidia GPU (even the mobile Tegra GPU), the decoding process uses it in order to increase its speed [8]. Nvidia releases GameStream software that works directly on GeForce GTX hardware; unfortunately, the same software does not operate directly on Nvidia GRID cards although Nvidia does release Software Development Kits (SDKs) to allow developers to create their own software.

Steam In-Home Streaming uses a similar approach. This is apparent in its conceptual design diagram [10]. One exception is that Steam In-Home Streaming, primarily designed for the home user, focuses on the local network. Therefore, servers and clients must be within the same network (e.g. broadcast domain), potentially requiring

Virtual Private Network (VPN) capabilities if not. This becomes important when considering streaming from a cloud-based source as VPN may be required to make the two sides of the connection appear as a single network.

During initial functionality testing, the performance of both GameStream and Steam In-Home Streaming was evaluated through just qualitative user experience ("Does it feel good enough?"). These early anecdotal results show comparable performance between GameStream and Steam In-Home Streaming although GameStream seems slightly superior. In addition, open source clients that use GameStream have been developed, which allows the support of additional thin client hardware. For example, Moonlight [11] has a number of GameStream-compatible clients including ones for iOS, Android, and even the Raspberry Pi. A Java-based Chrome browser plug-in is also available.

1.2 Thin Clients

The streaming protocol (and capability) from the cloud server to a thin client is important, but no discussion of reducing the hardware footprint would be complete without some discussion of the client hardware itself. Some of the more commercially-supported approaches have specialized clients available. Nvidia's Shield product implements the client-side of GameStream, and Valve's SteamLink product similarly implements the client-side of Steam In-Home Streaming. As alluded to earlier, the open-source GameStream client, Moonlight, is available on multiple platforms including iOS, Android, and Raspberry Pi, and even runs within the Chrome browser using an extension [11]. The latter allows any old desktop or laptop computer (regardless of operating system) to extend its lifespan by use as a thin client. This aspect may be particularly useful to many domains where a wide range of computers are available throughout.

2 Computational and Network Utilization

While the game streaming protocols and thin clients appear promising, their computational and network utilization must be measured to determine if they can address the needs for virtual training. To evaluate the client footprint, four very inexpensive thin clients were studied: the Nvidia Shield ($\sim$ $200), the Valve Software SteamLink ($\sim$ $50), the Dragon Touch X10 Android tablet ($\sim$ $100), and the Raspberry Pi 3 ($\sim$ $50). The experiment used two scenarios within Unreal Tournament 4. First, the Weapons Training course was used as a 10-min, fixed path scenario; second, a "death match" exercise was used as a 20-min, random combat scenario. The four thin clients were each tested individually with both scenarios. The Nvidia Shield used its own proprietary GameStream software, the SteamLink ran its own proprietary Steam In-Home Streaming software, and the Dragon Touch X10 and Raspberry Pi used the Moonlight client, an open-source application compatible with GameStream.

2.1   Computational Load

Given the limited capabilities of these thin clients, we studied the computational load within each thin client during each scenario in the experiment. The Nvidia Shield and the Dragon Touch X10 run the Android operating system, and the Valve SteamLink and the Raspberry Pi run Linux. Each operating system reports load on the central processing unit (CPU) differently, making a direct comparison difficult.

The Android-based clients reported data as a percentage of the CPU capacity actually used. Table 1 shows the results for those clients. The Nvidia Shield performed well and still had ample capacity for other tasks; conversely, the Dragon Touch X10 (using the Moonlight open source client) devoted more CPU to the streaming task although did not reach maximum utilization. Both clients used less of the CPU for the "Death Match" condition than for the "Weapons Training." We have not explored the cause, but note that both clients perform within capacity under both conditions.

Table 1. CPU load for Android-based clients

CPU Load

	Weapons Training	Death Match
Nvidia Shield	24.000	20.173
DragonTouch X10	89.867	43.205

The Linux-base clients report data as a value of CPU over/under utilization. The value is an average number of processes executing or waiting in the queue over time (one second). Table 2 shows the results. The Raspberry Pi performed well and reported little load. The SteamLink load is higher than desired; however, observations have shown that the SteamLink also maintains a load around 0.9 even when idle. Both clients had increased load under the "Death Match" condition, contrary to the results seen in the Android-based clients. However, both perform within capacity.

Table 2. CPU load for Linux-based clients

CPU Load

	Weapons Training	Death Match
Valve SteamLink	2.161	2.459
Raspberry Pi	0.273	0.313

These results show the thin clients considered perform adequately for streaming game content for virtual training. While this is not surprising for the Nvidia Shield and Valve SteamLink (since they are designed and built for such streaming), this is an important result for the Dragon Touch X10 and Raspberry Pi, which are general-purpose devices being utilized as thin clients.

2.2 Network Bandwidth

All streaming protocols, of course, use some quantity of network bandwidth. As far as bandwidth, the requirements depend on screen resolution. For example, Nvidia's GameStream approach requires 10 Mbps, and it recommends 20 Mbps for 720p/60 fps quality and 50 Mbps for 1080p/60 fps quality. Network capability will clearly be an important issue as virtual training moves to cloud-based approaches. Training centers may vary from very heavily used sites with ample network capability to only medium-duty sites with still only a 100 Mbps network. Careful consideration of network capability will be important, as it will drive potential location of cloud servers.

If we assume Nvidia's recommendations and the use of 1080p displays, each thin client will use up to 50 Mbps. Within a local location, this should be addressable. Even an older 100 Mbps network will support that requirement. However, if the servers are at a remote location, careful consideration is required as multiple clients may funnel through one or few links to the servers. Designing and implementing a network with an appropriate bandwidth (and topology) will allow servers and clients to transmit the data necessary.

Local Condition. To test bandwidth utilization, as discussed earlier, we used Unreal Tournament 4 and tested two scenarios, and tested in a local setting. Each scenario was run on the thin clients, each in their default settings. Results for the average bandwidth were as shown in Table 3.

Table 3. Network bandwidth in local condition (server on the local network)

Network Bandwidth

Mbps	Weapons Training		Death Match	
	Transmit	Receive	Transmit	Receive
Nvidia Shield	0.145	35.313	0.152	37.200
Valve SteamLink	0.060	13.340	0.090	15.640
Raspberry Pi	0.056	10.988	0.065	12.096
DragonTouch X10	0.081	42.968	0.053	44.048

Obviously, the bandwidth for received data is significantly larger. Of note, both the SteamLink and the Raspberry Pi had significantly reduced bandwidth utilization due to the lower frame rate of the streamed video. However, this works very well for virtual training and should allow upwards of 8 clients within a 100 Mb/s network. The Nvidia Shield and Dragon Touch Android tablet results show the potential cost of increasing to 60 frames/sec; however, both devices support lowering down to 30 fps, which may be worth reducing for the potential bandwidth savings.

Remote Condition. Since the Steam In-Home Streaming software can work on rack-mount servers with GPUs (in this case, an Nvidia GRID card), we also performed the same bandwidth test by running the same two scenarios but within a virtual machine running on an Amazon Web Services (AWS) instance. Recall that Steam In-Home Streaming requires a VPN connection due to a limitation that server and client must be on the same Layer 2 network. The results were as shown in Table 4.

Table 4. Network bandwidth in remote condition (server on the remote network)

Network Bandwidth

Mbps	Weapons Training		Death Match	
	Transmit	Receive	Transmit	Receive
Valve SteamLink (30fps)	0.098	15.181	0.116	16.441

While bandwidth utilization increased running from AWS, it is a very slight increase. Therefore, it certainly seems possible that a cloud-hosted training regimen could function and provide many enhancements for virtual training. Throughout both sets of bandwidth data, it is clear that the utilization is of an adequate level to allow streaming even on a 100 Mbps network and should work well within a limited network, provided that multiple installations "funnel" into larger connections.

2.3   Network Latency

For interactive virtual training, network latency is also an important issue. Depending on the source quoted, to provide a satisfactory experience for human use, the latency must be somewhere less than 60 ms 7 or less than 150 ms [12]. We take the "tougher" 60 ms figure here. Of course, locally within a given facility it is a given to achieve latencies under this recommendation. In the remote data center scenario, we used Amazon as a model of cloud data centers. Amazon runs four main data centers within the United States. As an informal study on latency, we collected latency ping times from various colleges and universities (both small and large) across the nation (see Table 5).

Each campus had at least one Amazon region within the 60 ms latency threshold recommended. These campuses are fairly dispersed and of various sizes. While not a definitive result, we feel this shows it is likely capable to design a network that can meet the latency threshold needed.

Given the findings on bandwidth and latency, we have found that both requirements can be met. Bandwidth utilization of both GameStream and Steam In-Home Streaming are reasonable and sufficiently low, and a network that provides latency to regional data centers that is within the 50 ms recommended limit is possible. The numbers found here provide guidance on the design requirements of such a network. Special consideration should be given to local facilities and how multiple instances funnel into any such data center.

Table 5. Ping times of various college and university campuses to Amazon regions.

Amazon region	University of Central Florida (large, metropolitan university)	University of Maryland (large, metropolitan university)	University of Minnesota (large, metropolitan university)	Bowdoin College (small, liberal arts college)	St. Olaf College (small, liberal arts college)
US-East (Virginia)	32 ms	15 ms	30 ms	29 ms	37 ms
US-West (California)	110 ms	89 ms	87 ms	91 ms	61 ms
US-West (Oregon)	91 ms	94 ms	52 ms	85 ms	49 ms
Europe (Ireland)	119 ms	105 ms	113 ms	125 ms	111 ms
Europe (Frankfurt)	136 ms	108 ms	111 ms	91 ms	113 ms
Asia Pacific (Mumbai)	253 ms	297 ms	388 ms	300 ms	438 ms
Asia Pacific (Seoul)	200 ms	205 ms	217 ms	215 ms	175 ms
Asia Pacific (Singapore)	261 ms	328 ms	292 ms	282 ms	309 ms
Asia Pacific (Sydney)	226 ms	229 ms	272 ms	251 ms	280 ms
Asia Pacific (Tokyo)	197 ms	176 ms	195 ms	220 ms	142 ms
South America (Sao Paulo)	147 ms	351 ms	208 ms	186 ms	178 ms

3 Conclusions and Future Work

The use of cloud-based systems and thin clients for virtual training addresses many concerns in cost, security, maintenance, and point of need. However, streaming interactive, 3-D graphical content to thin clients requires those clients possess sufficient computational capability and requires the network to handle the bandwidth requirements with appropriate latency for consumption by users. We have explored two streaming protocols built for video games and verified the computational load, network latency and network bandwidth utilization across four representative thin clients. We parameterized the CPU and network needs and these metrics show the viability of cloud-based virtual training.

Unfortunately, due to the limitation that Nvidia's GameStream software does not directly work on their GRID cards, we could only test Valve's Steam In-Home Streaming (via the SteamLink thin client) in the remote condition. We are currently exploring options for hosting GameStream-compatible approaches on AWS nodes.

In addition, to this point we have focused on single displays per user. Some virtual training (such as vehicle simulators) require multiple displays for a single user. Would a single thin client or multiple clients drive these? If the latter, how would they be synchronized? Similarly, we have also focused on keyboard and mouse input. What issues arise from other peripherals such as steering wheels?

References

1. VBS3 Release Notes (Version 3.9.2). https://manuals.bisimulations.com/vbs3/3-9/manuals/ #Release_Notes/Release_Notes.htm%3FTocPath%3DVBS3%2520Release%2520Notes% 7C_____0. Accessed 18 Jan 2017
2. Dumanoir, P., Willoughby, M., Grippin, B., Crutchfield, R., Wittman, R., Barie, S.: Live synthetic training and test & evaluation infrastructure architecture (LS TTE IA) prototype. In: Interservice/Industry Training, Simulation and Education Conference, Orlando (2015)
3. Virtual Network Computing (VNC). https://en.wikipedia.org/wiki/Virtual_Network_ Computing. Accessed 13 July 2017
4. Microsoft Remote Desktop Connection (RDC). https://www.microsoft.com/en-us/cloud-platform/desktop–virtualization?WT.srch=1&WT.mc_id=AID622874__SEM_inbb38GL& utm_source=Google&utm_medium=CPC&utm_term=microsoft%20remote%20desktop& utm_campaign=Enterprise_Mobility_Suite&gclid=EAIaIQobChMI06O02bWG1QIVj4KzCh1 NYwxnEAAYAiAAEgI5DfD_BwE. Accessed 13 July 2017
5. Apache Guacamole Manual. http://guacamole.incubator.apache.org/doc/gug/. Accessed 18 Jan 2017
6. Huang, C., Chen, K., Chen, D., Hsu, H., Hsu, C.: GamingAnywhere: the first open source cloud gaming system. ACM Trans. Multimedia Comput. Commun. Appl. **10**(1), 10 (2014)
7. GameStream. http://shield.nvidia.com/game-stream?utm_campaign=Oct_sale&utm_medium= Owned&utm_source=nvidia.com. Accessed 18 Jan 2017
8. Nvidia, Inc.: Cloud gaming with Nvidia GRID technologies. In: Game Developer's Conference (2014)
9. Steam In-Home Streaming. http://store.steampowered.com/streaming/. Accessed 18 Jan 2017
10. Steam In-Home Streaming Architecture. https://support.steampowered.com/kb_article.php? ref=3629-RIAV-1617. Accessed 6 July 2017
11. Moonlight. http://moonlight-stream.com/. Accessed 18 Jan 2017
12. Tolia, N., Andersen, D., Satyanarayanan, M.: Quantifying interactive user experience on thin clients. In: IEEE Computer, vol. 39, no 3 (2006)

"YUE Virtual Park"

Visualizing the National Voice

Ting Liang[(⊠)] and XiaoYing Tang[(⊠)]

Guangdong University of Technology, No. 729 Dongfeng Road, Yuexiu District,
Guangzhou, Guangdong, China
136956957@qq.com, 1009415641@qq.com

Abstract. This study presents a mobile technology was used to build an app for
the promotion of regional Chinese culture. We used traditional Cantonese
nursery rhymes as the basis for our work. These were recorded as sound files,
illustrated and combined with Augmented Reality technology to create a multi-
sensory experience for the user.

We used Android Studio to build the application and implement the main
functions. Unity3D was used to implement the AR functions. From a global
perspective, the popularity of Cantonese in foreign countries is higher than that
of Mandarin. It has a strong influence in overseas Chinese communities, and
Cantonese nursery rhymes are easy to understand, integrating local special
activities. Our app has use, therefore, both overseas and within China.

Cantonese nursery rhyme culture is multifaceted and for this reason it was
selected as the subject of our research. The linkage of the different forms of
presentation creates multi-sensory stimulation, which promotes the display of
traditional Cantonese values in the modern era. In the visual design of the
product, the traditional patterns of Cantonese culture were extracted, combined
with the illustration styles on the textbooks of the Chinese National Period, and
the illustrations and base maps of the Republic of China were drawn.

Keywords: Education games · Sound interaction · Cultural exchange

1 Introduction

The app was evaluated in a primary school classroom teaching environment. More than
1,000 students were exposed to it over a period of five days. The teacher's classroom
feedback was very positive and we were told that we had greatly improved the learning
situation of Cantonese nursery rhymes. After a week of trials we returned to the school
to conduct a return visit survey. We also produced a return visit video. We are constantly making changes and improvements to the app following feedback from schools
(Fig. 1).

This is a screenshot of the English version of the interface, this learning software
has three small games, designed around the Cantonese nursery rhymes. They are Music
Games, Fun Singing and Creating New Songs (Fig. 2).

© Springer Nature Switzerland AG 2019
C. Stephanidis (Ed.): HCII 2019, CCIS 1033, pp. 25–30, 2019.
https://doi.org/10.1007/978-3-030-23528-4_4

Fig. 1. Part of English interface

In order to fully reflect the cultural charm of China, all the illustrations used in the page refer to the illustration style of the Chinese National Period, and the color selects the gray tone of the Republic of China. The content of the graphic design is painted in the traditional singing environment and the scenes used by the children (Fig. 3).

One of the highlights of this project is to use the animated way to upgrade the teaching of Cantonese virginity, integrate AR technology, give children a new educational experience, improve the learning of learning, and inject a new era into traditional culture. At the same time, the crowd classification was carried out on the design of the online use scene and supporting teaching aids.

Designed for children in the school, greeting cards and postcards are designed. Because of the fun of hands-on production and the emotional development of children, products such as greeting cards and postcards can be produced and presented to others with uniqueness and creativity (Fig. 4).

Designed for foreign students is a bookmark. The pattern on the bookmark is in the form of ink painting, which is used to express Chinese color and ethnic representation. Providing a strong regional cues for foreigners also consolidates the influence of traditional culture (Fig. 5).

The design logic of the project is divided into three parts, namely online AR display, online APP interaction and joint interaction. In each part, the corresponding content design is done. For example, online AR display is a design that uses cards for augmented reality experience; online APP interaction is designed for three different levels of participants, namely primary participation, progressive participation and deepen participation; joint interaction is to increase the user's social sharing and attract more potential users to participate (Fig. 6).

The user usage scenarios for teens are broken down into three: classrooms, interclasses, and families. In the classroom learning is the primary form of penetration, the main function is entertainment; the learning in the inter-class is a progressive level of

Fig. 2. Interface illustration

Fig. 3. Learning card for primary school students

Fig. 4. Learning card for foreign students

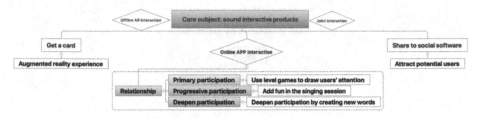

Fig. 5. Design logic diagram

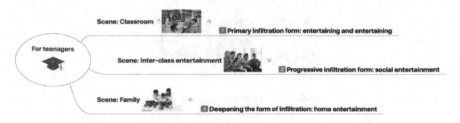

Fig. 6. Use scene and form diagram—for teenagers

penetration, the main function is social; the learning in the family is deep learning, the main function is to promote the family Integration of entertainment and learning. In this process, children are passively aware of active proximity and integration into life. This is a benign progression (Fig. 7).

Fig. 7. Use scene and form diagram—for international friends

There are also three user usage scenarios for international friends: Cantonese classes, Chinese and foreign exchange students, and interest learning. Learning in Cantonese classrooms is primary infiltration, progressive infiltration is the participation of recreational activities, and deeper penetration is self-study (Fig. 8).

The usage scenarios for potential users are mainly based on the sharing and attraction of social platforms, expanding the scope of contacts to attract potential users, and allowing potential users to learn independently.

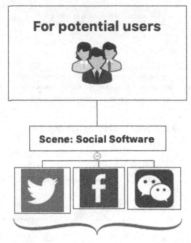

Fig. 8. Use scene and form diagram—for potential use

2 Conclusion

The purpose of this project is to visualize the voice of the nation through modern new technologies, and introduce the Chinese elements with traditional cultural colors into the development of the new era. In the process of design, we will carefully consider the needs of different levels and carefully divide them. Give the best possible communication to traditional culture as much as possible.

Improving Mobile Gaming Experience with User Status Detect System

Shieh-chieh Liao[1,2]($\boxtimes$), Fong-Gong Wu[1], and Shu-Hsuan Feng[2]

[1] National Cheng Kung University, No. 1, University Road,
Tainan City 701, Taiwan (R.O.C.)
P38041083@ncku.edu.tw
[2] Southern Taiwan University of Science and Technology, No. 1,
Nan-Tai Street, Yungkang District, Tainan City 710, Taiwan (R.O.C.)

Abstract. As the technology progresses, many of the popular personal computer games are ported to mobile platforms. Those games features complex and precise control method compare to those found on smart phones, this difference leads to more difficult control on those mobile ports and highly affects the users' experience. This research attempts to introduce a new way for users to interact with their mobile devices and improve their gaming experience. Using the gyroscope and camera found on the smart phones, the new user status detect system can collect the users and their devices' current condition (including the users' posture, body movement, and the distance and angle to their devices) and use those data to predict what the users are going to do, showing the interface before the users directly touching the screen, avoiding the problem that users' thumb obscuring often their vision.

Keywords: User-interface · User status · Mobile games

1 Introduction

With the advances in technology, the price of smart phones has been decreasing year by year, paired with the increasing popularity of mobile networks and mobile games, the spread of smart phones and player base of mobile games has increased exponentially. In recent years, mobile games are become more and more complex and have more functions than ever before, which requires more virtual buttons and clutter the screen, making the game difficult to control and obscure vision, resulting the readability being over 50% lower on a mobile display than on a desktop display [1].

Since the announce of smart phones back in 2008, the functions which smart phones provide have evolved greatly, but the user interface has not changed in significant way other than aesthetic. In recent years, many of the flagship smart phones even replace their physical buttons with virtual ones, making the screen cluttering problem worse than ever.

Motion detection is usually used as a direct game control method found in driving games and simulation games, but there is little usage of motion detect and status detect in action games. In this study, we will focus on using motion detect feature found in

© Springer Nature Switzerland AG 2019
C. Stephanidis (Ed.): HCII 2019, CCIS 1033, pp. 31–36, 2019.
https://doi.org/10.1007/978-3-030-23528-4_5

smart phones to let users interact with the user interface and improve their gaming experience.

In the introduction chapter, the theoretical notions and foundations of this research will be explained. including:

1. Current Use of Motion Detection in Mobile Gaming
2. Competitive Mobile Gaming
3. User Status Detect System

1.1   Current Use of Motion Detection in Mobile Gaming

Due to the limited screen space found on smart phones, many of the mobile games use motion control as their primary way of input. Though these games uses motion control to their advantages, making the game more immersive and easy to play [2], this control method also limits the number of actions user can perform, results in most of the games utilizing this control method being simpler games which don't require precise control.

1.2   Competitive Mobile Gaming

In recent years, esports is becoming a growing market. Having more players, more spectators and sponsors than ever. With mobile games being one of the largest division in video game market, many of the competitive games are ported to mobile platforms, results in mobile gaming being a part of esports now. [3]

With these many esports players and professional players, a lot of companies have make their effort designing peripherals to improve the control of mobile gaming, such as additional on-screen joysticks and buttons, some companies even developed gaming oriented smart phones to suit the market and help those high level gamers get an edge on their games.

1.3   User Status Detect System

We have found that in a long period of game session, users will maintain similar operating postures in order to have a comfortable gaming experience, and these postures have many common points between different platforms and different users; We have also found that some users will perform similar limb movements when performing certain functions, such as lifting the hand slightly and make their faces closer to the screen.

Using gyroscope and cameras found on modern smart phones, we are able to observe the users' current status with their devices including the distance between the user and screen, the device's position, and angle of the user holding the device, the user's posture and the way the user is holding the device. With these data, the system can interpret what the user is going to do, and perform the action before the user touches the screen (Fig. 1).

Fig. 1. Screen cluttering is a serious problem in mobile gaming.

2   Backgrounds

Since the advent of the first iPhone, smart phones have become an inseparable part of our daily life. With the help of more affordable smart phones hitting the market one after another, there is over 2.5 billion smart phones user around the globe, meaning that over third of the world's population owns a smart phone. A recent study done in Taiwan shows that over 51% of the population in Taiwan spend 2 to 5 h interacting with their smart phone, and over 28% of the users spend over 5 h every single day [4]. With these many users boosting the popularity of mobile networks and mobile games, many of the household names in game industry such as Blizzard shift their attention to mobile games development, some companies are even porting popular computer games directly to mobile platforms, making these new mobile games more complex then ever. In the beginning, mobile games mostly make use of motion control as their main way of input due to their more simple nature, but in order to access to those many complex functions, those ported mobile games mimics the control scheme on the computer with virtual buttons, making the screen clutter up with those virtual buttons, obscuring the user's vision.

2.1   Motion Control in Video Games

Playing video game with the player's own body is a concept that developers have been trying to achieve for years. But until Nintendo's Wii debut in 2006, they are always considered a gimmick. Nintendo's console provide an affordable package with accurate and easy control scheme suited for family-oriented users [5].

After the Wii's success, other big names in gaming industry soon follow up with their own take on motion control. Though most of these products end up with mixed results due to many problem such as lack of accuracy and quality game. The most unique one is Xbox's Kinect, which features a control method that doesn't require any controller.

2.2 Touch Screen and Gyroscope

Since the first smart phone hit the market, touch screen and gyroscope have been a staple for these devices. Game developers soon realize what they can achieve in game design with these functions built in the phone already, especially racing games and puzzle games [2]. As a result, many mobile games features unique control method and a unique system designed around it, differentiate them from conventional video games.

2.3 Mobile Ports of PC Games

As the technology continuously improves, mobile phones are becoming more capable than ever. With this power, developers started to port popular PC games to mobile platforms. Those games features slightly modified and simplified features found on their PC counterparts, but the lack of physical buttons means that users can only control their game with virtual buttons on screen, which is often not the optimal way to enjoy the game.

3 Materials and Method

3.1 Participants

We chose college students as our participants, since they are right in the target demographic of mobile games users. The requirements for participants are as below: fluent in Chinese, being 18 to 30 years of age, having played at least 3 mobile games in recent 6 month and having over 3 years of experience in action shooter genre games, gender is not restricted. Initially, 18 participants joined the experiment, 2 of them were excluded from the experiment due to the lack of experience in action shooter genre games, making the participant number 16.

3.2 System Structure

The user status detect system utilize gyroscope and front-facing camera to analyze the user's current status. The gyroscope provides data such as the position of the device, the angle user is holding the device and device's movement. With the help of True-Depth front-facing camera found on iPhone X, we can not only measure the distance between device and user but can also detect the user's facial expressions to let user further customize his or her experience.

3.3 Materials

For this experiment, we developed a prototype test environment based on one of the most popular mobile action shooter game "Player Unknown's Battle Grounds Mobile" [6], which has over 200 million current users. Participants will have to complete a few challenges including collecting items, examining map, aiming weapon and peeking corner. In order to utilize TrueDepth front-facing camera and maintain the consistency of experiment, all the participants will be using iPhone X exclusively.

During the experiment, we will use eye tracking device to monitor participant's vision, monitor participant's body motion with video camera and web cams to capture the changes in participant's face expression.

3.4 Procedures

The experiment will be conducted in the laboratory, and will be a 3 h procedure, all participants will be using iPhone X as their test device. In the beginning, participants will be requested to create an account for the experimenters' online testing system, and the demographic questionnaires will be distributed. After registration procedure, participants will be introduced to the functions this user status system provides and the testing program. In the experiment phase, participants are asked to finish specific actions in the testing program to represent the change in using user status detect system during gameplay session. After the participants finished all the requested tasks, the experiment ended and participants are required to finish a posttest questionnaire asking them about their experience with the system.

4 Results

In this study, we found that using both front-facing camera and gyroscope to detect user's status and utilize these data to reduce direct hand control in mobile gaming session can greatly improve user's gaming experience. In the posttest questionnaire, we found that over 80% off the participants agree that user status detect system provides a more pleasant gaming experience, but some participants have addressed that this method is not intuitive enough for them to grasp at a glance (Table 1).

Table 1. Posttest questionnaire summary

Posttest Questionnaire Summary
Number of Entry : 16

Question 1: Does User Status Detect System provide you a more pleasant user experience?

YES	13
NO	3

Question 2: Do you find playing mobile games with User Status Detect System more intuitive?

YES	10
NO	6

Question 3: How comfortable do you feel when playing a game with User Status Detect System?

1(Very Uncomfortable)	0
2	1
3	8
4	6
5(Very Comfortable)	1

5 Conclusion

The result of this study shows that using user status detect system to support traditional mobile game control method greatly improve user's gaming experience. This system doesn't require users making complex and specific gesture which may be inconvenient in many mobile gaming session and reducing the dependence of direct hand control, with a bit of practice, the users can quickly access many typically hard to reach features with ease.

Because of limited time and resource, we only have 16 legitimate subjects. In future research, to further improve the scope, including more test subject will be our first priority. Other than that, the system itself still have space for improvement, some of the participants addressed that while in the experiment, they accidentally triggered some unwanted function at the wrong time due to their head movement or change of posture, which can be annoying when playing games. In the next iteration, compensating the changes in user's posture will be our focus.

References

1. Rauch, M.: Mobile documentation: usability guidelines, and considerations for providing documentation on Kindle, tablets, and smartphones. In: IEEE International Professional Communication Conference (2011)
2. Gilbertson, P., Coulton, P., Chehimi, F., Vajk, T.: Using "tilt" as an interface to control "no-button" 3-D mobile games. Comput. Entertain. 6(38), 1–13 (2008)
3. Mitchell, F.: Esports Essentials: Mobile Esports are Here to Stay. The Sports Observer (2018)
4. Tien-Tse, C.: 2017 Taiwan Broadband Network Usage Survey Report. Taiwan Network Information Center (2017)
5. Andrews, S.: Is this the Rebirth of Motion Controls? Trusted Reviews (2018)
6. Shepherd, H.: Fortnite vs. PUBG: Player Count, Map, Weapons – Which is Better? PCGamesN (2019)

Freedom in Video Game Dialog: An Improvement on Player Immersion

Christopher J. Martinez[✉] and Matthew Ciarletto

University of New Haven, West Haven, CT 06516, USA
cmartinez@newhaven.edu

Abstract. Video game dialog generally consist of giving a player a few scripted options to choose from at an interaction point in the game. Allowing players to enter their own dialog can enhance player immersion. There is difficultly in allowing for natural language to drive the narrative of a game. Conceptual dependency theory, which gives a simple representation of natural language that is independent of its original syntactic representation, makes it easy to represent multiple semantically-similar sentences in the same way. Using this theory, a dialog engine was designed to allow game developers to write a small set of rules on player input for every interaction to determine an appropriate response.

Keywords: Video game narrative · Story dialog ·
Conceptual dependency theory · Natural language processing · HCI

1 Introduction

Player immersion is an important factor in the enjoyment of a video game [1]. While much progress has been made in visual and audio immersion, relatively little has been done to improve player immersion through dialog. Currently, in most games, an interaction with an non-playable character (NPC) consists of choosing from a small set of predetermined dialog options, some of which the player may not have thought to say on their own. The scripted dialog is a hindrance in two ways:

1. It removes the player from the immersion by minimizing the control they have over the character during a dialog interaction with an NPC.
2. It may prompt the player with a solution to a puzzle before the player has had sufficient opportunity to solve the puzzle intellectually.

One of the most notable video games using natural language processing is Façade [2], which allows the player to type their own dialog. This game focuses significantly on tone, which may not be suitable for a dialog engine intended to be applicable to a wider variety of games genres. The work done in this paper looks at how to expand natural language processing (NPL) to be used in any genre of video games.

© Springer Nature Switzerland AG 2019
C. Stephanidis (Ed.): HCII 2019, CCIS 1033, pp. 37–44, 2019.
https://doi.org/10.1007/978-3-030-23528-4_6

2 Past Work

In Dubbelman's paper, *Designing Stories: Practices of Narrative in 3D Computer Games*, two narrative structures are presented: *representation* and *presentation* [1]. A representational narrative structure entails recounting a story as something that happened in the past, as in a typical Charles Dickens or Jane Austen novel. The distinctive presence of a narrator facilitates this representational tone. The narrator's description allows for the player to feel immerse in the video game world.

A presentational narrative structure the audience is made to feel present in the story. Examples of this include live action role-playing, augmented reality, and reenactments. The audience becomes "embodied participants." The presentational narrative can have a player feel immerse by having a realistic dialog structure which we hope to address in this paper.

The Augmented Conversation Engine

Chris Swain discusses video game dialog through the Augmented Conversation Engine (ACE) that allows a player a great deal more freedom when interacting with NPCs [3]. It addresses a major challenge facing player immersion. Video games limit the player to a fix number of verbs: run, jump, throw, etc. Swain argues that to feel more immersive, the player should feel a greater degree of control over the character than is currently the standard.

The Sims achieves a wide verb variety by associating a set of actions with each object. The game designers bypassed NPL by implementing a nonsense language called Simlish. This avoided the difficulties associated with implementing NPL.

The designers set out to accomplish three goals in the creation of ACE:

- To provide a set of verbs to choose from so broad that it feels unlimited.
- All choices should lead to a scripted, relevant response for the NPC in order to avoid AI or parser difficulties.
- All verb choices should have an impact on the game state, moving toward or away from a goal.

The intention was to make the purpose of any given interaction clear to the player. The ACE still functions by making the player choose from such a predetermined list, and while it is an improvement over the typical four-choice style dialog implemented by many games, the freedom it provides is still limited in the same way.

For a given verb choice, the NPC has a set of twelve scripted responses. The responses are laid out in a matrix, with four degrees consisting of the level of trust between the player and the NPC and three degrees being based on chance, as the example in Fig. 1. Each interaction the player encounters is different depending on the current trust level and chance involve. The player feels that interaction is unlimited and feels more immerse in the game play.

	Chance 1 - 5	Chance 6 - 10	Chance 11-15	Chance 16+
Trust -3-0	"You maybe able to enter via the sewer."	"The sewer entrance was destroyed."	"I don't know anything."	"I wish I could trust you."
Trust 1-5	"Its not appropriate to ask about such things."	"What makes you think its not a food processing plant?"	"I'm impressed you know about the curse."	"Stay away from it because of the curse."
Trust 6+	"Let us talk about other things."	"One day I'll tell you."	"Theres a curse on the plant so stay away."	"Theres a hidden entrance by the river."

Fig. 1. ACE matrix

Discourse Act Rule	Meaning
DAAgree ?char	Agree with character
DADisagree ?char	Disagree with character
DAExpress ?char ?type	Express an emotion
DACriticize ?char ?level	Give a character light or harsh criticism
DAExplain ?param ?char	Explain a situation to a character

Fig. 2. Façade discourse acts. ?param refers to potential parameter and ?char refers to a potential character.

Inner Workings of Facade

Façade [2] handles NLP in a manner befitting a single domain. The designers divided the interpretation of NPL into two phases:

- Phase 1 maps surface text into discourse acts representing the pragmatic effects of an utterance.
- Phase 2 maps discourse acts into one or more (joint) character responses.

The NLP for this game is geared towards a dramatic nature. It uses discourse acts, such as agreeing with a character or opposing a character, to change the game state. Samples of discourse act rules and their meanings are described in Fig. 2.

In mapping input to the discourse acts a wide variety of potential input sentences are mapped to a small number of discourse acts. To perform the mapping, templates that consist of logical rules applied to combinations of specific words are used. For instance, "love" followed by "it," "that" or "to" will assert an *iAgree* fact. A fact is an intermediary between the raw input and a discourse act. Multiple facts are combined to compose a discourse act. In this example, the *iAgree* fact can be combined with another fact indicating a character, which can be null, to form the discourse act *DAAgree*. To form the intermediate facts, the logical rules in Fig. 3 are applied to combinations of words.

In creating Facade, the writers had to write ~800 template rules. They were surprised with the robustness rules set, and found that the game does in fact guide the player to use whatever language fits a given situation. In that way, the writers successfully implemented a NPL dialog interface in place of the traditional scripted dialog options while maintaining two crucial features:

- the set of rules was simple enough to be practical to implement in a real game, as contrasted by the difficulty of creating a NPL interface capable of human-like reasoning [4]; and
- the implementation is simple and efficient enough to run on any typical video game computer.

The Façade NPL implementation works well for a tone-based interpretation but would not be appropriate as a universal dialog engine.

Primitive	Meaning
ATRANS	Transfer of possession, ownership or control
PTRANS	Transfer of physical location of an object
PROPEL	Application of a physical force to an object
MTRANS	Transfer of information between agents or within an agent
MBUILD	Construction of a thought or of new information by an agent
INGEST	Taking in of an object by an animal
GRASP	To grasp an object
ATTEND	To focus a sense organ on an object
SPEAK	To make noise
MOVE	Movement of an agent's own body part
EXPEL	To push an object out of an agent's own body

X and Y: matches an input string in which X is followed by Y
X or Y: matches an input string containing X or Y
[X]: matches an input string containing X or nothing
Match all: matches any quantity of words
Match one: matches any one word
Template And X Y: matches template X followed by Y
Template Or X Y: matches template X or Y
Template Occurrence X: matches if X occurs
Template not X: matches if X doesn't occur

Fig. 3. Façade intermediate facts logical rules examples

Fig. 4. Conceptual dependency primitives and meanings

3   Conceptual Dependency

Conceptual dependency theory is an idea developed that serves to represent natural language in a format independent of syntactic representation or diction [5–7]. Rather than represent any given sentence, the purpose of conceptual dependency is to represent the meaning that underlies the sentence. This theory is based around two core assumptions:

- Two sentences that have the same meaning should be represented in the same way; and
- Any information that is implied should be explicitly expressed in its representation.

The first assumption concludes that the representation is general: words with the same meaning are represented in the same way, such as *get* and *receive* in many contexts. The second assumption implies that the representation supports inferences, and supports inference rules so that the same inferences can be made consistently and systematically. Accordingly, the foundation of conceptual dependency consists of the following components: (1) **Primitives** that represent actions, (2) **States** used to represent environmental conditions before and as a result of actions, and (3) **Dependencies** that are potential relationships between primitives, states, and objects.

A primitive is a general representation of an action to which many verbs can apply. The primitives in Fig. 4 can represent most actions. The primitives have different *slots*, or conceptually interdependent pieces of information. For instance, in PTRANS, these slots are as follows: (1) ACTOR: The initiator of the PTRANS, (2) OBJECT: The object being PTRANSed, (3) FROM: The starting location of the OBJECT, and (4) TO: The ending location of the OBJECT.

The major inference at play in PTRANS is that the object moves from a starting location to an ending location. This is true for any type of PTRANS, whether it be flying, running, jumping, buying, etc. Other primitives have different slots and corresponding implications.

4 Dialog Engine Design

In creating a system that allows NPL input the design shall meet the following criteria:

1. An NPC shall be able to process any short, one-sentence NPL meaningfully, minimizing the frequency that an NPC may give a response that doesn't fit the player's dialog entry.
2. NPC responses shall guide the player along the plot of the game and avoid tangential conversation.
3. Player input shall cause appropriate changes to the game state.
4. It shall be easy and simple for game developers to interface with and implement the dialog engine.
5. The engine shall be simple, running with minimal memory and processor requirements in order to make it technologically feasible to implement.

Designing a dialog system that could account for all possible language input is infeasible with set resources and impractical in terms of human effort.

The simplest way to allow the player input to progress the game state would be to search for keywords. If the player says one specific word such as "digging" then the NPC gives a scripted response and the game progresses. However, this could lead to NPC responses that don't fit the semantics of the player's input as a whole.

Conceptual dependency theory breaks a sentence down according to a set of **primitives** (generalizations of verbs). For example, ATRANS represents a transfer of possession described by verbs such as "give," "take," "sells," etc. The remaining parts of the sentence are **slots**, which may include locations, an object, or even another conceptualization. By restructuring natural language according to conceptual dependency theory, many input sentences can yield the exact same representation.

By establishing rules for the conceptual dependency representation rather than a set of keywords, a few rules can appropriately process a large number of potential input sentences leading to a robust dialog system. To allow the dialog engine to progress the game state, it must account for variables and flags so that dialog output can follow various paths according to the game state.

A problem with the use of conceptual dependency theory is its dependence on accurate interpretation of the pivotal verb in an input sentence, since the verb determines the ACT. An idealistic solution would be to programmatically account for every possible verb. The best tradeoff is to use a thesaurus to account for uncategorized verbs.

In order to allow game designers complete decisive control over how to determine the appropriate output, each element of the conceptual dependency representation can be tested with game state variables. For example, the designers can test whether the primitive is MTRANS, the object is "book," the starting location is "you" and the ending location is "me," or simply if the object is "book." In testing the conditions of the input representation and the game state, conditions can be tested and combined using common logical operators. Additionally, conditions can be nested.

5 Implementation

For demonstrative purposes, Java code was written to implement core dependency theory. First, Stanford NLP was used to convert player input into a dependency tree. For example, the input "Give me the book" yields:

$\rightarrow$ Give/VB (root)
$\rightarrow$ me/PRP (iobj)
$\rightarrow$ book/NN (dobj)
$\rightarrow$ the/DT (det).

Then, the dependency tree is searched to find the ACT at play. In this example, "give" is the verb. Analytically, it can be seen that this is an instance of PTRANS. If "give" were not in the list of precategorized verbs, thesaurus entries would have been searched until the nearest categorized verb were found, and its ACT would be used as the ACT for "give."

PTRANS implies the transfer of an object's location. So, the following slots must be filled: (1) Starting Location, (2) Ending Location and (3) Object.

The direct object is "book," so it is stored as the Object. Since "me" is the indirect object, it is stored as the Ending Location. The Starting Location has not been found since it does not exist in the input sentence. We can safely assume that the Starting Location refers to the NPC, and so that information is stored in Starting Location.

Then, the engine has completed the construction of the conceptual dependency representation. Control can then go to the code to test the input and determine the appropriate output. The conceptual categories and their corresponding slots are described in Fig. 5. For each of these primitive ACTs, the engine searches for the words that correspond to the relevant slots in the conceptual dependency representation and stores them accordingly.

The process of forming a conceptual dependency representation of a sentence given a dependency tree is as follows: (1) Find the root verb, (2) Determine the corresponding primitive, (3) Iteratively assign the other words from the input to the appropriate slots and (4) Replace pronouns and other references with their literal meanings, such as "him" with an actual name.

Some verbs may apply to multiple primitives. In such a case, the presence or absence of words to assign to the slots of each primitive serve to indicate which primitive matches the semantic intent of the input. For example, "tell" can fall under the SPEAK or the MTRANS primitives. However, the differences between "I talked to him" and "I told him about the plan" make the distinction clear: the latter refers to an indirect object, the "plan," and so it falls under the MTRANS category. The former, which lacks any word to fit in that slot, cannot be an instance of MTRANS and is therefore an instance of SPEAK.

Figure 6 shows example of inputs being transform into a conceptual dependency representation. Additionally, pronouns are implicitly converted to absolute references: the engine uses the most recent Object and Subject, Starting Location, Ending Location, and Agent from previous sentences to resolve pronouns to the nouns they represent. To accomplish this, each respective slot is stored persistently and updated with each dialog, regardless of whether it is input or output. So, output must be run through the dialog engine in addition to input.

Primitive	Slots
ATRANS	Object, Starting Location, Ending Location
PTRANS	Object, Starting Location, Ending Location
PROPEL	Subject, Object
MTRANS	Object, Starting Location, Ending Location
MBUILD	Agent, Conceptualization
INGEST	Subject, Object
GRASP	Subject, Object
ATTEND	Subject, Object
SPEAK	Subject, Object, Ending Location
MOVE	Subject, Object
EXPEL	Subject, Object

Fig. 5. Primitive ACTs and their corresponding slots

"He went to Iceland."
-> went/VBD (root)
-> He/PRP (nsubj)
-> Iceland/NNP (prep_to)
Primitive: PTRANS
Start: ?, End: Iceland, Object: He

"Tell me about Plato's Lost Dialogue."
-> Tell/VB (root)
-> me/PRP (dobj)
-> Dialogue/NNP (prep_about)
-> Plato/NNP (poss)
-> Lost/NNP (nn)
Primitive: MTRANS
Start: You, End: Me, Object: Plato's Lost Dialogue

"I learned how to tie my shoes."
-> learned/VBd (root)
-> I/PRP (nsubj)
-> tie/VB (ccomp)
-> how/WRB (advmod)
-> to/TO (aux)
-> shoes/NNS (dobj)
-> my/PRP$ (poss)
Primitive: MBUILD
Agent: I, Conceptualization: How to tie my shoes

Fig. 6. Examples of dialog in a conceptual dependency representation

6 Conclusion

In this paper, we have presented a mechanism for creating a video game dialog engine that allows free response by the player through natural language. The conceptual dependency representation allows for a simple deconstruction of an input sentence that can progress the game narrative forward. In the future, a dialog engine will be created to show how a game can use our dialog engine design for better user immersion.

References

1. Dubbelman, T., Designing stories. Practices of narrative in 3D computer games. In: Proceeding of the 2011 ACM SIGGRAPH Symposium on Video Games. Vancouver, pp. 37–41. ACM, August 2011
2. Procedural Arts: Façade. Procedural Arts (2005)
3. Swain, C.: The augmented conversation engine. In: International Conference on Advances in Computer Entertainment Technology, pp. 213–218. ACM, New York, December 2008
4. Turing, A.: Computing machinery and intelligence. Mind **49**, 433–460 (1950)
5. Schank, R.: The Cognitive Computer: On Language, Learning, and Artificial Intelligence. Addison-Wesley Publishing Company, Boston (1984)
6. Lytinen, S.L.: Conceptual dependency and its descendants. Comput. Math. Appl. **23**(2–5), 51–73 (1992)
7. Shank, R.C., Tesler, L.: A conceptual dependency parser for natural language. In: International Conference on Computational Linguistics (1969)

Combining Personality and Physiology to Investigate the Flow Experience in Virtual Reality Games

Lazaros Michailidis[1,2], Jesus Lucas Barcias[2], Fred Charles[1],
Xun He[1(✉)], and Emili Balaguer-Ballester[1(✉)]

[1] Bournemouth University, Bournemouth, UK
{lmichailidis, fcharles, xhe,
eb-ballester}@bournemouth.ac.uk
[2] Sony Interactive Entertainment, London, UK
Jesus.Lucas.Barcias@sony.com

Abstract. Immersive experiences are typically considered an indicator of successful game design. The ability to maintain the player's focus and enjoyment in the game lies at the core of game mechanics. In this work, we used a custom virtual reality game aiming to induce flow, boredom and anxiety throughout specific instances in the game. We used self-reports of personality and flow in addition to physiological measures (heart rate variability) as a means of evaluating the game design. Results yielded a consistently high accuracy in the classification of low flow versus high flow conditions across multiple classifiers. Moreover, they suggested that the anticipated model-by-design was not necessarily consistent with the player's subjective and objective data. Our approach lays promising groundwork for the automatic assessment of game design strategies and may help explain experiential variability across video game players.

Keywords: Flow · Immersion · Virtual reality · HRV · Game design · Tower Defense · Classification

1 Introduction

The experience of flow in video games has attracted considerable interest in recent years. Flow is a multi-faceted construct that emerges under sufficient challenge and it is characterized by intense concentration. Video game players often experience loss of time perception, loss of self-reflective thoughts, and a merging of action and awareness, during which their actions feel as being automatic [1]. Research has shown that flow's onset may be facilitated by personality traits [2, 3]. For example, agreeableness, conscientiousness, extraversion and openness have been positively linked to flow, due to their connection to well-being, social desirability and active lifestyle [4]. However, neuroticism has been found to have a negative relationship with flow [2, 4, 5], as it relates to a tendency in experiencing anxiety and negative emotions [6], both being counterproductive to flow.

© Springer Nature Switzerland AG 2019
C. Stephanidis (Ed.): HCII 2019, CCIS 1033, pp. 45–52, 2019.
https://doi.org/10.1007/978-3-030-23528-4_7

Flow is regarded as a highly desirable experience in video games and it is well documented that individuals are much more likely to replay a game during which they experienced flow [7]. Hence, it is a state highly sought by game designers [8]. In this work, we evaluated game design choices by classifying the physiological changes across a game session in response to challenge modifications. Results suggest that game design strategies could be improved with the approach proposed in this work.

2   Background

2.1   Influencing Flow Through Game Design

The flow experience is concededly an assortment of criteria [1]. Previous theoretical models attempted to cluster them into three ancillary categories, thereby separating them into preconditions, dimensions and outcomes of flow [9]. Hence, to influence the flow experience experimentally, one would have to turn to the preconditions, which precede the experience. The most common way of accomplishing this is by modifying the difficulty of the game, which results in a balance or discrepancy between the game's demands and the player's skills [10]. When such a balance is introduced, players are more likely to experience flow, whereas an incompatibility thereof may engender boredom (low challenge) or anxiety (high challenge) [1, 10]. Adaptive gameplay can elicit compelling experiences, regardless of the player's expertise, and it is perceived as more immersive compared to gameplay with predefined difficulty settings [11].

2.2   Flow and Heart Rate Variability (HRV)

Although there is considerable evidence in the physiological correlates of flow, evaluating game design, based on the flow experience, remains mostly unexplored [12]. Heart rate variability (HRV) is a conglomerate of statistical measures that aim to identify the differences between successive heartbeats as a function of time [13]. The raw signal of electrocardiography (ECG) is decomposed into the R-wave peaks, where an inter-beat interval (IBI) marks the time difference between a pair of consecutive R-Rs. These beats are also expressed as N-N or *Normal* beats, signifying that abnormal occurrences (e.g., ectopic beats) have been corrected [14].

Flow has been shown to present differential physiological patterns compared to anxiety and boredom. The relationship of the three states, with respect to sympathetic arousal, appears to be curvilinear, where flow hovers at the peak of an inverted U shape; low arousal indicates boredom and high arousal indicates anxiety [15]. Typically, heart rate increases in proportion to the difficulty of the game [16], with flow being associated with reduced HRV, allegedly as a result of mental load [15, 17].

3 Methods

3.1 Participants

Twenty-nine volunteers took part in the study (mean age = 31.5, SD = 7.0), all of who were employees in Sony Interactive Entertainment in London, United Kingdom. The sample comprised 19 males and 10 females with an average video games experience of 19.5 years (SD = 8.7). The study was approved by the Bournemouth University Research Ethics Committee (ref: 17333).

3.2 Materials

Data Collection. Electrocardiography recordings were obtained with BIOPAC BSL MP45 (BIOPAC Systems Inc., California, USA), using the proprietary software Student Lab 4.0. The data were acquired at a sampling rate of 1 kHz and the placement of the electrodes followed Einthoven's triangle principle in a LEAD I configuration [18]. The ground electrode was attached on top of the right ankle, the positive electrode on the left wrist and the negative on the right wrist. The data were imported into MATLAB R2018a (The MathWorks Inc., Natick, USA) for trial segmentation and analysis. In addition to the physiological data, two self-reports were used: the Dispositional Flow State Scale (DFS-2) [19] for flow and the Big Five Inventory (BFI) [20] for personality.

Game Stimulus. A Tower Defense (TD) virtual reality (VR) game for PlayStation VR[1] was developed in Unity 3D 2017.3.1p2 (Unity Technologies, San Francisco, CA). Tower Defense has been deemed a reliable genre for research [21]. A typical TD game features waves of enemies who spawn at a fixed rate. The enemies move along a path, from a starting point towards an exit, and the player's goal is to prevent as many of the enemies escaping as possible. To achieve this, the player can build towers, which automatically attack any enemy in proximity. Each new enemy wave is stronger than its preceding wave; hence, the towers can be upgraded into stronger types.

The game comprised 30 rounds (trials) grouped into three consecutive blocks with an overall average duration of 28.77 min (SD = 0.35 min). Each block included rounds designed to induce flow, anxiety and boredom (ordered as mentioned). The experimental variables were the health of the enemy units as well as the currency reward magnitude bestowed whenever the player eliminated an enemy. Reward manipulation served to hinder or to facilitate game progression and by extension player performance, thus adding to the perceived difficulty of the game.

---

[1] Disclaimer: The game used in this study was developed for the purpose of the study alone and is not intended for commercial release.

Flow-designed rounds featured an adaptive difficulty scaling mechanism that was inspired from earlier work in TD games [22]. The ratio of enemies escaping over enemies originally spawned was indexed through a predefined table of ratio ranges (e.g., {0.4–0.6}). The lower the ratio, the higher the difficulty of the next round and the lower the reward bonus. Conversely, the higher the ratio, the lower the difficulty of the succeeding round and the higher the reward bonus. On the other hand, anxiety and boredom round-types featured bosses. Unbeknownst to the player, those enemies were programmatically modified to be invincible. The bosses first appeared very early in the game (rounds 4 and 5), but they were vulnerable and easily eliminated. This was done to prevent players from apprehending the experimental manipulation at later stages of the game. Anxiety rounds featured a fast-moving boss with a high reward promised, whereas boredom rounds featured a slow-moving boss with very high health, but a low reward in return. Anxiety and boredom rounds were repeated three times in a row. Fleeing bosses did not precipitate difficulty adjustment for subsequent rounds – only flow rounds did.

3.3 Procedure

Participants were first asked to sign a consent form, informing them about the purpose of the study and their right to withdraw from the study at any point. The BFI was filled out and then a training stage to help familiarization with the controls of and the game. Once they reported confidence with handling the game, a resting baseline was recorded for one minute. Participants then played the full game and finally filled out the DFS-2 questionnaire.

3.4 Preprocessing

The raw ECG data were exported from Student Lab 4.0 and converted into MATLAB-compatible files. Date-time stamps from a text file created during the game were used to demarcate the beginning and end of each round, as well as the beginning and end of the game. These data were used to segment the continuous ECG signal into 30 data structures (as many as the trials). Further, each round was segmented into five epochs. The raw data were then processed using an algorithm proposed by Pan and Tompkins [23], which has been implemented in MATLAB and is publicly available [24]. The resulting data are inter-beat intervals (IBI), which were examined for ectopic beats using a threshold of 0.2, i.e. intervals changing by more than 20% of the previous [25].

HRV metrics comprised seven time-domain measurements[2], calculated for each epoch: mean IBI (ms), minimum IBI (ms), maximum IBI (ms), SDNN (ms), mean HR (count/min), pNN50 (%) and RMSSD (ms). Features comprised {28 participants × 30

---

[2] SDNN: Standard deviation of NN. HR: Heart Rate. pNN50: The percentage of adjacent NNs that have a distance of more than 50 ms. RMSSD: The root mean square of successive NNs. For a review, see [14].

trials × 5 windows} samples. Each row of features was first subtracted from the resting baseline of the corresponding participant [26]. All features were scaled by the sum of the personality traits of agreeableness, extraversion, conscientiousness and openness and then subtracted from neuroticism scores. All data were standardized using z-score transformation, in order to control for personality scaling and inter-feature numerical dominance, and provided the input to three standard classifiers separately – Support Vector Machine (SVM), CART Decision Tree (CART DT) and k-Nearest Neighbors (kNN). Among radial basis function (RBF), polynomial and linear kernels, RBF performed better in SVM. K-Nearest Neighbors classifier was trained using three nearest neighboring points and Euclidean distance metric. The trained and cross-validated model was then used to predict high-flow/low-flow binary categories for each game window (150 in total) on a different test dataset consisting of one participant not previously used during cross-validation. This enables the approach to provide a more realistic insight on how flow varied throughout the game.

4   Results

The self-report data were originally divided into low- and high-flow groups, based on the overall flow score obtained from the DFS-2, using k-means clustering with squared Euclidean as a distance metric. The low-flow group had an average flow score of 28.14 (45 being the maximum mean score) and $SD = 2.1$. The high-flow group had an average flow score of 34.93 and $SD = 2.14$. The clustered group indices were used as ground truth for the data classification. Rank analysis of covariance [27] showed that the low-flow group presented increased HRV compared to the high-flow group; all features were significantly higher in the low-flow group ($p < .01$), when pre-trial baseline was added to the model as a covariate. Conversely, the mean inter-beat intervals presented the opposite trend of heart rate ($p < .01$), as expected.

Leaving one participant out, SVM, CART DT and kNN were trained and then 10-fold cross-validated. The classifiers were able to discriminate between the low-flow and high-flow groups with a mean comparable accuracy of 94.3%, 93.6% and 95.4% respectively. The area under the receiver operating characteristic curve was AUC = 0.997, 0.999 and 0.998 respectively, indicating a nearly perfect prediction in all cases. This high accuracy suggests that the approach could be used to assess the physiological underpinnings of the original game design. Next, as a proof of feasibility, the optimal classifiers were applied to the test dataset from the left-out participant. As an example, predicted categories (crosses) compared with the original game design categories (squares) during the course of the game are shown in Fig. 1.

The plots show that the predicted categories present some overlap (squares and crosses of matching color) with the hypothesized categories in game windows wherein the flow experience was to be attenuated or accentuated. CART DT was proportionally the closest to the proportion of flow rounds in the original design. Predicted high-flow windows (black crosses) constituted 51.3% against 53.3% flow windows initially set by design. However, the timing of the predicted states was not always consistent with the timing they were designed to be elicited. These preliminary observations will be investigated in detail in future studies using larger datasets.

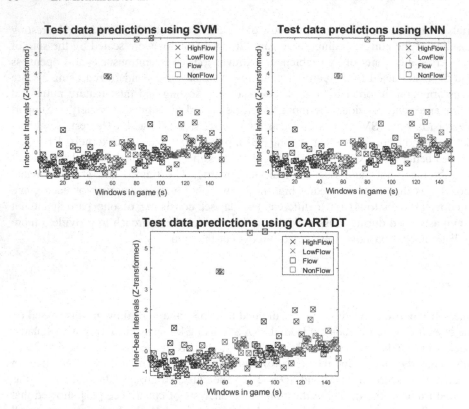

Fig. 1. Example of predicted flow categories (crosses) for one participant across three classifiers (Support Vector Machine, k-Nearest Neighbors and CART Decision Tree) during game rounds as a function of the inter-beat intervals. High-Flow and Low-Flow categories (the "ground truth") were acquired using k-means clustering on the self-reported overall flow experience. Black and red crosses show the classifier predictions for these ground truth labels. Flow and Non-Flow (Anxiety and Boredom, i.e., squares) categories are based on the design choices made in the game. Color congruence (High-Flow/Flow or Low-Flow/Non-Flow) suggests that the physiological responses were in line with the original design choices for the game rounds. The windows have an average duration of 10.3 s ($SD = 2.2$ s). (Color figure online)

5   Discussion

In this work, we explored the feasibility of an evaluative approach that allows game designers to identify the effectiveness of their design. Using self-reports as a guide for interpreting and predicting design outcomes in arbitrary segments of a game has a promising potential to be extrapolated to other video games and real-time applications. Such a data-driven approach is safer to employ in presence of tentative ground truth. We should stress that players react differently to the same game events [28], especially in presence of a hidden mechanic such as the indomitable bosses.

Using a previously optimized classifier, game designers may enquire a prediction in real time and thus uncover successful as well as problematic areas in their game. For example, boredom is typically an unwanted player state, whereas anxiety or frustration may not be inherently destructive to an engaging experience [29]. These affective states may be more pronounced in virtual reality games [30]. Perhaps, the players blamed themselves instead of the game for being unable to eliminate the bosses, thereby maintaining their motivation to play [31]. On the other hand, if the player fails to recuperate from anxiety during prolonged game playing, it may indicate that the design choices or game difficulty should be remediated [32]. Notably, HRV in the low-flow group may be entangled with other emotions during game playing, such as fear in horror games. Hence, the approach can be extended multimodally, with several physiological measures, to compensate for contextual heterogeneity.

Acknowledgements. The authors wish to thank Jeremy Hogan (Worldwide Studios, London), Fabio Capello (Sony Interactive Entertainment, London) and Charlie Hargood (Bournemouth University) for their guidance, and Bournemouth University, EPSRC, Centre for Digital Entertainment and Sony Interactive Entertainment for funding Mr. Michailidis's studentship.

References

1. Csikszentmihalyi, M.: Flow: The Psychology of Optimal Experience. Harper&Row, New York (1990)
2. Ullén, F., et al.: Proneness for psychological flow in everyday life: associations with personality and intelligence. Pers. Individ. Differ. **52**(2), 167–172 (2012)
3. Bassi, M., Steca, P., Monzani, D., Greco, A., Delle Fave, A.: Personality and optimal experience in adolescence: implications for well-being and development. J. Happiness Stud. **15**(4), 829–843 (2014)
4. Ullén, F., Harmat, L., Theorell, T., Madison, G.: Flow and individual differences – a phenotypic analysis of data from more than 10,000 twin individuals. In: Harmat, L., Ørsted, Andersen F., Ullén, F., Wright, J., Sadlo, G. (eds.) Flow Experience, pp. 267–288. Springer, Cham (2016). https://doi.org/10.1007/978-3-319-28634-1_17
5. Heller, K., Bullerjahn, C., von Georgi, R.: The relationship between personality traits, flow-experience, and different aspects of practice behavior of amateur vocal students. Front. Psychol. **6**, 1901 (2015)
6. Gray, J.A., McNaughton, N.: The Neuropsychology of Anxiety: An Enquiry into the Functions of the Septohippocampal System, 2nd edn. Oxford University Press, Oxford (2000)
7. Liu, C.C.: A model for exploring players flow experience in online games. Inf. Technol. People **30**(1), 139–162 (2017)
8. Nacke, L., Lindley, C.A.: Flow and immersion in first-person shooters: measuring the player's gameplay experience. In: Proceedings of the 2008 Conference on Future Play: Research, Play, Share, pp. 81–88. ACM (2008)
9. Nah, F.F.H., Eschenbrenner, B., Zeng, Q., Telaprolu, V.R., Sepehr, S.: Flow in gaming: literature synthesis and framework development. Int. J. Inf. Syst. Manag. **1**(1–2), 83–124 (2014)
10. Sherry, J.L.: Flow and media enjoyment. Communication theory **14**(4), 328–347 (2004)
11. Denisova, A., Cairns, P.: Adaptation in digital games: the effect of challenge adjustment on player performance and experience. In: Proceedings of the 2015 Annual Symposium on Computer-Human Interaction in Play, pp. 97–101. ACM
12. Michailidis, L., Balaguer-Ballester, E., He, X.: Flow and immersion in video games: the aftermath of a conceptual challenge. Front. Psychol. **9**, 1682 (2018). https://doi.org/10.3389/fpsyg.2018.01682

13. McCraty, R., Shaffer, F.: Heart rate variability: new perspectives on physiological mechanisms, assessment of self-regulatory capacity, and health risk. Glob. Adv. Health Med. **4**(1), 46–61 (2015)
14. Shaffer, F., Ginsberg, J.P.: An overview of heart rate variability metrics and norms. Front. Publ. Health **5**, 258 (2017)
15. Peifer, C., Schulz, A., Schächinger, H., Baumann, N., Antoni, C.H.: The relation of flow-experience and physiological arousal under stress—can u shape it? J. Exp. Soc. Psychol. **53**, 62–69 (2014)
16. Chanel, G., Rebetez, C., Bétrancourt, M., Pun, T.: Boredom, engagement and anxiety as indicators for adaptation to difficulty in games. In: Proceedings of the 12th International Conference on Entertainment and Media in the Ubiquitous Era, pp. 13–17. ACM (2008)
17. Keller, J., Bless, H., Blomann, F., Kleinböhl, D.: Physiological aspects of flow experiences: skills-demand-compatibility effects on heart rate variability and salivary cortisol. J. Exp. Soc. Psychol. **47**(4), 849–852 (2011)
18. Gargiulo, G., et al.: On the Einthoven triangle: a critical analysis of the single rotating dipole hypothesis. Sensors **18**(7), 2353 (2018)
19. Jackson, S.A., Eklund, R.C.: Assessing flow in physical activity: the flow state scale–2 and dispositional flow scale–2. J. Sport Exerc. Psychol. **24**(2), 133–150 (2002)
20. John, O.P., Srivastava, S.: The big-five trait taxonomy: history, measurement, and theoretical perspectives. In: Pervin, L.A., John, O.P. (eds.) Handbook of Personality: Theory and Research, vol. 2, pp. 102–138. Guilford Press, New York (1999)
21. Avery, P., Togelius, J., Alistar, E., Van Leeuwen, R.P.: Computational intelligence and tower defence games. In: 2011 IEEE Congress of Evolutionary Computation (CEC), pp. 1084–1091. IEEE (2011)
22. Sutoyo, R., Winata, D., Oliviani, K., Supriyadi, D.M.: Dynamic difficulty adjustment in tower defence. Procedia Comput. Sci. **59**, 435–444 (2015)
23. Pan, J., Tompkins, W.J.: A real-time QRS detection algorithm. IEEE Trans. Biomed. Eng. **32**(3), 230–236 (1985)
24. Sedghamiz, H.: MATLAB implementation of Pan Tompkins ECG QRS detector (2014). https://uk.mathworks.com/matlabcentral/fileexchange/45840-complete-pan-tompkins-implementation-ecg-qrs-detector
25. Malik, M., Camm, A.J.: Heart Rate Variability. Futura, New York (1995)
26. Vicente, J., Laguna, P., Bartra, A., Bailón, R.: Drowsiness detection using heart rate variability. Med. Biol. Eng. Compu. **54**(6), 927–937 (2016)
27. Quade, D.: Rank analysis of covariance. J. Am. Stat. Assoc. **62**(320), 1187–1200 (1967)
28. Grodal, T.: Video games and the pleasures of control. In: Media Entertainment: The Psychology of Its Appeal, pp. 197–213 (2000)
29. Kaye, L.K., Monk, R.L., Wall, H.J., Hamlin, I., Qureshi, A.W.: The effect of flow and context on in-vivo positive mood in digital gaming. Int. J. Hum. Comput. Stud. **110**, 45–52 (2018). https://doi.org/10.1016/j.ijhcs.2017.10.005
30. Pallavicini, F., Pepe, A., Minissi, M.E.: Gaming in virtual reality: what changes in terms of usability, emotional response and sense of presence compared to non-immersive video games? Simul. Gaming (2019). https://doi.org/10.1177/1046878119831420
31. Juul, J.: Fear of failing? The many meanings of difficulty in video games. Video Game Theory Reader **2**, 237–252 (2009)
32. Gilleade, K.M., Dix, A.: Using frustration in the design of adaptive videogames. In: Proceedings of the 2004 ACM SIGCHI International Conference on Advances in Computer Entertainment Technology, pp. 228–232. ACM (2004)

How Tour Video Games Benefit Students: Study Case Freshman Engineering School

Leticia Neira-Tovar[(✉)], Sergio Ordoñez[(✉)],
and Francisco Torres-Guerrero[(✉)]

Universidad Autónoma de Nuevo León, San Nicolás de los Garza, Mexico
leticia.neira@gmail.com, sergio.ordonezg@hotmail.com,
franciscot@gmail.com

Abstract. This work presents a practical application of using virtual reality platforms beyond gaming. In this case, this video game aims to help students in locating facilities of an engineering school. In order for people to better know their area of work or study, situations have arisen in which students or workers do not know some departments or some important areas where they are, and this creates problems for them. There are many problems of this type, the solution that is presented can change the way to look for places, not only for students or facilities, but for people who does not know the place.

The target of this work is to present the analysis of a tour game, that consists of an interface which both the 3D-modeled institution area and a map of it, so is easier for any user to locate a specific place. The VR interface uses a game pad controller to choose a facility where students want to go, and then start moving.

Keywords: Tour · Points of interest · Video games

1 Introduction

In the world of entertainment, are had many options to choose from, but currently there is one that is taking a wide change in every concept that it previously had: video games. Videogames have always been a negative thing for the world, but today these thoughts have been changing, rather than something negative, now it is seen as an option to expand the things that people can do. There are all kinds of playable video games. Not only those for fun with recreational purposes, but those oriented to health, biology, physics, mathematics and even for people with disabilities. In the world of entertainment, are had many options to choose from, but currently there is one that is taking a wide change in every concept that it previously had: video games. Videogames have always been a negative thing for the world, but today these thoughts have been changing, rather than something negative, now it is seen as an option to expand the things that people can do. There are all kinds of playable video games. Not only those for fun with recreational purposes, but those oriented to health, biology, physics, mathematics and even for people with disabilities. Video games are changing young people habits, so it is very important to take advantages of this technological approach and apply their capabilities in improving results in learning process [1].

In consequence of the many applications video games have, they can be used in many industries. One of those industries is tourism. Different areas of tourism like

C. Stephanidis (Ed.): HCII 2019, CCIS 1033, pp. 53–60, 2019.
https://doi.org/10.1007/978-3-030-23528-4_8

planning, entertainment, education, and accessibility may prove benefited from the use
of VR technologies [2]. Both virtual and augmented reality can be used to improve user
experience and motivation, as a guide route while people are in the tour [3]. These tours
often refer to landmarks, but tours may refer to other kind of places, such as a campus.

Campus tour video games are important and very dynamic because in a simple
interactive way people can give themselves and idea how the building internally looks
like, or how they can guide on their way when lost. These games offer solutions to
many problems which occur in school year. Before starting college, many students and
their parents come to check what the campus offers, which involves time and money
[4]. It would be easier if those families could see the campus without going out from
their homes, so they avoid the stress of walking or coming to campus just to tour the
campus [5]. After that, once the student started college, in his freshman year, he does
not know the entire facilities, so is sometimes hard to located specific places. Both
situations can be solved by the guidance in a VR tour. However, when speaking of VR
tours is needed to indicate different studies have shown that a 3D environment turns out
to be more assertive than a 2D one [6]. 3D environments have shortened the distances
between what the user sees in a real place and what he sees in a virtual world [7]. These
similarities between real and virtual places is an explicit need of a VR project with a
learning approach, which means is observable and the more consideration to those
needs, the more meaningful learning is [8]. As a virtual campus looks quite similar to
the real campus, the tool and what the user learns from it seems more meaningful than
what the user would learn from 2D map.

When designing a video games, usability is a key aspect to consider. Usability
involves and interaction of the user with the platform in which interface seems
attractive for the user and is easy to learn and navigate [9]. Those aspects are external to
the game, but these interactions define if a VR tool is useful to its purpose or its not.
Although the game has the quality it required, interaction has always and effect on the
use of technology [10]. However, even if quality and usability are accomplished, it is
needed to see user experience in order to test a video game. By testing video games
with user experience, it is possible to see and analyze satisfaction of the user and
improvements to the gameplay [11].

The user emotional state is a factor which affects results in testing, so it should be
monitored. Many VR solutions are usually designed so the user is able or learn how to
do expensive or dangerous task Performance and reactions of a user in many situations
vary depending on how he is feeling. By using virtual reality, user emotions can be
used without taking any risks [12]. There are different tools that can be used in
monitoring what the user is feeling, such as Emotiv EPOC. This device and interface
allow to record brain activity so there is a channel of information about the emotional
state of a user [13]. This technology provides an explanation about how the user feels,
and where improvements are required.

The final product of this work is a game that consists of an interface which both the
3D-modeled institution area and a map of it, so is easier for any user to locate a specific
place. The VR interface uses a gamepad controller to choose a facility where students
want to go, and then start moving. As it can be seen, the proposed app required to 3D-
model each building, as well as any other components which help as reference when

using the map. Also, there are included several events which can guide a tour around the facilities of the institution.

Another benefit of this project is to raise awareness on location of places, at the field of video games that has not been fully investigated and, thanks to advances in current technology, some options are generated to make employees or students to feel there is always someone who can guide you, and what better way to do it in a fun and dynamic way.

2 Methodology

Virtual Tour allows the user to train in finding the most effective route to a specific place. In both virtual o real scenario, user look for information in their surrounding in order to find that route. When a student starts freshman year, he is challenged to arrive on time to all his courses. If the student went lost because of not knowing how to get to those courses, he would probably not arrive on time This virtual tool aims to help students in knowing the facilities of the university campus, composed by 10 buildings, several sport areas, study areas, and a library, so he takes advantage of those resources. User interaction must be studied, and experience must be evaluated in two different levels: looking for information in a virtual scenario so different routes are identified, and timing in moving from one place to a target one.

2.1 Method Steps

The method was divided into four steps to optimized the team work.

Phase 1: Virtual Map Concept, where the map requirements are defined.
Phase 2: Test and analysis design, in which needed resources. Both technological and human, are identified.
Phase 3: Virtual Map tour design by defining priority events in app outcome. This phase includes 3D-modelling of the institution.
Phase 4: Models construction and tour interaction. This phase includes buildings and objects images recording, as well as programming and functional options definition.
Phase 5: testing and Analysis.

2.2 Test and Analysis

Specific tests were carried out which will be mentioned below

- Survey
- Timing Tour
- Recording

The types of Test are linked to each other, which ensures 3 samples from a single person; The plan that was organized was to apply these 3 tests to an exact amount of 40 people, which were all students from first semester to eighth semester, this in order to obtain different points of view, both of people more experienced with the surroundings and people who are not. Of course, both genders were taken into account, thus obtaining a total of 10 Female samples and 30 Male samples.

Timed Tests. These focused-on timing the times people made from Point A to Point B and then to Point C and continued, thus with the 10 Points that were established, this in order that the route covered a large part of the facilities and will not leave any blind spot.

Recording Test. This test consisted of using the Eye Tracker device to measure and record sight of people. In this way points of interest can be located and analyzed, so there is a chance for changing or improving routes in a more significant way (Fig. 1).

Fig. 1. Sample of what is shown in the program when recording what user sees, in which he sees plants.

Survey Test. This test is responsible for collecting opinions on the route. These data can be used to improve the information provided in Tutorials and thus give better guidance to students.

2.3 Infrastructure and Equipment

Eye Tracker. This device is to analyze the interest of people through their eyes and gives another approach when analyzing more results.

Gazepoint Analysis. Software provided by the Eye Tracker provider.

Xbox 360 Gamepad. Controller used to move inside the interface of the app.

Unity Engine. This engine was used as VR interface. Once 3D-modelled, all the buildings were used to create the virtual map of the institution as a Unity asset.

3 Results

In order to share the results obtained from the 40 samples, it was sought to gather the most accurate information. It was required in recording time intervals, so accuracy helped this work to have more control over the data collected.

Table 1, shows the results obtained from the first 15 samples only, all the times are measured in seconds.

Table 1. This table contains, targets, the locations of the Institution and the recorder time of the people that were applied the test.

E	S	SMT	CAR	1	2	3	4	3108	Cafeteria	4112	Building 8	Auditorium Rene Montante	CIDET	9102
18	M	3	IME	9.6	22.6	26.79	49.79	17.94	15.79	21.79	27.49	7.94	16.98	25.47
19	M	3	IMTC	23.49	24.82	28.93	49.91	21.64	11.91	11.81	20.48	13.48	16.86	31.46
21	M	8	IMTC	10.72	24.94	28.89	37.86	24.85	18.69	18.95	18.92	16.95	18.75	24.97
24	M	10	IMTC	9.86	21.78	41.91	30.94	16.79	14.8	38.74	27.78	12.57	16.64	25.95
23	M	M	IMTC	7.89	19.87	23.92	31.86	15.84	13.85	15.93	16.47	5.97	15.32	23.48
16	F	1	IMTC	8.92	33.64	39.86	33.82	17.84	15.86	19.88	29.64	6.93	18.47	37.82
21	M	5	ITS	9.7	16.7	22.7	32.1	31.8	12.1	13.2	26.2	10.2	21.5	27.7
18	M	5	IMTC	12.5	21.7	26.9	52.2	22.1	17.3	34.9	40.2	12.2	14.1	25.36
17	M	1	IMTC	13.4	23.8	45.1	49.8	22.3	14.9	23.4	18.6	16.9	22.9	26.6
18	M	4	IME	20.9	33.8	37.2	53.5	29.7	17.9	35.4	22.4	25.4	22.4	43.8
21	M	8	ITS	11.2	21.8	26.8	34.9	18.1	13.8	14.8	18.7	9.4	18.9	26.5
17	M	1	IMTC	10.4	28.9	37.2	55.9	32.7	18.9	27.4	35.7	19.7	25.8	40.5
20	M	5	IMTC	10.8	25.7	28.2	48.1	34.9	15.4	26.3	17.6	18.9	19.2	28.1
17	M	1	IMTC	44.3	20.4	32.4	52.8	17.2	35.4	26.9	37.8	12.9	24.9	58.7
19	M	3	IAS	10.1	20.8	31.4	36.2	20.9	15.3	24.1	26.4	18.9	25.9	29.8

These time intervals indicate that there is some loss of orientation for first semester students. On the other hand, later semester students shown a better orientation around the facilities, this is due to the same induction that was obtained in the beginning or in turn, to the experience that is obtained throughout his stay at his institution.

Using the Virtual Tour, it was possible to improve the orientation of the first semester students, which favored this work since it indicated that there were benefits for the students when using this method of learning.

Some people found hard not knowing some of the facilities of the institution, which gave them a trouble when it came to timing. However, they found eventually the indicated areas and they could proceed with the other points.

Experience caused very unequal time intervals between people, but still data was relevant and reliable.

3.1 Students with Experience

Experienced results were obtained with people that were cataloged with experience already in the institution, this means that they are of advanced semesters and it could be verified that if they can stare at any object, this helped us to find points of interest throughout the facilities of the institution.

As shown in Fig. 2, these points are located in different structures, walls, halls or even doors. While testing, several users said things like "How well the buildings are designed", and "This looks so realistic with all the details there are" and indicated this helped them in routes. Based on that, it was possible to identify points of interest.

Fig. 2. Points of interest representation from students who have experience at the facilities of the institution.

3.2 Students Without Experience

In the case of people with less experience, Fig. 3, results were harder to analyze, since people observed too many things all the time and could not establish an intermediate

Fig. 3. Points of interest representation from students who have not experience with the facilities of the institution.

point between all those things, for which it was chosen to keep them, but look for some key point. There are also shown three points for this case, but this data can not be as easily analyzed as the case where people already knew the facilities.

Next, are summarized surveys results (Fig. 4):

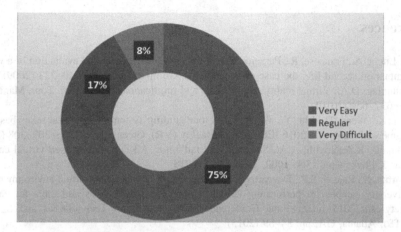

Fig. 4. Surveys results from people who participated in Virtual Tour test, in which is shown most of them already knew the facilities of the institution.

It was found that for the 75% (30 people out of 40) it was "Very Easy" to reach each of the proposed objectives. On the other hand, especially for first semester students, there were cases, 17% (6 People), where they say there was a "regular" difficulty locating the places, or even 8% (4 People) who said it was "Very Difficult" for them. This can give the work an idea of how well young people are oriented in their Tutorials classes and by the same institution.

4 Conclusions and Recommendations

Based on all obtained results and previous analysis, it can be established that people whom applied these tests have had a remarkable improvement in finding locations around the institution. They were asked if they would recommend using video games for their learning and more than 80% of them said they would recommend it.

This leads to the conclusion that video games, depending on how they are executed, can be beneficial for the people who try them, this with different purposes, but always the main one: the educational purpose. It would be recommended to place this type of modules in different locations, whether within the same institution or for casual use by employees or students, either at the entrance of the same or in a crowded place.

With the aim of being able to automate tests and find factors that allow restructuring scenarios it is necessary to find patterns of interaction variables through diffuse methods to be able to reinforce or eradicate vices in the interaction, the use of that method will be next step for this research.

Acknowledgments. The research work reported here was made possible by participation of Graduate and Under-graduate students at the Engineering School: Oscar Leal and Fredy Lucho.

References

1. De Lucia, A., Francese, R., Passero, I., Tortora, G.: Development and evaluation of a virtual campus on second life: the case of SecondDMI. Comput. Educ. **52**, 220–233 (2009)
2. Guttentag, D.A.: Virtual reality: applications and implications for tourism. Tour. Manag. **31** (5), 637–651 (2010)
3. Wei, X., Weng, D., Liu, Y., Wang, Y.: A tour guiding system of historical relics based on augmented reality. In: 2016 IEEE Virtual Reality (VR), Greenville, SC, pp. 307–308 (2016)
4. Sulthana, R.A., Jovith, A.A., Saveetha, D., Jaithunbi, A.K.: A game based virtual campus tour. J. Phys.: Conf. Ser. **1000**, 1108–1112 (2018)
5. Sharma, S., Rajeev, S.P., Devearux, P.: An immersive collaborative virtual environment of a university campus for performing virtual campus evacuation drills and tours for campus safety. In: 2015 International Conference on Collaboration Technologies and Systems (CTS), Atlanta, GA, pp. 84–89 (2015)
6. Barrera, S., Takahasi, H., Nakajima, M.: Hands-free navigation methods for moving through a virtual landscape. In: Proceedings of IEEE 2004 Computer Graphics International, Crete, Greece, pp. 388–394 (2004)
7. Wang, J., Lin, Z.: A general 3D campus navigator system. In: 2009 Eighth IEEE/ACIS International Conference on Computer and Information Science, Shanghai, pp. 1074–1078 (2009)
8. Torres-Guerrero, F., Neira-Tovar, L., Martinez Garcia, I.: Methodology for the estimation of effort for a project of virtual reality–a case study: ennui. In: Lackey, S., Chen, J. (eds.) VAMR 2017. LNCS, vol. 10280, pp. 82–93. Springer, Cham (2017). https://doi.org/10.1007/978-3-319-57987-0_7
9. Torres, F., Tovar, L.A.N., Egremy, M.C.: Virtual interactive laboratory applied to high schools programs. Procedia Comput. Sci. **75**, 233–238 (2015)
10. Chiao, H., Chen, Y., Huang, W.: Examining the usability of an online virtual tour-guiding platform for cultural tourism education. J. Hosp. Leisure Sport Tourism Educ. **23**, 29–38 (2018)
11. Neira-Tovar, L.A., Venegas-Rodríguez, A.: Propuesta de Diseño de Pruebas para Videojuegos Aplicados En La Salud. Revista Daena (Int. J. Good Consci.) **13**(1), 283–294 (2018)
12. Borisov, V., Syskov, A., Kublanov, V.: Functional state assessment of an athlete by means of the brain-computer interface multimodal metrics. In: Lhotska, L., Sukupova, L., Lacković, I., Ibbott, G.S. (eds.) World Congress on Medical Physics and Biomedical Engineering 2018. IP, vol. 68/3, pp. 71–75. Springer, Singapore (2019). https://doi.org/10.1007/978-981-10-9023-3_13
13. Ben Abdessalem, Hamdi, Boukadida, Marwa, Frasson, Claude: Emotional state and behavior analysis in a virtual reality environment: a medical application. In: Nkambou, Roger, Azevedo, Roger, Vassileva, Julita (eds.) ITS 2018. LNCS, vol. 10858, pp. 287–293. Springer, Cham (2018). https://doi.org/10.1007/978-3-319-91464-0_29

Automatic Generation of Homophonic Transformation for Japanese Wordplay Based on Edit Distance and Phrase Breaks

Jiro Shimaya[1]([⊠]), Nao Hanyu[2], and Yutaka Nakamura[1]

[1] Graduate School of Engineering Science, Osaka University, Toyonaka, Osaka, Japan
shimaya.jiro@irl.sys.es.osaka-u.ac.jp
[2] Graduate School of Frontier Biosciences, Osaka University, Suita, Japan

Abstract. Humor is important to establish more natural and enjoyable human–computer interactions. This research aims to understand the humor mechanism of "soramimi," which is a typical wordplay in Japan. Soramimi denotes a wordplay of replacing words in a well-known text with different words of similar pronunciation. It is empirically known that the humorous effect of soramimi is enhanced for a case where the vocabulary to be used is limited to a particular category. Although psychological and neuroscience studies focus on how speech misperceptions such as soramimi occurs, it is still unclear why a humorous effect is achieved. As a first step to understand the mechanism of soramimi humor, we developed a system called "soramimic," that can automatically transform Japanese input text into a similar-sounding sequence of words from a particular vocabulary category using dynamic programming. The dissimilarity of phoneme estimated from the edit distance and concordance rate of phrase breaks were chosen as a parameter to be optimized. Forty-six test subjects evaluated the similarity of pronunciation between the output sequence composed of only country names and its original input sentence. Results suggest that both the edit distance and concordance rate of phrase breaks are correlated with a subjective evaluation of the similarity.

Keywords: Homophonic transformation · Soramimi · Humor · Wordplay · Speech misperception · Natural language processing · Dynamic programming

1 Introduction

Humor is important to establish more natural and enjoyable human–computer interactions. Researchers have been interested in understanding the mechanism of humor [1,2], evaluation [3] and the automatic generation of humor [4].

Previous studies suggest that the humor of computer agents can improve the quality of interaction with the agent [5,6]. Ptaszynski et al. reported that conversations with computer agents expressing humor felt more natural and increased

C. Stephanidis (Ed.): HCII 2019, CCIS 1033, pp. 61–68, 2019.
https://doi.org/10.1007/978-3-030-23528-4_9

the motivation of human participants to prolong the conversation [5]. Mashimo et al. suggested that information felt interesting and could be understood easily when it was provided by a system of two robots exhibiting a humorous dialog called manzai [6].

The goal of this research is to understand the mechanism of humor called "soramimi," which is typically known humor type in Japan, and implement it in a human–computer interaction system. Soramimi is a wordplay by replacing words in a well-known text into different words of similar pronunciation. It is similar with puns in terms of causing a humorous effect arising from the near-homophonity between different words. It has been accepted as a popular form of humor in Japan for decades. For example, "Soramimi Hour," which is a short segment of the television program "Tamori Club," [7] introduces humorous soramimi and has been broadcast for over 25 years since its inception.

An equivalent English word for soramimi is mondegreen. Mondegreen denotes the misperception of speech and is sometimes recognized as humor. An example of mondegreen is as follows: "There's a bad moon on the rise" is misheard as "There's a bathroom on the right." When an original text to be misheard is a song phrase, mondegreen is occasionally called misheard lyrics. Mondegreen and misheard lyrics are accepted as humor in US. Videos involving misheard lyrics are uploaded to video sharing web platforms and are occasionally viewed over one million times. (e.g. [8,9]).

Two popular types of soramimi exist. The first type is the soramimi of rephrasing a text in one language with a similar-sounding text in different language. In Japan, English speech or song lyrics are typically rephrased in Japanese. A few Japanese researchers have investigated the automatic generation of such types of soramimi, especially in case of rephrasing English speech or text with Japanese [10,11]. Hajika et al. analyzed databases that include pairs of original English texts and proposed using the edit distance of their phonetic symbols as a measure to be optimized [11]. Sakakima et al. applied a Japanese speech recognition system for the automatic generation of soramimi [10]. They input an English speech file to the Japanese speech recognition software and obtained the output as soramimi.

The second type is soramimi by rephrasing a text with different words in the same language. In this type of soramimi, it is empirically known that the humorous effect is enhanced when the vocabulary of words to be used for soramimi is limited to a particular category. For example, many parody songs using only names of baseball players are generated and some of them have garnered more than one million views (e.g. [12,13]).

As a first step to understand the mechanism of soramimi humor, we develop an automatic generation system of the latter type of soramimi, i.e., soramimi using words from a particular vocabulary category. Although psychological and neuroscience studies focus on how speech misperception such as soramimi occurs [14–16], it is still unclear why the humorous effect is achieved. We expect that near-homophony is important for the humorous effect of soramimi. According to incongruity-resolution theory [17], humor occurs when a gap that renders a situation difficult to be understood is resolved. In soramimi, the gap is considered to be generated by a situation where different words or sentences that are semantically unrelated to each other are displayed side by side. In addition, the resolution of the gap may occur by perception to near-homophonity between the displayed words. Thus, we consider that it important to create soramimi having near-homophony with its original text and examine the relationships between near-homophony and fun.

Two reasons for focusing on the latter type of soramimi are as follows. First, because the latter type is considered simple compared to the former type as the language of the original and that of soramimi is the same; further, the latter type of soramimi can be generated as merely a sequence of noun that does not include other lexical category words. This simplicity is expected to be useful to examine its humor because the characteristics of soramimi is easy to be expressed quantitatively. Next, few studies are conducted regarding the latter type of soramimi even though it is accepted as a culture on the Internet. Developing an automatic generation system of the latter type of soramimi could be beneficial for creators and listeners of soramimi parody songs.

2   Soramimic – A System to Generate Humorous Homophonic Transformation Systematically

This section explains our proposed system called "soramimic" (soramimi + mimic), which is a text converter to generate soramimi using only words in a particular vocabulary category. An expected input is a Japanese text while the output is a word sequence that is considered to sound similarly as the input. It consists of four parts: word database (WDB), sentence structure analyzer (SSA), similarly sounded word selector (SWS).

WDB is a database of words to be used for soramimi. To generate a humorous effect, it contains words of a particular vocabulary category (e.g., baseball players, country names, etc.). For example, if one prepares a WDB of country names, it would appear as "Afgani-stan, Albania, Algeria, etc.".

An SSA is used to detect the position of phrase breaks in the input text. MeCab is used for the morphological analysis of the Japanese language. It divides sentences into words and assigns their lexical categories. Phrase breaks are defined as places before an independent word. In addition, if the input includes kanji, which is a Japanese ideogram, the SSA converts it into Japanese phonograms called kana by MeCab.

An SWS is a part that chooses a word from the WDB, and is expected to be the most similarly sounded with a certain division of the input. The similarity is evaluated based on the edit distance between the kana text of the division and that of the chosen word. The edit distance is defined as the minimum number of single-character edits (insertions, deletions, or substitutions) required to change one string into another string [18]. It is considered to represent string metrics.

After the word with the smallest edit distance with the input division is chosen, the SWS assigns a similarity score for optimization based on the following formula:

$$similarity = -w_{ed} \cdot E + -w_{pb} \cdot B \tag{1}$$

where E is the edit distance between the *kana* text of the division and that of the chosen word. B is a penalty assigned when the position of the phrase (word) breaks of the output is different from that of the input. w_{ed} and w_{pb} are the weight parameters for E and B, respectively.

Finally, the SWS outputs the word sequence by optimizing the *similarity* score using dynamic programming. The output characteristics can be controlled by changing weight parameters w_{ed} and w_{pb}. If w_{ed} is larger, the edit distance between the input and output should be small but the position of the phrase breaks in the output might be different from that in the input. Meanwhile, if w_{pb} is larger, the position of the phrase breaks should be concordant between the input and output, but the edit distance between them might be large.

Table 1 shows an example of the input and output of soramimic. The input text is the lyrics of a traditional Japanese song, "moshimoshi kameyo." The three types of output results under different weight parameters, i.e., the edit distance (ED), phrase breads (PB) and combined condition uses the parameter $(w_{ed}, w_{pb}) = (1,0), (0,1)$, and $(0.5, 0.5)$, respectively. The result appears to be consistent with the weight parameters in that edit distance (ED) is the smallest in the ED condition (34) while it is the largest in the PB condition (41). Meanwhile, concordance rate of phrase breaks (CRPB) is the largest in the PB condition (.00) while is the smallest in the ED condition (.56). The combined condition is in the middle of the other two conditions in terms of ED (36) and CRPB (.25).

3   Subjective Experiment

A purpose of the experiment was to verify whether soramimi generated by Soramimic was evaluated subjectively to sound similarly with its original. Hence, three types of conditions to generate soramimi were prepared:

ED condition. The weight parameter of soramimic is set to $(w_{ed}, w_{pb}) = (1, 0)$ such that its ED with the original text is small.

PB condition. The weight parameter is set to $(w_{ed}, w_{pb}) = (0, 1)$ such that its CRPB with the original text is small.

Combined condition. The weight parameter is set to $(w_{ed}, w_{pb}) = (1, 1)$ such that both ED and CRPB are small.

3.1   Method

Forty-six participants (34 males and 12 females) answered questionnaires for the evaluation. Informed consent was obtained from all participants before beginning the questionnaires.

Eleven original texts for evaluation were prepared. Five of them were lyrics of traditional Japanese songs while the other six were nonlyrics sentences chosen from ATR503, which is a spoken Japanese language database developed by the

Table 1. Example output of soramimic for the input lyrics of traditional Japanese song, "moshimoshi kameyo": condition and its weight parameters, the output text, its edit distance (ED) and concordance rate of phrase breaks (CRPB) with the input. "/" is the position of the phrase breaks

Condition (w_{ed}, w_{pd})	Line		Result	ED	CRPB
PB (0,1)	L1	input	Mo shi mo shi / ka me yo / ka me sa n yo	41	.00
		output	Mo ru do ba / ka na da / Ka me ru u n		
			(Moldova) (Canada) (Cameroon)		
	L2	input	Se ka i no / u chi de / o ma e ho do		
		output	A fu ga ni su ta n / po o ra n do		
			(Afghanistan) (Poland)		
	L3	input	A yu mi no / no ro i / mo no wa / na i		
		output	A n do ra / a ru ze n chi n / ta i		
			(Andorra) (Algentine) (Thailand)		
	L4	input	Do o shi te / so n na ni / no ro i no ka		
		output	Bu u ta n / a n do ra / su ro ba ki a		
			(Bhutan) (Andorra) (Slovakia)		
ED (1,0)	L1	input	Mo shi mo shi / ka me yo / ka me sa n yo	34	.56
		output	Ro shi a / i e me n / ka me ru u n		
			(Russia) (Yemen) (Cameroon)		
	L2	input	Se ka i no / u chi de / o ma e ho do		
		output	Ta i / i n do / chi ri / ta i / i n do		
			(Thai- (India) (Chili) (Thai- (India) land land)		
	L3	input	A yu mi no / no ro i / mo no wa / na i		
		output	A ru ba ni a / ta i / mo na ko / ta i		
			(Albania) (Thai- (Monaco) (Thai- land land		
	L4	input	Do o shi te / so n na ni / no ro i no ka		
		output	do i tsu / be na n / gi ni a / ta i / ta i		
			(Ger- (Benin) (Guinea) (Thai- (Thai- many) land) land)		
Combined (0.5,0.5)	L1	input	Mo shi mo shi / ka me yo / ka me sa n yo	36	.25
		output	Mo ru do ba / ka na da / Ka me ru u n		
			(Moldova) (Canada) (Cameroon)		
	L2	input	Se ka i no / u chi de / o ma e ho do		
		output	Ni ka ra gu a / chi ri / po o ra n do		
			(Nicaragua) (Chili) (Poland)		
	L3	input	A yu mi no / no ro i / mo no wa / na i		
		output	A ru ba ni a / ta i / mo na ko / ta i		
			(Albania) (Thai- (Monaco) (Thai- land) land)		
	L4	input	Do o shi te / so n na ni / no ro i no ka		
		output	Bu u ta n / sa n ma ri no / ga i a na		
			(Bhutan) (San Marino) (Guyana)		

Advanced Telecommunications Research Institute International. Three soramimi texts corresponding to three conditions (ED, PB, and combined) were generated from each input. Thus, 33 soramimi texts were used for the evaluation.

The questionnaire included 11 items. In each item, the set of input text and its three soramimi texts were displayed side by side. Participants ranked the three soramimi texts in terms of pronunciation similarity with its original. Thus, 11 rank data sets were obtained from one participant.

3.2 Result

3.3 Manipulation Check

First, we verified whether the ED and CRPB of soramimi are different based on condition.

The relative ED between the *kana* text of the input and that of the output are calculated as the ratio of the ED to the *kana* text length of the input. The relative ED instead of the ED is used because the ED tends to be long when the input text length is long.

The means (and SDs) of the relative EDs of the output are .722 (.043), .846 (.053), and .727 (.052) in the ED, PB, and combined condition, respectively. One-way repeated measure analysis of variance (ANOVA) revealed the significant main effect of conditions ($F(2, 10) = 87.365, p < .0001$). A post-hoc paired t-test with the Holm method revealed a significant difference in the pair of both ED and PB ($t(10) = 6.100, p = .0001$) and combined vs. PB ($t(10) = 5.496, p = .0003$).

The CRPB is calculated as the ratio of number of phrase breaks in the output whose position is the same as that in the input to the total number of phrase breaks in the output.

The means (and SDs) of the CRPB of the output are .383 (.146), 1.000 (0.000), and .626 (.151) in the ED, PB, and combined conditions, respectively. The mean CRPB in the PB condition is one because the soramimic merely divides the input at the phrase breaks when w_{ed} is zero. The post-hoc paired t-test revealed a significant difference between the ED and combined conditions ($t(10) = 8.232, p < .0001$).

It is considered that soramimi from the three conditions differed consistently with its corresponding weight settings.

3.4 Scores of the Subjective Evaluation

The means (and SDs) of the rank score for eleven soramimis in each condition are 2.045 (.342), 2.267 (.384), and 1.692 (.237) in the ED, PB, and combined conditions, respectively. One-way repeated measures ANOVA revealed the significant main effect of the conditions ($F(2, 45) = 24.143, p < .0001$). A post-hoc paired t-test with the Holm method revealed a significant difference in all possible pairs ($t(45) = 2.174, p = .0350$ for ED vs. PB, $t(45) = 5.347, p < .0001$ for ED vs. combined, and $t(45) = 7.325, p < .0001$ for PB vs. combined). This suggests that soramimi in the combined condition is evaluated as the most similarly sounded while that in the PB condition is evaluated as dissimilarly sounded.

Figures 1(a) and (b) show the relationships of the average rank score of subjective similarity with the ED and CRPB of soramimi, respectively. The rank correlated significantly with both the ED $(pearson's\ r = .466, t(31) = 2.936, p = .0062)$ and CRPB $(pearson's\ r = -.476, t(20) = 2.420, p = .0251)$. Note that data from the PB condition were eliminated in the correlation test for Fig. 1(b) because the CRPB in the PB condition is always one.

These results suggest that it is important to consider both the ED and CRPB to generate a similarly sounded soramimi. The ED is considered to contribute to the improvement in subjective similarity because of the high probability that the same phonon with the original is included in soramimi when the EDs among them is small. The CRPB is considered to be important because it might represent the rhythms of the sentence.

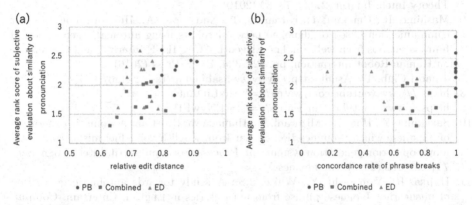

Fig. 1. Relationships of the subjective phonic similarity of soramimi with its (a) relative edit distance and (b) concordance rate of phrase breaks

4   Conclusion

We developed a system to automatically generate homophonic transformation (soramimi) for Japanese wordplay based on dynamic programming. ED and CRPB were chosen as parameters to be optimized. The results of subjective experiment suggested that optimization considering both the ED and CRPB were important to improve the subjective similar sounding of soramimi.

This result presented several limitations. First, only 11 original sentences for soramimi were evaluated. These sentences are not guaranteed to represent most types of general Japanese sentences. Next, only a subjective similarity of pronunciation was evaluated in this study, regardless of whether the soramimi generated by Soramimic was recognized as humor.

Examining the relationships between phonic similarity and humor in soramimi, improving humor in soramimi, and investigating the method to implement it in human–computer interaction systems are potential future studies.

Acknowledgement. This research was supported by "Program for Leading Graduate Schools" of the Ministry of Education, Culture, Sports, Science and Technology, Japan.

References

1. Ritchie, G.: Developing the incongruity-resolution theory. Technical report (1999)
2. Osaka, M., Yaoi, K., Minamoto, T., Osaka, N.: Serial changes of humor comprehension for four-frame comic Manga: an fMRI study. Sci. Rep. **4**, 5828 (2014)
3. Sulejmanov, F., Spasovski, O., Platt, T.: The development of the humor structure appreciation scale and its relation to sensation seeking inventory and need for closure scale. Eur. J. Humour Res. **6**(1), 124–140 (2018)
4. Yoshida, K., Minoguchi, M., Wani, K., Nakamura, A., Kataoka, H.: Neural joking machine: humorous image captioning (2018). arXiv preprint arXiv:1805.11850
5. Ptaszynski, M., Dybala, P., Rzepka, R., Araki, K.: An automatic evaluation method for conversational agents based on affect-as-information theory. J. Jpn Soc. Fuzzy Theory Intell. Inform. **22**(1), 73–89 (2010)
6. Mashimo, R., Umetani, T., Kitamura, T., Nadamoto, A.: Human-robots implicit communication based on dialogue between robots using automatic generation of funny scenarios from web. In: The Eleventh ACM/IEEE International Conference on Human Robot Interaction, pp. 327–334. IEEE Press (2016)
7. Tamori Club, TV Asahi. http://www.tv-asahi.co.jp/tamoriclub/
8. https://www.youtube.com/watch?v=VZhxLjDLu6Y
9. https://www.youtube.com/watch?v=iefStFNywPE
10. Sakakima, Y., Hori, K., Mizutani, Y., Hamakawa, R., et al.: Automatic generation of Japanese which pronunciation is near from English voice file: mishearing automatic operation generation system. Inf. Process. Soc. Jpn (Artif. Intell. Cogn. Sci.) **71**, 101–102 (2009). (in Japanese)
11. Hajika, R., Yamanishi, Y., White, J.S.: A study towards automatic generation of mishearing Japanese phrase from music lyrics in English. Entertain. Comput. **2016**, 114–119 (2016). (in Japanese)
12. https://www.youtube.com/watch?v=5LzZHHsnJD0
13. https://www.youtube.com/watch?v=H_TamoTCUJo
14. Ferber, R.: Slip of the tongue or slip of the ear? On the perception and transcription of naturalistic slips of the tongue. J. Psycholinguist. Res. **20**(2), 105–122 (1991)
15. Blank, H., Davis, M.H.: Prediction errors but not sharpened signals simulate multivoxel fMRI patterns during speech perception. PLoS Biol. **14**(11), e1002577 (2016)
16. Blank, H., Spangenberg, M., Davis, M.H.: Neural prediction errors distinguish perception and misperception of speech. J. Neurosci. **38**(27), 6076–6089 (2018)
17. Suls, J.: Cognitive processes in humor appreciation. In: McGhee, P.E., Goldstein, J.H. (eds.) Handbook of Humor Research, pp. 39–57. Springer, New York (1983). https://doi.org/10.1007/978-1-4612-5572-7_3
18. Levenshtein, V.I.: Binary codes capable of correcting deletions, insertions, and reversals. Soviet physics doklady **10**, 707–710 (1966)

Card-Collection Mechanics in Educational Location-Based AR Games: Transforming Learning Goals to Virtual Rewards

Eric Cesar E. Vidal Jr.[1]([✉]) [iD], Jaclyn Ting Ting M. Lim[1],
Jonathan D. L. Casano[1,2], and Ma. Mercedes T. Rodrigo[1] [iD]

[1] Ateneo de Manila University, Katipunan Avenue,
1108 Quezon City, Philippines
ericvids@gmail.com
[2] Ateneo de Naga University, Ateneo Avenue, 4400 Naga,
Camarines Sur, Philippines

Abstract. Location-based AR (LBAR) games offer a potentially viable learning platform for history-related content, but the experience is impaired by player fatigue due to compulsory movement between real-world locations, causing engagement to drop as the length of the game increases. This paper proposes incorporating card-collection mechanics (virtual collectibles/achievements in contemporary games) into an existing history-related, narrative-based LBAR game, *Igpaw: Loyola*, to counter the effect of fatigue to player engagement while increasing their capacity to absorb educational content.

Participants, divided into control and experimental batches, were tasked to play *Igpaw: Loyola* without and with the collection mechanic, respectively, under logged observation. Both versions of the game included required and optional locations. The control and experimental batches reported only minor differences in application usability, but a majority of the experimental batch visited the optional locations as opposed to none from the control batch. In the post-quiz, the experimental batch scored the same or better (on average and on each individual question) than the control batch. This leads to the conclusion that the card-collection mechanic significantly and positively impacts both the engagement and learning retention of players, and it is recommended for future LBAR games.

Keywords: Augmented reality · Educational game design · Usability ·
Game-based learning · Learning motivation · Location-based apps

1 Introduction

Location-based AR (LBAR) games are a form of digital entertainment that utilizes two novel elements: AR (*augmented reality*) technology, which forms the illusion of the player physically interacting with virtual 3D objects and characters superimposed on a real environment; and, *location tracking*, which is used in conjunction with AR to deliver customized content depending on where the player is currently situated.

© Springer Nature Switzerland AG 2019
C. Stephanidis (Ed.): HCII 2019, CCIS 1033, pp. 69–75, 2019.
https://doi.org/10.1007/978-3-030-23528-4_10

Since 2010, the number of AR applications for education has been increasing. In a review of 32 publications, Bacca and colleagues [1] found that the majority of these applications were created to carry science, humanities, and arts content. AR applications are used to provide supplementary information. AR is increasingly used for educational games and simulations and laboratory experiments. AR has been shown to increase achievement, motivation, and engagement, but it is challenging to deploy. Applications sometimes lose tracking information, hence digital content is not displayed properly, if at all. Because AR is still quite novel, digital information or the technology itself can be too distracting, undermining educational goals.

One of LBAR's theoretical foundations is *situated learning* [2]. It refers to the embedding of the learning experience within a relevant context to enable learners to interact with the world and build meaning as a result. Because smartphones are AR-capable, they create opportunities for learning while interacting with the physical world. The quality of the LBAR experience depends on a number of factors such as location, narrative, and experience mechanics. The location has an effect on the learning objectives, the experience design, and the overall player experience. Subjects such as history, geography, and architecture lend themselves to highly place-dependent LBAR. They are location specific and cannot be transferred in any meaningful way. The narrative or story that drives the interaction is also critical as it sets the structure and rationale for the AR experience. Finally, design of the experience refers to the balance between competition and collaboration, between interacting with the handheld and interacting with the environment, and providing an open-ended, inquiry-based experience and a closed experience with a definite win state.

There is some evidence to support the use of LBAR as a platform for history-related content. The out-of-laboratory experiences foster greater enjoyment and mitigate boredom, possibly because immersion in the context heightens relevance and realism of the subject matter [3]. However, the effectiveness of this platform is offset by factors such as fatigue (players exert more physical effort to travel from one location to another) and environmental hazards (such as inclement weather and risks to personal safety) [4, 5]. These impediments keep LBAR game authors from realizing the full potential of these games, as this imposes constraints on the scope and length of a game; typically, these games usually may not last longer than an hour or two before player fatigue sets in and the level of player engagement drops.

This paper proposes a method to keep players engaged in a history-related, narrative-based LBAR game despite the onset of fatigue, while attempting to increase players' capacity to absorb the educational content: *collection mechanics*. This idea is borrowed from the typical implementation of rewards in contemporary smartphone/mobile games such as Pokémon GO and Fate/Grand Order: namely, a game presents to the player virtual items (such as cards or other tokens), and gives the player the ulterior motive of collecting these virtual items in exchange for rewards, which may be virtual (in-game advantages, supporting information or narrative elements, etc.) or real (physical prizes, social recognition, etc.). In many of these games, the collection mechanic is designed so that items are not exclusive to each player, meaning, every player has an equal chance of collecting any given item. Collection mechanics of this form can thus be considered as an experience mechanic [2] that provides good balance between competition and collaboration (players may compete in terms of the quantity of items they have collected, but may also collaborate in the discovery and attainment of these items due to their non-exclusive nature) and between an open-ended or closed experience (players may finish the game without having collected every item but still accomplishing the baseline learning objectives; however, collecting all items is a definite win state).

2 Methodology

A card-collection mechanic is introduced in an existing history-related LBAR game, *Igpaw: Loyola.* [5] On top of the game's existing narrative designed to impart to its players general information about the Ateneo de Manila University's campus buildings (intertwined with facts about Jesuit history, Philippine mythology, and campus lore), players now also collect virtual cards (see Fig. 1) that are placed in various real-world campus locations. Some cards can be attained with little to no effort (such as automatic rewards for defeating an in-game enemy), while others require more effort (the player may need to look around the AR scene to discover a hidden card, or perform unconventional tasks to obtain them, such as repeatedly talking to characters).

Fig. 1. (clockwise from left) A virtual card being picked up by the player, the same card turned over, and the card album with collection in progress.

The cards themselves contain facts that strictly recap only what has happened in the same AR scene, meaning, the cards do not have any additional educational content besides what was already created initially for the game. This allows the developers to easily reuse existing game assets to prepare the cards themselves, making the addition of the collection mechanic a low-cost way to upgrade the existing game. By placing the specific information that we want players to recall in a card that players want to collect, we effectively transform an explicit learning goal into a player reward.

3 Evaluation

An experiment was held to determine the efficacy of this card-collection mechanic. 49 female students, aged 16–19, were tasked to play the first three chapters of *Igpaw: Loyola*. The participants were all senior high school students from a single grade level and are all participating in STEM studies, that is, they were previously judged to be of higher aptitude in science, technology, engineering and mathematics compared to their peers in the same grade level. They were divided into a control batch (33 students) and an experimental batch (16 students).

The control batch used the original version of the game for the experiment, while the experimental batch performed the same experiment two weeks later with the altered version of the game that has the card-collection mechanic implemented for the first three chapters. (The temporal separation was necessary to prevent the exchange of gameplay information between the control and experimental batches, because they are both required to play the game at the same physical locations, and players of one batch would encounter and possibly engage with players of the other batch otherwise.) Both versions of the game included a chapter wherein two locations are "optional", meaning, the player does not need to visit those locations to advance the narrative and complete the said game chapter.

Each of the control and experimental batches is further subdivided into groups of 5 to 8 players each, and members of a given group played the game together while accompanied by an observer that takes down notes and a facilitator that maintains order and helps the group navigate to the next location that the group unanimously chooses, in order to facilitate the duration of the experiment (while taking care not to influence the gameplay decisions of the players in any manner). After the gameplay session, each participant is asked to fill out a HARUS usability questionnaire (consisting of 8 questions pertaining to manipulability, M1 through M8, and 8 questions pertaining to comprehensibility, C1 through C8, on a 7-point Likert-type scale) [6], followed by a 10-question multiple-choice post-quiz that tests what facts they have retained after playing the game. The post-quiz contains questions that are all answerable by visiting only the required locations.

4 Results

In terms of the game's usability, no significant differences were found between the control (without card mechanic) and experimental (with card mechanic) batches for the majority (14 out of 16) of the questions in the usability survey, after applying, on a per-question basis, a Welch t-test [7] on the mean and variance of each batch's responses, then finding the probability associated with each t-test using a standard two-tailed distribution significance level of $a = 0.05$ (See Fig. 2). For the two questions that breach the significance level, namely, M1 = "I think that interacting with this application requires a lot of body muscle effort", and M3 = "I found the device difficult to hold while operating the application", the sample mean and variance of the experimental group is actually lower in both instances, which means that the experimental batch likely found the game to use less muscle effort and the device less difficult to hold, respectively, despite the addition of more game elements (i.e., the card-collection mechanic), which may indicate that the mechanic exhibits an illusory negating effect on perceived fatigue.

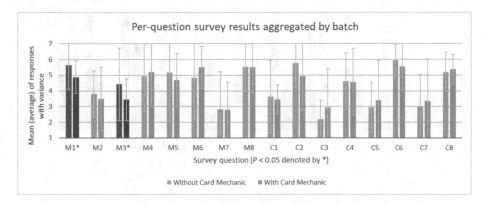

Fig. 2. Comparison of usability survey test results between control and experimental batches.

This finding, while not particularly noteworthy in and of itself, is coupled with another peculiarity observed during the experiment: None of the students in the control batch opted to visit either of the two optional locations, but 11 out of the 16 total students (2 groups out of 3) in the experimental batch visited *both* optional locations, without any external prodding. The observers of the experimental batch report that it is due to willingness on the part of the players to explore more of the campus and their desire to not miss the collectible cards in these optional locations. Thus, it is highly probable that the modified game's collection mechanic increased the players' engagement to the critical point of willingness to do optional tasks.

In the post-quiz, players of the control batch scored an average of 66.4% (variance 0.0255), while players in the experimental batch scored an average of 86.3% (variance 0.0145), with a Welch's t-test probability of $P < 0.001$, making it a significant score improvement that is highly unlikely to have been introduced by random chance. A per-question breakdown (see Fig. 3) reveals that the experimental batch consistently got the correct answer on each individual question at either an equal or higher rate than students in the control batch. The improvement in the percentage of correct responses for half of these questions (Q3, Q4, Q8, Q9 and Q10) were shown via t-test ($\alpha = 0.05$) to be unlikely random. Thus, we assert with high confidence that the modified game's card-collection mechanic is likely to increase players' retention of facts.

Observers also noted an increased tendency for players within the same experimental group to engage with each other, e.g., to compare card collections, to compete for the most cards collected, and to share strategies for obtaining particularly hard-to-find cards. While the experiment was not explicitly designed to monitor for these observations, their occurrence affirms card collection as an effective experience mechanic.

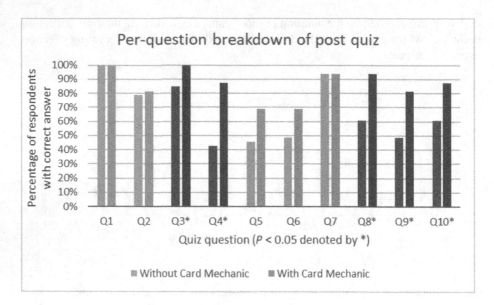

Fig. 3. Post quiz per-question results.

5   Conclusion

This study implemented a virtual-card-collection mechanic on top of an educational AR game; one that mimics the reward mechanics of popular smartphone/mobile games but is specifically designed to reiterate learning points previously presented earlier within the game. Evaluation shows that this mechanic significantly and positively impacts both the engagement and learning retention of players. Further studies may explore psychological reasons as to why collection mechanics increase player engagement in these games, and it is recommended that future location-based AR games be built with collection mechanics up front in order to improve player engagement and retention. For future work, an updated version of *Igpaw: Loyola* is currently being prepared that includes card collection for all 8 of its chapters, as well as real-world rewards (e.g., a physical gift in exchange for collecting all of the cards in the game); player analytics may be collected from this updated version to further expand this study.

References

1. Bacca, J., Baldiris, S., Fabregat, R., Graf, S.: Augmented reality trend in education: a systematic review of research and applications. Educ. Technol. Soc. **17**(4), 133–149 (2014)
2. Dunleavy, M., Dede, C.: Augmented reality teaching and learning. In: Spector, J., Merrill, M., Elen, J., Bishop, M. (eds.) Handbook of Research on Educational Communications and Technology, pp. 735–745. Springer, New York (2014). https://doi.org/10.1007/978-1-4614-3185-5_59

3. Harley, J.M., Poitras, E.G., Jarrell, A., Duffy, M.C., Lajoie, S.P.: Comparing virtual and location-based augmented reality mobile learning: emotions and learning outcomes. Educ. Technol. Res. Dev. **64**(3), 359–388 (2016)
4. Rodrigo, M.M., Vidal, E.C., Caluya, N.R., Agapito, J.L., Diy, W.D.: Usability study of an augmented reality game for Philippine history. In: Proceedings of the 24th International Conference on Computers in Education, Asia-Pacific Society for Computers in Education, Mumbai, India (2016)
5. Vidal, E.C., et al.: Igpaw: Loyola—design of a campus-wide augmented reality game using MAGIS. In: Proceedings of the 26th International Conference on Computers in Education, Asia-Pacific Society for Computers in Education, Philippines (2018)
6. Santos, M.E., Taketomi, T., Sandor, C., Polvi, J., Yamamoto, G., Kato, H.: A usability scale for handheld augmented reality. In: Proceedings of the 20th ACM Symposium on Virtual Reality Software and Technology (VRST 2014), pp. 167–176 (2014)
7. Welch, B.L.: The generalization of "student's" problem when several different population variances are involved. Biometrika **34**(1–2), 28–35 (1947)

Research on Evaluation Model of Social Game Advertising Effect Based on Eye Movement Experiment

Han Wang and Rongrong Fu[✉]

East China University of Science and Technology, No. 130 Meilong Rd,
Shanghai 200237, China
525034195@qq.com, Muxin789@126.com

Abstract. The rapid development of technology constantly changes the way advertising is transmitted. In recent years, more and more brands have chosen to use game advertising on social media to spread brand information. Faced with this new form of advertising, the industry is still adopting the existing evaluation system and method, lacking the research and application of the supporting effect evaluation system, ignoring the analysis of the special attributes of such advertisements, leading to the lack of accuracy in evaluation of advertising effects. In view of the current problem, this paper adopts the method of eye movement experiment, taking social game advertisement as an example, establishes the effect evaluation model of social game advertisement, and obtains the design principle of social game advertisement. It is verified by the second experiment that the result shows that the effect evaluation model is effective, and the proposed design principles are feasible. This helps advertisers to accurately and effectively grasp the communication advantages and disadvantages of social game advertising when measuring the effectiveness of advertising, and provide objective data support for the later adjustment of advertising delivery strategy. It is expected to provide an empirical reference for the industry to measure the effectiveness of social game advertising, enrich the theoretical research on the evaluation of social game advertising effectiveness, and provide reference for the application of eye movement experiment in social game advertising research.

Keywords: Eye movement experiment · Social game advertising · Effect evaluation model

1 Introduction

With the help of mobile internet technology, the social media platform has developed rapidly. More and more brand owners choose to place game advertisements on social platforms. The novel interaction mode and cool interface attract the attention of enterprises and individual consumers. The mobile social attributes not only enhance the communication advantage of advertising, but also improve the conversion rate of social game advertisements. However, there are still many gaps in the research on the evaluation system of social game advertisements.

© Springer Nature Switzerland AG 2019
C. Stephanidis (Ed.): HCII 2019, CCIS 1033, pp. 76–84, 2019.
https://doi.org/10.1007/978-3-030-23528-4_11

For the study of advertising effectiveness evaluation, the academia is shifting from early qualitative research to scientific quantitative research, in order to measure objective advertising effects through scientific data. Although eye tracking technology has been widely used in the field of advertising effects research, the application research in the field of interactive advertising effects is still not mature, and there has not formed an evaluation model for social game advertising. Therefore, this paper uses eye tracking technology to construct a social game advertising effect evaluation system and evaluation model, based on which the optimization design and its effect verification.

The research content of this paper mainly includes four parts: The first part determines the preliminary evaluation indicators through theoretical research. The second part uses eye tracking experiments and questionnaire data for statistical analysis, establishes the indicator proportion, and reconstructs the evaluation model. The third part optimizes the advertising design and validates the effect based on the effect evaluation model. The fourth part summarizes the research results.

2 Constructing Social Game Advertising Effect Evaluation System

2.1 Determining Social Game Advertising Effectiveness Evaluation Index

Through the teasing and analysis of related literatures, this study takes the attention of consumers' exposure to advertising as the objective research basis of advertising effects, and stands on the advertising level effect model, which uses advertising cognition, emotion and behavioral tendency as the three dimensions of evaluation indicators. Starting from the evaluation index of social media advertising, combined with the characteristics of game advertising, the effect evaluation index with significant game advertising characteristics is constructed (Fig. 1):

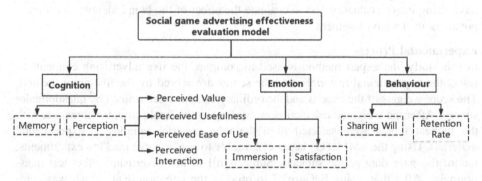

Fig. 1. Social Game advertising effect evaluation index system.

2.2 Determining the Advertising Elements

After constructing the effect evaluation index system by using the literature method, it is necessary to select typical social game advertisements as experimental materials, in order to compare the objective attention data with the subjective effect data. After combing and summarizing the literature, entertainment, information, usefulness, interface design and interactive experience are used as social game advertising elements, and used as indicators for experts to measure eye movement experimental materials.

After questionnaire survey and statistical analysis, it is found that the five elements of social game advertising will have a positive impact on the effect of the advertisement, thus determining that these five advertising elements can be used as filter conditions for experimental stimulation, ensuring the typicality of experimental materials and effectively improving the accuracy of the experimental results.

3 Eye Tracking Experiment

3.1 Experimental Design

Purpose of the Experiment
In different advertisements for different delivery periods, the brand identity is same. Consumers' memory and attitude towards brand identity can better represent their attitude towards the whole brand. Therefore, if you want to improve the brand communication effect, you should still study the consumers' attention and attitude of brand identity to enhance the effectiveness of brand communication.
In this experiment, the eye tracker was used to record the gaze data of subject's net dwell time, fixation point. Through data analysis, the influence of brand identity at different positions on the attention of subjects was found. At the same time, the degree of memory, cognition, emotion, and behavior of the brand was examined by the advertising effect evaluation test to evaluate the effect of the brand identity in different positions in the advertisement.

Experimental Process
In this study, the expert method is used to compare the five advertising elements to select the experimental materials, and the scores are scored by the five-point method. The score weights of the experts and the ordinary users are determined by questionnaire survey. After the weighted calculation, according to the final score, the three ads with the highest scores were selected from the nine material samples as experimental materials. Using the SMI ETG glasses eye tracker to perform eye tracking experiments, record the gaze data of the subjects. Subjects fill in the advertising effect test questionnaire. After that, using BeGaze3.7 to process the attention data, which was compared with the questionnaire data by SPSS, and finally the effect evaluation model of social game advertising was obtained.

Selection of Experimental Materials

After looking for a large number of game advertisements, it was found that the brand identity mainly appeared in three positions of the advertisement page: the home page, the last page and the other advertisement content pages. These three types of positions were respectively expressed as the beginning, the end and the middle. In order to make the experimental materials have a certain typicality, according to the multi-factor interactive experiment method, the three kinds of brand identification position in advertisements at the beginning, middle and end are divided into: "beginning"(B), "middle"(M), "end"(E), "beginning, middle"(B,M), "beginning, ending"(B,E), "beginning, middle, ending"(B,M,E), "middle, ending"(M,E), "none"(N). But only for three types of ads that have actual meaning: "end", "beginning, ending" and "beginning, middle and end" are studied, as shown in Table 1.

The current social game advertisements can be roughly divided into three types of scenes. Each advertisement of the three types is marked and scored, and weighted calculation is performed according to the score weights obtained by the questionnaire, and the comprehensive score of each advertisement is obtained. The highest score of each type is used as an experimental material for eye movement experiments.

Table 1. Experimental materials.

Scene use	Ad name	Logo position	Comprehensive score
	Jay Chou can read the mind	E	27.648
Internet/Service	Flying up	E	28.577
	Finding a dream journey	B,M,E	29.753
Product / Brand promotion	Party artifact	B,M,E	26.457
	Fix feel	B,M,E	26.292
	Draw your summer car	E	27.330
Hotspot / Festival event	Shape of love	B,E	29.565
	Brave spring festival	B,E	24.630
	Weather changes fate	B,E	26.154

3.2 Research and Analysis on the Effect of Social Game Advertising

Brand Identity Location and Attention

After data analysis, the location of the brand identity in social game advertising has a significant impact on the consumer's attention. According to the statistical results in Fig. 2, in terms of attention, the experimental material 1 obtained the longest gaze time and the most fixation point, which was called to obtain the high attention effect, and so on, the experimental material 3 obtained the medium attention effect, and the experimental material 2 was obtained the lowest attention effect. The data shows that the more times and the longer the brand identity appears, the easier it is to attract the attention of the participants, that is, the brand identity appears at the beginning, middle and end to get the most attention of the consumers.

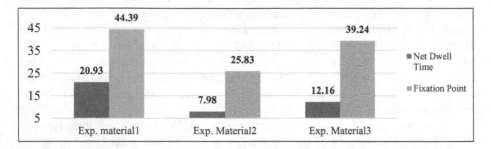

Fig. 2. Differences in attention between social game ads with different brand locations

Although the long-term exposure of the brand identity will attract the attention of the users, whether the brand identity will affect the influence of other advertising information on the user's perception, whether the positive effect brought by the attention of the brand identity will positively promote the communication effect of the advertisement needs further research and analysis.

Attention and Advertising Effects
According to Fig. 3, the most attention-grabbing experimental material 1 did not achieve the best advertising effect, but the experimental material 3 that gained the second attention obtained the best advertising effect, and the experimental material 2 that get the least attention obtained the lowest advertising effect. It can be seen that the content that attracts consumers' attention does not necessarily achieve the corresponding advertising effect. According to cognitive load theory, there are more content in game ads that require high level of interaction. This information will attract more attention from consumers. Therefore, more attention to these contents will affect the audience's handling of other surrounding information and consume cognitive resources for non-interactive information processing.

3.3　Construction of Social Game Advertising Effect Evaluation Model

According to the above analysis, it is known that the experimental material 3 has obtained moderate attention, but the highest advertisement effect data. Therefore, the effect data of the experimental material 3 is used as the basic data for constructing the effect evaluation model of the social game advertisement. Since the questionnaire adopts the calculation method of the five-point scale, and the average value of the attention times is 39.241, the data of the attention times is normalized, so that the eye movement data and the questionnaire data are in the same numerical range to perform data analysis. By using SPSS for regression analysis and weight calculation, the evaluation model of social game advertising is summarized as follows:

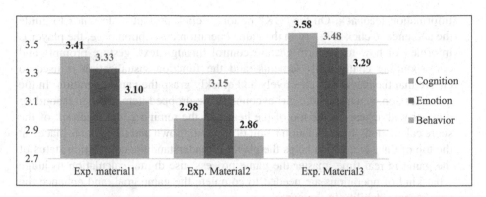

Fig. 3. Differences in effects of social game ads with different brand locations

Perception Level = 0.282 * Perceived Value + 0.227 * Perceived Ease of use
+ 0.257 * Perceived Usefulness + 0.234 * Perceived Interaction
Cognitive Effect = 0.488 * Memory + 0.512 * Perception Level
Emotional Effect = 0.461* Immersion +0.539* Satisfaction
Behavioral Effect = 0.483 * Sharing Will + 0.517 * Retention rate.

4 Optimized Design and Verification of Social Game Advertising

Based on the constructed effect evaluation model and analysis results, this study takes the brand activities in real life as the main design subject, proposes the principle of advertising optimization design, completes the optimization design of social game advertisements, and applies on the WeChat platform to validate the effectiveness of optimization principles and design.

4.1 Optimization Design of Social Game Advertising

Specific Design Process

(a) Scene settings. The overall selection of the blue swimming pool's light and shadow effect is the same as the "Bubble Show" event. The center of the page is placed with a cartoon girl as the main body, which can attract the player's first gaze. The brand logo is placed in the bubble in the hand of the little girl. It becomes the focus of the little girl's gaze and finger pointing, and also guides the player's gaze point to the brand logo. Dropped water guns, cold drinks, swim rings, cameras, sunglasses and the sun are also compatible with the items involved in the bubble show, from interface design to element selection to create a scene that is close to real events. These elements are arranged in order, so that the theme of the activity can be attached to the interface design to help consumers form a basic scene awareness of the activity.

(b) Information feedback. On the "OK" button, a click prompt is designed to guide the audience to click (Fig. 4). In the game operation description page, the player is informed of how to perform gesture control through text, gesture prompts and corresponding changes of elements, and the function visualization is used to ensure that the player can effectively and quickly grasp the game operation. In the game session, when the little girl encounters the dropped item, the corresponding number will appear on the top of the head. As the reminder and feedback of the score calculation, the calculation result of the countdown and the score is placed at the top of the page, which helps the player to understand the completion status of the game in real time, master the game process, use digital calculation to judge what kind of operations are needed to complete the game goal, and enhance the user's controllability to the game.

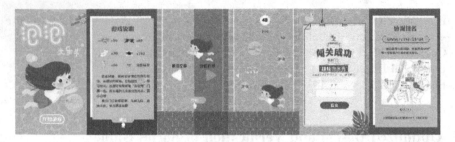

Fig. 4. Social game advertising effect picture

(c) Design consistency. This optimization design, from the choice of elements, including the little girl, falling items and transparent bubbles; color choices, including sky blue, pink, yellow and other cute colors and advertising interface design, have maintained the highly consistency of real activities, and it also realizes the consistency of online advertising screen design and offline activity scene layout in content and scene.

4.2   Validation of Social Game Optimization Ads

Data Evaluation for Social Game Optimization Ads
The optimized social game advertisement is published on the WeChat platform of Yueda 889 Plaza in the form of embedded WeChat headline graphic information. As of October 21, 2018, the ad generated a total of 1258 views. Since the embedded publishing limits the scope of propagation to a certain extent, the exposure effect of the advertisement will also be affected. Therefore, when evaluating the effect of optimizing the advertisement, it is also necessary to take into account the propagation effect of the graphic information carrying the game advertisement. According to the WeChat background data record, the graphic information obtained 732 readings on the day of August 14th. Although the reading volume decreased significantly with the pass of time, it still showed a slow growth trend.

Evaluation of Eye Movement Effects of Social Games Optimization Advertisements

The optimized design of social game advertisements was used as experimental material for eye movement experiments and advertising effectiveness questionnaire, containing 50 participants. The experimental results are as follows (Figs. 5 and 6):

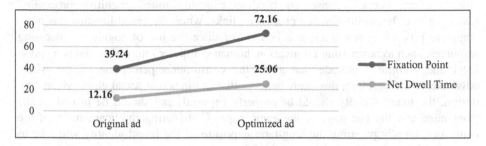

Fig. 5. Comparison of eye movement data between original and optimized ads

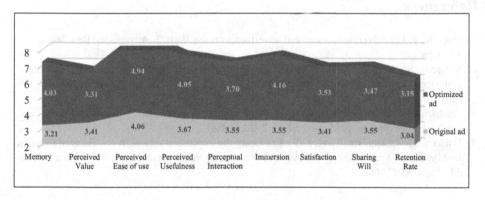

Fig. 6. Comparison of questionnaire data between original and optimized ads

Compared with the original advertisement, the optimized design has significantly improved the number of gaze points and net dwell time, and the effects in advertising cognition, emotion and behavior have also been significantly improved, in addition to perceived value and sharing will that the average score of the indicators is slightly lower than the original advertisement, and the optimized advertisement has better performance in other aspects. The reason for this result is: First, the target audience of the "bubble show" advertisement has limitations, children and their parents are more sensitive to advertising information, which reduces the willingness of the target audience to share ads with friends. Second, "Yueda 889 Plaza" does not gain high enough brand awareness, which is not conducive to consumers' perception of brand value. Therefore, the impact of optimized advertisements on users' perceived value and sharing intentions will be slightly lower than that of original advertisements.

5 Conclusion

Different brand identification positions in social game advertisements will affect the attention effect of advertisements, but there is no significant positive influence relationship between attention effect and advertising effects. The experimental results show that the advertisements with medium attention effect produce the best advertising attitude effect, because consumers need to allocate limited cognitive processing resources to different information processing links, when the brand identity gets more cognitive processing resources, it is bound to reduce the use of cognitive processing resources, such as advertising information, human-computer interaction, the perception level and emotional attitude that affect the consumer's perception of the whole advertisement. Therefore, this study believes that in the actual social game advertising design, the brand identity should be properly exposed, and should be placed on the front page and the last page of the game page. Considering the adaptability of the consumer, blindly pursuing the long-term exposure of the brand identity will lead to consumers' resentment.

References

1. Ducoffe, R.H.: Advertising value and advertising on the Web. J. Advertising Res. **36**(5), 21–35 (1996)
2. Sreejesh, S., Anusree, M.R.: Effects of cognition demand, mode of interactivity and brand anthropomorphism on gamers brand attention and memory in advergames. **70**, 575–588 (2017)
3. Zeithaml, V.A.: Consumer perceptions of price, quality, and value: a means-end model and synthesis of evidence. J. Market. **52**(3), 2–22 (1988)
4. Hsiao, C.H., Chang, J.J., Tang, K.Y.: Exploring the influential factors in continuance usage of mobile social Apps: satisfaction, habit, and customer value perspectives. Telematics Inform. **33**, 342–355 (2016)

Towards a Narrative Driven Understanding
of Games User Experience

Henrik Warpefelt[1]([⊠]) and Björn Stråå t[2]

[1] Department of Game Design, Uppsala University, 62157 Visby, Sweden
henrik.warpefelt@speldesign.uu.se
[2] Department of Computer and Systems Sciences, Stockholm University,
16450 Kista, Sweden
bjor-str@dsv.su.se

Abstract. Over the last two decades, there has been an expansion of the field of human-computer interaction to move from a functionalist viewpoint to a viewpoint more focused on the user's experience of an artifact. At the same time, the field of game studies has emerged as a way of understanding the user experience of games. Over the years, researchers have studied games as user experience artifacts, but as of yet there seems to be a dearth of frameworks that can be used to analyze the user experience of games from the perspective if game studies. In this paper, we take initial steps to provide such a framework by describing how the game narrative can be used to understand how users interpret games.

Keywords: Situation · Character · Narrative · Games user experience

1 Introduction

Over the last two decades, the field of Human-Computer Interaction (HCI) has seen an expansion into User eXperience (UX). This broadened focus has allowed us as researchers to view the artifacts that we interact with and use in a different light, focusing not only on the necessities of interaction but also on the user's experience of the product. By extension this also allows us to better understand the needs and motivations of our users. It also provided us with many useful theories on how we can view the user experience of digital products, for example the concept of character introduced by Janlert and Stolterman [4] and the separation between the designer's intention with their artifact and how it actually appears for the user as described by Hassenzahl [3].

At the same time the field of game studies has grown from its media studies roots into a vast and diverse field, focused on many different aspects of games. In particular, understanding the player's experience has been a core focus for the field, and many researchers have spent countless hours trying to describe how players perceive their gaming experience [5, 7, 10]. Similarly, we have seen the rise of the concept of Game eXperience (GX) [9], which is UX applied to games. The concept sees a large amount of use in the industry, where larger game developers now have teams of user researchers who try to improve the UX of their games. However, as of yet there seems

© Springer Nature Switzerland AG 2019
C. Stephanidis (Ed.): HCII 2019, CCIS 1033, pp. 85–89, 2019.
https://doi.org/10.1007/978-3-030-23528-4_12

to be no framework for how to holistically examine GX issues, and much of the research being done seems to focus primarily on working with artifacts to solve singular problems. In this paper, we propose a theoretical framework that helps us integrate the understanding created by game studies literature with the UX knowledge present in the HCI field, with the aim of improving the way we examine GX issues.

2 Situated Understanding of the User's Experience

Successful game design is to a large extent dependent on understanding how the user will interpret a certain design, and how that interpretation differs from the interpretation intended by the designer [11]. Hassenzahl [3] used the concept of character [4] to provide a model for how this difference between the intended product character created by the designer, and the apparent product character perceived by the user. Character, as described by Janlert and Stolterman [4], is the user's holistic perception of the different characteristics of an object. These characteristics are interrelated and inform each other, and integrate into a cohesive whole. This means that by knowing some of the characteristics (but not necessarily all of them) users can infer the remaining characteristics of an object. As described by Hassenzahl, the user's understanding of a product is situated in the context in which the user acts, as well as their previous experience with similar artifacts. Thus, the user will infer characteristics based on similar artifacts that they have encountered previously. As described by Janlert and Stolterman [4] we all build what they call a repertoire of character, which is a collection of different characters against which we compare new things that we encounter. Note, however, there may exist a mismatch between the character as apparent to the user, and the one intended by the designer. Hassenzahl [3] terms these two states the apparent product character, which is the character as it is interpreted by the user in their situated space, and the intended product character, which is the character as it was intended by the artifact's designer. Thus, when we encounter new artifacts, we may interpret them in ways that are different to what the designer intended, and many problems related to both UX and GX are related to a mismatch between these two types of character.

Fortunately, the field of game studies has engaged in a thorough exploration of what constitutes the GX, which can be used to inform a more in-depth understanding of the user's situation when they are interacting with the game. By utilizing the findings from the fields of user experience research and game studies we will be able to achieve a more in-depth understanding of how we should develop and evaluate games, and how that process can be augmented to improve the end products. For example, by better understanding how the game narrative [2, 6, 8] influences the game experience. This then informs our understanding of how the player's knowledge is situated [3], and how they understand the character of the game, as well as how this differs from the intended design of the game [11].

As described by Strååt [11] the game experience extends beyond the play session, and essentially starts when the player first encounters the game, e.g. reads about it online, or sees an advertisement about it [7]. However, the game experience is also influenced as the player plays the game. Not only do they encounter new interaction possibilities within the game, but the narrative of the game also acts as a framing for their experience. As mentioned by Strååt and Verhagen [12] the player's situation is altered as the player plays the game. This has the effect of altering the apparent product character [3] of the game, which means that the player perceives the game differently.

As the player plays the game, they are exposed to various stimuli that make up the gaming experience. As a part of the game, the narrative is therefore part of these stimuli and thus help build the player's understanding of the game's character, constantly altering the expectations the player has on the game. These expectations may be mundane, like that falling from a great height may injure the player's character, but can also be used to tell the player about how things work differently in this world.

3   Situation from Narrative

To understand how users of games perceive and interpret narratives we will use the theory of cognitive narrative in film developed by Bordwell [1]. This provides us with a basic framework on which to base our reasoning about how narratives are interpreted by humans. In his book, Bordwell introduced two concepts central to a constructivist understanding of narrative: fabula and syuzhet, both derived from Russian narrative formalism. Fabula is the understanding a perceiver has of a narrative they have experienced, or in the words of Bordwell: *[t]he fabula is thus a pattern which perceivers of narratives create through assumptions and inferences* [1]. Note here that the fabula need not necessarily be the "true" version of the narrative, but instead is how the perceiver has interpreted the individual events that make up the narrative. Fabula are in turn constructed from the perceiver's interpretation of a number of schemata, each a separate unit of information that helps the perceiver understand and interpret what they are perceiving. It is important to note that schemata are constructs that exist within the perceiver's cognition, and not necessarily in the game as an artifact. They are thus of the perceiver, not of the artifact. Syuzhet is described by Bordwell as the "architectonics of the film's presentation of the fabula", or what is actually shown to the perceiver of the narrative. Within the realm of the syuzhet, we find specific camera angles, editorial choices, costume and set design, spoken lines, music, and the myriad of other details that can be found in a film. Together, these details make up the details that the perceiver uses to create their schemata, and by extension their fabula of the narrative.

Together, fabula, syuzhet, and schemata allow us to describe the perception of narrative from the perspective of the perceiver. However, many of the specifics for the theories presented by Bordwell [1] are strongly tied to the medium of film. Although the concepts of fabula, syuzhet, and schemata are transferable between media, the same is not true for the details that pertain to them. If we view this theory from the perspective of games, where the perceiver is the player of the game, we can let Bordwell's cognitive narrative theory act as a framing for our understanding of the specifics pertaining to games and play.

As stated by Calleja [2] the player will create a story of their experience in the game, called the alterbiography. This is the story of the events that happened during their playthrough of the game, and how these were perceived by the player, told from a first-person perspective, which is very similar to the fabula described by Bordwell [1].

Jenkins [6] describes a similar construct, the emergent narrative, which is the narrative that emerges as the player plays the game. The key difference here is that the alter-biography is by definition of and from the player, whereas the emergent narrative exists disconnected from the player's perception. The difference here can be likened to the difference between the intended and apparent product character of the game [3] where the alterbiography and fabula are essentially the apparent product character of the narrative, whereas the emergent narrative can be seen as the intended product character of the game. By extension, we can then use Bordwell's concept of syuzhet - the "architectonics of the film's presentation of the fabula" - as a cognate to the concept of the intended product character of the narrative. It represents the various atoms of the story as told to the player of the game, for example the appearance of the characters in the game, the set pieces, the story beats that the player experiences, or the spoken lines and written text in the game. By understanding these various atoms as characteristics not only of the narrative but also of the game, we can expand our existing under-standing of character and better understand the player's situation process.

4 Conclusion

The theoretical framework presented in this article is a first step towards a more complete understanding of the game experience. It is by no means complete, but provides us with the basic building blocks we need to broaden our understanding of the player's gaming experience, be it in terms of UX or GX. Part of this is understanding how the narrative of the game informs the UX and GX, and how they in turn inform the narrative.

Using this theoretical framework, we can expand our understanding of the GX to encompass things that are very difficult to analyze using traditional UX methods, for example the narrative of a game. By considering the narrative as another layer on top of the GX and UX, that is both framed by and acts as a framing to the gaming experience, we can reason about how the traditional GX components such as user interaction and in-game challenges are affected by the stories we tell the player, and how these stories help frame the player's understanding of the things with which they are presented by the game. This would in turn allow us as researchers to discuss and dissect how the player interprets the things with which they are presented in the game, and allows us to better characterize processes such as player onboarding.

The framework is not yet easily applied as an analytical tool, but would need some kind of supporting construct that lets us as researchers deconstruct what Bordwell [1] would refer to as the syuzhet of the game, or what in UX research is known as the character and characteristics of the game. Combining the framework with a list of common characteristics and characters would allow us to meaningfully do a more encompassing deconstruction of the GX, and thus allow us to reason about the nar-rative in terms of these characteristics and how these are understood by the player, which in turn allows us to apply Hassenzahl's [3] and Stråât's [11] theories to better understand the how the player experiences the game.

References

1. Bordwell, D.: Narration in the Fiction Film. Routledge, Abingdon (1987)
2. Calleja, G.: In-Game: From Immersion to Incorporation. MIT Press, Cambridge (2011)
3. Hassenzahl, M.: The Thing and I: understanding the relationship between user and product. In: Blythe, M.A., Overbeeke, K., Monk, A.F., Wright, P.C. (eds.) Funology. Human-Computer Interaction Series, vol. 3, pp. 301–313. Springer, Heidelberg (2003). https://doi.org/10.1007/1-4020-2967-5_4
4. Janlert, L.-E., Stolterman, E.: The character of things. Des. Stud. **18**(3), 297–314 (1997)
5. Jennett, C., et al.: Measuring and defining the experience of immersion in games. Int. J. Hum.-Comput. Stud. **66**(9), 641–661 (2008)
6. Jenkins, H.: Game design as narrative architecture. In: Harrigan, P., Wardrip-Fruin, N. (eds.) First Person. New Media as Story, Performance, and Game, pp. 118–130. MIT Press, Cambridge (2004)
7. Kultima, A., Stenros, J.: Designing games for everyone: the expanded game experience model. In: Proceedings of the International Academic Conference on the Future of Game Design and Technology, pp. 66–73. ACM, May 2010
8. Murray, J.H.: Hamlet on the Holodeck: The Future of Narrative in Cyberspace. MIT Press, Cambridge (2017)
9. Nacke, L.E., Drachen, A., Göbel, S.: Methods for evaluating gameplay experience in a serious gaming context. Int. J. Comput. Sci. Sport **9**(2), 1–12 (2010)
10. Sánchez, J.L.G., Vela, F.L.G., Simarro, F.M., Padilla-Zea, N.: Playability: analysing user experience in video games. Behav. Inf. Technol. **31**(10), 1033–1054 (2012)
11. Strååt, B.: Extending game user experience - exploring player feedback and satisfaction. Ph.D. thesis. Stockholm University (2017)
12. Strååt, B., Verhagen, H.: Exploring video game design and player retention-a longitudinal case study. In: Proceedings of the 22nd International Academic Mindtrek Conference, pp. 39–48. ACM, October 2018

Application of Archery to VR Interface

Masasuke Yasumoto[1](✉) and Takehiro Teraoka[2]

[1] Faculty of Information Technology, Kanagawa Institute of Technology,
1030 Shimo-ogino, Atsugi, Kanagawa 243-0292, Japan
yasumoto@ic.kanagawa-it.ac.jp
[2] Department of Computer Science, Faculty of Engineering, Takushoku University,
815-1 Tatemachi, Hachioji, Tokyo 193-0985, Japan
tteraoka@cs.takushoku-u.ac.jp

Abstract. A game controller that imitates a real object can provide a realistic experience. For example, a gun-type controller and a handle-type controller can give players a realistic experience of shooting and racing, respectively. In this paper, we present multiple interfaces comprising a bow and its components that we have developed and enhanced for application to different games and playing styles. Through these explanations, we demonstrate the potential of these interfaces for game application to xR.

Keywords: VR · Interface · Bow

1 Introduction

Various interfaces have been developed in the game field so far. In general, these interfaces are not generic but are limited to special use. For example, there is a gun-type controller for a shooting game, a handle-type controller for a racing game, and so on. These days in the xR field, applications for games are constantly coming out, but in the case of VR using HMD, the general purpose controller is mostly used. The reality offered by the controller is increased by supplementing it with images.

With AR and MR, it is difficult to compensate with CG images because players can actually see the handheld controller. They can also see the surrounding environment in the real world, so the reality of the controller itself needs to be enhanced in order to achieve an immersive experience.

In light of this background, we have focused on the bow as an instrument of reality and have developed various bow-shaped interfaces. Bows have been used all over the world for eons, so most people are familiar with the basic operation without having ever touched one. Also, the bow requires analog operation, in contrast to, say, a gun, which makes it safer than a gun, and people tend to feel it is fun to operate. To enhance the reality of the bow-shaped interface, in addition to the appearance, the force reality and force feedback are important; therefore, we have applied a bow and bow components to multiple bow-shaped interfaces by measuring parameters based on a real bow.

© Springer Nature Switzerland AG 2019
C. Stephanidis (Ed.): HCII 2019, CCIS 1033, pp. 90–95, 2019.
https://doi.org/10.1007/978-3-030-23528-4_13

Fig. 1. Bow-shaped interfaces in use. (Left: "Light Shooter". Center: "3rd Electric Bow Interface". Right: "VAIR Bow".)

Our multiple bow-shaped interfaces are shown in Fig. 1. The "Light Shooter" with Electric Bow Interface [1] is based on a traditional Japanese bow and is used in combination with a projector. The "3rd Electric Bow Interface" [2] is based on a western recurve bow and is a standalone system incorporating a mobile projector and a computer. The "VAIR Bow" is a VAIR Field device [3] that is part of the new physical e-Sport trend; it has been developed with a smartphone and an HTC VIVE Tracker.

In this paper, we describe the characteristics of the bow and the systems that implement these interfaces.

2   Bow-Shaped Interfaces

2.1   Bow Form

The bow-shaped interfaces that we developed are divided into a Japanese bow type (e.g., the Light Shooter) and an archery type (e.g., the 3rd Electric Bow Interface and VAIR Bow), as shown in Fig. 1. The Japanese bow has a structure in which the limb and the grip are integrated, while the archery bow's limb and grip are divided. These bows also have a different way of setting the arrow: if the shooter is right-handed, the arrow needs to be set on the right side with the Japanese bow and on the left side with the archery bow. The Japanese bow has no attachments (e.g., scope), while the archery bow can be attached with a stabilizer, a clicker, a damper, and so on to enable stable shooting. In light of these features, the archery type is the more suitable device for a VR environment.

However, using these devices in the VR environment poses several difficult problems. First, they do not have a rigid body, as they are designed to curve and bend. It is not easy to fix various sensors to this type of structure, so durability is a problem in areas with strong movement. In fact, our initial prototype bow-shaped interface, which had sensors on the string and electrical wires, was not durable enough and the string broke after only a few shots. This happened not only because the string was tensioned but also because the string vibrated violently after shooting. In addition, for safety reasons our device used an air shot without an arrow, and this air shot also contributed to the low durability.

Another problem is the impact that the bow itself receives when a player draws and shoots. This impact actually disables the sensors attached to the

Fig. 2. Depiction of player drawing a VAIR Bow. HTC vive tracker and strain gauges are integrated into the bow's grip and bottom of the limb, respectively.

device. For example, an inexpensive acceleration sensor can obtain data with a margin of plus or minus two grams; however, there is much more acceleration than that when a bow is used, so it is easy to damage the sensors. Therefore, the 3rd Electric Bow Interface uses a 9-axis IMU, which has high durability with a margin of plus or minus 16 grams.

2.2 Bow Information

The requirements of bow-shaped interfaces vary depending on whether the application is for game playing or sports training. In the case of game playing, the most important thing for players is to feel good and have fun, while for sports training, it is more important for the players to feel like they're using something real. Our interfaces were developed for game devices, but the information they obtain during usage is accurate enough to be used in sports.

Our bow-shaped interfaces obtain three items of information: the direction of player's aiming, the position of the device, and the degree of player's drawing the string. First, the direction of aiming is the direction of shooting a virtual arrow. When a player aims with the scope attached on the device, the point that the scope reticle shows is the shooting direction.

The player's position can be calculated by the angle of the bow and the direction of shooting, assuming that the player's position is fixed. The 3rd Electric Bow Interface utilizes this approach by using a sensor integrated into the device to obtain the parameters of the device's position. However, different players have different heights, different arm lengths, and different ways of holding the bow, so the relative position of the device from a fixed point (such as the ground) should be measured in order to calculate more precise parameters. The absolute position is also required if the player moves with the device on while playing the

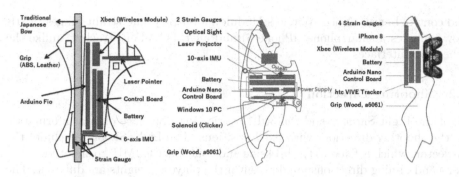

Fig. 3. Construction of interfaces. (Left: "Light Shooter". Center: "3rd Electric Bow Interface". Right: "VAIR Bow".)

game. When the player draws and shoots the bow from a fixed position, this positional information is required. The VAIR Bow, which is our latest interface, obtains the positional information by integrating an HTC vive tracker, as shown in Fig. 2.

The degree of player's drawing the bow is related to the flight distance and speed of the arrow. The larger this degree, the stronger force that the arrow receives. As mentioned above, it is difficult to set a sensor on the string or around the limb. To circumvent this, we focus on the fact that the metal in the grip is slightly distorted after drawing the string and transmitting this force to the grip. By measuring the relation between this amount of distortion and the degree of drawing the string, the flight distance and speed of the virtual arrows can be calculated. Our interfaces therefore obtain the parameters of the distorted amount with a strain gauge and then calculate them.

By using this information, our interfaces can provide an experience like a real simulation. However, as shown in Fig. 2, our devices use an air shot without a real arrow when players use them. When using a real bow and arrow, the player's hand touches the bow and arrow, and this friction also needs to be considered. Therefore, to enhance our interfaces, information on the friction should be measured and integrated in VR.

3 System

3.1 Construction

As shown in Fig. 3, the Light Shooter and the 3rd Electric Bow Interface are based on a traditional Japanese bow and an archery bow, respectively. The Light Shooter consists of a laser pointer, a microcomputer (Arduino Fio and control board), 6-axis IMU, Xbee (Wireless Module), and strain gauges. The 3rd Electric Bow Interface consists of a mobile laser projector, Windows 10 PC, 10-axis IMU, a microcomputer (Arduino Nano and control board), Solenoid, Optical Sight, and strain gauges. In addition to a microcomputer (Arduino Nano and control board), Xbee (Wireless Module), a battery, and strain gauges, VAIR Bow includes a smartphone (iPhone 8) and an HTC VIVE Tracker, unlike the other two interfaces.

3.2   Shooting Direction

Both the Light Shooter and the 3rd Electric Bow Interface obtain information on the shooting directions with fixed positions. The Light Shooter excludes the projector, which is fixed to the backside and contains the IMU, so shooting directions and aiming directions are different if the players' heights are different. The 3rd Electric Bow Interface includes the projector, which is set in the same direction as the sensor, so the differences of those directions are smaller than those of the Light Shooter. When a player holds this interface, an image determined from the parameters of the sensor and the player's height and arm length is projected in the shooting direction, as shown in the center of Fig. 1.

VAIR Bow obtains positional information with the HTC VIVE Tracker and is used in combination with an attached iPhone that displays the shooting direction, which makes it possible to create a more accurate simulation than the other two interfaces. However, the positional relation of the player's eyesight and the iPhone is unknown, so there is gap between the viewing angle of the image and the actual viewing angle. In the VAIR Field in which this interface is used, the player can see the display with a wider viewing angle than the actual one because the iPhone's display is so small that the player can barely see it if both angles are adjusted.

Therefore, to enhance the realism of the simulation, the iPhone should be replaced with a tablet, which has a wider display, and then the player's face position can be obtained with the internal camera.

3.3   Device Position

As mentioned above, in both the Light Shooter and the 3rd Electric Bow interfaces, fixed parameters related to each device position are used to obtain the position, but different players see different gaps between the shooting direction and the aiming direction.

In contrast, VAIR Bow obtains the device position with an HTC VIVE Tracker. The typical device using "AR Kit" with a camera is not accurate enough to obtain the device position. This device also loses the tracking when the player moves violently. Compared to the typical device, our VAIR Bow can obtain the device position with higher accuracy. Furthermore, its function is not affected at all if the player suddenly moves.

Therefore, we can apply this VAIR Bow to physical e-Sports applications such as "VAIR Field", where multiple players move around and shoot with a gun-type or bow-type device.

4   Conclusion

In this paper, we have described the construction and characteristics of several bow-shaped interfaces used as game controllers and simulators. We also demonstrated how to obtain necessary information and prospects. In the future, by using information that we cannot obtain currently and calculating it, we will apply these interfaces to sports training applications.

References

1. Yasumoto, M., Ohta, T.: The electric bow interface. In: Shumaker, R. (ed.) VAMR 2013. LNCS, vol. 8022, pp. 436–442. Springer, Heidelberg (2013). https://doi.org/10.1007/978-3-642-39420-1_46
2. Yasumoto, M., Teraoka, T.: Electric bow interface 3D. In: SIGGRAPH Asia 2015 Emerging Technologies, SA 2015, pp. 11:1–11:2 (2015)
3. Yasumoto, M., Teraoka, T.: VAIR field - multiple mobile VR shooting sports. In: Chen, J.Y.C., Fragomeni, G. (eds.) VAMR 2018. LNCS, vol. 10910, pp. 235–246. Springer, Cham (2018). https://doi.org/10.1007/978-3-319-91584-5_19

What Drives Female Players' Continuance Intention to Play Mobile Games? The Role of Aesthetic and Narrative Design Factors

Qiangxin Zheng[(⊠)] and Lili Liu

College of Economics and Management,
Nanjing University of Aeronautics and Astronautics, Nanjing, China
zhengqxl998@163.com, llili85@nuaa.edu.cn

Abstract. Many scholars have suggested that video games predominantly target at male players. However, with the proliferation of mobile games in recent years, evidence shows that the gap between male players and female players are closing. Report from Entertainment Software Association 2015 indicates that Women (48%) and Men (52%) play video games in approximately equal numbers. Therefore, it is very important to pay more attention to female players' preferences and design mobile games for them. Compared with male players who prefer more complex and competitive games, female players exhibit less dedication and skill with respect to gaming. Yet, research on mobile games generally ignore the female group and the female-orientated game design factors. To fill this gap, this study identifies the aesthetic and narrative game design factors and investigate how these design factors influence female players' continuance intention to play mobile games. Focus group discussions were conducted to explore the aesthetic and narrative design factors they preferred. Our findings provide suggestions for future female-orientated game developers regarding the aesthetic character design and narrative design, thus help them to retain and attract more female game players, improve the overall experiences, gain a broader market, and improve their profitability.

Keywords: Mobile game · Female players · Aesthetics ·
Narrative · Continuance intention

1 Introduction

Many scholars have suggested that video games predominantly target at male players [7]. However, with the proliferation of mobile games in recent years, evidence shows that the gap between male players and female players are closing [3]. Mobile games specifically targeting female players are gaining popularity and the number of female game players is rapidly growing. As a result, report from Entertainment Software Association 2015 indicates that Women (48%) and Men (52%) play video games in approximately equal numbers [3]. In mainland China, female made up 53% of all mobile game players in 2013 [16], while the mobile game design remains male-centric and unfriendly to female players [2]. Compared with male players who prefer more complex and competitive games, female exhibit less dedication and skill with respect to

© Springer Nature Switzerland AG 2019
C. Stephanidis (Ed.): HCII 2019, CCIS 1033, pp. 96–103, 2019.
https://doi.org/10.1007/978-3-030-23528-4_14

gaming [12]. Yet, research on mobile games has generally ignored the female group and the female-orientated game design factors. To fill this gap, this exploratory study identifies the aesthetic and narrative game design factors and investigate how these design factors influence female players' continuance intention to play mobile games.

Different from male-centric games, female-orientated games pay more attention the aesthetic and narrative design. Aesthetic refers to the perceived visual appeal of a digital character in mobile games [1]. Many female players consider the visual appeal (e.g., clothes, shoes, and hats) of a character and aesthetics (e.g., background skins) of a game as very important for them to keep playing a game. For example, the Chinese mobile game "Love and Producer" attracted 7 millions of players within one month after launched in December 2017, with females representing 90% of the downloads [8]. Love and Producer is a dating simulation game for mobile, which lets players develop romantic relationships with one of the anime boys shown in Fig. 1. The male characters in the game are good-looking and dressed appropriately in different occasions. The visual appeal is very bright, fresh, soft, and natural.

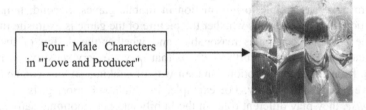

Four Male Characters in "Love and Producer"

Fig. 1. Male Characters in Love and Producer (Source: https://supchina.com/2018/01/16/)

Additionally, an engaging narrative is provided. Female players are allowed to interact with the male characters in various ways. Players are able to date with male characters in different scenarios and have conversations with a particular male character in the game anytime, with customized responses from them (e.g. Figure 2). After launching, "Love and Producer" became successful immediately. Its monthly revenue in January 2018 surpassed $31 million [4].

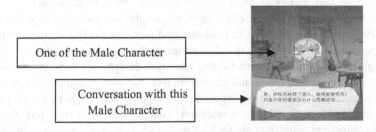

One of the Male Character

Conversation with this Male Character

Fig. 2. Interaction with Character in Love and Producer (Source: https://supchina.com/2018/01/16/)

Inspired by the game love and producer, this study seeks to investigate what drives female players' continuance intention to play mobile games, focus on the role of aesthetic and narrative design factors. An interview with 8 female mobile game players was conducted to explore the aesthetic and narrative design factors they prefer. Based on the interview conclusions, we provide suggestions for future game developers regarding the aesthetic character design, visual appeal design, and narrative design, thus help them to retain and attract more female game players, improve the overall experiences, gain a broader market, and improve their profitability.

2 Literature Review

2.1 Differences Between Male and Female Players

There is a big gap between the needs of female players and those of male players. First, females are more sensitive to information compared with males. Nii Yasuyun, a well-known expert in Human Sciences states: "In general, men are better at spatial cognition, while women are better at language and nuance." Female's aptitude for language makes them more susceptible to information in mobile games. Second, females pay more attention to details, such as whether the picture of the game is exquisite in details, whether the color collocation is reasonable, and whether the design of the role is exquisite and beautiful, which further reflects that they are very sensitive to information. Third, female are more emotional in their way of thinking, so they can be attracted by narrative design more easily. For example, in childhood, most girls like to play *playing house*, they play different roles in the family and get emotional satisfaction by interacting with other members of the family. Boys like the exciting game such as horse riding and fighting, but girls prefer narrative games. Love and producer is designed as a love forming game with rich storyline, which gains instant popularity among female game players in Mainland China. In the game, players can interact with four male protagonists, with the increased time devoted to the game and upgrade of game level, the plot will be further developed. The prevalence of Love and producer indicates that females are more sensitive, they prefer to indulge in fantasy and ideal world. Therefore, if the game designer intends to better retain female players, he/she should better understand contemporary women, and find the design factors that can trigger their fantasy, and improve their game experience. In general, male players care more about the competitive and technical aspects of the game, they want to get a sense of excitement and conquer difficult challenges while playing games. On the contrary, female players pay more attention to aesthetic and narrative design, they want to relax themselves and have a better emotional experience during game playing.

Female players prefer the aesthetic and narrative design factors in games not only because they have unique emotional characteristics, but also because their purpose of playing games differ from male players [15]. Most female players focus more on entertainment and emotional communication, hence, they may not pay too much attention to numerical achievements such as the attack power of characters in the game and the experience gained in each game. Our questionnaire also proves this point.

Therefore, aesthetic design and narrative design must be considered in order to bring better visual experience, participation and satisfaction to female players.

2.2 Aesthetic

Beauty is a psychological feeling that people can fully experience and enjoy. Beauty could affect people's emotions from the appearance, environment and moral aspects [9]. Aesthetic design is an applied science. An aesthetic feeling is enjoyable, which could be stimulated by colors, textures, lines, and shapes [18]. Mobile game consists of comprehensive elements such as music, art, film, literature and so on. While playing games, players will be attracted by the view point of the screen at the beginning, following by the fun of game play, and finally by the experience of virtual aesthetics [5]. A game with better visual appeal will provides players with better aesthetic experience. Therefore, an attractive video game must be capable to incur aesthetic experiences in different ways, e.g., character model design, map details, action effects, magic effects and so on. For example, in the game, costume is the soul of the game character design. Many female players like to change costumes for game characters, which gives the character a fresh feeling, makes it more enjoyable to play a game, and eventually affect their intention to continue game playing.

2.3 Narrative

Scholars argue that the whole process of a game is consisted of a series of problems and events to be solved by the players. Therefore, this process can be treated as narrative [11]. For example, On December 6, 2017, Hit-point, a Japanese game company, launched a game *traveling frog*, which became the Top 1 free game in the App Store within two months. The protagonist of the game is a cute little frog, players can give it a name, buy presents like food, lucky charm, and props for it, the frog will have a trip to different scenic spots with these presents, and then it will bring some local specialties and postcards back for their caregivers (the players). Many female players were addicted to the game and posted pictures of their frogs on their social network sites. The narrative of *traveling frog* (process of raising frogs) can arouse players' maternal feelings, which is very distinctive [13].

3   Methodology

In this study, we employed the focus group discussion method. We recruited eight female players who had played at least one mobile game, and then assigned them to two groups (four players in each group). The group is "focused" on the mobile game experiences [14], leading to the development of a theoretical understanding of cognitive, behavioral, situational, and environmental factors in this context [6]. All participants met the focus group moderator in the same room, participants in group 1 were invited at first and then group 2 members [7]. Before the discussion, all participants were asked to provide their demographic information (see Table 1). Each discussion lasted for one hour, discussions were moderated by the same instructor. During the discussion, we asked six questions in the brainstorming discussion: (1). Which mobile game do you play? Why do you play it? (2). While deciding whether continue to play a mobile game, which factor you care about most? (3). Do you prefer games that have a rich storyline? (4). Would you play a game because of its graphic design, character design, costume design, etc.? (5). Do you buy skins or props to dress up your favorite characters? (6). Why would you like to dress up a character? Based on participants' approval, the moderator recorded the discussions. Next, we sorted and categorized their answers.

Table 1. Participant demographics

Group No.	Participant ID	Gender	Age	Frequency of playing per week	Average duration of play	Favorite game	Focused factor
1	1-A	F	21	Everyday	4–5 h	Happy elimination	The plot design (N)
	1-B	F	21	Everyday	1–2 h	Onmyoji	Game scene Design(A)
	1-C	F	21	Twice per week	3–4 h	Thrill battlegrounds	Game scene Design, Operation design(A)
	1-D	F	22	Everyday	2–3 h	Thrill battlegrounds	Operation design(A)
2	2-A	F	20	Everyday	2–3 h	Honor of kings	Operation design(A)
	2-B	F	23	3 times per week	1 h	Thrill battlegrounds	Character design(A)
	2-C	F	21	Everyday	1–2 h	Love and producer	The plot design (N)
	2-D	F	22	Everyday	2–3 h	Honor of kings, Thrill battlegrounds	Character design(A)

4   Results

4.1   Aesthetic

Based on the answers from participants, we extracted three aspects of aesthetic design factors that female players care about most: character design, game scene design, and operation design.

Character Design. The design of game characters is very important. Game characters are the protagonist in the game world, they are usually the first object depicted by a game construct [17]. Players are able to select a game character to represent themselves and interact directly with other characters, which makes them more willing to continuously play the game in the future. Participant 2-B said, "Playing thrill battlegrounds takes up most of my game play time, the critical reason is that I can play with my friends, which may improve my playing experiences. As for my personal preference, I will love this game even more if they can beautify the game characters and design more beautiful clothes. I hope I can change different kinds of clothes for my character in the game, and I want to be distinctive." Participant 2-D added, "The design of characters and the skin of characters are what I care most about, and I have bought a lot of skins (e.g. Figure 3) for my favorite game characters."

Fig. 3. The character and its skin in Honor of kings (Source: a game screenshot provided by Participant 2-D)

Game Scene Design. Game sense design refers to all object modeling design, such as game scenario design (e.g., flowers, mountains, rivers, or trees in the game environment) [10]. Participant 1-B said, "The key reason I like Onmyoji is that its interface is very delicate and designed in Japanese comic style." Participant 1-C said, "If a game graphic design is particularly rough, then my experience of playing the game will be very poor. The game scene design of Thrill battlegrounds is very authentic and vivid. For example, every blade of grass on the ground is very vivid. In the snow mode, the sound that the characters walk on the snowfield is almost the same with natural sound."

Operation Design. Operation design enables players to interact with the game environment (e.g., game characters). Compare with a game that is difficult to manipulate, female players prefer cool operating interfaces and functions, such as effective visualization of attack. Whether the operation design is cool influences female players' game experience. Participant 2-A said, "The most important reason that I don't play Thrill battlegrounds is that the interface is not cool enough when attacking, so it could not attract me." Participant 1-D added, "Because the operation is complex, when I play Thrill battlegrounds with my friends, I can only carry out simple attacks and cannot constitute high damage."

4.2 Narrative

Narrative design of the game mainly refers to the plot settings in the game. Among existing mobile games, narration design generally follows two methods: (1) the storyline cannot be changed. Regardless of the player's choice and operation, the storyline can only develop in one predefined direction eventually; (2) the storyline that can be changed. Depending on the player's choice, the story could be re-developed and goes to different directions. In this case, the players perform as a narrative creator rather than a passive receiver. Participant 1-A said, "There are various types of elimination games in the APP store now, but I prefer the one with a storyline, which is not too boring." Participant 2-C said, "I've been playing *Love and Producer* for a year, and I usually spend one or two hours every day on the game. In the game, I met Xu Mo (a hero in the game) and fell in love with him. Every step of the story development impressed me deeply." Participant 1-A added, "I like playing *Love and Producer* too. Because my story in the game is not exactly the same as others, the result becomes different because of our different choices, that's why I like it." Results of focus group discussion indicate that, among similar games, female players prefer those with detailed and editable plot design.

5 Discussion

The number of female mobile game players is increasing rapidly, who have different preferences on game design factors compared with male players. According to our focus group discussion, we find that female players paid little attention to improve their fighting skills and complete complicated tasks. On the contrary, they focus more on narrative design and aesthetic design factors of games, such as game scene design, character design and operation design. For instance, participants in the group discussion frequently reported two favorite mobile games: Glory of Kings and thrills battlefield, and 5 participants like them. Their discussion about these two games support that female players pay more attention to the aesthetic design. For example, participant 2-D said, "Compared with thrills battlefield, the character design of Glory of Kings is more delicate and beautiful. According to the current universal world view, the designer positions the roles and designs heroes with different attributes, such as Su Daji is sexy, has strong explosive force and weak vitality. In terms of characters' skins, the design is also very delicate and pretty. For example, the outfits for Su Daji are sexy, and the movements and special effects of her fighting skills will change when the skin changes, which makes the game more diverse and flexible."

The future of female mobile game market is promising. In order to attract more female users, game designers should better understand female players' preferences. First, designers should pay more attention to the aesthetic design in terms of character design (e.g., provide diverse characters, emphasize details of characters), game scene design (allow players to adjust the game scene according to their own preferences, such as background colors), and operation design (e.g., enhance the visual effect of attack). Besides, the designer should be aware that female players' operational skill is relatively weak, thus they should simplify the operation as much as possible without reducing the entertainment of the game. Finally, designers should enhance the narrative of the game, as interesting plot can help a game to attract more female players. We hope above suggestions are useful for game designers to retain and attract female players, further expand its player base, improve its profitability and sustainability.

Acknowledgement. This study was supported by the Fundamental Research Funds for the Central Universities: No. NR2018002 awarded to second author and the Creative Studio of Electronic Commerce in Nanjing University of Aeronautics and Astronautics.

References

1. Cai, S., Xu, Y., Yu, J., De Souza, R.: Understanding aesthetics design for E-commerce web sites: a cognitive-affective framework. In: Proceedings of 16th Pacific Asia Conference on Information System (2008)
2. Cote, A.C.: Writing "Gamers" the gendered construction of gamer identity in Nintendo power (1994–1999). Games Culture. https://doi.org/10.1177/1555412015624742 (2015)
3. Entertainment Software Association. Essential facts about the computer and video game industry (2015). http://www.theesa.com/wp-content/uploads/2015/04/ESAEssential-Facts-2015.pdf
4. Feng, J.Y.: Love and Producer, the Chinese Mobile Game That Has Millions of Women Hooked (2018). https://supchina.com/2018/01/16/love-and-producer-the-chinese-mobile-game-that-has-hooked-millions-of-women/
5. 黄天益, 赖守亮.: 浅析游戏设计中的虚拟美学及体验.才智·Ability and Wisdom **18**, 270 (2017)
6. Kidd, P.S., Parshall, M.B.: Getting the focus and the group: enhancing analytical rigor in focus group research. Qual. Health Res. **10**(3), 293–308 (2000)
7. Kocurek, Carly A.: Coin-Operated Americans: Rebooting Boyhood at the Video Game Arcade. University of Minnesota Press, Minneapolis (2015)
8. Liu, T.: Video games as dating platforms: exploring digital intimacies through a Chinese online dancing video game. Telev. New Media **20**(1), 36–55 (2019)
9. 李晓鲁, 邓子月.: 浅析美学与设计美学的"同"与"不同". 美术与设计 **20**, 97 (2016)
10. Li, Y.: Art design in the application of mobile games and research. Postgraduate Dissertation. Harbin Normal University, Harbin (2016)
11. Liu, Y.C.: Playably story: interactive narrative of electronic game. Postgraduate Dissertation. China Academy of Art, Beijing (2015)
12. Paaßen, B., Morgenroth, T., Stratemeyer, M.: What is a true gamer? The male gamer stereotype and the marginalization of women in video game culture. Sex Roles **76**(7–8), 421–435 (2017)
13. 沈茵菲.: 对抗性电子游戏的多重叙事模式.视听 **7**, 152–153 (2018)
14. Thomas, L., Macmilian, J., Mccoll, E., Hale, C., Bond, S.: Comparison of focus group and individual interview methodology in examining patient satisfaction with nursing care. Soc. Sci. Health **1**(4), 206–220 (1995)
15. 吴采融, 陆峰. 情感化设计在手机游戏中的应用.理念传递 **02**(023), 83–84 (2018)
16. Wu, D.: Mobile games emotional design for female players. Postgraduate Dissertation. Central China Normal University, Wuhan (2014)
17. 王思惠.: 中国传统服饰美学对网络游戏角色设计的影响.美术视点 **05**, 193 (2015)
18. 徐恒醇. 设计美学.清华大学出版社 (2006)

Human Robot Interaction

Simultaneous Dialog Robot System

Takuya Iwamoto[✉], Kohtaro Nishi, and Taishi Unokuchi

Cyberagent, Inc., Abema Towers 40-1 Udagawacho, Shibuya-ku,
Tokyo 153-0042, Japan
{iwamoto_takuya_xa,kohtaro_nishi,
taishi_unokuchi}@cyberagent.co.jp

Abstract. Various types of communication robots have been used in practical applications. Cases where robots are utilized as receptionist, among others, are increasing. However, this trend is not new nowadays. Generally, robots that are used for reception and customer services are developed on the assumption of one-on-one customer service. Thus, when one user interacts with the robot, other customers have to wait for their turn. In this research, we propose a system that can simultaneously serve many people by using one robot with multiple directional microphones and speakers.

Keywords: Robot · Humanoid · Information · Hospitality

1 Introduction

Currently, Amazon and Jindong operate as unmanned stores [1, 2]. In these stores, a user can do smooth shopping without using an accounting system. Henn-na Hotel [3] and Hama Sushi [4] in Japan have introduced a robot that allows users to experience hospitality. These robots are connected via a network to access big data in real time, answer user questions, and perform tasks.

Currently, customer service robots installed in department stores and information centers become common [5]. However, these robots can only speak to one user at a time, and people who want to talk/use the robot have to wait for their turn. Therefore, in this research, we develop a robot system wherein directional speakers are installed in the robot and can be set in pairs. Then, we describe its use case.

2 General System

This system can provide customer service not only from the front but also from the direction where the microphone and directional speaker are installed (Fig. 1). Through this directional speaker, the robot speaks at the same time. However, the user can hear only the voice directed to him/her, thereby enabling a one-to-many communication.

C. Stephanidis (Ed.): HCII 2019, CCIS 1033, pp. 107–111, 2019.
https://doi.org/10.1007/978-3-030-23528-4_15

Fig. 1. System overall

3   System Components

Figure 2 shows the configuration of this system. The components of this system are a robot, two microphones, two directional speakers, and a personal computer (PC). The robot uses Pepper, which is a model for corporate use. Two USB microphones are attached on the front shoulders of Pepper. The directional speakers (Tristate, parametric speaker experiment kit) are fixed on to the two tripods behind the back of Pepper and are then attached to its head. The height was adjusted to ensure that the sound was heard from a close position (Fig. 3).

First, the microphone and speaker were connected to the PC. Second, the voice recorded from the microphone was sent to DialogFlow for voice recognition. Third, the answer registered in advance was collected, and the acquired character string was subjected to speech synthesis using Google Cloud text-to-speech application programming interface (API), which is a speech synthesis software as service. Finally, the answers to the questions were speech synthesized using Google's Cloud text-to-speech API, and the output was released from the speaker.

The microphone and speaker were installed separately on the left and right, respectively, and the answer to the voice spoken on the left microphone is heard from the left speaker (the same for the right). This setup works in parallel.

4   Exhibition and Use Cases

This system was demonstrated and presented at Yahoo! JAPAN Hack Day 2018 which was held at Akihabara UDX on December 15–16, 2018. A user stated that "it can be used in various situations" and "waiting for practical use." Hence, we considered the use case scenario of this system based on our experience at and opinion on the exhibition.

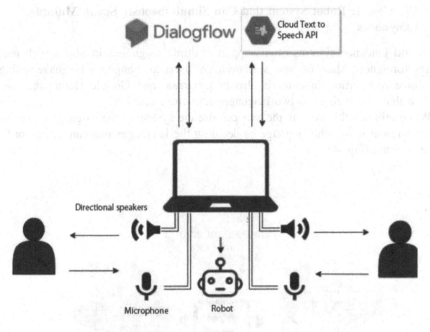

Fig. 2. System components

Fig. 3. Installation of the microphone and directional speakers

4.1   Use Case 1: Robot System that Can Simultaneously Speak Multiple Languages

Robot and guidance systems often support multiple languages in places with many visiting foreigners. Many of these systems allow users to change the language settings. The voice recognition function is also in progress, and Google Homepage has a function that can distinguish two languages set beforehand [6].

When utilizing this system, the user can use the system in the language that he/she prefers without setting the language by deciding the languages that can talk according to the position (Fig. 4).

Fig. 4. Robot system that simultaneously speaks multiple languages

4.2   Use Case 2: Individual Approaching System

Robots approach pedestrians with voice and motion. By employing an omnidirectional speaker, the same message can be delivered to everyone in a room. When a robot announces an advertisement, such as introducing a product, only a few people need this message. Therefore, adding a function that can estimate personal attributes using the camera of this system and rendering a directional speaker movable can be useful, enabling an approach similar to the pedestrian attributes (Fig. 5).

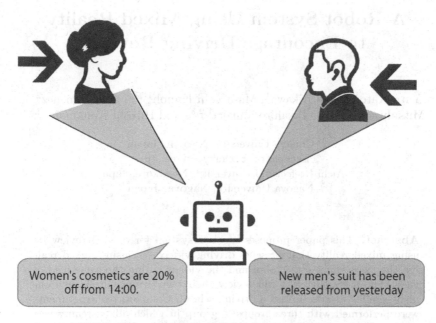

Fig. 5. Schematic of the Individual Approaching System

5 Future Work

In this study, we proposed a customer service robot by using multi-directional speakers. In the future, we will design an interaction that allows a user to feel that the system or robot is "speaking to her or him" only despite the robot speaks simultaneously to multiple people. Moreover, we will examine the feasibility of the use case scenario discussed in this paper.

References

1. Amazon Go. https://www.amazon.com/b?ie=UTF8&node=16008589011. Accessed 27 Mar 2019
2. Jian24. http://www.jian24.com/. Accessed 27 Mar 2019
3. Hen-na Hotel. https://www.hennnahotel.com/en/. Accessed 27 Mar 2019
4. Hama Sushi Roboto. https://www.softbank.jp/robot/biz/case/hamazushi/. Accessed 27 Mar 2019
5. Watanabe, M., Ogawa, K., Ishiguro, H.: Field study; can androids be a social entity in the real world? In: Human-Robot Interaction (HRI), pp. 316–317 (2014)
6. Talk to the Google Assistant in multiple languages. https://support.google.com/googlehome/answer/7550584?hl=en. Accessed 27 Mar 2019

A Robot System Using Mixed Reality to Encourage Driving Review

Yuta Kato[1], Yuya Aikawa[1], Masayoshi Kanoh[1(✉)], Felix Jimenez[2],
Mitsuhiro Hayase[3], Takahiro Tanaka[1,2,3], and Hitoshi Kanamori[1,2,3]

[1] Chukyo University, Nagoya, Japan
mkanoh@sist.chukyo-u.ac.jp
[2] Aichi Prefectural University, Nagakute, Japan
[3] Nagoya University, Nagoya, Japan

Abstract. This paper proposes a robot system for driving review by using mixed reality that presents driving videos. By using mixed reality, the users can see the robot and the videos within the same field of view. The users therefore can review their own driving in an environment similar to a lecture at a driving school. Comparative experiments were performed with three groups; a group in which mixed reality was used to display driving situations (proposed system), a group in which tablet terminals were used, and a group in which only a robot was used (no video). The results show that using the proposed system for driving review may increase attachment to the robot.

Keywords: Driving review · Mixed reality · Human-robot interaction

1 Introduction

The number of traffic accidents has been steadily decreasing recently, however, the traffic accident rate for elderly drivers is increasing each year. To address this problem, it is necessary for elderly people to look back and review their driving behavior. At present, elderly people can review their own driving behavior by going to a driving school and attending driving classes. In order to improve driving behavior, it is necessary to learn repeatedly from the mistakes in one's driving. Therefore, elderly drivers have to take courses many times and go to the driving schools at the specific hours. This time restraint and the obligation to attend classes poses a burden on elderly people. Therefore, a system is needed to encourage elderly drivers to review their driving behavior at their convenience, without having to go to a driving school.

Tanaka et al. [1] have proposed to use an agent to support elderly drivers. As a result of a survey, robots received the second high evaluation following driving instructors. In our research, we have been developing a system that allows to review various driving situations with a robot [2]. In the proposed system, mixed reality is used. By using mixed reality, users can observe the robot, view the video, and ask questions simultaneously. The system displays the answers with

C. Stephanidis (Ed.): HCII 2019, CCIS 1033, pp. 112–117, 2019.
https://doi.org/10.1007/978-3-030-23528-4_16

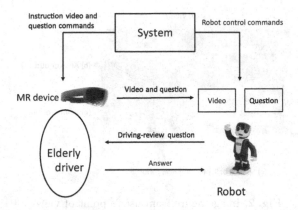

Fig. 1. System overview

a video, with the robot commenting on the video. When using this system, it is possible to reflect on one's driving experience just like students do in a lecture at a driving school, so we assume that a high learning effect can be obtained. In fact, mixed reality is used in various fields of learning and education [3–5]. In order to confirm the effectiveness of the proposed system, comparative experiments were conducted with three groups; a group using mixed reality, a group using a tablet, and a group using a robot with no video.

2   Proposed System

Figure 1 shows the outline of the system. The system transmits to the mixed reality device a video of a scene judged to be dangerous taken from the video recording of a driver; the action to be taken for the scene is displayed in the form of a question. The mixed reality device displays the video and the question on its lens. The system also sends motion and utterance information to the robot to facilitate intuitive understanding of the displayed video and the question. The elderly drivers, while watching the video displayed on the mixed reality device, receive a lesson from the robot by reviewing the driving situations and answering the questions.

Figure 2 shows an image of mixed reality from the viewpoint of the elderly driver. The mixed reality device presents the (a) video, (b) answer buttons, and (c) a speech balloon. These are created by computer graphics. The elderly drivers look back at their own driving by operating the buttons displayed in (b) in response to the question, while viewing the video presented in (a). The speech balloon (c) is an auxiliary information presentation interface when the elderly drivers cannot hear the robot's utterance. The robot (d) shares the presented video, the robot's utterance contents, and the button pressing status with the system.

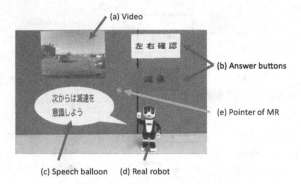

Fig. 2. Image figure from user's point of view

3 Experiment

3.1 Experimental Method

The following three methods are used in three groups and are compared in terms of displaying the video; the effects and impressions of the proposed system are investigated.

1. "Proposed system" group uses a display device to create mixed reality. The subject can see the robot and the video within the sweep of his/her eye. When reviewing the driving, the robot gives explanations about the video by utterance.
2. "Tablet" group uses a tablet terminal as a display device. In this group, the subject can freely hold the tablet terminal. As is the case with the proposed system group, when reviewing the driving, the robot gives explanations about the video.
3. "Robot alone" group only uses a robot and no display device. Because no video is used in this group, the subject reviews his/her driving only with the robot's utterance.

The experimental procedure is as follows. First, as prior explanation, we tell the subject about the flow of the experiment and the equipment used. After that, as a simulated driving, the subject watches a 15-min video of assumed driving. After watching the video, the subject looks back on five driving scenes using one of the methods. The subjects in the proposed system group and tablet group do it while watching the video of each scene. The five videos used for the review of driving were created from the 15-min video of the simulated driving. After the review, the impressions from the robot and the learning effects are evaluated by the impression evaluation questionnaire and the review effect confirmation test.

Figure 3 shows the impression evaluation questionnaire. Each question item is given on a 7-point Likert scale; the higher the score, the better the evaluation. Figure 4 shows the review effect confirmation test. The test has five questions.

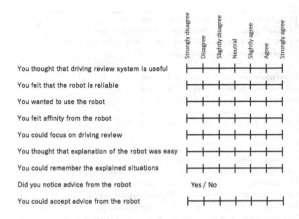

Fig. 3. Impression evaluation questionnaire

In each question, the subject answers whether each scene was praised or lectured by the robot and selects a situation of each scene from seven options (A) to (G). Since two questions (answering "praised/lectured" and selecting the situation) are set up for one review scene, a full mark is 10 points. The total of 30 people participated in the experiment, ten subjects in each group.

3.2 Experimental Results

Figure 5 shows the results of the impression evaluation questionnaire. Kruskal-Wallis test was performed, and Tukey test was adopted for multiple comparison. In the figure, (**) and (*) are combinations that become significant at the significance levels 1% and 5%, respectively, and (+) is a combination in which significant tendency ($p < 0.1$) is recognized. Figure 6 shows the results of the review effect confirmation test. The score was 9.0 ± 1.8 points for the proposed system group, 8.5 ± 2.1 points for the tablet group, and 7.1 ± 1.9 points for the robot alone group. As a result of performing one-factor analysis of variance and multiple comparison Tukey's test, significant difference was recognized between the proposed system group and the robot alone group ($p < 0.1$).

3.3 Discussion

According to the results of the impression evaluation questionnaire, the evaluation of the robot alone group was the lowest in seven items out of eight. When interviewing the subjects in the robot alone group, many answered "I could not understand even if the robot explained the driving situation by referring the time of situation." It is assumed that the reason for low evaluation was that the subjects could not accurately review the driving with just the robot's utterance, even if the video was only about 15 min long. There was no significant difference between the proposed system group and the tablet group. We consider that this

Five situations were displayed in driving review with the robot.

1. In each situation, answer whether you got praised or lectured.

2. Which content was praised/lectured; choose from the seven options A to G below.
   You may choose the same option multiple times.

Content

First review situation   Praised / Lectured

Second review situation   Praised / Lectured

Third review situation   Praised / Lectured

Fourth review situation   Praised / Lectured

Fifth review situation   Praised / Lectured

Options

A About your car's speed when a bicycle passes in front of your car

B About your car's speed when a pedestrian passes in front of your car

C About the distance between a passing bicycle and your car

D About the distance between a passing pedestrian and your car

E About the distance between roadside zone and your car

F About safety confirmation at the time of right turn in intersection

G About safety confirmation at the time of left turn in intersection

Fig. 4. Review effect confirmation test

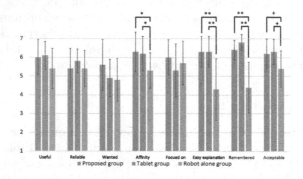

Fig. 5. Results of impression evaluation questionnaire

is because each group has its advantages and disadvantages. In the proposed system group, the robot and the video can be viewed within the same field of view, it is therefore possible to review the driving in a situation similar to a lecture at a driving school. However, in the interview after the experiment, there were answers like "Part of the video displayed on the lens disappeared." A part of the video may disappear from the view if the subject moves his/her head due to the performance of the device, so the subject's movement was restricted during the review. On the other hand, in the tablet group, there is no restriction on how to hold the tablet for displaying the video, so the burden on the subject from watching the video is reduced. However, subjects tended to always watch the screen of the tablet, and there were opinions that "the robot may not be necessary."

In the results of the review effect confirmation test, the proposed system group earned the highest score, and the robot alone group earned the lowest

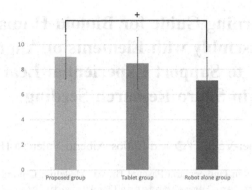

Fig. 6. Results of review effect confirmation test

score. These results suggest that the presentation of the video affects the establishment of memory.

Attachment to the robot may increase if it is used frequently, so mixed reality is better suited for the purpose than the tablet terminal.

4 Conclusion

In this paper, we proposed a robot system using mixed reality in order to encourage driving review. To confirm its effectiveness, comparative experiments were conducted with three groups; a group using a video presentation device with a robot and mixed reality, a group using a robot and a tablet, and a group using only a robot. Experimental results suggest that using mixed reality is better than using tablets in the environment where humans and robots coexist. As future work, we are planning to conduct experiments in a situation close to the actual driving environment using a drive simulator.

References

1. Tanaka, T., et al.: Driver agent for encouraging safe driving behavior for the elderly. In: 5th International Conference on Human-Agent Interaction (2017)
2. Aikawa, Y., et al.: Comparison of gesture inputs for robot system using mixed reality to encourage driving review. In: International Conference on Soft Computing and Intelligent Systems and International Symposium on Advanced Intelligent Systems (2018)
3. Takahashi, Y.: A trial and verification of video teaching material for lifelong learning for the elderly. J. Bunka Gakuen Univ. Stud. Fashion Sci. Art Des. **46** (2015). (in Japanese)
4. Matsuoka, K., Obara, H., Kubota, M.: Learning support system for guitar playing using wearable devices. In: 77th National Convention of IPSJ (2015). (in Japanese)
5. Fujisawa, Y., Ito, S., Kobayashi, K.: Development of learning support system for fingerspelling by augmented reality. In: 5th International Conference on Intelligent Systems and Image Processing (2017)

Self-learning Guide for Bioloid Humanoid Robot Assembly with Elements of Augmented Reality to Support Experiential Learning in Sauro Research Seeding

Karen Lemmel-Vélez[(⊠)] [iD] and Carlos Alberto Valencia-Hernandez

Institución Universitaria Pascual Bravo, Medellín, Colombia
karen.lemmel@pascualbravo.edu.co,
carlos.valencia@pascualbrabo.edu.co

Abstract. A self-learning guide for assembly robots BIOLOID PREMIUM in human form is presented, where elements of augmented reality are included in order to facilitate the process of assembly and manipulation of prototypes. This guide was evaluated with students belonging to the research seeding SAURO (research seeding in Automation and Robotics) of the Institución Universitaria Pascual Bravo.

For the design of the guide was necessary the 3D model of the humanoid robot and the creation of augmented reality markers, all with the aim of promoting the interaction of students with technological objects and robotic platforms; for this the software Google sketchup and Build AR Pro were used.

It was achieved that the process of assembling the BIOLOID PREMIUM humanoid robot at the time of execution decree. The students using the guide manifested who had fun learning how to put together the robot, who had flexibility in learning and could manage their own time. Likewise, the use of this guide facilitated the understanding of the parts of the robot and the function that each of them fulfills and even the students declared the control of the self-learning process.

On the other hand, students externalized that their interpretation skills of 3D models and their spatial location got better with the use of the guide with elements of augmented reality.

Keywords: Augmented reality · Engineering education · Self-learning

1 Introduction

According to [1] augmented reality (AR) can be defined as "a technology which overlays virtual objects (augmented components) into the real world" where these virtual objects appear to coexist as objects in the real world. AR, usually enable layering of information over 3D space and creates new experiences of the world. [2] says AR offer opportunities for teaching, learning, research, or creative inquiry.

Also augmented reality offers several advantages in the educational context as: (1) it has encourage kinesthetic learning, (2) it can support students by inspecting the

© Springer Nature Switzerland AG 2019
C. Stephanidis (Ed.): HCII 2019, CCIS 1033, pp. 118–125, 2019.
https://doi.org/10.1007/978-3-030-23528-4_17

3D object or class materials from a variety of different perspectives or angles to enhance their understanding, (3) it increases the student level of engagement and motivation in academic activities, and (4) it allows to provide contextual information [1, 3]. In addition, AR juxtaposes real objects, virtual text, and other symbols, which reduces cognitive load in the limited working memory [1].

[1] says that clearly AR's most significant advantage is its "unique ability to create immersive hybrid learning environments that combine digital and physical objects, thereby facilitating the development of processing skills such as critical thinking, problem solving, and communicating through interdependent collaborative exercises." what allows the development of self-learning process by increases students' motivation and helps them to acquire better investigation skills.

On the other hand AR is used today in every level of schooling, from K-12 to the university level [1, 4]. Several examples like [5–11] can confirm it. The fields of education in which the AR has been used are science education, storytelling, health education, geography education, engineering education, art education, foreign languages education, native language education, architecture education, mathematics education, culture education, computer education, library and information science and history education as well as informal education [4].

The research seeding sauro is working on improving the learning and research skills of its members, proof of this is [12, 13]. At the same time one of the most important topics in the Research seeding is robotics, in which have been developed different jobs like [14]. Along with all this is also the development of soft skills through projects as shown [15] and [16], reason why the need to design guidelines that allowed the experiential learning in the laboratory in an autonomous or self-learning way was saw and given the advantages of the AR, the guide for Bioloid humanoid robot assembly were created.

2 Methodology

The general methodology used is show in Fig. 1.

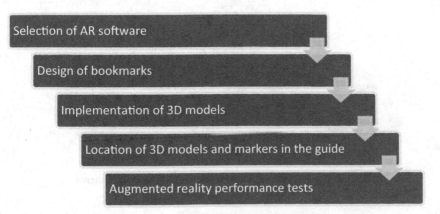

Fig. 1. General methodology for the construction of the Guide for Bioloid Humanoid Robot Assembly.

2.1   Selection of AR Software

For the selection of the AR software several criteria were taken into account, such as: (1) Stability, a system is stable when its level of failure decreases below a certain threshold. In this case, the number of failures obtained in the tests carried out for the software was considered. Faults can be defined such as misidentification of markers, oscillations in the virtual object, and losses of the virtual object at close range of the marker. (2) Multiplatform, ability to install software in more than one operating system. (3) Accessibility to the source code, ability to access or decompose a software in the programming language that was written, for example C++, Basic, Assembler, etc. (4) Low cost, refers to the cost of the license, in this case the lower the cost the better. (5) Programmer experience, knowledge that the user of augmented reality software must have in the specific use of a programming language to be able to implement their applications. (6) Available documentation: refers to the existence and easy access of information regarding software such as tutorials, user manuals and technical charac-teristics and at last (7) Friendly environment: refers to the ease of use of the pro-gramming environment or software development.

Figure 2 shows the comparison of three development environments evaluated in their main characteristics on a scale of 0 to 5. It's observed that the BuildAR software obtained a high qualification in documentation, around friendly, stability, and low cost; however, the ARToolkit obtained higher scores for multiplatform and accessibility to the source code. Despite all the above, the BuidAR Pro exceeds the previous two, since it obtains the highest rating in 4 out of 7 criteria (stability, friendly environment, available documentation, developer experience and low cost), then BuildAR Pro software was chosen for the implementation of the AR.

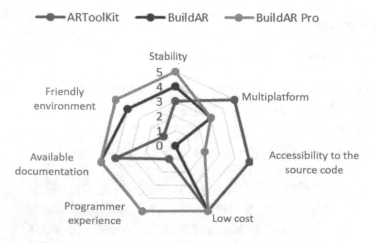

Fig. 2. Comparison of three AR development environments.

2.2 Design of Marks

For the design of the markers, several criteria observed in the literature were taken into account, the majority based on morphological characteristics; They are: (a) The image contained within the box must have a single centroid. (b) The solidity of the image contained within the box must be less than 0.5. (c) The convex area of the image contained within the box must be greater than 35%. (d) The centroid of the image contained within the box should be as close as possible or coincide with the centroid of the marker. (e) It should be avoided to use images with some level of symmetry for the markers since this generates problems in the orientation of the represented objects.

2.3 Implementation of 3D Models

For the implementation of the 3D objects we used the software Google sketchup. A free software that offers libraries of predesigned objects, among them some models of Bioloid robots. The last ones were taken, modified and cut into pieces for the implementation of this project (See Fig. 3).

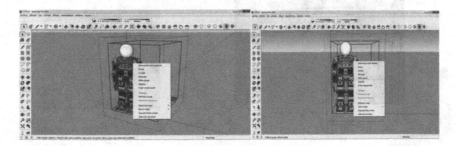

Fig. 3. 3D model of Bioloid Humanoid robot

2.4 Location of 3D Models and Markers in the Guide

For the location of the 3D objects in the manual (Fig. 4), the pages where more complexity was evidenced were chosen so that the 3D models increased in the document would serve as support for the correct assembly of the respective models described in the manual.

Fig. 4. Markers and 3D model in BuildAR Pro.

2.5   Augmented Reality Performance Tests

Finally, it was validated that all the models increased in the document were consistent with the flat illustrations and that both their location and their orientation with respect to the physical manual were correct and pertinent.

3   Results

The robot was downloaded from the library from Google sketchup, the head is created (see Fig. 3) and cutting in pieces were carried out. The markers with their respective QR code were created and generated to be attached to the robot's assembly guide.

Markers were created and evaluated for both arms (Fig. 5), legs and trunk (Fig. 6). All of them in two different positions, in addition the complete packaging of the robot (Fig. 7) performance test was make.

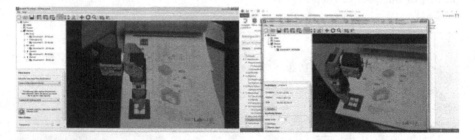

Fig. 5. AR left and right arm in the Guide for Bioloid Humanoid Robot Assembly

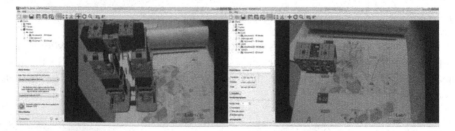

Fig. 6. AR Legs and trunk in the Guide for Bioloid Humanoid Robot Assembly

On the other hand, as a test for the guide, three groups of two students each were taken in order to carry out the assembly of the robot with the help of the guide. Three students had previously made the robot assembly using the traditional manufacturer's guide. In this regard, the following assessments were obtained.

- The interaction of students with technological objects and robotic platforms is promoted.
- The students who had already made the robot's assembly noticed a decrease in the time needed to complete the activity.
- All the students stated that the use of augmented reality was easy and they enjoyed it.
- The students liked the graphic content and the interaction with it.
- The participants said that the understanding of the parts and their functionality in the robot was easy, those who had already done the assembly added that they had better use of their own time given that they depended less on the tutors' help.
- The participants mentioned that the use of the guide with AR allowed them a better understanding of the 3D models.
- The students stated that they felt motivated and that they liked being able to carry out the activity as a team since they were able to share with their classmates.

Fig. 7. AR Full Robot using the Guide for Bioloid Humanoid Robot Assembly.

4 Conclusions

The use of AR promoted the interaction of students with technological objects and robotic platforms.

It was achieved that the process of assembling the BIOLOID PREMIUM humanoid robot at the time of execution decree.

The students using the guide manifested who had fun learning how to put together the robot, who had flexibility in learning and could manage their own time. Likewise, the use of this guide facilitated the understanding of the parts of the robot and the function that each of them fulfills and even the students declared the control of the self-learning process.

On the other hand, students externalized that their interpretation skills of 3D models and their spatial location got better with the use of the guide with elements of augmented reality.

References

1. Akçayır, M., Akçayır, G.: Advantages and challenges associated with augmented reality for education: a systematic review of the literature. Educ. Res. Rev. **20**, 1–11 (2017). https://doi.org/10.1016/j.edurev.2016.11.002
2. Chen, P., Liu, X., Cheng, W., Huang, R.: A review of using Augmented Reality in Education from 2011 to 2016. Innovations in Smart Learning. LNET, pp. 13–18. Springer, Singapore (2017). https://doi.org/10.1007/978-981-10-2419-1_2
3. Montoya, M.H., Díaz, C.A., Moreno, G.A.: Evaluating the effect on user perception and performance of static and dynamic contents deployed in augmented reality based learning application. Eurasia J. Math. Sci. Technol. Educ. **13**, 301–317 (2017). https://doi.org/10.12973/eurasia.2017.00617a
4. Yilmaz, R.M.: Augmented reality trends in education between 2016 and 2017 Years. In: State of the Art Virtual Reality and Augmented Reality Knowhow. intechopen, pp. 81–97 (2018)
5. Alhumaidan, H., Lo, K.P.Y., Selby, A.: Co-designing with children a collaborative augmented reality book based on a primary school textbook. Int. J. Child-Comput. Interact. **15**, 24–36 (2018). https://doi.org/10.1016/j.ijcci.2017.11.005
6. Koonsanit, K., Sc, M., Lan, P.V.U., Ed, D.: iCreate : 3D Augmented Reality Painting Book for Vocabulary Learning, pp. 29–33 (2017)
7. Jeffri, N.F.S., Awang Rambli, D.R.: Design and development of an augmented reality book and mobile application to enhance the handwriting-instruction for pre-school children. Open J. Soc. Sci. **05**, 361–371 (2017). https://doi.org/10.4236/jss.2017.510030
8. Radu, I., Antle, A.: Embodied learning mechanics and their relationship to usability of handheld augmented reality. In: 2017 IEEE Virtual Real Work K-12 Embodied Learn through Virtual Augment Reality, KELVAR 2017, pp. 3–7 (2017). https://doi.org/10.1109/kelvar.2017.7961561
9. Fonseca Escudero, D., Redondo, E., Sánchez, A., Navarro, I.: Educating Urban Designers using Augmented Reality and Mobile Learning Technologies/ Formación de Urbanistas usando Realidad Aumentada y Tecnologías de Aprendizaje Móvil. RIED Rev Iberoam Educ a Distancia **20**, 141 (2017). https://doi.org/10.5944/ried.20.2.17675
10. Bendicho, P.F., Mora, C.E., Añorbe-Díaz, B., Rivero-Rodríguez, P.: Effect on academic procrastination after introducing augmented reality. Eurasia J. Math. Sci. Technol. Educ. **13**, 319–330 (2017). https://doi.org/10.12973/eurasia.2017.00618a
11. Montoseiro Dinis, F., Guimaraes, A.S., Rangel Carvalho, B., Pocas Matrins, J.P.: Virtual and augmented reality game-based applications to civil engineering education. In: 2017 IEEE Global Engineering Education Conference (EDUCON), pp. 1683–1688 (2017)
12. Vélez, K.L., Hernandez, C.A.V.: PBL applied to graduation projects that demand incorporate new academic knowledge. In: International Symposium on Project Approaches in Engineering Education (2016)
13. Lemmel-Vélez, K., Valencia-Hernandez, C.A.: Kit based on xbee and arduino type micro controllers for support in skills development on programming, electronics and automation in decentralized offer programs. In: International Symposium on Project Approaches in Engineering Education (2018)
14. Lemmel-Vélez, K., Valencia-Hernandez, C.A.: Design of a robotic hand controlled by electromyography signals using an arduino type microcontroller for people with disabilities. In: Figueroa-García, J.C., López-Santana, E.R., Villa-Ramírez, J.L., Ferro-Escobar, R. (eds.) WEA 2017. CCIS, vol. 742, pp. 289–299. Springer, Cham (2017). https://doi.org/10.1007/978-3-319-66963-2_26

15. Lemmel-Vélez, K., Rivero-Mejía, S.E., Ocampo-Quintero, C.A.: Experiences of the SICAP research seeding in the development of soft skills. In: Zaphiris, P., Ioannou, A. (eds.) LCT 2018. LNCS, vol. 10925, pp. 446–460. Springer, Cham (2018). https://doi.org/10.1007/978-3-319-91152-6_34

16. Tobón, C., Patiño-arcila, I.D., Lemmel-Vélez, K.: Análisis por elementos finitos del desempeño estructural de jaula de seguridad para vehículo Renault Logan bajo normatividad FIA Finite element analysis of the structural performance of safety roll cage of Renault Logan vehicle under FIA regulations. Cintex **23**, 35–52 (2018)

Developing a Behavior Converter to Make a Robot Child-Like for Enhancing Human Utterances

Saeko Shigaki[1]($\boxtimes$), Jiro Shimaya[2], Kazuki Sakai[2], Atsushi Shibai[3], Mitsuki Minamikawa[4], and Yutaka Nakamura[2]

[1] Graduate School of Information Science and Technology,
Osaka University, Suita, Japan
`s-sigaki@ist.osaka-u.ac.jp`
[2] Graduate School of Engineering Science, Osaka University, Suita, Japan
[3] RIKEN Center for Biosystems Dynamics Research, Saitama, Japan
[4] Graduate School of Medicine, Osaka University, Suita, Japan

Abstract. We proposed a child-like filter to promote conversation and a storytelling system that asks users to read books aloud to a robot whose behavior is converted by the filter. In this study, we conducted two subjective experiments to verify the effect of the filter; one experiment was to verify whether the robot displays the behavior of a child when the child-like filter is applied, and the other was to verify an increase in the number of times of speaking when they read a book aloud to the robot with the filter. Our results suggest that when the age of the robot with the filter was younger than the one without, a higher number of times of speaking was demonstrated for the robot with the filter.

Keywords: Human robot interaction · Storytelling ·
Robot motion generation · Care-receiving robot

1 Introduction

The action "speaking" is a fundamental behavior in human communication. In some nursing homes for elderly people, there are areas where the staff actively speak to the elderly and perform recitation as recreation to encourage speech. However, due to the relative shortage of care workers in the current world where the population is aging and there is an increase in the number of elderly people living alone, providing ample opportunities for speaking to each elderly person is not easy.

Therefore, partner robots are expected to communicate with the elderly to encourage speech. In the field of human-robot interaction, it is known that robots can encourage people to perform specific actions through communication [1,2]. By spreading the use of such robots, the burden on human staff can be alleviated at settings where there is a shortage of labor. In addition, by using robots with

C. Stephanidis (Ed.): HCII 2019, CCIS 1033, pp. 126–135, 2019.
https://doi.org/10.1007/978-3-030-23528-4_18

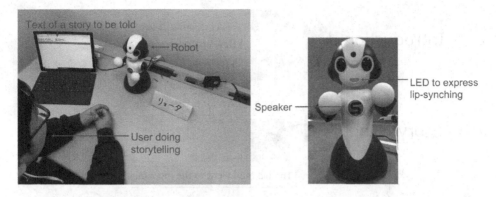

Fig. 1. The storytelling robot system   **Fig. 2.** Sota, a table-top doll-like robot

less interpersonal pressure, it is possible to promote the performance of specific actions while providing a comfortable communication place that human partners can hardly afford.

On the other hand, it has been reported that people are less likely to follow instructions from robots than from people [3], and in an implementation where robots simply ask people to do something, it is concluded to be difficult to effectively encourage people to take specific actions. Therefore, we considered an approach to implement a robot with appearance and function that people actively want to interact with.

One of the approaches used to make people think that they want to interact with robots, is to implement a robot with "weakness" that makes people think that they want to assist in the robot's task achievement [4,5]. We focused on "child-likeness" as a useful weakness to encourage people to speak actively. We expect to realize a robot that encourages people to speak actively by giving such child-like characteristics to the robot and setting scenes that can be taken care of by speaking. In this research, we developed a filter (child-like filter) that adds human-like characteristics to the robot's speech. We also implemented a storytelling robot system that means "storytelling from a human to a robot" as one of the situation where people speak to robots actively. We conducted two experiments; one is to verify that the robot's age feels younger while using the child-like filter, the other is to verify the number of active utterances increases while using the filter.

2 System Implementation

2.1 The Child-Like Filter

We developed a child-like filter that gives child-like characteristics to the robot in order to promote active speech from the user to the robot. The child-like filter firstly replace honorific words and difficult words with appropriate words. Then, the system performs morphological analysis on the character string obtained in

Fig. 3. The flow of the dialogue

the first step to divide it into words and acquires lexical categories and inflected forms of the words. Here, we used MeCab. Based on the result of morphological analysis, honorific words are replaced into non-honorific expression so as to be child-like.

In addition, the system let the robot repeat the periodic movements according to the length of the morpheme. The periodic movement is selected from movements such as shaking hands back and forth, shaking the body sideways, shaking hands in front of the body, and shaking the neck sideways. Lastly, the speech speed of the robot is reduced into 0.9 times of the original speed.

2.2 The Storytelling Robot System

The storytelling robot system promotes storytelling behavior in a human by recognizing the text read by the user and indicating whether the robot has understood the content or not while using communication to promote the next utterance. The situation of the storytelling dialogue performed using the system is shown in Fig. 1. The system consists of a robot communicating with a user, a recognizer for the user's speech, a computer for determining the robot's action based on the contents of the robot's speech, and a database of the story information (the robot's reaction to the story and the story itself). As the robot that communicates with a user, we used a 28 cm tall table-top doll-like robot called Sota, from Vstone Co., Ltd. (Fig. 2).

The speech of a user is acquired through a microphone placed near the user, is transcribed by speech recognition software, and is used for the subsequent behavior determination of the robot. In the database, story information is registered as prior knowledge to smoothly engage in storytelling dialogue with the user.

Figure 3 shows the flow of the dialogue in the system. The dialogue consists of three phases: introduction, storytelling, and closing. The introduction phase is a simple robot-led dialogue such as self-introduction. In the storytelling phase, every time the user reads a story sentence, the mismatch rate between the read sentence and the correct sentence registered in the system is calculated. The dialogue progresses after selecting either "promote the user to utter the same sentence again" or "promote the user to utter the next sentence" as the action of the robot according to the mismatch rate. The dialogue shifts to the closing phase when the user reads the story sentences towards the end. In the closing phase, the robot gives an impression or thanks for the storytelling based on the registered sentences.

3 Experiment 1: How the Robot's Age Is Felt by Applying the Child-Like Filter

The purpose of Experiment 1 is to apply the child-like filter to verify whether the age of the robot that's made to speak feels younger. Therefore, we conducted a questionnaire evaluation to estimate the robot's age after showing subjects a video where the robot speaks with and without the child-like filter.

3.1 The Experimental Method of Experiment 1

27 people (12 men and 15 women) in 20s to 50s answered the questionnaire. In the questionnaire, subjects watched a video in which the robot speaks and picked the option they thought represented the age range of the robot. There are 11 options for the age ranges (from 0–2 years old to 18–20 years old, and over 20 years old). In the analysis, the average value of the age range of each option is taken as the estimated age when the option is selected. The estimated age when a subject chooses "over 20 years old" is 21 years old.

In order to verify the influence that the contents of the speech have on the estimated age, we prepared two types of videos with different speech content for the robot, both with and without the child-like filter. The contents of the speech had two parts: a greeting including self-introduction, and some talk about the robot's favorite things. We prepared four different videos consisting of a matrix of filter factors (with and without) and speech content factors (greetings, favorite things), and each subject answered with what they thought the robot's age range was for all the videos. After that, the subject was asked in the form of a choice of multiple answers about what characteristics of the robot were considered important in estimating age (Table 1).

3.2   The Results of Experiment 1

Figure 4 shows the results of the robot's estimated age with respect to speech content factors (greetings, favorite things) and child-like filter factors (with, without).

As a result of the two-factor within-subject analysis of variance, a significant main effect of the filter factor was recognized ($F(1,26) = 93.6$, $p < .05$). In addition, significant main effects of speech content factors were recognized ($F(1,26) = 18.2$, $p < .05$). The interaction between the child-like filter factor and the speech content factor was not significant ($F(1,26) = .452$, n.s.).

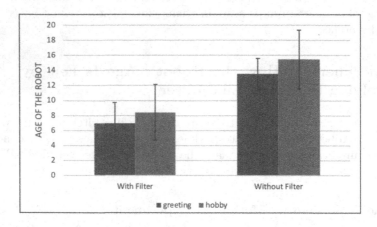

Fig. 4. Estimated age of the robot with regard to the speech content and with and without the child-like filter

Table 1 shows the results of how many subjects used each characteristic of the robot as clues to estimate the robot's age. The largest number was of subjects (25 out of 27) who based their perception on the presence or absence of honorifics, followed by the number of subjects who based their perception on the presence or absence of fillers (19 out of 27).

3.3   Consideration on the Results of Experiment 1

The fact that a significant main effect of the child-like filter factor was recognized for the robot's estimated age is considered to suggest that using the child-like filter makes the robot feel younger than when it is not used. In this experiment, the child-like filter applied movements of the arm and neck to the robot, slowed down the voice speed, removed honorific expressions from speech, and inserted fillers. These changes are thought to contribute to making the robot's age feel younger. At least 22% of subjects answered that they used the robot's movement, voice speed, and presence or absence of honorifics as clues for age estimation, and this suggests that the speech characteristics converted by the child-like filter

Table 1. Characteristics focused on robot age estimation

Characteristics	The number of subjects who focused on each characteristic of the robot (and their proportion)
The appearance	3 (11%)
The movement	6 (22%)
The voice pitch	6 (22%)
The voice speed	13 (48%)
The spoken content	13 (48%)
The presence or absence of honorifics	25 (93%)
The presence or absence of fillers	19 (70%)

affected age estimation. Also, regarding the estimated age of the robot, the fact that a significant main effect of the speech content factor was recognized and that about half of the subjects answered that what the robot said was a clue for age estimation was thought to suggest that not only the use of the child-like filter but also the content the robot speaks affects how people feel about the robot's age. Thus, while several factors are suggested to affect the robot's age estimation, the characteristics that affect age estimation are not clear from Experiment 1. The contribution of each characteristic will become clear by conducting experiments in which the characteristics are changed one by one and conditions are set in detail, leading to the development of a more effective child-like filter.

4 Experiment 2: Active Speech Promotion Effect by Using Child-Like Filter

The purpose of Experiment 2 is to verify whether the child-like filter promotes the user's active speech to the robot. To achieve this purpose, we performed a subject experiment to set up a storytelling scene for a robot that speaks with and without the child-like filter, and measured how many times the subjects repeat the storytelling to the robot in situations where the subjects can freely stop the storytelling. Moreover, in order to verify what aspect of the impression change of the robot by the child-like filter affects the reading behavior, we conducted a questionnaire survey on the impression of the robot itself and the robot's dialogue.

4.1 The Experimental Method of Experiment 2

15 people in their 20s (8 men and 7 women) participated. The experiment was carried out with the within-subject design of two conditions; the condition with the child-like filter and the condition without the filter. Written informed consent was obtained from all participants.

After that, the subjects narrated two stories of 10 sentences each to the robot. Of the two, one was the condition with the child-like filter, and the other was the one the without filter condition. The order of execution of the conditions was randomized for each subject. In the with-filter condition the robot interacts using speech sentences converted by the filter and the gesture given in the filter, and in the without-filter condition the robot interacts with the speech sentence that is not converted by the filter. The storytelling dialogue consisted of three phases: introduction, storytelling, and closing. In the introduction phase, a simple greeting-like dialogue including self-introduction from the robot took place, and the robot told the subject the title of the story to be read at the end. The story to be read was the opening part of Momotaro and Urashima Taro. They are famous Japanese fairy tails. In the storytelling phase, the robot was teleoperated by the experimenter to behave like speech recognition had failed for a predetermined number of repetitions for each sentence. In other words, the robot requested the subject to repeat the same sentence for a predetermined number of times. Although it was possible to operate the robot autonomously using the voice recognition function on the system, in that case, there was concern that the behavior of the robot may greatly differ depending on the individual characteristics of the subject such as the clarity of the pronunciation. Therefore, we teleoperated the robot in Experiment 2.

The subjects repeated the sentence for a predetermined number of times or skipped the dialogue to the next sentence by pressing the "Next" button on the tablet placed in the laboratory. The "Next" button was provided to the subjects with the explanation that they could use it when they felt difficult to read the same sentence again and when they wanted to move forward. The default number of repetitions of the last three sentences was set to a large number, and the number of times the subject spoke before pressing "Next" was counted for those sentences. The average value of the number of utterances of the subject in the last three sentences was defined as the number of active utterances of the subject and was used as an index to compare between the conditions. The predetermined number of repetitions for each sentence was a random number of 14 or less for the first seven sentences and 22 for the last three sentences. After finishing the reading of 10 sentences, in the closing phase, simple dialogue took place in which the robot expressed thanks to the subject.

After the storytelling dialogue, a questionnaire was presented with questions about the dialogue and the robot's impression. Specifically, the following items were asked under the seven-point scale method (1. I do not think so at all–7. I strongly think so). Specific questions are shown below.

Boredom The dialogue with the robot was boring.
Fatigue The dialogue with the robot was fatiguing.
Motivation I wanted to tell the robot a story.
Experienced accuracy The speech recognition accuracy of the robot was good.

In addition to the above, we asked how old the robot was felt to be with the same options as in Experiment 1.

4.2 The Result of Experiment 2

The analysis was conducted on the number of active utterances of 14 people, except one woman who could not measure the number of utterances at the time of reading the last 3 sentences due to system trouble. The average value and the standard deviation of the number of utterances at each level (with, without) of the child-like filter factor are shown in Table 2. The mean value of the condition with child-like filter was significantly larger than that of the condition without child-like filter. In order to confirm the influence of the order effect in addition to the presence or absence of the child-like filter, a two-factor analysis of variance was performed with the child-like filter factor and the condition execution order factor as factors. As a result, the interaction between the condition execution order and the child-like filter factor was not significant ($F(1,12) = 1.2$, n.s.). The main effect was not significant with respect to conditional performance factors ($F(1,12) = .59$, n.s.) and was significant for child-like filter factors ($F(1,12) = 4.8$, $p < .05$).

Table 2. The number of active utterances ($*p < .05$)

Average (Standard deviation)		F-value
With filter	Without filter	
9.6(6.8)	9.2(7.1)	4.8*

In addition, the questionnaire response results for the condition with child-like filter and the condition without the child-like filter were compared by the within-subjects t-test. The results are shown in Table 3. There were no significant differences between the conditions for any of the items. In order to verify the possibility that the robot's perceived young age contributed to the change in the number of utterances, correlation analysis of the estimated age of the robot and the number of utterances was conducted under the condition with child-like filter and the condition without child-like filter. As a

Table 3. The questionnaire results ($*p < .05$)

	Average (Standard deviation)		t-value
	With child-like filter	Without child like filter	
Estimated age	5.4(2.2)	6.3(2.8)	−1.5
Boredom	4.3(1.8)	4.6(1.9)	−1.3
Fatigue	5.2(1.5)	5.2(1.9)	0
Motivation	3.5(2.2)	3.1(2.1)	1.1
Experienced accuracy	2.4(1.8)	2.3(1.8)	0.14

result of Pearson's correlation test, no significant correlation was found (With child-like filter: $r = -.26$, $t = -.92$, n.s., without child-like filter: $r = -.078$, $t = -.27$, n.s.).

4.3 Consideration on the Results of Experiment 2

The average value of the number of utterances in the condition with child-like filter is larger than the condition without child-like filter, and the main effect of the child-like filter factor is recognized. These facts are thought to suggest that the user's active speech to the robot is promoted by the change of the speech characteristics and the insertion of gestures by using the child-like filter. By using the child-like filter, the system is expected to contribute to the realization of storytelling dialogue with the robot which users can continue actively and easily.

On the other hand, in the questionnaire results, there was no significant difference in the estimated age of the robot by the presence or absence of the child-like filter, and the correlation between the estimated age and the number of active utterances was not significant. We could not confirm whether the increase in the number of active utterances in this result is due to the child-like filter feeling that the robot was young. The fact that the robot's estimated age did not change significantly with the presence or absence of the child-like filter is considered to mean that the results of Experiment 1 were not duplicated in Experiment 2. The reason for this is that in Experiment 2, because the robot only made a compelling utterance in the storytelling phase, which occupies most of the time of the dialogue, it became difficult for the subject to clearly recognize the behavior change of the robot by the child-like filter. By setting the timing of the questionnaire in the middle of the dialogue or devising the manner of involvement so that the robot's speech in the storytelling dialogue increases, it is possible to deeply examine the relationship between the subjective index and the behavioral index to the impression of the robot.

5   Conclusion

We considered that it is effective to give a robot child-like characteristics which make surrounding people want to take care of it. Therefore, we developed a child-like filter that converts the robot's speech and movement to child-like. Questionnaire evaluation suggests that the application of the child-like filter makes the robot seem significantly younger than when the child-like filter was not applied. In addition, it was suggested when the situation of a storytelling from a person to the robot is set by applying the child-like filter, the number of times of storytelling to the robot increased. On the other hand, since a significant change in the robot's estimated age could not be observed parallelly with a change in the number of active utterances, to deepen an examination of the relationship between the robot's impression change and its action by increasing the robot's utterance opportunities during the storytelling dialogue is a future work.

Acknowledgment. This research was supported by Program for Leading Graduate Schools, Ministry of Education, Culture, Sports, Science and Technology.

References

1. Watanabe, T., et al.: Clinical and neural effects of six-week administration of oxytocin on core symptoms of autism. Brain **138**(11), 3400–3412 (2015)
2. Uchida, T., Takahashi, H., Ban, M., Yoshikawa, Y., Ishiguro, H.: A robot counseling system -what kinds of topics do we prefer to disclose to robots? In: 2017 26th IEEE International Symposium on Robot and Human Interactive Communication (RO-MAN), pp. 207–212. IEEE (2017)
3. Geiskkovitch, D.Y., Cormier, D., Seo, S.H., Young, J.E.: Please continue, we need more data: an exploration of obedience to robots. J. Hum.-Robot Interact. **5**(1), 82–99 (2015)
4. Yamaji, Y., Miyake, T., Yoshiike, Y., De Silva, P.R.S., Okada, M.: STB: child-dependent sociable trash box. Int. J. Soc. Robot. **3**(4), 359–370 (2011)
5. Tanaka, F., Matsuzoe, S.: Children teach a care-receiving robot to promote their learning: field experiments in a classroom for vocabulary learning. J. Hum.-Robot Interact. **1**(1), 78–95 (2012)

Can We Recognize Atmosphere as an Agent?

Pilot Study

Hideyuki Takahashi[1(✉)], Midori Ban[1], Naoko Omi[1,2], Ryuta Ueda[1,2],
Sanae Kagawa[2], Hisashi Ishihara[1], Yutaka Nakamura[1],
Yuichiro Yoshikawa[1], and Hiroshi Ishiguro[1]

[1] Osaka University, Osaka, Japan
takahashi@irl.sys.es.osaka-u.ac.jp
[2] Daikin Industries, Ltd., Osaka, Japan

Abstract. There are many environment control systems such as air conditioning systems for providing suitable environment to users. However, there are significant individual differences in the sense of suitable environments among users. Hence, a recommendation system indicating personally suitable environments for each user is extremely important. For this purpose, we are now developing an interactive human–machine interface system that dynamically recommends a suitable room environment for users. In this study, we investigated how the anthropomorphic appearance of the recommending system affected the satisfaction of the users. The results showed that the intellectual impression of the appearance was more important than the emotional impression when using the recommendation system.

Keywords: Environment control system · Interactive recommendation system

1 Introduction

Environment control systems like air conditioning systems are intended to create a suitable environment for users. However, the estimation of a "suitable environment" is not easy because the subjective comfortableness of environments is qualitative and huge different among users. Currently, there are two representative methods for manipulating environment control systems. One is direct manipulation and the other is autonomous manipulation. In direct manipulation, users set the precise parameters of the system by themselves for creating their desired environment. Meanwhile, in autonomous manipulation, artificial intelligent systems estimate the environment desired by users from a pre-learned database and autonomously control the environment based on this estimation. Each manipulation method has both of merits and demerits. Direct manipulation helps reflect individual traits in the environmental state. However, manipulating the precise parameters of the system is considerably difficult for users. Furthermore, if users do not have enough knowledge about the system, there is a risk the manipulation becomes short-sighted and the system cannot perform at its full potential. In contrast, autonomous manipulation is quite effortless for users.

© Springer Nature Switzerland AG 2019
C. Stephanidis (Ed.): HCII 2019, CCIS 1033, pp. 136–140, 2019.
https://doi.org/10.1007/978-3-030-23528-4_19

However, most of these methods cannot consider the individual traits of users (for example, being sensitive to heat or cold).

To solve this dilemma during manipulation, we developed an interactive robot as an interface for environment control systems (Fig. 1 left). This robot can act as if it controls the environmental setting based on an intimated interaction between users and the robot. We are assuming that this type of anthropomorphic interface enables users to feel that the manipulation of the environment is interactive, and this feeling improves the satisfaction of users.

Fig. 1. Interactive robot (left) and room with visual projection walls (right)

In our project, we prepared a room with walls such that animated visual stimuli could be projected on entire surfaces (Fig. 1 right). Our ongoing research has so far indicated that the content of the visual stimuli projected on walls strongly affects subjective feeling of the users regarding the environment in the room [1]. We are expecting are study to contribute toward the development of next-generation air conditioning systems that can provide qualitative atmosphere control that could improve user satisfaction. For accomplishing this project, our interactive robot was assumed to recommend a visual stimulus suitable for the mental state of users by interacting with the user on this room.

In this pilot study, we investigated how the anthropomorphic appearance of the robot affected user satisfaction based on the wall images recommended by the system.

2   Overview of the Pilot Experiment

In our pilot experiment, participants were asked to suggest their preference toward the system by touching one image from the two options displayed on the touch panel screen. Participants selected their preferred image three times and then the system displayed one recommended wall-projected image for participants. Actually, the recommended image was determined randomly and the system did not estimate participant preference at all. We prepared two types of system appearances as the experimental conditions, systems with and without anthropomorphic appearances. In the system with an anthropomorphic appearance, the robot was set beside the touch panel display, and it pretended as if it observed the user's behavior. However, in the system without an anthropomorphic appearance, the robot was not present. The only difference between the two conditions was the appearance (Fig. 2), and the recommendation algorism did not differ between the two conditions.

**With anthropomorphic
appearance condition**

**Without anthropomorphic
appearance condition**

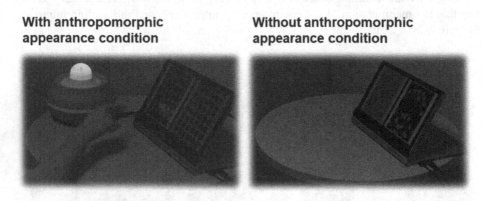

Fig. 2. Systems with (left) and without (right) anthropomorphic appearance

A participant experienced each condition twice alternately (within design). Immediately after seeing the recommended wall images projected by the system, he or she was asked to answer questions regarding four aspects of the system using a seven-scale Likert questionnaire ("suitability of recommended wall image", "satisfaction of recommend system", "intellectual impression of the system" and "emotional impression of the system").

Twelve university students participated the pilot experiment (average age 23.8 yrs., 6 females). Figure 3 presents the mean scores of the questionnaire in the two conditions. Although we could not find a significant score difference for "suitability of recommended wall image" between the conditions, we found a difference for "satisfaction of recommended system" (paired t-test p = 0.052). This result implied that the satisfaction of the recommendation provided by the system with the robot was higher than that that in the condition without the robot. Furthermore, we found that the scores for both "intellectual impression of the system" and "emotional impression of the system" in the system with the robot were higher than those in the condition without the robot.

Figure 4 shows scatter plots between intellectual/emotional impression of the system and system satisfaction degree (one plot indicates one participant). The correlation coefficient between the intellectual impression and system satisfaction degree was higher than that between the emotional impression and satisfaction. This result implied that the intellectual impression formed because of the anthropomorphic appearance might have improved the satisfaction of the participants.

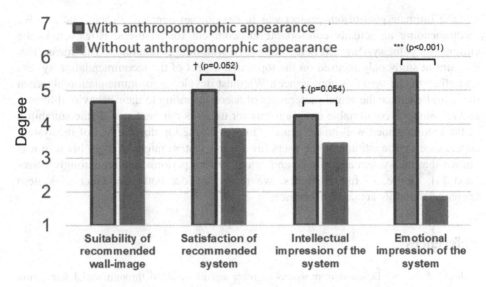

Fig. 3. Mean scores of the questionnaire under the two conditions

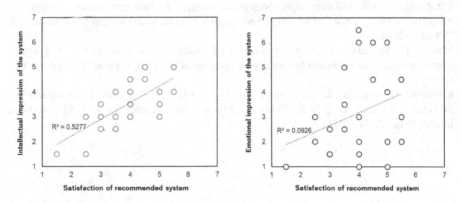

Fig. 4. Scatter plots between intellectual/emotional impression of the system and the system satisfaction degree (one plot indicates one participant)

3 Future Work

The results of our pilot experiment suggest that the appearance of the system interface strongly affects our attitude toward the system and satisfaction levels. This result is consistent with previous similar studies [2, 3]. Interestingly, our findings showed that the intellectual impression of the appearance was more important than the emotional impression when using the recommendation system. Moreover, Matsui and Yamada claimed that the emotional impression regarding the recommendation system was also important [3]. In future studies, we must analyze how these two different impressions of the system affect user behaviors and satisfaction more precisely.

The ultimate goal of our project was to develop an interactive robot that enabled recommending an actually comfortable environment for all users. However, in the current study, the system merely recommended wall images randomly. This means that the current study only focused on the top-down aspect of the recommendation system (the effect of the system's appearance). We must develop a recommendation algorism that could estimate the actual preferences of users according to their behavioral history and recommend comfortable environments for users as our next step. If the suitability of the recommended wall image actually improves, the top-down effect of the system appearance on the attitude of the users toward the system might change, because it is known that the system appearance and actual system performance are strongly correlated [4]. Hence, in future studies, we must consider both the effect of system appearance and its actual performance.

References

1. Ban, M., et al.: Different impressions of other agents obtained through social interaction uniquely modulate dorsal and ventral pathway activities in the social human brain. In: Proceeding of HCII 2019 (2019)
2. Takahashi, H., et al.: Different impressions of other agents obtained through social interaction uniquely modulate dorsal and ventral pathway activities in the social human brain. Cortex **58**, 289–300 (2014)
3. Matsui, T., Yamada, S.: Designing trustworthy product recommendation virtual agents operating positive emotion and having copious amount of knowledge. Front. Psychol. **10**, 675 (2019)
4. Komatsu, T., Yamada, S.: Adaptation gap hypothesis: how differences between users' expected and perceived agent functions affect their subjective impression. J. Syst. Cybern. Inform. **9**(1), 67–74 (2011)

GEC-HR: Gamification Exercise Companion for Home Robot with IoT

Wei-Feng Tung[✉]

Department of Information Management, Fu-Jen Catholic University,
New Taipei City, Taiwan
076144@mail.fju.edu.tw

Abstract. BACKGRUND: A growing number of home robots were developed by many robot industries (i.e., iRobot, HACHI) In modern society, more people are used to utilize wearable device to transmit amount of exercise to their APP on smart phone by Bluetooth transmission; nevertheless, the research tends to connect smart watch to home robot to provide a robotic system for exercise companion service and a game of progression.

OBJECTIVE: The research is to propose and develop a 'gamification exercise companion for home robot; GEC-HR' that can accompany people exercise or physical fitness in front of the home robot at home anytime and anywhere. GEC-HR can synchronize to estimate attainment rate of exercise by robotic movement recognition technology when they exercise. Next, the users can play an interactive game afterwards, which can enhance interesting for the users.

METHODOLOGY: GEC-HR will be implemented by Android APPs for ASUS Zenbo. It needs a built-in camera to detect and photograph user's motion to detect by Zenbo SDK. In addition, a smart watch will transmit amount of exercise (i.e., heart rate, exercise time) to Google cloud platform for data acquisition of home robot. GEC-HR can detect, acquire, and analyze user's exercise data by IoT and recognition technology. The users watch the exercise videos robot recommended and finish its exercise or physical fitness along with the video play, and then user obtains accomplishment points (i.e., flower diagram) based on movement recognition (Robotic API) and smart watch (Wear OS) (Fig. 1).

CONCLUSION: This is a cross-disciplinary research (Sports science, AI) that is to propose and develop a robotic system integrating IoT (wearable device) A recommendation system will be implemented into the GEC-HR system to provide an on-demand exercise service and a reward game afterwards. For the verification, the amount of exercise can be further analyzed to verify the performance and benefits of GEC-HR.

Keywords: GEC-HR · Home robots · Zenbo · IoT · Companion robot

1 Introduction

Artificial intelligence has made numerous advancements over the past few years. AI is able to perform tasks normally requiring human intelligence, such as visual perception, speech recognition, decision-making, and translation between languages. Some

© Springer Nature Switzerland AG 2019
C. Stephanidis (Ed.): HCII 2019, CCIS 1033, pp. 141–145, 2019.
https://doi.org/10.1007/978-3-030-23528-4_20

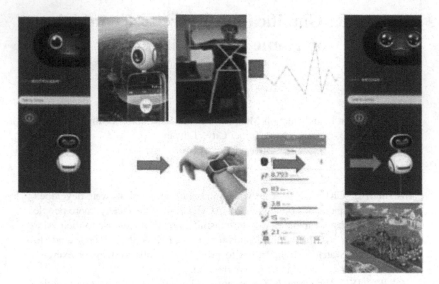

Fig. 1. The Robotic system integrating IoT for GEC-HR

well-known features or AI developments involve the Apple personal assistant, Siri, automobiles from Tesla, customer support services from Cogito, Drones and Echo from Amazon. With the advancement of robotics and artificial intelligence, social companion robots have started to take shape: these human or animal shaped, smaller or bigger mechanic creatures are able to carry out different tasks and have interactions with humans and their environment. Robots' sensors can respond to environmental changes (movements, sounds et.al.) simulating interaction with the patient. They can monitor patients or be used in the therapy. Other potential benefits of therapy with robots are that there are no known adverse effects, specially trained personnel are not required and they can repeat the script in the same way as many times as it is required.

The research is to develop Android applications and Unity for a gamification exercise companion for home robot (GEC-HR) that provides exercise companionship and interaction game. Especially, the exercise's motion detection can be used to really detect users' motions. Our robot provides the users do the exercise along with some videos played on robots, and a synchronous movement detection can be used to detect the users' real motions to check whether follow and complete the exercise videos. In the robot's market, there are few products that can accompany with exercise besides of fitness apps of mobile phones. However, it is common for people to have no regular exercise, which in turn has a negative impact on physical health for elder adults. Thus, the goal of GEC-HR is to accompany the exercises for elder adults anytime at home (Fig. 1).

2   Related Work

The related work describes two relative topics: (1) companion robots; (2) exercise and health functions by companion Robot.

2.1   Companion Robots

Palro is a robot developed by FujiSoft. The name of Palro comes from "PAL" (friends) and "RO" (the first two letters of the robot). Palro combines intelligent technology. It is mostly used in nursing homes, elderly health centers, etc. in Japan. Institution, PALRO is used as a care prevention support robot. Ludwig is a boy robot developed by the university of Toronto. Raro can tilt his head, make eye contact and cry. Scientists at the University of Amsterdam in the Netherlands and Hansen Robots of the United States have developed the companion robot "Alice" for spiritual care research. Papper's development platform can be used to develop application software for dementia, and evidence from nursing agencies, application software for assisting care staff is expected to increase. Elli Q will also know how to use the user's past and more personal suggestions to make the proposal more likely to be adopted. Finally, using the robot's body motion, sound, lighting, screen display and other dimensions, the interaction is very natural in a way similar to human body language. Elli Q can decide whether it is appropriate to wake up and suggest users to perform an activity, such as listening to music or watching a movie. (The lens recognizes that elderly users are depressed, they can suggest them to watch children's videos, photos, and video calls with their children. Listen to music or watch drama). The next step of robot is creating a new relationship between people and robots: helpful companionship. Think of the qualities in a friend – empathy, playfulness and fun. MIT social roboticist Cynthia Breazeal will share how Jibo, an attentive and expressive home helper, and social robots are creating space for humanized engagement with technology that makes consumers feel as if they're interacting with someone, and not something (Eresha et al. 2013).

These robots were designed for companion. These robots enable self-learning and big data analysis (Balkin 2016), so they can do research and remember what you like, and provide the more friendly and better interactions with people.

2.2   Exercise and Health Functions by Companion Robot

Several studies, trials and experiments have been done all over the world around companion robots. In particular, they have been centered on how this application of artificial intelligence can be used effectively with exercise and health functions to aid people, specifically the elderly. It is evident, however, that for these robots to be successful in application for real-life exercise and health functions (Dahl 2013). Another key study based out of the School of Informatics at Indiana University involved researchers monitoring and increasing exercise adherence in older adults by robotic intervention. This involved 10 participants in an exercise program improving older adults physical range of motion in a controlled experiment with 3 conditions: a personal trainer robot, a personal trainer on-screen character, and a pencil-and-paper exercise plan to demonstrate the perceived benefits of humanoid robots to older adults.

When the vision-processing unit detects the presence of a user, it signals this information to the exercise adherence unit, which begins the interaction. If the user consents to begin an exercise, the robot first demonstrates it. Based on information from the vision-processing unit, the exercise adherence unit determines whether the user has completed an exercise correctly and, if the user has not, give the user an opportunity to be guided through the exercise again (Gadde 2011).

In summary, older adults, especially those aging in place, are subject to physical and mental problems that drastically diminish their quality of life (Cutchin 2003). To reduce these problems, an interactive system could instruct, monitor, and encourage older adults during the performance of physician-prescribed exercises (Fig. 2).

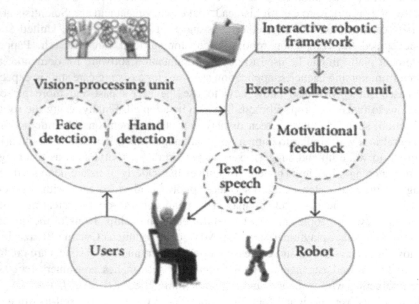

Fig. 2. An interaction loop links the older adult user and the personal trainer robot (Gadde 2011)

Within this loop, the robot leads the user through each exercise move by physically demonstrating it and giving encouragement and feedback on the user's adherence through synthesized speech (Gadde 2011).

3   GEC-HR Robot System Developments

GEC-HR will be implemented into ASUS Zenbo. First. Zenbo play exercise video and motion detection using Zenbo SDK API and create hands detections by OpenCV simultaneously. Second IoT part is to use TecWatch to transit the amount of exercises to cloud database and can access data by Zenbo system. Finally, a simulated-garden game can be provided for users to play according to the results of motion detections and IoT feedback data (i.e., amount of exercises). The proposed robot as a 'fitness coach' to check the user's exercise performance and then provide an interactive game of planting flowers in virtual garden (design by Utility) according to the previous results of exercise (Fig. 3).

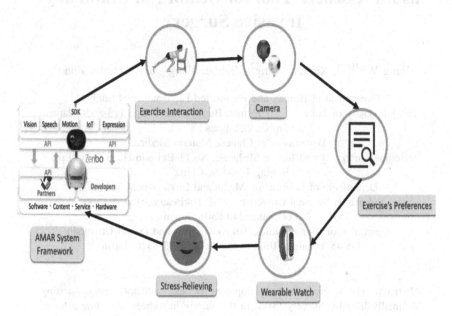

Fig. 3. Exercise companion service process (Source: This Research)

References

Balkin, J.M.: The Three Laws of Robotics in the Age of Big Data. Social Science Research, Rochester (2016)

Choo, A., May, A.: Virtual mindfulness meditation: virtual reality and electroencephalography for health gamification. In: IEEE Games Media Entertainment, pp. 1–3 (2014)

Cutchin, M.P.: The process of mediated aging-in-place: a theoretically and empirically based model. Soc. Sci. Med. **57**(6), 1077–1090 (2003)

Dahl, T.S., Boulos, M.N.: Robots in Health and Social Care: A Complementary Technology to Home Care and Telehealthcare? https://www.mdpi.com/2218-6581/3/1/1. Accessed 30 Dec 2013

Eresha, G., Häring, M., Endrass, B., André, E., Obaid, M.: Investigating the influence of culture on proxemic behaviors for humanoid robots. In: The 22nd IEEE International Symposium on RO-MAN, pp. 430–435 (2013)

Gadde, P., Kharrazi, H., Patel, H., MacDorman, K.F.: Toward monitoring and increasing exercise adherence in older adults by robotic intervention: a proof of concept study (2011). https://www.hindawi.com/journals/jr/2011/438514/abs/

Gardiner, C., Geldenhuys, G., Gott, M.: Interventions to reduce social isolation and loneliness among older people: an integrative review. Health Soc. Care Community **26**, 147–157 (2016)

Gardiner, B., Martin, R.L., Sunley, P., Tyler, P.: Spatially unbalanced growth in the British economy. J. Econ. Geogr. **13**, 889–928 (2013)

Kennedy, A.B., Resnick, P.B.: Mindfulness and physical activity. Am. J. Lifestyle Med. **9**(3), 221–223 (2015)

Discussion on the Feasibility of Soft Actuator as an Assistive Tool for Seniors in Minimally Invasive Surgery

Jiang Wu[1]([⊠]), Xinnan Wang[2], Zizhou Wang[3], and Longfei Zhao[4]

[1] Department of Human and Engineered Environmental Studies,
The University of Tokyo, 7-3-1 Hongo, Bunkyo-ku, Tokyo 113-8656, Japan
leon901221@gmail.com
[2] Department of Chinese Materia Medica,
Beijing University of Chinese Medicine, No.11 Bei San Huan Dong Lu,
Beijing 10-0029, China
[3] Department of Information Media and Environment Sciences,
Yokohama National University, 79-1 Tokiwadai, Hodogaya-ku,
Yokohama 240-8501, Japan
[4] Department of Biomechanics, Tokyo Medical and Dental University,
1-5-45 Yushima, Bunkyo-ku, Tokyo 133-8510, Japan

Abstract. The research and development of soft actuators for supporting Minimally Invasive Surgery (MIS) in the elderly have been attracting a lot of interest in recent years. However, most of them contain rigid structures, such as cable driving mechanisms. Moreover, their Range of Motion (RoM) and bi-directional control of motion is quite limited. This work presents a new elastomeric pneumatic actuator with air chambers for the purpose of MIS support. A prototype of the actuator was made for a comparison with a traditional cable driven structure. The prototype could be equipped with some medical devices in its central silicone tube. The outer diameter of the designed actuator was about 8.5 mm. The results showed that the proposed actuator achieved a 180° bending angle readily, with a small sweeping area when going through a narrow cavity.

Keywords: Minimally Invasive Surgery · Elderly · Range of Motion · Bi-directional control of motion · Elastomeric pneumatic actuator

1 Introduction

Minimally Invasive Surgery (MIS) was actually taken into wide use in the 80's. The technology has a multitude of advantages over open surgery, such as smaller incisions, less pain, lower risk of infection, shorter hospital stays and recovery time, less scarring, and reduced blood loss, even in extremely old patients [1]. These advantages have improved patients' quality of life (QOL) radically.

© Springer Nature Switzerland AG 2019
C. Stephanidis (Ed.): HCII 2019, CCIS 1033, pp. 146–153, 2019.
https://doi.org/10.1007/978-3-030-23528-4_21

The introduction of the MIS technology has been followed by the development of robotics around the world. These systems, for example the "Da Vinci" [2], have dealt with several types of problems inherent to the essential differences in surgical approach, such as reduced dexterity. A needle insertion manipulator for robotically-assisted laparoscopic surgery was designed and tested [3]. Also, force control was realized for a robot called MC^2E [4], based on organ–instrument interaction forces.

On the other hand, the research and development of soft actuators have been attracting a lot of interest in recent years [5]. Marchese et al. [6] provided a recipe for soft fluidic elastomeric robots analysis which differentiated by their internal channel structure, namely ribbed, cylindrical, and pleated. Martinez et al. [7] developed a robotic tentacle with three-dimensional mobility based on flexible elastomers. It has the advantage of being soft and multiple-DOF, the shape can be changed quite easily for purposes, but it cannot control its radial expansion according to the target position and need.

Some soft actuators have been developed for supporting MIS. For example, Rateni et al. [8] developed a soft robotic cable driven gripper that has three fingers for grabbing objects flexibly. Each finger of gripper can be bent up to 45°, but it is unclear whether the wrist of the gripper can be bent or not for reaching a big Range of Motion (RoM). Chen et al. [9] developed a visual servo control for a cable driven soft robotic manipulator made from silicone rubber. It uses eight non-abrasive fiber cables for controlling multiple Degrees of Freedom (DoF), and has ablation tools and a micro CCD camera. However, its diameter (30 mm) is too large for some specific MIS tasks.

In our previous studies, we prototyped a guide frame with rigid structure (Fig. 1) for surgery support [10]. In this paper, we introduce a novel elastomeric pneumatic actuator design with two air chambers that can be used for a 180° RoM and bi-directional control of motion with a 8.5 mm outer diameter for the purpose of MIS support.

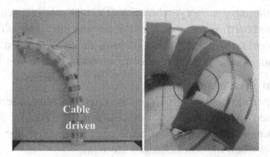

Fig. 1. A first prototype of guide frame was made of polyacetal driven by cable mechanisms.

2 Methods

We designed our actuators targeted at two typical MIS cases in mind: kidney stone surgery (Fig. 2(a)) and nasal surgery (Fig. 2(b)). Thus, we expect to access both wide spaces and narrow cavities with them to reach lesion locations. Based to the two MIS cases, we identified the following four features of the soft actuators:

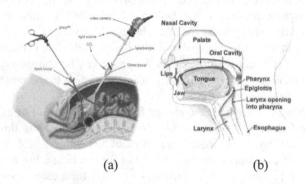

(a)   (b)

Fig. 2. Imaging of two typical MIS case: (a) kidney stone surgery [11], (b) nasal surgery [12].

Wide Range of Motion (RoM)
For instance, in nasal surgery, in order to reach the bottom of maxillary sinus, soft forceps need to be bent to nearly 180°. Currently, without such devices, sometimes surgeons need to open a hole in the patient's face to do the necessary procedure. A completely soft body with pneumatic driving chambers could make this wide RoM possible.

Controllable Softness
Considering again the nasal surgery, when a soft actuator is inserted into the nose, it should be straight and hard. When it reaches the turning site, it should be controlled to bend with an appropriate softness, while keeping its radial size in control to avoid getting stuck. An antagonistic structure was designed to realize this feature.

Usable for Medical Treatment
In MIS, in order to perform navigation, or see the internal cavity, a series of endoscopic surgical tools are used, but these medical devices cannot be bent by themselves. When these medical instruments are inserted into the central silicone tube of the prototype, they can be bent too when the soft actuators are bent.

Bi-directional Control of Motion
During kidney stone surgery, it is necessary to rotate left and then right to go through some paths, or avoid some organs in the abdominal cavity. A soft pneumatic actuator containing two antagonistic chambers should be able to realize this function.

Based on the aforementioned requirements, we explored the possible actuator structures (Fig. 3). Our designs include two 2 mm air chambers and a 2 mm silicone tube in its center, which can be used for inserting medical devices (e.g. endoscope). We also studied three different external structures (Fig. 4): flat cylindrical, helix cylindrical, and a reinforced surface with embedded 0.7 mm cotton string. The outer diameter of the designed actuators was about 8.5 mm.

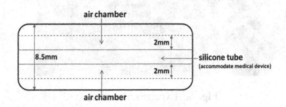

Fig. 3. Illustration of the internal structure: 2-chambers to realize antagonism.

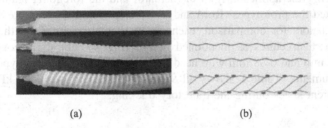

(a)   (b)

Fig. 4. The external structure: (a) three different surfaces on prototypes, (b) line graph of the same structures.

3   Performance Evaluation

To test whether the prototypes would achieve the aforementioned requirements, we set up the following experiment. As shown in the control block diagram (Fig. 5), pressure is applied to the two chambers by using an air compressor which was controlled by the voltage to the pressure controller, and monitored by pressure gauges during the process of the experiment (Fig. 6).

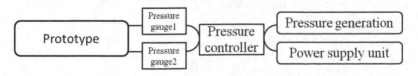

Fig. 5. Control block diagram of experiment.

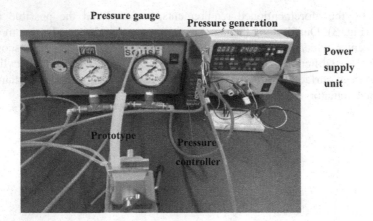

Fig. 6. Experimental setup.

3.1   Trajectory Test

In order to verify the applicability of the actuator and the foregoing features, the first test investigated the prototypes' RoM and its corresponding air pressure. Using three groups of actuators for comparison, each group of which contained three different external support structures as mentioned before (Fig. 4). For the second and third group, a 0.66 mm and 0.88 mm wire need to be inserted into the prototypes to imitate medical instruments. Table 1 shows all 9 prototypes angle at 40–70 kPa. Figure 7 shows 6 different states during the trajectory tracking.

Table 1. Angle at different pressures (40–70 KPa).

Shape of prototype	40 kPa	50 kPa	60 kPa	70 kPa
1. Flat cylinder	0°	21° ± 3°	60° ± 5°	130° ± 10°
2. Helix cylinder	20° ± 14°	190° ± 30°	340° ± 20°	–
Reinforced cylinder	0°	30° ± 2°-	42° ± 2°	53° ± 3°
3. Flat cylinder (0.66 mm)	0°	20° ± 5°	60° ± 8°·	100° ± 14°
4. Helix cylinder (0.66 mm)	21° ± 20°	73° ± 30°	145° ± 15°	178° ± 10°
Reinforced cylinder (0.66 mm)	0°	30° ± 1°	40° ± 3°	50° ± 2°
5. Flat cylinder (0.88 mm)	0°	0°	9° ± 5°	40° ± 2°
6. Helix cylinder (0.88 mm)	0°	0°	55° ± 5°	62° ± 5°
Reinforced cylinder (0.88 mm)	0°	0°	0°	30° ± 2°

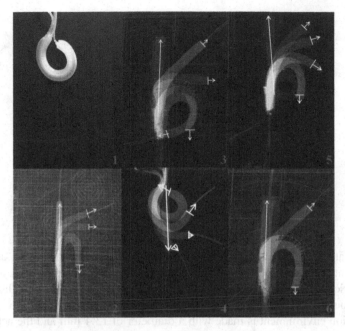

Fig. 7. 6 different states during the trajectory tracking.

From the experimental data, we can see that:

- Inserting an internal wire to simulate a surgical device increased the required driving pressure.
- The helix cylinder prototype requires the lowest input pressure to reach a rotation of 180° but the output is difficult to control accurately.
- Cotton string reinforcement stabilizes the control, but requires a greater air pressure.

3.2 Narrow Space Test

To evaluate whether the designed actuators can work in narrow spaces or not, we used a perforated cork to imitate the nasal surgery in a narrow environment. Figure 8 shows the all experimental states when the prototype passes through the cork hole and carries on the 180° turning.

Fig. 8. 5 possible configurations of the prototype.

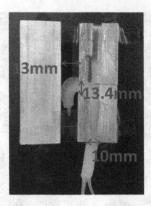

Fig. 9. 180° turning state.

In the state of rough inner wall, prototype can still penetrate the hole, advancing, and turning at the hole, reaching 180° (Fig. 9) with a small sweeping area. According to a cadaveric study [13], height of the anterior (sagittal) of dentate maxillary sinuses and edentulous maxillary sinuses are about 14.39 ± 6.35 mm and 16.37 ± 3.29 mm. Our simulation environment is made with a diameter of 13.4 mm and the actuator can pass and reach an angle of 180. It satisfies the range of 14.39 ± 6.35 mm, therefore in the actual operation, the actuator is basically can through the sinus ostium.

4   Conclusion and Future Work

In this study, a new elastomeric flexible pneumatic actuator with two antagonistic air chambers is proposed. Test results are promising for meeting the requirements for MIS support. That proposed actuator achieved a 180° bending angle readily driven by air pressure, with a small sweeping area when going through a narrow cavity.

Meanwhile, accuracy of pressure instruments and error caused by fabrication methods cannot be ignored, and more experiments are needed to prove the actuators' validity and reliability. In order to solve these problems, for the reconstruction of the control system, as well as the automatic fabrication of the actuator is the work need to be solved. The effectiveness of the proposed actuators will be validated in animal surgeries fully functional actuators will be produced to be developed into a product for clinical use.

In the future, we will analyze how changing the internal and external structure of the actuator affects its response by using Finite Element Analysis, for achieving a better performance.

Acknowledgement. The authors would like to thank the JSPS Program for Leading Graduate School (Graduate Program in Gerontology, Global Leadership Initiative for an Age Friendly Society, The University of Tokyo) for providing financial support to Jiang Wu.

References

1. Kwon, I.G., Cho, I., Guner, A., et al.: Surg. Endosc. **29**, 2321 (2015). https://doi.org/10.1007/s00464-014-3955-2
2. Broeders, I.A.M.J., Ruurda, J.: Robotics revolutionizing surgery: the intuitive surgical "da Vinci" system. Ind. Robot.: Int. J. **28**(5), 387–392 (2001)
3. Kobayashi, E., et al.: A new safe laparoscopic manipulator system with a five-bar linkage mechanism and an optical zoom. Comput. Aided Surg. **4**(4), 182–192 (1999)
4. Zemiti, N., et al.: Mechatronic design of a new robot for force control in minimally invasive surgery. IEEE/ASME Trans. Mechatron. **12**(2), 143–153 (2007)
5. Shen, H.: The soft touch. Nature **530**, 24–26 (2016)
6. Marchese, A.D., Katzschmann, R.K., Rus, D.: A recipe for soft fluidic elastomer robots. Soft Robot. **2**(1), 7–25 (2015)
7. Martinez, R.V., et al.: Robotic tentacles with three-dimensional mobility based on flexible elastomers. Adv. Mater. **25**(2), 205–212 (2013)
8. Rateni, G., et al.: Design and development of a soft robotic gripper for manipulation in minimally invasive surgery: a proof of concept. Meccanica **50**(11), 2855–2863 (2015)
9. Wang, H., et al.: Visual servo control of cable-driven soft robotic manipulator. In: 2013 IEEE/RSJ International Conference on Intelligent Robots and Systems (IROS). IEEE (2013)
10. Wu, J., Yu, W.: Development of flexible movable guide frame for supporting the water-filled-laparo- endoscopic surgery. In: The Proceeding of 2015 International Symposium on InfoComm Medical Technology in Bio-Medical & Healthcare Application, p. 92, Chiba, Japan (2015)
11. Veligeti, R.C.: Minimally invasive surgery for cancer: the best alternative to open surgery. http://www.continentalhospitals.com/blog/minimally-invasive-surgery-for-cancer-the-best-alternative-to-open-surgery/. Accessed 15 Mar 2017
12. By Illu01_head_neck.jpg: Arcadian derivative work: Prof. Squirrel. https://upload.wikimedia.org/wikipedia/commons/f/f8/Head_neck_vsphincter.png. Accessed 15 Mar 2017
13. Gandhi, K.R., Wabale, R.N., Siddiqui, A.U., Farooqui, M.S.: The incidence and morphology of maxillary sinus septa in dentate and edentulous maxillae: a cadaveric study with a brief review of the literature. J. Korean Assoc. Oral Maxillofac. Surg. **41**(1), 30–36 (2015)

Recognition of Listener's Nodding by LSTM Based on Movement of Facial Keypoints and Speech Intonation

Takayoshi Yamashita[1(✉)], Maya Nakagawa[1], Hironobu Fujiyoshi[1], and Yuji Haikawa[2]

[1] Chubu University, Kasugai, Japan
takayoshi@isc.chubu.ac.jp
[2] Honda Research Institute Japan, Wako, Japan

Abstract. Communication between humans and robots is crucial to achieve successful cooperation in real-life scenarios. The robot must understand not only linguistic expressions, but also non-linguistic expressions such as nodding and gestures. In this research, we examine whether a listener nods in response to a speaker's utterance. Our proposed method judges nodding based on the movement of the listener's facial keypoints and the speaker's speech intonation. The proposed method achieves approximately 84.4% recognition accuracy when we input the movement and intonation simultaneously. This improves nodding recognition accuracy by 8.8% over movement only approach. This result indicates that the movement of the listener's facial keypoints and the speaker's intonation are important information in nodding recognition.

Keywords: Nodding · Speech intonation · RNN · Facial keypoint

1 Introduction

Robots are already widely used in industrial applications and their fields of active use will continue to expand. Some potential future uses are information robots in shopping malls and support robots for nursing. It is important for robots to understand not only verbal expressions but also non-verbal gestures. Non-verbal expressions by way of subtle body movements such as smiling are part of normal conversation flow and facilitate communication [1]. In this paper, we recognize the listener's nodding within a conversation. The listener's nod is triggered by the speaker's intonation. We propose a method to recognize a listener's nodding using the inflection of the speaker's speech and the change in position of the listener's facial keypoints. Our proposed method achieves the following.

- Recognition of listener nodding using speaker intonation
- Improvement of recognition accuracy by simultaneously considering the speaker's intonation and the listener's change in facial keypoint positions

C. Stephanidis (Ed.): HCII 2019, CCIS 1033, pp. 154–160, 2019.
https://doi.org/10.1007/978-3-030-23528-4_22

2   Related Works

Human communication includes non-verbal cues. Therefore, a robot must understand non-verbal expressions to improve its communication with humans. Human head movement detection is a method for recognizing non-verbal expressions.

Head movement detection can be roughly divided into two categories: using a wearable device and using a camera-based approach. The method of using a wearable device equipped with an acceleration sensor performs feature extraction by principal components analysis (PCA) on the time-series data to recognize head movements such as "nodding" and "swing". Motion recognition is performed using the k-nearest neighbor method or a neural network [5]. The wearable device approach requires the subject to wear a sensor during communication, which entails a physical burden.

One of the camera-based methods uses a convolutional neural network (CNN) to recognize human actions from RGB and optical flow data [4] In this method, the recognition accuracy is improved by dividing the data into two streams: spatial and temporal. Although this camera-based method is highly accurate, it is dependent on the camera viewpoint.

3   Nodding Dataset

The listener's gesture is induced by the speaker's speech. Using the speech information elucidates the timing of the listener's nodding. Therefore, we consider that the speech information input can effectively improve recognition accuracy. We collect our own nodding dataset consisting of movies of approximately 10 min of human-to-human conversation via video chat. In addition, we annotate the sequence with the following labels: "utterance content", "expression", "gaze", "nodding", "target of nodding", and "continuity of nodding". Figure 1 shows example image frames from the dataset.

Fig. 1. Examples of image frames from our dataset

4   Proposed Method

We propose a nodding recognition method that combines the information of the listener's movement acquired from the camera with the speaker's speech. Our method begins by extracting the facial keypoint movement information of the recognition target and speaker's speech information. This information obtained in each frame of the video is sequentially input to the recurrent neural network (RNN) [2]. The RNN outputs the nodding probability for each frame.

4.1   Motion Information

The position differences of the facial keypoints between the current frame and the previous frame are used as the movement information. When we extract the feature of the entire face image, this forms appearance features, thereby capturing information that may not be necessary for nodding recognition. It is possible to capture motion information and remove unnecessary appearance information by using the motion difference of the facial keypoints. We use Dlib for face detection and facial keypoint detection [6]. As shown in Fig. 2, Dlib detects 68 facial keypoints. The amount of movement $d_{x,i}$ in the x direction and $d_{y,i}$ in the y direction at time t of the facial keypoint i is given by Eq. (1). Because the total number of facial keypoints is 68, the feature vector of the motion information has 136 dimensions when combining $d_{x,i}(t)$ and $d_{y,i}(t)$.

$$\begin{cases} d_{x,i}(t) = x_i(t-5) - x_i(t) \\ d_{y,i}(t) = y_i(t-5) - y_i(t) \end{cases} \tag{1}$$

Fig. 2. Facial keypoint detection using Dlib

4.2   Speech Information

Because the listener's nodding is induced by the speaker's speech, we can use the speech information as an additional cue for the timing of the listener's nodding. We consider two types of speech information: the presence or absence of speech and the speech intonation. We represent the presence or absence of speech by a binary value indicating whether the speaker is speaking. We calculate the speech intonation based on speech waveform data, which we record as 16-bit discrete data. We measure the speech intonation by the amplitude of the speech waveform data. However, because voice waveform data has negative values, we calculate the voice power from the waveform data in preprocessing. In addition, the sampling frequency is different between the video image sequence and the voice data. Thus, we use the value obtained by summing the voice power of 10 samples before and after time t as the feature $S(t)$ of the speech information, as indicated by Eq. (2).

$$S(t) = \sum_{10}^{i=-10} s(t+i)^2 \tag{2}$$

Nodding Label. In general, there are two types of nodding: nodding in response to the other person's speech (represented by the label "you") and nodding during one's own speech (represented by the label "me"). We focus on nodding in response to the other person's speech, therefore, we use only "you" samples for training and evaluation.

4.3 Network Architecture

Figure 3(a) shows the network structure when the input comprises only speech information, and Fig. 3(b) shows the network structure when the input comprises only the change in position of the facial keypoints. Figure 3(c) shows the network structure when the input to the long short-term memory (LSTM) layer [3] comprises both the change in position of the facial keypoints and the intonation information. We normalize each input value to between 0 and 1. All of the

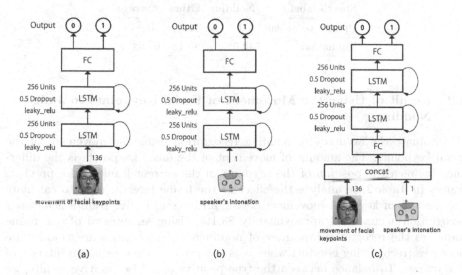

Fig. 3. Network architecture

networks have two LSTM layers and one fully-connected (FC) layer to output the nodding probability. Figure 3(c) shows the concatenation of the movement and the intonation feature values before inputting them into the LSTM layer. We apply weights to these feature values during concatenation. For training, we use RMSprop as the optimizer and we train for 300 epochs with a batch size of 32.

5　Evaluation

We begin by evaluate only the speech information as the input feature by using the network structure shown in Fig. 3(a). We then evaluate the movement of facial keypoints and experiment with the frame interval used for calculating the amount of movement using the network structure shown in Fig. 3(b). Finally, we evaluate the combination of both of the aforementioned features as in Fig. 3(c) to demonstrate the resulting improvement in the recognition accuracy.

5.1　Relationship Between Intonation and Nodding

Table 1 shows the accuracy of judging nodding based on speech information. Simply the presence or absence of speech as input does not enable judgment of nodding. The speech intonation information achieves a recognition accuracy of approximately 42.0%. The average recognition rate is approximately 63.6%. This result indicates that the speaker's speech intonation is important for judging whether the listener is nodding.

Table 1. Recognition accuracy by speech label [%]

Speech label	Nodding	Other	Average
Present or absent	0.0	100.0	50.0
Intonation	42.0	85.1	63.6

5.2　Result of Using the Movement of Facial Keypoints to Judge Nodding

We evaluate the accuracy of nodding recognition using the movement of the facial keypoints. The amount of movement of the facial keypoints is the difference between the position of the keypoint in the current frame and a previous frame. In Table 2 we analyze the effect of the frame interval used to calculate the amount of keypoint movement. Using an interval of five frames achieves a recognition accuracy of approximately 83.1%. Using an interval of one frame improves the recognition accuracy of nodding, but also introduces more false positives (recognizing nodding when it is not present) than using an interval of five frames. To balance between the true positive and false positive results, we use an interval of five frames for the final experiment.

Table 2. Recognition accuracy by frame interval [%]

Interval	Nodding	Other	Average
1 frame	81.7	84.4	83.1
5 frame	72.6	91.7	82.2

5.3 Result of Using both Keypoint Movement and Intonation for Nodding Recognition

We aim to improve the nodding recognition accuracy by simultaneously training the model on both the intonation features and the keypoint movement information. As shown in Table 3, using both of these feature types simultaneously achieves an 84.4% overall accuracy to judge whether nodding is present. This result is more accurate than that achieved by using each feature type alone. However, using both features simultaneously training reduces the accuracy of judging the absence of nodding by approximately 4.3% compared to using only the amount of keypoint movement. This is balanced by the substantial improvement (8.8% points higher) in the detection of nodding (true positives). Thus, the simultaneous use of both features is promising for nodding recognition.

Table 3. Recognition accuracy by feature type [%]

Interval	Nodding	Other	Average
Speech intonation	42.0	85.1	63.6
Facial keypoints movement	72.6	91.7	82.2
Intonation and movement	81.4	87.4	84.4

6 Conclusion

We proposed a method to recognize a listener nodding based on the speaker's speech intonation and the amount of listener facial keypoint movement. Simultaneously using both the speaker's intonation and the amount of listener facial keypoint movement significantly improves the detection of nodding (approximately 8.8% points higher than using only the amount of keypoint movement). In future work, we will consider nodding recognition for multiple people, end-to-end network training, and recognition of nonverbal expressions other than nodding.

References

1. Kobayashi, N., et al.: Quantitative evaluation of infant behavior and mother infant interaction. Early Dev. Parent. **1**(1), 23–31 (1992)
2. Graves, A., et al.: Speech recognition with deep recurrent neural networks. In: Acoustics, Speech and Signal Processing (ICASSP), pp. 6645–6649 (2013)
3. Hochreiter, S., et al.: Long short-term memory. Neural Comput. **9**(8), 1735–1780 (1997)
4. Simonyan, K., et al.: Two-stream convolutional networks for action recognition in videos. NIPS (2014)
5. Wu, L., et al.: In Vivo evaluation of wearable head impact sensors. Ann. Biomed. Eng. **44**(4), 1234–45 (2015)
6. King, D.E.: Dlib-ml: a machine learning toolkit. J. Mach. Learn. Res. **10**, 1755–1758 (2009)

AI and Machine Learning in HCI

AI-Based Technical Approach for Designing Mobile Decision Aids

Kiana Alikhademi[1]([✉]), Brianna Richardson[1], Kassandra Ross[2],
Jihyun Sung[2], Juan E. Gilbert[1], Wi-Suk Kwon[2],
and Veena Chattaraman[2]

[1] University of Florida, Gainesville, FL 32611, USA
{kalikhademi, richardsonb, juan}@ufl.edu
[2] Auburn University, Auburn, AL 36849, USA
{mkr0028, jzs0157, kwonwis, vzc0001}@auburn.edu

Abstract. Conversational Voice User Interfaces (VUIs) help us in performing tasks in a wide range of domains these days. While there have been several efforts around designing dialogue systems and conversation flows, little information is available about technical concepts to extract critical information for addressing the users' needs. For conversational VUIs to function appropriately as a decision aid, artificial intelligence (AI) that recognizes and supports diverse user decision strategies is a critical need. Following the design principle proposed by Kwon et al. [1] regarding the conversational flow between the user and conversational VUI, we developed an AI-based mobile-decision-aid (MODA) that predictively models and addresses users' decision strategies to facilitate users' in-store shopping decision process. In this paper, technical details about how MODA processes users' natural language queries and generate the most appropriate and intelligent recommendations have been discussed. This developmental approach provides broad implications to conversational VUIs for diverse complex decision-making contexts and decision-makers with a critical need for decision assistants.

Keywords: Decision aid systems · Conversational agent ·
Voice User Interface · Artificial intelligence

1 Introduction

Conversational Voice User Interfaces (VUIs) have become fairly popular in a wide array of fields, including in-home assistants, mobile-assistants, and even online assistants. With the increased presence of these agents, there has been a surge in research dealing with how to optimize their functionality and in which settings they are most appropriate.

Within the shopping domain, there has been a concerted effort towards optimizing agents for online shopping. Qiu et al. [4] suggests that in virtual environments, like online shopping, intelligent agents are one of the four major contributors to users'

© Springer Nature Switzerland AG 2019
C. Stephanidis (Ed.): HCII 2019, CCIS 1033, pp. 163–169, 2019.
https://doi.org/10.1007/978-3-030-23528-4_23

feelings of social presence. Much of the attention in the realm of shopping conversational VUIs has been on optimizing them so that the user is interested in engaging with them and willing to re-use them. Qiu and Benbasat [3] found that human voice-based communication in intelligent agents could greatly influence the user's perceptions of social presence, which could in turn enhance trust, enjoyment, and decision to use the agent. Furthermore, Anderson et al. [6] observed participants interacting with an embodied interface and found that intelligent agents must be rule-based and incorporate natural language parsing to be useful and effective for users. Gnewuch et al.'s [7] suggestions for more effective customer service intelligent agents also required complex natural language processing and flexible conversation flow so that users might respond more optimistically towards them.

In particular, shopping-based intelligent agents deal with a specialized issue that extends from the relations between consumer and supplier: trust. With trust being the most important factor consumers rely on when interacting with their supplier [5], it is especially fragile between consumers and agents because these consumers worry about opportunistic biases within agent recommendation [6]. In an attempt to address this trust concern, we developed MODA, a novel conversational VUI, which was built to assist in the in-store shopping experience by suggesting products based on users' decision-making strategies. Kwon et al. [1] designed principles of conversational flow for in-store decision-aid based on the H-E-O-C framework designed by Chattaraman et al. [2]. These principles helped design MODA with the ability to identify the decision-making strategies and preferences and tailor the nature of its assistive tasks to user strategies and preferences. In doing so, MODA's assistive intent becomes transparent to the user, which may help alleviate the trust concern. MODA consists of separate subsystems that work to understand and process the natural language and finally respond appropriately to user needs.

2   AI-Based Technical Approaches and Components

Our AI-based conversational agent attains its functionality through three different components: the model, dialog, and data subsystems. In the following section, brief introductions to the goal of each component are given. This will be followed by detailed technical approaches to the construction of each component.

2.1   Model Subsystem

The model subsystem acts as MODA's brain and plays the main role of recognizing the decision-making strategies proposed in [1] and constructing the conversation flow. After the dialog subsystem receives the query, it is passed to the model subsystem to extract the necessary information. The model subsystem contains rules and inferences for labeling and segmenting the natural language input based on consumer-elaboration, context-abstraction, and decision-making strategies discussed in [2]. One of the most important capabilities of a VUI is whether it distinguishes relevant from non-relevant information which helps to classify a correct step within a conversation flow, commonly referred to as Natural Language Understanding (NLU). NLU is the procedure of parsing a raw query into the structured data and storing it in the predefined variables. Dialogflow agents use supervised intent classifications and rule-based entities matching within NLU. *Intents* are mappings between user queries and appropriate responses, whereas *entities* are the procedure for recognizing and parsing useful data out of the natural language queries. There are two different sets of entities, including user-defined and system entities. System entities are general types of entities such as location, scale, and time. Developers can define their own entities which match with their goal and the context that the VUI will be used in. In MODA, we used entities to define different options in three types of parameters: product attributes, brands, and decision criteria. Attributes, brands, and criteria data collected by Chattaraman et al. [2] through shopping website content analysis and user observation studies have been utilized to define entities.

During the human-to-human natural dialog, contextual information related to previous dialog(s) is perceived, stored, and retrieved as needed. Within Dialogflow, the context parameter is used to show the current state of the VUI and store the previous states similar to natural dialog between humans. Context management is hence a vital tool for managing dialogs between users and the VUI efficiently. Within MODA, we used context in each intent to store the corresponding parameters and use it whenever it is needed in the conversational flow so that users do not repeat the same information again. Contexts are used to identify the next steps within the conversational flow which is influential in dialog management. To apply the design principle discussed by Kwon et al. [1], the natural language query is assessed continuously to verify existence and number of parameters such as attributes, brands, and criteria with the goal of recognizing the accurate intents and their corresponding contexts and entities. This information helps predict the appropriate decision-making flow and rules to address the user's needs.

By using the features discussed above, we are able to extract the requisite information from users' natural language queries. However, besides acquiring essential information, MODA needs to generate appropriate responses to recommend a product that matches the user's needs. Responses could either be fixed type messages or more intelligent ones coming from outside servers. Fulfillment is the procedure that allows the Dialogflow agent to call the backend server to process the information and generate dynamic and intelligent responses. In the MODA project, a NodeJS server was developed, which processed the raw JSON request file, which made the necessary connections with the data subsystem to retrieve information and generate the proper response object, and send it back through REST API procedures (see Fig. 1).

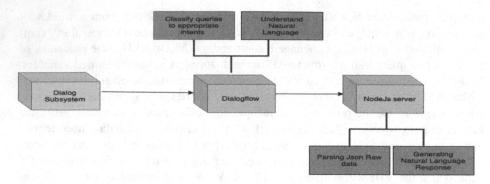

Fig. 1. Overview of model subsystem structure

2.2 Dialog Subsystem

The dialog subsystem consists of the mobile interface, similar to common messaging applications, where conversation history is displayed and user input is retrieved, via voice or text modalities. As an Android application, MODA was built with Java and Android SDK.

Several libraries were included to expand the functionality of MODA. Dialogflow's API.AI allows a connection between the dialog subsystem and the model subsystem. When users open the app, Dialogflow sends the generic welcome message that can be seen in the screenshot to the left in Fig. 2. Once a user sends a message back, the message is shown on the screen and is sent to Dialogflow via the API.AI package for processing. EyalBira's LoadingDots, which can be seen in action in Fig. 2 in the screenshot to the right, is used to display to the user that MODA is preparing a response. Once a message is returned, the text is printed in its own speech bubble and Google's Text-to-Speech API is implemented to voice MODA's responses.

The modality of the app is optimized so that physical requirements are minimized while accessibility is maximized. Users have the option to use the text or voice modal. If the voice modal is chosen, MODA will automatically start up the mic each time the system awaits a response, and it will send the message as soon as the user is done speaking. This reduces the monotonous and, for some, exhausting motion of repetitively tapping the mic and send buttons. Furthermore, MODA contains the keyword inquiry, 'Repeat,' that will get MODA to verbally repeat the last message sent.

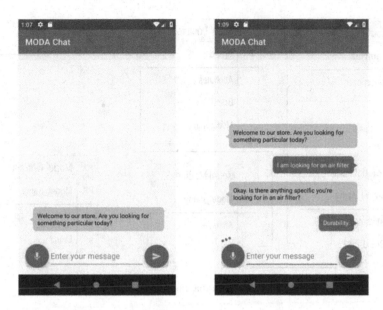

Fig. 2. MODA Android application interface

2.3 Data Subsystem

Knowledge is an important part of human beings as they refer to it for completing many tasks including making conversation. The same rule also exists for the conversational agents as they intend to facilitate conversation and assist users. Without proper data knowledge about the domain, it is impossible for a VUI to achieve meaningful goal-oriented conversations. MODA as a conversational, goal-oriented assistant needs enough information about the products to respond to users appropriately, and this is why the data subsystem is needed. This subsystem, a MySQL database, encompasses products and related information including specifications, reviews, and ratings in different relational data tables as shown in Fig. 3. After the user's requests are processed by the model subsystem to extract the appropriate information, MODA's model subsystem sends queries (via NodeJS) to the data subsystem to retrieve the most appropriate product models that match the user's expectations. Model locations within the store can also be queried to provide a final step of assistance by identifying where the user should find their items of interest. *Model_criteria* and *Model_medium* are the databases used to gain information about the medium level (i.e., generally acceptable level) products, whereas *Model_rank* helps to find the best available product for each attribute. In Fig. 3 Private keys and entity relationships between the tables have been defined. Although in developing the current MODA prototype, we used static databases described above. When implementing MODA in a real-world retail store, a dynamic data subsystem that organically connects multiple sources of real-time data to generate and update the aforementioned databases is highly recommended.

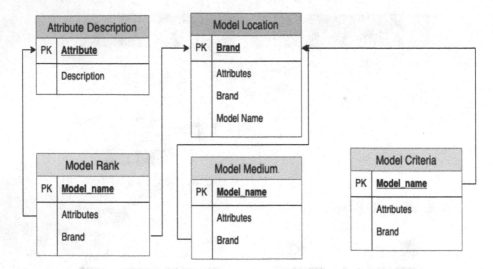

Fig. 3. Entity relation diagram of data subsystem

3 Conclusion

Conversational VUIs are accommodating us in many different tasks and settings of our daily lives including, but not limited to, shopping. However, there are not many conversational VUIs developed for in-store shopping scenarios. We developed MODA, an intelligent mobile decision aid system which accommodates users in shopping by intelligently retrieving information based on the users' voiced needs. Technical details within each subsystem of MODA have been shared to guide other researchers through possible methods of extracting information from similar natural language queries. Our future works are focused on evaluating the MODA system using large-scale data including different queries and assess the usability of MODA.

Acknowledgements. This material is based in part upon work supported by the National Science Foundation under Grant Numbers IIS-1527182 and IIS-1527302; the Alabama Agricultural Experiment Station; and the Hatch program of the National Institute of Food and Agriculture, U. S. Department of Agriculture. Any opinions, findings, and conclusions or recommendations expressed in this material are those of the authors and do not necessarily reflect the views of the funding agencies acknowledged above.

References

1. Kwon, W.-S., Chattaraman, V., Ross, K., Alikhademi, K., Gilbert, J.E.: Modeling conversational flows for in-store mobile decision aids. In: Stephanidis, C. (ed.) HCI 2018. CCIS, vol. 852, pp. 302–308. Springer, Cham (2018). https://doi.org/10.1007/978-3-319-92285-0_42
2. Chattaraman, V., Kwon, W.-S., Eugene, W., Gilbert, J.: Developing and validating a naturalistic decision model for intelligent language-based decision aids. Hum. Factors Ergon. Soc. Annu. Meet. **61**(1), 176–177 (2017)

3. Qiu, L., Benbasat, I.: Evaluating anthropomorphic product recommendation agents: a social relationship perspective to designing information systems. J. Manag. Inf. Syst. **25**(4), 145–182 (2009). https://doi.org/10.2753/MIS0742-1222250405
4. Qiu, L., Jiang, Z., Benbasat, I.: Real experience in a virtual store: designing for presence in online shopping. In: Proceedings of the PACIS 2006, p. 93 (2006)
5. Andersen, V., Hansen, C.B., Andersen, H.H.K.: Evaluation of agents and study of end-user needs and behaviour for e-commerce. COGITO focus group experiment (2001)
6. Benbasat, I., Wang, W.: Trust in and adoption of online recommendation agents. J. Assoc. Inf. Syst. **6**(3), 4 (2005)
7. Gnewuch, U., Morana, S., Maedche, A.: Towards designing cooperative and social conversational agents for customer service (2017)

Human Learning in Data Science

Anna Beer$^{(\boxtimes)}$, Daniyal Kazempour$^{(\boxtimes)}$, Marcel Baur$^{(\boxtimes)}$,
and Thomas Seidl$^{(\boxtimes)}$

LMU Munich, Munich, Germany
{beer,kazempour,seidl}@dbs.ifi.lmu.de,
marcel.baur@campus.lmu.de

Abstract. As machine learning becomes a more and more important area in Data Science, bringing with it a rise of abstractness and complexity, the desire for explainability rises, too. With our work we aim to gain explainability focussing on correlation clustering and try to pursue the original goals of different Data Science tasks,: Extracting knowledge from data. As well-known tools like Fold-It or GeoTime show, gamification is a very mighty approach, but not only to solve tasks which prove more difficult for machines than for humans. We could also gain knowledge from how players proceed trying to solve those difficult tasks. That is why we developed *Straighten it up!*, a game in which users try to find the best linear correlations in high dimensional datasets. Finding arbitrarily oriented subspaces in high dimensional data is an exponentially complex task due to the number of potential subspaces in regards to the number of dimensions. Nevertheless, linearly correlated points are as a simple pattern easy to track by the human eye. *Straighten it up!* gives users an overview over two-dimensional projections of a self-chosen dataset. Users decide which subspace they want to examine first, and can draw in arbitrarily many lines fitting the data. An offset inside of which points are assigned to the corresponding line can easily be chosen for every line independently, and users can switch between different projections at any time. We developed a scoring system not only as incentive, but first of all for further examination, based on the density of each cluster, its minimum spanning tree, size of offset, and coverage. By tracking every step of a user we are able to detect common mechanisms and examine differences to state-of-the-art correlation and subspace clustering algorithms, resulting in more comprehensibility.

1 Introduction

Unsupervised data mining is reliving a revival due to the lack of explainability in most supervised machine learning algorithms. Correlation clustering algorithms are easily explainable, and most functional principles are obvious for users. Nevertheless, they intrinsically do not work fully unsupervised and automatically: at some point a developer must have defined some criteria for a good correlation cluster, or how to proceed looking for one. For that usually one of many definitions is applied. But those definitions of a correlation cluster can differ significantly in regards to many aspects:

© Springer Nature Switzerland AG 2019
C. Stephanidis (Ed.): HCII 2019, CCIS 1033, pp. 170–176, 2019.
https://doi.org/10.1007/978-3-030-23528-4_24

- A correlation can be linear or non-linear
- A correlation cluster can be defined by a limited or unlimited space in which all points belong to the cluster. It can also be defined by the points belonging to it.
- Density connectivity can be mandatory or not
- A correlation cluster can exist only in a subspace of the data space or the points could correlate in every dimension.

To gain knowledge about users' perception of a correlation cluster, we designed "Straighten it up!", a game in which users can denote correlation clusters in an easy way, looking at two-dimensional projections of high dimensional data. We do not only want to learn which criteria most of the users estimate as most important, but also want to learn about their approach. *Straighten it up!* allows to collect data about, e.g., which projections are most often chosen as the first ones, in which projections the "optimal" clusters are the same for all users and in which projections they differ. Also, different groups of users can be detected and analysed. Users are motivated to play by getting points according to a score, which the scientist interested in their data is able to adjust accordingly. Our main contributions are as follows:

- We develop *Straighten it up!*, a game in which users have to find linear correlations
- *Straighten it up!* allows to collect data on which points are perceived as correlation clusters by users. With that, the definitions of correlation clusters can be critically reconsidered.
- The approach of how to find correlation clusters can be analyzed.
- We developed a scoring function which rates users' solutions depending on density of clusters, accuracy and precision of the linear approximations
- The scoring function can be adjusted by the researcher.

The paper is structured as follows: Sect. 1.1 gives a brief overview over related work in the field of gamification as well as linear correlation clustering. Section 2 describes *Straighten it up!* in detail with respect to the setup of the game, the scoring function, and the data which can be extracted. Section 3 concludes this paper.

1.1   Related Work

We approach work related to *Straighten it up!* from two sides. At one hand, we look at current gamification systems, while on the other hand, we regard state-of-the art correlation clustering methods.

Gamification. One of the most prominent games from the domain of protein structure elucidation is FoldIt! [1] which lets the players fold a set of given proteins after accomplishing a tutorial. Computing tertiary structures of proteins which have a conformation resulting in minimum energy is a computationally challenging and still unsolved task. There are methods to predict tertiary structures from a given protein but these heuristics may lead to local but not necessarily to global minima. A protein with a low energy conformation is desirable, since this ensures a structure by which it is most stable. By FoldIt! the tertiary structure of a protein has been discovered which has been unknown to the protein-biochemistry community [2] until that point. Another approach is Phylo DNA [3] which puts the task of multiple sequence alignment into a game. The task of determining an alignment of multiple sequences is also computationally challenging. Since this problem is NP-hard, heuristics exist, which may also lead to a local, but usually not to a global optimum.

Correlation Clustering. Similar to tasks often solved by gamification, clustering is also known to be NP-hard and as a consequence a wealth of heuristics exist. Besides various models of clustering (partitioning like k-means [4], density based like DBSCAN [5] or hierarchical like single-link [6]) there are also subspace clustering methods working on high-dimensional data space, which are tailored to detect subspaces in which the data objects of a cluster are most similar within each of their respective clusters [7]. These subspaces may be axis-parallel or arbitrary oriented. The latter is also known in the literature as correlation clustering which comes with a rich body of literature. Most of the methods can be subsumed in the three categories: local (e.g. 4C [8]), global (e.g. CASH [9]) and hierarchical (e.g. HiCO [10]) correlated clusters. Being aware that there also exist non-linear correlation clustering methods (e.g. HCC [11]) we refer here with the term correlation clustering to linearly correlated clusters throughout this work. Embedding the task of correlation clustering into a gamification context, serves the following purposes:

- The design of scoring functions
- Gaining insights from the way the players approach the tasks
- Using the obtained insights to develop new correlation clustering methods.

2   Straighten It Up!

Straighten it up! is designed to gather many different aspects of user behaviour as well as intuitive definitions of correlation clusters. The scoring used as incentive for users rewards linear correlated clusters, which are defined by the space in which cluster members lie. To define that space, users can create lines between two dots set by mouse clicks, and change the width of each with an additional offset handle. All two-dimensional projections of the data are given in an overview. Based on this overview, one can choose which projection to regard first in detail and create linear correlation clusters in it.

2.1   Scoring

User retention, activity and motivation is one of the key problems gamification aims to solve [12–14]. To keep users engaged in our application we implemented a scoring system. A high-score is tracked for every dataset, and the top ten scores are displayed in the application. Players can then compete to break each others high score. Their current score on their active game can also be calculated which then might trigger the feedback loop, where the player might try to improve on their result before submission (See Fig. 1).

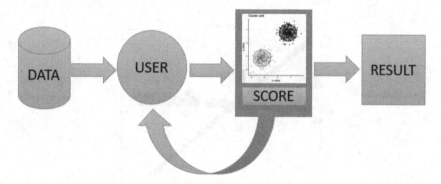

Fig. 1. The feedback loop a user will go through in our game. After checking their score, the player can try to improve on their solution or submit it to the database.

Another key reason for a scoring system is the ability to evaluate the discovered clusters. A higher score indicates a "better" set of found lines by users. Since the quality of found clusters depends on the application we developed an adaptable base for a score function. It rewards good clusterings and offers replayability at the same time. Players should feel engaged to try to improve their submissions for the same dataset, using different approaches. We looked at several parameters to achieve this:

1. **Cluster density.** The number of points belonging to a line w.r.t. its offset is divided by the according area. High density leads to a high score.
2. **Minimum spanning tree.** A minimum spanning tree is calculated for the points belonging to the line. Even though it could, as shown in Fig. 2, lead to undesired approaches getting a high score, it enables handling non-linear clusters.
3. **Offset.** A large offset is considered an indicator for lower cluster quality, as it increases the probability of defining noise as a cluster.
4. **Dataset coverage.** Depending on the dataset, a high coverage of points can be desired, so that most of the points belong to any cluster. Nevertheless, this could mislead users to create clusters containing only noise. If only the most obvious clusters are wanted, a low coverage could be desired.

Combining those points leads to the following scoring function:

$$SCORE = h_0 * density + h_1 * \frac{1}{span} + h_2 * \frac{1}{offset} * coverage \qquad (1)$$

Note the inverted value for the score from a minimum spanning tree and offset. Lower values in those categories mean a better cluster, which means their score should be higher. h_0, h_1 and h_2 are hyperparameters, which can be set according to the desired results gamers should try to achieve. For example, if it is important that users try to find especially very dense clusters, h_0 could be set high in relation to h_1 and h_2.

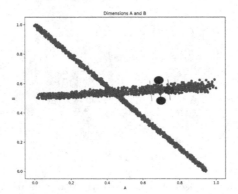

Fig. 2. An example for an objectively bad line that would yield a good score regarding only the minimum spanning tree.

2.2   Penalties

With the above scoring, malicious users could still produce undesired results. To retain some of those, penalty points can be used. To prevent disproportionate penalties if the overall scoring is already low, a relative penalty is subtracted from the original score. Empirically, a logarithmic scale delivered the desired results: like that, penalty points for the first unwanted behaviours are weighted heavier. Equation 2 shows a way to calculate the fraction of the score that is subtracted for p penalty points, with h_p being a hyperparameter scaling the penalty.

$$\frac{log(p+1)}{h_p} \tag{2}$$

Also, behaviours like generating more lines than necessary for a single correlation, as shown in Fig. 3, should be punishable. For example, the penalty could depend on the number of lines in a projection.

2.3   Knowledge Discovery

To be able to analyze as much as possible from every game played, we gather a plethora of data: Every move has a time stamp. A move can be the creation, deletion, or change of a line. With the time stamp we can gather insight of how single lines are refined in order to receive a higher score and also analyze in which

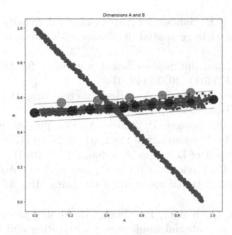

Fig. 3. Splitting one correlation into many smaller lines could yield a higher score, thus a penalty for too many lines in one projection can be introduced.

order different projections are processed by users. Also, the time needed for a move can deliver valuable insights. We store all lines set by users, i.e., starting point, end point, and bandwidth, as well as the projection in which the line was set. The post-processing file containing which points are lying in the bandwidth of which line delivers all information needed to calculate the scores.

3   Conclusion

In summary, we developed a game which allows to gather data on how linear correlation clusters are defined intuitively and on how users proceed to find them. Based on this, existing definitions for linear correlation clusters can be analyzed in future work and frequently used approaches can be transferred to new automatic linear correlation clustering algorithms.

Acknowledgement. This work has been funded by the German Federal Ministry of Education and Research (BMBF) under Grant No. 01IS18036A. The authors of this work take full responsibilities for its content.

References

1. Cooper, S., et al.: Predicting protein structures with a multiplayer online game. Nature **466**(7307), 756 (2010)
2. Khatib, F., et al.: Crystal structure of a monomeric retroviral protease solved by protein folding game players. Nat. Struct. Mol. Biol. **18**(10), 1175 (2011)
3. Kawrykow, A., et al.: Phylo: a citizen science approach for improving multiple sequence alignment. PLoS ONE **7**(3), e31362 (2012)
4. Lloyd, S.: Least squares quantization in PCM. IEEE Trans. Inf. Theory **28**(2), 129–137 (1982)

5. Ester, M., Kriegel, H.P., Sander, J., Xu, X., et al.: A density-based algorithm for discovering clusters in large spatial databases with noise. In: KDD, vol. 96, pp. 226–231 (1996)
6. Sibson, R.: SLINK: an optimally efficient algorithm for the single-link cluster method. Comput. J. **16**(1), 30–34 (1973)
7. Kriegel, H.P., Kröger, P., Zimek, A.: Subspace clustering. Wiley Interdiscip. Rev.: Data Min. Knowl. Discov. **2**(4), 351–364 (2012)
8. Böhm, C., Kailing, K., Kröger, P., Zimek, A.: Computing clusters of correlation connected objects. In: Proceedings of the 2004 ACM SIGMOD International Conference on Management of Data, pp. 455–466. ACM (2004)
9. Achtert, E., Böhm, C., David, J., Kröger, P., Zimek, A.: Global correlation clustering based on the hough transform. Stat. Anal. Data Min. ASA Data Sci. J. **1**(3), 111–127 (2008)
10. Achtert, E., Böhm, C., Kröger, P., Zimek, A.: Mining hierarchies of correlation clusters. In: 18th International Conference on Scientific and Statistical Database Management (SSDBM 2006), pp. 119–128. IEEE (2006)
11. Kazempour, D., Mauder, M., Kröger, P., Seidl, T.: Detecting global hyper-paraboloid correlated clusters based on Hough transform. In: Proceedings of the 29th International Conference on Scientific and Statistical Database Management, p. 31. ACM (2017)
12. Deterding, S., Dixon, D., Khaled, R., Nacke, L.: From game design elements to gamefulness: defining gamification. In: Proceedings of the 15th International Academic MindTrek Conference: Envisioning Future Media Environments, pp. 9–15. ACM (2011)
13. Zichermann, G., Cunningham, C.: Gamification by Design: Implementing Game Mechanics in Web and Mobile Apps. O'Reilly Media Inc., Sebastopol (2011)
14. Hamari, J., Koivisto, J., Sarsa, H.: Does gamification work?–A literature review of empirical studies on gamification. In: 2014 47th Hawaii International Conference on System Sciences (HICSS), pp. 3025–3034. IEEE (2014)

How to Achieve Explainability and Transparency in Human AI Interaction

Joana Hois[✉], Dimitra Theofanou-Fuelbier, and Alischa Janine Junk

Group Research, Future Technologies, Daimler AG, Stuttgart, Germany
{joana.hois, dimitra.theofanou-fuelbier,
alischa_janine.junk}@daimler.com

Abstract. It is typically not transparent to end-users, how AI systems derive information or make decisions. This becomes crucial, the more pervasive AI systems enter human daily lives, the more they influence automated decision-making, and the more people rely on them. We present work in progress on explainability to support transparency in human AI interaction. In this paper, we discuss methods and research findings on categorizations of user types, system scope and limits, situational context, and changes over time. Based on these different dimensions and their range and combinations, we aim at individual facets of transparency that address a specific situation best. The approach is human-centered to provide adequate explanations with regard to their depth of detail and level of information, and we outline the different dimensions of this complex task.

Keywords: Transparency · Explainability · Human AI interaction

1 Introduction

The number of artificial intelligence applications that are available on the business and consumer market have increased over the last years (Das et al. 2015). In some areas, more tasks have even been taken over by intelligent algorithms. Also, the future impact of AI is expected to become further pervasive and encompassing. One such example is a lifelong personal assistant (Gil and Selman 2019) that supports and tutors humans. These systems will highly affect social lives and influence human decisions. Trusting and relying on such systems to make correct (or 'good') suggestions or decisions is inevitable for these AI systems to achieve their full functionality (Mohseni et al. 2018).

AI systems can provide explanations together with their decisions and suggestions or interact with users when questions about their decisions and suggestions arise: in human-computer-interaction – or rather human-AI-interaction – explainability provides transparency and contributes to trust (Miller 2019). Even though trust itself is influenced by a variety of other aspects, e.g., human, robotic, and environmental factors (Schaefer et al. 2016), we focus here on aspects regarding explainability when interacting with artificial intelligence systems and how this can yield transparency. Also, the need for explainability of AI systems' decisions and behaviors has grown in general (Gunning 2017), and explainability is seen as a toolset to understand the underlying technicalities and models (Ribeiro et al. 2016 and Štrumbelj and Kononenko 2014).

© Springer Nature Switzerland AG 2019
C. Stephanidis (Ed.): HCII 2019, CCIS 1033, pp. 177–183, 2019.
https://doi.org/10.1007/978-3-030-23528-4_25

For more adaptive, continuously learning AI systems that closely collaborate with human end-users and that may change their behavior over time, transparency and understanding of the AI systems' behavior is inevitably, e.g., to increase user acceptance. The exact way, how to achieve this transparency and explainability is still an open question and ongoing research shows the complexity of the entire topic (Miller 2019 and Mohseni et al. 2018). For example, users may vary the detail of transparency they wish to see, or users may react more seamlessly to the system's behavior with higher understanding.

In this paper, we discuss different levels of transparency both from the perspective of human end-users and AI systems. In the next section, we show the different dimensions of transparency both from a human and an AI perspective. We next address potential roles and relationships during the human-AI-interaction, followed by aspects of situational awareness and time. As a result, we highlight the complexity when aiming at an appropriate level of explanations with regard to transparency in a specific situation.

2 Facets of Transparency

The existing body of research concerned with transparency and explainability of AI focus on different aspects of transparency, see Sect. 3. In this paper we will use a three-facetted-model of transparency based on the work of (Endsley 1995) and (Chen et al. 2014) regarding the situation awareness model and agent transparency.

As shown in Fig. 1, we identify three key facets of transparency. One aspect being the transparency about the behavior and the underlying intentions of the system. The second facet is concerned with the decision making mechanism of the system, including an understanding about the underlying algorithm and the integrated variables. The third facet adds an understanding about potential limitations of the system which includes an estimation of the probability of errors in a given situation.

When determining the level of transparency in a given situation, characteristics of the system as well as the user have to be taken into account: the system can provide explanations actively or on-demand and the system can also interact in a specific way that may be interpreted as social cues by the user. The user has certain preferences and prior experience with systems and potential expectations. A facet of transparency can be achieved by the interaction of both system and user.

The adequacy of an explanation, however, can hardly be determined without taking into account personal characteristics of the user. Depending on the general technical knowledge, the time of usage and the situation awareness of the user, the required quality and quantity of the explanation to reach a certain level of transparency might vary. This effects possible relationships during interaction (Sect. 4) and is influenced by specific situations (Sect. 5).

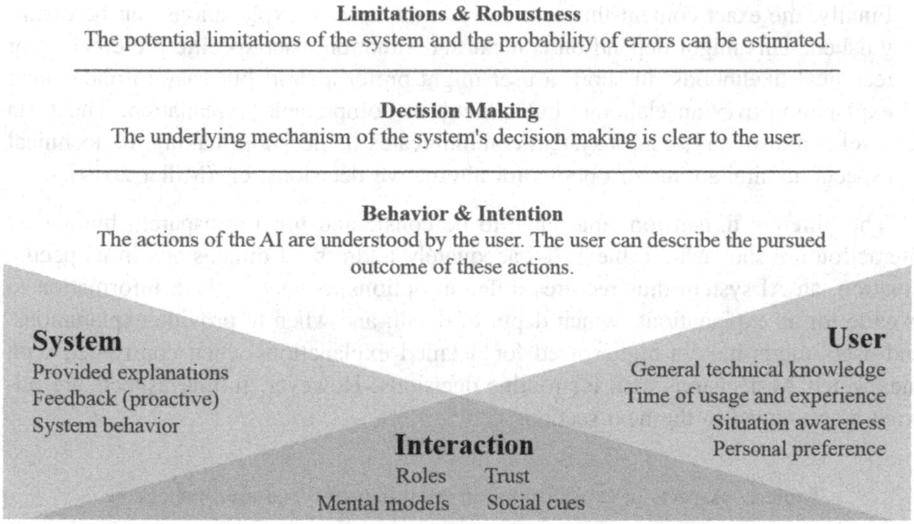

Limitations & Robustness
The potential limitations of the system and the probability of errors can be estimated.

Decision Making
The underlying mechanism of the system's decision making is clear to the user.

Behavior & Intention
The actions of the AI are understood by the user. The user can describe the pursued outcome of these actions.

System
Provided explanations
Feedback (proactive)
System behavior

User
General technical knowledge
Time of usage and experience
Situation awareness
Personal preference

Interaction
Roles   Trust
Mental models   Social cues

Fig. 1. Facets of transparency

3 Aspects of AI Explainability

AI functionalities are nowadays often enabled by machine learning models that have been trained with large data sets and that may learn when interacting with users and change their behavior over time. It has been argued that certain models intrinsically entail explanations in their decisions, e.g., decision trees, and are thus more easy to interpret, though also decision trees can become rather complex for humans to perceive and understand them (Štrumbelj and Kononenko 2014 and Došilovic et al. 2018). Complex machine learning models are difficult to interpret, and several approaches for explainability have been discussed (Ribeiro et al. 2016 and Samek et al. 2017).

It can be distinguished, whether explainability is primarily seen as a method that aims at analyzing trained machine learning model results or as a method that aims at making machine learning model results transparent for end-users. Analyzing an AI system according to all aspects is recommended (Mohseni et al. 2018). In this paper, we focus on those aspects directly related to interaction with end-users, who are not experts in technical details or the developers of the AI system.

Explainability of AI systems have several different aspects:

- The system can use different channels to communicate explanations, such as text, speech, graphical, visualizations, or auditive signals.
- Measures to evaluate explainability for non-expert users vary between measuring user mental models, task performance, user satisfaction, or trust, according to (Mohseni et al. 2018).
- The main purpose to provide explainability of a model also varies, e.g., the goal might be to support trust, causality, transferability, informativeness, or ethical reasons, according to (Lipton 2016).

– Finally, the exact content that is used to communicate explanations can be distinguished. This might depend on context and situation, user-specific preferences, or technical likelihoods. In short, a user might prefer a short but easy to understand explanation over an elaborate but difficult to comprehend explanation. The meta level can also vary, e.g., a system communicates its decision making, its technical aspects, its limitations, or options for alternative decisions, cf. (Miller 2019).

The different dimensions that have to be considered for a transparent human AI interaction are shown in Table 1. To adequately address all dimensions in a specific situation, an AI system thus requires different options to select, which information to provide for an explanations, which depth of detail, and when to provide explanations. End-users might have a higher need for detailed explanations when confronted with unexpected AI decisions than for routine decisions. However, further aspects are relevant as presented in the next sections.

Table 1. Aspects of explainability in AI systems for end-user interaction

Content	Channel	Evaluation	Purpose
Detailed	Visual (text)	Mental model	User acceptance
Brief	Visual (graphics)	Task performance	Trust
Individualized	Auditive	User satisfaction	Causality
General	Movement	Trust measures	Information
…	…	…	…

4 Relations Between Humans and AI During Interaction

(Fitts 1951) characterized the human-machine interaction by describing the relative strengths and limitations of humans and computers, sometimes referred to as what "men are better at" and what "machines are better at" lists (MABA-MABA). Since the classification includes the full range between "only human" and "only machine", a description of different levels of automation (LOA) became necessary, e.g. (Sheridan and Verplank 1978, Parasuraman et al. 2000), see Table 2. Despite the wide body of research in the field of LOA of the last 60 years, the question of how the human decision making process could be implemented in autonomous systems has not been answered yet. While systems with integrated machine learning algorithms are developed, that are able to learn and change their behavior over time, the situation becomes even more complex. E.g., while a certain limitation of a system (e.g., sensor fusion) might lead to the presentation of the full set of decision alternatives at the beginning, it might change over time to the next higher level of automation where only one alternative is suggested. A different facet of transparency (see Sect. 2) might be needed to ensure a suitable interaction after a certain time of usage.

When interacting with an intelligent systems, yet another aspect comes into play: the attribution of roles, such as the AI system being a tutor or a personal assistant. Further research will have to clarify, if different roles of the intelligent system might have implications for the recommended level of automation, action selection, and

Table 2. Levels of automation of decision and action selection (Parasuraman et al. 2000, p. 287)

HIGH
10. The computer decides everything, acts autonomously, ignoring the human.
9. informs the human only if it, the computer, decides to
8. informs the human only if asked, or
7. executes automatically, then necessarily informs the human, and
6. allows the human a restricted time to veto before automatic execution, or
5. executes that suggestion if the human approves, or
4. suggests one alternative
3. narrows the selection down to a few, or
2. The computer offers a complete set of decision/action alternatives, or
1. The computer offers no assistance: human must take all decisions and actions.
LOW

transparency. (Karapanos et al. 2009) has shown that human expectations towards a product changes over time. In terms of a personal intelligent assistant, for instance, this may also be applicable, and the way a human perceives and interacts with an intelligent system may shift over time as the user makes experiences with the system.

5 Situational Awareness and Context

As argued before, the personal characteristics of the user as well as the characteristics of the system have an impact on the recommended type of explanation and the interaction quality. Additionally, the context in which the interaction takes place is expected to have a significant influence on the interaction in general and the need for explanation and transparency in particular. The situation awareness of the user and the time of usage are key factors to influence the need for transparency and explanation in order to create trust.

According to (Endsley 1995), situation awareness encompasses the perception of the situation, the comparison of the situation, and the anticipation of a future state. In this paper, the term situation awareness will be used to refer to the characteristics of the situation as well possible consequences of the decision making. The relationship between the situation awareness and the need for transparency and explanation however is not linear.

The situation characteristics further impacts the trust level a user places in the AI system or its explanation. Studies have shown that explanations can increase trust or the lack of explanation can decrease trust, e.g., (Holliday et al. 2016). Trust aspects are more relevant though, when dealing with severe situations. Particularly, when situational awareness is rather low, trust becomes more relevant (Wagner and Robinette 2015). On the one hand, humans may still trust and rely on systems making poor decisions (Wagner and Robinette 2015). Ideally in these situations of overtrust, a system would be able recognize its own limitations and make it transparent. On the other hand, humans also tend to disbelieve explanations given by an already untrusted systems (Miller 2019).

6 Summary and Outlook

An intelligent system that aims at making its behavior, decisions, and suggestions transparent to human users in a specific situation has to take into account various facets and dimensions, as described above. In this paper, we highlighted the various topics that lead to the complexity of such an endeavor.

Further research is needed with regard to long-term studies that show how the interaction between learning systems and users may change over time and thus vary with regard to transparency. In this respect, the impact of trust and changes in trust with the support of transparency is also an open topic.

Furthermore, transparency is not only complex and cost- or time-expensive, its wide variations with regard to a specific situation is particularly influenced by consequences of the interaction. Routine situations may not rely on transparency, while severe situations heavily depend on it. Transparency could also be offered after interaction has taken place, e.g., the situation and the underlying mechanisms how decisions were made by the system could be presented to the user after a critical situation. Such adequate ways, however, need to be studied.

Personality traits could be of interest for a situation-adequate human AI interaction: users with a need for cognition might have a higher need for explanations or technically averse users may need additional explanations. However, in severe situations, this might not be as relevant.

References

Chen, J.Y.C., Procci, K., Boyce, M., Wright, J., Garcia, A., Barnes, M.: Situation awareness–based agent transparency. Technical report, Army Research Laboratory ARL-TR-6905 (2014)

Das, S., Dey, A., Pal, A., Roy, N.: Applications of artificial intelligence in machine learning: review and prospect. Int. J. Comput. Appl. **115**(9), 31–41 (2015)

Došilović, F.K., Brčić, M., Hlupić, N.: Explainable artificial intelligence: a survey. In: Proceedings of the 41st International Convention on Information and Communication Technology, Electronics and Microelectronics MIPRO, pp. 210–215. IEEE Xplore (2018)

Endsley, M.R.: Toward a theory of situation awareness in dynamic systems. Hum. Factors J. **37**(1), 32–64 (1995)

Fitts, P.M.: Human engineering for an effective air navigation and traffic control system. Technical report, National Research Council (1951)

Gunning, D.: Explainable artificial intelligence (XAI). DARPA Program (2017). https://www.darpa.mil/program/explainable-artificial-intelligence. Accessed 18 Mar 2019

Gil, Y., Selman, B.: A 20-year community roadmap for artificial intelligence research in the US executive summary. https://cra.org/ccc/wp-content/uploads/sites/2/2019/03/AI_Roadmap_Exec_Summary-FINAL-.pdf. Accessed 18 Mar 2019

Holliday, D., Wilson, S., Stumpf, S.: User trust in intelligent systems: a journey over time. In: Proceedings of the 21st International Conference on Intelligent User Interfaces, pp. 164–168. ACM, New York (2016)

Karapanos, E., Zimmerman, J., Forlizzi, J., Martens, J.-B.: User experience over time: an initial framework. In: CHI 2009 Proceedings of the SIGCHI Conference on Human Factors in Computing Systems, pp. 729–738. ACM, New York (2019)

Lipton, Z.C.: The mythos of model interpretability. Commun. ACM **61**(10), 36–43 (2016)

Miller, T.: Explanation in artificial intelligence: insights from the social sciences. Artif. Intell. J. **267**, 1–38 (2019)

Mohseni, S., Zarei, N., Ragan, E.D.: A survey of evaluation methods and measures for interpretable machine learning. Computing Research Repository (CoRR) (2018). http://arxiv.org/abs/1811.11839. Accessed 18 Mar 2019

Parasuraman, R., Sheridan, T.B., Wickens, C.D.: Model for types and levels of human interaction with automation. IEEE Trans. Syst. Man Cybern. – Part A: Syst. Hum. **30**, 286–297 (2000)

Ribeiro, M.T., Singh, S., Guestrin, C.: "Why should i trust you?" Explaining the predictions of any classifier. In: Proceedings of the 22nd ACM SIGKDD International Conference on Knowledge Discovery and Data Mining, pp. 1135–1144. ACM, New York (2016)

Samek, W., Wiegand, T., Müller, K.-R.: Explainable artificial intelligence: understanding, visualizing and interpreting deep learning models. ITU J.: ICT Discov. Impact Artif. Intell. (AI) Commun. Netw. Serv. **1**(1), 39–48 (2017)

Schaefer, K.E., Chen, J.Y.C., Szalma, J.L., Hancock, P.A.: A meta-analysis of factors influencing the development of trust in automation: implications for understanding autonomy in future systems. Hum. Factors: J. Hum. Factors Ergon. Soc. **58**(3), 377–400 (2016)

Sheridan, T.B., Verplank, W.: Human and computer control of undersea teleoperators. Man-Machine Systems Laboratory, Department of Mechanical Engineering, MIT, USA (1978)

Štrumbelj, E., Kononenko, I.: Explaining prediction models and individual predictions with feature contributions. Knowl. Inf. Syst. **41**(3), 647–665 (2014)

Wagner, A., Robinette, P.: Towards robots that trust: human subject validation of the situational conditions for trust. Interact. Stud. **16**(1), 89–117 (2015)

Data on RAILs: On Interactive Generation of Artificial Linear Correlated Data

Daniyal Kazempour$^{(\boxtimes)}$, Anna Beer$^{(\boxtimes)}$, and Thomas Seidl$^{(\boxtimes)}$

Ludwig-Maximilians-University Munich, Oettingenstr. 67, 80538 Munich, Germany
{kazempour,beer,seidl}@dbs.ifi.lmu.de

Abstract. Artificially generated data sets are present in many data mining and machine learning publications in the experimental section. One of the reasons to use synthetic data is, that scientists can express their understanding of a "ground truth", having labels and thus an expectation of what an algorithm should be able to detect. This permits also a degree of control to create data sets which either emphasize the strengths of a method or reveal its weaknesses and thus potential targets for improvement. In order to develop methods which detect linear correlated clusters, the necessity of generating such artificial clusters is indispensable. This is mostly done by command-line based scripts which may be tedious since they demand from users to 'visualize' in their minds how the correlated clusters have to look like and be positioned within the data space. We present in this work RAIL, a generator for *R*eproducible *A*rtificial *I*nteractive *L*inear correlated data. With RAIL, users can add multiple planes into a data space and arbitrarily change orientation and position of those planes in an interactive fashion. This is achieved by manipulating the parameters describing each of the planes, giving users immediate feedback in real-time. With this approach scientists no longer need to imagine their data but can interactively explore and design their own artificial data sets containing linear correlated clusters. Another convenient feature in this context is that the data is only generated when the users decide that their design phase is completed. If researchers want to share data, a small file is exchanged containing the parameters which describe the clusters through information such as e.g. their Hessian-Normal-Form or number of points per cluster, instead of sharing several large csv files.

Keywords: Linear correlations · Interactive · Data generator · Artificial datasets

1 Introduction

Artificial data has its purpose in a variety of cases. Given scenarios where no data is available, scientists can use their current knowledge about their models and generate artificial data. If there are privacy aspects which prevent the usage

© Springer Nature Switzerland AG 2019
C. Stephanidis (Ed.): HCII 2019, CCIS 1033, pp. 184–189, 2019.
https://doi.org/10.1007/978-3-030-23528-4_26

of real-world data, synthetic data sets enable evaluating developed methods as elaborated in [3]. Especially in the field of data mining, artificial data poses a solid baseline where the effects of e.g. hyperparameters can be evaluated. Further it enables scientists to apply the *ceteris paribus* principle to create several data sets where a subset of conditions (e.g. density, number of data points, relative distances etc.) are fixed, except precisely one, which is modified to study the effects of this particular property without any side effects.

Consulting the Google scholar website with the search term "artificial data sets" yields over 8750 articles which include this term. More articles are found with the term "synthetic data sets" with around 22300. However, taken together they only contribute a small fraction of 0.7% of the 4.220.000 search results with the term "data sets". Considering that we have been missing a lot of other terms under which synthetic data can be found, we may still observe that the scientific articles using synthetic data are by far in minority. In the following we elaborate in the related work section on some currently popular data set platforms and some domain specific ones. We then proceed to elaborate on our concept regarding a generator for artificially constructed, linear correlated data sets addressing also potential pitfalls and challenges which can arise. We then conclude our work by a brief summary and outlook.

2   Related Work

There exists a variety of platforms hosting artificial and real-word data, e.g., the UCI Machine Learning repository [1] which maintains currently approximately 450 data sets categorized by tasks, attribute types, data types, domains, number of dimensions and number of data points. A by far larger repository of data sets is given by the Harvard Dataverse [2]. This platform includes over 80.782 data sets where a search can be performed by publication year or author name and author affiliation, providing not only the data set but also corresponding publications. Regarding the number of offered data sets the kaggle platform [4] contains with 12.992 data sets much fewer than the Harvard Dataverse. However, it provides a forum for discussions enabling scientific exchanges. Further it provides so called "Kernels" which are jupyter notebooks [7] containing source code. This concept introduces an aspect of interactiveness and exploration. As an interesting part a ranking of data sets is provided and competitions are offered. The aspect of competitiveness stimulates researchers to test their developed methods on data sets, accepting the data sets implicitly as a benchmark. One domain specific example is MRBrainS [5] which provides Grand Challenges on magnet resonance brain images. One aspect which motivates the necessity of synthetic data and a platform for such, is the Skluma [6] tool which provides a statistical learning pipeline for cleansing and ordering data repositories. In [6] the authors mention that there remains a large number of repositories where the description of data is poor. A synthetic data set which is generated through a unified interactive generator would reduce the risk of bad-documented data and enhance reproducibility as well as facilitate its exchange.

3   On Interactive Generation of Linear Correlated Data

In our setting we are specialized on (hyper)linear correlated data for which we designed a tool, which enables scientists to generate their own data sets interactively. The settings of the created data can be easily contributed to a platform which hosts the artificially created data. A simple tool for interactively generating artificial data sets may foster scientific exchange in a form in which the strengths and weaknesses of, e.g., clustering methods can be discussed on. The scientific exchange component serves the purpose to facilitate the collaborative exploration of the performance of different methods on synthetic data sets. Here scientists can exchange experiences they made like, e.g., successful hyperparameter settings as well as unsuccessful ones.

To further unify and facilitate not only generating reproducible synthetic data but also reproduce synthetic data used in different publications, we encourage the creation of interactive and easy to use data generators. For a reproducible generation of linear correlation clusters we introduce a first prototype. With that, we exemplarily depict the main requirements we elaborated for generic data generators:

1. Easy to use: We do not want to make scientist waste their time on playing around with numbers in abstract formulas until they obtained an intuitively accessible example. Thus we consider an interactive setting with intermediate visual feedback as appropriate.
2. Reproducible: The data sets generated should be easily reproducible, preferably and especially for large data sets without having to store the whole data set, but, for example, rather only the necessary settings and random seeds.
3. Flexible: Versatile types of data should be creatable, and it should not be limited by, e.g., the number of clusters or the amount of noise.
4. Uniform: We encourage to elaborate a minimum standard for data in regard to different aspects: The range and accuracy of numbers can for example, easily be unified. The accuracy is especially important due to technical properties of different data types.

RAIL (*R*eproducibile *A*rtificial *I*nteractive *L*inear correlated data) is a first prototype of a generator specialized on building linearly correlated clusters in demonstrative three dimensions. It is planned to extend it to arbitrary many dimensions and other convenient functions we will elaborate in this section. The code is available under https://gitlab.cip.ifi.lmu.de/beera/RAIL.git. Even though real world data sets are available, it is often more effective to test some special cases on explicitly designed data than real world data which either does not cover those special cases at all or are not as evident as one would wish. Such special cases cover, e.g., situations where linear correlated clusters intersect, or overlap mostly, or are explicitly orthogonal to each other etc. However, the creation of such specific constellations of linearly correlated clusters demands either doing some time consuming calculations or trying out different parameter settings until the desired case is constructed. To circumvent these issues, a visual, interactive generator like RAIL can augment to reach exactly those constellations

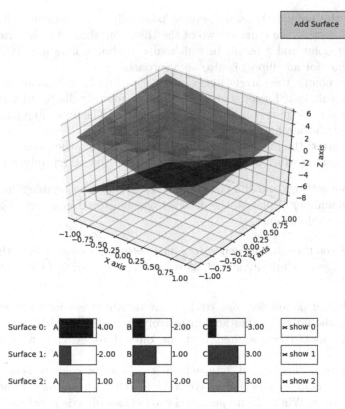

Fig. 1. Screenshot of RAIL. The initial parameters are randomly generated to simplify starting. (Color figure online)

without having to invest a substantial amount of time. In Fig. 1 we see the GUI of RAIL. The user can choose the number of linear correlations freely and change the parameters of every correlation independently with easy to use sliders. The feedback is immediate and the coherence of parameters and planes is color coded. Correlations can be added or hidden (but are kept for a possible later use). Sliders enable easy change of the parameters A, B, and C so that the plane is defined by:

$$Z = AX + BY + C$$

Changing A leads to a rotation around the y axis, changing B leads to a rotation around the x axis, and changing C leads to a perpendicular shift of the plane along the z axis. All these changes are performed immediately. When the desired constellation of planes is achieved, data points along these planes can be generated, which is not implemented yet in this work in progress. Therefore the user should have again several interactively eligible settings:

1. Range of the points: there are several possibilities to implement that, for example, selecting the range of two of the three variables. The determination of a center point and a radius in which surrounding points may lay (or two center points for an ellipse) is also an approach.
2. Number of points: the correlations can consist of differently many points.
3. Type of distribution: for some purposes an, e.g., uniform distribution of points on a plane may be more suitable than a Gaussian. The according parameters to each distribution have to be stored.
4. Degree of jitter: the maximum deviation of points from the plane itself
5. The random seed which is used is important to be able to reproduce the data.

With those settings and the parameters A, B, and C describing each plane as well as the number of planes, the data set can be stored in a very effective as well as reproducible manner.

Challenges. Even though such generators may seem to be easy at first, they offer diverse challenges, technically as well as regarding the design of the interface to keep it simple:

1. The number of parameters one could want to adjust is enormous, still such generators should be simple and intuitively usable. In which sequence the parameters should be inquired best, or offered to be chosen is an open question.
2. Regarding high dimensional data, which is one of our goals to generate, the human mind comes to its limits. We have to fall back on lower dimensional representations. While two dimensional projections on axis parallel subspaces do not offer very much information, three dimensional presentations, as RAIL uses, which are rotatable, offer a faster interpretation of data, but mostly if users interact. These interactions cost time again, which we originally aim to reduce.
3. The human factor: How to convince people to use and extend such a generator instead of coming up with their own home-brew scripts?

4   Concluding Remarks

In this work-in-progress we have briefly elaborated on our concept of an interactive system for generating linearly correlated data sets where scientists can upload the model including settings like number of data points, number of clusters, and the seeds for generating the clusters instead of sharing the whole data set. With this work, we strive to create a tool for scientific exchange, reproducibility, as well as a chance to validate results and reveal hidden properties of newly developed methods. Finally we hope to set with our work the rails for interactive generation, modification and distribution of artificial data sets.

Acknowledgement. This work has been funded by the German Federal Ministry of Education and Research (BMBF) under Grant No. 01IS18036A. The authors of this work take full responsibilities for its content.

References

1. Dheeru, D., Taniskidou E.K.: UCI Machine Learning Repository. School of Information and Computer Sciences, University of California, Irvine (2017)
2. King, G.: An introduction to the dataverse network as an infrastructure for data sharing. J. Sociol. Meth. Res. **36**, 173–184 (2007)
3. Bellovin, S.M., Dutta, P.K., Reitinger, N.: Privacy and synthetic datasets. LawArXiv (2018) (osf.io/preprints/lawarxiv/bfqh3/)
4. Goldbloom, A.: Data prediction competitions - far more than just a bit of fun. In: IEEE International Conference on Data Mining Workshops, pp. 1385–1386 (2010)
5. Mendrik, A.M., et al.: MRBrainS challenge online evaluation framework for brain image segmentation in 3T MRI scans. J. Comput. Intell. Neurosci. **2015**, 1–16 (2015)
6. Beckman, P., Skluzacek, T.J., Chard, K., Foster, I.: Skluma: a statistical learning pipeline for taming unkempt data repositories. In: Proceedings of the 29th International Conference on Scientific and Statistical Database Management, pp. 41:1–41:4, Chicago, IL, USA (2017)
7. Kluyver, T., et al.: Jupyter Notebooks-a publishing format for reproducible computational workflows. In: ELPUB, pp. S.87–S.90 (2016)

Adaptation of Machine Learning Frameworks for Use in a Management Environment
Development of a Generic Workflow

Christian Roschke[1]([✉]), Robert Manthey[2], Rico Thomanek[1], Tony Rolletschke[1], Benny Platte[1], Claudia Hösel[1], Alexander Marbach[1], and Marc Ritter[1]

[1] University of Applied Sciences Mittweida, 09648 Mittweida, Germany
roschke@hs-mittweida.de
[2] University of Technology Chemnitz, 09110 Chemnitz, Germany

Abstract. The combination of person and location recognition provides numerous new fields of possible applications, such as the development of approaches for detecting missing persons in public spaces using real-time monitoring. It is necessary to use frameworks of both domains on given data sets and to merge the acquired results. For this purpose Thomanek et al. [11] developed an evaluation and management system for machine learning, which allows the interconnection of different frameworks and the fusion of result vectors [11]. This paper discusses the EMSML in terms of interfaces and components to develop a generic workflow that supports the integration of different frameworks for people and location recognition. In this context, the focus is on the required adaptation of existing frameworks to the implemented infrastructure. A generic workflow concept can be deduced from the analysis results. This concept can be applied to two typical frameworks for evaluation and implemented as prototypes. Subsequently, developed test cases are used to demonstrate the functional validity of the prototypes and the applicability of the concept.

Keywords: Generic workflow · Machine learning · Recognition

1 Introduction

The automatic detection and recognition of people in videos has many applications in multiple areas. This includes, for example, advantages for securing websites, for password-free computer login and also for the analysis of behavior of individuals in surveillance areas. Location recognition in audiovisual media can also be used to implement video-based navigation in buildings or to adequately annotate non-annotated data records afterwards. The combination of the two described areas of application provides new possible applications. For example, this leads to the problem area of person and location recognition in real-time surveillance data. Thereby, approaches are needed to find missing persons

© Springer Nature Switzerland AG 2019
C. Stephanidis (Ed.): HCII 2019, CCIS 1033, pp. 190–197, 2019.
https://doi.org/10.1007/978-3-030-23528-4_27

in public places. In order to address this problem, the international evaluation campaign TRECVid included the task of Instance Search, which has been in progress for eight years [2]. This campaign is organized by the National Institute of Standards and Technology (NIST, USA) and aims to support research in the field of robust multimedia information retrieval. In this environment, on the basis of a defined data set of 464 h of video material from the long-standing BBC series EastEnders, various systems and approaches were developed and tested [1].

Approaches from the domains of person and location recognition like Peng et al. [8], Chen et al. [3], Mokhayeri et al. [6] and Zeng et al. [13] are mostly problem-specific and difficult to transfer to other domains. Furthermore existing frameworks are used as well as own CNNs trained, whereby the determined characteristics can be used exclusively for the direct evaluation in the context of the problem to be solved. A standardized storage, administration and application to other problem fields is usually not intended. Thomanek et al. [11] describes an approach in which an evaluation and management system for machine learning (EMSML) was developed to evaluate and easily combine existing frameworks [10]. The resulting system aims to standardize the complete workflow, to make resources available in a suitable way, to persistently store research data as well as to prepare them for further processing and to merge all obtained results. In this respect, a complex infrastructure was created, which can also be used in other application domains. A deficit of the resulting system currently consists in the need to adapt existing frameworks for integration into the infrastructure [11].

This paper presents a generic workflow that is necessary to integrate frameworks for person and location recognition into the EMSML. Existing interfaces are examined and in detail the adaptations of existing frameworks and technologies to the requirements of the implemented infrastructure are discussed.

2   Methods

For the integration of existing frameworks as well as feature extractors from the domains of person and location recognition into the EMSML, it is necessary to analyze the EMSML with regard to interfaces and components and to derive a generic workflow conceptually. This concept has to be applied to selected frameworks and implemented prototypically. The prototypes are used to evaluate whether the generic concept works. The holistic system including the prototypes is applied to a given annotated data set. This allows to look at memory structures of the EMSML over time and to determine whether the system behaves as expected. In this respect, it must be checked whether partial results can be saved and whether at the end of the process chain the annotations appear comparable with the determined final results.

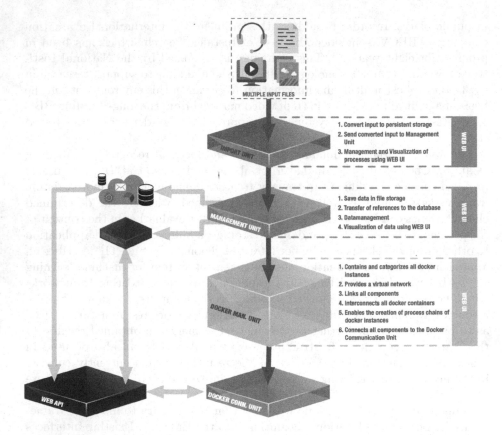

Fig. 1. Schematic representation of the system architecture of the EMSML

2.1 EMSML Architecture

EMSML is a tool for setting up holistic process chains in the context of machine learning. Multiple components are stored decentralized, networked with each other and the data flow is provided via standardized interfaces. It can be used to map existing processes or to develop new ones. The basic structure ensures parallelization, scalability and distributability. This allows different frameworks to be combined with each other and the processing can be distributed to other computers with less resources. Figure 1 shows the basic structure of EMSML. Basically, the system consists of several core components described below for the execution of processes and a database server for the permanent storage of all results and raw data.

Import and Datamanagement. The *Import Unit* is used to import multiple files such as images, texts and audiovisual media. In this respect, these files can be transferred individually or collectively into the system. All imported data are packed, processed and forwarded to the *Management Unit*. Especially the import processes are arbitrarily adaptable. The *Management Unit* is the central unit for data management. The files provided by the *Import Unit* are transferred to a central storage and all references are saved in corresponding database structures. Both the data and the database can be viewed via web interfaces. All files are stored on a central server and made accessible via various protocols such as SMB, NFS, HTTP and FTP. This means that access to the storage is also possible via other tools. Afterwards, only the absolute references and not the data itself are transferred into the database system (PostreSQL).

Docker Management Unit. In addition to the *Import Unit* and the *Management Unit*, which basically include data management and import mechanisms, the *Docker Management Unit* provides logic to add additional functionality in the form of docker containers. This unit is based on PortainerIO, a simple management UI for docker, where containers can be managed and categorized. It is also possible to build a virtual network and link containers with each other. This enables the regulated exchange of information between individual components. In addition, process chains can be created and managed. Another central function of this unit is the management and linking of the sub-areas *Machine Learning Frameworks*, *Processing Scoring* and *Export*.

Connection of Data Management and Docker Management. The EMSML has an api to enable the filterable and individualized transfer of data from the database. This api is able to receive and process HTTP requests as well as specific requests to the database. In addition, this component allows data records to be combined as desired and transferred in any exchange format. In addition, files can be obtained directly from the file storage. The *Docker Connection Unit* exists for the communication of all docker containers with other tools outside the virtualized environments and the api. It retrieves data records for processing via HTTP, forwards results and interfaces with the *Docker Management Unit*.

2.2 Adjustment of Multiple Frameworks

Based on the architecture of the EMSML, the following steps can be identified, which have to be performed to add another framework to the EMSML. These steps are shown in the Fig. 2 and described below.

Step 1: Import the data sets to be processed. The data record to be processed must be transferred to the system using the *Import Unit*. A set of auxiliary tools can be used. Database tables are created for all imported and preprocessed data and a data record label is assigned, which enables each imported element to be assigned to a data record. As an alternative to the import, already created data records can be processed.

Step 2: Creating a docker container for the framework. If a framework is not already available as a docker container, a new docker image must be created and added to the *Docker Management Unit*. Depending on the used

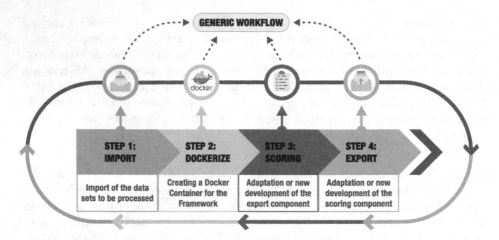

Fig. 2. Generic workflow for adapting a framework to integrate into EMSML

HOST operating system and required libraries the use of a suitable base image has to be considered. Based on this, all other tools and the framework itself can be installed in the Docker container.

After the general setup of the container and the test whether the framework works in the virtualized environment, adjustments must be made to the EMSML infrastructure. A component must be added that can communicate with the web api using HTTP. In this context, the container makes a request and transmits the data record and the required exchange format using a POST request. The web api prepares the references to the files as requested and forwards them to the container. The framework must be adapted in such a way that the exchange format will be read and the files can be referred to the prepared references for further processing using GET requests. The output of the framework must also be modified so that the generated data is sent to the web api in JSON format using HTTP. The processing of the data within the frameworks can be omitted, since only the interfaces have to be adapted. After adapting the interfaces within the container, a connection to the web api must be established in the *Docker Connection Unit* to enable communications. In addition, a database table must be created in the database for the corresponding framework, which can map the data to be transferred. The attributes of the table are automatically created from the transmitted JSON. The results are set in relation to the data record to enable subsequent processing using a scorer.

Step 3: The scoring component. After the data processing of the framework, the results are available in the corresponding table. A performance evaluation (scorer) is required to evaluate these results. A scorer in the form of a docker container is already integrated in the system and can be adapted as required. By means of the container it is possible to use several result tables, whereby all results of a table are represented on a point scale. A result gets at least 0 points and a maximum of 100 points. In addition, further approaches of machine learning, which are provided by the *Machine Learning Component*, can be used for data fusion to calculate a score. The results generated by the scorer are stored in a corresponding table and set in relation to the data sets.

Step 4: The export component. Based on the result table created by the scorer, the export component can export the results in an exchange format. A docker container is already integrated in the system, which formats the scorer results using an XML Schema Definition (XSD) and exports them as XML.

2.3   Application of the Developed Workflow

Two records are selected for both Location Recognition and People Recognition and imported into the system in step 1. For location recognition, the data set *Places 2nd generation* and the framework *ResNet152-places365* are used. *Places 2nd generation* is a scene centered database with 205 scene categories and 2.5 million annotated images [14]. For resource reasons, 10,000 intellectually selected images are selected for testing. Basis for the person recognition is the data set *SCface - Surveillance Cameras Face Database* with 4160 static images of 130 persons [12]. The *Import Unit* is needed to transfer the data into the system. After execution, it is expected that the EMSML has copied 14,160 images from both data sets into created directories and that two tables filled with references have been created in the database. It is particularly important to ensure that all images are provided with the correct data record label.

Frameworks selected for the test are *ResNet152-places365* for the location recognition domain *and FaceNet* for the face recognition domain from the person recognition domain. *ResNet152-places365* allows ten classifications to be determined for each image with decreasing accuracy [4]. In addition, the first ten found attributes of the *Sun Attributes* dataset [5,7] are provided for each processed image. *FaceNet* is a one-shot model that directly learns a mapping of images to a compact Euclidean space in which distances directly correspond to the measure of facial similarity [9]. Currently, several implementations of *FaceNet* are available. The Tensorflow implementation by David Sandberg will be used. For both frameworks a docker container already exists, which has to be adapted and can be integrated into the EMSML. *ResNet152-places365* and *FaceNet* have PythonAPIs for the application of the frameworks. These apis are easily extensible and customizable in both implementations, so that a routine can be integrated to load data directly from the web api and transfer results as JSON to it. For both frameworks two database tables have to be created. After linking the docker containers with the *Docker Connection Unit* it is expected that both database tables are filled with framework specific attributes and with detected results. There must also be a relational link between the dataset images and the generated data. In both cases, the scoring component available in the system is used for the performance evaluation. The syntax of the scoring component must be checked to ensure that the results are transferred to the scoring system and that a final results table is generated. An XSD is used to specify a schema for the system to export the data. A valid XML must be generated based on the scoring results and the transferred schema.

3   Results and Discussion

All expectations of the test were converted into standardized test cases. In the underlying naming scheme, the ID is composed of T for test case, S for step, {1–4} for the number of the respective step, and $C1$–$C9$ for case number. All steps of the workflow could be executed. An excerpt from the resulting test document is shown in Fig. 3. All test cases could be executed correctly. The generic workflow was applicable for the selected frameworks. When using the workflow, several advantages and disadvantages explained below were noticed. The modular structure of the workflow allowed a structured processing and individual adjustments of the transfer process of the frameworks into the EMSML. By the modular view on the complete process it is now possible to carry out optimizations step by step and to examine the workflow in the context of the automatability. This would be necessary because the intellectual processing of the process is error-prone and time-consuming. In particular the transfer of the frameworks into a docker container or the connection to the standardized interfaces of the system is not trivial and remains with framework specific. In this context, the workflow must be examined using further frameworks.

ID	EXPECTATION	STATUS
TS1C1	Two directories are created.	✓
TS1C2	14,160 images are split between both directories.	✓
TS1C3	Two tables are created in the database.	✓
TS1C4	Both tables are filled with references.	✓
TS1C5	All images are provided with the correct data record label.	✓
TS2C1	Framework specific attributes have been created	✓
TS2C2	All relations are available.	✓
TS3C1	Two database tables were created.	✓
TS3C2	All attribute-based data was inserted and linked.	✓
TS4C1	A scoring table was created.	✓
TS4C2	All results were converted into points.	✓
TS4C3	An XSD can be passed and an XML is created.	✓
TS4C4	The generated XML is valid and contains scoring data.	✓

Fig. 3. EMSML test results with customized frameworks

4   Conclusion

In this paper a generic workflow could be developed to integrate frameworks from the domain of facial recognition and location recognition into the EMSML. By means of several exemplary selected frameworks it was possible to implement and test this workflow prototypically. The investigation shows that the developed workflow works and can be used as a methodical guide. The modular structure of the workflow allows further investigations in the context of automatability in order to develop a generic and automated integration component for the EMSML. This would optimize the intellectual adaptation of individual frameworks in terms of efficiency. Furthermore, the findings can be used to adapt further frameworks and iteratively improve the previously rudimentarily implemented scoring component or to compare several scoring procedures with each other.

References

1. Awad, G., et al.: TRECVID 2017: evaluating ad-hoc and instance video search, events detection, video captioning and hyperlinking—the insight centre for data analytics. In: Proceedings of TRECVID 2017 (2017)
2. Awad, G., et al.: TRECVID 2016: evaluating video search, video event detection, localization, and hyperlinking. In: Proceedings of TRECVID 2016. NIST, USA (2016)
3. Chen, C., Huang, J., Pan, C., Yuan, X.: Military image scene recognition based on CNN and semantic information. In: 2018 3rd International Conference on Mechanical, Control and Computer Engineering (ICMCCE), pp. 573–577. IEEE, September 2018
4. Chen, X., Ji, Z., Fan, Y., Zhan, Y.: Restful API architecture based on laravel framework. J. Phys: Conf. Ser. **910**, 012016 (2017)
5. Grgic, M., Delac, K., Grgic, S.: SCface - surveillance cameras face database. Multimedia Tools Appl. **51**, 863–879 (2011)
6. Mokhayeri, F., Granger, E., Bilodeau, G.A.: Domain-specific face synthesis for video face recognition from a single sample per person. IEEE Trans. Inf. Forensics Secur. **14**(3), 757–772 (2019)
7. Patterson, G., Hays, J.: SUN attribute database: discovering, annotating, and recognizing scene attributes. In: Proceedings of the IEEE Computer Society Conference on Computer Vision and Pattern Recognition (2012)
8. Peng, Y., et al.: PKU_ICST at TRECVID 2018: instance search task. In: Proceedings of TRECVID Workshop Proceeding (2018)
9. Schroff, F., Kalenichenko, D., Philbin, J.: FaceNet: a unified embedding for face recognition and clustering. In: Proceedings of the IEEE Computer Society Conference on Computer Vision and Pattern Recognition (2015)
10. Thomanek, R., et al.: University of applied sciences Mittweida and Chemnitz university of technology at TRECVID 2018. In: Proceedings of TRECVID Workshop (2018)
11. Thomanek, R., et al.: A scalable system architecture for activity detection with simple heuristics. In: IEEE Winter Conference on Applications of Computer Vision (WACV) (2019)
12. Tome, P., Fierrez, J., Vera-Rodriguez, R., Ramos, D.: Identification using face regions: application and assessment in forensic scenarios. Forensic Sci. Int. **233**, 75–83 (2013)
13. Zeng, J., Zhao, X., Gan, J., Mai, C., Zhai, Y., Wang, F.: Deep convolutional neural network used in single sample per person face recognition. Comput. Intell. Neurosci. **2018**, 1–11 (2018)
14. Zhou, B., Lapedriza, A., Xiao, J., Torralba, A., Oliva, A.: Learning deep features for scene recognition using places database. Advances in Neural Information Processing Systems 27 (2014)

Software to Support Layout and Data Collection for Machine-Learning-Based Real-World Sensors

Ayane Saito[1(✉)], Wataru Kawai[2], and Yuta Sugiura[1,3]

[1] Keio University, Yokohama, Japan
ayane-3110@keio.jp
[2] The University of Tokyo, Bunkyo, Japan
[3] JST PRESTO, Kawaguchi, Japan

Abstract. There have been many studies of gesture recognition and posture estimation by combining real-world sensor and machine learning. In such situations, it is important to consider the sensor layout because the measurement result varies depending on the layout and the number of sensors as well as the motion to be measured. However, it takes time and effort to prototype devices multiple times in order to find a sensor layout that has high identification accuracy. Also, although it is necessary to acquire learning data for recognizing gestures, it takes time to get the data when the user changes the sensor layout. In this study, we developed software that can arrange real-world sensors. In this time, the software can handle distance-measuring sensors as real-world sensors. The user places these sensors freely in the software. The software measures the distance between the sensors and a mesh created from measurements of real-world deformation recorded by a Kinect. The classifier is generated using the time-series of distance data recorded by the software. In addition, we created a physical device that had the same sensor layout as the one designed with the software. We experimentally confirmed that the software could recognize the gestures on the physical device by using the generated classifier.

Keywords: Sensor layout · Machine learning · Distance-measuring sensor

1 Introduction

Physical changes in the real world can be measured by deploying the real-world sensors in daily life. For such measurements, the number and layout of the sensors have to be determined, taking into account the real-world changes we want to capture, the associated costs, device sizes, and so on. However, it is difficult to design an optimal sensor layout in consideration of these various limitations. In addition, gesture recognition and posture estimation can be performed by combining real-world sensors and machine learning. For example, Touché [1] identifies touch gestures by machine learning of the frequency response when the sensor is touched. In this way, complicated actions can be identified by learning in advance, but it is necessary to generate a classifier using unique sensor data according to the state to be identified. However, the number, position, and angle of sensors that can acquire such unique sensor data are

© Springer Nature Switzerland AG 2019
C. Stephanidis (Ed.): HCII 2019, CCIS 1033, pp. 198–205, 2019.
https://doi.org/10.1007/978-3-030-23528-4_28

often determined by trial and error. Moreover, it takes time and effort to accumulate learning data in the real world every time the number and layout of the sensors are changed.

In this study, we developed software that helps to arrange real-world sensors and support learning data collections. At present, the software handles distance-measuring sensors as real-world sensors. The user places models of the sensors freely in the software, and the software measures the distance between the placed sensors and real world objects recorded by an RGB-D camera (a Kinect). The obtained distance data is recorded as time series data to identify real-world changes such as gestures. Furthermore, in this study, to confirm that the software can accumulate learning data, we used a classifier generated from gesture data acquired by the software to identify gesture data acquired by sensors placed in the real world.

2 Related Works

2.1 Simulation of Real-World System on a Computer

There have been many studies to simulate by restoring the shapes and conditions of the real world on a computer. Ino et al. produced a CG model of a human hand on the computer by using motion capture data and software called Dhaibaworks which can generate digital models of the human body [2]. They estimated a grasping hand pose by performing learning with a convolutional neural network on a photographed image of a CG model and three-dimensional position data such as hand joints. Kanaya et al. developed a human-mobility sensing system simulator, called Humans, that uses map data, human agent information, sensor information, and network information [3]. They simulated the walking behavior of people in a city while simulating changes in the kind or arrangement of sensors on the map. Yuan et al. learned virtual egocentric video and posture of a humanoid model walking in a virtual world [4]. They estimated walking postures of people in the real world by combining data in images of the real world shot by a camera mounted on the head of a pedestrian and learning data in the virtual world. Since these studies are computer simulations, there is an advantage that it is not necessary to accumulate learning data in the real world and it does not take much money and time.

In this study, the target of simulation was a real-world sensor. We developed software that helps user to avoid the trial and error involved in setting up physical sensors and that also accumulates learning data.

2.2 Measuring Motion with Photo Sensors

We developed software that can handle distance-measuring sensors, which are a kind of photo sensor. There have been many studies on measuring and identifying human body movements by using photo sensors. For instance, AffectiveWear is a device for recognizing facial expressions that measures the distance between the skin and the frame of a pair of glasses by using an array of photo-reflective sensors on the frame [5]. EarTouch recognizes gesture using the ear as an input surface by using photo-reflective sensors attached to earphones to measure skin deformation inside the ear [6]. iRing measures the distance between the skin of the finger and photo-reflective sensors attached to a ring-shaped device to recognize bending of a finger [7]. Miyata et al. estimated the grasping posture of a hand by attaching a band-type device with embedded distance-measuring sensors to the grasped object [8].

In this study, we detected and identified hand gestures made in front of distance-measuring sensors.

3 System Implementation

3.1 Overview

We developed software for arranging the placement of distance-measuring sensors which are often used as real-world sensors. The flow of our system incorporating this software, shown in Fig. 1, is divided into a phase of accumulating learning data by the software and a phase of gesture recognition using data acquired by distance-measuring sensors in the real world. In the learning phase, the user makes gestures in front of a Kinect and acquires time-series distance data with sensors placed on the software. The acquired data is converted into image data from which the histograms of oriented gradients (HOG) feature is then extracted. The classifier is generated by learning with a support vector machine (SVM) that takes the obtained HOG feature as input. In the gesture recognition phase, the same kind of gesture as one performed in front of Kinect is performed in front of distance-measuring sensors arranged in the real world in the same layout as in the software, and sensor data is acquired. The acquired sensor data is converted in order of distance value and image, and the HOG feature is extracted. The obtained HOG feature performs gesture recognition by referring to the classifier generated from the data acquired in the software.

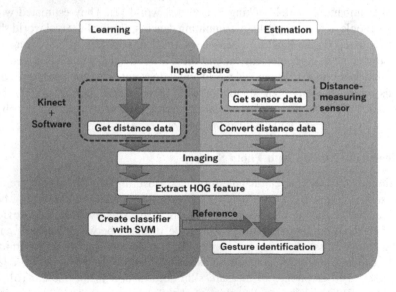

Fig. 1. Flow of our system.

3.2   Configuration of Software

We used Unity to create the software. The real-world changing data was acquired as 3D depth information with a Kinect v2, and the shape of the real world was restored in the virtual world with Unity. First, we converted the Kinect depth coordinate system into a real-world space coordinate system (Unity's coordinate system). The 3D depth information was converted into a 3D mesh on Unity. In order to construct a high-resolution mesh on Unity, we used depth information from the center of a 1/4 × 1/4 range of the image taken with Kinect. The simulated distance-measuring sensors were placed in the virtual world holding the mesh and the distances between the sensors and the mesh were measured, as shown by the black cylindrical object in Fig. 2.

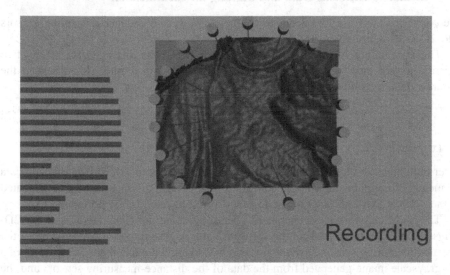

Fig. 2. Overview of developed software.

The distance value was calculated by using a binary search algorithm using a Raycast function that can determine collision with the collider (we set up a 3D mesh is a collider). The binary search was continued down to the resolution of Kinect's depth (1 mm), and when there was no 3D mesh in the measurable range of the sensor, we set the distance value to the maximum measurable distance of the sensor. The acquired distance values were displayed as graphs on Unity's game screen (Fig. 2) and saved as a CSV file.

3.3   Real-World Sensor Data Acquisition

The distance-measuring sensors in the real world were GP2Y0E02A developed by Sharp Corporation. Each sensor consisted of an infrared LED and a position detector (PSD) and measured the distance to the target object based on an incident position of the reflective infrared light. They could detect distances from 4 cm to 50 cm. Since the relationship between the sensor value and the distance value is linear, the distance value was calculated from the sensor value (1) and recorded as time-series data.

$$Distance = 4.0 + (2.2 - SensorValue * 5/1023)/0.036 \tag{1}$$

The sensors were connected to a microcontroller (Arduino Pro Mini, 3.3 V). The sensor data were sent to a PC. Since the time intervals for acquiring the distance data differed between the software and the distance-measuring sensor, the data of the distance-measuring sensor was extracted according to the time interval of the software, which was the longer time interval, and saved as a CSV file.

3.4 Obtaining Learning Data and Making an Identification

We converted the CSV files acquired by the software and distance-measuring sensors into 2D-grayscale image data.

The start timing of imaging was taken to be when the distance data of any two sensors became smaller than 30 cm. We applied a low-pass filter (RC filter) to the distance data, as follows:

$$y[i] = 0.4x[i] + 0.6y[i - 1] \tag{2}$$

(x: present data, y: time series data frame)

After obtaining the filtered distance data, we converted it into 2D-grayscale image data by means of normalization. In the converted image, each distance value was allocated to the vertical axis, and the time-series data were allocated to the horizontal axis.

The SVM classifier was generated by learning using the HOG features of the 2D-grayscale image generated from the software data. A gesture performed in front of the distance-measuring sensors in the real world was identified using the HOG features of a 2D-grayscale image generated from the data of the distance-measuring sensors and the classifier generated with the data of the software.

4 Evaluation

4.1 Overview

We conducted experiments to determine whether the learning data accumulated by our software can be used to identify data measured with distance-measuring sensors in the real world. Seventeen distance-measuring sensors were attached around the perimeter of a Hue Go light developed by Philips. The distance between adjacent sensors was about 2.5 cm (Fig. 3 (left)). The sensors in the software were arranged in the same layout as those in the real world (Fig. 3 (right)). Next, we performed several gestures in front of the Kinect and acquired distance data. After that, the same gestures were

Fig. 3. Sensor layout (Left: in the real world, Right: in the software).

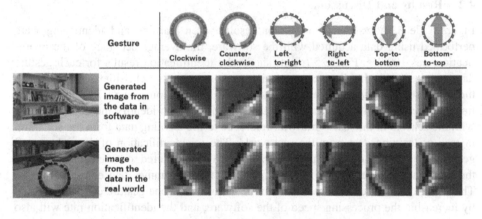

Fig. 4. Types of identified gesture and examples of generated images.

performed in front of distance-measuring sensors placed in the real world, and the distance data were acquired from the sensor data. Figure 4 shows the types of identified gesture and examples of generated images. Each gesture was performed ten times in front of the Kinect and ten times in front of the distance-measuring sensors; 15 frames were acquired per gesture and imaged. Leave-one-out cross-validation was performed on the dataset acquired with the software to calculate the identification rate, and a classifier was generated. Then, we identified each gesture acquired by the distance-measuring sensors using the classifier generated with the data acquired on the software.

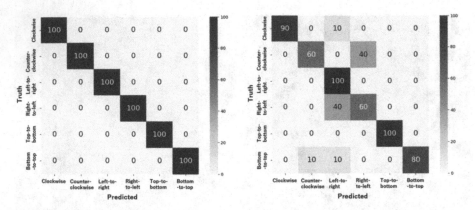

Fig. 5. Identification results (Left: using data acquired with the software, Right: using data acquired by the distance-measuring sensors).

4.2   Results and Discussion

Figure 5 (left) shows the identification results when learning and identifying were performed using data acquired with the software; the average accuracy of the identification was 100.0%. Figure 5 (right) shows the identification results for each gesture data acquired with the distance-measuring sensors using the classifier generated with the software data; the average accuracy of the identification was 81.7%. This identification rate was high enough to show that it is possible to identify the data measured with the sensors in the real world with reference to the learning data from the software, instead of learning data from the real world. The misidentification of the right-to-left gesture as the left-to-right gesture in Fig. 5 (right) is considered to have been caused by the fact that the gesture has been completed before all frames had elapsed (Fig. 4). Therefore, the number of frames that can be acquired for one gesture can be increased by increasing the processing speed of the software, and the identification rate will also increase.

5   Limitations and Future Work

The simulated sensors placed in the software are not affected by ambient light, but the actual distance-measuring sensors are affected by it; the ambient light adds noise to the sensor data. The identification was performed on relatively slow gestures because the processing speed of the software was slow in the experiment and the distance data were acquired at intervals of about 0.30 s. Since the distance-measuring sensor can obtain data at a higher speed, it is considered possible to identify faster gestures by increasing the processing speed of the software. In future work, we will develop a system that presents a sensor layout that increases the identification rate when the user specifies the number of sensors.

6   Conclusion

We developed software for designing the layout of real-world sensors and verified the identifiability of the data acquired with the sensors placed in the real world by using a classifier generated from the data acquired on the software. The software acquires distance data by measuring the distance in the virtual world based on depth information from a Kinect and sensors placed in the virtual world. Data acquired with sensors in the real world can be identified using a classifier generated from data acquired on the software. We found that the average accuracy of the identification was 81.7%. In future work, we will increase the processing speed of the software and develop a system that presents a sensor layout having a high identification rate.

Acknowledgments. This work was supported by JST AIP-PRISM JPMJCR18Y2 and JST PRESTO JPMJPR17J4.

References

1. Sato, M., Poupyrev, I., Harrison, C.: Touché: enhancing touch interaction on humans, screens, liquids, and everyday objects. In: Proceedings of the SIGCHI Conference on Human Factors in Computing Systems (CHI 2012), pp. 483–492. ACM, New York (2012)
2. Ino, K., Ienaga, N., Sugiura, Y., Saito, H., Miyata, N., Tada, M.: Grasping hand pose estimation from RGB images using digital human model by convolutional neural network. In: 9th International Conference and Exhibition on 3D Body Scanning and Processing Technologies, pp. 154–160. HOMETRICA CONSULTING, Lugano, Switzerland (2018)
3. Kanaya, T., Hiromori, A., Yamaguchi, H., Higashino, T.: Humans: a human mobility sensing simulator. In: 2012 5th International Conference on New Technologies, Mobility and Security (NTMS), pp. 1–4. IEEE, Istanbul, Turkey (2012)
4. Yuan, Y., Kitani, K.: 3D ego-pose estimation via imitation learning. In: Ferrari, V., Hebert, M., Sminchisescu, C., Weiss, Y. (eds.) ECCV 2018. LNCS, vol. 11220, pp. 763–778. Springer, Cham (2018). https://doi.org/10.1007/978-3-030-01270-0_45
5. Masai, K., Sugiura, Y., Ogata, M., Kunze, K., Inami, M., Sugimoto, M.: Facial expression recognition in daily life by embedded photo reflective sensors on smart eyewear. In: Proceedings of the 21st International Conference on Intelligent User Interfaces (IUI 2016), pp. 317–326. ACM, New York (2016)
6. Kikuchi, T., Sugiura, Y., Masai, K., Sugimoto, M., Thomas, B.: Eartouch: turning the ear into an input surface. In: Proceedings of the 19th International Conference on Human-Computer Interaction with Mobile Devices and Services (MobileHCI 2017), pp. 27:1–27:6. ACM, New York (2017)
7. Ogata, M., Sugiura, Y., Osawa, H., Imai, M.: iRing: intelligent ring using infrared reflection. In: Proceedings of the 25th Annual ACM Symposium on User Interface Software and Technology (UIST 2012), pp. 131–136. ACM, New York (2012)
8. Miyata, N., Honoki, T., Maeda, Y., Endo, Y., Tada, M., Sugiura, Y.: Wrap sense: grasp capture by a band sensor. In: Proceedings of the 29th Annual Symposium on User Interface Software and Technology (UIST 2016), pp. 87–89. ACM, New York (2016)

Visualization and Exploration
of Deep Learning Networks
in 3D and Virtual Reality

Andreas Schreiber[1(✉)] and Marcel Bock[1,2]

[1] German Aerospace Center (DLR), Linder Höhe, 51147 Cologne, Germany
andreas.schreiber@dlr.de
[2] University of Koblenz-Landau, Universitätsstraße 1, 56070 Koblenz, Germany

Abstract. Understanding of *artificial intelligence* (AI) systems becomes more important as their use cases in real-world applications growth. Today's AI systems are increasingly complex and ubiquitous. They will be responsible for making decisions that directly affect individuals. *Explainable AI* can potentially help by explaining actions, decisions and behaviours of AI systems to users. Our approach is to provide a tool with an interactive user interface in 3D. The tool visualizes deep learning network layers and allows interactive exploration on different levels of detail. The visualization then improves transparency and opacity of AI systems for experts and non-experts.

Keywords: Explainable artificial intelligence · Deep learning · Interpretable machine learning · Interactive exploration · Visualization

1 Introduction

Neural networks and deep learning models are useful techniques for machine learning applications as natural language processing, image recognition, or autonomous systems. For example, Google DeepMind developed ALPHAGO, which taught themselves to play Go and beat the current world champion. Because of the size of such neural networks and its complexity, is difficult to understand what is going on and how the neural network reaches a result.

Our approach shows that one can visualize large neural networks in a three-dimensional space and that the network becomes more accessible because of the interactive and user-friendly interface. We present our implementation based on the UNREAL ENGINE [2] using MNIST [6] as an example network (Sect. 2). For this visualization, we give an overview about user study results (Sect. 3). To understand the context, we discuss related work (Sect. 4). We conclude our results and describe future work that we derived from our findings (Sect. 5).

C. Stephanidis (Ed.): HCII 2019, CCIS 1033, pp. 206–211, 2019.
https://doi.org/10.1007/978-3-030-23528-4_29

2   Neural Network Visualization in 3D

The visualization of neural networks can help to understand and interpret deep learning models. Nevertheless, the variety of models and the size of real-world data sets has many design challenges [4]. We focus on interactive 3D visualization for deep learning models, which are implemented with TENSORFLOW [1].

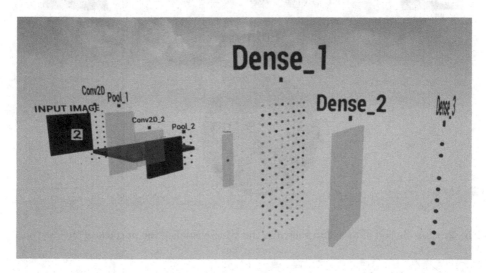

Fig. 1. The MNIST-network visualized in the UNREAL ENGINE. Different layers and neurons are displayed.

We created a 3D scene to visualize the neural network (Fig. 1). The UNREAL ENGINE creates the network automatically. It needs the name of the layer and the number of neurons. For each layer, the neurons can be displayed separately which allows the application to run in real-time. The type of layer (e.g., *convolutional*, *pooling*, or *dense*) determines which information the neurons provide. A neuron of a convolutional layer shows information of its related layer, so the user knows to which layer the neuron belongs to. Beside displaying the output of the neuron, one can apply the convolutional mask of it to the test data (Fig. 2). This provides deeper understanding of its function and purpose.

TENSORFLOW provides many detailed information for neural networks. That is why the user interfaces should be designed overseeable and information should be reducible at any time. Changes of results and values—such as the bias values— are displayed. For a better performance, information is not being updated as long as the user does not open the specific menu.

Each neuron has its own user interface, which would be divided into categories. That should help to give the user a better overview. A main-menu should provide the possibility to start the training process of the model and to adjust training parameters.

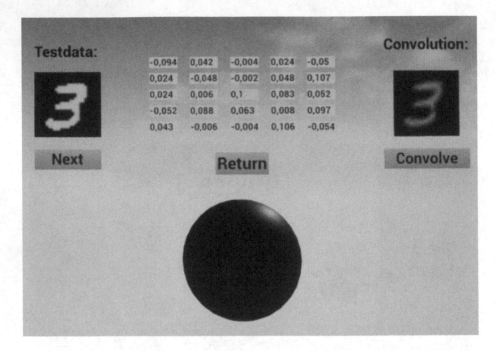

Fig. 2. Convolution of test data shown in the UI to visualize the purpose of the neuron.

2.1 Visualization of Large Neural Networks

Large neural networks consist of thousands or more neurons per layer, which is a challenge for real-time applications. For large networks, we visualize the MNIST-network in another way. Instead of visualizing the whole network, we encapsulate the layers and neurons. First, the user sees one big cube which represent the whole network. As the user approaches the cube, it will vanish when he reaches a certain distance and more layers will be visible (Fig. 3). This way the UNREAL ENGINE displays just a certain part of the network and the application can run in real-time, even when the network is larger than the shown example.

3   Evaluation

For evaluating the understandability and usefulness of our visualization approach, we conducted a user study.

Evaluation Setup. We presented the neural network visualization to machine learning experts as well as non-experts. The visualization and its interaction techniques were presented to the participants via a large display. In a first step, the study conductor explained each step of the interaction with neural networks, such as training and exploration. After that, the participants filled out an online questionnaire. In a second step, participants where able to create and change the network layout using PYTHON scripts. The study conductor gathered feedback using interviews.

Results. The main *expectations* of participants on a neural network visualization, especially for learning about neural networks, were:

- It should be visible whether a neuron is activated or not.
- It should be possible to inspect how a neuron activation changes due to changed parameters.
- It should be possible to visualize the architecture of the neural network (i.e., the network layers).

The major results of our study showed, that expectations were fulfilled. The participants reported some findings and remarks, including the following:

1. Participants mentioned, that there should be a general interface for other machine leaning libraries than TENSORFLOW.
2. Participants like the ability to filter in the input data and test data and to inspect neurons.
3. Participants did not like the visualization of neuron's weights.
4. Participants demanded a more concise summary of a layer's state.

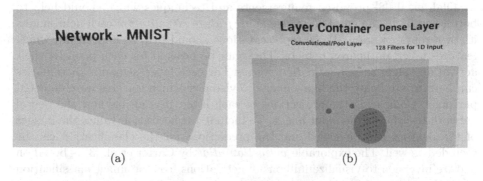

      (a)   (b)

Fig. 3. Levels of detail for large neural network visualization: (a) the network is visualized as a cube first; (b) more details of the model are visible after zooming in.

4   Related Work

There are several techniques to visualize results of neural networks. *Saliency maps* are a method of segmentation and are used to highlight certain areas in a picture. Simonyan et al. [10] use saliency maps to project the activation of neurons onto the input picture. This way they can verify that the correct object on a picture is used for the classification. The picture can be altered to watch changes in the classification progress, as well. Methods such as *Guided BackProp* [11] or *DeConvNet* [12] project activation of neurons, too, but they are used to visualize activation patterns and to create *feature maps*.

Kindermans et al. [5] point out that those projections are not convenient enough for explanations of results because this techniques would just visualize the signal-to-noise ratio of the input. Their own method, *PatternNet*, replaces the weights of the model for the projection which enhances the results. *PatternAttribution* can visualize the effect of the classification process for each neuron with *heat maps*.

Class Activation Mapping (CAM) by Zhou et al. [13] uses a heat map such as *PatternNet* but enhances this map with information which class was detected in a certain region and with its probability. *t-SNE* [7] plots are used to visualize and cluster data points. The dimensions are reduced and the points are placed in a 2D- or 3D-space based on their similarity. For neural networks, used vectors can be visualized and wrongly placed data points are visible. This provides hints for possible errors.

Kahng et al. [4] presented different design requirements for software which should visualize neural networks. Different kind of data should be supported such as text, audio, or images. The amount of data should be reducible and a software should be capable of visualizing complex model architectures. It would be important that the software is generalizable to extend the kind of models. For a user it should be possible to choose the dataset and keep track of the input through the whole neural network.

Olah et al. [8] proposed requirements and techniques which should help to better comprehend neural networks. With *feature visualization* each neuron gets its own representation. These representations should help to understand which features a certain neuron detects. They can be ordered for each pixel by their activation values as *semantic dictionaries*. For each layer, semantic dictionaries can be projected onto the input image to visualize which features were detected per pixel. Comparing the projections of each layer, it is visible how the neural network transforms the input image. To include the activation values the images of the neurons can be scaled and the predictions for the classification can be included as well. The explorable *activation atlas* by Carter et al. [3] is based on feature inversion to visualize millions of activations from an image classification network.

5   Conclusions and Future Work

Our goal was to develop an application which visualizes a neural network to enhance its comprehensibility. We developed a prototype for such a visualization, which visualizes a *convolutional neural network* and allows users to view results and to watch the classification process.

Based on the evaluation the prototype will be enhanced in the future. Each layer could get a user interface which displays results of the contained neurons. For example, the average of the activation values could be computed or all result images could be added together. KERAS models provide methods for saliency maps and class activation maps. Those methods could be used to enhance the visualization. More types of models and data will be supported in the future, such models which work with audio files. The challenge will be to display results in an appropriate way.

Support for standard exchange format for machine learning models—such as the *Open Neural Network Exchange* (ONNX) format [9]—will be integrated which allows a user to pass a file to the application and the model and data will be loaded automatically. *Augmented Reality* headsets (e.g., MICROSOFT HOLOLENS) will be supported in the future, too. Therefore, the interaction with the model in the scene has to be adjusted and the benefit to use these headsets will be evaluated.

References

1. Abadi, M., et al.: TensorFlow: large-scale machine learning on heterogeneous systems (2015). https://www.tensorflow.org/
2. Bock, M., Schreiber, A.: Visualization of neural networks in virtual reality using unreal engine. In: Proceedings of the 24th ACM Symposium on Virtual Reality Software and Technology, VRST 2018, pp. 132:1–132:2. ACM, New York (2018). https://doi.org/10.1145/3281505.3281605
3. Carter, S., Armstrong, Z., Schubert, L., Johnson, I., Olah, C.: Activation atlas. Distill (2019). https://distill.pub/2019/activation-atlas
4. Kahng, M., Andrews, P.Y., Kalro, A., Chau, D.H.P.: ActiVis: visual exploration of industry-scale deep neural network models. IEEE Trans. Vis. Comput. Graph. **24**(1), 88–97 (2018)
5. Kindermans, P.J., et al.: Learning how to explain neural networks: patternnet and patternattribution. In: 6th International Conference on Learning Representations (2018)
6. Lecun, Y., Bottou, L., Bengio, Y., Haffner, P.: Gradient-based learning applied to document recognition. Proc. IEEE **86**(11), 2278–2324 (1998)
7. van der Maaten, L., Hinton, G.: Visualizing data using t-SNE. J. Mach. Learn. Res. **9**(Nov), 2579–2605 (2008)
8. Olah, C., et al.: The building blocks of interpretability. Distill (2018). https://distill.pub/2018/building-blocks
9. ONNX: Open neural network exchange format (2018). https://onnx.ai/
10. Simonyan, K., Vedaldi, A., Zisserman, A.: Deep inside convolutional networks: visualising image classification models and saliency maps (2013). http://arxiv.org/abs/1312.6034v2
11. Springenberg, J.T., Dosovitskiy, A., Brox, T., Riedmiller, M.: Striving for simplicity: the all convolutional net (2014). http://arxiv.org/abs/1412.6806v3
12. Zeiler, M.D., Fergus, R.: Visualizing and understanding convolutional networks (2013). http://arxiv.org/abs/1311.2901v3
13. Zhou, B., Khosla, A., Lapedriza, A., Oliva, A., Torralba, A.: Learning deep features for discriminative localization (2015). http://arxiv.org/abs/1512.04150v1

Machine Learning Enhanced User Interfaces for Designing Advanced Knitwear

Martijn ten Bhömer[(⊠)], Hai-Ning Liang, and Difeng Yu

Xi'an Jiaotong-Liverpool University, Suzhou 215123, People's Republic of China
{Martijn.Tenbhomer,HaiNing.Liang}@xjtlu.edu.cn,
Difeng.Yu14@student.xjtlu.edu.cn

Abstract. The relationship between visual appearance and structure and technical properties of a knitted fabric is subtle and complex. This is an area that has been traditionally problematic within the knitting sector, understanding between technologists and designers is hindered which limits the possibility of dialogues from which design innovation can emerge. Recently there has been interest from the Human-Computer Interaction (HCI) community to narrow the gap between product design and knitwear. The goal of this article is to show the potential of predictive software design tools for fashion designers who are developing personalized advanced functionalities in textile products. The main research question explored in this article is: "How can designers benefit from intelligent design software for the manufacturing of personalized advanced functionalities in textile products?". In particular we explored how to design interactions and interfaces that use intelligent predictive algorithms through the analysis of a case study, in which several predictive algorithms were compared in the practice of textile designers.

Keywords: User Interface · Machine learning · Knitwear

1 Introduction

Developments of advanced textile manufacturing techniques—such as 3D body-forming knitwear machinery—allows the production of almost finalized garments, which require little to no further production steps to finalize the garments [17]. Moreover, advanced knitting technology in combination with new materials enable the integration of localized functionalities within a garment on a 'stitch by stitch level', such as moisture management, compression, and abrasion resistance [16]. Knitted constructions provide remarkable diversity and a range of potential end products, however, currently the market is not fully able to absorb and utilize the technological advances [4]. One of the possible reasons for this problem is that the advanced knitting machines require highly skilled programmers and designers with technical understanding. The relationship between

© Springer Nature Switzerland AG 2019
C. Stephanidis (Ed.): HCII 2019, CCIS 1033, pp. 212–219, 2019.
https://doi.org/10.1007/978-3-030-23528-4_30

visual appearance and structure and technical properties of a knitted fabric is subtle and complex [5].

Recently there has been interest from the Human-Computer Interaction (HCI) community to narrow the gap between product design and knitwear. For example, by developing a compiler that can automatically turn assemblies of high-level shape primitives and even 3D models into low-level machine instructions [13,14]. Other research have looked at developing computational parametric tools for digitally designing and industrially producing knitted fabrics, which created a more direct link between design and manufacturability [8]. In the field of Computer Science there have been instances were techniques such as data mining and machine learning were applied to aid the design process of complex garment manufacturing [19]. This led to advantages such as better prediction of parameters, for example fabric elongation [15] and air permeability [12]. Another benefit is enhanced sustainability due to reduction of consumption of textile-related materials, such as fabrics, yarns, dyes, and sewing threads [7]. Better sizing could be achieved by analyzing textile data, leading to improved customer satisfaction [6].

2   Case Study

The design process of knitwear garments consists of several sequential steps, requiring multiple translations between different media (such as sketches, patterns and machine code) and between different people (fashion designer, knitwear designer, knitting engineer and machine technician). The final result can only be evaluated by the designer and wearer after the manufacturing. Therefore, the integration of specialized functionalities (such as compression, breathability of the textiles, and areas used for sensing vital signs) require many cycles of product development and manufacturing, for example in the case of smart garments [2]. This leads to a challenge, because in the design process it is often beneficial to be able to have rapid iterations in which potential directions can be explored and evaluated. In the case of knitwear, we have previously attempted to bridge this gap using prototyping techniques such as on-the-body paper prototyping and 3D printing [1]. In this project we hypothesize that knitwear designers can have increased creative freedom when they have direct feedback about the intended functionalities during the design process (without actual manufacturing).

This project focuses exclusively on *functionalities* in knitted garments, more precisely we focus on a specific type of knitting called *circular knitting*. The term 'circular' covers all knitting machines whose needle beds are arranged in circular cylinders and can knit a wide range of fabric structures, garments, hosiery and other articles in a variety of diameters [18]. Circular knitting technology has evolved and enables designers to create sleek bodywear and performance active wear. It allows ready-to-wear three-dimensional (3D) tubular garments to be created directly from yarns without any seams, for example in underwear, swimwear and sportswear [10].

This project aims to predict the functionalities of a manufactured fabric product, without the need of actually producing the product. To this end, one of the most popular and powerful approaches is *machine learning*. Machine learning enables us with the help of computers to predict certain outcomes, or new samples, by "training" mathematical models using example data or past experience [9]. The trained model can generate accurate predictions or decisions without being explicitly programmed to perform the task [3]. Because of its usefulness, machine learning has been widely applied in many domains such as healthcare, fraud detection, personalized recommendation, etc. In this project, we consider multiple machine learning techniques including linear, non-linear, and tree-based models to predict various target variables collected from empirical testing.

3   Machine Learning for Knitwear

In this article we will present our exploratory process based on three steps when applying machine learning algorithms: (1) data collection and preparation; (2) model building, evaluating, and selecting; (3) prediction.

Fig. 1. Example of pattern files that represent the knitting machine instructions. The colors on the pattern in the left represent the different material or surfaces as described by the designer. The pattern on the right represents the different knitting structures that the machine has to make (each pixel represents a stitch by the needle).

The main property of circular knitting technology is that all the constructions are restricted by a tubular shape, variations in shape and functionality can be realized by making changes in the materials (the yarns) and structures (the specific knits) within this tube [11]. These variations are normally expressed using patterns which can be converted in machine-readable instructions (Fig. 1 shows an example of these type of patterns). In our data model we express these two parts using predictor variables (the parameters that potentially have an impact on the result) and the target variables (the desired outcomes). In order to simplify the data model for the first try-out of our approach we decided to limit the variation of materials, and instead focus on the combination of different knitting structures. To make variations of the knitting structures we defined three parameters that would serve as the predictor variables: stitch type, stitch structure and tube coverage. As target variables we focused on basic parameters (such as weight and diameter), dynamic parameters (such as unload force and elongation) and performance parameters (such as comfort and energy).

In order to train the machine learning algorithms, it was necessary to create a dataset which the algorithms could use to base the predictions on. Creating this training data consisted from two steps, first it was necessary to create physical samples of fabric with different predictor variable combinations, and secondly, it was necessary to devise a set of testing protocols to evaluate the performance of the target variables within these samples. We used circular knitting machines to knit 36 tubular fabric structures, which cover all the variations of different predictor variables. Figure 2 shows all the physical samples ordered by variation. Finally, testing methods were used to measure the target variable results for each of the fabric structure.

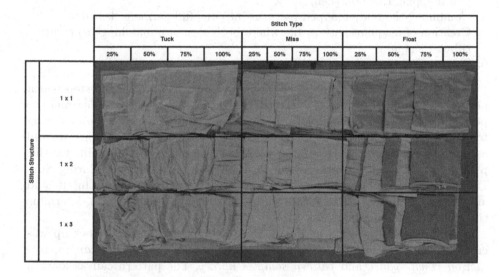

Fig. 2. Overview of the 36 samples ordered by variation.

In order to model the relation between the predictors and target variables, we compared a set of eight algorithms. These algorithms can be divided into three groups: linear regression models, non-linear regression models, and tree-based models. We built the eight models and evaluated them in two sets of analysis; first with the data generated from the tests in our own lab, and in a second analysis with the data provided by an external testing lab. Two methods that were used for measuring the effectiveness of the algorithms are $RMSE$ (root-mean-square error) and R^2 (coefficient of determination). Based on the two analysis, we finally selected six models by eliminating Robust Linear Regression and Elastic Net due to their similar poor performance with Linear Regression.

4   Designing the User Interface

The User Interface (UI) design was a process in collaboration with the knitwear designers, who would be eventually using the interface. The design of the interface started by understanding how the predictive capabilities of this tool can play a role in the design process of functional knitwear. We asked our knitwear design partners how their current process looks like, and which tools they used in each step of the process. Summarized this process contains the following steps:

1. Creating the concept based on the visual direction, gathering inspiration for patterns and graphics (for example by manipulating and combining patterns).
2. Creation of a pattern library. Several patterns that can be tested for different knit combinations, and through trial and error achieve the right functionality.
3. Subjective assessment of the visual and functional aspects of the test results, and mapping them on them body.
4. Combining the body mapped patterns into one full garment design.
5. Creation of a square pattern file where both sides are matching (to create a tubular shape).
6. Start engineering process to integrate the design onto a 3D form.

Based on this process our initial aim was to use the tool in the step which normally require iterative testing (Step 2). The tool should offer the designer the possibility to evaluate and explore the changes in functionality, without having to physically knit each sample. This could result in faster explorations, as well as more flexibility in the exploration process. The main starting point for this process is the visual patterns which have already been designed during Step 1. Therefore, the tool should be able to use the visual patterns as input, and allows the designer to make variations of the knitting structures, to determine the values of the functionalities.

Based on the directions set-out in the requirements phase, a mock-up was created. The main interface (Fig. 3 left) consists from the *pattern canvas, prediction results panel*, and *pattern samples library*. The pattern canvas loads a vector visual pattern, and separates the different objects in separate layers onto the canvas. The property adjustments panel gives a quick overview of the prediction results for the designed fabric. The pattern samples library panel let the users re-use patterns they have created before. Clicking on one of patterns will load the *pattern design window* (Fig. 3 right). This window allows the designer to change knitting parameters of the pattern, such as stitch type and stitch structure. The window shows a visual representation of how the knitting pattern will look like, as well as an overview of the direct feedback about the predicted functional values (such as breathability, elongation, weight and evaporation, etc.).

The main interface of the tool (Fig. 4) was divided in two main areas. The *pattern design area* shows the representation of the fabric by a rectangle consisting of two areas. A draggable line allows the designer to change the coverage percentage. The knitting type and knitting structure can be adapted by using the dropdown lists. When manipulating the pattern values, the software will calculate the predicted values of the functionalities in real-time, and display them

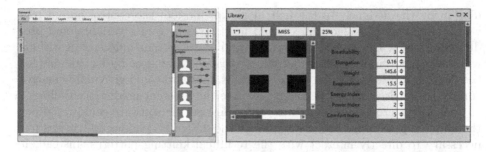

Fig. 3. The window on the left shows the proposed main window of the software. The window on the right shows the pattern design window.

in the *predicted values table* on the right side of the interface. The designer has the possibility to switch between different Machine Learning algorithms in order to see how this will change the predicted values of the target variables. The software will also display the reliability score in the form of colored stars which is based on the RMSE and R^2 values, this enables the designer to make a decision on the design based on the reliability of the intended functionalities.

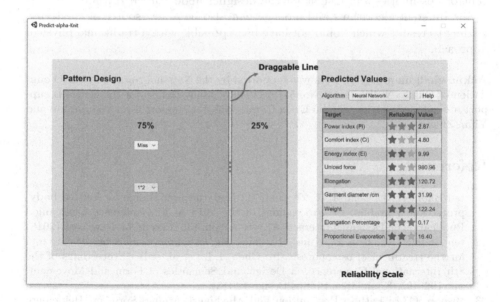

Fig. 4. Screenshot of the working prototype.

5   Conclusion

One of the challenges of designing the User Interface was to find a balance between how much of the Machine Learning features should be open for manipulation by the designer. In the first mock-up, most of the control parameters were hidden, and the algorithms would just show the target variables and predictor variables. During the process, as we discovered that different algorithms will have some variety in their output, we realized that it could be valuable for the designer to show the different algorithms, and also could give more creative control to the designers to be able to explore the different prediction results.

One of the crucial decisions was to decide how the software could represent the knitting pattern in the software. From the designer's perspective, it was not necessary to directly interact with the technical knitting patterns. Instead, it would be preferred to use a more abstract visual representation that focuses on the visual and functional qualities. However, for the algorithm to work accurately, it is necessary to work with a pattern representation and predictor variables which come as close as possible to the final manufactured fabric. Based on our current exploration we think there is an interesting tension here, where future research can help to find new opportunities.

One of our concerns is related to the process of replacing physical sampling with virtual sampling. By eliminating cycles of iterative physical manufacturing (one of the goals of developing this software), the designer might lose the chance to gain inspiration from manufacturing "accident". On the other hand, new control possibilities and insight for the designer about the algorithms (such as trying different algorithms and models) can also be a new source of creativity, leading to results which would not have been possible with a traditional physical approach.

Acknowledgments. This work was supported by the National Natural Science Foundation of China (NSFC, Grant No. 51750110497). Many thanks for the generous support of Santoni Shanghai, Studio Eva x Carola, and the support from Yuanjin Liu and Yifan Zhang.

References

1. ten Bhömer, M., Canova, R., de Laat, E.: Body inspired design for knitted body-protection wearables. In: Proceedings of the 2018 ACM Conference Companion Publication on Designing Interactive Systems, pp. 135–139. ACM, New York (2018)
2. ten Bhömer, M., Jeon, E., Kuusk, K.: Vibe-ing: designing a smart textile care tool for the treatment of osteoporosis. In: Chen, L.L., et al. (eds.) Proceedings of the 8th International Conference on Design and Semantics of Form and Movement, pp. 192–195. Koninklijke Philips Design (2013)
3. Bishop, C.M.: Pattern Recognition and Machine Learning. Springer, Heidelberg (2006)
4. Black, S.: Innovative knitwear design utilising seamless and unconventional construction, London, UK (2002)
5. Eckert, C.: The communication bottleneck in knitwear design: analysis and computing solutions. Comput. Support. Coop. Work **10**(1), 29–74 (2001)
6. Hsu, C.H., Wang, M.J.J.: Using decision tree-based data mining to establish a sizing system for the manufacture of garments. Int. J. Adv. Manuf. Technol. **26**(5), 669–674 (2005)

7. Jaouachi, B., Khedher, F.: Evaluation of sewed thread consumption of jean trousers using neural network and regression methods. Fibres Text. East. Eur. **23**, 91–96 (2015)
8. Karmon, A., Sterman, Y., Shaked, T., Sheffer, E., Nir, S.: KNITIT: a computational tool for design, simulation, and fabrication of multiple structured knits. In: Proceedings of the 2nd ACM Symposium on Computational Fabrication, pp. 4:1–4:10. ACM, New York (2018)
9. Kuhn, M., Johnson, K.: Applied Predictive Modeling. Springer, New York (2013). https://doi.org/10.1007/978-1-4614-6849-3
10. Lau, F., Yu, W.: Seamless knitting of intimate apparel. In: Yu, W. (ed.) Advances in Women's Intimate Apparel Technology, pp. 55–68. Woodhead Publishing (2016)
11. Matković, V.M.P.: The power of fashion: the influence of knitting design on the development of knitting technology. Textile **8**(2), 122–146 (2010)
12. Matusiak, M.: Application of artificial neural networks to predict the air permeability of woven fabrics. Fibres Text. East. Eur. **23**, 41–48 (2015)
13. McCann, J., et al.: A compiler for 3D machine knitting. ACM Trans. Graph. **35**(4), 49:1–49:11 (2016)
14. Narayanan, V., Albaugh, L., Hodgins, J., Coros, S., Mccann, J.: Automatic machine knitting of 3D meshes. ACM Trans. Graph. **37**(3), 35:1–35:15 (2018)
15. Ogulata, S.N., Sahin, C., Ogulata, R.T., Balci, O.: The prediction of elongation and recovery of woven bi-stretch fabric using artificial neural network and linear regression models. Fibres Text. East. Eur. **14**(2), 9–46 (2006)
16. Power, E.J.: Advanced knitting technologies for high-performance apparel. In: McLoughlin, J., Sabir, T. (eds.) High-Performance Apparel, pp. 113–127. Woodhead Publishing (2018)
17. Sayer, K., Wilson, J., Challis, S.: Seamless knitwear - the design skills gap. Des. J. **9**(2), 39–51 (2006)
18. Spencer, D.J.: Knitting Technology: A Comprehensive Handbook and Practical Guide, 3rd edn. Woodhead Publishing, Sawston (2001)
19. Yildirim, P., Birant, D., Alpyildiz, T.: Data mining and machine learning in textile industry. Wiley Interdiscip. Rev. Data Min. Knowl. Discov. **8**(1), e1228 (2018)

Physiological Measuring

Emotion Recognition System Based on EEG Signal Analysis Using Auditory Stimulation: Experimental Design

Catalina Aguirre-Grisales[1,2]([envelope]), Edwin Gaviria-Cardenas[1],
Victor Hugo Castro-Londoño[3], Hector Fabio Torres-Cardona[4],
and Jose Luis Rodriguez-Sotelo[1]

[1] Electronic Engineering Department, Universidad Autónoma de Manizales,
Old Train Station, Manizales, Colombia
catalina.aguirreg@autonoma.edu.co
[2] Universidad del Quindío, Cra. 15 #12N, Armenia, Quindío, Colombia
[3] Universidad de Caldas, Cl. 65 #26-10, Manizales, Caldas, Colombia
[4] Department of Music, Universidad de Caldas, Cl. 65 #26-10,
Manizales, Caldas, Colombia
http://www.uam.edu.co/

Abstract. In this document the design of an emotion recognition system based on the EEG signals analysis based on auditory stimulation is proposed. Here, an auditory emotion recognition protocol using the International Affective Digitalized Sounds (IADS) second edition database is introduced, in which the database is divided into three groups: Negative, Positive and Neutral sonorous stimuli according to their normative mean valence and arousal ratings. The protocol was implemented through the psychopy3 stimulation libraries, and the signal acquisition is made using the Emotiv EPOC+ device through a software developed in the python environment. The stimulation protocol and the acquisition process are synchronized through pulses allowing to carryout stimulus register and to control the experiment.

Keywords: Emotion recognition · Electroencephalogram · Auditory stimulation · Stimulation protocol

1 Introduction

Emotion is defined as an episode of interrelated and synchronized changes in the organism in response to the evaluation of an external or internal stimulus event [1]. Emotions are the reason for our desire to survive and our inspiration, and they represent the premotor platform that drives or restrains most of our actions [2].

Currently, the affective computing area seeks to improve the human experience through the balance between emotion and cognition, allowing a natural

© Springer Nature Switzerland AG 2019
C. Stephanidis (Ed.): HCII 2019, CCIS 1033, pp. 223–230, 2019.
https://doi.org/10.1007/978-3-030-23528-4_31

communication amid humans and machines, being the elicitation and recognition of human emotions one of the most important research fields in this area [3], in which human emotional states can be evoked by external stimuli (e.g., auditory, visual and audiovisual stimuli) and be identified by physiological changes [1, 3–7]. Some of the physiological measures that have been employed for emotion recognition are facial expression, heart rate, blood pressure, among others [4]. However, the brain signals through the electroencephalogram (EEG) provides a direct path for emotion recognition with a high classification accuracy [3, 4].

Typically, any pattern recognition system is composed by two phases, the experimental one and the off-line analysis (composed by features extraction and pattern recognition). The success of the off-line analysis phase lies in the quality, and the control degree of the experiment, being this the way to provide a neuroanatomical respond that reflects the expected changes in the brain signals [4, 10].

In this paper, the design of the experimental phase of an emotion recognition system based on EEG signal analysis using auditory stimulation is proposed. Here, the EEG data acquisition and the emotion elicitation are made through a software developed in the Python programming environment, in which the emotive EPOC+ is used as a Brain-Computer Interface device and the psychopy3 as the stimulation library [11]. In order to have an standard experiment, the elicitation protocol uses the International Affective Digitized Sound (IADS) database second edition [13] as stimuli. Therefore, the aim of this experimental process design is to provide a brain signal that may be able to process efficiently and to prove the stimulation protocol, in order to have the tools to develop a real time emotion recognition system using sonorous stimulation.

The layout of the paper is as follows. In Sects. 2, the stimuli protocol, data acquisition, data preprocessing and signal visualization are presented. Results and Discussion follows in Sect. 3, and finally, conclusions and future research are presented.

2   Design of the Experimental Phase

The experimental phase relates the primary step for a correct emotion recognition system, since it involves the data acquisition, emotions elicitation, and visualization. The experimental phase works in a parallel way, in which the signal acquisition and the stimulation are synchronized by pulses allowing to carry a register and control of the experimental phase (Fig. 1). All the experiment was developed in python platform using the EEG interface proposed by [18] and the library Psychopy3 proposed by [11].

2.1   Stimulation Protocol

Stimuli Database: In order to develop an emotion induction protocol that allows to perform a large number of trials, and which would be easily used in general populations, the international affective digitized sound (IADS) 2nd edition [13] was used. The IADS is a standardized database of everyday sounds designed to evoke emotions. The database was created by the Center for Emotion and Attention (CSEA) at the University of Florida, with the aim to provide a stimulation tool able to create standard experiments in the field of emotion induction and detection research. For developing the stimulation protocol, the IADS database was divided into three groups according to the mean valence ratings following the instructions of [13]. The auditory stimulation groups are Negative (mean valance ratings lower than 4), Neutral (Mean valence rating between 4 and 6), and Positive (mean valence rating upper than 6).

Protocol Design: The stimulation protocol is able to evoke three different emotion groups divided into positive, neutral, and negative. This protocol is based on the Sourina's auditive protocol [6], developed in 2012. The protocol was made in python environment using psychopy3 library [11] as follows (Fig. 2): 10 se for experiment preparation, six seconds of sound exposure followed by 15 s of silence in which is verified the participant feeling of each stimulus through a self assessment emotion wheel develop by [14].

2.2 Data Acquisition

The EEG signal was recorded using the Emotiv Epoc+ system, which is a wireless low cost EEG system composed by 16 wet saline electrodes, distributed in 14 EEG channels and 2 references. The 14 electrodes are placed at the positions AF3, F7, F3, FC5, T7, P7, O1, O2, P8, T8, FC6, F4, F8, AF4 according to the 10–20 international standard [15], and the 2 references are located in the position P3 and P4 (Fig. 3). Each channel data has been digitalized using an embedded 16 bit ADC with a 128 Hz sampling frequency, all data were send to the computer receptor via Bluetooth [16]. The EEG signals were filtered using a bandpass FIR filter with a cutoff frequency of 0.3 Hz to 50 Hz in order to reference and reduce the high-frequency noise. In this experiment, 8 EEG channels were selected (T8, FC5, P8, T7, F3, F7, FC6 and P7) in order to reduce the computational effort, this reduction was made according to Zheng's work [17].

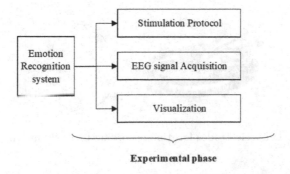

Fig. 1. Emotion recognition system, experimental phase

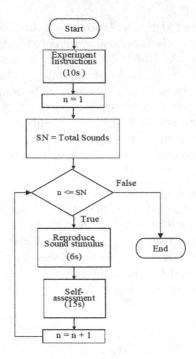

Fig. 2. Stimulation protocol flow chart

2.3   Visualization

The signal visualization was designed as a cyclic process based on the EEG interface developed by Hurtado-Rincón et al. [18] in which a window is created to locate the acquired signal and the synchronization pulse, and it is set its colors and labels up. All the signals come in a temporal matrix conformed by 9 vectors, the first 8 are the EEG signals and the last one is the synchronization pulse generated in the stimulation protocol process. This window is updated according to the temporal matrix refresh in the acquisition signal process.

Fig. 3. Emotiv EPOC+ electrodes location according to 10–20 international standard [16]

Table 1. Some auditory stimuli and its normative valence and arousal ratings in the IADS2 database

Category	Sound	Valence mean	Arousal mean
Negative	Growl	3.37	6.39
	Buzzing	3.02	6.51
	Vomit	2.08	6.59
Neutral	Cat	4.63	4.91
	Heart beat	4.83	4.65
	Restaurant	5.36	5.01
Positive	Brook	6.62	3.36
	Beethoven	7.51	4.18
	RockNRoll	7.90	6.85

3   Results and Discussion

The auditory stimuli were divided into three emotions categories (Negative, Neutral and Positive) according to the valence mean level. It is important to note that the arousal level was not taken into account, since conforming to the database specifications the arousal degree level has nonlinear distribution respect to the pleasantness of the sound [13]. Table 1 describes a brief summary of the auditory stimuli distribution of the IADS2 database; as it can be seen, the negative sounds have low valence ratings (less than 4) and in this case high arousal levels. On the other hand, the neutral category presents sounds with valence rating between 4 and 6, and lower arousal compared with the negative category. Finally, the positive category presents sound with valence levels higher than 6 and wide-ranging of arousal ratings. Figure 4 illustrates the auditory stimuli distribution made for the development of the stimuli protocol. Furthermore, in order to use all the auditory stimuli, it was necessary to resample all the sound stimuli to 48kHz, otherwise the psychopy library will not reproduce the sounds in the stimulation process.

In order to test the operation of the experimental phase, the connection, acquisition, stimulation and visualization were tested with the laboratory members. As specified above, it was necessary to reduce the EEG channels from 14 to 8, with the aim to decrease the computational effort, since the acquisition, stimulation, and visualization processes were done in a parallel way in the same computer. To guarantee the synchronization between the acquisition and stimulation process, the signal pulses from the stimulation code were generated to indicate the temporal stimulus execution. Both the acquisition and pulses are shown in the visualization interface developed to carry an experimental record and to control the experiment procedure. The visualization interface is presented in Fig. 5. This interface is composed by two elements, the first is a record of the user during the experiment, and it is located in the upper right side of the interface; the second element presents the EEG and synchronization signal on the left

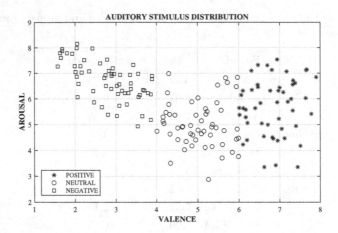

Fig. 4. IADS2 distribution for an discrete emotion experiment

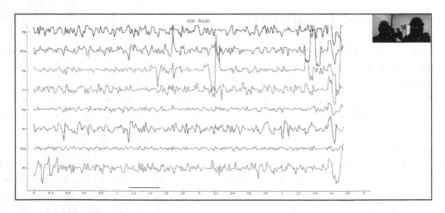

Fig. 5. Interface acquisition developed in python environment

side of the interface. The synchronization signal can vary according to the experiment requirements, in this case as the proposed experiment uses three discrete emotions categories, it was necessary to create three different synchronization signals that allow to know the kind of stimulus and the elicitation moment according to the stimulation protocol.

4   Conclusions

In this paper, experimental emotions elicitation design using sonorous stimulation was proposed, with the aim to provide brain signals with specific patterns that allow an automatic emotions recognition. For this, the stimuli characteristics and the signals acquisition were taken into account to develop the stimulation protocol and signals acquisition system, as a way to control the experiment process and to provide a brain signal with expected patterns in order to be able to use into the off-line analysis phase (signal features extraction, and pattern recognition process). Here, all the stimulation, acquisition and visualization algorithm was developed in a python environment. Finally, this experimental design aims to provide a standard emotion induction experiment able to be used in the study of emotional response to auditory stimulation. The future research works include the EEG signals analysis and feature extraction, and the development of an automatic emotion recognition system using artificial intelligence.

References

1. Scherer, K.R.: What are emotions? And how can they be measured? Soc. Sci. Inf. **44**(4), 695–729 (2005)
2. Llinás, R.R.: El cerebro y el mito del yo: el papel de las neuronas en el pensamiento y el comportamiento humanos. Editorial Norma (2003)
3. Liu, Y.J., Yu, M., Zhao, G., Song, J., Ge, Y., Shi, Y.: Real-time movie-induced discrete emotion recognition from EEG signals. IEEE Trans. Affect. Comput. **9**(4), 550–562 (2018)
4. Al-Nafjan, A., Hosny, M., Al-Ohali, Y., Al-Wabil, A.: Review and classification of emotion recognition based on EEG brain-computer interface system research: a systematic review. Appl. Sci. **7**(12), 1239 (2017)
5. Koelstra, S., et al.: DEAP: a database for emotion analysis; using physiological signals. IEEE Trans. Affect. Comput. **3**(1), 18–31 (2012)
6. Sourina, O., Liu, Y., Nguyen, M.K.: Real-time EEG-based emotion recognition for music therapy. J. Multimodal User Interfaces **5**(1–2), 27–35 (2012)
7. Teo, J., Chia, J.T.: Deep neural classifiers for EEG-based emotion recognition in immersive environments. In: 2018 International Conference on Smart Computing and Electronic Enterprise (ICSCEE), pp. 1–6. IEEE (2018)
8. Sanei, S.: Adaptive Processing of Brain Signals. Wiley, Hoboken (2013)
9. Amari, S., et al.: The Handbook of Brain Theory and Neural Networks. MIT Press, Cambridge (2003)
10. Luck, S.J.: An Introduction to the Event-Related Potential Technique. MIT Press, Cambridge (2014)
11. Peirce, J., et al.: PsychoPy2: experiments in behavior made easy. Behav. Res. Methods **51**, 1–9 (2019)
12. Bradley, M., Lang, P.J.: The International affective digitized sounds (IADS): stimuli, instruction manual and affective ratings. NIMH Center for the Study of Emotion and Attention (1999)
13. Bradley, M.M., Lang, P.J.: The international affective digitized sounds (IADS-2): affective ratings of sounds and instruction manual. Technical report B-3. University of Florida, Gainesville, FL (2007)
14. Mendez-Alegria, R., Yenny, C.C., Granollers, T.: Rueda de emociones de ginebra+: instrumento para la evaluación emocional de los usuarios mientras participan en una evaluación de sistemas interactivos. Rev. Ing. Dyna, vol. En prepara (2015)
15. Homan, R.W., Herman, J., Purdy, P.: Cerebral location of international 10–20 system electrode placement. Electroencephalogr. Clin. Neurophysiol. **66**(4), 376–382 (1987)
16. Emotiv (2019)

17. Zheng, W.L., Lu, B.L.: Investigating critical frequency bands and channels for EEG-based emotion recognition with deep neural networks. IEEE Trans. Auton. Ment. Dev. **7**(3), 162–175 (2015)
18. Hurtado-Rincón, J.V., Martínez-Vargas, J.D., Rojas-Jaramillo, S., Giraldo, E., Castellanos-Dominguez, G.: Identification of relevant inter-channel EEG connectivity patterns: a kernel-based supervised approach. In: Ascoli, G.A., Hawrylycz, M., Ali, H., Khazanchi, D., Shi, Y. (eds.) BIH 2016. LNCS (LNAI), vol. 9919, pp. 14–23. Springer, Cham (2016). https://doi.org/10.1007/978-3-319-47103-7_2

3D Eye Tracking for Visual Imagery Measurements

Kenta Kato[✉], Oky Dicky Ardiansyah Prima[✉],
and Hisayoshi Ito[✉]

Graduate School of Software and Information Science,
Iwate Prefectural University, Takizawa, Japan
g231q010@s.iwate-pu.ac.jp,
{prima,hito}@iwate-pu.ac.jp

Abstract. Experiences of visual imagery, the ability to see in the mind's eye, occur in various situations. The Vividness of Visual Imagery Questionnaire (VVIQ) has been widely used to subjectively measure the vividness of visualizers based on its score. For objective measurements, studies show that functional Magnetic Resonance Imaging (fMRI) can be used to measure individual variabilities of the vividness of visual imagery. However, questions are remained on how the visualizers see the images spatially. This study proposes a method to measure the spatial distribution of gaze in 3-dimensional space of an object seen by a visualizer using a glass-typed 3D eye tracker. The eye tracker estimated gaze in 3D based on vergence eye movements. Thus, if the visualizer reports good visual imagery of a given image, the eye tracker will be able to estimate the location of the object in 3-dimensional space. The eye tracker is equipped with polarizing lenses to enable the visualizer to see the given stimuli in both virtual and real worlds. Here, a 3D television (3DTV) is used to present the stimuli virtually. Ten introductory students completed the VVIQ and divided into two groups: high and low vividness visualizers, based on total scores of the VVIQ. Experiment results show that 3D gaze fixations of subjects who reported good visual imagery were relatively distributed around the location of the given stimuli.

Keywords: Visual imagery · VVIQ · 3D-gaze · Eye tracking

1 Introduction

Studies on visual imagery have a very long history. The visual imagery system can be described as an independent system which connect the verbal system with human cognition. Visual imagery is an effective tool for improving listening and reading comprehension. For students with reading disabilities, a combination of visual imagery and verbal rehearsal may be an effective strategy [1].

There are differences between individuals in their abilities in the recall of pictures. The widely used standard measure of imagery vividness is the Vividness of Visual Imagery Questionnaire (VVIQ) [2]. VVIQ measures mostly object imagery based on the user's subjective claim on his imagery vividness. Objective measurement of imagery vividness has been developed based on relative changes in brain activity of visual cortex measured by functional magnetic resonance imaging (fMRI) [3].

C. Stephanidis (Ed.): HCII 2019, CCIS 1033, pp. 231–237, 2019.
https://doi.org/10.1007/978-3-030-23528-4_32

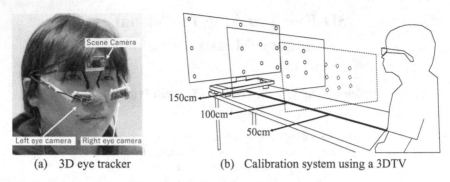

(a)   3D eye tracker   (b)   Calibration system using a 3DTV

Fig. 1. Our glass-type 3D eye tracking.

Since individuals tend to process imagery information using either spatial imagery or object imagery, eye trackers have been used to analyze the relationship between eye movements and visual imagery [4]. Experiments have been shown to have highly correlated patterns of gaze between perception and imagery of the same visual object [5]. However, currently available eye trackers are not capable to measure eye gaze in 3-dimensional, hence measured patterns of gaze in 2-dimensional may not reflect spatial processing as it would occur in the real world.

This study proposes a new measure to reveal vividness of mental imagery by correlating the user's VVIQ score and the spatial distribution of eye gaze pattern in 3-dimensional space when he was looking at a given object. A glass-typed 3D-gaze eye tracker was developed and used in the visual imagery experiments. The eye tracker is equipped with a 3D television (3DTV) and polarizing lenses to enable stimuli presentation in both virtual and real worlds.

2   Materials and Methods

2.1   Participants and Subjective Vividness Rating

Ten students from Iwate Prefectural University (average age = 22.4) participated in the study. Each participant voluntarily gave written informed consent in accordance with ethical guidelines and had normal or corrected-to-normal vision. Each participant completed VVIQ to measure vividness of visual imagery with a standardized battery of visualization questions [2]. The average of the vividness ratings on a 5-point Likert scale against the 16 questions was used. Participants with the highest and lowest VVIQ scores were grouped, resulting in a high vividness group ($N = 5$) and a low vividness group ($N = 5$).

2.2   3D Gaze Measurement: Experimental Task

Our glass-typed 3D eye tracker is composed of three webcams: a camera for capturing the scene viewed by the participant and the other for capturing pupils from both eyes. Infrared (IR) filter of cameras for capturing pupils have been replaced with IR-Pass

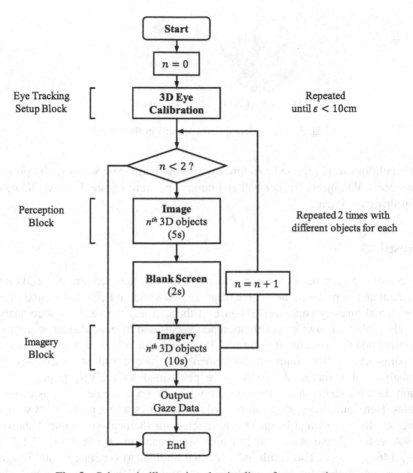

Fig. 2. Schematic illustrating the timeline of our experiment.

filter to allow IR imaging. Two IR LEDs were aligned off axis to the cameras to create dark pupil effects. The shape of each pupil is estimated by contouring the pupil image. Pupil center is then estimated by fitting an ellipse to the contour using least-squares regression. Polarizing lenses were attached to the frame glasses to enable the participant see 3D objects displayed on the 3DTV. 3D eye gaze calibration was measured by correlating 2D coordinates of both center of pupils and 3D coordinates of stimuli on the 3DTV. Figure 1 shows our glassed-type 3D eye tracker and its calibration system.

Each participant wore an eye-tracker and completed the eye gaze calibration. The calibration routine was repeated until the accuracy achieved less than 10 cm. The experiment consisted of two conditions: visual perception and visual imagery conditions. In the visual perception condition, the participant viewed a 3D object displayed on the 3DTV in 5 s. In the visual imagery condition, the participant was asked to generate vivid and detailed mental images corresponding to previously shown 3D object in 10 s. The interval time between two conditions was 2 s to completely turn off the display. Figure 2 shows a schematic illustrating the timeline of our experiment.

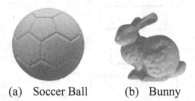

(a) Soccer Ball   (b) Bunny

Fig. 3. 3D models used as stimuli in this study.

These conditions were repeated two times where the participant was visually presented with different 3D objects (soccer ball and bunny) per run. Figure 3 shows 3D models used in this experiment.

3 Results

Distances of 3D gaze points for each condition against the location of the 3D object were calculated to measure the degree of generated vivid and detailed mental images. For the visual imagery condition, 3D gaze of the first and the next 5 s were analyzed separately. Table 1 shows eye calibration accuracies and average distances among 3D gaze points and the location of presented 3D objects for two groups of vividness. All participants achieved the minimum requirements for the eye calibration accuracy. Two-way analysis of variance (ANOVA) were performed with VVIQ (high, low) and duration during generation of mental imagery (the first 5 s, the next 5 s) as dependent variables. Here, only 3D gaze points towards a 3D object where participants were able to generate the best mental images were selected for the analysis. Table 2 shows the ANOVA result. There was a statistically significant main effect of VVIQ, $F(1, 16) = 7.146$, $p < 0.05$. This result indicates that abilities to generate mental images in 3D spaces are higher for participants having higher VVIQ score. Figure 4 shows samples of 3D gaze points during visual perception and visual imagery conditions for two group of vividness.

4 Discussion

To our knowledge, this study is the first attempt to use a 3D eye tracker in visual imagery experiment. The 3D eye calibration routine was difficult for many participants because during this process, the participant had to generate proper eye vergence which is a rare act in daily life. Before conducting the experiment, participants were trained to perform the 3D eye calibration properly.

Our findings based on the results of this study extend the fact [4, 5] that individuals which have vivid visual imagery tend to generate better mental images in a 3-dimensional space. As illustrated in Fig. 4, the distribution of fixations for participants having higher VVIQ appeared to concentrate their gaze points close to the location of previously presented 3D object.

Table 1. Eye calibration accuracies and average distances among 3D gaze points and the location of presented 3D objects for two groups of vividness. Only 3D gaze points where participants were able to generate the best mental imagery were selected for the analysis.

Subject ID	VVIQ	Average difference in distance (cm)		Eye calibration accuracy (cm)
		First 5 s	Next 5 s	
1	High vividness	0.10	0.57	6.72
2		35.42	36.65	6.50
3		75.04	72.61	7.45
4		2.41	0.91	5.52
5		5.19	3.48	7.52
6	Low vividness	46.25	45.03	5.88
7		31.71	30.23	2.39
8		42.85	42.27	5.74
9		79.50	79.92	3.42
10		114.19	106.67	5.96

Table 2. ANOVA results

Effect	DF	Sum Sq.	F-value	p-value
VVIQ	1	7,459	7.146	0.0167
Duration	1	10	0.010	0.9223
VVIQ × Duration	1	2	0.002	0.9651
Residuals	16	16,700		

Appendix

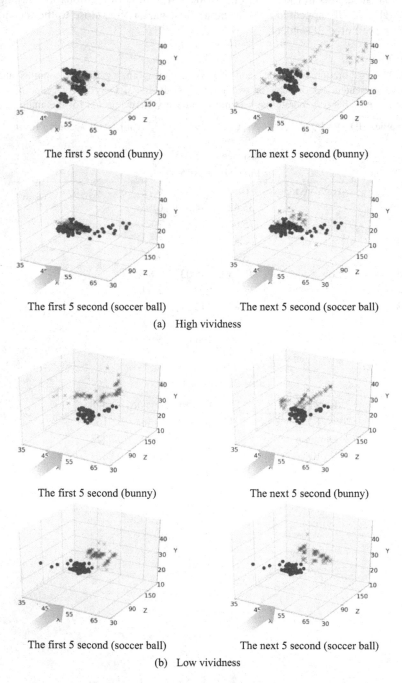

The first 5 second (bunny)   The next 5 second (bunny)

The first 5 second (soccer ball)   The next 5 second (soccer ball)

(a)   High vividness

The first 5 second (bunny)   The next 5 second (bunny)

The first 5 second (soccer ball)   The next 5 second (soccer ball)

(b)   Low vividness

Fig. 4. Distributions of 3D gaze points on generating mental imagery.

References

1. Kelly, K.P.: The Power of Visual Imagery: A Reading Comprehension Program for Students with Reading Difficulties, 1st edn. Corwin, Thousand Oaks (2006)
2. Marks, D.F.: Visual imagery differences in the recall of pictures. Br. J. Psychol. **64**, 17–24 (1973)
3. Cui, X., Jeter, C.B., Yang, D., Montague, P.R., Eagleman, D.M.: Vividness of mental imagery: Individual variability can be measured objectively. Vis. Res. **47**, 474–478 (2007)
4. Johansson, R., Holšánová, J., Holmqvist, K.: What do eye movements reveal about mental imagery? Evidence from visual and verbal elicitations. In: Proceedings of the 27th Annual Conference of the Cognitive Science Society, pp. 1054–1059 (2005)
5. Laeng, B., Bloem, I.M., D'Ascenzo, S., Tommasi, L.: Scrutinizing visual images: the role of gaze in mental imagery and memory. Cognition **131**, 263–283 (2014)

Poincaré Plot Indexes of Heart Rate Variability: Pattern II Responses and Mental Workload

Chi'e Kurosaka$^{(\boxtimes)}$, Hiroyuki Kuraoka, and Shinji Miyake

University of Occupational and Environmental Health, Japan, Kitakyushu, Japan
chie-k@health.uoeh-u.ac.jp

Abstract. We investigated the difference in the Poincaré plot indexes between Pattern I and Pattern II responses related to the sensory intake/rejection hypothesis. ECG s were recorded from 34 healthy participants during two resting periods and four mental tasks, i.e., mental arithmetic (MA), mirror tracing (MT), Embedded Figures Test (EFT), and Raven Progressive Matrix Test (RAVEN). MA tasks were performed in two conditions, i.e. machine-paced (MA-m) and self-paced (MA-s). The experimental procedure was divided into two sessions. Both began with a rest period and machine-paced MA task. In Session 1 this was followed by EFT and MT while in Session 2 this was followed by RAVEN and a self-paced MA task. NASA-TLX was used after each task to evaluate subjective mental workload. Mean RR interval, two parameters from Poincare plot, i.e. SD1 and SD2 were calculated. All indexes were standardized across eight blocks for each participant and were analyzed by repeated measures from ANOVA and the Tukey's HSD method. In results, NASA-TLX scores in MA-m1, MAm2, and MT were significantly higher than in other tasks, and were lower in MA-s and RAVEN ($p < .05$). RRIs were longer in MT than in other blocks. Poincaré plot parameters in MT showed distinctive changes in which SD1 was longer while SD2 was shorter. The combination of SD1 and SD2 in the Poincaré plot may be useful in the evaluation of mental workload for tasks including a specific attribute such as sensory intake characteristics.

Keywords: Poincaré plot · Mental workload · Heart rate variability

1 Introduction

The sensory intake/rejection hypothesis proposed that task induced physiological responses depend on the task characteristics [1]. Sensory rejection tasks such as mental arithmetic (MA) affect cardiac activity resulting in heart rate (HR) and blood pressure increase (Pattern I response). Contrastingly, sensory intake tasks such as mirror tracing (MT) tasks induce peripheral vascular contraction and HR decrease, (Pattern II response) [2]. Poincaré plot analysis may evaluate autonomic nervous system (ANS) activity [3]. We investigated the difference in Poincaré plot indexes between Pattern I responses and Pattern II responses by using four mental tasks with different task characteristics.

© Springer Nature Switzerland AG 2019
C. Stephanidis (Ed.): HCII 2019, CCIS 1033, pp. 238–243, 2019.
https://doi.org/10.1007/978-3-030-23528-4_33

2   Methods

2.1   Participants

Thirty-four healthy males ages 20–26 (mean 22.6 ± 1.9 yrs.) participated in this study. All participants provided written informed consent. This study was approved by the Ethics Committee of the University of Occupational and Environmental Health, Japan.

2.2   Physiological Measurement

ECG signals were recorded from the CM_5 lead throughout the experiment and RR intervals (RRI) were obtained by 1 kHz sampling.

2.3   Mental Workload

Mental Arithmetic Task (MA)
The MA task is based on the MATH algorithm proposed by Turner et al. [4]. A numerical calculation is displayed on a computer screen for 2 s, after which the target number is displayed following the word "EQUALS." Participants are required to press the left mouse button if the target number is correct and to click the right mouse button if not.

The MA tasks were performed in two conditions: machine-paced (MA-m) and self-paced (MA-s). In the MA-m condition, the next equation automatically appears after 1.5 s, whether participants responded or not. In the MA-s condition, the next equation will not be displayed until participants respond. The MA task contains five levels of difficulty as shown in Table 1. The initial question is always level 3. The next question level increases if the prior answer was correct and decreases if not.

Table 1. MA task level.

Level	Formula
1: easy	2-digit + 1-digit
2	2-digit ± 1-digit
3	2-digit ± 2-digit
4	3-digit + 2-digit
5: difficult	3-digit − 2-digit

Mirror Tracing Task (MT)
Participants are required to trace a zig-zag pathway on a computer screen with a mouse whose horizontal and vertical control elements are interchanged (Fig. 1). All participants were instructed to trace "as precisely as possible without deviating from the path way, but never hurry."

Fig. 1. Screen shot of MT.

Embedded Figures Test (EFT)
Participants are shown a simple figure and then required to find the simple figure in a complex design that is so patterned that each component of the simple figure is made part of a clear-cut sub whole of the pattern; the simple figure is thereby effectively hidden [5, 6].

Raven Progressive Matrix Test (RAVEN)
Eight abstract patterns are displayed in a picture and the ninth must be filled in. Participants are required to identify the rules on which the pattern is based and then select the appropriate pattern from eight given options [7].

2.4   Subjective Assessment

The National Aeronautics and Space Administration Task Load Index (NASA-TLX), a widely used subjective workload assessment technique, was used. It consists of six subscales: Mental Demand (MD), Physical Demand (PD), Temporal Demand (TD), Own Performance (OP), Effort (EF), and Frustration level (FR). The weighted workload (WWL) is calculated from the individual subscale scores and their respective weights obtained from the paired comparisons [8].

2.5   Procedure

The experimental procedure was divided into two sessions as shown in Fig. 2, and MA-m tasks were performed in both sessions following the 5-min resting periods. All tasks were performed for 5 min. The session order was randomized. NASA-TLX was used after each task to measure subjective mental workload.

2.6   Statistics Analysis

One participant was excluded from the analysis due to an incomplete data set. We calculated RRI averages and two Poincaré Plot parameters - the length of the transverse axis (SD1), and the length of the longitudinal axis (SD2) [3] in eight 5-min blocks: PRE-A, MA-mA, EFT, MT, PRE-B, MA-mB, RAVEN, and MA-s. All parameters

	PRE-A	MA-mA	EFT	MT
Session-A	5 min	5 min	5 min	5 min

	PRE-B	MA-mB	RAVEN	MA-s
Session-B	5 min	5 min	5 min	5 min

Fig. 2. Experimental procedure.

were standardized in each participant. Two resting periods and two MA-m blocks were calculated depending on the session order such as PRE-1, PRE-2, MA-m1 and MA-m2.

The results were analyzed by repeated measures of analysis of variance (ANOVA) in each block (SPSS statistics 19). The degree of freedom was adjusted using the Greenhouse-Geisser correction. Tukey's honestly significant difference (Tukey's HSD) test was used in the post-hoc analysis.

3   Results

Figure 3 shows the results for RRI in each block. Although there were no significant differences between MT and resting period, RRIs did increase in MT blocks relative to resting period blocks supposing that the MT task induced Pattern II responses.

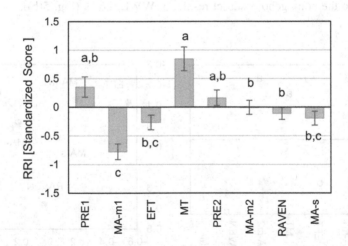

Fig. 3. RRI averages in each block. Bars indicated the standard errors of the mean. Letters indicate homogenous subset results by Tukey's HSD ($p < .05$).

Poincaré plot parameters, SD1 and SD2, in each block are shown in Fig. 4. The result of SD1 in MT was significantly longer than in the EFT ($p < .05$). SD2 in PRE2 was significantly longer than in several task blocks such as MA-m1, EFT, and MT ($p < .05$).

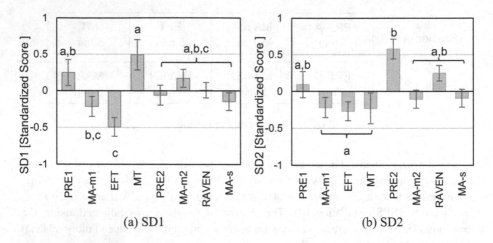

Fig. 4. Poincaré plot parameters in each block. The bars indicated the standard errors of the mean. Letters indicate homogenous subset results by Tukey's HSD.

Figure 5 shows NASA-TLX scores and scattergram of SD1 and SD2. Poincaré plot parameters were re-standardized in only six task blocks. WWL scores in MA-m1, MA-m2, and MT were significantly higher than in other tasks, and were lower in MA-s and RAVEN (Fig. 5(a)). The pair of SD1 and SD2 were plotted in each quadrant proportionate to the homogenous subset results in WWL scores (Fig. 5(b)).

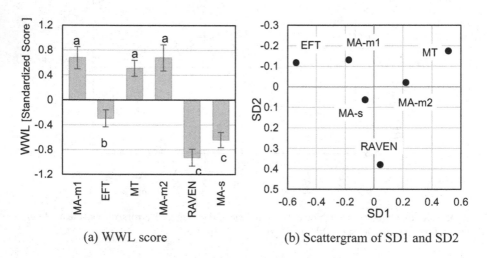

Fig. 5. WWL scores and scattergram of SD1 and SD2 in each task block.

4 Conclusion

It has been reported that SD2 was longer during relaxation and shorter during tension [9]. It is supposed that participants felt tension before the experiment. Contrastingly, participants adapted to the experiment's environment and were more relaxed in PRE-2, resulting in the longest SD2 in this study in PRE-2. Generally, the length of SD2 is short when the deviation of RRI is small, thereby the length of SD1 also shortens as shown in the result of EFT in Fig. 4. However, we found that the length of SD1 was longer when SD2 was shorter in MT. RRI was a sensitive physiological index to distinguish between Pattern I responses and Pattern II responses. However, it did not correspond to the subjective assessment such as WWL scores. Although subjective workload (WWL) scores in MT and MA are high, HR in MT is lower than in a resting period. Therefore, HR itself cannot be used to evaluate mental workload. As shown in this research, the combination of SD1 and SD2 from a Poincaré plot may be a valuable tool to evaluate mental workload when tasks include a specific attribute such as sensory intake characteristics.

References

1. Lacey, J.I.: Psychophysiological approaches to the evaluation of psychotherapeutic process and outcome. In: Rubinstein, E.A., Parloff, M.B. (eds.) Research in Psychotherapy, pp. 160–208. American Psychological Association, Washington, DC (1959)
2. Schneiderman, N., McCabe, M.: Psychophysiologic strategies in laboratory research. In: Schneiderman, N., Weiss, S.M., Kaufmann, P.G. (eds.) Handbook of research method in cardiovascular behavioral medicine, pp 349–364. Plenum Press, Berlin (1989)
3. Toichi, M., Sugiura, T., Murai, T., Sengoku, A.: A new method of assessing cardiac autonomic function and its comparison with spectral analysis and coefficient of variation of R-R interval. J. Auton. Nerv. Syst. 62(1–2), 79–84 (1997)
4. Turner, J.R., Heiwitt, J.K., Morgan, R.K., Sims, J., Carrol, D., Kelly, K.A.: Graded mental arithmetic as an active psychological challenge. Int. J. Psychophysiol. 3(4), 307–309 (1986)
5. Witkin, H.A., Goodenough, D.R.: Cognitive Styles: Field Dependence and Field Independence, p. 15. International Universities Press Inc., Madison (1981)
6. Wu, C.: Short-term memory and subjective evaluation on dynamic characters. Master Thesis, National Cheng Kung University (2003)
7. SCHUHFRIED website. https://www.schuhfried.com/assets/en/APM/APM.pdf. Accessed 15 Mar 2019
8. Hart, S.H., Staveland, L.E.: Development of NASA-TLX (task load index): result of empirical and theoretical research. In: Hancock, P.A., Meshkati, N. (Eds.) Human Mental Workload, North Holland, New York (1988)
9. Matsumoto, Y., Mori, N., Mitajiri, R., Jiang, Z.: Study of mental stress evaluation bases on analysis of heart rate variability. J. Life Support Eng. 22(3), 19–25 (2010)

The Characteristics and Modeling of the Surface Electromyography and Electrocardiogram of Human Fatigue During Pedaling

Zhongqi Liu[1,2], Xiaoze Yu[1,2], and Qianxiang Zhou[1,2(✉)]

[1] Key Laboratory for Biomechanics and Mechanobiology of the Ministry
of Education, School of Biological Science and Medical Engineering,
Beihang University, Beijing 100191, China
zqxg@buaa.edu.cn
[2] Beijing Advanced Innovation Centre for Biomedical Engineering,
Beihang University, Beijing 102402, China

Abstract. The fatigue of the pedaling exercise was studied in order to establish a fatigue analysis and evaluation model of the human pedaling. Twelve subjects participated in the pedaling test and the subjects completed six types of pedaling tasks at frequencies of 20, 30, 40, 50, and 60 times/min. Subjective fatigue, ECG signals, and surface EMG signals of subjects were measured. Principal component analysis (PCA) was used to extract the important indicators related to fatigue in sEMG signals and ECG signals, and the sEMG signal and ECG signal fatigue evaluation index were combined with the subjective fatigue evaluation data to establish the radial basis model of fatigue evaluation. The model based verification results show that the radial basis model has good accuracy and can effectively evaluate the pedaling fatigue.

Keywords: Pedaling movement · sEMG · ECG · Mechanical characteristics · Modeling

1 Introduction

Stepping and running are the process of continuous contraction and relaxation of the lower limb muscles of the human body based on gait movement. It is the premise of various production tasks, sports and daily life, and is one of the basic activities of the human body [1]. During long-term exertion or strenuous exercise, the number of muscle fibers recruited and the frequency of contraction increase, and the accumulation of metabolites, muscle soreness and swelling, and increased fatigue in the legs even cause leg muscle spasm occurring. If a reasonable rest is not arranged in time, the body function will take a long time to recover and even cause a permanent damage to the body and mind. How to effectively reduce the functional damage of the human body in the process of being forced, reasonable scheduling of intensity and time of task has always been one of the focused issues in occupational safety and health research.

© Springer Nature Switzerland AG 2019
C. Stephanidis (Ed.): HCII 2019, CCIS 1033, pp. 244–249, 2019.
https://doi.org/10.1007/978-3-030-23528-4_34

Surface electromyography signals and ECG signals are commonly used to evaluate human fatigue. Surface electromyography (sEMG) is the result of cumulative accumulation of action potentials in multiple spatial and temporal units of muscle tissue, reflecting movement of recruited fiber of muscles. With unfiltered raw EMG signals, Usama constructed an evaluation model by means of genetic algorithm and fuzzy logic theory to assess muscle force and fatigue [2]. Lorenz et al. applied six kinds of sEMG signal fatigue detecting algorithms for upper limb contraction motion fatigue detection [3]. Electrocardiogram (ECG) is the superposition of action potentials in the excitation of many cardiomyocytes, reflecting the level of comprehensive activity of cardiomyocytes. The changes of operator's heart rate are often used to characterize physical fatigue. Physical fatigue is measured by comparing the degree of changes of heart rate during the resting period, exercise period and recovery period. The ECG monitoring equipment developed in recent years has the characteristics of small size, high portability, convenient wearing, etc. It is convenient for ECG signal acquisition and analysis, and does not cause interference to the operator and can be used for continuous dynamic ECG monitoring and fatigue analysis. These two physiological signal acquisition processes do not cause harm to the human body, and thus are widely used in biomedicine, ergonomics, sports science, rehabilitation engineering and other fields. Through the detection of sEMG signals and ECG signal characteristics, effective physiological indicators could be obtained for fatigue evaluation [4, 5].

This study focused the fatigue problem of pedaling and running, and fatigue evaluation model would studied to makes reasonable arrangements for the workload and working time of physical labor in producing activity, and provide a theoretical basis for the design of sports training tasks making it more in line with ergonomic requirements.

2 Method

2.1 Participants

Twelve healthy male college students were screened as subjects by online recruitment. The subjects were (22.3 ± 2.55) years old, weight (72.56 ± 2.87) Kg, and height (173.13 ± 2.29) cm. The subjects were often running, without hypertension, diabetes and other serious medical history. There was no strenuous exercise 24 h ago before the experiment and have sufficient sleep and good mental state.

2.2 Apparatus and Task

During the experiment, the sEMG signal, ECG signal, pedaling time, temperature and humidity of laboratory, and subjective fatigue degree scores of the subjects were collected. The equipment to be used is as follows:

(1) sEMG signal acquisition device
    JE-TB0810 was selected to obtain sEMG and it was wireless. Its sampling frequency was 1000 Hz.

(2) ECG signal acquisition equipment

The MP150 was selected to collect the ECG signal. The ECG100C ECG module was used in this experiment, and the sampling rate was set to 1000 Hz.

(3) Power bicycle

A magnetically controlled horizontal lower limb power bicycle was selected as the pedaling device.

2.3 Experimental Tasks

As shown in Fig. 1, according to the fixed frequency rhythm of the metronome, the subjects completed 6 sets of pedaling tasks on the power bicycle in the frequencies of 20, 30, 40, 50, 60 times/min. The bicycle power of pedaling load was fixed, and each group pedaling time was 5 min. After completing a group of pedaling tasks, rest for 5 min and then proceed to the next group of pedaling task. According to the Borg scale of Table 1, the subject answered the feeling of his fatigue every 1 min. The sEMG signals and ECG signals were collected during the pedaling and rest periods.

Fig 1. The subject's pedaling exercise experiment

Table 1. Borg scale

Score	Qualitative description
0	Nothing
0.5	Extremely light
1	Very light
2	Weak (light)
3	Mild
4	Slightly stronger
5	Strong
6	Middle strong
7	Very strong
8	Extremely strong

3 Results

3.1 sEMG Index

Taking 10 s as a signal segmentation, the sEMG signals of the two states of pedaling, running exercise and post-exercise rest were calculated and analyzed, and the average value of the test data of the time domain, frequency domain, and nonlinearity of the myoelectric signal such as the gastrocnemius muscle, the rectus femoris, biceps femoris, lateral femoral muscle, tibialis anterior muscle, etc.

(1) Time domain indicator
   The index raised in the process of dynamic force exertion. After long-term force exertion of high load, the IEMG and RMS decreased.
(2) Frequency domain indicators
   During the rest period after exercise, MPF and MF decreased.
   The trend of the frequency domain index in the exercise phase was consistent with the trend of rest period. MF value and the MPF value both declined, and the declining trend of MF index was more obvious than the MNF indicator.
(3) Wavelet packet transform
   After the exercise, the total energy value of the wavelet packet increased. In the state of motion, the energy value of the wavelet packet raised in a stepwise manner.
   In the last group of pedaling exercise, the wavelet packet energy value of the thigh muscle muscles of the rectus femoris, lateral femoral muscles and biceps femoris showed a downward trend. In the post-exercise resting and exercise state, the wavelet packet energy value of the thigh muscle was larger than that of the calf muscle index.
(4) Nonlinear indicators
   During the rest period, the LZC complexity decreased. The LZC complexity of the rectus femoris, biceps femoris, and lateral femoral muscles of the thigh muscles had more obvious change than that of the calf muscles. The Lyapunov exponent and Renyi entropy showed a decreasing trend, but the change was not obvious.
   During the exercise phase, the LZC complexity decreased. The Lyapunov exponent and the Renyi entropy decreased in a stepwise manner. However, the entropy of the tibialis anterior and lateral mandibular muscles decreased obviously.

3.2 ECG Signal Index

(1) Time domain indicator
   At rest, the SDNN, SDANN and NN50 increased gradually. The RMSSD, PNN50, and SDNNI decreased, but the trend was not obvious.
   During the exercise state, The SDNN, SDANN, and NN50 indicators gradually increased. The SDNNI index gradually decreased. The change of RMSSD and PNN50 indicators was unstable with the exercise time.

(2) Frequency domain indicators
    In the rest period after exercising, the LF, LF/HF and LFnorm, increased.
    During the exercise phase, the LF, LF/HF increased, and the HF showed a downward trend.

3.3 Subjective Fatigue Data

As showed in Table 2, as the exercise process continuing, the subjective fatigue evaluation value increased. In the early exercise process, the subjects were relaxed, and the breathing was steady and slow, and the human perception ability, exercise ability and work efficiency were at a high level. Meanwhile, the subjective fatigue evaluation average was 1.4. At this time, the subjects were in an indefatigability state.

As the exercise progressed, the body's metabolism was accelerated; the respiratory rate and sweat secretion increased, and the fatigue was enhanced. When the exercise reaches the final stage, the fatigue evaluation score was 7.6. After six stages of exercise, the subjects themselves felt tired subjectively, and sense of fatigue appeared.

Table 2. One-way ANOVA data of subjective fatigue assessment

Statistical indicators	Mean value	Variance	Significant level
Stage1	1.4	0.548	0.004
Stage2	2.8	0.837	0.001
Stage3	4	1	0.001
Stage4	5.4	0.548	0.001
Stage5	6.6	0.894	0.001
Stage6	7.6	0.578	0.001

3.4 Fatigue Feature Index Extraction

Correlation analysis between EMG and ECG signal and subjective fatigue evaluation showed that with the progress of exercise process, EMG signal time domain index, IEMG, RMS, frequency domain index MPF, MNF, wave packet energy, wavelet packet Entropy, 60–90 Hz band energy ratio, 90–120 Hz band energy ratio, LZC complexity, Lyapunov exponent, Renyi entropy and other changes are related to subjective fatigue evaluation. There were correlations between SDN, SDANN and LF in ECG signal indicators and subjective fatigue evaluation. Therefore, the physiological signal index described above was selected as objective physiological data for fatigue evaluation.

4 Fatigue Modeling

According to the subjective fatigue evaluation data, the fatigue level was divided, and the corresponding fatigue state of the physiological index was obtained. The Borg scale scores 0–3 for the relaxed state, 4–6 for the mild fatigue state, and 7 points or more for the fatigue state. The sEMG signal was integrated with the ECG signal fatigue evaluation index, and combined with the subjective fatigue evaluation classification label corresponding to the physiological index, 70% of the data was randomly selected as the training data, and the remaining 30% data was used as the test set data for verifying the generalization ability of the model. The polynomial kernel function, the radial basis kernel function and the Sigmoid kernel function were selected to map the training data set. Meanwhile, Three kinds of three-class supporting vector machine models with different kernel functions were trained, and the classification effect was judged by the classification accuracy rate. The results were as follows. As shown in Table 3, the model constructed by the radial basis kernel function had the highest accuracy. Using the pedaling motion testing set data to verify the generalization performance of the model, the classification accuracy rate for pedaling exercise fatigue was 89%.

Table 3. Training results of classification model

Kernel function	Loss function parameter (c)	Regularization parameter (g)	Accuracy rate
Polynomial	5.015	0.568	91.2%
Radial basis	5.278	0.574	92.2%
Sigmiod	4.285	0.536	90.4%

References

1. Yuan, Y.C., Wan, L.H., et al.: Principles of rehabilitation for common chronic neurologic diseases in the elderly. J. Clin. Gerontol. Geriatr. **3**, 5–13 (2012)
2. Usama, J.N.: Artificial intelligence methods to estimate muscle force and muscle fatigue in human arm based on EMG signal. Huazhong University of Science & Technology, Wuhan, China (2013)
3. Kahl, L., Hofmann, U.G.: Comparison of algorithms to quantify muscle fatigue in upper limb muscles based on sEMG signals. Med. Eng. Phys. **38**(11), 1260–1269 (2016)
4. Zhuang, J.J., Huang, X.L., Ning, X.B., et al.: Spectral analysis of heart rate variability applied in the exercise of professional shooting athletes. In: The 7th Asian-Pacific Conference on Medical and Biological Engineering, APCMBE, Beijing, China, pp. 326–328 (2008)
5. Kiryu, T., Motomiya, N., Ushiyama, Y., et al.: Snapshot evaluation of fatigue during skiing exercise. In: Proceedings of the 20th Annual International Conference of the IEEE Engineering in Medicine and Biology Society, IEMBS, Hong Kong, China, pp. 2775–2778 (1998)

EEG Acquisition During the VR Administration of Resting State, Attention, and Image Recognition Tasks: A Feasibility Study

Greg Rupp[1]([✉]), Chris Berka[1], Amir Meghdadi[1],
Marissa C. McConnell[1], Mike Storm[2], Thomas Z. Ramsøy[2],
and Ajay Verma[3]

[1] Advanced Brain Monitoring Inc., Carlsbad, CA, USA
grupp@b-alert.com
[2] Neurons Inc., Taastrup, Denmark
[3] United Neuroscience, Dublin, Ireland

Abstract. The co-acquisition of EEG in a virtual environment (VE) would give researchers and clinicians the opportunity to acquire EEG data with millisecond-level temporal resolution while participants performed VE activities. This study integrated Advanced Brain Monitoring's (ABM) X-24t EEG hardware with the HTC Vive VR headset and investigated EEG differences in tasks delivered in two modalities: VE and a desktop computer.

EEG was acquired from 10 healthy individuals aged 24–75 with a 24-channel wireless EEG system. This was synchronized with a resting-state eyes open/closed task in both dark and bright environments, a sustained attention task (3-Choice Vigilance Task, 3CVT) and an image memory task. These tasks, along with resting data, were collected in a VR-administered VE as well as on a desktop computer. Event-related potentials (ERPs) were investigated for target trials for SIR and 3CVT. Power spectral analysis was performed for the resting-state tasks.

A within-subject comparison showed no differences in the amplitudes of the Late Positive Potential (LPP) in 3CVT when comparing tasks administered in the VE and the desktop. Upon visual inspection, the grand average waveforms are similar between the two acquisition modalities. EEG alpha power was greatest during resting state eyes closed in a dark VR environment.

This project demonstrated that ABM's B-alert X24t hardware and acquisition software could be successfully integrated with the HTC Vive (programmed using Unreal Engine 4). This will allow high quality EEG data to be acquired with time-locked VR stimulus delivery with temporal resolution at the millisecond level. As expected, a within-subjects analysis of cognitive ERPs revealed no significant differences in the EEG measures between Desktop and VR AMP acquisitions. This shows that the task administration in a VE does not alter the neural pathways activated in sustained attention and memory tasks.

Keywords: EEG · Event related potential · Virtual Reality (VR) ·
Attention and memory · Integration

C. Stephanidis (Ed.): HCII 2019, CCIS 1033, pp. 250–258, 2019.
https://doi.org/10.1007/978-3-030-23528-4_35

1   Introduction

A growing number of virtual reality (VR) devices are commercially available and deliver an immersive experience to the end-user. This technology was developed primarily for gaming and has been scaled such that the price point is not unreasonable for much of the population. The potential application of these VR systems to the research and clinical domains is considerable. Specifically, the potential co-acquisition of EEG and VR is of great importance as it would give researchers and clinicians the opportunity to acquire EEG data with millisecond level temporal resolution while the participant is immersed in a virtual environment (VE). Today's VR technology allows for delivery of a realistic VE allowing comparisons of EEG metrics and responses evoked by VEs versus similar presentations on desktop or other 2D environments.

The amount of research involving EEG and VR is growing steadily. The efficacy of using VEs to enhance simulated environments has been demonstrated in a wide range of fields, from psycholinguistics to education to driving simulation [1–6]. In one study, VR and EEG were integrated into a Virtual Reality Therapy System that used EEG to measure VR-induced changes in brain states associated with relaxation [6]. It is clear that VR, used in combination with EEG, can be a tool for delivering and creating novel and enhanced environments designed for assessments or therapeutic interventions.

Advanced Brain Monitoring (ABM) has developed a collection of neurocognitive tests collectively referred to as the Alertness and Memory Profiler (AMP). AMP is a neurocognitive testbed designed to be administered while simultaneously recording EEG/ECG with a wireless and portable headset that acquires 20 channels of EEG and transmits digitized data via Bluetooth to a laptop. AMP consists of sustained attention, working memory, and recognition memory tests that are automatically delivered and time-locked to the EEG to generate event-related potentials (ERPs). In prior work ABM demonstrated the potential utility for ERP measures acquired with AMP as sensitive early stage biomarkers indicative of the cognitive deficits associated with Mild Cognitive Impairment.

In the present study, the integration potential of ABM's B-Alert X24t headset with the HTC Vive™ VR headset was assessed. This was done in two ways: the physical integration of the hardware and software, and the EEG measures collected during the AMP tasks. The aim was to achieve millisecond level time syncing between the EEG and VR headsets, ensure comfort for the user, and ascertain whether or not there were significant EEG differences between tasks administered on the desktop computer and tasks administered in the VR environment.

2   Methods

2.1   Participants

Ten healthy individuals ranging from 24 to 75 years old were recruited and screened to serve as participants. Data was acquired at the study site at 9:00 am. The VR AMP and Desktop AMP acquisition were done at least one week apart (in no particular order) to minimize any practice and or/memory effects.

2.2   B-Alert® X24 EEG Headset

EEG was acquired using the B-Alert® X24 wireless sensor headset (Advanced Brain Monitoring, Inc, Carlsbad, CA). This system has 20-channels of EEG located according to the International 10–20 system at FZ, FP1, FP2, F3, F4, F7, F8, CZ, C3, C4, T3, T4, T5, T6, O1, O2, PZ, POz, P3, and P4 referenced to linked mastoids. Data were sampled at 256 Hz.

2.3   VR EEG Acquisitions

The participants were administered AMP that had been adapted to the HTC Vive™ Steam Software (Fig. 1). The participants were given a few minutes to acclimate themselves to the virtual reality room that simulated the room in which the acquisition was occurring.

Fig. 1. The B-Alert/HTC Vive integrated system

Fig. 2. The 3CVT task in the VE. A NonTarget image is being presented.

The protocol for the VR AMP acquisition was as follows:

- Resting State Eyes Open in a VE with normal indoor lighting (RSEO-Bright, 5 min)
- Resting State Eyes Closed in a VE with normal indoor lighting (RSEC-Bright, 5 min)

- 3-Choice Vigilance Task (3CVT test of sustained attention, 20 min)
- 10 min break
- Resting State Eyes Open in a VE without any lighting (RSEO-Dark, 5 min)
- Resting State Eyes Closed in a VE without any lighting (RSEC-Dark, 5 min)

The 3CVT requires participants to discriminate between Target, frequent stimuli (right side up triangle), from NonTarget and Interference infrequent stimuli (upside down triangle and diamond, Fig. 2). Afterwards, the original EO and EC tasks were repeated, but were performed within a darkened virtual room.

2.4 Desktop EEG Acquisition

The procedure was the same for the desktop EEG AMP acquisition. The only difference is that there were no RSEO or RSEC dark tasks, as light could not be effectively controlled in the room where the acquisitions occurred.

2.5 Power Spectral Density and Event Related Potential Calculation

For 3CVT, raw EEG signals were filtered between 0.1 and 50 Hz using a Hamming windowed Sinc FIR filter (8449 point filtering with a 0.1 Hz transition band width). For each event type, EEG data were epoched from 1 s before until 2 s after the stimulus onset. The baseline was adjusted using data from 100 ms before the stimulus onset. Trials were rejected if the absolute value of EEG amplitude in any channel during a window of −50 ms to +750 ms (compared to the stimulus onset) was larger than a threshold level of 100 µV. Independent component analysis (ICA) was performed using EEGLAB software to detect and reject components classified as having sources other than the brain. Moreover, epochs with abnormally distributed data, improbable data, or with abnormal spectra were also removed using Grand average of ERPs in each condition and trial type was calculated by using a weighted average using the number of ERPs in each condition as the weights.

For the resting state tasks, Data was bandpass filtered (1–40 Hz) Power spectral densities were computed using Fast Fourier Transform with Kaiser Window on one second windows with 50% overlap. The total power in each frequency bin 1 to 40 Hz and 9 frequency bandwidths were computed for each epochs and were averaged across all the epochs during each session. Artifact was detected using ABM's proprietary artifact detection algorithms, and epochs contained more than 25% bad (having artifact) data points were excluded from analysis.

3 Results

3.1 Signal Quality

The signal quality during the VR EEG acquisition was comparable to that of the desktop acquisitions. Table 1 summarizes this data.

Table 1. Average number of clean epochs (or clean trials for ERP tasks) compared between VR and Desktop during each task

Task	RSEO Bright	RSEC Bright	3CVT
VR	154	194	177
Desktop	186	204	209

3.2   EEG Differences Between Desktop and VR Resting State in a Bright Environment

In all three conditions of resting state (Desktop Bright, VR Bright and VR Dark), as expected, alpha power was significantly greater (p < 0.01) at all channels during RSEC (eyes closed) compared to RSEO (eyes open). Figure 3 depicts this finding for Desktop Bright – VR Bright and Dark are not shown).

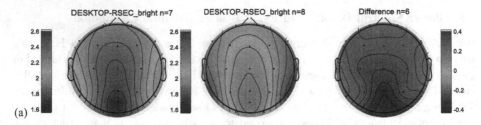

Fig. 3. Alpha power during resting state eyes closed compared to resting state eyes open for the desktop bright modality

When comparing resting state EEG during VR and Desktop acquisitions, there was no within subject significant difference in Alpha power during RSEO (Fig. 4) and RSEC (not pictured).

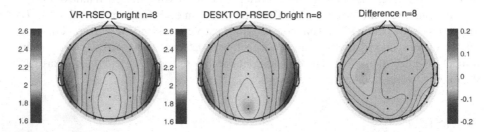

Fig. 4. Alpha power during VR (left) and desktop (center) RSEO. The rightmost figure displays a difference map

3.3   Resting State Alpha Power in a Bright vs. Dark VR Environment

In VR during the eyes open task, alpha power was significantly greater ($p < 0.01$) in the dark environment compared to the bright environment at all channels (Fig. 5). There was no significant difference between the dark and bright environments with eyes closed.

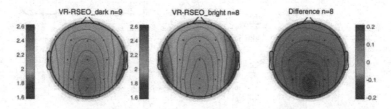

Fig. 5. Differences in Alpha power between Dark and Light VEs for RSEO

3.4   Event Related Potentials and Performance During 3CVT

There were no significant performance differences between Desktop and VR 3CVT (Fig. 6).

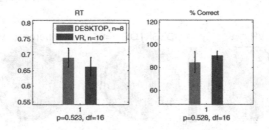

Fig. 6. The performance metrics shown are reaction time (left) and percent correct (right)

Figure 7 displays the grand average for the two 3CVT modalities examined in this study. Upon visual inspection, the 3CVT ERP waveforms from the Desktop and VR acquisitions do not significantly differ.

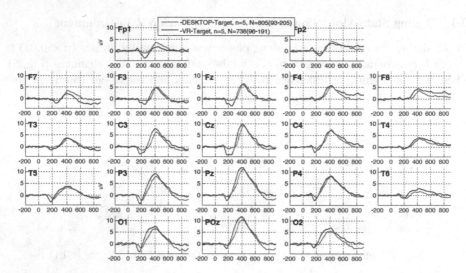

Fig. 7. Grand average plots for all participants for desktop and VR 3CVT Target (frequent) trials.

A within-subject comparison of the amplitude of the late positive potential (LPP) was computed for both Desktop and VR 3CVT Target (frequent) trials. There was no significant difference at any channel between VR and Desktop acquisitions (Fig. 8).

Fig. 8. LPP differences between VR and Desktop 3CVT Target (frequent) trials.

Additionally, the target effect, which is the difference in LPP amplitude between Target and NonTarget trials for each participant, is shown in Fig. 9. There was no significant difference in target effect between the VR and Desktop 3CVT.

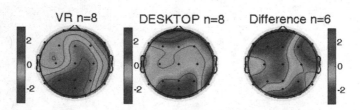

Fig. 9. Target effect for VR and Desktop 3CVT

4 Discussion

This project demonstrated that ABM's B-alert X24 hardware and acquisition software could be successfully integrated with the HTC Vive (programmed using Unreal Engine 4) to allow high quality EEG data to be acquired with time-locked VR stimulus delivery with temporal resolution at the millisecond level. As expected, a within-subjects analysis revealed no significant differences in the EEG measures between Desktop and VR AMP acquisitions.

This preliminary evaluation suggests the integrated systems could prove useful for numerous clinical and research applications. However, there are several issues that will need to be addressed prior to widespread adoption of VR-EEG. The HTC Vive weighs 1.04 lb and exerts significant pressure on a subject's face, causing discomfort and in some cases neck strain. The device is bulky with several heavy wires, making it somewhat difficult to be mobile while wearing the device. An improvement in form factor of the HTC Vive could ameliorate these problems and increase the comfort of the participant, allowing for longer acquisitions. There is also potential for further integration with the ABM EEG headsets. For example, the capability of integrating the EEG electrodes with the Vive headset would result in a lighter and more comfortable system.

Thus, the HTC Vive appears to be a promising tool for future research as it allows participants to be fully immersed in a given environment without changing the core neurological signatures associated with attention, learning and memory. There are many potential applications of VR as it offers realistic 3-D experiences, for example the measurement of Optic flow. Optic flow (OF) refers to the perception and integration of the visual field as one moves through a physical environment. Specifically "radial optic flow" involves the perception of motion around a central visual field when there is change in scenery from self-directed movement or from objects moving towards or away from the observer [7, 8].

Radial OF has been extensively studied in association with neurodegenerative disease, particularly Alzheimer's disease (AD) and amnestic MCI (aMCI) [7–10, 11, 12]. Psychophysical testing confirmed OF impairment in AD but not in aMCI, however the neurophysiological studies revealed sensory (early components P100 and N130), perceptual and cognitive ERP component differences for OF tasks in AD and differences in the cognitive ERP components for aMCI during a variety of experimental paradigms designed to stimulate OF [7, 9]. The primary finding across studies of AD patients is longer latency and reduced amplitude of the P200. In one study of aMCI patients the latency of the P200 was inversely correlated with MMSE suggesting a link to cognitive decline.

These ERP changes are also highly correlated with impairments in navigational abilities in AD [7, 9, 11]. Interestingly, not all AD or MCI patients show the ERP changes and there have been several reports that older adults with no neurodegenerative disease evidence ERP change in OF and impaired navigational capabilities. Additional research is required to further delineate the differences across AD, MCI and controls, associate the findings with regional differences in structure or function (MRI, fMRI and

PET) and to better understand the relationships with cognitive decline and navigational abilities.

There is currently no standardized method for testing patients for OF although OF deficiencies may be inferred following a comprehensive ophthalmological work-up [8]. There are multiple computerized tests as well as OF training protocols reported in the literature however, there is no consensus on the size, color, shape or other dimensions of the visual stimuli used to evoke OF. All these approaches are administered to non-mobile participants and thus can only evaluate the perceived movements within the display. In contrast, the virtual reality (VR) environment offers a rich array of potential test environments for simulating the 3-dimensional characteristic of true OF as encountered during locomotion.

However, this application of an integrated VR/EEG headset is not the only use case. VEs could also provide an opportunity to assess "skill in activities of daily living" embedding various tests of attention and memory such as recalling shopping lists, finding items in the store and adding up dollar amounts prior to check-out.

References

1. Baka, E., et al.: An EEG-based evaluation for comparing the sense of presence between virtual and physical environments. In: Proceedings of Computer Graphics International 2018, pp. 107–116. ACM, Bintan Island (2018)
2. Tromp, J., et al.: Combining EEG and virtual reality: the N400 in a virtual environment. In: The 4th Edition of the Donders Discussions (DD 2015), Nijmegen, Netherlands (2015)
3. Lin, C.-T., et al.: EEG-based assessment of driver cognitive responses in a dynamic virtual-reality driving environment. IEEE Trans. Biomed. Eng. **54**(7), 1349–1352 (2007)
4. Makransky, G., Terkildsen, T.S., Mayer, R.E.: Adding immersive virtual reality to a science lab simulation causes more presence but less learning. Learn. Instr. **60**, 225–236 (2017)
5. Slobounov, S.M., et al.: Modulation of cortical activity in 2D versus 3D virtual reality environments: an EEG study. Int. J. Psychophysiol. **95**(3), 254–260 (2015)
6. Slobounov, S.M., Teel, E., Newell, K.M.: Modulation of cortical activity in response to visually induced postural perturbation: combined VR and EEG study. Neurosci. Lett. **547**, 6–9 (2013)
7. Tata, M.S., et al.: Selective attention modulates electrical responses to reversals of optic-flow direction. Vis. Res. **50**(8), 750–760 (2010)
8. Albers, M.W., et al.: At the interface of sensory and motor dysfunctions and Alzheimer's disease. Alzheimers Dement **11**(1), 70–98 (2015)
9. Yamasaki, T., et al.: Selective impairment of optic flow perception in amnestic mild cognitive impairment: evidence from event-related potentials. J. Alzheimers Dis. **28**(3), 695–708 (2012)
10. Kim, N.G.: Perceiving collision impacts in alzheimer's disease: the effect of retinal eccentricity on optic flow deficits. Front Aging Neurosci. **7**, 218 (2015)
11. Hort, J., Laczó, J., Vyhná Lek, M., Bojar, M., Bureš, J., Vlček, K.: Spatial navigation deficit in amnestic mild cognitive impairment (n.d.)
12. Kavcic, V., Vaughn, W., Duffy, C.J.: Distinct visual motion processing impairments in aging and alzheimer's disease. Vis. Res. **51**(3), 386–395 (2012). https://doi.org/10.1016/j.visres.2010.12.004

HCI Design for Mobile Devices with a Sensor System for Performance Diagnostic in Sports

Matthias Stecker, Robin Nicolay$^{(\boxtimes)}$, and Alke Martens

IEF, IFI, University of Rostock,
Albert-Einstein-Str. 22, 18119 Rostock, Germany
{robin.nicolay, alke.martens}@uni-rostock.de

Abstract. Newly designed sport sensors and health applications provide many new information on vital parameters, such as oxygen saturation of muscles, tissue hemoglobin, and pulse index. So far there are only visualizations which show sophisticated vital parameters after workout. In this paper we describe constraints on parameter visualization during workouts and introduce a new mobile visualization concept allowing live adjustment of workouts.

Keywords: HCI in sport · Mobile devices · Sensor feedback

1 Introduction

HCI design for mobile device and the investigation of interaction scenarios related to sport activities are comparably new fields for scientific research. Nonetheless, a lot has happened here in the last years. Several system developers have appeared on the market with different sport tracking systems, including additional health information [1–3]. The additional information can be separated into hard parameters, which are measured by the mobile device, (e.g. pulse), and soft parameters, which are algorithmically estimated, (e.g. sleeping time). A comparison can be found in [4]. In contrast, the combination of mobile devices with a specialized sensor system, e.g. for performance diagnostic in sports, is an area, which has been barely been exploited in its possibilities so far, for neither industry nor HCI Design research at Universities. A very recent development is the integration of an ECG App in the Apple WatchOS5.2 [3a], which is in use primarily for healthcare. However, there might be a broad range of possible users and many potential applications – one leading to masses of new data for exploring the potential usage in new fields and the quality of usage of mobile devices in everyday settings. We have learned all of this over several years of research, working together with the industrial partner OXY 4 and the University of Applied Sciences in a funded research project called Train4U. In this research project, OXY4 developed a sensor, which measured four crucial vital parameters: oxygen saturation of the muscle (SmO_2), tissue hemoglobin index, pulse rate and pulse index. All of which are very important and helpful measurements for an athlete to improve his/her workout. So far, there are only visualizations, which show the results after the workout is done. Currently in mobile devises there exists rudimentary visualization of these important parameters in real time during training activity and in a non-laboratory setting. For example, the

© Springer Nature Switzerland AG 2019
C. Stephanidis (Ed.): HCII 2019, CCIS 1033, pp. 259–264, 2019.
https://doi.org/10.1007/978-3-030-23528-4_36

classical way to investigate blood parameters like oxygen saturation is the blood test or by using a spirooxymetrie both of which are preformed in a lab and are not available under real conditions. Results are sometimes shown to the athlete, but are usually interpreted by the trainer or the physician and thus, in most cases, not designed for instant real-time feedback for the athlete at training time. Our partners developed a sensor which should, in the end, give the same insights as a blood test or spiro-test, but are non-invasive and deliver the results in real time. The sensor itself is small and can be carried in a sleeve or pouch and easily worn by the athlete during training [5].

Therefore, in this project we decided to develop a visualization for mobile devices according to the measurements of a sensor system for performing diagnostic in sports. The mobile devices used for our application were either a smartphone and/or a smart watch. The visualization on the mobile device shows all of the vital parameters mentioned above. After an empirical investigation of athletes of different areas, we decided on a traffic light system to show, for example, the range of SmO_2 during performance. Our application consisted of the visualization and an underlying expert system [6], which analyses the constantly submitted sensor data, takes additional soft parameters into account, and calculates the threshold of the range. All these aspects will be explicated in more detail in the following sections.

2 HCI Design Decision for Mobile Devices in Sports

Development for a mobile platform has a completely different focus than development for a desktop platform (e.g. [1, 2]). On mobile devices, the soft- and hardware challenges are entirely different. The software-challenges include the limitation of the operation system (OS), including design guidelines given by the OS, differing menu structure and navigation, the limitation of icons and images, as well as the software implementation. The hardware-challenges include the display limitation, input- and output capabilities and the requirement for mobility designing. These challenges are further extended by tracking sport activities. To allow for a scientific analysis of the field we decided to distinguish two forms of usage of sport applications: active mode and passive mode. Necessarily, the design of the HCI has to be different in both cases: during the active mode when the athlete preforms the workout and gets a visualization of his/her vital parameters at training time (i.e. in real-time), and during the passive mode when the workout is analyzed by the trainer or the athlete post-performance. Problems can arise during the active mode- it is difficult to capture all of the information in a short time. We find here the situation classified by Dunlop [1] as "Design for limited in- and output". The athlete needs quick information and can, in most cases, not extensively interact with the devise or has no interest to investigate any menus or similar navigation activities during a workout. Additionally, especially for smart watches, sweat on the display can cause further issues. During a sports activity, the athlete is focused on the performance of their body and not on information processing or interaction. Professional athletes claimed in our interviews that too much information from the mobile device during training was distracting. Thus, a smaller level of detail and an instant recognition of information, in the form of alarms for example, is needed. Subsequently, more detailed information can be shown in the passive use of the application. The athlete, his/her trainer, or physician can look at the analyzed data, compare it, discuss is, and take different snapshots at different points in time. Moreover, comparison with other soft parameters (e.g. food, sleep, etc.) can be easily reflected in the data analysis in the passive mode.

Another challenge of the sports sector is the development of stand-alone-devices. Moreover, there are only a few sensors that currently support performance diagnostics in the sport sector. Most of the sensors that have already been developed are used in laboratories [7, 8]. Our sensor system is based on OXY4's system (DR2) which contains a near-infrared spectroscopy (NIRS) [9]. The sensor measures vital parameters and the application calculates, analyzes, visualizes and saves the measurements. Furthermore, the sensor can be used for professional as well as amateur athletes. Additional challenges appeared to bring the visualization for these two groups in line. The HCI design is different for professional and amateur athletes. They have, for example, completely different training goals and workflows. Moreover, the sensor has to be designed for many types of amateur and professional athletes. A cyclist may desire to fix the mobile device in front of him/her on the bicycle, whereas a runner carries the device in a pocket or on his arm. If this position is not occupied by the sensor the measurements would be inadequate for the athlete. To solve this specific problem OXY4 made it possible for the sensor to be mounted at various locations (e.g. on the leg or arm). Additionally, we decided to develop the application for a smart watch as well. The interaction with the sensor was realized with Bluetooth, and later with ANT+.

To lay the foundation for our development we investigated current smart watches and fitness or health apps as well as interviewed professional and amateur athletes, including those who, from time to time, train or participate in sports. We have investigated most of the fitness apps and all available smart watches in 2016 and 2017 [4]. Through the investigation of current sport medical practices and a questionnaire with 130 amateur athletes we examined these differences between amateur and professional athletes in relation to devise and system design. In our questionnaire, we asked the participants what their experience is with influencing parameters. We found that a majority of the participants believe that parameters of sleep, weather and nutrition influences the quality of their training. Furthermore, they identified the consumption level of protein, alcohol and caffeine as key factors that influence athletic performance. As a result, we reflected these insights in a rule system on the expert system level, where the professional or amateur athlete can decide, which items affect his/her training quality. We have integrated this in the app in the form of a pre-workout evaluation - see Fig. 2. Both can be done on the mobile device, preferably a smart phone, or on a stationary computer.

We developed two mobile interfaces, which can both be used on a smart phone and smart watch. The display is separated into four parts, which reflect the sensor parameters - see Fig. 1. The application provides a feedback system, which informs the user of a critical performance level by warnings and alarms - see Fig. 2. Immediately following the completion of activity, the user receives feedback in various ways. One of which may be a text to their smart phone devise. Another form is the traffic light color system which has been extended to an alert mode: red meaning the pre-set parameters have been surpasses, yellow meaning the pre-set parameters are close to being exceeded, and green meaning the athlete is under or within the pre-set parameters. The second level of information for the athlete then is the number in percent or direct (pulse rate), alternatively a text, telling the user that the value is too high/too low. This was due to the application scenario, where we have the requirement to realize a pure visual feedback (as acoustic and haptic is not working). In larger displays, we can combine the traffic light alerts and text information - see Fig. 2.

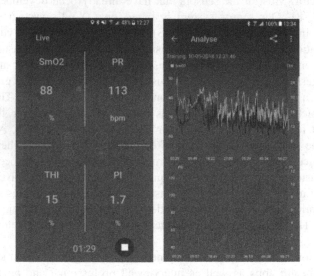

Fig. 1. (Color figure online)

The passive mode tracks the sensor information on a finer grained level - this can be seen in Fig. 1. Here, the system shows the trajectory of each parameter during each training, for several trainings and in different comparative modes.

The programmed application was then tested by a small group of amateur athletes who responded positively to the device and corresponding application. We found out that for example runners wearing the smart watch on the wrist were in most cases able to react to sensor feedback (haptic). In contrast to that, cyclists didn't use a watch, and had the device fixed on their bike. Thus, they didn't want to have haptic feedback during their workout. The most interesting result was that football players, who tested the device, didn't feel the haptic signal during training time. Surprisingly we found that most athletes didn't want to have acoustic feedback and, in most cases did not recognize it, during training time. Additionally, tests with different design alternatives showed in our case, that the cyclic display (used for example by Apple Watch 4 Activity Tracker [12]) with the traffic light system is perceived to be confusing and not easy to read during sport activities.

In the development and testing of the device, there arose some problems in regard to the connection between the devices. Here, these problems were in relation to the preciseness of data exchange and limited battery range of either sensor and/or mobile device. Our results were then used by OXY4 to further improve the quality of their sensor.

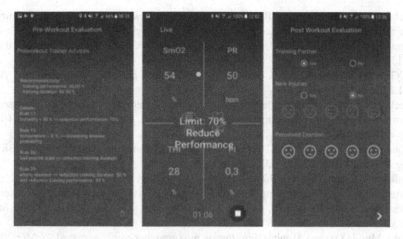

Fig. 2. (Color figure online)

3 Conclusion and Outlook

In the project Train4U we have investigated a field, where a new sensor is used in sport activity with the goal to give real-time feedback to professional and amateur athletes. Research and development of sensors are at the forefront of professional and amateur sports – they are integrated directly in mobile devices (count of steps, heart rate and even pulse or most modern ECG). Recently the trend has been towards the development of special mobile watches for sport applications, called fitness watches. However, regarding the broad range of possibilities which are now available for "normal" smart watches, we predict that fitness watches will not be a future project. The combination of a health sensor and a mobile device, e.g. a smartphone or smart watch, leads to new demands regarding HCI.

The most interesting result from the HCI design perspective has been the different ideas amateur athletes had about the design and feedback. Our application is currently developed for Android, but can be transferred to all platforms. Additional examination of the system is needed since the device has yet to be get tested by professional athletes.

Acknowledgement. Our research project has been funded by the EU, The European Fond for Regional Development, under the project number TBI-V-1-120-VBW-042. We thank the funders and our partners for the support and cooperation in this project.

References

1. Dunlop, M., Brewster, S.: The challenge of mobile devices for human computer interaction. Pers. Ubiquitous Comput. **6**(4), 235–236 (2002). https://doi.org/10.1007/s007790200022
2. Xu, C., Lyons, K.: Shimmering smartwatches: exploring the smartwatch design space. In: Proceedings of the Ninth International Conference on Tangible, Embedded, and Embodied Interaction (TEI 2015) (2015)

3. Bieber, G., Kirste, T., Urban, B.: Ambient interaction by smart watches. In: Proceedings of the 5th International Conference on PErvasive Technologies Related to Assistive Environments (PETRA 2012). ACM, New York (2012). Article 39. http://dx.doi.org/10.1145/2413097.2413147

4. ECG on Apple Watch OS 5.2. https://www.apple.com/apple-watch-series-4/health/. Accessed 28 Mar 2019

5. Stecker, M.: Generisches Framework für die Darstellung von Messergebnissen im Anwendungsgebiet Leistungsdiagnostik im Sportbereich. Masterproject and thesis University of Rostock (2016)

6. Mohammed, R., Hornberger, C.: Muscle oxygenation monitoring using OXY DR2. Biomed. Eng.-Biomed. Tech. **62**(s1), S33 (2017)

7. Waßmann, I., von Malotky, N.T.G., Martens, A.: Train4U - mobile sport diagnostic expert system for user-adaptive training. In: 12th International Symposium on Computer Science in Sport (Peer Reviewed Paper), IACSS, 8–10 July 2019, Moscow, Russia (2019). https://iacss2019.ru/

8. Moxy Muscle Oxygen Monitor. http://www.moxymonitor.com/. Accessed 28 Mar 2019

9. Ear Sensor. https://www.cismst.org/en/loesungen/im-ohr-sensor/. Accessed 28 Mar 2019

10. Hornberger, C., Wabnitz, H.: Approaches for calibration and validation of near-infrared optical methods for oxygenation monitoring. Biomed. Tech. (Berl). **63**(5), 537–546 (2018). https://doi.org/10.1515/bmt-2017-0116

11. Harrison, R., Flood, D., Duce, D.: Usability of mobile applications: literature review and rationale for a new usability model. J. Interact. Sci. **1**(1), 1 (2013)

12. Huang, K.Y.: Challenges in human-computer interaction design for mobile devices. In: Proceedings of the World Congress on Engineering and Computer Science, vol. 1, pp. 236–241 (2009)

13. Apple Watch 4 Activity Tracker. https://www.apple.com/apple-watch-series-4/activity/. Accessed 28 Mar 2019

Testing of Exoskeletons in the Context of Logistics - Application and Limits of Use

Gabriele Winter[1]([⊠]), Christian Felten[2], and Jörg Hedtmann[2]

[1] German Social Accident Insurance Institution for Commercial Transport, Postal Logistics and Telecommunication (BG Verkehr), Mina-Rees-Str. 8, 64295 Darmstadt, Germany
gabriele.winter@bg-verkehr.de
[2] German Social Accident Insurance Institution for Commercial Transport, Postal Logistics and Telecommunication, Ottenser Hauptstraße 54, 22765 Hamburg, Germany

Abstract. Lifting, carrying and lowering of loads are still essential activities of logistics today, for example in order picking and sorting jobs. So-called exoskeletons are intended to physically relieve employees of manual load handling. Such devices are designed to decrease the load on the back by taking over a part of the required momentum. The devices are worn on the body and are intended to provide the employees with strength support during load manipulation in order to reduce the load on the spine. Individual operating experiences under real working conditions concerning the suitability and effectiveness of exoskeletons in load handling are now available. In an intervention study a passive back-supporting exoskeleton was tested with experienced staff.

This poster shows the main results of the study with eight male workers, lifting and carrying parcels with and without a passive exoskeleton in a familiar working environment. Some key questions of this study were: Does the use of these assistance systems create additional health risks for employees? Which safety aspects have to be taken into account and which have to be considered in the risk assessment? For this purpose, measurements of the electric muscle activity of stressed back muscles, recording of kinematic data as well as employee interviews (e.g. subjective feeling of discomfort, acceptance) were carried out. The results show only moderate relief effects for the analyzed workplace. Adverse effects caused by wearing the exoskeletons require careful consideration of the application of the examined exoskeleton.

Keywords: Manual material handling · Musculoskeletal complaints · Body-supported devices

1 Introduction

Manual material handling in order picking, which is characterized by increased physical strain, a high repetition rate and/or unfavourable working postures, still are a health hazard to employees today. According to BKK statistics from 2016, work-related diseases of the musculoskeletal system and connective tissue in particular still

© Springer Nature Switzerland AG 2019
C. Stephanidis (Ed.): HCII 2019, CCIS 1033, pp. 265–270, 2019.
https://doi.org/10.1007/978-3-030-23528-4_37

account for a considerable proportion of days of incapacity to work (over 30%, see [1]). A number of companies are trying to find ergonomic solutions to reduce the load on the spine. The use of assistance systems worn on the body could have positive effects on the lower part of the back due to load redistribution when bending the torso (see [2–4]). For picking in warehousing and handling operations, where lifting and lowering heavy loads can be seen as the cause of increased strain on the spine an assistance system should be used in a selected work area. A company from the logistics industry wants to use exoskeletons to lower the load on employees at working places, where it is very difficult to transfer loads with other technical lifting devices.

From the types of exoskeletons currently available on the market (cf. systematization according to [5, 6]), a passive system was chosen to support the erection of the back during load handling. When the upper body is bending forward, the device supports back and chest with flexible tubes. In this way it transfers part of the load from the lower back to the chest and to the legs. The restoring force of a spring-damper system assists in raising the upper body upright (see [7, 8]). A major objective of the intervention study is to quantify the degree of support provided by a passive exoskeleton and to examine the advantages and disadvantages from the point of view of the employees in the selected work area. Ultimately, the use of such assistance systems should result in positive developments with regard to back health (e.g. possible reduction of physical complaints and diseases in the lower back area, see [2]).

2 Methodology

Work process analysis: The analyzed activities in the member company in the logistics work area include the picking of goods. The goods to be transferred were delivered in the form of individual parcels on pallets. Manual handling included lifting the load from the pallet, carrying the parcel (alone or in pairs; with or without transport cart) and placing the load in a transport trolley.

Figure 1 shows various typical postures and movements: The removal of a parcel from the lower pallet level (Fig. 1, left) or the carrying of a parcel on a shoulder (Fig. 1, right). In addition, data were collected on secondary activities (e.g. walking without a load). In total, the data of eight employees, who performed the activities as a couple over a period of two hours, could be collected. The test persons worked in pairs with and without exoskeletons (i.e. one with and one without an assistance system for one hour each).

The project partner, the "Institute for Occupational Safety and Health of the German Social Accident Insurance" (IFA) supports the German Social Accident Insurance Institutions e.g. in workplace measurements and advice. In order to record kinematic data on postures and body movements over the entire measurement period, four three-component acceleration sensors (AX3 type) from Axivity were used by IFA. For the documentation of the activities, time-synchronized video recordings were used. From the sensor data, the torso bending angle and the exoskeleton bending angle (both for the right and left side) were calculated.

The evaluation was activity-based, with each measuring interval being assigned to the corresponding work execution - documented by video. In order to quantify the

Fig. 1. Left: Lifting of a parcel from a pallet (lower area); Right: Carrying a parcel with exoskeleton (parcel on shoulder)

muscle physiological load changes in the back area (due to the expected reduction due to redistribution of the load) by the exoskeleton in the field, electromyographic measurements (EMG) were carried out on the stressed back muscles (Musculus erector spinae (longissimus) and Musculus erector spinae (iliocostalis)).

Laboratory measurements carried out in advance at the IFA with the exoskeleton concerned provided comparative data for lifting loads up to a maximum of 25 kg. The measurement system developed at the IFA with the evaluation program WIDAAN is described including further references to the literature [9]. Immediately after the measurement phase, a test person survey took place: In addition to the subjective perception of stress during the activities, data were collected on the perceived support and wearing comfort of the assistance system used.

3   Results

In connection with the exoskeleton support used, the differentiated activity analysis revealed the relevant partial activities of lifting the load, carrying the load single, carrying the load in pairs, placing the load and walking without load. Other partial or secondary activities such as sitting or bending with static torso support [10] did not occur during the period under study. According to the workflow analyses, the average weight per parcel was approx. 24 kg (range from 3 kg to a maximum of approx. 50 kg) per employee. The distance covered when carrying the load ranging from 5 m to a maximum of about 15 m.

On average, 46 lifting, carrying and placing operations were carried out per hour. Depending on the number of employees, between 0.8 and approx. 1.1 tons of load are moved per hour. All eight test persons who took part in the tests were professionally experienced (on average approx. 2.7 years) and on average approx. 29 years old at the time of the examination (standard deviation 5.7 years). Wearing the exoskeleton did not fundamentally influence the torso postures or torso movements based on the median of the torso bending angle. However, a tendency towards strong bending and upright to slightly overstretched torso postures was observed more frequently.

Due to its function, the passive exoskeleton can only have a positive supporting effect in this working environment when lifting and lowering loads. According to the manufacturer, the torque support at hip joint level is between 15 Nm and 30 Nm depending on the direction. As a result, the system can only compensate approx. 6% of the total torque to be applied at the level of the hip joints when lifting and lowering heavy loads (here 25 kg). In the survey, the test persons confirmed that the exoskeleton used here provided noticeable support (mean value 29%, relief effect on the visual analogue scale of maximum 50%), especially when lifting loads and in a supporting posture.

The wearing comfort of the system was rated rather negative. Five test persons complained of pressure points on the chest and thighs after one hour of use (see Fig. 2) - three test persons did not. Overall, the test persons rated the support as moderate with regard to the job requirements given.

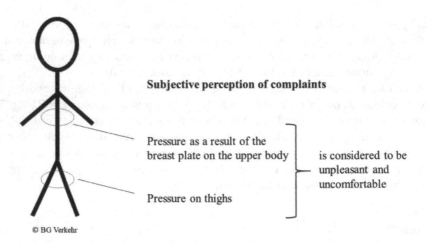

Subjective perception of complaints

Pressure as a result of the
breast plate on the upper body

Pressure on thighs

is considered to be
unpleasant and
uncomfortable

© BG Verkehr

Fig. 2. Complaint regions where the exoskeleton is perceived as uncomfortable (e.g. pressure points)

4 Discussion and Conclusion

The results show a substantial relief effect caused by a supported posture when lifting and placing parcels. The level of the relief effect is, however, only moderate in terms of muscle activity (EMG reduction) (5–10% MVC, MVC: Maximum Voluntary

Contraction). With regard to the hip joint moment to be applied when lifting heavy parcels (25 kg), the balance is similar, so that the biomechanical efficiency can only be described as moderate here. The time required for lifting and lowering at the workplace is on average under six minutes per hour. The other considerably longer lasting activities such as carrying the load and walking without load rather cause a disturbing effect of the system and therefore the suitability of the exoskeleton used here is clearly relativized. Since very heavy parcels weighing more than 25 kg have to be transported relatively frequently in the work area, the use of a passive exoskeleton system generally appears to be of little use, as only a portion of the basic load is removed here and thus the overall effectiveness decreases. The subjectively perceived discomfort in the chest and thighs also shows the need for optimization of such exoskeletons. If the results of field studies are compared with exoskeletons in industry, the results of the employee interviews show a similar rating of discomfort. According to [7], the test persons (n = 18) felt an increase in complaints in the chest region and on the thighs when wearing an exoskeleton of the same structure. The principle of load redistribution means that an increasing discomfort is perceived for the additional burdening body regions chest and thighs [7].

5   Outlook

Although it was found that a passive exoskeleton of this type is not appropriate, especially in the field of work under investigation, companies should continue to seek and test assistance systems to lower the burden on employees. Until now exist no long-term studies on the use of the exoskeletons in industry [3]. Since no long-term studies on the use of the exoskeleton tested here exist to date, possible long-term consequences cannot be ruled out. For example, the facilitation of work could result in a loss of coordination, which could lead to increased strain on the back when working without an assistance system. Basically it has to be considered that the use of such an exoskeleton when lifting and setting down loads can lead to a redistribution of the back load, but a change in behaviour in favour of a more back-friendly work (with regard to the posture) cannot be assumed.

References

1. BKK 2016: AU-Kennzahlen nach Wirtschaftsgruppen, Bundesländern, Altersgruppen, Berufsgruppen und Diagnosehauptgruppen, Januar 2016. https://www.bkk-dachverband.de/fileadmin/gesundheit/monatsauswertungen/Summen_Gesamtergebnis_01_Januar_2016.pdf
2. Hensel, R., Keil, M., Bawin, S.: Feldstudie zur Untersuchung des Laevo-Ergoskelettes hinsichtlich Usability, Diskomfort und Nutzungsintention. In: Tagungsband des 64. Frühjahrskongresses der Gesellschaft für Arbeitswissenschaft. GfA-Press, Dortmund (2018)
3. Steinhilber, B., Seibt, R., Luger, T.: Einsatz von Exoskeletten im beruflichen Kontext – Wirkung und Nebenwirkung. Zeitschrift ASU Arbeitsmed Sozialmed Umweltmed 53, 662–664 (2018)

4. Bosch, T., van Eck, J., Knitel, K., de Looze, M.: The effects of a passive exoskeleton on muscle activity, discomfort and endurance time in forward bending work. Appl. Ergon. **54**, 212–217 (2016)
5. BGHM 2017: Einsatz von Exoskeletten an (gewerblichen) Arbeitsplätzen. Fach-Information Nr. 0059
6. DGUV 2018: Fachbereichs-Information. Fachbereich Handel und Logistik, BGHW. FBHL 006
7. Hensel, R., Keil, M.: Subjektive Evaluation industrieller Exoskelette im Rahmen von Feldstudien an ausgewählten Arbeitsplätzen. Zeitschrift für Arbeitswissenschaft **72**(4), 252–263 (2018)
8. Hensel, R., Keil, M., Mücke, B., Weiler, S.: Chancen und Risiken für den Einsatz von Exoskeletten in der betrieblichen Praxis. ASU Arbeitsmed Sozialmed Umweltmed **53**, 654–661 (2018)
9. IFA: CUELA-Messsystem und Rückenmonitor. Webcode d5128, 10 January 2019. https://www.dguv.de/ifa;/fachinfos/ergonomie/cuela-messsystem-und-rueckenmonitor/index.jsp
10. Baltrusch, S.J., van Dieën, J.H., van Bennekom, C.A.M., Houdijk, H.: The effect of a passive trunk exoskeleton on functional performance in healthy individuals. Appl. Ergon. **72**, 94–106 (2018)

Object, Motion and Activity Recognition

A Novel Picture Fingerprinting Technique to Provide Practical Indoor Localization for Wheelchair Users

Jicheng Fu[1(✉)], Paul Wiechmann[1], Marcus Ong[1], Gang Qian[1], and Daniel Yan Zhao[2]

[1] University of Central Oklahoma, Edmond, OK 73003, USA
{jfu, pwiechmann, mong, gqian}@uco.edu
[2] University of Oklahoma Health Sciences Center, Oklahoma City, OK 73104, USA
daniel-zhao@ouhsc.edu

Abstract. Although GPS-based localization systems are widely used outdoors, they are inapplicable in indoor settings, where GPS signals are mostly unavailable. Existing research, however, has not found a feasible solution to obtain indoor positioning information. Existing indoor localization approaches either suffer from low accuracy or rely on expensive infrastructure and dedicated devices. In this study, we propose a novel picture fingerprinting-based indoor localization approach for power wheelchair users, who suffer from more restricted mobility. A location is represented by pictures (i.e., picture fingerprints) taken from different angles at the location. Localization is achieved by matching a locating picture, taken during wheelchair navigation, with the picture fingerprints of locations in a building. State-of-the-art deep learning techniques were employed to match locating and fingerprinting pictures. Experimental results showed that the proposed approach achieved accurate location recognition. Compared to existing indoor localization approaches, our proposed approach neither relies on dedicated infrastructures and devices nor requires labor-intensive maintenance and, therefore, provides a new direction for achieving feasible and accurate indoor localization.

Keywords: Convolutional neural network · Deep learning · Indoor localization · Picture fingerprint · Wheelchair

1 Introduction

Research has shown that people spend 90% of their time indoors [1]. Therefore, it is important and meaningful to help people explore unfamiliar indoor settings, e.g., shopping malls, subways, etc. Although GPS-based localization systems are widely used outdoors, they are inapplicable in indoor settings, where GPS signals are mostly unavailable [2]. As a result, indoor localization has attracted extensive investigations and become an important research area.

Indoor localization is especially important for wheelchair users because they face significant challenges when traveling outside their homes. The challenges arise from

© Springer Nature Switzerland AG 2019
C. Stephanidis (Ed.): HCII 2019, CCIS 1033, pp. 273–278, 2019.
https://doi.org/10.1007/978-3-030-23528-4_38

the inherent limitations of wheelchair usage, e.g., avoiding stairs, finding dropped curbs, ramps, automatic doors, elevators, etc. Without appropriate assistance, wheelchair users may be confined to their homes, which may segregate them from society and lead to an inactive lifestyle.

Despite extensive research efforts on indoor localization, no widely adopted approaches are readily available to wheelchair users. Existing approaches either rely on infrastructures and dedicated devices [3, 4] or can only roughly estimate indoor positioning information [5]. To overcome these challenges, we propose a novel picture fingerprinting approach for indoor localization. A location is represented by pictures (i.e., picture fingerprints) taken from different angles at the location. Localization is achieved by matching a locating picture, taken during wheelchair navigation, with the picture fingerprints of various locations within a building. We have explored different approaches to measure the similarity between a locating picture and fingerprint pictures. Specifically, we attempted to achieve localization by upgrading the well-known FaceNet [6], which was very accurate in face recognition. As FaceNet is specialized for facial recognition, it cannot be directly used for location recognition. We employed the transfer learning technique to derive a deep convolutional neural network based on FaceNet. Experimental results showed that the proposed picture fingerprinting-based approach could achieve accurate location recognition. Compared to existing approaches, our proposed approach neither relies on dedicated infrastructures and devices nor requires labor-intensive maintenance, and, therefore, provides a new direction to achieve feasible and accurate indoor localization.

2 Related Work

The challenge of indoor localization lies in how to establish the relationship between a person's current location and some known information. Existing fingerprinting approaches achieve indoor localization by comparing a newly sampled signal (e.g., Wi-Fi, GSM, Bluetooth, etc.) with signal fingerprints [2]. A signal fingerprint refers to the unique signal identity and strength associated with a particular indoor location. Unfortunately, Wi-Fi and GSM signals are notoriously unstable, which require intensive computation to achieve reasonable accuracy [4]. Geomagnetism has been proven reliable for obtaining location information because building structures can twist geomagnetism to form local variants of the Earth's magnetic field [2]. However, our experimental experience with geomagnetism indicates that the sensor readings vary greatly between different mobile devices. Even for the same device, if it is oriented to different directions, it would generate very different sensor readings. Therefore, to achieve accurate localization, expensive dedicated equipment has to be used for geomagnetic solutions [7, 8]. Similarly, the Bluetooth-based solution also needs dedicated devices to emit signals [9]. Furthermore, the collection and maintenance of signal fingerprints require significant specialized expertise and extensive efforts. As a result, volunteers are normally recruited to report signal fingerprints [2, 10]. However, volunteer-based signal collection is not reliable and may lead to inaccurate results [2].

Another related work that achieves localization by matching images captured by a smartphone with pre-stored images is through the use of Barcode or QR-Code [11].

This approach, however, is inappropriate for wheelchair users. It is difficult for wheelchair users to find the Barcodes within a building. Even if they can find the Barcode, it will be very challenging for handicapped wheelchair users to use their smartphones to scan the Barcode to identify the current location.

3 Method

In this study, a wheelchair is equipped with a smartphone holder as it is inconvenient for wheelchair users to operate the smartphone while driving. We have developed an Android smartphone app that can control the smartphone's camera to take locating pictures. Once a locating picture is taken, the smartphone app sends it to a server to recognize the location.

In order to recognize locations, we need to compare the similarity between a locating picture and pre-recorded fingerprint pictures. We investigated three different approaches to compare the likeliness of pictures. First, we attempted to perform picture matching using FaceNet [6] in the hope that FaceNet could distinguish pictures of the same locations from those of different ones. FaceNet was chosen because it achieved very accurate face recognition (about 99%). As shown in Fig. 1, the network of FaceNet consists of convolutional layers and fully connected layers, which transform a picture into a Euclidean embedding of size 128. The convolutional layers are responsible for image processing and feature extraction. The fully connected layer is responsible for performing high-level reasoning to generate the Euclidean embedding for a given picture. The similarity of two pictures is measured by the Euclidean distance in a 128-dimensional space, i.e., pictures of the same location should have a small Euclidean distance, and a large distance otherwise.

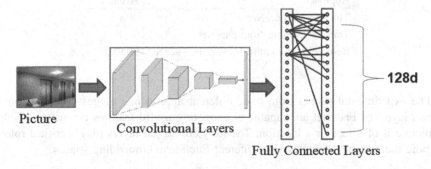

Picture   Convolutional Layers

Fully Connected Layers

128d

Fig. 1. Network structure

Second, we employed the transfer learning technique to avoid constructing the deep convolutional neural network (CNN) from scratch. Transfer learning refers to using existing knowledge in a neural network to solve different, but related problems [12]. By using transfer learning, we derived a deep CNN for location recognition from FaceNet to leverage its existing discriminative capabilities. Specifically, the convolutional layers were frozen while a new fully connected layer was developed to generate the Euclidean embedding for pictures in order to determine how effectively the existing filters could be repurposed for location recognition.

Third, we retrained the entire network of FaceNet, including the convolutional layers and fully connected layers. For the second and third approaches, we used a training set of 1,310 indoor pictures (for 95 different locations) to train the network and used a testing set of 91 pictures (for 12 different locations) to evaluate the trained network.

4 Results

Experimental results are shown in Table 1. It is clear that the original FaceNet was unable to accurately measure the similarity between pictures of locations. Its accuracy was only 59%. In comparison, the CNN obtained through transfer learning achieved an accuracy of 90.17%. As the new CNN reused FaceNet's convolutional layers, the performance improvement lay in the new fully connected layers, which mapped a given picture into a different 128-dimensional Euclidean embedding space. Therefore, we could reasonably infer that the reason for the poor performance of the original FaceNet is that its embedding space was specialized only for the facial domain. Although the CNN obtained by re-training the entire network of FaceNet achieved the best accuracy (90.91%), the effort of training the entire network has outweighed the benefit compared to the use of transfer learning, which only retrained the fully connected layers while reusing the existing convolutional layers.

Table 1. Experimental results

Approach	Accuracy
The original FaceNet	59%
Transfer learning from FaceNet	90.17%
Re-training the entire network of FaceNet	90.91%

The experimental results from three different approaches suggest that the convolutional layers of FaceNet are capable of extracting useful features no matter whether the picture is of a face or a location. The fully connected layers play a critical role in mapping the extracted features into different Euclidean embedding spaces.

5 Conclusion and Future Work

In this paper, we proposed a new picture fingerprinting-based indoor localization approach. Different from signal fingerprints, an indoor location is now represented by pictures taken at that location. Indoor localization is achieved by matching a newly taken picture with pre-recorded fingerprint pictures of various locations. In order to measure the similarity between two pictures, we first attempted to use the well-known

FaceNet. However, experimental results showed that FaceNet was unable to accurately recognize locations as its embedding space was specialized for facial recognition. Then, we tried to derive a deep convolutional neural network from FaceNet by freezing the convolutional layers and developing new fully connected layers through training. As a result, we improved the accuracy of location recognition to 90.17%. Finally, we retrained the entire network and achieved an accuracy of 90.91%. The experimental results suggest that transfer learning is a better choice because significant efforts can be saved from training the entire network, while still achieving similar accuracy. Compared to existing indoor localization solutions, our proposed approach does not rely on dedicated infrastructures or devices. The picture collection and subsequent maintenance do not require specialized expertise or labor-intensive efforts. Therefore, our proposed approach provides a new direction to achieve feasible and accurate indoor localization.

In the next step, we will continue to improve the accuracy of our location recognition system by using a larger training set of location pictures. In addition, we will improve the robustness of the proposed approach by training it using blurry pictures as well as pictures with unexpected objects, e.g., pedestrians.

Acknowledgement. This work was supported by the National Institute of General Medical Sciences of the National Institutes of Health under award number P20GM103447. The content is solely the responsibility of the authors and does not necessarily represent the official views of the National Institutes of Health.

References

1. Jiang, Y., Pan, X., Li, K., Lv, Q., Dick, R.P., Hannigan, M., et al.: Ariel: automatic wi-fi based room fingerprinting for indoor localization. In: Proceedings of the 2012 ACM Conference on Ubiquitous Computing, pp. 441–450 (2012)
2. Zafari, F., Gkelias, A., Leung, K.: A survey of indoor localization systems and technologies. arXiv preprint arXiv:1709.01015 (2017)
3. Kumar, P., Reddy, L., Varma, S.: Distance measurement and error estimation scheme for RSSI based localization in Wireless Sensor Networks. In: 2009 Fifth International Conference on Wireless Communication and Sensor Networks (WCSN), pp. 1–4 (2009)
4. Zhang, C., Subbu, K.P., Luo, J., Wu, J.X.: GROPING: geomagnetism and crowdsensing powered indoor navigation. IEEE Trans. Mob. Comput. **14**, 387–400 (2015)
5. Link, J.A.B., Smith, P., Viol, N., Wehrle, K.: FootPath: accurate map-based indoor navigation using smartphones. In: 2011 International Conference on Indoor Positioning and Indoor Navigation (IPIN), pp. 1–8 (2011)
6. Schroff, F., Kalenichenko, D., Philbin, J.: FaceNet: a unified embedding for face recognition and clustering. In: Proceedings of the IEEE Conference on Computer Vision and Pattern Recognition, pp. 815–823 (2015)
7. Haverinen, J., Kemppainen, A.: Global indoor self-localization based on the ambient magnetic field. Robot. Auton. Syst. **57**, 1028–1035 (2009)
8. Storms, W., Shockley, J., Raquet, J.: Magnetic field navigation in an indoor environment. In: 2010 Ubiquitous Positioning Indoor Navigation and Location Based Service, pp. 1–10 (2010)

9. Ahmetovic, D., Murata, M., Gleason, C., Brady, E., Takagi, H., Kitani, K., et al.: Achieving practical and accurate indoor navigation for people with visual impairments. In: Proceedings of the 14th Web for All Conference on the Future of Accessible Work, p. 31 (2017)
10. Ganti, R.K., Ye, F., Lei, H.: Mobile crowdsensing: current state and future challenges. IEEE Commun. Mag. **49**, 32–39 (2011)
11. Carboni, D., Manchinu, A., Marotto, V., Piras, A., Serra, A.: Infrastructure-free indoor navigation: a case study. J. Locat. Based Serv. **9**, 33–54 (2015)
12. Pan, S.J., Yang, Q.: A survey on transfer learning. IEEE Trans. Knowl. Data Eng. **22**, 1345–1359 (2010)

Motion Estimation of Plush Toys Through Detachable Acceleration Sensor Module and Machine Learning

Kaho Kato[✉], Naoto Ienaga, and Yuta Sugiura

Keio University, Yokohama, Japan
kaho_0128@keio.jp

Abstract. We propose a system that estimates motion in a plush toy by means of an attached sensor device and gives the user a sound feedback corresponding to the predicted motion. We have created several different types of detachable acceleration sensor modules as an accessory for the toy. This module can be attached at any position on a commercially available plush toy. The user can create original motions by teaching through demonstration, and the captured sensor data is converted into 2D image data. We extracted the histograms of oriented gradients (HOG) features and performed learning with a support vector machine (SVM). In an evaluation, we decided the attaching parts and motions in advance, and participants moved a plush toy in accordance with these. Results showed that it was possible to estimate the plush toy's motion with high accuracy, and the system was able to register a sound for each motion.

Keywords: Machine learning · Interactive plush toy ·
Teaching by demonstration

1 Introduction

Most of us have owned plush toys at some point in our lives. Such toys are familiar to us, and they are often displayed at home as a form of interior decoration. Many people played with such toys in their childhood and have the desire for plush toys to be given a new breath of life. In anime and movies, such wishes sometimes come true. To achieve this in the actual world, we propose a system that animates plush toys by means of a computer.

Interactive plush toys have already been on sale for a while. These toys have built-in electronic devices such as sensors, speakers, and microphones. Our objective in this study, however, is to develop a commercially available plush toy with no built-in electronic devices. Our system can be used with any plush toy and does not require slitting open a toy to attach anything. Essentially, we want to make wishes come true not with an interactive plush toy but rather with an attached interactive plush toy.

In this paper, we propose a system that estimates motion in a plush toy by means of an attached sensor device. We have created several different types of detachable acceleration sensor modules. We introduce three of them here: a band type, a ribbon type, and a skirt type. Their appearances match that of a plush toy, so users can attach

© Springer Nature Switzerland AG 2019
C. Stephanidis (Ed.): HCII 2019, CCIS 1033, pp. 279–286, 2019.
https://doi.org/10.1007/978-3-030-23528-4_39

them as accessories. The microcontroller is packaged in a bag that the toy carries on its shoulders like a backpack. The sensor data is converted into 2D grayscale image data and is learned with a support vector machine (SVM). We conducted an experiment in which participants performed a predetermined set of motions and found that it was possible to estimate the plush toy's motion with high accuracy (Fig. 1).

Fig. 1. A plush toy with our modules.

2   Related Works

2.1   Interactive Plush Toy

There have been many studies on interaction with plush toys.

Ikeda et al. developed an operating system in which SNS and e-mail are utilized to operate a plush toy. They combined an acceleration sensor and a photo-reflective sensor (PRS) inside a plush toy and activated it using voice recognition technology [1]. Yonezawa et al. combined various sensors inside a plush toy and developed Com-music to create music corresponding to the intensity of the inter-action between the toy and the user [2]. Takase et al. proposed a soft-driving mechanism using threads, cloth, and cotton and used it to develop a plush toy robot [3].

In another work, a system that moves a plush toy in a display as an interface has been developed. Munekata et al. developed this system in order to make a user's attachment to a plush toy stronger [4].

However, in the above studies, devices must be installed inside the plush toy, which means they are only applicable for a specific toy.

In this research, we aim to make a plush toy interactive by using items that can be attached.

2.2 Making Existing Objects Interactive

In our system, we make a plush toy interactive by attaching devices to it. In a similar study, Sugiura et al. developed a plush toy that can be turned into an interactive robot by means of an attachable device that the user can fix onto the toy's limbs, thus enabling it to move freely [5]. Our research is different in that we focus on motion recognition from within the toy.

Kosaka et al. combined sensors with a vacuum cleaner as a game application [6]. In the game, the user collects monsters by sucking up dust. This is an interesting application of entertainment to cleaning that can enhance daily life.

2.3 Motion Estimation by Real-World Sensors

We need to obtain real-world information for estimating a plush toy's motion. The easiest way to do that these days is to collect the information by means of low-cost sensors and estimate the real-world data by machine learning.

Kikui et al. used convolutional neural networks (CNNs) to recognize time series data collected from photosensors and to identify time series gestures [7]. Fukui et al. developed a wristband-type device equipped with photo reflective sensors that can detect hand gestures by measuring changes to the wrist contour that occur while gesturing [8]. The obtained time series sensor data is then converted into image data and identified by extracting the HOG features and performing learning by SVM.

Our system learns the data from acceleration sensors by SVM and then inputs various motions to the toy.

3 System Implementation

3.1 Overview

In this research, we estimate a plush toy's motions by attaching acceleration sensors and obtain sound feedback corresponding to the predicted motion. We attach acceleration sensor modules to each part of a plush toy, such as the paws or the head, and obtain sensor data for every motion. The obtained time series sensor data are converted into image data, and the system then extracts the HOG features from the image data and learns by SVM. After registration of the motions, the user can play using the same motions (Fig. 2).

3.2 Acceleration Sensor Module

We developed several detachable acceleration sensor modules, three of which are introduced here: a band type, a ribbon type, and a skirt type (Fig. 3). Their appearances match that of a plush toy, so users can attach them as accessories. The user attaches a module to any part of a commercially available plush toy and then can define some original motions and teach by demonstration.

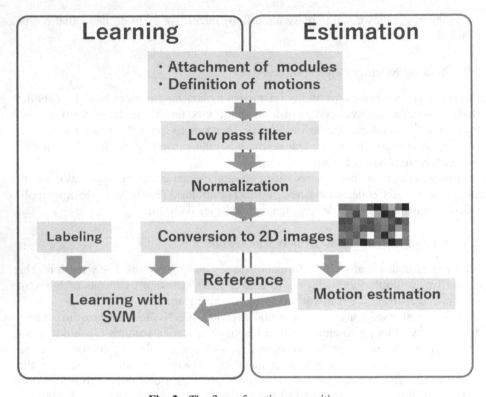

Fig. 2. The flow of motion recognition.

The acceleration sensor in the module has three axes, so we can obtain data from three directions (x, y, and z). Each sensor is connected with a microcontroller (Arduino Pro Mini), and sensor data is sent to a PC through the XBee module. The microcontroller is packaged in a bag that the toy carries on its shoulders like a backpack.

3.3   Obtaining Learning Data and Motion Estimation

SVM is used for making a classifier in the Python 3.0 environment.

In this research, we estimate motions through learning by SVM after converting the time series sensor data into 2D grayscale image data and obtaining the HOG·features. First, the system judges if a gesture has been made. We calculate differential values between the current sensor data and the one before it and convert them into absolute values. Then, we sum up these values. If the total value passes a certain threshold, data collection is started. Sensor data is often unstable due to gravity or subtle shaking, so we apply a low pass filter (LPF) (specifically, an RC filter) to the obtained sensor data. The formula is as follows:

$$y[i] = a * y[i-1] + (1-a) * x[i], \tag{1}$$

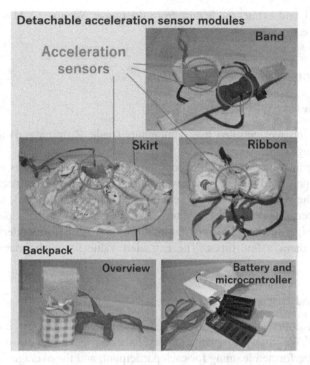

Fig. 3. Acceleration sensor module.

where a is a filter value, x is current data, and y is a time series data frame. At this time, we obtain information on gesture changes by the time series and get the sensor data of the last 60 frames. We then convert them into 2D grayscale image data by means of normalization. In the converted image, each sensor value is allocated in the vertical axis direction and the time series data of 60 frames is allocated in the horizontal axis direction. We convert all sensor data into image data (Fig. 4).

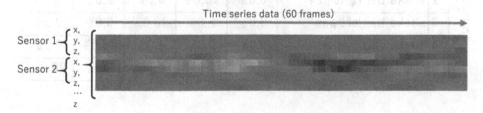

Fig. 4. Example of image data.

We extract the features from images by using the HOG features. At this time, the size of an image is $3 \times n$ [px] height $\times$ 60 [px] width (n: number of sensors). We extend the image data in two directions by four times in order to set the HOG parameters more easily. We define cell size as 4 [px] $\times$ 4 [px] and block size as 3

[cell] × 3 [cell], and extract the feature from the image. We use SVM as the classifier for the motion estimation.

4 Evaluation

4.1 Overview

In the experiment, we recruited five participants (male: 2, female: 3) aged 22 to 24 years old (average: 23.2 years).

The participants interacted with a teddy bear that had three devices attached to the head, the right paw, and the left paw. Five motions had already been decided: 'nod the head', 'shake the right paw', 'shake the left paw', 'shake both paws', and 'clap both paws'. They performed the five motions 20 times, so each participant made 100 motions. The experimenter explained the motions to them before collecting data, and they practiced them a few times. The extracted value for each image was 32,886 dimensions.

4.2 Result and Discussion

The total data collected in the experiment was 5 gestures × 20 times × 5 people = 500 data. We show the evaluation results using leave-one-out cross-validation (Table 1). We performed learning for each participant, and the average accuracy of the identification was about 97.2%.

Table 1. Results of the experiment.

	Motions	Predicted 1	2	3	4	5
	1 nod the head	98.0%	2.0%	0.0%	0.0%	0.0%
	2 shake the right paw	0.0%	98.0%	0.0%	2.0%	0.0%
Truth	3 shake the left paw	0.0%	2.0%	98.0%	0.0%	0.0%
	4 shake both paws	0.0%	0.0%	4.0%	96.0%	0.0%
	5 clap both paws	2.0%	0.0%	0.0%	2.0%	96.0%

The results showed that the accuracy of the identification declined when the number of sensors attached to the plush toy increased.

Moreover, the system sometimes detected a motion incorrectly, such as a combination of 'nod the head' and 'shake the right paw'. This occurred by the right paw slightly moved together when a user moved the head hard.

5 Application

We made an application to apply sounds for a plush toy. After registration of motions, our system can identify the plush toy's motion. In our application, the user can register any sound for each motion of the toy. The user can then interact with the toy by using the registered motions.

6 Limitation and Future Work

In our system, we can move the plush toy freely without having to be connected to a PC. The device is powered by a battery that is packaged inside a bag that the toy carries as an accessory. However, as this bag is rather large, smaller plush toys are not able to carry it. In the case of small plush toys, we should hang the bag from the toy, so we cannot move it completely free.

In this research, we decided on the attaching part and motions in advance. However, individual users will want to play with their plush toys differently. We will explore this through a user study experiment in future work.

7 Conclusion

In this paper, we proposed a motion estimation system for a plush toy. We fabricated an acceleration module and attached it to various parts of a plush toy. This module obtains the plush toy's motion information as sensor data. The obtained time series sensor data is converted into 2D grayscale image data, and the system identifies motions by extracting the HOG features from the image data and performing learning by SVM. The results of experiments with participants showed that the system could identify motions with the average accuracy of 97.2%. In the future, we will perform further testing with a user study experiment.

Acknowledgments. This work was supported by JST AIP-PRISM JPMJCR18Y2.

References

1. Ikeda, A., Chiba, Y., Haneda, H.: Stuffed toy as non-display interaction devices. In: Proceedings of the SIG Ubiquitous Computing Systems (UBI) 2013, IPSJ, 2013-UBI, vol. 40, no. 16, pp. 1–5 (2013)
2. Yonezawa, T., Clarkson, B., Yasumura, M., Mase, K.: A music expressive communication with sensor-doll interface. In: Proceedings of the SIG Human Computer Interaction (HCI) 2001, IPSJ, pp. 17–24 (2001)
3. Takase, Y., Mitake, H., Yamashita, Y., Hasegawa, S.: Motion generation for the stuffed-toy robot. In: Proceedings of the Annual Conference on the Society of Instrument and Control Engineers (SICE 2013), pp. 213–217 (2013)

4. Munekata, N., Komatsu, T., Matsubara, H.: Marching bear: an interface system encouraging user's emotional attachment and providing an immersive experience. In: Ma, L., Rauterberg, M., Nakatsu, R. (eds.) ICEC 2007. LNCS, vol. 4740, pp. 363–373. Springer, Heidelberg (2007). https://doi.org/10.1007/978-3-540-74873-1_43
5. Sugiura, Y., et al.: PINOKY: a ring that animates your plush toys. In: Proceedings of the ACM Annual Conference on Human Factors in Computing Systems (CHI 2012), pp. 725–734. ACM (2012)
6. Kosaka, T., Matsushita, M.: Monster cleaner: a serious game to learn cleaning. Laval Virtual ReVolut. "Transhumanism++" (ReVo), EPiC Eng. **1**, 50–59 (2018)
7. Kikui, K., Itoh, Y., Yamada, M., Sugiura, Y., Sugimoto, M.: Intra-/inter-user adaptation framework for wearable gesture sensing device. In: Proceedings of the ACM International Symposium on Wearable Computers (ISWC 2018), pp. 21–24 (2018)
8. Fukui, R., Okishiba, S., Karasawa, H., Warisawa, A.: Dynamic hand motion recognition based on wrist contour measurement for a wearable display. In: Proceedings of the Robotics and Mechatronics Conference (Robomech 2017), pp. 2A2–L02 (2017)

An Exploratory Inspection of the Detection Quality of Pose and Object Detection Systems by Synthetic Data

Robert Manthey[1]([✉]), Falk Schmidsberger[1], Rico Thomanek[2],
Christian Roschke[2], Tony Rolletschke[2], Benny Platte[2], Marc Ritter[3],
and Danny Kowerko[1]

[1] Junior Professorship Media Computing, Technische Universität Chemnitz,
09107 Chemnitz, Germany
{robert.manthey,falk.schmidsberger,
danny.kowerko}@informatik.tu-chemnitz.de
[2] Faculty Media Sciences, University of Applied Sciences, Technikumplatz 17,
09648 Mittweida, Germany
{rthomane,roschke,rolletsc,platte}@hs-mittweida.de
[3] Faculty Applied Computer Sciences and Biosciences,
University of Applied Sciences, Technikumplatz 17, 09648 Mittweida, Germany
marc.ritter@hs-mittweida.de

Abstract. Many modern systems use image understanding components to inspect, observe and react. Often, the training is realized and limited to manually annotated real world data, but dangerous or resource expensive scenarios are rare. We create a solution to overcome these limitations and reduce the manual annotation process by producing synthetic scenarios of arbitrary content and composition.

Keywords: Pose detection · Object detection · Quality analysis ·
Testing · Synthetic data

1 Introduction

Nowadays, several systems exist to detect objects, persons and their pose. They observe drivers of cars to prevent microsleep or incidents with pedestrians, count visitors of exhibitions, inspect the products at the assembly lines, or search for people loading trucks. But the training of the system being able to detection and to identify these tasks is realized by some images and videos captured from real world like [1,3] and slightly annotated by a manual, error-prone and slow process. At the same time, some scenarios are nearly impossible to produce because of the high costs of manufacture, the danger of physical injury or danger of life to the performers. For instance, a fire detection system should know the visual appearance of fire at a chair inside a room as shown in Fig. 1a. The shortcomings restrict the training and the detection of events and objects as

© Springer Nature Switzerland AG 2019
C. Stephanidis (Ed.): HCII 2019, CCIS 1033, pp. 287–294, 2019.
https://doi.org/10.1007/978-3-030-23528-4_40

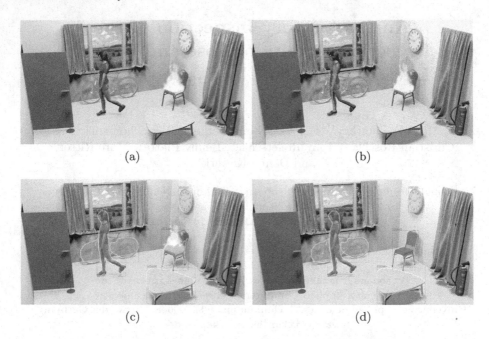

(a)   (b)

(c)   (d)

Fig. 1. Scene with (a) person, different objects and a burning chair. (b) with highlighted elements of the detected person. (c) with the classification of the detected and identified objects with their class label and confidence value and (d) the identical scene without the burning chair but increased confidence of the table from 0.72 to 1.0.

well as the inspection of the performance of the detection systems. To overcome these shortcomings in the field of training the systems as well as the checking of correctness, we create a system to produce visual data and there ground truth annotations with a minimum of resources. In this way, a huge amount of scenes could be created and processed without danger or expensive equipment. We apply our scenes to different open-source detection systems to determine there properties. Technical and visual conspicuous effects are recorded, inspected and compared to ground truth.

Similar developments like the research of [2,8,9] use modified game engines to create synthetic data to fulfill their requirements. In most cases they create geometric primitives added with task dependent textures mapped to the surface which allow a fast but sometimes imperfect data creation process. They train and test aerial reconnaissance systems with these data and show the gap between fully synthetic trained detection systems and fully real world data trained detection systems, but also remark the problem of data collection and annotation for real world data.

Additionally, existing real world datasets represent the technological properties and constraints of the time they were captured. For instance, they were recorded by mono cameras with old NTSC, PAL or HD-ready resolution, 25 frames per second, interlacing and 256 colors. But today, Full HD, 4k and 8k UHD will be needed with 200 frames per second, High Dynamic Range and stereo cameras are required, which need a recreation of the full, expensive capturing process in reality. As opposed to this, synthetic datasets are created from mathematically defined structures being independent of resolution, framerate or the amount of cameras capturing them.

2   System Architecture and Workflow

Based on our experience with synthetic data for testing of multimedia workflows from [4] and [5], we further developed our solution to the *Synthetic Ground Truth Generation for Testing, Technology Evaluation and Verification* (SyntTEV) framework [6]. Those uses the open source 3D modelling tool Blender[1] to generate the scenarios, the ground truth and the corresponding images sequences as shown in Fig. 2. With the tool MakeHuman[2] we setup 3D humanoids like in Fig. 3, being imported and used in Blender and animated by captured activities like walking, jumping, etc. With the embedded version of the universal programming language Python[3] and the Blender-provided Programming Interface[4] we realize the task-dependent modification and creation process of our scenes in Blender. The combination of the desired scene with some objects, some humanoids, the desired activities and other environment specifications like camera and light positions, is stored and processed by Blender to synthesize the designated images and ground truth data.

3   System Application and Data

We produce multiple scenarios like in Fig. 1 to get object detections from different perspectives or like in Fig. 4 to test the detection quality of simulated visual stereo sensors from different locations relative to the detected instances. The second idealized scenario contains a textureless plane as ground, a female humanoid with 163 bones and common clothes and hairstyle, as well as a slightly colored gray bike. The light setup produces only few shadows just like a sunny day. The humanoid is executing a captured forward-walking activity of 234 steps while the bike is moving side by side. Nine simulated visual stereo sensors are positioned in a line orthogonal centered above the center of the path. Each rectangle sensor contain two cameras with a spacing of around 0.16 blender coordinate units and with a focal length of 35.0. We conduct three series with a sensor spacing of 0.1,

---

[1] https://www.blender.org.
[2] https://www.makehumancommunity.org.
[3] https://www.python.org/.
[4] https://docs.blender.org/api/2.79/.

0.3 and 0.5 units each and with five angle adjustment of -40, -20, 0, $+20$ and $+40°$ to the vertical line and along the direction of movement. The position of each bone of the humanoid was stored in a SQLite-database[5] at each frame of the series with global coordinates as well as local coordinates relatively to the perspective and position of each camera. As result we obtained 63.180 images and $(\#\text{Bones} \times \#\text{Frames}) \times (\#\text{Sensors} \times \#\text{Cameras}) \times (\#\text{Series} \times \#\text{Angles}) = 163 \times 234 \times (9 \times 2) \times (3 \times 5) = 10,298,340$ annotations as ground truth.

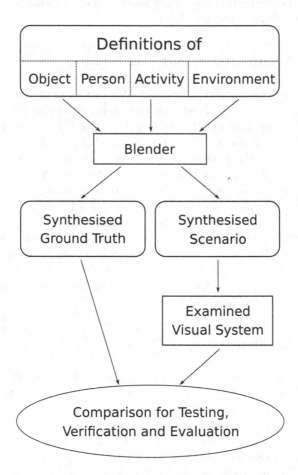

Fig. 2. Workflow for the generation of synthetic scenes and the analysis of existing visual detection systems. The definitions of objects, persons, activities and environment representing the scene are used by Blender to combine the components and to render visual data for a input of the examined system as well as ground truth. A later comparison of both sets shows the properties of this system [7].

---

[5] https://www.sqlite.org/.

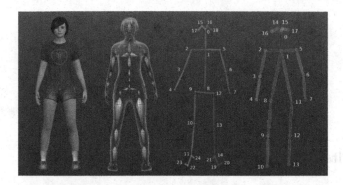

Fig. 3. Example of a MakeHuman humanoid, a skeleton with 163 bones and the keypoints of the *BODY25* and the *COCO* output format [6].

Fig. 4. View to the scenario with the line of rectangle virtual stereo sensors at the top left, the walking humanoid and a bike following the clarifying red line. (Color figure online)

These images are processed by the open-source pose detection tool Openpose[6] which detects up to 18 COCO-based keypoints of a human skeleton in a presented image as shown in Fig. 3. A approximately matching of the 18 keypoints to the 163 bones is used to inspect the quality of the tool at the different settings.

For each image i we calculated the point misplacement error M_i between a detected keypoint $p_{d,i}$ and the matching bone $p_{o,i}$ from the ground truth, normalized with the amount of detected keypoints $|k_{d,i}|$ as well as the maximum distance error e, representing the image diagonal, as shown in Eq. 1. The entire confidence C_i of each frame is the confidence $c_{d,i}$ of each detected keypoint normalized by the total amount of all 18 keypoints $|k|$, as in Eq. 2. As result we obtain the detection error D_i by Eq. 3.

---

[6] https://github.com/CMU-Perceptual-Computing-Lab/openpose/.

$$M_i = \frac{\sum \frac{p_{o,i} - p_{d,i}}{|k_{d,i}|}}{e} \qquad (1)$$

$$C_i = \frac{\sum c_{d,i}}{|k|} \qquad (2)$$

$$D_i = M_i * (1 - C_i) \qquad (3)$$

4   Results

The detection results and the error were inspected to find salient effects as shown in the diagrams of Figs. 5, 6 and the images of Fig. 7. The detection frameworks working on the synthetic data like on real world datasets and the detection rate depends also on the perspective and the alignment of the respective camera. The best results were achieved with the cameras at the center of the line as expected.

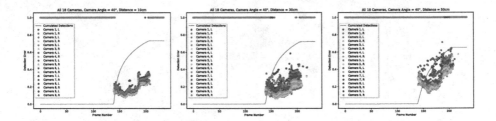

Fig. 5. Increasing the distance of the sensors simultaneously increase the variance of the detection error, as well as slightly decreasing the overall amount of detections.

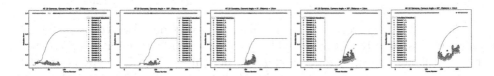

Fig. 6. Changing the angle adjustment from −40 to 40 show a later detection because of the movement of the humanoid, but also their increased variance. The overall amount of detections decrease with the convergence of the angle to the vertical line corresponding to the amount of occultation of keypoints by the humanoid body itself.

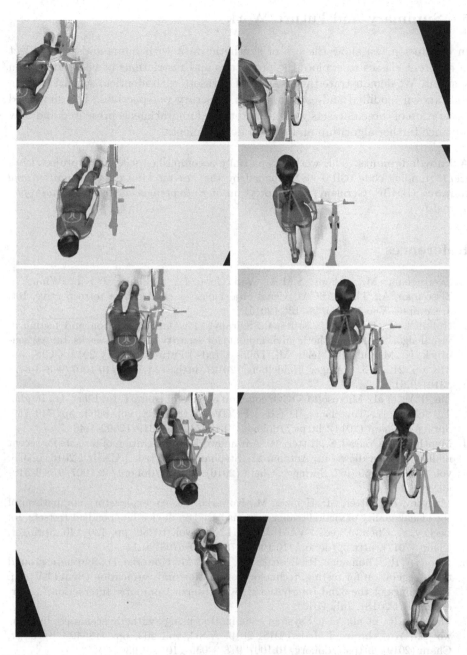

Fig. 7. Each rows show the images of the left camera of sensor 1, 3, 5, 7 and 9 with a angle adjustment of −40 and +40, respectively. The left column represent the frontal perspective at frame 60 and the right column the back perspective at frame 165 with nearly the same position of the humanoid relative to the camera. Clearly visible are the stable and nearly complete detections from the back and the heavy shortcomings of the frontal detections.

5   Summary and Future Work

In conclusion, we show the use of synthetic data with humanoids and object of different classes to explore the properties and restrictions of visual detection systems. We demonstrate the creation of datasets with identical scenarios being well known modified and captured from arbitrary perspectives. The simplified generation of these datasets with ground truth annotations is presented and may advance further algorithm and system developments.

Acknowledgments. This work was partially accomplished within the project *localizeIT* (funding code 03IPT608X) funded by the *Federal Ministry of Education and Research* (BMBF, Germany) in the program of *Entrepreneurial Regions InnoProfile-Transfer*.

References

1. Everingham, M., Eslami, S.M.A., Van Gool, L., Williams, C.K.I., Winn, J., Zisserman, A.: The PASCAL visual object classes challenge: a retrospective. Int. J. Comput. Vis. **111**(1), 98–136 (2015)
2. Hummel, G., Kovács, L., Stütz, P., Szirányi, T.: Data simulation and testing of visual algorithms in synthetic environments for security sensor networks. In: Aschenbruck, N., Martini, P., Meier, M., Tölle, J. (eds.) Future Security 2012. CCIS, vol. 318, pp. 212–215. Springer, Heidelberg (2012). https://doi.org/10.1007/978-3-642-33161-9_31
3. Lin, T.Y., et al.: Microsoft COCO: common objects in context. In: Fleet, D., Pajdla, T., Schiele, B., Tuytelaars, T. (eds.) ECCV 2014. LNCS, vol. 8693, pp. 740–755. Springer, Cham (2014). https://doi.org/10.1007/978-3-319-10602-1_48
4. Manthey, R., Conrad, S., Ritter, M.: A framework for generation of testsets for recent multimedia workflows. In: Antona, M., Stephanidis, C. (eds.) UAHCI 2016. LNCS, vol. 9739, pp. 460–467. Springer, Cham (2016). https://doi.org/10.1007/978-3-319-40238-3_44
5. Manthey, R., Ritter, M., Heinzig, M., Kowerko, D.: An exploratory comparison of the visual quality of virtual reality systems based on device-independent testsets. In: Lackey, S., Chen, J. (eds.) VAMR 2017. LNCS, vol. 10280, pp. 130–140. Springer, Cham (2017). https://doi.org/10.1007/978-3-319-57987-0_11
6. Manthey, R., Thomanek, R., Roschke, C., Ritter, M., Kowerko, D.: Synthetic ground truth generation for testing, technology evaluation and verification (SyntTEV). In: Proceedings of the 32nd International BCS Human Computer Interaction Conference, (HCI 2018), July 2018
7. Manthey, R., et al.: Visual system examination using synthetic scenarios. In: Karwowski, W., Ahram, T. (eds.) IHSI 2019. AISC, vol. 903, pp. 418–422. Springer, Cham (2019). https://doi.org/10.1007/978-3-030-11051-2_63
8. Richter, S.R., Vineet, V., Roth, S., Koltun, V.: Playing for data: ground truth from computer games. CoRR abs/1608.02192 (2016). arXiv:1608.02192
9. Sadeghi, F., Levine, S.: CAD2RL: real single-image flight without a single real image. CoRR abs/1611.04201 (2016). arXiv:1611.04201

Synthetic Ground Truth Generation for Object Recognition Evaluation

A Scalable System for Parameterized Creation of Annotated Images

Benny Platte[1]([✉])(iD), Rico Thomanek[1], Christian Roschke[1], Robert Manthey[2],
Tony Rolletschke[1], Frank Zimmer[1], and Marc Ritter[1]

[1] Hochschule Mittweida, Technikumplatz 17, 09648 Mittweida, Germany
platte@hs-mittweida.de
[2] Chemnitz University of Technology, 09107 Chemnitz, Germany

Abstract. The number of application areas for object recognition are on the rise. Usable data are often limited or not well prepared to adapt to research. For image-based recognition, extensive training data is required in order to achieve precise object recognition with good repeatability.

In order to generate training data with a high variance of individual parameters required for indoor localization, we developed a pipeline for Synthetic ground truth generation. This pipeline can be used to generate specific training data for object recognition in large amounts. Another field of application is the testing of the behavior of trained networks against specific parameters.

Keywords: Object recognition · Ground truth generation · Annotated data

1 Introduction

For image-based orientation, powerful object recognizers and feature extractors are essential. To train them, extensive amount of training data are required for precise object recognition with good repeatability. If the publicly accessible databases are filtered according to preferred features for indoor localization, the amount of data available is significantly reduced. Further criteria, such as the wish for several images of the same object under different conditions with complete annotation, complicate the search for previously annotated data.

For these reasons we reduced the effort of collecting and annotating. By using openly accessible 3D-CAD models as a basis, the required data can be generated automatically. Collecting Pixel-wise annotated images with objects from all spatial perspectives including depth information is still a challenging task that involves massive resources.

To take a further step in increasing the precision of these imaging systems, we develop a synthetic generation of a large amount of object images in conjunction

C. Stephanidis (Ed.): HCII 2019, CCIS 1033, pp. 295–302, 2019.
https://doi.org/10.1007/978-3-030-23528-4_41

with corresponding annotation data like [1,2]. These synthetic generated images with associated metadata provides universal pixel perfect ground truth data for image recognition.

2   Related Work

A few approaches for synthetic of furniture can be found in publicly accessible databases including 3D objects and annotations [3,4] or SceneNet [5].

Tiburzi et al generated in [6] ground truth data with small step parameters for human poses. Fisher et al. provides in [7] procedural placement for furniture combinations. Armeni et al. already comes very close to our approach by showing the procedural arrangement of objects in contexts [8]. Other datasets offer many images with annotations like SceneNet [9,10].

What we have generally missed in all these datasets is the presence or the possibility of generating small-step changes to individual parameter combinations.

3   Presented Toolchain

3.1   Overview

For this purpose, 3D design data of objects - here office furniture - are combined with scene parameters (Fig. 1 ⓐ) and rendered using *blender* [11] (Fig. 1 ⓑ). The references to the images and the metadata calculated independently from rendering are written to the database.

This toolchain runs, once started, autonomous completely bypassing manual annotations as illustrated in Fig. 1.

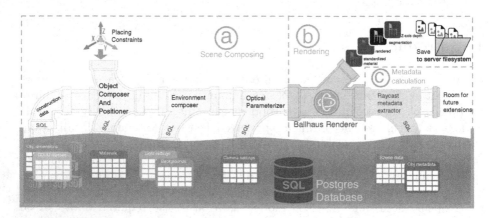

Fig. 1. Workflow overview: all data handling based on Postgres database. The tool chain consists of two parts. The scene composer ⓐ and the two-split output stage, consisting of the ballroom renderer ⓑ and the raycast metadata calculator ⓒ. (Color figure online)

3.2 Scene Build: Parameter Combination

Each scene is composed of a combination of parameters. The basis for the szenes are publicly available 3D CAD models These are equipped with modular parameters in different categories

- object parameters texture, material, reflectivity, object informations based on COCO Dataset [9].
- ambient parameters such as lighting situation, distance to object
- technical specifications of the image sensor like focal length, depth of field, aperture and sensor size

Lighting Situations. In our area of application for indoor navigation, an existing lighting situation doesn't change much. The main lighting is fixed and is provided by windows and lamps. However, the basic lighting can be very different. A room can be bright or dark. While the sun is shining in, the human eye can see objects very well with a high brightness range and distinguish bright from dark [12] without problems. A camera suffers from a much lower dynamic range and is less able to distinguish these contrasts, especially if the contrast divides the object, i.e. one part is light and the other dark. This can be addressed using the Light Situation parameter.

Scene Composer. The toolchain of the *Scene Composers* (Fig. 1 ⓐ) consists of three parts *Object Composer and Positioner*, *Environment composer* and *Optical Parameterizer*. These are shown in Fig. 1 in yellow. Each of the components processes one of the above parameter categories. The *Object composer* assembles the scene from the 3D data. The object or in further stages several objects are placed and aligned. For later analyses, it is essential to assign location attributes to objects so that they are comparable across different instances.

The *Environment composer* equips the finished objects with lighting and background. A floor was initially omitted in order to render the objects from all spatial directions, even from below. At the end of the composing pipeline ⓐ in Fig. 1 the adjustment of the image sensor takes place considering the visibility corridor, shown in blue in Fig. 2. The sample images from Fig. 3 were recorded with a starting focal length of $f_0 = 50\,mm$ and a camera distance of $d_0 = 4500\,mm$. With this combination, all objects are fully visible at any spatial angle.

Further focal length distance pairs for the existing scenes are derived from this using the relationship

$$tan\frac{\delta}{2} = \frac{s}{2f} = \frac{g_p}{2d} \quad \longrightarrow \quad d = \frac{fg_p}{s} \tag{1}$$

where:

$s = s_w = s_h$ = sensor width and height(same for quadratic sensor)
f = focal length (f_0 = initial = $50\,mm$)
δ = visual angle, $\frac{\delta}{2}$ for both sides of the optical axis (δ_0 = initial)
d = distance from lens to object (d_0 = initial = $4500\,mm$)

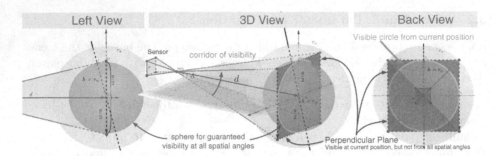

Fig. 2. Calculation of the envelope sphere for the object size and placement (Eq. 1). (Color figure online)

g_p = projected object size in perpendicular plane (flat size, see the circle with the yellow border in Fig. 2)

Future objects are constrained to be within the enveloping sphere of visibility in order to use the same focal length-distance pairs. The envelope sphere is determined by the largest possible sphere that fits into the blue visibility corridor in Fig. 2. The visibility corridor is spanned by sensor size s and visibility angle *delta*. The center of this sphere is located at the intersection of the optical axis with the normal plane spanned by the initial distance d_0. The radius is 3048 mm and is determined by

$$r_m = d_0 \cdot sin\left(\frac{\delta}{2}\right) = d_0 \cdot sin\left(tan^{-1}\left(\frac{s}{2f_0}\right)\right) \qquad (2)$$

Scene Variations. Each of the possible parameter combinations will produce new representations of the rendered object. The number of finished scenes to be rendered factorially increases with the number of parameters. In the current version, 7 selected materials are combined with 5 light situations and 2 focal length distance pairs. This results in 70 variations per scene:

$$z = n_{\text{lights}} \cdot n_{\text{materials}} \cdot n_{\text{focallengths}} \qquad (3)$$

3.3   Scene Rendering and Metadata Calculation

Single Rendering Run. After assembling the scene, the camera is set to the starting position (φ_0, θ_0), shown in Fig. 3. The render resolution was set to 896 pixels in x and y direction. Rendering the scene creates an output image that is stored in the server's file system (Fig. 1 ⓑ). The reference to the image is stored in the database, where it is linked to the source parameters.

Metadata Calculation. After rendering the 2D object annotations are determined (Fig. 1 ⓒ) from the virtual screen using a raycast [13,14] method.

Therefore non-recursive virtual beams are traced backward through each pixel of the rendered image back into the scene for ray–surface intersection

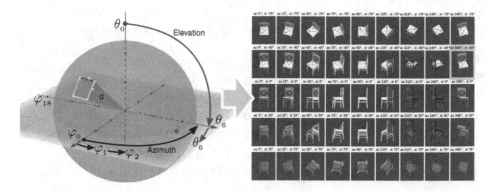

Fig. 3. "Ballhaus-Kreisel" around the object in 24 azimuthal positions $\varphi_n \in [0\,23]$ with 13 elevation angle positions $\theta_n \in [0\,12]$ per φ_n. For clarification one random position is marked: the yellow camera position corresponding to the adjacent rendered picture. (Color figure online)

tests with scene models [15]. The transmitted beam does not bounce off or pass through surfaces. This method excludes the possibility of obtaining false results from reflections, refractions or the natural fall of shadows.

Process Whole Scene Orbitals. In order to make an object detector to be trained resistant to the position of objects in space or to check their sensitivity to the spatial position of objects when testing object detectors, the objects from all spatial angles are treated equally.

The spatial angles of the recording should be discretely evenly distributed at a spacing of $\frac{\pi}{12}$ in the interval

$$\varphi \in [0\,2\pi] \qquad\qquad \theta \in [-\pi\,\pi]$$

$$\varphi_n = \sum_{n=0}^{23} \frac{1}{12} n\pi \qquad\qquad \theta_n = \sum_{n=0}^{12} \frac{1}{12} n\pi - \frac{\pi}{2} \qquad (4)$$

4   Outcome: First Run

In the first run 458640 images were generated for 21 objects in all combinations. This corresponds to 70 complete Ballhaus orbitals with 21840 images per scene.

Table 1 shows the statistical values of the first run for one pair of focal length and distance. Figure 4 also shows the distribution of the boundingboxes for the different COCO object classes. Here the value of $\overline{x}_{w,chair} = 0.19$ and $\overline{x}_{h,chair} = 0.28$ with a standard deviation of $(\sigma_{w,chair}, \sigma_{h,chair}) = (0.03, 0.06)$ from Table 1 is shown in the high concentration of the chairs in the bottom area of the left part of Figure 4. This characteristic also occurs in Figure 4 on the right part: the distribution of the boundingbox widths and heights of the COCO label "chair" shows a significant characteristic with a clear shift of the heights compared to the widths in the compressed first distribution chart.

Table 1. Statistical values of bounding boxes of the corresponding COCO category ($\overline{x}_w, \overline{x}_h$ = arithmetic mean, $\widetilde{x}_w, \widetilde{x}_h$ = median, σ_w, σ_h = standard deviation)

COCO	bbox	Bounding box width					Bounding box heigth				
Label	Count	$\overline{x}_w$	$\widetilde{x}_w$	σ_w	Min	Max	$\overline{x}_h$	$\widetilde{x}_h$	σ_h	Min	Max
Chair	98280	0.19	0.19	0.03	0.11	0.27	0.27	0.28	0.06	0.11	0.44
Desk	21840	0.72	0.67	0.18	0.31	1.00	0.60	0.56	0.19	0.27	1.00
Lamp	10920	0.19	0.20	0.06	0.09	0.27	0.23	0.23	0.05	0.09	0.32
Monitor	10920	0.26	0.27	0.09	0.08	0.42	0.27	0.27	0.09	0.09	0.47
Table	87360	0.48	0.48	0.16	0.23	1.00	0.43	0.41	0.13	0.16	0.75

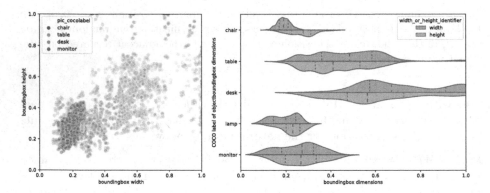

Fig. 4. Distribution of boundingbox dimensions for various COCO labels

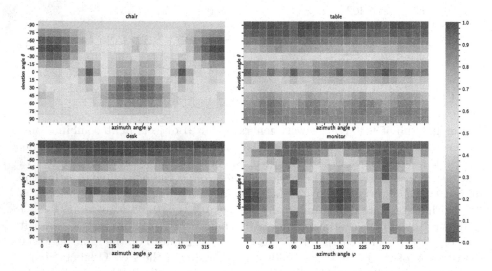

Fig. 5. Average visibility $\overline{v}(\varphi, \theta)$ for several object classes. Every segment shows the visibility value based on the max projection area of a whole render orbital ($v_{max} = 1$).

Figure 5 shows visibility maps of 4 COCO classes. The average value for all chairs shows that they have the highest visibility from the front diagonally below and behind diagonally above. The visibility mask of the monitor is also very clear: it is best seen frontally and dorsally, very little from the side. This corresponds to the reality of looking at a monitor.

5 Conclusion and Future Work

The focus for our field of application is the generation of complete object orbitals with annotation of each single image. The ground truth generator presented here generated a data set of 458640 completely annotated images in the first run. This data set is now available for training purposes or evaluation of object detectors. The inclusion of all partial modules from Fig. 1 ⓐ–ⓒ on a database ensures generic access and simple expandability of the entire system.

Individual components can be equipped by additional instances of existing parameters such as material, light settings and environment. The modules also provide a basic framework for further parameters. It is conceivable for example that visibility can be gradually reduced by depth of field limitations, blurred areas (simulation of dirty lenses of smartphones) or noise due to low illuminance. In a next step, more complex scenes with several objects and mutual covering could be created.

The integration of automatic training and test set synthesis technologies into interactive systems offers another opportunity for continuing further work. Users could manipulate higher-level meta-parameters, such as the illumination of a room by sunlight according to the sun position during a day. This room is then filled with synthetically generated and illuminated objects.

We are convinced that these artificially generated scenes have a great future, especially with applications with particular requirements.

References

1. Feng, G., et al.: Abstract: an indoor localization simulation platform for localization accuracy evaluation. In: 2018 15th Annual IEEE International Conference on Sensing, Communication, and Networking (SECON), June 2018, pp. 1–3 (2018). 10/gftk9s
2. Ceriani, S., et al.: Rawseeds ground truth collection systems for indoor self-localization and mapping. Auton. Robots 27(4), 353–371 (2009). https://doi.org/10.1007/s10514-009-9156-5. 10/bvt398
3. IKEA Planer & Planungshilfen - IKEA (2018). https://www.ikea.com/, https://www.ikea.com/ms/de_DE/campaigns/services/planer_und_ratgeber.html#/
4. Roomeon - Die Erste Interior Design Software. Fotorealistisch Und in 3D (2018). http://de.roomeon.com/
5. Handa, A., Patraucean, V., Badrinarayanan, V., Stent, S., Cipolla, R.: SceneNet: understanding real world indoor scenes with synthetic data, 22 November 2015. arXiv:1511.07041 [cs]

6. Tiburzi, F., Escudero, M., Bescos, J., Martinez, J.M.: A ground truth for motion-based video-object segmentation. In: 2008 15th IEEE International Conference on Image Processing, San Diego, CA, USA, pp. 17–20. IEEE (2008). 10/fn5ks2, http://ieeexplore.ieee.org/document/4711680/

7. Fisher, M., Ritchie, D., Savva, M., Funkhouser, T., Hanrahan, P.: Example-based synthesis of 3D object arrangements. ACM Trans. Graph. **31**(6), 1 (2012), 10/gbb6sf. http://dl.acm.org/citation.cfm?doid=2366145.2366154

8. Armeni, I., Sax, A., Zamir, A.R., Savarese, S.: Joint 2D–3D-semantic data for indoor scene understanding, p. 9, 6 April 2017

9. Lin, T.-Y., et al.: Microsoft COCO: common objects in context, 1 May 2014. arXiv:1405.0312 [cs]

10. McCormac, J., Handa, A., Leutenegger, S., Davison, A.J.: SceneNet RGB-D: can 5M synthetic images beat generic ImageNet pre-training on indoor segmentation? In: 2017 IEEE International Conference on Computer Vision (ICCV), October 2017, pp. 2697–2706. IEEE, Venice (2017). 10/gftpgx, http://ieeexplore.ieee.org/document/8237554/

11. Blender Foundation. Blender. Org - Home of the Blender Project - Free and Open 3D Creation Software. https://www.blender.org/

12. Radonjić, A., Allred, S.R., Gilchrist, A.L., Brainard, D.H.: The dynamic range of human lightness perception. Curr. Biol. **21**(22), 1931–1936 (2011). pmid: 22079116. 10/d735svhttps://www.ncbi.nlm.nih.gov/pmc/articles/PMC3244211/

13. Roth, S.D.: Ray casting for modeling solids. Comput. Graph. Image Process. **18**(2), 109–144 (1982). 10/cn2kkv, https://linkinghub.elsevier.com/retrieve/pii/0146664X82901691

14. Gilbert, E.G., Johnson, D.W., Keerthi, S.S.: A fast procedure for computing the distance between complex objects in three-dimensional space. IEEE J. Robot. Autom. **4**(2), 193–203 (1988). 10/d7q7k3

15. Cameron, S.: Collision detection by four-dimensional intersection testing. In: IEEE Trans. Robot. Autom. **6**(3), 291–302 (1990). 10/c942g2, http://ieeexplore.ieee.org/document/56661/

Generation of Individual Activity Classifiers for the Use in Mobile Context-Aware Applications

Tony Rolletschke[1]($\boxtimes$), Christian Roschke[1], Rico Thomanek[1], Benny Platte[1], Robert Manthey[2], and Frank Zimmer[1]

[1] University of Applied Sciences Mittweida, 09648 Mittweida, Germany
{tony.rolletschke,christian.roschke,rico.thomanek,benny.platte,
frank.zimmer}@hs-mittweida.de
[2] Chemnitz University of Technology, 09107 Chemnitz, Germany
robert.manthey@informatik.tu-chemnitz.de

Abstract. In recent years, various methods for the automated recognition of human activities based on the analysis of sensor data using machine learning approaches have been researched. The continuously increasing hardware performance of mobile devices such as smartphones and wearables and the ongoing development of existing algorithms have resulted in steadily higher recognition rates. These latest advances resulted in an growing demand for intelligent and context sensitive mobile applications. However, the generation of valid ground truth information with a suitable quality remains a major challenge. In addition, there is currently no standardized procedure for generating an activity classifier for the use in custom application areas. The holistic workflow introduced in this paper focuses on the recognition of activities using mobile devices. For this purpose, the generation of a ground truth information by recording and annotating sensor data is described. The generated data set is used for transfer learning in a machine learning framework and the resulting model is the basis for a mobile real-time classification application. The data source is a current study of the University of Applied Sciences Mittweida.

Keywords: Mobile sensing · Activity recognition · Machine learning

1 Introduction

Due to the ongoing development into a world of ubiquitous portable computers, the domain of mobile activity monitoring has become one of the major trends over the past few years. There are currently various scientific approaches in the area of activity recognition that prefer camera-based solutions [13] in addition to usual sensory systems [7]. On the basis of these technologies, applications are being developed for a wide variety of areas, such as health monitoring [15], fitness games [9] and evaluation of vehicle telemetry data [6]. Furthermore, large

© Springer Nature Switzerland AG 2019
C. Stephanidis (Ed.): HCII 2019, CCIS 1033, pp. 303–310, 2019.
https://doi.org/10.1007/978-3-030-23528-4_42

companies are exploring ways to support workers in complex working tasks to minimize errors and increase manufacturing efficiency [12]. In these cases, the focus concentrates on identifying, distinguishing and qualitatively rating different types of movements. Critical in this context is a high detection accuracy in almost real-time.

To achieve this precision, annotated data sets of high quality are required. Some past research studies use existing data sets for this purpose. However, these usually contain measurements of context-specific activities that can only rarely be transferred to other areas. Other researchers, such as Ward et al. [19] and Yang et al. [20], rely on complex measurement installations in which special sensors are attached to the body parts of study participants in order to determine the various activity characteristics. But the long wearing of these sensors is uncomfortable for the participants and not suitable for everyday usage. Furthermore, the acquisition and initialization of such complex measuring systems are associated with high overall costs and therefore unsuitable for use in real applications.

With the increasingly powerful hardware, the onboard interfaces provided by widely available mobile operating systems can now be used for deep learning techniques [16]. This allows the implementation of context-aware applications that adapt their behavior to the current environment of a user. We describe a holistic workflow that enables the recognition of activities with sensors from typical mobile devices. For the training of an activity classifier, we generate a data set in an ongoing research study.

2 Methodology

The following section describes a holistic workflow shown in Fig. 1 for classifying activities. For this purpose, a method for generating ground truth information using a mobile application for smartphones and wearables is introduced. Afterward, the created data set is used to train a machine learning algorithm. The resulting model is used for real-time classification of activities on mobile devices.

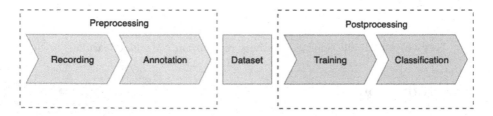

Fig. 1. Holistic workflow for activity recognition consisting of four steps

2.1 Recording

As part of the study, a group of students will be equipped with state of the art hardware. These include an Apple Watch Series 3, an iPhone 7 and a GoPro

Hero 5. The carrying position of the devices is fixed and must be checked by the test person using a checklist at the beginning of every measurement. This ensures that the individual measurement series can be easily reproduced.

The Apple Watch, for example, should be worn on the wrist of the dominant hand. Another important aspect is the orientation of the watch. The display of the Apple Watch aligned to the top of the wrist and the digital crown to the elbow. Additionally, Apple emphasizes that an accurate measurement of the heart sensors can only be guaranteed by an optimal fit [5]. Therefore, the back of the watch must touch the skin directly.

Fig. 2. iOS and watchOS user interface of the developed app

Furthermore, it is important to ensure that the Apple Watch is neither too loose or too tight. Because this would not only corrupt the measurement results but can also result in skin irritation [5]. Related requirements must also be followed during the positioning of the smartphone. This should be placed in the front trouser pocket with the display towards the thigh and the lightning connector facing upwards. The action cam is visibly attached to the test person's body with the help of a chest strap. In this way, the subject's field of vision is recorded widely in a first-person view. After the checklist has been correctly processed, the participant is allowed to perform the measurement. For this purpose, an app specially implemented for this study is installed on the hardware.

Inside the user interface shown in Fig. 2, a login screen is implemented on which the user enter an anonymous identification number at the beginning of each measurement. This links the series of measurements with the individual participant and enables the evaluation of user-dependent and user-independent recognition accuracy. The remaining handling of the app is managed via the Apple Watch user interface. This offers the user the possibility to start or stop the measurement and displays further status information such as the previous measurement duration. This has the advantage that the user only interacts with one device during the measurement and can, therefore, concentrate on performing activities. In addition, the sensor values are prevented from being falsified because the iPhone does not have to be removed or put in the trouser pocket.

Apple's *Core Motion* Framework enables access to different types of sensors. For this reason, the framework is used to capture relevant sensor data during the measurement shown in Table 1. There is a distinction between hardware sensors, which allow to readout raw data, and software sensors, which provide an already processed version of the raw values. Noise and other external influences, such as the impact of gravity, are already removed from the data of the software sensors. This allows analyzing only the forces applied by the user in further evaluation. The measurement of the sensor data is additionally done in relation to a predefined world coordinate system so that the rotation of the device about any axis in three-dimensional space can be exactly followed [11]. This minimizes the dependence on the orientation of the device. For example, it is irrelevant whether the telephone is placed in the trouser pocket with the connections pointing downwards or upwards.

2.2 Annotation

The workflow described in this section uses a form of supervised learning. The aim of this technique is to train a model using labeled data and known features. Afterward, predictions about unknown or future data can be calculated [18]. To generate a training data set, it is required to allocate the recorded sensor data with the corresponding activity classes. For this purpose, the annotation of the video stream simultaneously recorded to the sensor data acquisition follows in a specially developed web-based application. The user interface of this web application displays a preview of the video material and also includes a functional timeline for an overview of the annotation progress. In addition, a list of the key mappings for using the tool is shown. A further motivation for the use of a video-based annotation procedure is the workload reduction during the execution of activities. This avoids the overhead of simultaneous handwritten documentation. Besides a falsification of the sensor data recording by the movement of the hand, as it would occur with a written protocol, is prevented. Furthermore, the recorded video contains a significant part of the original information, which eliminates the possibility of vague information from the subjects memory laps while collecting activities. In this way, the disadvantages resulting from a retrospective approach are minimized.

Table 1. Simplified overview of the recorded sensor data (cf. [8])

Sensor	Type	Data	Description
Accelerometer	Hardware	Acceleration	Deliver accelerometer data for all three axes of the device
Gyroscope	Hardware	Rotation Rate	Deliver the raw gyroscope data
Magnetometer	Hardware	Magnetic Field	Provide compass-level orientation data and raw magnetometer data
Altitude	Hardware	Pressure	The recorded pressure, in kilopascals
	Software	Relative Altitude	The change in altitude (in meters) since the first reported event
Pedometer	Software	Pedometer Data	Information about the distance traveled by a user on foot
Device Motion	Software	Attitude	The attitude of the device
		Rotation Rate	The rotation rate of the device relative to the current reference frame
		Gravity	The gravity acceleration vector expressed in the device's reference frame
		User Acceleration	The acceleration that the user is giving to the device
		Magnetic Field	Returns the magnetic field vector with respect to the device
		Heading	The heading angle (measured in degrees) relative to the current reference frame
Heart Sensor	Hardware	Heart Rate	A quantity sample type that measures the users heart rate

2.3 Training

The function of an activity classifier is to distinguish between different activities performed by humans based on sensor data. There are different learning methods for the analysis of the sensor data. Akhavian and Behzadan [1] tested five different approaches for the classification of sensor data during the execution of human activities and achieved the best results with artificial neural networks Ordóñez et al. [17] also showed with their publication that the use of *CNNs* and *LSTMs* achieves high accuracy in the detection of human activity. They outperformed by an average of 4% other methods which don't use recurrent neural networks. Furthermore, in their research, they describe an approach for a generic deep learning framework. Based on this publication, Apple has integrated the functionality for creating activity classifiers into their own machine learning framework called *Turi Create*. This framework was released by Apple in 2017 under an open source license on GitHub and is designed for developers with little experience in machine learning. For this reason, only a few lines of code are required to create a user-defined machine learning model [4]. For processing of the several sensor data in *Turi Create* they are merged and converted into a suitable input format (*SFrame*). The sensor data must be sorted in ascending order and the several values must be arranged in a row. Each recording corresponds to a set of measured values and is called a session. The activity classifier expects that each measured value is assigned to a session and has an activity label. For the quantitative evaluation of the classifier, the generated data set is randomly split into training and test data. Then the model will be trained and its generalizability determined by an evaluation function. A test on just training data would only correspond to retrieval of stored data [10]. Once the model reaches satisfactory results, the training process is completed, the resulting model will be saved and exported to a format appropriate for iOS (*MLModel*). Then it can be used for real-time classification on the iPhone.

2.4   Classification

In the middle of 2017, when iOS 11 was rolled out, Apple introduced a new framework called *Core ML*. This framework offers powerful functions to integrate machine learning into applications for iOS, macOS, watchOS and tvOS. For example, it enables computationally intensive classification procedures performed locally on a mobile device using artificial neural networks. This eliminates the requirement of sending data to a server and significantly reduces processing speed by eliminating transmission times. [3]

First implementations with *Core ML* have already shown promising results in the classification of images, text, and recognition of human poses [14]. In our case, the focus is on the use of a model created with *Turi Create* (cf. Section 2.3) to classify activities. For this it is necessary to activate the sensors listed in Table 1 on the mobile device and to query them with the desired sampling frequency.

The temporary storage of the resulting measured values takes place in an array with the capacity of the desired window size. This size corresponds to the length of the prediction interval used to classify the activities. If the array is filled with sensor data, its contents are committed to the prediction function of the model. Finally, the model returns a prediction. This contains the recognized activity with the highest probability. [2]

3   Results

In a first beta test, the mobile iOS application was tried out by students as part of a research project. The group recorded several activities and logged their experiences and insights. The results show, that after a short familiarization phase, the app can be used without technical knowledge. Initial difficulties related to incorrect positioning of the hardware and wrong operation of the application. These obstacles were solved during the test period by increasing familiarity with measurement technology and the introduction of the checklist mentioned in Sect. 2.1. Also a bug caused by an expired developer certificate, which made the app disappear, was quickly fixed. A longterm problem resulting in connection problems between iPhone and Apple Watch disappeared after a bugfix during an update of the watchOS operating system.

During one semester, about 24 h of sensor and video data were collected. In the process, it was possible to store the various pieces of information in a common database and link them together using time stamps. Activities such as lying, sitting, standing, running, climbing stairs and the transitions between the forms of these movements were included. In addition, measurements in different modes of transport such as car, bus, and train were performed. Approximately 10% of the recordings are unusable or only partially usable due to the above-mentioned challenges. The remaining part of the data set is currently evaluated with the annotation tool described in Sect. 2.2 and will be labeled with the corresponding activity.

4   Conclusion

In this paper, we introduced a holistic workflow that is already being used in an ongoing study. The first recordings of the smartphone app are already in a central database and are currently being annotated according to the procedures described in Sect. 2.2. The result shows that the generation of an activity data set with commercially available smartphones and wearables is possible. In the future, the training of the activity classifier and the evaluation of the resulting model will follow. Finally, it is planned to analyze the quality of the model during the classification of activities in a real-time application. In addition, the handling, scalability, and reliability of the workflow will be optimized in a further field and long-term tests. We also intend to generate comparable test data sets for other activities and compare the performance of the activity classifier with other methods.

Acknowledgments. This work was written in the junior research group "Agile Publika" funded by the European Social Fund (ESF) an the Free State of Saxony.

References

1. Akhavian, R., Behzadan, A.H.: Wearable sensor-based activity recognition for data-driven simulation of construction workers' activities In: Winter Simulation Conference, pp. 3333–3344 (2015)
2. Apple: Deployment to Core ML GitBook (2018). https://apple.github.io/turicreate/docs/userguide. Accessed 15 Jan 2019
3. Apple: Machine Learning - Apple Developer (2018). https://developer.apple.com/machine-learning. Accessed 15 Jan 2019
4. Apple: Turi Create - User Guide (2018). https://apple.github.io/turicreate/docs/userguide/. Accessed 21 Jan 2019

5. Apple: Wearing your Apple Watch - Apple Support (2018). https://support.apple.com/en-us/HT204665. Accessed 28 Jan 2019
6. Cardoso, N., Madureira, J., Pereira, N.: Smartphone-based transport mode detection for elderly care. In: HealthCom, pp. 1–6 (2016)
7. Chen, Y., Shen, C.: Performance analysis of smartphone-sensor behavior for human activity recognition. IEEE Access **5**, 3095–3110 (2017)
8. Dev, A.: Core Motion Framework - Apple Developer (2018). https://developer.apple.com/documentation/coremotion. Accessed 21 Aug 2018
9. Direito, A., Jiang, Y., Whittaker, R., Maddison, R.: Smartphone apps to improve fitness and increase physical activity among young people: protocol of the Apps for IMproving FITness (AIMFIT) randomized controlled trial. BMC Public Health **15**(1), 635 (2015)
10. Ertel, W.: Grundkurs Künstliche Intelligenz. Springer Fachmedien Wiesbaden, Wiesbaden (2016). https://doi.org/10.1007/978-3-658-13549-2
11. Henpraserttae, A., Thiemjarus, S., Marukatat, S.: Accurate activity recognition using a mobile phone regardless of device orientation and location. In: BSN, pp. 41–46 (2011)
12. Hitachi: DFKI and Hitachi jointly develop AI technology for human activity recognition of workers using wearable devices (2017). http://www.hitachi.com/New/cnews/month/2017/03/170308.html. Accessed 13 Sept 2018
13. Jalal, A., Kim, Y., Kim, Y.J., Kamal, S., Kim, D.: Robust human activity recognition from depth video using spatiotemporal multi-fused features. Pattern Recogn. **61**, 295–308 (2017)
14. Li, K.: Awesome CoreML Models - GitHub (2018). https://github.com/likedan/Awesome-CoreML-Models. Accessed 18 Jan 2019
15. Moser, L.E., Melliar-Smith, P.M.: Personal health monitoring using a smartphone. In: 2015 IEEE International Conference on Mobile Services (MS), pp. 344–351. IEEE (2015)
16. Newnham, J.: Machine Learning with Core ML: An iOS Developer's Guide to Implementing Machine Learning in Mobile Apps. Packt Publishing, Birmingham (2018)
17. Ordóñez, F., Roggen, D.: Deep convolutional and LSTM recurrent neural networks for multimodal wearable activity recognition. Sensors **16**(1), 115 (2016)
18. Raschka, S.: Python Machine Learning. Packt Publishing Ltd., Birmingham (2015)
19. Ward, J.A., Lukowicz, P., Troster, G., Starner, T.E.: Activity recognition of assembly tasks using body-worn microphones and accelerometers. IEEE Trans. Pattern Anal. Mach. Intell. **28**(10), 1553–1567 (2006)
20. Yang, A.Y., Iyengar, S., Kuryloski, P., Jafari, R.: Distributed segmentation and classification of human actions using a wearable motion sensor network. In: 2008 IEEE Computer Society Conference on Computer Vision and Pattern Recognition Workshops (CVPR Workshops), pp. 1–8. IEEE (2008)

Observation Planning for Identifying Each Person by a Drone in Indoor Daily Living Environment

Koki Sakata[1]($\boxtimes$), Koh Kakusho[1], Masaaki Iiyama[2],
and Satoshi Nishiguchi[3]

[1] School of Science and Technology,
Kwansei Gakuin University, Nishinomiya, Japan
{fzj92496,kakusho}@kwansei.ac.jp
[2] Academic Center for Computing and Media Studies,
Kyoto University, Kyoto, Japan
iiyama@mm.media.kyoto-u.ac.jp
[3] Faculty of Information Science and Technology,
Osaka Institute of Technology, Osaka, Japan
satoshi.nishiguchi@oit.ac.jp

Abstract. This article discusses observation planning for identifying each person in indoor living environment such as office space using a mobile camera mounted on a drone. Since many people in the environment often keep their positions and postures during their work, it is difficult to observe the face of all the people by a fixed camera installed in the environment to identify each of them, when some of them keep orienting their faces toward the directions opposite to the camera. In this article, it is proposed to observe each person's face with a mobile camera mounted on a small drone, which flies around the ceiling in the environment. Assuming that the position and orientation of each person has already been obtained by the fixed camera, the proposed method observes each person's face from the front with an appropriate distance in turn while minimizing the total cost for changing the position and the orientation of the drone before completing the observation for all the people.

Keywords: Human identification · Face recognition · Observation planning · Drone · Traveling Salesman Problem

1 Introduction

Recently, various IoT devices such as smart speakers and smart TVs are widely used in our indoor daily living environment such as homes or offices [1]. In this environment, if it is known who is where, it is possible to provide various user-specific services such as presenting incoming urgent messages or favorite news to different users in different places using IoT devices placed there. However, it is not realistic to assume that the position of each user is obtained by his/her smartphone, because we are not usually keep carrying our own smartphones in our homes. If some cameras are installed in the environment, it is possible to grasp the current position and orientation of each person

© Springer Nature Switzerland AG 2019
C. Stephanidis (Ed.): HCII 2019, CCIS 1033, pp. 311–319, 2019.
https://doi.org/10.1007/978-3-030-23528-4_43

[2], yet it is not easy to know who he/she is by observing the face because people do not necessarily orient their faces toward any camera [3]. Moreover, they usually keep their positions and postures especially in indoor daily living environment, unlike in outdoor public environment such as on a street.

In this article, it is proposed to identify each person by observing his/her face in turn with a camera mounted on a small drone, which flies around the ceiling in the environment. Assuming that the position and the orientation of each person has already been obtained by a camera fixed in the environment, the proposed method plans continuous motion of the drone so that its mounted camera observes the face of each person most efficiently from the front with an appropriate distance to identify the person, while minimizing the total cost for changing the position and the orientation of the drone before completing the observation for all the people.

In the remainder of this article, the position and the orientation of a mobile camera suitable for observing the face of each person will be first discussed in Sect. 2. In Sect. 3, a planning method for observing each person's face in turn while minimizing the total cost for changing the position and the orientation of the drone will be proposed. Some experimental results for evaluating the proposed method will be presented in Sect. 4. Finally, the summary and some discussion on possible future steps of this work will be given in Sect. 5.

2 Position and Orientation of Camera for Observing Each Person

2.1 Acquiring Current Positions and Orientations of Each Person and the Drone

Recently, RGB-D cameras are widely used for various purposes, and it becomes easy to obtain 3D positions objects including human bodies in the observed scene together with its color image. Many methods for detecting human bodies in the scene are also proposed in conventional work [4]. Thus, it is assumed in the following discussion that RGB-D cameras are installed around the ceiling in the environment so that the upper part of the body of each person in the environment can be observed without occlusion from the camera, and the position and the orientation of each person's body are obtained from, for example, the 3D positions of the head and the shoulders. Here, let N be the number of persons in the environment where their faces cannot be observed from the fixed camera. The position and the orientation of i-th person denoted by H_i ($i = 1, 2, \ldots N$) among the N persons is denoted by h_i and g_i respectively. Whensome markers are attached to the drone, its position and orientation denoted by m and l can also be obtained. The relations between person H_i and the drone equipped with a camera in the positions and orientations denoted above are illustrated in Fig. 1.

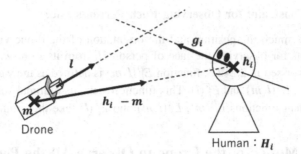

Fig. 1. Geometric constrains for the positions and the orientations of person H_i and the drone equipped with a camera.

2.2 Geometric Constraint for the Distance Between Each Person and the Drone

To observe the face of person H_i using the camera on the drone, it is necessary to keep an appropriate distance from the person so that the facial region in the image obtained by the camera appears in a size suitable for recognizing the face. Let us denote the most appropriate distance by d. Based on the difference between the two distances of d and $h_i - m$, which is the actual distance of the drone from H_i, the function that evaluates the departure of the distance between the positions of the drone and H_i from d can be defined. This function is denoted hereafter by $E_i^D(m)$, which takes its minimal value 0 when the drone is located exactly in the distance of d from H_i.

2.3 Geometric Constraint for the Angle Between the Orientations of Each Person's Face and the Drone

For observing a person's face to identify him/her by a camera, it is necessary to observe the face from its front as much as possible. To satisfy this condition for observing the face of person H_i by the camera on the drone, the camera first of all needs to be oriented toward the person so that his/her face is properly captured within the field of view of the camera and the face actually appears in the image obtained by the camera. The departure of the orientation of the camera from this condition is evaluated by the function denoted by $E_i^A(l, m)$ based on the angle between l and $h_i - m$, which are the orientation of the drone itself and the direction from the drone to the person H_i, respectively. This function takes its minimal value 0 when both l and $h_i - m$ are in the same direction.

Moreover, to observe the face of person H_i from the front, its orientation g_i and the camera orientation l need to be in opposite directions to each other. The departure of the camera orientation l from the above condition is evaluated by function $E_i^F(l)$ based on the angle between the vectors g_i and l. The function takes its minimal value 0 when the angle is 2π.

2.4   Overall Constraint for Observing Each Person's Face

To evaluate how much the position and the orientation of the drone violate the geometric constraints for observing the face of person H_i from its front with appropriate distance d as discussed in 2.2–2.3, function $E_i^O(l,m)$ is defined as the weighted sum of functions $E_i^D(m)$, $E_i^A(l,m)$ and $E_i^F(l)$. This function stake its minimal value 0 when all the tree component functions $E_i^D(m)$, $E_i^A(l,m)$ and $E_i^F(l)$ take their minimal value 0.

3   Planning Motion of the Drone to Observe All the Persons

3.1   Cost for Changing Geometric Configurations of the Drone to Observe Different Persons

The position and the orientation of the drone for observing each person from its front at the most appropriate distance as discussed above differs for different persons. Thus, to observe the faces of all the N persons in the environment, the drone needs to change its geometric configuration, which consists of the position and the orientation, in turn. Considering the cost for moving the drone as well as the risk for disturbing the activity of each person by the drone flying around the person, it is preferable to minimize the total cost for changing the configuration of the drone before completing the observation for all the persons, as well $E_i^O(l,m)$ for each person H_i. Whereas the configuration that minimizes $E_i^O(l,m)$ is determined only by the position and the orientation of H_i, the total cost for changing the configuration of the drone depends on the order for observing all the persons.

Let $H_{i(n)}$ denote the person who are the n-th to be observed by the drone, and let $m_{i(n)}$ and $l_{i(n)}$ denote the position and the orientation of the drone when it observes person $H_{i(n)}$. The cost for changing the configuration of the drone to observe $H_{i(n+1)}$ after $H_{i(n+1)}$ is evaluated by the function denoted by $C(m_{i(n)}, l_{i(n)}, m_{i(n+1)}, l_{i(n+1)})$, where its value is calculated as described below.

The amount of translation of the drone from its position $m_{i(n)}$ to $m_{i(n+1)}$ can be evaluated by the distance between $m_{i(n)}$ and $m_{i(n+1)}$. This amount is denoted by $M(m_{i(n)}, m_{i(n+1)})$. Similarly, the amount of rotation of the drone from its orientation $l_{i(n)}$ to $l_{i(n+1)}$ can be evaluated by the angle between $l_{i(n)}$ and $l_{i(n+1)}$. This amount is denoted by $R(l_{i(n)}, l_{i(n+1)})$. Since usual drones can translate and rotate independently at the same time, it is assumed in this work that the drone can perform the translation from $m_{i(n)}$ to $m_{i(n+1)}$ and the rotation from $l_{i(n)}$ to $l_{i(n+1)}$ independently at the same time, too. If the time spent for completing the motion constituted by these translation and rotation is considered for the cost for changing the configuration of the drone by the motion, the cost is determined by the larger value between $M(m_{i(n)}, m_{i(n+1)})$ and $R(l_{i(n)}, l_{i(n+1)})$, where those values are assumed to be preliminarily normalized into the same range. Then, the value of function $C(m_{i(n)}, m_{i(n+1)}, l_{i(n)}, l_{i(n+1)})$ is calculated as max $\{M(m_{i(n)}, m_{i(n+1)}), (l_{i(n)}, l_{i(n+1)})\}$ in this work.

3.2 Determining Configurations of the Drone for Observing All the Persons in a Given Order

Let us assume that the order to observe all the persons is temporarily given as $H_{i(1)}, \cdots, H_{i(N)}$. To suppress the total cost for changing the configuration of the drone for the observation as much as possible, configurations $m_{i(1)}, m_{i(1)}, \cdots, l_{i(N)}, l_{i(N)}$ of the drone to observe each person's face in the given order are required to minimize the sum of $C\big(m_{i(n)}, m_{i(n+1)}, l_{i(n)}, l_{i(n+1)}\big)$ over $H_{i(1)}, \cdots, H_{i(N)}$. Moreover, each of these configurations is also required to minimize $E_{i(1)}^{O}\big(m_{i(1)}, l_{i(1)}\big), \cdots, E_{i(N)}^{O}\big(m_{i(N)}, l_{i(N)}\big)$ to satisfy the geometric constraints discussed in Sect. 2 for observing each person's face from its front with an appropriate distance as much as possible. To represent the degree of violation for these two requirements for observing all the persons in the given order, function $E\big(m_{i(1)}, l_{i(1)}, \cdots, m_{i(N)}, l_{i(N)}\big)$ is defined as the weighted sum of the above two kinds of functions as follows:

$$
E\big(m_{i(1)}, l_{i(1)}, \cdots, m_{i(N)}, l_{i(N)}\big) = w_1 \sum_{n=1}^{N} E_{i(n)}^{O}\big(m_{i(n)}, l_{i(n)}\big)
$$
$$
+ w_2 \sum_{n=1}^{N-1} C\big(m_{i(n)}, m_{i(n+1)}, l_{i(n)}, l_{i(n+1)}\big) \quad (1)
$$

where w_1 and w_2 are the weights for the functions of the two kinds. The configurations that minimize the above function are denoted by $\hat{m}_{i(1)}, \hat{l}_{i(1)}, \cdots, \hat{m}_{i(N)}, \hat{l}_{i(N)}$, respectively.

3.3 Planning the Order for Observing All the Persons

Since the motion of the drone taking configurations $\hat{m}_{i(1)}, \hat{l}_{i(1)}, \cdots, \hat{m}_{i(N)}, \hat{l}_{i(N)}$ obtained above just minimizes the total cost for observing persons $H_{i(1)}, \cdots, H_{i(N)}$ in this order, it is necessary to find the best order with the minimal value for the total cost among all the possible orders for observing all the persons. This problem can be formulated as so-called *Traveling Salesman Problem* (TSP) [5], by regarding the total costs for observing all the persons with different orders as the cost for travelling all the cities with different orders in TSP.

Whereas only a single location is considered for visiting each city in usual formulation of TSP, more than a single configuration are allowed for the drone to observe each person's face in our problem. Of course, it is most preferable for the drone to take the best configuration with which the camera on the drone can observe the face exactly from its right front with the distance exactly the same as d when each person is observed. However, it is sufficiently possible to recognize the person from facial images obtained by observing his/her face with other configurations slightly different from the best configuration. The TSP with the extension that a certain area is allowed for visiting each city has been discussed in a previous work [6], in which first the best order for visiting all the cities with the shortest distance is first determined for the locations each of which is tentatively chosen among the area allowed for each city, and then modify the location chosen for each city within the area so that the distance for visiting all the cities is further minimized.

Since the degree of violation for the requirements to observe each person's face by the drone with its configuration constituted by position l and orientation m is represented by function $E_i^O(l, m)$ in our problem, configurations allowed to observe each person is not given as an area but the degree. Thus, in our method, the best order for observing all the persons is obtained by finding the order $H_{i(1)}, \cdots, H_{i(N)}$ that gives the minimal value for $E\left(\hat{m}_{i(1)}, \hat{l}_{i(1)}, \cdots, \hat{m}_{i(N)}, \hat{l}_{i(N)}\right)$, which attains minimal values for both $E_i^O(l, m)$ and $C\left(m_{i(n)}, m_{i(n+1)}, l_{i(n)}, l_{i(n+1)}\right)$ for the given order.

4   Experimental Results

4.1   Result for Simulated Environment

For the experiment to verify the actual behavior of the drone by the method described above, simulated environment with different arrangement of the people is first employed. Since various layouts can be considered for usual office environment [7], some typical layouts among them are employed for the experiment. Figure 2 shows an example of the result. The arrangement of the people working with the desks and chairs is shown in figure (a), where 10 persons are working in the room in the size of 8×8 m. In the figure, the position and the orientation of each person in the given layout is indicated by a small black square with a short line, respectively. The position and the orientation of the drone at each moment of its planned configuration is indicated by a circle with a short line in figure (b). As shown in this result, the configurations of the drone reasonable to observe all the persons are planned by the proposed method. Similar results were obtained for various layouts in the experiment.

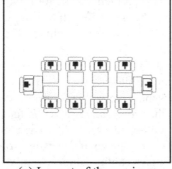
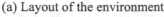
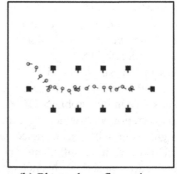

(a) Layout of the environment   (b) Planned configurations

Fig. 2. Experimental result for simulated environment.

4.2 Result for Real Environment

Second, a drone is moved by the proposed method in real environment. Tello EDU of Ryze Technology is employed for the drone and Kinect v2 of Microsoft for the camera fixed in the environment. OpenCV is employed for image processing. To avoid the risk for colliding with humans by accident, a toy mask is hung around the standard standing height of humans. The image obtained by observing the drone in the environment with the fixed camera is shown in Fig. 3(a). Figure 3(b)–(d) show the images taken by the camera on the drone when it took off from the floor, moved to observe the face of the mask and reached the aimed configuration.

As shown in figure (a), the mask was not captured in the field of view of the camera on the drone when it took off from the floor. After the motion of the drone planned by the proposed method, the mask was captured in the image as shown in (b), and then the face of the mask was observed from its front with an appropriate distance as shown in (c). Although there is only a single face in the environment in this experiment, it could be confirmed that the drone move to properly in real environment by the proposed method.

(a) Sample image of the fixed camera   (b) When the drone took off

(c) When the face was captured   (d) When the face was observed properly

Fig. 3. Experimental result in real environment.

5 Conclusions

This article discussed a method for planning observation for each person's face by a camera on a drone to identify the person in an indoor living environment. To identify each person by observing his/her face, it is required for the face to be observed from its front at an appropriate distance so that the frontal face is captured in an appropriate size in the observed image. In addition, it is also required that the cost for changing the geometric configuration of the drone for observing all the face is minimized. In order to fulfill these two requirements, the functions for evaluating the violation of those requirements by geometric configurations possibly taken by the drone when it observes all the persons in a given order is defined to be minimized. Although the problem for finding the best order that gives the smallest value for the minimized value of the function among all the possible orders can be formulated as a kind of TSP, more than a single configurations are allowed for the configuration to be taken for observing each person's face, unlike usual TSP. Thus, the solution of the problem was obtained by searching for the best order while determining the configuration to observe each person by minimizing the weighted sum of the above functions by referring to the previous work for an extension of TSP similar to our problem. It was also verified that the drone shows appropriate behavior by the proposed method in the experiments in simulated and real environment.

As one of the possible future steps of our work, it needs to be considered how to reduce the possibility of disturbing the work of each person by continuously flying around the person. Moreover, although this article assumes identification of each person for the possible application of the proposed method, it can be viewed in more broader sense as the technique for surveillance by a mobile camera for indoor daily living environment. Since the previous work for surveillance has employed fixed cameras because the observed environment is public space where almost all the people are moving around. However, for the environment where people are not moving, the camera needs to move instead. It is also another important future step of this work to discuss how to apply the proposed method for observation of human behavior in that environment.

References

1. Vinay Sagar, K.N., Kusuma, S.M.: Home automation using internet of things. Int. Res. J. Eng. Technol. (IRJET) 02(03), 1965–1970 (2015)
2. Xia, L., Chen, C.C., Aggarwal, J.: Human detection using depth information by Kinect. In: International Workshop on Human Activity Understanding from 3D Data (in Conjunction with CVPR), pp. 15–22 (2011)
3. Tan, X., Chen, S., Zhou, Z.-H., Zhang, F.: Face recognition from a single image per person: a survey. Pattern Recogn. 39(9), 1725–1745 (2006)
4. Cao, Z., Simon, T., Wei, S.-E., Sheikh, Y.: Real multi-person 2D pose estimation using part affinity fields. In: The IEEE Conference on Computer Vision and Pattern Recognition (CVPR), pp. 7291–7299 (2017)

5. Zhang, J.: Natural computation for the traveling salesman problem. In: 2009 Second International Conference on Intelligent Computation Technology and Automation, vol. 1, pp. 366–369 (2009). (in Japanese)
6. Noguchi, Y., Takemura, A., Ohta, H., Nakamori, M.: A heuristic algorithm for the region covering salesman problem. The Special Interest Group Technical Reports of IPSJ, vol. 2012-MPS-91, no. 18, pp 1–5, December 2012
7. Office Layout Plans. https://www.conceptdraw.com/solution-park/building-office-layout-plans. Accessed 28 Mar 2019

Use of Multiple Distributed Process Instances for Activity Analysis in Videos

Rico Thomanek[1(✉)], Benny Platte[1], Christian Roschke[1], Robert Manthey[2],
Tony Rolletschke[1], Claudia Hösel[1], Marc Ritter[1], and Frank Zimmer[1]

[1] University of Applied Sciences Mittweida, 09648 Mittweida, Germany
{rico.thomanek,benny.platte,christian.roschke,tony.rolletschke,
claudia.hosel,marc.ritter,frank.zimmer}@hs-mittweida.de
[2] Chemnitz University of Technology, 09107 Chemnitz, Germany
robert.manthey@informatik.tu-chemnitz.de

Abstract. Video surveillance of security-relevant areas is being used
ever more frequently. Because of limited human resources, they are usually only checked for the presence of problematic activity after a specific
event has occurred. An approach to the solution is provided by automated systems that are capable of detecting and analyzing movement
sequences of objects including persons. Even though solutions already
exist for scene recognition [3,4,8,9], their architecture, their problem-
specific domain and the nature of the systems make it difficult to integrate new activities or better algorithms. A system structure based
on decentralized process instances and their communication via defined
interfaces would instead enable a simpler expansion of the system. This
paper describes the determination of activities in videos using decentralized frameworks and their interconnection via standardized interfaces.
All components act autonomously and provide their data via a central
location. Based on this approach, the modular system can be used for a
wide variety of applications in the context of machine learning.

Keywords: Activity analysis · Machine learning · Distributed process

1 Introduction

In recent years, the number of surveillance cameras has increased worldwide.
CCTV (Closed Circuit Television) cameras are constantly capturing ever larger
amounts of image data, which due to limited personnel resources are usually
only checked for signs of problematic activity after a certain event has occurred.
An approach to the solution offers automated systems, which in the sense of the
"predictive police work" are able to capture and evaluate motion sequences of
objects including persons.

For an automated image-based analysis, regarding the objects contained
in the video and their characteristics, different implementations of algorithms
already exist (e.g. Mask R-CNN, Faster R-CNN, RetinaNet, ...). However, a

© Springer Nature Switzerland AG 2019
C. Stephanidis (Ed.): HCII 2019, CCIS 1033, pp. 320–327, 2019.
https://doi.org/10.1007/978-3-030-23528-4_44

direct concatenation of these algorithms is not possible due to a lack of interfaces between the different frameworks.

The automatic activity detection involves various subtasks, which range from the extraction of the individual frames to the object detection, the tracking up to the detection of the activity. Here it becomes clear that these different system blocks have to provide their services via defined interfaces. The contribution of this paper describes the structure of the process sequence shown in Fig. 1 for the detection of simple activities in videos. For the management and interconnection of the individual subtasks, a self-implemented management system (EMSML evaluation and management system for machine learning) was used, which was developed in the context of the international evaluation campaign TRECVid 2018 (Maryland USA) [1, 10]. In order to ensure interoperability of the system, the use of established and standardized technologies for interprocess communication is in the foreground. At the centre of the system is a central database, which can be used by the frameworks as database and data storage. The aim is to design the process chain in such a way that it can be used in future real-time environments. For this purpose, all components should act autonomously and provide their data via a central location. The communication between the instances takes place via standardized data exchange formats and protocols.

Fig. 1. Process chain to be implemented for activity detection.

2   System Architecture

In the context of scene recognition, solutions already exist that can detect selected activities [3, 4, 8, 9]. The disadvantage is the proprietary of the systems, which makes it difficult to integrate new activities or better algorithms. Regarding this disadvantage, the process chain (Fig. 1) to be developed should enable the simple and inexpensive exchange of single blocks.

2.1   The Management System

The EMSML environment aims to decentralize the individual components and connect them via standardized interfaces. This allows to distribute the workload of different processes to several network nodes. Parallelized process processing can also be realized, for example object detection in several thousand images can be distributed to several processors. An overview of the EMSML environment is shown in Fig. 2 and contains the core functionalities listed below.

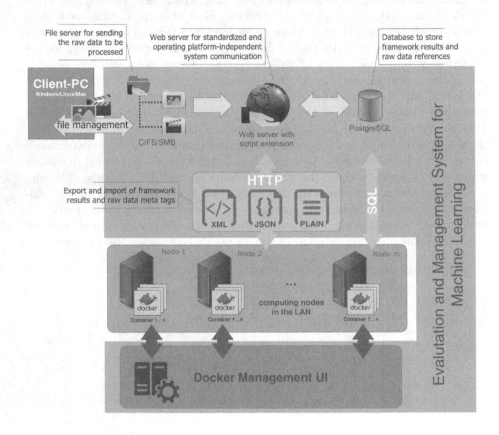

Fig. 2. System environment of EMSML.

Storage and Administration: The central storage and provision of all required raw data (images, videos) is carried out via the LAN. The protocols CIFS (Common Internet File System) and SMB (Server Message Block) are available for the storage of the files. The processing frameworks get the images and videos to be processed via *HTTP*. For this a *GET-Request* with the parameters *from* and *to* must be transmitted to the web server integrated in EMSML. The parameters *from* and *to* define the number of desired files. The metadata of the requested files are specified in the corresponding response as *XML* or text can be provided. The results extracted from the frameworks can be send to EMSML in the form of *JSON* or *XML*. Alternatively, the results can be stored in the database during processing using *SQL*.

Process Control: The required frameworks can be managed and controlled as docker containers. EMSML uses the software *Portainer* under the zlib license as management environment. It provides a web-based interface for the administration of different computing nodes and their docker containers.

Pre- and Post-processing: Videos can be split into frames using a docker container. All frames are stored, referenced in the database and are available for further processing via *HTTP* download. In addition to the raw data, already saved framework results can also be retrieved for further processing in the form of *JSON* and *XML*.

Analysis and Evaluation: The framework data stored in EMSML can be obtained in the standardized data exchange formats *JSON* and *XML* for their analysis or evaluation.

2.2 Used Frameworks

For the determination of simple activities, the following free-available or self-implemented frameworks will be combined with the EMSML environment.

Detectron is a framework developed by Facebook, based on the Deep Learning Framework *Caffe2* and offers a high quality and powerful code base for object recognition. *Detectron* is to be used for the detection of objects and their boundary frames. In addition to the x-,y-coordinates of the starting point, the height and width of the box are stored in addition to the object classification [2].

YOLO9000 is a network for real-time classification and localization of objects within an image and has been trained with over 9000 different object categories. To increase the performance of object recognition, *YOLO9000* is used together with *Detectron* for object recognition. The object class and values of the bounding box are also stored in the database [7].

Object Tracking is realized with our own implemented framework. [6, 11] It places the objects merged by *YOLO9000* and *Detectron* in a temporal relation, based on the Euclidean distance and the corresponding object history in previous frames. As a result, each tracked object in the database is assigned an object ID.

Activity Detection is realized by simple heuristics. The activities to be identified are based on the activities defined in the Task ActEV within the scope of the international evaluation campaign TRECVid (Maryland USA). These are "Opening", "Closing", "Entering", "Exiting","Vehicle_turning_left", "Vehicle_turning_right", and "Vehicle_u_turn".

Although the EMSML environment provides essential interfaces for system communication, the frameworks *Detectron* and *YOLO9000* do not provide corresponding interfaces. An adaptation of the source code is therefore necessary.

Integration of *Detectron*: *Detectron* is implemented in Python. Classes for *HTTP*, for *XML* and *JSON* processing and for database communication are available. The following functionalities have been added for integration into EMSML.

By default, *Detectron* provides the ability to batch process all images in a local folder. The image download from the web server and the subsequent classification is not part of the implementation. A *HTTP* component has been added for this purpose. The passed URL returns as resource a text document listing the URLs of the images to be processed, which are then loaded using the *HTTP* component and classified. The number of images can be specified in the *HTTP* request. By default, 100 images are requested.

A direct SQL communication with the EMSML database was implemented for the immediate storage of the results. To reduce the protocol overhead, the results of 100 classified images in the block are transferred to the database.

Figure 3 shows the integration of a framework into the EMSML environment.

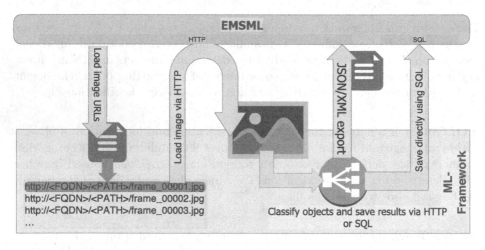

Fig. 3. Integration of an image processing ML framework into the EMSML environment

Integration of *YOLO9000*: *YOLO9000* was implemented in *C*. Based on this, the integration of parsers for *JSON* or *XML* and database communication is more difficult. Even a *HTTP* communication is more complex to realize.

With regard to the reasons mentioned above, the *YOLO9000* source code has only been extended by the function of image download. For this purpose,

the text document with the corresponding image URLs will be transferred as
a parameter when *YOLO9000* is started. The download of the text document
was realized by the Linux command line program "wget", outside of *YOLO9000*.
YOLO9000 then interprets this file, loads the images and classifies them.

In addition to the SQL interface, EMSML also offers data import as *JSON*
or *XML*. The *Yolo9000* results are stored as *JSON* files in the local file system.
These files can then be imported into EMSML.

Integration of Object Tracking: The self-implemented framework for tracking classified objects across multiple frames already provides an interface to the
JSON import. The *JSON* Document is created by EMSML specifying the video
ID and object class. It contains all recognized objects, including their coordinates, size, and URL to the corresponding frame.

Activity Recognition. The heuristics for scene recognition are executed for
the activities "Opening", "Closing", "Entering" and "Exiting" directly in the
EMSML database. Here the boundary frames are analyzed with regard to their
size change and overlap with other objects. Figure 4 illustrates this fact for
the activity "Entering". The detected object positions are compared with other
objects (e.g. door, vehicle) according to their temporal course. If the last occurrence of an object was associated with an overlap, the activity "Entering" is
concluded.

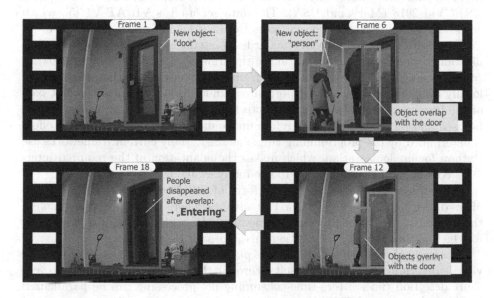

Fig. 4. Determination of "Entering" by comparing the bounding boxes

For the other activities the corresponding direction vectors were determined
from the movements of the objects. To determine the activity, the direction vec-

tors were accumulated over successive frames from a starting point. If a defined threshold value is exceeded, a corresponding motion pattern is present. The minimum angle defined for left and right motion is $\pm40°$. For a rotation, the minimum cumulative angular amount was set to $\pm170°$. A "Vehicle_u_turn" can only be triggered if this minimum sum of angles is exceeded and at least two left or right vectors have occurred before.

The determined activities were also stored in the database using SQL.

2.3 Framework Management

All used frameworks were realized as independent Docker-Images and are managed by *Portainer*. The available *Docker* images can be installed and started on all managed compute nodes. For distribution of load it is also possible to execute resource-intensive frameworks simultaneously on different compute nodes. The session management integrated in EMSML then provides each computing node with only a part of the raw data. The raw data is distributed linearly based on the number of processing framework instances. The processing time can thus be reduced by the number of instances.

3 Results and Discussion

The process chain 1 shown in Fig. 1 could be realized with the EMSML environment and was successfully used for the international evaluation campaign TRECVid 2018 (Maryland USA). The data set used is VIRAT V1 [5], which consists of 455 different video sequences from the field of video surveillance.

Even with the availability of standardized interfaces for interprocess communication, a programmatic adaptation of the frameworks *YOLO9000* and *Detectron* was necessary. By default, these frameworks only allow the processing of locally available images. Data export into standardized formats is also not part of the frameworks. An incorporation into the source code of the frameworks to be used and its adaptation is therefore unavoidable. The implementation effort is determined by the programming language used. Many current frameworks use Python for implementation, which makes the adaptation of the required interfaces correspondingly simple due to the many available classes.

In addition to data import in the form of *JSON* and *XML*, EMSML also offers direct data storage via SQL. The advantage here is the direct provision of the results, which can be processed immediately by other frameworks. Especially for the real-time activity recognition this approach is essential.

The derivation of the activities takes place exclusively on the basis of the previously determined framework results stored in the database, which leads to very short detection times. More time-consuming pre-processing can be parallelized by the architecture of EMSML.

Furthermore, the aim is the real-time-capable interconnection of the frameworks using the EMSML environment. For this purpose, the session layer rudimentarily available in EMSML must be extended by functionalities for session control, parameter negotiation and error handling.

4 Conclusion

This paper presented a system for managing and interconnecting distributed frameworks in the area of object recognition, object tracking, and activity detection. This workflow could be prototypically implemented and used on the basis of different exemplarily selected frameworks. The modular structure of the system allows the simple integration of further frameworks or the development of other domains.

References

1. Awad, G., et al.: Trecvid 2018: benchmarking video activity detection, video captioning and matching, video storytelling linking and video search. In: Proceedings of TRECVID 2018. NIST, USA (2018)
2. Girshick, R., Radosavovic, I., Gkioxari, G., Dollár, P., He, K.: Detectron (2018). https://github.com/facebookresearch/detectron
3. Jalal, A., Kamal, S., Kim, D.: A depth video-based human detection and activity recognition using multi-features and embedded hidden Markov models for health care monitoring systems. IJIMAI (2017)
4. Miguel, J.C.S., Bescs, J., Martnez, J.M., Garca,: DiVA: a distributed video analysis framework applied to video-surveillance systems. In: 2008 Ninth International Workshop on Image Analysis for Multimedia Interactive Services, pp. 207–210, May 2008. https://doi.org/10.1109/WIAMIS.2008.29
5. Oh, S., et al.: A large-scale benchmark dataset for event recognition in surveillance video. In: CVPR 2011. IEEE, June 2011. https://doi.org/10.1109/cvpr.2011.5995586
6. Platte, B., Thomanek, R., Rolletschke, R., Roschke, C., Ritter, M.: Person tracking and statistical representation of person movements in surveillance areas. Int. J. Des. Anal. Tools Integr. Circuits Syst. **7**, 6
7. Redmon, J., Farhadi, A.: YOLO9000: Better, Faster, Stronger. arXiv:1612.08242, December 2016
8. Song, Y., Kim, I.: DeepAct - a deep neural network model for activity detection in untrimmed videos. JIPS (2018)
9. Sultani, W., Chen, C., Shah, M.: Real-world anomaly detection in surveillance videos. arXiv.org (2018)
10. Thomanek, R., et al.: University of applied sciences Mittweida and Chemnitz university of technology at TRECVID 2018, Gaithersburg, Maryland, USA, November 2018
11. Thomanek, R., et al.: A scalable system architecture for activity detection with simple heuristics. In: WACV (2019)

Video-Surveillance System for Fall Detection in the Elderly

Koudai Yano[1(✉)], Yusuke Manabe[1], Masatsugu Hirano[1],
Kohei Ishii[2], Mikio Deguchi[1], Takashi Yoshikawa[1],
Takuro Sakiyama[1], and Katsuhito Yamasaki[3]

[1] Niihama College, National Institute of Technology, Niihama, Ehime, Japan
Koudai.yano0128@gmail.com
[2] Kagawa College, National Institute of Technology, Takamatsu, Japan
[3] Eikokai Ono Hospital, Ono, Hyogo, Japan

Abstract. Recently, the number of households comprising only elderly people (60 years old or older) has increased because of the falling birth rate and the aging population. According to a recent Japanese Statistics Bureau report, the total population was estimated to be 126.59 million among which 35.22 million people were elderly. Furthermore, the Ministry of Health, Labor, and Welfare predicted a shortage of approximately 380,000 nursing care staff in Japan by 2025 [1], which is the year in which the baby-boomer generation is expected to become more than 75 years old. As the number of users of nursing care services increases, 2.53 million nursing staff will become necessary by 2025; however, it is expected that only 2.15 million staff will be present based on the current rate of increase. According to the official release of the sufficiency rate associated with the number of nursing care staff actually required to serve the number of people who requires them, which increase with the aging population, there will be a shortage of care workers of approximately 200,000 in 2020 and of approximately 380,000 in 2025. Therefore, we have developed a video-surveillance system capable of detecting an elderly person falling in the absence of care workers.

Keywords: Video-surveillance system · Fall detection · Feature-point matching

1 Introduction

Recently, the number of households comprising only elderly people has increased because of the falling birth rate and the aging population. According to a recent Japanese Statistics Bureau report, the total population was estimated to be 126.59 million among which 35.22 million people were elderly. Furthermore, the Ministry of Health, Labor, and Welfare predicated that there will be a shortage of approximately 380,000 future nursing care staff in Japan by 2025 [1], which is the year in which the baby-boomer generation is expected to be more than 75 years old. This shortage is predicted to considerably impact a substantial amount of care recipients. Although an expected shortage of approximately 330,000 with respect to the nursing care staff was

© Springer Nature Switzerland AG 2019
C. Stephanidis (Ed.): HCII 2019, CCIS 1033, pp. 328–333, 2019.
https://doi.org/10.1007/978-3-030-23528-4_45

announced in February 2018, a further shortage of 50,000 was announced recently to create extensive concern about nursing care in the aging society.

As the number of users of nursing care services increases, 2.53 million nursing staff will be necessary by 2025; however, it is expected that only 2.15 million staff will be available at the current rate of increase. According to the official release of the sufficiency rate associated with the nursing care staff actually required to serve the number of people who require them, which increase with the aging population, there will be a shortage of approximately 200,000 care workers in 2020 and a shortage of approximately 380,000 care workers in 2025.

According to the Ministry of Health, Labor, and Welfare, the elderly who are in need of care mainly suffer from brain disease or stroke (17.2%), dementia (16.4%), old-age infirmity (13.9%), and fractures and/or falling (12.2%) (Fig. 1). If a young person has a minor fall and is hurt, he/she will heal with rest. However, in the elderly, extended rest leads to weakening of the muscular strength and physical ability, resulting in the worsening of symptoms. Even if they have no fractures or injuries, their body will increasingly resist movement if they lose self-confidence by falling or because of fear of moving by themselves, and their muscular strength and physical function will gradually decline.

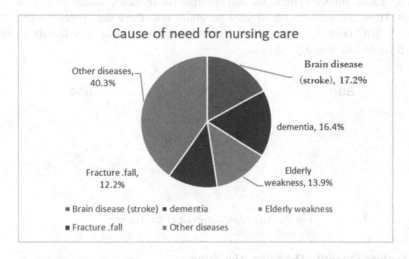

Fig. 1. Results of survey conducted by the Japanese Cabinet Office

If a system is established for monitoring the elderly and informing the nursing care staff when an abnormal situation occurs, caregivers may be able to take action before the elderly people actually fall or before the situation becomes more serious (Fig. 2). The deterioration in the quality of life of such elderly persons can be minimized by introducing a video-surveillance system. Thus, we are convinced that this research is considerably meaningful in the field of nursing care.

To apply our fall-detection method, feature-point matching is initially performed for each successive frame using the AKAZE algorithm to derive the feature values.

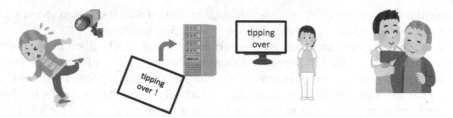

Fig. 2. A video-surveillance system for elderly persons

Two consecutive frames are arranged on the left and right, and the corresponding points are connected by a line. Fall detection is further performed by detecting the negative slope of the drawn line. The details are described in the following section.

2 Methods

2.1 Feature Value

To set up a surveillance system, we first describe the features, which are central to this research. Here, the features are divided generally into three data types, "edge," "corner," and "flat" (Fig. 3). The assigned feature values are important factors in all the research related to image processing.

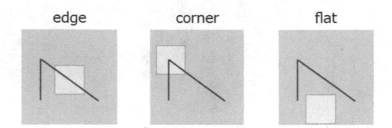

Fig. 3. The edge, corner, and flat features

2.2 Feature-Quantity-Detection Algorithm

- **SIFT (Scale Invariant Feature Transform)** [3]. This algorithm makes it possible to extract the robust feature quantities by rotation, scale, lighting change, etc. It is used for recognition and detection of objects, creation of panoramic photos, etc.
- **SURF (Speeded Up Robust Features)** [4]. SIFT was relatively slow while trying to use it in practice (in real time), and a high-speed version is required. SURF is a faster version of SIFT.
- **ORB (Oriented FAST and Rotated BLIEF)** [5]. ORB is a good alternative to SIFT and SURF in terms of the computational cost, matching performance, and patents.

- **HOG (Histograms of Oriented Gradients)** [6]. HOG is a histogram of the gradient direction of the luminance of the local region or cell, and it is set as a feature quantity by the combination. It can express the rough shape of an object.
- **Haar-like.** The Haar-like method combines the local brightness differences of an object into a feature value used for face detection. For example, if it is an image of a person's face, a bright color is assigned to the neighborhood of the cheek than to the eyes. The Haar-like feature quantities are those that use features based on such contrasts.
- **KAZE** [7]. KAZE was named based on the imaginary Japanese "kaze." A major characteristic is its extreme robustness to image disturbance. Filtering is performed using a nonlinear diffusion filter (a Gaussian filter like SIFT) without smoothing.

2.3 Fall-Detection Method

In this research, we initially set up a web-connected camera and a compact-size PC to run the program in the home of an elderly person. Using our system, falls are first detected using video surveillance. Fall detection is currently performed using the AKAZE feature value, mainly because it is more robust than other features and boasts an operating speed comparable to that of the constrained SURF [2]. In addition, because it is a recently published feature quantity, we considered it to be of technical value to perform research based on AKAZE.

- **AKAZE (Accelerated KAZE).** This feature value overcomes the disadvantage that the operational speed of the KAZE feature acquisition is considerably slow. We are trying to significantly accelerate the processing using a mathematical method called fast explicit diffusion (FED). Furthermore, a unique feature-quantity descriptor called robust modified-local difference binary (M-LDB) is specified, and the gradient information in the image is effectively utilized. The application of AKAZE considerably increases the speed without reducing the advantage of high robustness of the KAZE feature value.

3 Results

The PC configuration used at this time exhibits the following characteristics:

OS Windows 10 (64-bit)
CPU Intel Core i5-2500
GPU NVIDIA GTX 550 Ti
Resolution 1600 × 1190 (pixels)

Based on the image resulting from the actual implementation of the AKAZE feature value (Fig. 4), we confirmed that the correspondence of the feature points was accurately conducted.

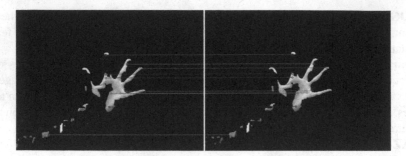

Fig. 4. The result of the adoption of the AKAZE feature value

4   Discussion

Currently, the method of fall detection is being studied using the AKAZE feature value. However, we have encountered a problem that the program forcibly terminates during operation. In the future, this problem should be rectified to ensure its reliable operation as an elderly watching system. There are two currently considered causes for this problem.

One possible cause is the lighting in the room where the experiment was conducted. Some error may have occurred when the object to be photographed blocked the lighting while the system was distinguishing the object from the background. If this is the cause, it can be dealt with by installing the camera near the ceiling lighting.

The second possible cause is simply a problem associated with the program. We consider that the threshold set while considering the background subtraction may not be appropriate.

5   Conclusions

Our system was not completely able to prevent falls as originally planned. Initially, it was trying to detect a fall using only optical flow. However, because the operation was slow, we used human intervention by which detection was performed based on the ideology that the speed may be improved by narrowing the range for calculating the optical flow. We also examined a method to use the optical flow while detecting people.

Based on such an examination, we judged that it is currently difficult to detect falling using optical flow at present. Therefore, we have begun and intend to continue investigating a method of fall detection using the AKAZE feature value.

References

1. Ministry of Health, Labor and Welfare Information. https://www.mhlw.go.jp/seisakunitsuite/bunnya/hukushi_kaigo/kaigo_koureisha/chiiki-houkatsu/dl/link1-1.pdf. Accessed 10 Feb 2019
2. Web site information. http://poly.hatenablog.com/entry/2014/01/06/063012. Accessed 4 Feb 2019
3. Lowe, D.G.: Distinctive image features from scale-invariant keypoints. Int. J. Comput. Vision **60**(2), 91–110 (2004)
4. Bay, H., Tuytelaars, T., Van Gool, L.: SURF: speeded up robust features. In: Leonardis, A., Bischof, H., Pinz, A. (eds.) ECCV 2006. LNCS, vol. 3951, pp. 404–417. Springer, Heidelberg (2006). https://doi.org/10.1007/11744023_32
5. Rublee, E., Rabaud, V., Konolige, K., Bradski, G.: ORB: an efficient alternative to SIFT or SURF, pp. 2564–2571 (2011)
6. Dalal, N., Triggs, B.: Histograms of oriented gradients for human detection (2005)
7. Alcantarilla, P.F., Nuevo, J., Bartoli, A.: Fast explicit diffusion for accelerated features in nonlinear scale spaces (2012)

Virtual and Augmented Reality

Size Perception of Augmented Objects
by Different AR Displays

Jong-gil Ahn[1], Euijai Ahn[2], Seulki Min[1], Hyeonah Choi[1],
Howon Kim[3], and Gerard J. Kim[1(✉)]

[1] Digital Experience Laboratory, Korea University, Seoul, Korea
{hide989,minsk327,hyonah09,gjkim}@korea.ac.kr
[2] Service Laboratory, Institute of Convergence Technology, KT, Seoul, Korea
euijai.ahn@kt.com
[3] SW-Content Research Laboratory, ETRI, Daejeon, Korea
hw_kim@etri.re.kr

Abstract. Augmented reality (AR) has positioned itself as one of main media technologies, and its further proliferation depends on its usability, ergonomics and perceptual qualities with respect to the effective and correct convey of information. However, there exists no established guideline as how to visualize augmented information properly for various types of AR displays. We investigate for one important perceptual quality in AR, correct size perception of the augmented object, for three representative AR displays. The AR displays considered are: (1) small hand-held mobile device, (2) closed video see-through HMD, and (3) optical see-through HMD. The augmented object, a nominally sized box, is visualized in three different styles: (1) as a texture mapped simple polygonal model, (2) as a bump mapped polygonal model with shadow, and (3) as a detailed scanned mesh model. The size perception was assessed in two viewing angles: (1) sitting down and looking straight and (2) standing and looking down in 45 degrees (1.5 m distance). The experimental results revealed significant effects by the display type, rendering style and viewing angle. E.g. users tended to overestimate the object size and took longer to complete the task, when the small hand-held display is used. We believe the findings can serve as one guideline for developing effective AR applications.

Keywords: Human perception and performance · Augmented reality ·
Mobile · Optical See-through HMD · Video See-through HMD · Rendering

1 Introduction

Augmented reality (AR) refers to the type of information media that overlays, through special display systems, useful information registered over real world objects and environments [1]. With the help of the various recent technological advancements such as in powerful mobile computers, robust tracking algorithms and lighter display devices, AR has positioned itself as a promising media technology with many possible application areas [2–5]. However, its further proliferation depends on its usability, ergonomics and perceptual qualities with respect to the effective and correct convey of information [6]. The design of usable interface and information visualization for AR

© Springer Nature Switzerland AG 2019
C. Stephanidis (Ed.): HCII 2019, CCIS 1033, pp. 337–344, 2019.
https://doi.org/10.1007/978-3-030-23528-4_46

will have unique requirements (in terms of situating and augmenting virtual objects over the real), as distinguished from those for the usual 2D graphical desktop or touch-screen platforms. However, there exists little such guidelines as how to visualize augmented information properly for various types of AR displays [7–9].

Thus, in this paper, we investigate for one important perceptual quality in AR, namely, the correct size perception of the augmented object, with respect to three possibly influential factors (see Fig. 1). First, we consider the AR display type. The AR displays considered are: (1) small hand-held mobile device, (2) closed video see-through HMD, and (3) optical see-through HMD. In addition, the visualization technique for the augmented object can equally affect the size perception. As such, the augmented object, a nominally sized box, is visualized in three different styles: (1) as a texture mapped simple polygonal model, (2) as a bump mapped polygonal model with shadow, and (3) as a detailed scanned mesh model. Finally, the size perception was assessed in two viewing angles: (1) sitting down and looking straight and (2) standing and looking down in 45 degrees (1.5 m distance). The findings should help establish the design guidelines for developing effective AR applications.

Fig. 1. Real object (left) and texture mapped simple polygonal model (right). Although the created virtual objects are made equal in consideration of the physical size of the actual objects, the visual perception varies depending on the augmented reality display and rendering style.

2   Related Work

As a media that involves the presentation of the 3D world, depth perception in AR has been an important issue. For example, Diaz et al. [10] has investigated how various factors such as the shading, shadows, aerial perspective, texture affect the depth perception. With the increased utility and availability of AR technology, its usability aspect has started to draw much more attention lately in the research arena. Specific topics might include the perceptual qualities such as the visibility and readability of the augmented scene, and naturalness and how harmonious the augmented object can be felt with respect to the real world backdrop and particularly the augmentation target [11–13]. A related topic is the size perception. Combe et al. compared the 1:1 scale perception of a cockpit through two different virtual reality systems: a Head Mounted Display (HMD), and a large cylindrical projection screen vs. the physical [14]. Sugano et al. assessed the user interaction performance and virtual object presence with respect to the existence of 3D cues like shadow [15]. In VR, it is generally regarded that HMD's can bring about underestimation of objects [16]. Livingston et al. conducted a detailed user study to examine a set of display attributes for used to visually conveying occlusion in outdoor, far-field AR [17]. However, there is not much such work in AR, especially for different types of displays. Note that the different AR displays we consider are not merely different in their components or manufacturing specifications, but have more fundamental differences with the collective factors of: e.g. how it is used (hand-held or worn), whether the display is open or closed, and whether video is used for the real world representation.

3 Experiment

3.1 Experiment Design

The experiment was designed as a three factor, $3 \times 3 \times 2$ within subject repeated measure, totaling 18 different test conditions. As already indicated, the three factors were: (1) AR display type, (2) augmentation object rendering style and (3) viewing angle. There were three AR displays considered: (1) small hand-held mobile device, (2) closed video see-through HMD, and (3) optical see-through HMD (see Fig. 2). The augmented object, a nominally sized box, was visualized in three different styles: (1) as a texture mapped simple polygonal model, (2) as a bump mapped polygonal model with shadow, and (3) as a detailed scanned mesh model (see Fig. 3). The size perception was assessed in two viewing angles: (1) sitting down and looking straight and (2) standing and looking down in 45 degrees (1.5 m distance). The main dependent variable was the extent to how much the augmented object was perceived over-estimated or under-estimated.

Table 1. Implementation details of the three AR displays.

Type	Device	Operating system	Content platform – AR tracking
Mobile	Samsung Galaxy S8	Android	Unity - ARCore
Video see-through HMD	Samsung Gear VR	Android	Unity – Vuforia
Optical see-through HMD	Microsoft HoloLens	Windows	Unity – HoloLens Toolkit

3.2 Experimental Set-Up

The experimental set-up was as follows. There were two tables: one placed with the actual box object and the other where the same box, but the virtual one, was to be augmented at the same position. To augment (track and register) the box object, a similar shaped box decaled with textured markers on their six sides was used. This marker box was slightly smaller than the augmented version so that it would not be visible while the augmented version was overlaid on it (also see Fig. 4). The implementation details of the three AR displays are shown in Table 1.

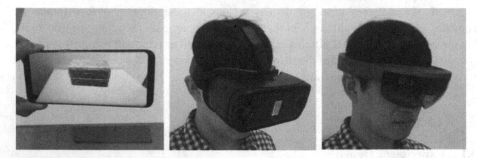

Fig. 2. Experiment AR device setup: small hand-held mobile device (left), closed video see-through HMD (middle), and optical see-through HMD – Microsoft HoloLens (right).

The augmented box object is visualized in three different rendering styles: (1) as a texture mapped simple polygonal model, (2) as a bump mapped polygonal model with the shadow effect, and (3) as a detailed scanned mesh model (see Fig. 3). All three objects were manually calibrated and matched to have the default scale as equal to the real object which had the dimensions of 28.5 cm × 19.5 cm × 16.5 cm. The bump map was created by a simple image analysis of the original 2D texture tool available from the Unity.

Fig. 3. Simple texture mapped (left) bump mapped (middle) and 3D scanned mesh box models (right).

Finally, to measure the user response in assessing the size (e.g. scale adjustment, see next subsection), we devised a simple hand-held button/joystick device. The size assessment was carried out 1.5 m away from the table in two viewing conditions: sitting down and standing.

3.3 Detailed Procedure

A total of 30 subjects participated in the experiment (20 males and 10 females) aged between 20 and 36 (mean: 27.8). The experiment proceeded as follows. First the participants were briefed about the purpose of the experiment and spend some time (10 to 15 min) familiarizing themselves with the display and how to use the response recording device. The subject then carried out the actual task, which was simply to view the real object on the real table first for 1 min to obtain and remember the feel for the actual object size. Then, the subject turned around to the other table on which an arbitrarily resized virtual object was augmented. The virtual object was resized in the range of −10% to +10% of the original, and presented in a random order. Given this augmented object, the subject was to use the input device to adjust its size (e.g. larger or smaller) until it matched the size of the real object one just saw a minute ago. The subject carried out this task for the 18 different conditions presented in a balanced order and sufficient rest times were given between the treatments (see Fig. 4). In each treatment, 5 different size assessments were performed and recorded. As a side note, task completion time was also recorded and a brief post interview was conducted to gather any user thoughts.

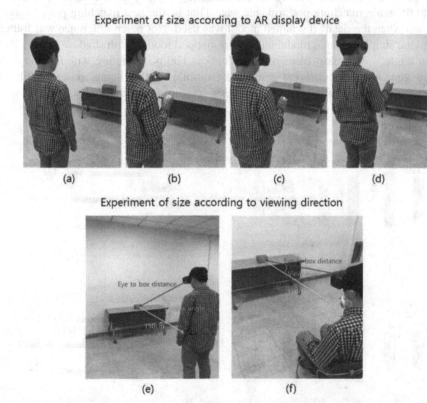

Fig. 4. (a) looking at the real object first, (b)–(d) assessing the size of the augmented object relative to the real in three different displays – hand-held, video see-through HMD and optical see-through (HoloLens), (e) user standing and (f) user sitting.

4 Results and Discussion

The experimental data were analyzed using one-way ANOVA and Tukey's Posthoc test. The results are illustrated in Fig. 5. Subjects were able to determine the relative scale and carry out the matching task the fastest with the video see-through display, and the slowest with the hand-held display. It seems that the size determination was difficult and caused time delay when a small mobile display was used. In terms of the size assessment, a statistically significant effect was found for the AR display type: between mobile and video see-through HMD, and between mobile and optical see-through HMD. Subjects generally over-estimated the augmented object when viewed through the mobile hand-held display, with a significant difference with the other two display types. On the other hand, the optical see-through display exhibited a significant level of under-estimation. The video see-through display resulted in the near 1–1 scale matching performance to the real reference object. This trend is mostly regardless of the rendering style and viewing angle, indicating very little interaction.

The only exception was when the augmented object was viewed sitting down (straight into the object), the rendering style affected the scale matching performance. But in general, better the quality of the rendering style was, the faster and more accurate the scale matching performance was. That is, the best matching performance was found when the detailed scanned model was used. Not much difference was found between the simple textured model and bump-mapped model (with shadow effect). The viewing angle was in most cases of no influence. The post-briefing with the subjects revealed generally the consistent results: the mobile display being most difficult to perform the scale matching task and the video see-through being the easiest.

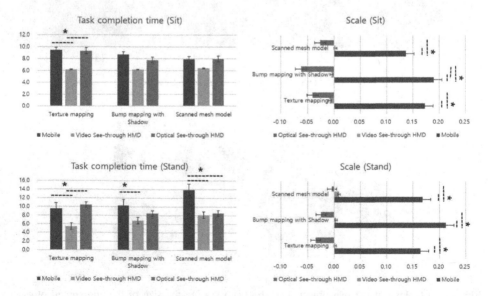

Fig. 5. Experimental results – Task completion time (left) and scale (right) - * indicate p < 0.05.

5   Conclusion

In this work, we investigated for one important perceptual quality in AR, correct size perception of the augmented object, for three representative AR displays. The effects of rendering style and viewing angle were also looked into. We have found that the video see-through display provided the most accurate and fastest size perception. The mobile display caused serious over-estimation and vice versa for the optical see-through display. The quality of the rendering was also a factor. In particular, the detailed 3D model helped for a more correct size perception as stereoscopic display was used from a near distance (1.5 m). In the future, we would like to continue and extend the experiment by considering more complex objects than a box, and study other perceptual qualities such as visibility, naturalness and environmental harmony. We hope that the results from this work can contribute to designing effective AR applications such as AR based shopping and product reviews in which size perception plays an important role.

Acknowledgements. This work was partially supported by the Global Frontier R&D Program on <Human-centered Interaction for Coexistence> funded by the National Research Foundation of Korea grant funded by the Korean Government (MEST) (NRF-2015M3A6A3076490), and by the MSIT (Ministry of Science, ICT), Korea, under the ITRC (Information Technology Research Center) support program (IITP-2019-2016-0-00312) supervised by the IITP (Institute for Information & communications Technology Promotion).

References

1. Billinghurst, M., Grasset, R., Looser, J.: Designing augmented reality interfaces. ACM SIGGRAPH Comput. Graph. **39**(1), 17–22 (2005)
2. Fuchs, H., et al.: Augmented reality visualization for laparoscopic surgery. In: Wells, W.M., Colchester, A., Delp, S. (eds.) MICCAI 1998. LNCS, vol. 1496, pp. 934–943. Springer, Heidelberg (1998). https://doi.org/10.1007/BFb0056282
3. Wu, H.K., Lee, S.W.Y., Chang, H.Y., Liang, J.C.: Current status, opportunities and challenges of augmented reality in education. Comput. Educ. **62**, 41–49 (2013)
4. Olsson, T., Lagerstam, E., Kärkkäinen, T., Väänänen-Vainio-Mattila, K.: Expected user experience of mobile augmented reality services: a user study in the context of shopping centres. Pers. Ubiquit. Comput. **17**(2), 287–304 (2013)
5. Azuma, R., Baillot, Y., Behringer, R., Feiner, S., Julier, S., MacIntyre, B.: Recent advances in augmented reality. IEEE Comput. Graph. Appl. **21**(6), 34–47 (2001)
6. Moere, A.V., Purchase, H.: On the role of design in information visualization. Inf. Vis. **10**(4), 356–371 (2011)
7. Wetzel, R., McCall, R., Braun, A.K., Broll, W.: Guidelines for designing augmented reality games. In: Proceedings of the 2008 Conference on Future Play: Research, Play, Share, pp. 173–180. ACM (2008)
8. Furmanski, C., Azuma, R., Daily, M.: Augmented-reality visualizations guided by cognition: perceptual heuristics for combining visible and obscured information. In: Proceedings of the International Symposium on Mixed and Augmented Reality, pp. 215–320. IEEE (2002)
9. Bengler, K., Passaro, R.: Augmented reality in cars: requirements and constraints, ISMAR 2006 industrial track (2006)

10. Diaz, C., Walker, M., Szafir, D.A., Szafir, D.: Designing for depth perceptions in augmented reality. In: Proceedings of the 2017 IEEE International Symposium on Mixed and Augmented Reality, pp. 111–122. IEEE (2017)
11. Kruijff, E., Swan, J.E., Feiner, S.: Perceptual issues in augmented reality revisited. In: Proceedings of the 2010 IEEE International Symposium on Mixed and Augmented Reality, pp. 3–12. IEEE (2010)
12. Avery, B., Sandor, C., Thomas, B.H.: Improving spatial perception for augmented reality x-ray vision. In: Proceedings of the 2009 IEEE Virtual Reality Conference, pp. 79–82. IEEE (2009)
13. Tatzgern, M., Kalkofen, D., Schmalstieg, D.: Dynamic compact visualizations for augmented reality. In: Proceedings of the 2013 IEEE Virtual Reality Conference, pp. 3–6. IEEE (2013)
14. Combe, E., Posselt, J., Kemeny, A.: 1: 1 scale perception in virtual and augmented reality. In: 18th International Conference on Artificial Reality and Telexistence, pp. 152–160 (2008)
15. Sugano, N., Kato, H., Tachibana, K.: The effects of shadow representation of virtual objects in augmented reality. In: Proceedings of the International Symposium on Mixed and Augmented Reality, pp. 76–83. IEEE (2003)
16. Knapp, J.L.J.: Visual perception of egocentric distance in real and virtual environments. In: Virtual and Adaptive Environments, pp. 35–60. CRC Press (2003)
17. Livingston, M.A., et al.: Resolving multiple occluded layers in augmented reality. In: Proceedings of the International Symposium on Mixed and Augmented Reality, pp. 56–65. IEEE (2003)

Increasing Virtual Reality Immersion Through Smartwatch Lower Limb Motion Tracking

Alix Angarita[1][✉], Alvaro Hernandez[1], Christopher Carmichael[2], Alvaro Uribe-Quevedo[2], Claudia Rueda[1], and Sergio A. Salinas[1]

[1] Universidad Pontificia Bolivariana, Bucaramanga, Santander, Colombia
{alix.angarita.2013,alvaro.hernandez.2014,claudia.rueda, sergio.salinas}@upb.edu.co

[2] University of Ontario Institute of Technology, Oshawa, ON, Canada
{christopher.carmichael,alvaro.quevedo}@uoit.ca

Abstract. Virtual reality locomotion has been a subject of study as it plays an important role that affects immersion and presence. Walking constitute a challenging interaction in virtual reality installments as it is a complex task to recreate. Some approaches have focused on input devices employing diverse technologies including robotics, omnidirectional treadmills, reorientation through tracking, and most recently, inertial measurement units, optical tracking, and low-friction surfaces. Amongst the various solutions, those targeting consumer-level VR products are gaining momentum as VR headsets become more affordable, creating the opportunity to mass impact content creation in entertainment, tourism, healthcare, training, education, and simulation applications employing VR. In this paper, we present the development of a lower limb virtual reality room-scale environment where users walk while using a Smartwatch as a tool to capture walking data without requiring external sensors or tracking systems. A preliminary study focused on a usability assessment to gather perceptions on the use of a smartwatch as a suitable tracking tool for VR installments.

Keywords: Virtual reality · Smartwatch · Gait tracking · Usability evaluation

1 Introduction

Locomotion in virtual reality (VR) can increase immersion and presence, reduce motion sickness, and improve the user experience [16]. Early approaches at VR walking had users moving within a limited tracking area employing optical trackers [3], where the spatial limitation raised the need for unlimited locomotion resulting in the prototypes employing unidirectional treadmills and elliptic or cycling devices [6]. VR walking devices have introduced complex systems for omnidirectional locomotion employing low-friction surfaces for users to walk

© Springer Nature Switzerland AG 2019
C. Stephanidis (Ed.): HCII 2019, CCIS 1033, pp. 345–352, 2019.
https://doi.org/10.1007/978-3-030-23528-4_47

while wearing low-friction rubber sandals, and motion tracking accomplished via six degrees of freedom (DOF) magnetic trackers [7]. Interestingly, a similar concept has been gaining popularity amongst VR Arcades in the form of omnidirectional treadmills offering semi-natural walking interactions. For example, the Virtuix Omni employs a low-friction surface and shoes that allow walking over a surface while being secured to a harness attached to a fully rotational waist hoop to avoid falls [2]. Although semi-natural walking interfaces have shown to provide inferior user experience when compared to real walking, a study conducted in [20] concluded that the intricate use of an omnidirectional treadmill (e.g., turning around, wearing the equipment, and fatigue from use) reduces the user experience when compared to game-pad-based VR locomotion.

Most recently, VR has been gaining momentum in the consumer electronics space with various forms of desktop and mobile VR technologies [5]. Common VR experiences take place in a seated or standing while being stationary or moving around within the tracking area. However, current VR systems lack more extensive areas of interactions as tracking systems are limited by the range of their sensors, resulting in the design of various locomotion mechanics based on teleportation, controller movement, tunnelling vision, and the human joystick [19]. Although innovative, such interactions aim at addressing the presence and reducing motion sickness effects caused by movement in VR, and advances in makerspace are enabling developers, researchers, and enthusiasts to create VR walking devices to close the gap between high-end omnidirectional treadmills and consumer-level solutions [17].

Despite the complexity of VR walking hardware, the impact of locomotive user interfaces in scenarios other than entertainment has seen studies associate to (i) health care where patients under physiotherapy are exposed to engaging VR scenarios while utilizing a treadmill assisting on recovering lower limb mobility [8], and (ii) training mobility, balance and fall risk in the elderly [15]. However, adopting large treadmills for general use can be expensive, consumer-level solutions have been driving advances in developing innovative forms of interactions such as Level-ups [14], a device that simulates stationary walking with haptic feedback for terrain height differences.

In this paper, we present the development of a VR scenario that employs a Smartwatch as a walking user interface. Smartwatches are currently being mass adopted because of their heart rate, motion, and electrocardiography tracking features [1]. The interactive scenario was developed by analyzing the four phases of gait to determine the signal processing requirements to capture the walking data adequately. Data from the wearable was streamed through Web-Sockets accessed by the game engine running the interactive scenario, producing movement based on walking. To understand and assess our solution usability perception, we conducted a preliminary study where participants walked in a VR room while moving a ball in front of them with their feet.

2   Development

To utilize the Smartwatch as a suitable user interface for VR walking, we designed our system to gather lower limb motion information at the ankle, and transfer the data to the game engine through a Local Area Network (LAN) comprised of an access point and a router as presented in Fig. 1.

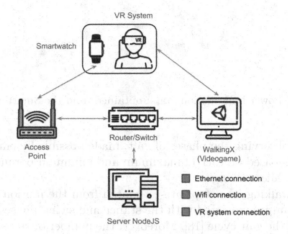

Fig. 1. System architecture.

The components of our system architecture include a Mobvoi Ticwatch E Smartwatch [9], a Vr-Ready computer desktop, and the HTV Vive VR headset. To enable the acceleration and angular velocity data transmission from the Smartwatch, we developed a Wear OS Android application (App) employing Android Studio capable of sampling data at a 100 Hz frequency. To receive the data from the Smartwatch, we implemented a Node.js server that allows synchronizing the data through the WiFi LAN, employing the Socket.io library that provides an event-based bidirectional communication merging AJAX and WebSockets into one robust API [12].

2.1   Gait Analysis

Gait is comprised of two main phases, stance and swing, each having unique events that define the walking pattern [10]. The stance phase involves: (i) the initial contact, (ii) loading response, (iii) mid-stance, and (iv) the terminal stance, while the swing phase involves: (i) pre-swing, (ii) initial swing, (iii) mid-swing, and (iv) the terminal swing. To capture gait while in VR, the horizontal angular velocity perpendicular to the user's sagittal plane was obtained from the Smartwatch as presented in Fig. 2. To visualize the peaks and valleys from the motion captured data, we employed a 4–5 Hz Butterworth band-pass filter [11].

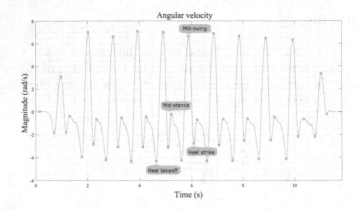

Fig. 2. Lower limb motion graph obtained from the Smartwatch.

Figure 2 allows observing the phases of gait, made possible by employing gener-alized thresholds based on each of maximum and minimum parameters detected from the users while walking.

To identify walking, the steps are estimated from the motion captured data by using timestamps associated with the stance and swing phases 60% and 40% duration during the gait cycle [18]. Moreover, the number of steps and frequency by monitoring the heel strike and foot-off events is monitored and informed to the user through the graphical user interface. The report also provides information about the percentage spent in both phases, the average stance, swing and stride times.

2.2   Smartwatch Gait Tracking

To increase embodiment during the VR experience, we created a virtual avatar that matches the captured walking movements. The gait tracking data received by the Unity game engine are transferred to a virtual avatar to define its anima-tion frames, for visualization of the walking motion. However, obtaining informa-tion about the gait phases is insufficient to determine the walking direction. The user's orientation in VR was obtained by calculating the orientation vector from the accelerometer and gyroscope information from the Smartwatch employing quaternions. Then, the quaternion information is sent to Unity where the avatar direction is changed.

2.3   Vive Tracker Gait Tracking

To compare the Smartwatch tracking data with one of a system used in VR, we integrated one HTC Vive Tracker to monitor gait interactions. The Vive Tracker allowed measuring the walked distance through the ankle's position and orientation. To compare the tracked data with that of the Smartwatch, the Vive tracker is located opposite to it and around the ankle.

2.4   VR Interactive Scenario

VR allows for highly immerse and interactive experiences, and most developments often display users within the computer-generated world as floating cameras with hands hanging in the air associated with the headset and controllers. As a solution to increase immersion, the avatar body movements are triggered by the Smartwatch information and adjusted to match the VR headset visual feedback. The interactive scenario was designed to match the tracking area of the HTC Vive's base station to guarantee adequate headset tracking during the interaction. The environment requires the user to find the ball and push it towards the goal area displayed in the scene. A total of four goal areas are presented, each displayed after completion of the previous one (Fig. 3).

Fig. 3. VR animated avatar from motion tracked data and first-person VR HMD view of the walking environment and interactive ball.

2.5   Preliminary Study

To understand the usability perception of employing a Smartwatch as a suitable user interface for VR walking, we conducted a preliminary study with seven volunteers from a Graduate program in Computer Science. The volunteers, five male and two female, wore the Smartwatch and a Vive Tracker around the ankle. The Vive Tracker was added to compare how both tracking systems compare to each other during the experience. After securing the tracking devices, volunteers were introduced to the VR environment and asked to interact with the virtual ball until completing the four tasks. Then, all volunteers completed the System Usability (SUS) questionnaire [4], a tool to measure ease of use in a quick manner.

3   Results

Data from the Smartwatch and Vive tracker were obtained from the interactions with the virtual ball within the VR experience. Figure 4 shows a comparison between the data collected from both tracking devices. Since the Vive Tracking samples data at 91 Hz, the graph was adjusted to map the 100 Hz sampling from the Smartwatch. From Fig. 4 it is worth highlighting the correspondence of gait events during the stance and swing phases. Both devices were able to measure the same amount of steps and steps per minute. However, data from two users presented a significant mismatch between motion captured information caused from occlusion of Vive Tracker sensor.

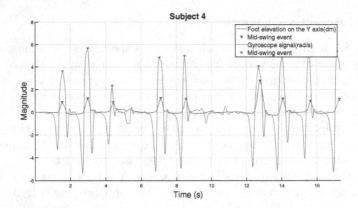

Fig. 4. Smartwatch and VIVE Tracker captured signals.

The SUS is comprised of ten questions covering usability aspects related to the need for support, training, and complexity. Responses are based on a 5-point Likert scale representing the composite measure of the overall usability on a 0–100 scale. The scale is calculated by subtracting 1 is from the score for each of the odd-numbered questions, while subtracting the resulting value from 5 for the even questions. A SUS score above a 68 is considered above average, and anything below 68 is considered below average [13]. The results from the SUS questionnaire are presented in Table 1.

Table 1. Table to test captions and labels

Questions	Rate	SUS score
I think that I would like to use this system frequently	3.2	2.2
I found the system unnecessarily complex	1.6	3.4
I thought the system was easy to use	4.2	3.2
I think that I would need the support of a technical person to be able to use this system	1.2	3.8
I found the various functions in this system were well integrated	4,2	3.2
I thought there was too much inconsistency in this system	1.6	3.4
I would imagine that most people would learn to use this system very quickly	4.6	3.6
I found the system very cumbersome to use	1.4	3.6
I felt very confident using the system	3.8	2.8
I needed to learn a lot of things before I could get going with this system	1.4	3.6
Average SUS		82/100

4   Conclusion

Here we have presented our preliminary work on developing a VR walking inter-action employing a Smartwatch. We created an interactive scene where users interact with a ball by walking through the HTC Vive defined tracking area while wearing a Smartwatch and a Vive tracker secured at their ankles. Gait data acquired from the Smartwatch allowed animating a walking avatar by mapping the stance and swing phases in conjunction with the walking orientation. Although the acquired signals from the Smartwatch allowed capturing gait infor-mation similar to the commercial Vive Tracker, further testing is required to understand the performance and reliability of the data, as some users experi-enced data capture bottlenecks. Future work will focus on studying different Smartwatches and signal processing algorithms and conducting a more exten-sive study focused on the performance and reliability of the data to walk in a VR installment effectively.

Acknowledgements. The financial support of the Emerging Leaders in the Americas Program in support of A. Hernandez and A. Angarita, and the Natural Sciences and the Engineering Research Council (NSERC) of Canada in support of A. Uribe Quevedo Discovery Grant, and Universidad Pontificia Bolivariana, Bucaramanga, Colombia are gratefully acknowledged.

References

1. Adapa, A., Nah, F.F.H., Hall, R.H., Siau, K., Smith, S.N.: Factors influencing the adoption of smart wearable devices. Int. J. Hum.-Comput. Interact. **34**(5), 399–409 (2018)
2. Avila, L., Bailey, M.: Virtual reality for the masses. IEEE Comput. Graph. Appl. **34**(5), 103–104 (2014)
3. Barrera, S., Romanos, P., Saito, S., Takahashi, H., Nakajima, M.: Real time detec-tion interface for walking on cave. In: Proceedings Computer Graphics Interna-tional 2003, pp. 105–110. IEEE (2003)
4. Brooke, J., et al.: SUS-a quick and dirty usability scale. Usability Eval. Ind. **189**(194), 4–7 (1996)
5. He, P.: Virtual reality for budget smartphones. Young Sci. J. **18**, 50–57 (2016)
6. Iwata, H.: Walking about virtual environments on an infinite floor. In: Proceedings IEEE Virtual Reality (Cat. No. 99CB36316), pp. 286–293. IEEE (1999)
7. Iwata, H., Fujii, T.: Virtual perambulator: a novel interface device for locomotion in virtual environment. In: Proceedings of the IEEE 1996 Virtual Reality Annual International Symposium, pp. 60–65. IEEE (1996)
8. Jung, J., Yu, J., Kang, H.: Effects of virtual reality treadmill training on balance and balance self-efficacy in stroke patients with a history of falling. J. Phys. Ther. Sci. **24**(11), 1133–1136 (2012)
9. Mobvoi: TicWatch S&E - A smartwatch powered by Wear OS by Google (2019). https://www.mobvoi.com/pages/ticwatchse
10. Muro-De-La-Herran, A., Garcia-Zapirain, B., Mendez-Zorrilla, A.: Gait analysis methods: an overview of wearable and non-wearable systems, highlighting clinical applications. Sensors **14**(2), 3362–3394 (2014)

11. Patterson, M.R., Johnston, W., O'Mahony, N., O'Mahony, S., Nolan, E., Caulfield, B.: Validation of temporal gait metrics from three IMU locations to the gold standard force plate. In: 2016 38th Annual International Conference of the IEEE Engineering in Medicine and Biology Society (EMBC), pp. 667–671. IEEE (2016)
12. Rai, R.: Socket. IO Real-Time Web Application Development. Packt Publishing Ltd., Birmingham (2013)
13. Sauro, J.: Practical Guide to the System Usability Scale: Background. Benchmarks & Best Practices. CreateSpace Independent Publishing Platform, Scotts Valley (2011)
14. Schmidt, D., et al.: Level-ups: motorized stilts that simulate stair steps in virtual reality. In: Proceedings of the 33rd Annual ACM Conference on Human Factors in Computing Systems, pp. 2157–2160. ACM (2015)
15. Shema, S.R., et al.: Clinical experience using a 5-week treadmill training program with virtual reality to enhance gait in an ambulatory physical therapy service. Phys. Ther. 94(9), 1319–1326 (2014)
16. Steinicke, F., Visell, Y., Campos, J., Lécuyer, A.: Human Walking in Virtual Environments. Springer, New York (2013). https://doi.org/10.1007/978-1-4419-8432-6
17. Sun, Q., et al.: Towards virtual reality infinite walking: dynamic saccadic redirection. ACM Trans. Graph. (TOG) 37(4), 67 (2018)
18. Umberger, B.R.: Stance and swing phase costs in human walking. J. R. Soc. Interface 7(50), 1329–1340 (2010)
19. Vlahović, S., Suznjevic, M., Skorin-Kapov, L.: Subjective assessment of different locomotion techniques in virtual reality environments. In: 2018 Tenth International Conference on Quality of Multimedia Experience (QoMEX), pp. 1–3. IEEE (2018)
20. Warren, L.E., Bowman, D.A.: User experience with semi-natural locomotion techniques in virtual reality: the case of the Virtuix Omni. In: Proceedings of the 5th Symposium on Spatial User Interaction, pp. 163–163. ACM (2017)

Data Center Physical Security Training VR to Support Procedural Memory Tasks

Eun Sun Chu[1](✉), Austin Payne[1], Jinsil Hwaryoung Seo[1](✉),
Dhruva Chakravorty[2], and Donald McMullen[2]

[1] Soft Interaction Lab, Texas A&M University,
College Station, TX 77843, USA
{chueunsony17, hwaryoung}@tamu.edu
[2] HPRC, Texas A&M University, College Station, TX 77843, USA

Abstract. The importance of physical security in a data center cannot be emphasized enough. Poor physical security would not only be out of compliance with government regulations, but also present an incredible risk to the integrity of the machines in question. Physical security means a set of policies, precautions, and practices must be adopted to avoid unauthorized access and manipulation of a data center's resources. Physical security practices in data centers cover a great number of steps to follow, such as locking up the server room, setting up surveillance, using rack mount servers, and many other security protocols. Existing physical security programs use traditional learning methods such as online classes, books and onsite training. However, these materials have limitations to provide trainees practical and hands-on experiences that are based on procedural tasks.

We developed CiSE-ProS (Cyberinfrastructure Security Education for Professionals and Students) VR, a virtual reality training application that supports students in learning physical security principles through various procedural tasks in a virtual data center environment. Since physical security training consists of various procedural tasks, CiSE-ProS VR could be an effective environment which can support people through embodied scenario-based activities. We investigate how a virtual reality training tool would benefit a trainee in remembering sequential tasks of physical security in a data center in comparison to a training video. The pilot study shows that CiSE-ProS VR enhances trainees' procedural memory formation of physical security concepts in the data center by allowing them to access the data center facility and dynamically interact with individual items in the data center.

Keywords: VR · VR training · Procedural memory · Data center security · Cyber security

1   Introduction

1.1   Virtual Reality-Based Training

Virtual Reality (VR) is a medium composed of interactive computer simulations that interactively respond to the participant's actions and augment the feedback to one or

© Springer Nature Switzerland AG 2019
C. Stephanidis (Ed.): HCII 2019, CCIS 1033, pp. 353–358, 2019.
https://doi.org/10.1007/978-3-030-23528-4_48

more senses. This usually provides the feeling of being mentally immersed or present in the simulation [1]. VR has been considered as an emerging training tool in many industry domains and proposed as a platform that supports embodied learning.

Through its immersive nature and movement tracking capabilities, VR can allow users to interact, practice and learn skills easily [2]. This makes VR training more effective than traditional training. Recently, VR based training has gained increasing attention in occupational training by delivering instructions through a more immersive and interactive arrangement [3–5]. For this reason, many companies are trying to adopt VR technologies for employee training, because VR-based training can be more effective than traditional training methods. Walmart is already training associates soft skills, such as empathy, customer service, and compliance using VR [6]. Also, Volkswagen created a VR training simulation that can train 10,000 employees to manipulate virtual vehicle parts that corresponded to real world actions [7]. Japan Airlines is using VR for trainees to work with life-sized virtual representations of aircraft engines and equipment from anywhere in the world [8]. Some research that examined the technology's effectiveness have found that it reduces the time taken to learn, decreases the number of trainee errors, increases the amount learned, and helps learners retain knowledge longer than traditional methods [9].

1.2 Virtual Reality and Memory

Recent research projects show that people remember information better when it is experienced in a VR environment. Harman et al. investigated immersive VR environments for memory recall by a boarding an airplane in a VR airport. The participants who experienced the virtual airport in an HMD had more accurate recall than those who used the desktop [10]. Krokos et al. presented that virtual memory palaces, a technique used to aid memory recall by using spatial mappings and environmental attributes, in HMD condition can provide superior memory recall ability compared to the desktop condition. In the study, participants stated that they could be more immersed and focused on the task [11].

Embodied actions in VR also support the recall of information. Brooks studied whether active participants in a 3D virtual house support memory recall compared to passive participants. Active participants controlled camera navigation via a joystick, while passive participants observed the navigation. They investigated that active participants had a superior environment layout recall compared to those who were in a passive setting. This suggests that memory was enhanced for those aspects of the environment that were interacted with directly—particularly the environment which was navigated [12].

In addition, other researchers present that VR supports procedural memory formation [13, 14]. Procedural memory is a type of long-term memory and concerned with how things are done with the acquisition, retention, and utilization of perceptual, cognitive, and motor skills [15–17]. Since VR technology offers embodied interactions, VR allows users to do kinesthetic activities in an environment. With real-time feedback, users can be engaged within a novel context that strongly relates to their actions. These kinesthetic activities in VR can support procedural memory formation through learning. Vázques et al. presented Words in Motion, a virtual reality language learning system, and conducted a user study which compares a text-only condition and a kinesthetic virtual reality condition [2]. Virtual kinesthetic learners showed significantly higher retention rates after a week of exposure than all other conditions and higher performance than non-kinesthetic virtual reality learners.

1.3   Physical Security Training in a Data Center

Within a data center environment, physical security and rigorous controls are very important. Software cybersecurity is built on a foundation of good physical security control. Therefore, physical access control to cyber systems remains a high-priority requirement. However, cybersecurity students usually do not have physical access to experience and learn physical security elements and procedure. Instead, they learn these concepts through lectures, videos, or web-based materials [18]. Considering that physical security training includes procedural tasks (physical access, replacing RAM, etc.), these traditional training methods are limited to provide trainees practical and hands-on experiences that consist of multiple procedural tasks.

1.4   The CiSE-ProS Virtual Reality Program

The CiSE-ProS VR (Fig. 1) program is developed to support users to learn cybersecurity principles through immersive and embodied tasks in the virtual data center environment. It offers a blend of cybersecurity and interactive visualization technologies to students in an innovative learning environment [19]. We chose VR technology because it is a participatory technology that provides an embodied environment that a user can learn through enacting scenario-based tasks.

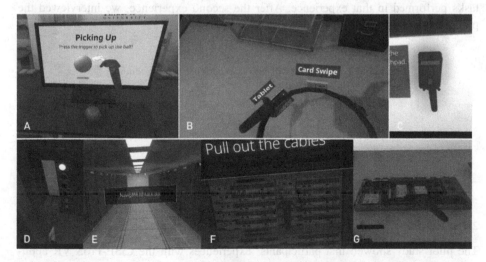

Fig. 1. (A) Tutorial room, (B) Virtual tool belt equipped with security items, (C) Thumb scanner, (D) Card Swipe at the elevator, (E) Server Room, (F) Taking cables out from the node, (G) Replacing a RAM, in the CiSE ProS VR

In the training program, the user has two tasks: entering the data center and replacing a node's RAM. To enter the data center, the user has to acquire virtual tools (key, card, and tablet), which is needed to complete the following protocols: entering the elevator, scanning their thumb, and entering the server room (Fig. 1B, C, D, E). To replace a node's RAM, the user has to find the appropriate server rack in the data center first. Then, the user has to remove the node, place it on the cart, take the cart to the workshop, replace the broken RAM, reconnect the node to the rack, and exit the data center. Throughout this process, the user will use HTC VIVE controllers for detailed actions, such as opening a rack door, manipulating cables, and replacing a RAM (Fig. 1F, G).

2 Pilot Study

2.1 Method

We conducted a pilot with six participants to investigate how participants remember series of information through embodied tasks in a VR environment in comparison to a non-interactive walk-through video of a data center. The participants were Texas A&M University students, mostly familiar with VR. However, they were not familiar with cybersecurity and data center concepts. They were divided into two groups: one (group A) viewed a video first on a laptop and then an interactive training with an HTC VIVE display; the other (group B) viewed information first with an HTC VIVE display and then on a laptop. Each group experienced five components: pre-study, experience 1 (video or VR), knowledge test, experience 2 (VR or video) and interview. In the pre-study session, we asked each participant's general experience with VR and cybersecurity. After the first experience, they had to answer two questions about a series of tasks performed in that experience. After the second experience, we interviewed the participants (Table 1).

Table 1. The orders of users' experiences in the studies

		Group A	Group B
Session 1	Pre-study		
	Video	VR	
	Knowledge test		
Session 2	VR	Video	
	Interview		

2.2 Results

The pilot study showed that participants' experiences with the CiSE-ProS VR application were very positive. All three participants that started with the VR application were able to answer correctly to questions about the procedure of following physical security protocol in a datacenter and fixing a node with a broken RAM. Two out of the three participants that started with the video walk-through answered correctly to the same questions. Since we had only three participants for each condition, it is hard to conclude that VR is better than a video for procedural training. However, five participants stated that they felt more immersed in the training environment and enjoyed the embodiment aspect of solving problems in the VR training than the video training. We include some of their responses from the interviews.

> "I prefer VR because I could easily be immersed in VR but video was distracting." ID01
> "I prefer VR because it is good for paying attention. And it's more interactive and I can feel I'm doing this. So, I could learn more." ID 02
> "I prefer VR because I was actually trying to solve the problem and had the physical sense of solving the problem." ID 06

However, one participant reported that she could pay more attention to video training because it took time to get used to controller interaction in the beginning.

In addition, participants acknowledged that virtual reality technology would be beneficial to education and training, and they were fascinated by interactive and immersive qualities of the technology.

Students also acknowledge that video materials might be good for simple memorization of repetitive information because the video environment is simple and doesn't have to deal with additional information that VR may have to address. However, they find benefits of using VR for practical information and training.

> "VR gives more hands on experiences. Therefore, it will be good for data center security training." ID 01
> "VR would be good for practicing movement-based tasks." ID 05

3   Conclusion and Future Work

In this paper, we examined how virtual reality would benefit students with procedural tasks and memory formation. We learned that CiSE-ProS provided users bodily interactions in a more engaging and interactive way compare to the video training. As a result, users could learn concepts of physical security in a data center and tasks in repairing hardware much easier and retain more information than watching a video. In the near future, we would conduct in-depth studies with more participants to validate the result that we found from the pilot study.

References

1. Sherman, W.R., Craig A.B.: Understanding Virtual Reality: Interface, Application, and Design (2002)
2. Vázquez, C., Xia, L., Aikawa, T., Maes, P.: Words in motion: kinesthetic language learning in virtual reality. In: 2018 IEEE 18th International Conference on Advanced Learning Technologies (ICALT), pp. 272–276. IEEE, IIT Bombay, India (2018)

3. Brough, J.E., Schwartz, M., Gupta, S.K., Anand, D.K., Kavetsky, R., Pettersen, R.: Towards the development of a virtual environment-based training system for mechanical assembly operations. Virtual Reality 11(4), 189–206 (2007)
4. Gavish, N., Seco, T.G., Webel, S., Rodriguez, J., Peveri, M., Bockholt, U.: Transfer of skills evaluation for assembly and maintenance training. In: BIO Web of Conferences, vol. 1, p. 00028. EDP Sciences (2011)
5. Langley, A., et al.: Establishing the usability of a virtual training system for assembly operations within the automotive industry. Hum. Factors Ergon. Manuf. Serv. Ind. 26(6), 667–679 (2016)
6. Zdnet. https://www.zdnet.com/article/walmart-deploys-17000-oculus-go-headsets-to-train-its-employees/. Accessed 20 Sept 2018
7. VRScout. https://vrscout.com/news/volkswagen-employee-training/. Accessed 05 Mar 2018
8. NetworkWorld. https://www.networkworld.com/article/3098505/japan-airlines-employs-micro soft-hololens-for-inspections-and-training.html. Accessed 22 July 2016
9. Deloitte Insights. https://www2.deloitte.com/insights/us/en/industry/technology/how-vr-train ing-learning-can-improve-outcomes.html. Accessed 14 Sept 2018
10. Harman, J., Brown, R., Johnson, D.: Improved memory elicitation in virtual reality: new experimental results and insights. In: Bernhaupt, R., Dalvi, G., Joshi, A., Balkrishan, D.K., O'Neill, J., Winckler, M. (eds.) INTERACT 2017. LNCS, vol. 10514, pp. 128–146. Springer, Cham (2017). https://doi.org/10.1007/978-3-319-67684-5_9
11. Krokos, E., Plaisant, C., Varshney, A.: Correction to: virtual memory palaces: immersion aids recall. Virtual Reality 23(1), 17 (2019)
12. Brooks, B.M.: The specificity of memory enhancement during interaction with a virtual environment. Memory 7(1), 65–78 (1999)
13. Ebert, A., Deller, M., Steffen, D., Heintz, M.: "Where did I put that?" – effectiveness of kinesthetic memory in immersive virtual environments. In: Stephanidis, C. (ed.) UAHCI 2009. LNCS, vol. 5616, pp. 179–188. Springer, Heidelberg (2009). https://doi.org/10.1007/978-3-642-02713-0_19
14. Stone, R.T., Watts, K.P., Zhong, P., Wei, C.S.: Physical and cognitive effects of virtual reality integrated training. Hum. Factors 53(5), 558–572 (2011)
15. Tulving, E.: Memory and consciousness. Can. Psychol./Psychologie canadienne 26(1), 1 (1985)
16. Anderson, J.R.: Language, Memory, and Thought. Lawrence Erlbaum Associates, Publisher, Hillsdale (1976)
17. Bobrow, D.G., Collins, A.: Representation and Understanding: Studies in Cognitive Science. Academic Press, Inc., Cambridge (1975)
18. Cone, B.D., Thompson, M.F., Irvine, C.E., Nguyen, T.D.: Cyber security training and awareness through game play. In: Fischer-Hübner, S., Rannenberg, K., Yngström, L., Lindskog, S. (eds.) IFIP International Information Security Conference, vol. 201, pp. 431–436. Springer, Boston (2006). https://doi.org/10.1007/0-387-33406-8_37
19. Seo, J.H., Bruner, M., Payne, A., Gober, N., Chakravorty, D.K.: Using virtual reality to enforce principles of cybersecurity. J. Comput. Sci. 10(1) (2019)

InNervate AR: Dynamic Interaction System for Motor Nerve Anatomy Education in Augmented Reality

Margaret Cook[✉], Austin Payne, Jinsil Hwaryoung Seo,
Michelle Pine, and Timothy McLaughlin

Texas A&M University, College Station, TX 77840, USA
atmgirl@tamu.edu

Abstract. Augmented reality applications for anatomy education have seen a large growth in its literature presence for 3D model education technology. However, the majority of these new anatomy applications limit their educational scope to the labelling of anatomical structures and layers, and simple identification interactions. There is a strong need for expansion of augmented reality applications, in order to give the user more interactive control of the anatomy education material. To meet this need, the mobile augmented reality application, InNervate AR, was created. This application allows the user to scan a marker for two distinct learning modules; one for labelling and identification of anatomy structures, the other one for interacting with the radial nerve of the canine forelimb. The first module matches other existing anatomy augmented reality structures. The second module is unique, because it allows the user to play an animation of the anatomy models, to show what the normal range of motion for the muscles of the limb is, based on the motor innervation of radial nerve. Next, the user can select where to make a cut along the length of the radial nerve, to cause a nerve deficit to one or more of the muscles of the limb. Based on this user input, the application will then play a new animation of the changed range of motion of the canine thoracic limb. A formal user study was run with this new application, which including pre- and post- knowledge assessments. Our initial data analysis showed that qualitative students' responses and quantitative data were significantly positive. This implies that the application may prove to be educationally effective. We are going to expand the scope of the application based on the analyses of user data and feedback, and develop educational modules for all of the motor nerves of the canine forelimb.

Keywords: Anatomy · Augmented reality · Educational technology

1 Introduction

Due to the increased accessibility of educational technologies, the curriculum for higher education anatomy has seen rapid reformation, (Biassuto et al. 2006). Traditionally, anatomy courses are primarily taught with the methods of didactic lectures and cadaver dissection. The anatomy classroom teaching materials are characterized by static, two- dimensional images. Laboratory involves dissection guides, animal

© Springer Nature Switzerland AG 2019
C. Stephanidis (Ed.): HCII 2019, CCIS 1033, pp. 359–365, 2019.
https://doi.org/10.1007/978-3-030-23528-4_49

cadavers, and aids such as plastinated anatomical models (Peterson 2016). However, decreased laboratory funding and laboratory time, and increased technology development, have led to limiting animal use to only teaching procedures which are considered essential (King 2004; Murgitroyd et al. 2015; Gurung et al. 2016). With the evolvement learning theories in the classroom, as well as the growth of 3D technology, there is a need for those who work in the anatomy higher education field to re-examine the learning tools that are used in anatomy courses (Azer et al. 2016).

One of several new trends to emerge in anatomy education technology is augmented reality applications for anatomy education. Augmented reality is defined as a technology that superimposes a computer-generated image on a user's view of the real world, thus providing a composite view. This technology is usually developed as an application, and can be used with mobile devices. However, the majority of these new anatomy applications only focus primarily on labelling of anatomical structures and layers, or simple identification interactions (Jamali 2015; Kamphuis 2014; Ma 2016).

It is important that anatomy content in augmented reality (AR) be expanded from simple identification questions, and labelled three-dimensional structures. As a step toward this expansion, the goal of this was to build an AR application for mobile devices, which explores the selected topic: deficits to canine muscle movement, in response to motor nerve damage. This concept is difficult for students, due to the requirement of mental visualization of the anatomical structures involved, and the need to employ critical thinking for exam questions involving clinical reasoning scenarios. Rather than making another simple interaction and labelling interface, is project allows the user to take a more interactive roll in what information is being presented by the anatomy AR application.

1.1 Visual Spatial Ability and Learning Anatomy

Visual-spatial ability has been defined as the mental manipulation of objects in three-dimensional space. When learning anatomy, spatial visualization is important, as students must learn spatial relationships and interactions between anatomical structures. This knowledge is crucial for surgical skills, because anatomy education gives the baseline skill set for accurate diagnosis in organs and body systems (Azer and Azer 2016). The amount of cadaver contact has been reduced in higher education, and so new three-dimensional models are being created to compensate. 3D modeling tools allow the user to the add or remove structures and observe them from different angles in three-dimensional space, thus enhancing the teaching process of complicated anatomical areas (Gurung et al. 2016).

1.2 Critical Thinking in Higher Education

One of the goals of InNervate AR is to deepen the learning that a student can gain from their interaction with the anatomy content in this application. By taking the anatomical material beyond pure identification, and into more complex and dynamic interaction, an element of critical thinking can possibly be introduced. According to Abraham et al. "critical thinking is the process of actively and skillfully applying, relating, creating, or evaluating information that one has gathered." The ability to think critically is vital to science education, and is crucial for life-long learning (Abraham 2004). Kumar and James support this argument by adding that critical thinking is a rational process, with personal reflection to reach a conclusion. This approach to learning has become a high focus in educational research (Kumar 2015).

1.3 Mobile Devices and Augmented Reality for Anatomy Education

Augmented reality (AR) has been granted a large literature presence in higher education. One example of mobile AR study was a multi-university study with a specific mobile application, HuMAR. The intent of implementing HuMAR was to teach general human anatomy to students. Overall, they hoped to measure the user experience of the application, in three different anatomy courses, across three different universities. They performed a pilot test, and after analyzing their pre- and post-surveys, they determined that this mAR application could be effective in motivating and improving student learning (Jamali 2015). Another research project tested to see if mobile augmented reality (mAR) could be implemented in a Turkish medical school anatomy class, as an educationally impactful tool. The researchers concluded that mAR decreases cognitive load, increases academic achievement, and can make the learning environment more flexible and satisfying (Küçük et al. 2016).

In terms of the user interface of AR, most projects seem similar in nature. The Miracle system is described as providing an identification of structures interaction and "a meaningful context compared with textbook description (Kamphuis 2014)". The work done by Chien et al. includes a system that has "pop-up labeling" and an interactive 3D skull model, that the users can rotate to view different angles of the model. They also found results showing that the 3D display of AR helped students improve their spatial memory of the location of anatomical structures, as compared to a traditional 2D display. (Chien 2010). The MagicMiror project of Ma et al. is mapped to the users own body, but it is still a simple point and click interface. The user is quizzed based on definitions and asked to identify structures (Ma 2016). There is a lack of understanding of how AR can support more complex learning in anatomy, and how to ensure that the AR system has strong usability in a classroom environment (Kamphuis 2014; Cuendet et al. 2013). But as seen in the review by Lee et al., this technology has a large potential to serve in education, as it can make the educational environment more engaging, productive, and enjoyable. Furthermore, it can provide a pathway for students to take control of their own learning and discovery process (Lee et al. 2012).

2 Methods

The focus of this application was the bones, intrinsic muscles, and motor nerves of the canine thoracic limb, with a specific learning module for the radial nerve. All of these concepts are included in the undergraduate VIBS 305 Biomedical Anatomy course curriculum at Texas A&M University. All of the anatomy content was created and animated with special attention to anatomical correctness. InNervate AR was designed as a marker-based system. This means that the camera of the mobile device detects a shape on a piece of paper, known as the marker, and then the application loads the programmed learning module that corresponds to that marker. To accomplish this marker recognition, InNervate AR was built on a Samsung Galaxy smart phone with Google ARCore software, utilizing image recognition developments from Viro Media. The first scannable marker brings up the labelling and identification module. The second scannable marker brings up the learning module that explores motor nerve deficits. The user is allowed to "cut" nerves on the limb with a swipe of the finger on the mobile device, with a corresponding animation following the user's action. This animation will demonstrate changes to motor innervation of the limb, based on where the nerve cut occurred. For example: the user will view the muscles and nerves on the limb, and an animation will demonstrate normal muscle movements for a healthy range of motion. Afterwards, the user will be able to cut the nerve supplying motor inner-vation to the limb, and then a new animation will play, demonstrating which muscle action deficits now exist, because the muscles will or will not move, depending on its location in relationship to the damaged/cut nerve (Fig. 1).

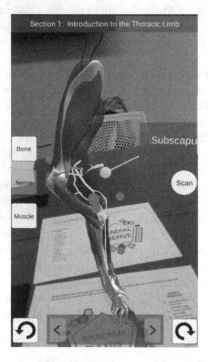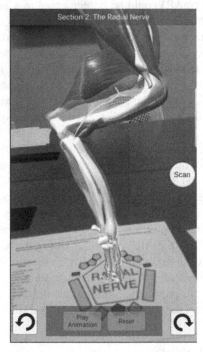

Fig. 1. Screen captures from the InNervate AR application show what the user sees during the labelling (left) learning module and the radial nerve animation (right) learning module.

2.1 Study of Knowledge Gain

Within the quasi-experimental design of this study, the non-equivalent groups design is being followed. This means that no randomized control group exists, but a pre- and post- test is given to groups of people that are as similar as possible, in order to determine if the study intervention is effective or not in learning. The pre- test was written to include anatomy knowledge questions, a free response question, demographics questions, and Likert-Scale based questions about their anatomy education experience. The post- test was written with five knowledge-based questions, three of which mirrored the anatomy knowledge questions of the pre-test, with the same concept being asked in a different way.

2.2 User Study Sequence of Events

Participants were eligible to participate in the user study as long as they had completed the Texas A&M VIBS 305 Anatomy course within the timeframe of the previous 2 academic years. All participants were given 90 min maximum to complete the activities of the user study. The participant was provided with a mobile device (SAMSUNG Galaxy) and a corresponding paper handout for how they were to proceed with interacting with InNervate AR. This handout asked them to perform specific tasks, in a defined sequence, in order to ensure that the user had interacted with all parts of the application. After completing their interaction with InNervate AR, the participant was asked to complete a post-activity questionnaire (Fig. 2).

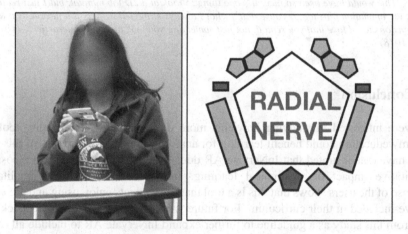

Fig. 2. A user study participant is scanning marker (left) for the radial nerve animation learning module. This marker is pictured on the right.

3 Results and Discussion

After the user study was completed, all of the data was compiled and analyzed. There was a total of 22 participants in the user study for the Innervate AR application. Five of the participants were male, and 17 were female. 11 of the participants obtained an "A" in the TAMU VIBS 305 Anatomy course, 9 of the participants obtained a "B" and 2 participants obtained a "C" in the course.

3.1 Participant Testing Results

In the pre-questionnaire, the participants had 3 anatomical knowledge test questions. In the post-questionnaire, the participant had 5 anatomical knowledge test questions, 3 of which were matched to the pre-questionnaire test questions. In other words, the same content was tested on in those 3 questions, but asked in a different way. The scores of the participants were analyzed, and 77.27% of the participants' scores improved on the 3 matched questions, after using the InNervate AR application. 18.18% of the participants made the exact same score on the matched anatomy questions, and 4.55% of the participants had a lower score in the post-questionnaire on the 3 matched questions. This data appears to suggest that the majority of the participants saw an improvement in their knowledge of the anatomical content.

The participants seemed to enjoy their use of InNervate AR, and all of them gave positive feedback about their user experience. Some of the verbal comments of the participants during their use of the InNervate AR application were:

> "Very interactive compared to other apps I've tried...You can't always go into the lab, and even then, you can't see through the muscles to see branching." (User ID:1008)
> "Nice way to look at the anatomy from different angles... Most apps don't have what would happen if something is wrong, they just have the structures" (User ID: 1009)
> "This would have been so nice. It's one thing to look at a 2D lab manual, but I just really like the animation part too, because that's what I always struggled with. Is it a flexion, is it an extension etc....I love that you scan it, not just something you look at, it's so interactive." (User ID:1018)

4 Conclusion

We were interested in studying how this more dynamic augmented reality tool for anatomy education could benefit learning for anatomy students. The results of this user study have demonstrated that InNervate AR does have the potential to have a positive quantitative impact on anatomical learning. In addition, the positive qualitative response of the users shows that this is a tool that the students enjoy using and are eager to have included in their curriculum. For future work, we plan to use the feedback and data from this study as a guideline to further expand InNervate AR to include all of the motor nerves of the limb as learning modules. In addition, we are going to conduct in-depth studies considering how spatial visualization and critical thinking affect learning anatomy using AR.

References

Biassuto, S.N., Caussa, L.I., Criado del Río, L.E.: Teaching anatomy: cadavers vs. computers? Ann. Anat. **188**(2), 187–190 (2006)

Peterson, D.C., Mlynarczyk, G.S.A.: Analysis of traditional versus three-dimensional augmented curriculum on anatomical learning outcome measures. Anat. Sci. Educ. **9**(6), 529–536 (2016)

King, L.A.: Ethics and welfare of animals used in education: an overview. Anim. Welf. **13** (SUPPL.), 221–227 (2004)

Murgitroyd, E., Madurska, M., Gonzalez, J., Watson, A.: 3D digital anatomy modelling - practical or pretty? Surgeon **13**(3), 177–180 (2015)

Gurung, P., Lukens, J.R., Kanneganti, T.: Using 3D modeling techniques to enhance teaching of difficult anatomical concepts **21**(3), 193–201 (2016)

Azer, S.A., Azer, S.: 3D anatomy models and impact on learning: a review of the quality of the literature. Health Prof. Educ. **2**(2), 80–98 (2016)

Jamali, S.S., Shiratuddin, M.F., Wong, K.W., Oskam, C.L.: Utilising mobile- augmented reality for learning human anatomy. Procedia – Soc. Behav. Sci. **197**(February), 659–668 (2015)

Kamphuis, C., Barsom, E., Schijven, M., Christoph, N.: Augmented reality in medical education? Perspect. Med. Educ. **3**(4), 300–311 (2014)

Ma, M., et al.: Personalized augmented reality for anatomy education. Clin. Anat. **29**(4), 446–453 (2016)

Abraham, R.R., et al.: Clinically oriented physiology teaching: strategy for developing critical-thinking skills in undergraduate medical students. Adv. Physiol. Educ. **28**(3), 102–104 (2004)

Kumar, R., James, R.: Evaluation of critical thinking in higher education in Oman. Int. J. High. Educ. **4**(3), 33–43 (2015)

Küçük, S., Kapakin, S., Göktaş, Y.: Learning anatomy via mobile augmented reality: effects on achievement and cognitive load. Anat. Sci. Educ. **9**(5), 411–421 (2016)

Chien, C.-H., Chen, C.-H., Jeng, T.-S.: An interactive augmented reality system for learning anatomy structure. In: International MultiConference of Engineers and Computer Scientists, vol. 1, p. 6 (2010)

Cuendet, S., Bonnard, Q., Do-Lenh, S., Dillenbourg, P.: Designing augmented reality for the classroom. Comput. Educ. **68**, 557–569 (2013)

Lee, K.: Augmented reality in education and training. TechTrends **56**(2), 13–21 (2012)

Ormand, C.J., et al.: Evaluating geoscience students' spatial thinking skills in a multi-institutional classroom study, 9995 (2018)

Ormand, C.J., et al.: The spatial thinking workbook: a research-validated spatial skills curriculum for geology majors. J. Geosci. Educ. **65**, 423–434 (2017)

Gagnier, K.M., Shipley, T.F., Tikoff, B., Garnier, B.C., Ormand, C., Resnick, I.: Training spatial skills in geosciences: a review of tests and tools. In: 3-D Structural Interpretation: Earth, Mind, and Machine: AAPG Memoir, vol. 111, pp. 7–23 (2016)

Trifone, J.D.: The test of logical thinking: applications for teaching and placing science students. Am. Biol. Teach. **49**(8), 411–416 (1987)

Animal Trail: An Augmented Reality Experience in the Amazon Rainforest

Cinthia Larissa da Costa[✉] and Wilson Prata

Sidia, Manaus, Brazil
{cinthia.costa,wilson.prata}@sidia.com

Abstract. Sidia, a Research and Development Institute, with the natural science park *"Bosque da Ciência"* (Forest of Science) have teamed up to develop a solution for the community of Manaus learn interactively about the Amazon Forest with support of scientific knowledge. This partnership was motivated because the park has an important structure but can't properly communicate about the diversity for its visitors. In other hand, Augmented Reality (AR) enables richer and immersive experience. Along with the context where it would be applied, AR brought many issues that needed to be directed, in this case: how can AR contribute to enriching the experience of users visiting the park? Considering that AR is a technology that allows the imposition of a layer of information on reality; first, we mapped the main opportunities of interaction within the journey of the visitors to improve their experience. To do so, Double Diamond British Design Council was chosen as a methodology to assist in discovery until delivery. The application started with the most interesting attraction for the visitants: the animals. They live loose in the forest and sometimes can't appear in visitors' journey but AR collaborates in these interactions by unveiling 3D virtual animal. The visitants can interact and consult all content whenever they want since it is stored in the application after unlocked inside the park. We concluded that AR had been prove to be a relevant solution for encouragement and support visitor's interaction in the park. This research was funded by Samsung by resources originated by Informatic Law.

Keywords: Design Research · Augmented Reality (AR) ·
Social & environmental · Amazon rainforest

1 Introduction

1.1 Context and Problematic

This article aims to expose the research and development process of an AR mobile application. It was developed in an environment with opportunity of investment, moreover it was important to improving collaboration with the local community and encourage it interaction and knowledge with the surrounding nature. The institution that this solution was implemented was the *"Bosque da Ciência"* (Forest of Science), a natural science public park with focus on Amazonian flora and fauna.

Forest of Science is located in Manaus, a capital in the Amazon in Brazil, its purpose is to preserve local biodiversity and to promote scientific diffusion program of

C. Stephanidis (Ed.): HCII 2019, CCIS 1033, pp. 366–373, 2019.
https://doi.org/10.1007/978-3-030-23528-4_50

INPA's (National Institute of Research of the Amazon), the maintainer of the park. Sidia is an institute of science and technology, also located in Manaus, that receives public and private support and seeks, between other things, to serve the local community.

The Forest of Science have thirteen hectares inside a metropolitan region and is a reference in a circuit of natural tourism in Brazilian Amazon.Circuit is a category which describes the exercise of a practice or the provision of a particular service through facilities, equipments and spaces that not necessarily have a spacial continuity, beside that, it keep being recognized by its end user for it whole [1]. The Forest of Science is a reference of recreation for the citizen, for Magnani [1] it is the concept of "piece": when space becomes a point of reference to distinguish certain group of visitors as belonging to a network of relationships. In Urbe, the citizens do not necessarily know each other through bonds built in the day-to-day of the neighborhood, but rather, are recognized as having the same symbols and references for tastes, orientations, values, consumption habits, and similar lifestyles.

Through the extensively research on AR, and their potential areas of application, the Sidia's designers identified the opportunity to apply and learn more about the usage of AR in open spaces by developing a smartphone application for Forest of Science visitants. Thus, this app could enhance the users' experience and knowledge about the forest, which aligns with INPA's objective to spread the knowledge about the Amazon and its value to the community.

After Sidia present the idea of the proposal for INPA and Forest of Science, the project was accepted and perceived as a social investment in the park from the Sidia and Samsung and a great learning opportunity for the institute (Figs. 1 and 2).

Fig. 1. Family in manatee tank in Forest of Science.

Fig. 2. Agouti walking in the park and the visitants.

Fig. 3. Sloth with her newborn (Source: Sidia, 2018)

1.2 Augmented Reality

Augmented Reality (AR) is a powerful technology that enables richer and immersive experience. Using a smartphone or specific device, AR blends its cues and digital graphic overlays with the real world as we perceive it [2]. This immersion has potential to create a deeper engagement when the user is performing a task in a device through an experience of presence, a sense of "being there" [3]. When we have the opportunity to apply user experience design approach and an emerging technology, such as AR, it becomes the perfect pair to exhibit the value of both.

AR is an emerging technology on the rise and Sidia's goal has started to research and develop AR solutions. The planning for the development of a PoC (Proof of Concept) was the use of a cross-platform game engine Unity to code the application with ARCore [4], the Google's platform for building AR experiences, using different APIs; it enables the phone to "sense" the environment and to interact with information. During development, it was choosing a collaborative and participatory approach with the development team.

1.3   Questions and Objectives

In view of the scenarios and tools described above, we raise the main question: **how to use AR to improve the discoverability and user engagement with Forest of Science main attractions?** From this questioning, we developed the research with the complement questions: who goes to the park? Why are they going in there? Where are they from? How do they orientate themselves in the park? What are the most popular attractions? How do they get information about the attractions? What do they like or dislike there? Would they use an app walking on the park? What applications they use? What type of smartphone they have? What kind of interactions are they familiarized to? How register the experiences the people? How to make into a given, something that initially seems individual and subjective?

These complementary questions are as important as the main one. The team can understand a technology is a tool to solve a problem but if the problem is not well framed the tool make no sense. We have a previous hypothesis that AR could contribute to improve the experience of the visitors, through those questions we can confirm it and exactly how.

Therefore, the general objective is using the ARCore Google's platform to create a solution to answer these questions and help the park structure to receive their visitants. And the specific objectives with this article is:

- Discover characteristics about the profile of the main visitors of the park;
- Identify the pains, needs and desires of visitors and park managers;
- Based on user research, raise the requirements to support the application development backlog.

1.4   Theoretical Grounding

In Radical Technologies, Adam Greenfield highlight the importance to reconsider our relationship with the networked objects, services and spaces that define people. The author talks about the new technologies like Augmented Reality that make life easier, more convenient and more productive also reinforce it limitations and constrains. In the book, there is a stress of the importance of the usage of AR considering questions like: What challenges does it present to us, as individuals and societies? Who benefits from their adoption? In this work we reinforce the importance of a human-centric development approach to proper respond to these questions. In this sense, The VR Book is a reference about this emergent technologies and human-centered design. Jason Jerald focus on Virtual Reality but brings the concepts about AR and the proximity and distance of these technologies. Technical aspects related with technology limits and human cognition are well defined by Jerald. About Design Research Jenny Preece *et al.* show a relevant discussion and best practices about the techniques to do in field, like Shadowing. This technique was chosen to understand the behavior of the visitants in the park. Those different and complementary recommendations and premises are considered for the definition of the methodology that was choose in the research.

Still on the initial discoveries within the Forest of Science, Ethnography is an important method of collecting data from Anthropology that is based on intense observation, contact and coexistence. The Magnani brings ideas about urban to understand the relationship the city and community with the park.

2   Methodology

2.1   Proof of Concept of Mobile Application

The main idea of development was to converged into a Proof of Concept (PoC). Through three months of intense development it was tested and proved that the proposed idea for the park was feasible. To make it happen the project used the double diamond framework (Fig. 4) as project's development methodology. The advantage of this approach was to consider the user perspective in beginning of the project, the possibility to approach a problem without a clear view of which kind of solution will be developed and clear moments for divergence and convergence. In those steps, the work of Greenfield, Jerald, Preece *et al.* and Magnani help the developers to take the decision according with user and stakeholders needs, technical feasibility and resources available.

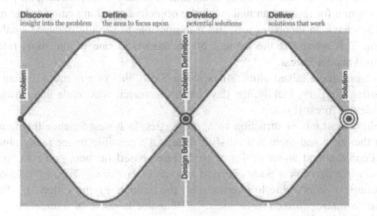

Fig. 4. Double Diamond British Design Council (Source: https://www.designcouncil.org.uk/news-opinion/design-process-what-double-diamond, 2019)

3   Results

3.1   Discovery Step: Design Research

The discovery phase aid us to identify the strength points and needs of the Forest of Science as an attraction. Semi-structured interviews and observations were important to mapping the visitors' profiles. According to Preece *et al.* [5], the observation offers information which helps in understanding the real context of activities. Based on that, it was used the Shadowing technique, an ethnographic method adapted to design, which, through direct observation it allows multiple interpretations of the reality of usage and gave us relevant insights to guide the application, such as: most used facilities, most frequent paths and journeys, reactions to attractions, attention spots and visitants complains.

The interview happened inside the Forest of Science in two different days, because the responsible of the park informed that there are two types of audience: one for weekdays, other for weekend. The designers team interviewed eighteen people, for the majority of them it was the third time that they visited the park. There were some responses that indicate that it was the first time that the visitors attended the park.

The team discovery that the main visitants in the Forest of Science are people that lives in Manaus. In this group, the most frequent and recurrent are families, followed by people who are hosting visitors and want to show the city for them; the third profile are groups of visitors like teachers with students from pre-elementary or elementary school and scouts.

They use the signaling boards to have orientation to walk in the park, if was not their first time, most of them already learned how to walk in the park and know the location of each attraction. However, when they were asked about information available they usually said that there was a lack of information: *"Pouca informação. Olhei o mapa da entrada e as placas, mas muitas estão danificadas."* ("Few information. I looked at the map of the entrance and the plates, but many are damaged.").

The main attractions inside the Forest of Science for these people are, first, the Manatee, the park has two big water tanks and it is easy to see them. The park has a support program for rescued animals with the objective of taking care for late return to nature. They have an incubator too, and it is possible to see the manatee's calves and feed them. This animal is the symbol of the park and one of the most referenced animals in Amazon Forest.

The second most talked attraction was the Sloth, this one is more difficult to see when visiting the park, luckily, the day that the research was made there was a sloth baby inside the forest (Fig. 3).

The third most talked attraction were the turtles, in Forest Science there are many turtles in the lakes and there is a building where it's possible to see many amazonian species. People talked about turtles and manatees based on being able to "interact": *"Lago das tartarugas, pois pode interagir com os bichos dando ração."* ("Lake of the turtles because it is possible to interact with the animals giving ration."), *"Peixe-boi por causa da interação com os animais."* ("Manatee because of interaction with animals."). The last attraction that the people talked about was the indigenous hut that also is an art-craft store and the giant otter, that have a tank too.

Most people cited attractions that are fixed in the park, which have their place, so that there is the chance to visualize them and create a minimal interaction. But as an interesting feature of the park is to see the diversity of animals loose, not always in a visit the person can enjoy this experience. Many doubted if there was an alligator in the lake, since it was static, resembling a statue. When asking about what they do not like in the Forest of Science: *"Cadê o macaco, a preguiça, o poço do poraquê vazio? Queria ver mais animais. A estrutura é excelente, mas estava sem guias mirins. Até a ilha da Tanimbuca foi tranquilo achar guia, mas lá embaixo não."* ("Where is the monkey? the sloth? the electric fish lake was empty? I wanted to see more animals. The structure is excellent, but it was without guides. Even the Tanimbuca's Island was easy to find a guide, but not down there."). Many people did not go in the far areas of the park, for lack of knowledge, lack of information or time of visitation. When applying the shadowing it was possible to perceive this behavior, followed by three different profiles, one family (mother and two children), one scout group (performing activity) and one tourist alone (Fig. 5).

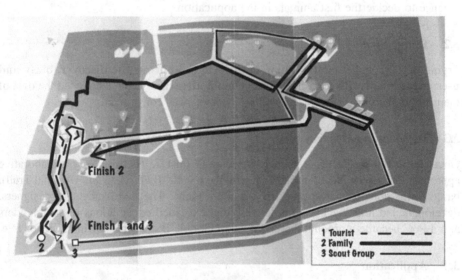

Fig. 5. Map of the Forest of Science with the visitant's journeys by the Shadowing observation technique (Source: Sidia, 2018)

Main Findings. There is a lot of information in the park that the visitor can interact to have a richer experience and a learning opportunity. There are many areas and trails not fully explored by visitor's due lack of clear information. People like to see the animals and the Forest of Science is a reference to find the animals of the Amazon. However, the guides are not enough, the boards do not bring much information and many spots lack for signalization. *"Ficamos três dias na mata fechada, mas não encontramos muitos animais, só jacaré e os botos. Nos informaram que o Bosque era uma reserva fechada com animais."* ("We stayed three days in the woods, but we did not find many animals, only alligators and porpoises. We were informed that the park was a closed reserve with animals.").

Some insights that the research provided: 1. It is important to see animals, a solution that enables observation in details when they do not appear will be high praised by the visitors; 2. Directions inside the park to easily find the attractions is another need, with this, people can discover more paths and trails in the Forest; 3. It's important have a map indicating the strategic points for discovery; 4. Besides the information available in the information spots and current signalization, the visitors would like to have more information about the attractions; 5. Forest visitors mostly use smartphones that are not on the ARCore list, despite being constantly updated. It's a point of attention to include more users. In addition to the Android system, the application needs to reach the iOS system.

To help the decision of what attractions the app could have in dealing with a PoC, the research helped to list the animals that are harder to find: sloth, monkey, electric fish, giant otter, alligator. As well the animals with greater contact and more reminders: manatee and turtles. With this list the team discussed with the responsible of Forest Science to decide the first animals in the application.

3.2   Define Step

Trying to answer the question: **how to use AR to improve the discoverability and user engagement with Forest of Science main attractions?** the team used the data of main findings to be assertiveness and the backlog was constructed.

3.3   Develop and Delivery Step

Once the development stage started, we worked on UX, UI in a very collaborative approach. One of the ideations came up with the name *"Trilha Animal"* (Animal Trail), based on its content that covers the Amazon's fauna. The involvement of designers, developers and artists achieved a delivery that exceeded expectations of stakeholders and a PoC became a product that today is on Google Play to be downloaded for free.

3.4   Application

The app needs to be downloaded in ARCore compatible smartphone in order to unlock the list of content in the strategic points of the park. The user can follow signaling boards or the digital map that comes with in the app. The boards have instructions of usage and an AR tag (a type of QR Code) where the user with the app makes smartphone's camera scan the tag to render an Augmented Reality 3D virtual model of the animal uncovered. Therefore, while walking around the target points, the visitor can virtually interact with the "animals" even when they are not hiding or less active (resting) and also learn more about the forest. The content is saved in the application gallery, as a collectable experience. It was developed seven contents, each one associated with one animal: manatee, giant otter, alligator, monkey, electric fish, agouti and sloth (Fig. 6).

Fig. 6. Trilha *Animal* (Animal Trail) screens in Google Play Store (Source: https://play.google.com/store/apps/details?id=br.org.sidia.TrilhaAnimal&hl=en, 2019)

4   Conclusion

For projects that deal with new technologies that lack a well based documentation and user guideline, choose the right methodology is a key point. In this sense, Design Council Double Diamond approach has been proved to be adequate to approach the challenge we had here. Augmented Reality is a new technology that enables new patterns of interactions, this is an opportunity at same time it is a risk. To explore the first and minimize the later, user research, in field exploration, collaborative and participatory development have been shown to be a secure procedure.

Although in its early stage, the app prides the team for providing a new tool and pathway for environmental education through the use of AR technology. Currently, a second phase of development is being under evaluation, with improvements to be identified in usability tests and new functions to add more value to the users.

Acknowledgement. This research was funded by Samsung by resources originated by Informatic Law.

References

1. Magnani, J.G.C.: De perto e de dentro: notas para uma etnografia urbana. Rev. bras. Ci. Soc. **17**(49), 11–29 (2002). ISSN 0102-6909. http://dx.doi.org/10.1590/S0102-69092002000200002

2. Greenfield, A.: Radical Technologies: the Design of Everyday Life. Verso, Brooklyn (2017). ISBN-13 978-1-78478-043-2

3. Jerald, J.: The VR Book: Human-Centered Design for Virtual Reality. ACM Books (2016). https://doi.org/10.1145/2792790

4. Google's ARCore (2019). https://developers.google.com/ar/discover/

5. Preece, J., Sharp, H., Rogers, Y.: Design de interação – Além da interação homem computador. Bookman, Porto Alegre (2013). ISBN 9788582600061

Equirectangular Image Quality Assessment Tool Integrated into the Unity Editor

Adriano M. Gil and Thiago S. Figueira[✉]

SIDIA Instituto de Ciência e Tecnologia (SIDIA), Manaus, AM, Brazil
{adriano.gil,t.figueira}@sidia.com

Abstract. Equirectangular images are captures in 360° of user surroundings. Virtual reality applications provide immersive experience
when using this type of media. However, in order to develop a 360 viewer
it is necessary to choose among different media formats, resolution configurations and texture-to-objects mappings. This work proposes to develop
a tool integrated into *Unity* editor to automatize the quality assessment
of different settings of 360 image visualization. Using objective metrics,
we compare the UV mapping of a procedural sphere, a *Skybox* rendering
and a *Cubemap*.

Keywords: Virtual reality · Image processing · Unity3D

360° pictures capture the surroundings of the user thus simulating the entire
information available from a single point. 360 cameras such as the Samsung Gear
360 capture panoramic photos and store it in a suitable format for 360 visualization. Amongst the several possible formats for 360° pictures, the equirectangular
one is widely adopted. Virtual reality applications provide an immersive experience when using 360 media and give users the feeling of being inside the 360
picture as the virtual world simulates the one captured in the picture.

Virtual reality (VR) devices render the virtual world with a different image
for each eye in order to emulate depth and as a result increase the feeling of presence within the context of the application. The technology behind VR headsets'
displays has evolved, but it still faces the challenge of offering a high density
of pixels per field of view (FoV) degree. According to Visual Acuity (1965), the
human eye has an estimated resolution of 60 pixels per degree which means
that an average 100-degrees device should render its content at 6k resolution to
provide the most realistic spacial emulation.

A 360 image viewer usually renders its contents in a sphere to mimic the
natural placement of visual elements as they would be perceived by the user in
the real world. A large amount of pixels is required to keep the quality of the
pictures though. The research for the best possible visual quality means picking
one in a given set of different exhibition formats each one with different distortion
degrees along the existing 360°. In order to decide the appropriate format and

© Springer Nature Switzerland AG 2019
C. Stephanidis (Ed.): HCII 2019, CCIS 1033, pp. 374–381, 2019.
https://doi.org/10.1007/978-3-030-23528-4_51

resolution for a 360 image it is necessary to take into consideration the device in which this picture will be displayed hence the necessity of a tool that is able to simulate devices and compare image settings so it provides the most suitable choice.

There are two approaches for image quality assessment: Subjective and Objective metrics. The first one employs human observers to evaluate and score a sequence of pictures and the second one makes automatic evaluations using mathematical models. In the context of tools, *Unity Editor* is a game development engine for computers, mobile, console, virtual and augmented reality. It is both used by small development groups as well as big corporations such as Microsoft and Disney, it is also the most used development tool for virtual reality.

In this paper, we developed an equirectangular image quality assessment tool which employs objective metrics integrated into the Unity Editor. To make assessments as close to real case scenarios, our tool is capable of simulating visualization with field of view and resolution values provided by the user. The Fig. 1 below presents the Unity Editor interface we built.

1   Related Work

VR applications differ from other applications due to their innate concern to provide content to all possible VR viewpoints. According to Fuchs (2017), VR headsets have the ability to isolate the spectator both visually and acoustically from the real world.

Zakharchenko et al. (2016) specifies that spherical panoramic content may be presented in different projection types: equirectangular (ERP), rectilinear, doughnut, cube map and multiview. According to Dunn and Knott (2017), the format of the 360 image has high impact on resolution and uniformity. Equirectangular images, for instance, have high resolution on the poles and high uniformity on the equator line whilst on a cubemap, there is high density on the edges and high uniformity in each face's diagonal.

Wang and Bovik (2006) categorize image quality assessment as subjective or objective. Objective metrics are defined as full-Reference (FN), No-Reference (NR) and Reduced-Reference (RR).

The most reliable strategy to evaluate image quality is through subjective metrics. In this case, human observers assess a set of pictures and score it in a scale from 1 (worst) to 5 (best), this technique is called MOS (Mean Opinion Score) and it calculates the average score given a set of scores for each sample.

Even though subjective tests are precise, they are inconvenient and expensive. Especially when a virtual reality environment is being evaluated because it is, by definition, more immersive. Thus, a complimentary objective metric would be useful and less expensive.

Prior work on 360 image quality assessment can be found on literature: Md et al. (2015) and Zakharchenko et al. (2016). Despite our focus on image quality assessment of 360 spherical panoramic images, our proposal only assesses screenshots obtained from texture projections inside Unity3D. Therefore, our final target are 2D images as the result of such projections.

2   Projecting 360 Images to UV Mapping

360 images comprehend the entire field-of-view of the user. Considering the equirectangular format, some mapping implementations are listed below:

1. Utilize a sphere *Mesh* to render the 360 image inside it
2. Utilize a *Skybox* to render the 360 image on the background
3. Map the 360 image to UV positions of a cubic *Mesh*.

Each mapping possibility has its own advantages and disadvantages in terms of resolution offered by angular direction and general distortion of the 360 image.

3   Mapping Equirectangular Images to a Sphere

We adopted the standard UV mapping technique for spheres which is based on the latitude/longitude approach.

Given N longitude values, the angular size T can be obtained by the Eq. 1:

$$T = \frac{2\pi}{N} \tag{1}$$

The overall angular size of an I quantity of longitude values can be obtained by the Eq. 2:

$$\alpha_i = i * T \tag{2}$$

The sine and cosine of the angle T define the X and Z positions of the sphere points which belong to the cross section of the sphere. In such manner, assuming a sphere of radius R, we can write Eqs. 3 and 4.

$$x_i = R * \sin(\alpha_i) \tag{3}$$
$$z_i = R * \cos(\alpha_i) \tag{4}$$

In a longitudinal cut, it is possible to perceive that the R-ray of a cross-section varies along the height of the sphere. K is the angular size of a sphere latitude given M latitude values as seen on Eq. 5:

$$K = \frac{\pi}{M} \tag{5}$$

The total amount of an i quantity of latitude values can be obtained by Eq. 6:

$$\alpha_{yi} = i * K \tag{6}$$

The Y position for each sphere point, considering unit radius, can be obtained by Eq. 7:

$$y_i = \cos(\alpha_{yi}) \tag{7}$$

The radius D_{yi} obtained in a cross section at latitude i is defined in Eq. 8 as:

$$R_{yi} = \sin(\alpha_{yi}) \tag{8}$$

Applying Eq. 8 in Eqs. 3 and 4 we get positions X and Z of the vertices of the sphere according to their longitude and latitude coordinates.

$$x_i = \sin(\alpha_{yi}) * \sin(\alpha_i) \tag{9}$$
$$z_i = \sin(\alpha_{yi}) * \cos(\alpha_i) \tag{10}$$

4 Mapping Equirectangular Images to a Skybox

A skybox is rendered when no 3D element is rasterized by the virtual camera. In the rasterization process, it is necessary to identify a UV coordinate for each pixel (or fragment) rendered on screen. Skybox shaders usually utilize 3D textures to store the six faces of a cube through a graphical function called $tex3D$.

Mapping an equirectangular image to a skybox involves finding the UV vector value given a normalized direction. Considering the vector (x, y, z) as the normalized direction, Eq. 11 can be used on a vertex shader.

$$uv = (\arctan(\frac{x}{y}), \arccos(y)) \tag{11}$$

Thus, when mapping to a sphere UV coordinates are projected into 3D space and when mapping to a skybox the opposite happens: normalized 3d space positions continuously seek equivalent UV coordinates.

5 Mapping Equirectangular Images to a Cubemap

The first step to use a Cubemap is to generate a cube. The standard cube generated by Unity, however, does not have enough vertices for precise UV mapping. It happens as UV mapping is a sine/cosine function whereas rasterization inside of a triangle obtains UV values through linear interpolation of its vertices, thus causing distortions.

For better results, we divided each triangle into four parts. From a cube of 10 vertices and 12 triangles, we obtained a 4090 vertices/4096 triangles cube.

As we generate each new vertex, it is possible to calculate its respective UV coordinate using Eq. 11. Noticeably, the cubemap view is equivalent to the discretization of the continuous UV mapping approach in a skybox, i.e., it is calculated per vertex instead of being applied on pixel basis.

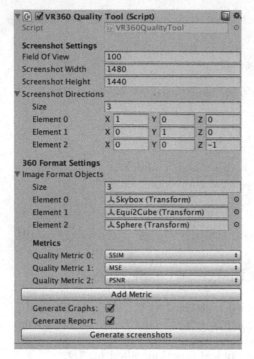

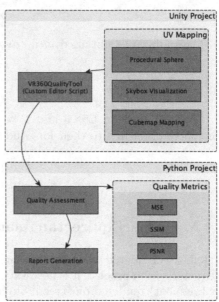

Fig. 1. Our tool as seen directly on the Unity Editor

Fig. 2. The architecture of our implementation.

The architecture of our implementation involves a C# configuration layer in *unity* and a *python* layer for calculating the objective metrics for each of the Unity-generated images. Cross-tiered communication takes place through the creation of new processes within the Unity editor. Figure 2 shows how the components are connected in our architecture.

For a friendlier use, an editor interface has been developed in the form of a custom *unity inspector*, that is, a custom view of our component in C#. In this component you can define the angle of the field of view, define width and height as well as directions of the screenshots to be generated, define the comparison metrics to be used, and define whether graphs or a report will be generated at the end of the process.

The *python* layer is responsible for evaluating the pairs of images generated by *unity*. Using the *scikit*, *numpy*, and *matplotlib* libraries, the images are evaluated and the result of each metric is saved in a report at the end, summarizing all results.

With regards to the metrics, the goal of the objective assessment is to develop a quantitative measure that can determine the quality of any given image. It is difficult, though, to find a single, objective, easy-to-calculate measurement that matches the visual inspection and is suitable for a variety of application requirements. As to address this problem, we are using three different metrics described below.

MSE or "Mean Square Error". The Eq. 12 as follows:

$$MSE = \frac{1}{MN} \sum_{m=0}^{M-1} \sum_{n=0}^{N-1} e(m,n)^2 \qquad (12)$$

SSIM is described by Wang et al. (2004) and can be calculated by the Eq. 13.

$$SSIM(x,y) = \frac{(2*\mu_x*\mu_y + C_1)*(2*\sigma_{xy} + C_2)}{(\mu_x^2 + \mu_y^2 + C_1)*(\sigma_x^2 + \sigma_y^2 + C_2)} \qquad (13)$$

Peak Signal-to-noise ratio (PSNR) is the most used metric for image quality assessment, the Eq. 14 is shown below:

$$PSNR = 10 * log_{10} \frac{(2^n - 1)^2}{MSE} \qquad (14)$$

We used *unity 2017.3.1 F* and *python 2.7* to implement the proposed tool. The tool can be imported into any *unity* project through a *unitypackage*, a standard format from *unity* to distribute resources and tools. To perform the quality assessment the button "Generate screenshots" is pressed and the value for each metric is calculated using the first image format as the default to evaluate the others. In Fig. 1, the reference image is the screenshot of the *skybox*, which are compared with those obtained with the *cubemap* and the spherical mapping. The results are summarized in the generated report, as demonstrated by the table below (Figs. 4, 5, 7, 8, 9, 10 and 11).

Fig. 3. Cubemap - direction 0   **Fig. 4.** Skybox - direction 0   **Fig. 5.** Sphere - direction 0

Fig. 6. Cubemap - direction 1

Fig. 7. Skybox - direction 1

Fig. 8. Sphere - direction 1

Fig. 9. Cubemap - direction 2

Fig. 10. Skybox - direction 2

Fig. 11. Sphere - direction 2

Based on the obtained results, we found that the *cubemap* pictures had better evaluation despite having an interpolation error. Such mapping error can be corrected by a *fragment shader* and it is visible in Figs. 3 and 6.

Metrics	MSE	SSIM	PSNR
Direction 0 - Cubemap	176,22	0,93	25,67
Direction 1 - Cubemap	125,63	0,93	27,14
Direction 2 - Cubemap	13,83	0,97	36,72
Direction 0 - Sphere	88,56	0,88	28,66
Direction 1 - Sphere	242,47	0,76	24,28
Direction 2 - Sphere	96,26	0,86	28,30

The SSIM metric analyzes structural distortions as well as luminance and contrast differences between a reference image and the processed image. According to this metric, the cubemap had the best results in all three directions.

Directions 2 and 5 had the best results according to PSNR and MSE. Direction 0 did not present good results and that is due to the mapping degradation which can be easily perceived subjectively. After quick subjective analysis, it would be understandable to conclude that sphere - direction 2 has better image quality when compared to the cubemap, but after a deeper investigation it is observable how the sphere has distortions all over its image while the cubemap has distortions in specific areas affected by the mapping degradation.

6 Conclusions

We proposed the development of an equirectangular image quality assessment tool which uses objective metrics such as MSE, SSIM and PSNR in order to facilitate choosing among different image resolutions and mapping solutions.

Our tool is integrated into the Unity Editor as Unity is the most used development engine for virtual reality applications. Different parameters were used to compare the quality of 360 images generated by three UV mapping techniques: latitude/longitude in a inverted sphere; skybox; and cubemap.

One of the disadvantages of our tool is that the user needs to know the metrics to be able to make the best parameters choice. For future work, we plan to use the current metrics to achieve a single and final evaluation value that should indicate the best result in an automated manner. Another improvement point identified is that the accuracy of the end result should be greater if the visualization is obtained directly from rendering on the mobile devices where VR applications can be executed. Thus, we also plan an embedded component in the application that allows you to reap results while running the application on the mobile device.

References

Dunn, C., Knott, B.: Resolution-defined projections for virtual reality video compression. In: 2017 IEEE Virtual Reality (VR), pp. 337–338. IEEE (2017)

Fuchs, P.: Virtual Reality Headsets - A Theoretical and Pragmatic Approach. CRC Press, Boca Raton (2017)

Md, S.K., Appina, B., Channappayya, S.S.: Full-reference stereo image quality assessment using natural stereo scene statistics. IEEE Sig. Process. Lett. 22(11), 1985–1989 (2015)

Visual Acuity (VA) (1965)

Wang, Z., Bovik, A.C.: Modern image quality assessment. Synth. Lect. Image Video Multimedia Process. 2(1), 1–156 (2006)

Wang, Z., Bovik, A.C., Sheikh, H.R., Simoncelli, E.P.: Image quality assessment: from error visibility to structural similarity. IEEE Trans.Image Process. 13(4), 600–612 (2004)

Zakharchenko, V., Choi, K.P., Park, J.H.: Quality metric for spherical panoramic video. In: Optics and Photonics for Information Processing X, vol. 9970, p. 99700C. International Society for Optics and Photonics (2016)

Prototyping User Interfaces for Mobile Augmented Reality Applications

Nicholas Harvel[1], Daniel W. Carruth[1(✉)] (iD), and Julie Baca[2]

[1] Center for Advanced Vehicular Systems, Mississippi State University,
Starkville, MS 39759, USA
{nh732,dwc2}@cavs.msstate.edu
[2] U.S. Army Corps of Engineers Engineering Research
and Development Center, Vicksburg, MS 39180, USA
julie.a.baca@usace.army.mil

Abstract. This paper presents a case study of the development and evaluation of user interfaces for mobile augmented reality applications. Two augmented reality applications were developed for Apple iPad using Unity and Apple's ARKit software. The applications were developed to demonstrate augmented reality capabilities on mobile devices to students, industry, and potential sponsors. During development and evaluation of the demonstration applications, world-anchored floating 3D text for presentation of information was often off-screen and difficult to read. Pairing 2D screen-anchored text with 3D augmented reality objects improved readability but at the cost of reduced immersion.

Keywords: Augmented reality · Usability · Mobile applications

1 Introduction

Recent advances in application programming interfaces (APIs) for computer vision, tracking, and scanning 3D geometry on mobile devices provide commonly available platforms for developing augmented reality (AR) applications. However, AR is still in its infancy and few precedents exist for how programmers should design the user interfaces for AR applications. At the Center for Advanced Vehicular Systems (CAVS) at Mississippi State University (MSU), we have developed prototype AR applications for marketing and outreach, education, and industry on iOS devices using Unity and Apple's ARKit. Each application implements different methods for user interaction with the AR environment. This paper focuses on how interaction with the 3D environment on a 2D touch screen presents challenges for AR application designers.

These applications are used to experiment on different tactics for the program to communicate to the user. One of the prototype applications provided users with multiple methods for interaction, including flat on-screen elements (e.g., 'Next' arrow) to supplement 3D interactive objects (e.g., lug nuts in the tire change applications). World-anchored floating 3D text presented challenges in both ensuring an aesthetically pleasing presentation and, more importantly, for ensuring that the information was easily visible and readable. As shown by the Labeled Electrical Box Application, this type of text is often large and gets in the way of the rest of the application. Screen-

© Springer Nature Switzerland AG 2019
C. Stephanidis (Ed.): HCII 2019, CCIS 1033, pp. 382–388, 2019.
https://doi.org/10.1007/978-3-030-23528-4_52

anchored 2D text, on the other hand, improves readability but fails to fit with the dynamic AR environments.

1.1 Related Work

Augmented reality (AR) is a rapidly developing field characterized by swiftly changing technology. As a field, AR platforms range from television and desktops to mobile systems (e.g., smart phones and tablets) to smart glasses and head-mounted displays (HMD). Application areas for AR systems include industry [1], context-based instruction [2], education [3], entertainment [4], navigation [5], health [6], and more. This paper focuses on mobile augmented reality (MAR) applications developed for a through-the-camera display on a tablet device.

In 2017, standard tools for developing advanced MAR were released by Apple (ARKit for iOS) and Google (ARCore for Android) [7, 8]. In 2018, Unity released AR Foundation tools that provide a common interface to both ARKit and ARCore, simplifying development for both iOS and Android MAR devices [9].

There is a growing literature on guidelines and principles for MAR development [10, 11]. Both Apple and Google provide human interface guidelines for design of MAR applications [12, 13]. A benefit of MAR is that the user's view of the real world is enhanced, albeit through a limited window [6]. MAR systems can help users to identify and locate key landmarks and features in the environment [1]. MAR can attach and display virtual information to landmarks, e.g., procedures to perform or a display indicating the safe areas near equipment [2]. A challenge for MAR application design is the combination of a 2D input interface (the tablet touchscreen) onto a 3D mixture of virtual and real environment elements. In addition to the 3D nature of the environment, the mobile nature of the device leads to an unpredictable variety of situations and environments in which the application may be used [11]. MAR may also slow user interaction with real world elements due to the pace at which the application provides instruction or its ability to process the environment [6].

2 Augmented Reality Applications

2.1 Tools

Our MAR applications were developed using Unity 2018.3.4f1 and the AR Foundation tools [9]. The applications were deployed to an Apple iPad Pro (Model No. A1893) running multiple versions of iOS over the course of development (11.1.2, 11.3.1, 12.0, and 12.1.4). Unity and the AR Foundation tools therefore provided a platform agnostic interface to Apple's ARKit (version 1.5) tools [7]. Scene mapping and object recognition was implemented using Vuforia libraries incorporated in Unity. Vuforia provides tools for both 3D object scanning and 3D object recognition. Vuforia was used in the labeled electrical box application to create a virtual version of and to recognize the electrical box.

2.2   Tire Change Application

The tire change application was developed as a continuation of an earlier MAR application designed for the Mississippi State University Formula SAE team. The previous application used MAR to create the appearance of a virtual model of the team's competition vehicle in the real world. This application was used to educate users on the features and design of the vehicle. The modified application provides interactive instructions for the process of changing a flat tire on the virtual vehicle by walking the user through the procedure step-by-step in MAR (see Fig. 1). In MAR, the user acts on the virtual vehicle with virtual parts and virtual tools presented at a 1:1 scale.

Fig. 1. Screenshot of the tire change application. The user must tap an unattached lug nut or the right arrow at the bottom of the screen to move to the next step.

Purpose. This prototype was developed as a demonstration that MAR can be used for purposes other than entertainment; more specifically, the Tire Change application was intended to serve as a demonstration of an instructional MAR application. The users can learn how to perform the procedures by using MAR on a full-size vehicle without requiring an actual vehicle to be present and minimizing the risks associated with working on an actual vehicle.

Function. The MAR environment supplements the learning experience by providing the user with the flexibility to view the process as if it were physically occurring in front of them. The mobility of MAR allows the user to review the actions from multiple angles. The interactive features enhance the procedure in a way that maintains the user attention while allowing the user to learn from their mistakes without risk to persons or equipment.

Review. When testing the application, it became clear that the user interface needed improvement. In some steps, the user is presented with an overwhelming amount of text that obscures the display of the MAR application. The application emphasized the text over the observation of the procedure. In other steps, the instructions were too vague and failed to explain to the user the required actions to move to the next step.

2.3   Labeled Electrical Box Application

The labeled electrical box application was developed to experiment with user interfaces tied to physical objects and to test the reliability and stability of object tracking in MAR. The demonstration box is a power supply for up to eight CCTV cameras. The box also includes a power switch and fuses for surge protection. The MAR application added labeled key features and landmarks on the exterior and interior of the electrical box (see Fig. 2). The application demonstrated how MAR could communicate helpful information about an object without the need of a manual. The application also communicated potential safety hazards of which the user should be aware while working with the electrical box. The application recognized both the inside and outside of the electrical box. It also distinguished whether the box is opened or closed and then labeled the box accordingly.

Purpose. This application was developed to provide an example of object-tethered user interface elements in a MAR application. The application is relatively simple but similar to the application described in [2]. The user is assisted during maintenance of the device using MAR. Key landmarks and features are identified and information about the box is provided without the need for a manual. The intent of the application is to provide ease of use and simplicity that will reduce intimidation and make it safer to do maintenance work on unfamiliar equipment.

Function. This program uses MAR to replace a traditional manual; it greatly reduces the linear search requirements imposed by a manual, enabling the user to quickly determine key information needed to perform tasks. It also reduces the risk of confusing the specifications of the components.

Review. Demonstrations of the application revealed flaws due to certain design decisions. For example, as the camera moves and the background changes, the floating text becomes more difficult to read. In addition, the application did not communicate to the user what elements were interactive or how to use them. As a result, users did not recognize that certain elements were interactive. However, once the user selected an object and made changes, the UI responded with alterations that led users to understand the interactive nature of the application. For example, the information and icons on the box changed after the lid was opened, providing the user with reassurance that they

Fig. 2. Screenshot of the labeled electrical box application. The user may tap on one of the color-coded sections to obtain additional information.

were moving in the right direction. This example highlighted another UI issue, however, as the electrical box is difficult to open and often requires two hands. Since the user is holding the device and has only one hand available, this made some users reluctant to put down the device and thus, continued to struggle to open the electrical box with one hand.

3   Lessons Learned

3.1   User Interface Design

A comprehensive analysis and discussion of issues encountered for all applications formed the basis of a refined UI design approach. This approach includes a mixture of visual cues and intuitive animations, paired with reduced and more precise text, all of which will simplify and enhance the user's experience. While proper balance of text and visuals is a common general user interface issue, this difficulty is heightened in augmented reality (AR) applications. In this environment, the need to maximize the user's view can lead to misuse of text in and overlaid on the camera view. As of this writing, the Apple guidelines recommend screen space text elements overlaid on the camera view [7].

3.2 Loss of Maneuverability

When using MAR one of the user's hands is dedicated to holding the device, leaving only one hand free for interacting with the physical world. This lack of mobility has no consequences in some applications but begins to cause issues when the MAR application is tailored to maintenance work. The programmer and designer identify these types of situations and prompt the user to put down the device whenever the issue may arise.

4 Augmented Reality Applications

We developed prototype mobile applications to demonstrate the benefits of MAR for two purposes: instructing users on procedures for a virtual vehicle and projecting technical and safety information onto a physical object. During development and review of the applications, we identified usability issues related to display of text on the mobile device and the need to continue to hold the device. As the focus for developing MAR technology moves from technology-driven to application-driven, user interface designers will continue to expand and apply understanding of how issues specific to MAR affect application usability.

References

1. Fraga-Lamas, P., Fernández-Caramés, T.M., Blanco-Novoa, Ó., Vilar-Montesinos, M.A.: A review on industrial augmented reality systems for the industry 4.0 shipyard. IEEE Access **6**, 13358–13375 (2018)
2. Mourtzis, D., Zogopoulos, V., Katagis, I., Lagios, P.: Augmented reality based visualization of CAM instructions towards industry 4.0 paradigm: a CNC bending machine case study. Procedia CIRP **70**, 368–373 (2018)
3. Chao, W.-H., Chang, R.-C.: Using augmented reality to enhance and engage students in learning mathematics. Adv. Soc. Sci. Res. J. **5**(12), 455–464 (2019)
4. Rauschnabel, P.A., Rossmann, A., TomDieck, M.C.: An adoption framework for mobile augmented reality games: the case of Pokémon Go. Comput. Hum. Behav. **76**, 276–286 (2017)
5. Sekhavat, Y.A., Parsons, J.: The effect of tracking technique on the quality of user experience for augmented reality mobile navigation. Multimed. Tools Appl. **77**(10), 11635–11668 (2018)
6. Aebersold, M., et al.: Interactive anatomy-augmented virtual simulation training. Clin. Simul. Nurs. **15**, 34–41 (2018)
7. Apple Inc: Apple Developer – ARKit. https://developer.apple.com/arkit/. Accessed 28 Mar 2019

8. Google: Google Developer – ARCore. https://developers.google.com/ar/. Accessed 28 Mar 2019
9. Unity Technologies: About AR Foundation. https://docs.unity3d.com/Packages/com.unity.xr.arfoundation@1.0/manual/index.html. Accessed 28 Mar 2019
10. Kourouthanassis, P.E., Boletsis, C., Lekakos, G.: Demystifying the design of mobile augmented reality applications. Multimed. Tools Appl. **74**(3), 1045–1066 (2015)
11. Irshad, S., Rambli, D.R.A.: User experience of mobile augmented reality: a review of studies. In: Proceedings of 3rd International Conference on User Science and Engineering (i-USEr), pp. 125–130. IEEE, Shah Alam (2014)
12. Apple Inc: Apple Developer - Human Interface Guidelines - iOS - System Capabilities - Augmented Reality. https://developer.apple.com/design/human-interface-guidelines/ios/system-capabilities/augmented-reality/. Accessed 28 Mar 2019
13. Google: Augmented Reality Design Guidelines. https://designguidelines.withgoogle.com/ar-design/augmented-reality-design-guidelines/. Accessed 28 Mar 2019

Studying Relationships of Muscle Representations and Levels of Interactivity in a Canine Anatomy VR Environment

Ben Heymann[✉], Preston White[✉], and Jinsil Hwaryoung Seo[✉]

Texas A&M University, College Station, TX 77840, USA
{benheymann,hwaryoung}@tamu.edu,
prestonthorpwhite@gmail.com

Abstract. Virtual Reality (VR) is at the forefront of modern technology; revolutionizing current methods for conducting activities such as gaming, training simulations, and education. When considering anatomy education specifically, students must learn form, function, and movement of various bones, muscles, muscle tendons, ligaments, and joints within the body. Historically, cadaver dissection is believed to be the most optimal method of study, but it is not always accessible. We created a VR canine thoracic limb application that allows students to learn about musculoskeletal movements, while dynamically interacting with anatomical visualization. We aimed at increasing memory retention in a more immersive and engaging way. In our study, three major factors were considered: (1) spatial visualization ability of learners, (2) visualization styles of muscles, and (3) levels of interactivity of the application. Participants of differing spatial abilities (high and low) studied a virtual thoracic limb in one of two visual conditions (realistic muscles or symbolic muscles) and one of two interactive conditions (interactive manipulation or non-interactive viewing). We tested these against each other to determine which method of muscle representation holds the most effective form of memory retention, and what role interactivity plays in this retention. Before the experiment, we gathered data pertaining to student's spatial visualization ability via a mental rotation test to create a baseline. After the experiment, we interviewed the participants to gather qualitative data about the application's effectiveness and usability. We observed through 24 user studies that low spatial visualization users gained an advantage through dynamic visualization learning to almost perform as well as their high spatial visualization counterparts. Realistic muscles assisted participants with identifying anatomical views more efficiently, and therefore had a significantly better average compared to the symbolic representation.

Keywords: Virtual reality · Anatomy education · Learning tool

1 Introduction

1.1 Background

Anatomy education is fundamental in life science and health education as well as visual studies. Students may use many study aids including diagrams, illustrations,

C. Stephanidis (Ed.): HCII 2019, CCIS 1033, pp. 389–397, 2019.
https://doi.org/10.1007/978-3-030-23528-4_53

animations, and 3D graphics (Albanese 2010). The current learning tools for anatomy can be enhanced by using technological innovations like virtual reality and augmented reality. Researchers have developed virtual reality and augmented reality for anatomy education. Seo et al. created ARnatomy and Anatomy Builder VR: ARnatomy aims to integrate a tangible user interface and augmented reality by using dog bones to control the display of information on a mobile device such as a smartphone or tablet (Seo et al. 2014). Anatomy Builder VR examines how a virtual reality system can support embodied learning in anatomy education. The backbone of the project is to pursue an alternative constructivist pedagogical model for learning canine anatomy. Direct manipulations in the program allow learners to interact with either individual bones or groups of bones, to determine their viewing orientation and to control the pace of the content manipulation.

This project is one branch of Anatomy Builder VR. It is a virtual reality application of a musculoskeletal thoracic limb model that supports students' understanding of form, function, and movement. We have formulated three hypotheses in conjunction with ones found during initial research to address the three major factors of the experiment: spatial visualization, quality of muscle representation, and interactivity.

1.2 Spatial Visualization

Spatial Visualization is the ability to mentally manipulate an object in three dimensions. Based on prior research, students with low spatial visualization ability can share similar memory retention to high spatial visualization students via dynamic visualization learning methods. This is called the compensating hypothesis (Berney et al. 2015). Spatial visualization was examined in a recent study concerning the effectiveness in methods of problem-solving strategies and was shown to be the strongest indicator in visuospatial anatomy comprehension, or in other words, visualizing the movement of the canine thoracic limb in VR enhances memory retention (Nguyen et al. 2016). Spatial awareness has been observed to boost understanding of anatomy education and using virtual reality as a physicality-based immersive application, learners can take advantage of spatial visualization (Lu et al. 2017). With active learning the promotion of mental manipulation and interaction leads to higher cognitive engagement creating a more suitable learning experience. Our application provides a 3D space that a user can walk around and manipulate components to support to spatial visualization.

1.3 Muscle Representation

We provide two muscle display modes: realistic mode and symbolic mode. Both muscle representations offer similar movement and function, with the symbolic muscle setup displaying a simplified visual representation however, the realistic form was the deciding factor on memory retention. Using the virtual canine thoracic limb is an example of artificial implementation where we rely on recreating a real form to convey a better understanding. Creating the spatial connection while immersed in the VR environment induces a perceptual outlook forcing the brain to evaluate the scene in which there is a direct promotion of spatial learning. There is a direct correlation between the sense of ownership, or sense that one's own body is the source of sensations, and the representation of the virtual model where there is an increase in ownership as the model more closely resembles its actual form (Argelaguet et al. 2016).

1.4 Interactive System

Based on our own preconceptions combined with a study done on interactivity and conceptual learning in virtual reality, we find that the interactive VR experience shows better results. Interactivity provides a truly immersive experience offering more connection to the study itself and promoting a higher learning setup. The study found that interactive VR aids children in problem solving, but the non-interactive version seemed to support greater indications of conceptual change (Roussou et al. 2006). When completing a cognitive based task, a user will have a higher advantage being exposed to a dynamic learning environment where they have the ability to manipulate objects for themselves based on their experience, prior knowledge. Direct manipulation, immersion, and interaction are some of the most important aspects to learn 3D anatomical info as it gives students a clear visual and physical understanding of form and spatial relationship.

2 Canine VR Muscle Simulation Room

2.1 Setup and Creation

The final application include one set of hyper realistic dog bones from the thoracic limb, two different representations of the biceps/triceps, a functional model stand that could include interactive buttons, and a lab setting to help immerse the participants. In terms of creating the bones, each bone went through a process that included laser scanning, 3D sculpting, retopology, and texturing. The realistic muscle models went through a similar process, but 1-on-1 sculpting sessions with our anatomy experts replaced laser scanning. Symbolic muscles were created through muscle effects in Autodesk Maya. The same program was used to create the model stand and lab environment. Rigging and animating had to be done on both thoracic limbs, so they could complete a walk cycle and show muscle contractions accordingly. Programming in Unity was also required to set up the VR equipment, and interactive actions, to run with the application.

The process of photogrammetry entails the use of photography to 3D map objects based on their distance. Our experimentation with photogrammetry resulted in poor quality scans that we were unable to use. This process did not allow us to achieve the level of anatomical accuracy that we desired. Laser scanning was found to be the most effective way for us to initially create the bones models, and we used the "XYZ Scan Handy" laser scanner. The scanner has a sensor built in and once the object is recognized and in focus it produces an OBJ file (a 3D digital model file). However, after the scan is complete and the model is created, there is still a touch-up process involved.

We used a 3D software called "Sculptris" (Fig. 1) that let us control and fix any problems with the topology of each bone. The topology refers to the 3D grid or mesh consisting of vertices, faces, and edges that shapes the object. We went through each of the five bones on the thoracic limb (the scapula, radius, ulna, humerus, and carpal bones) and assured there were no errors in the topology to avoid texture complications. For the scapula and carpal bones, we were forced to bring them into another application before Sculptris, called Autodesk Maya to repair holes in the mesh from the laser-scans.

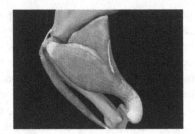

Fig. 1. Sculpting process   **Fig. 2.** Muscle texturing

Texturing was the final step to have finished muscle assets that could be rigged and animated. We strived to create a texture that would look like real muscles. Using software called Substance Painter, we created multiple layers to influence the texture of the models. This allowed us to get a two-toned, red/orange texture showing striations similar to a real muscle (Fig. 2).

2.2   Creating 4 Unique Conditions for Experimentation

Four unique versions of the application were created from the pieces that have been produced so far. The four different versions are realistic interactive (Fig. 3), realistic non-interactive, symbolic interactive, and symbolic non-interactive (Fig. 4). The interactive versions of our application had buttons that enabled the user to control the thoracic limb.

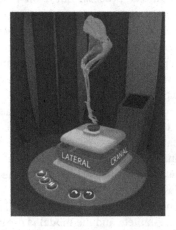

Fig. 3. Realistic interactive   **Fig. 4.** Symbolic non-Interactive

We programmed the interactive application to control the animation speed of the walk cycle, and the rotation of the thoracic limb and base. The rotation ability allows us to rotate the thoracic limb and also teach the user four different anatomical views (lateral, medial, cranial, and caudal). When the model rotates, part of the base rotates at the same rate to display the corresponding view. Playing and pausing the animation teaches the user about the reciprocal relationship between the bicep and triceps (Fig. 5).

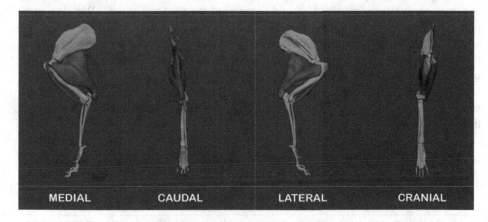

Fig. 5. Anatomical views

By pointing the VIVE hand-controller laser at a specific button, the user can press the trigger on the back of the controller to activate the function of that button. The non-interactive versions of our application consisted of no buttons, and the user did not receive a controller. Muscle representation is the only difference between the realistic and symbolic versions of our application. In the symbolic version emphasizes muscle contractions more easily, but the realistic version provides a realistic contraction.

3 User Studies

3.1 Participants

The user studies were conducted to give us a better understanding of how effective the different methods would be on musculoskeletal movement retention and anatomical identification. We used dynamic visualizations in our application to help engage spatial visualization. A dynamic visualization is a way to represent material that involves rotational movement and analysis for a more in-depth study. To learn the information represented in the teaching module, students must be able to mentally visualize the canine thoracic limb. We recruited 24 participants who had never studied a university level anatomy course before, and randomly assigned them 1 of 4 versions based on their Vz scores. Spatial Visualization, or Vz, is the ability to apprehend, encode, and manipulate mental representations. Before the experiment, participants' spatial visualization abilities were assessed using the Revised Purdue Spatial Visualization Test (). In addition, students' comprehension of anatomical information was assessed using a post-test involving anatomical views, joint locations, and muscle contractions.

3.2 Study Procedure

In this study, we collected data through quantitative and qualitative means along with recording the user experience to fully analyze the experiment. In the quantitative data, the main analyzations revolved around comparing the post-test scores. We also compared the users' Revised PSVT:R scores that determined if they had high or low Vz abilities. After that we compared the effectiveness of each of the applications by sorting the results respectfully. The qualitative data we received came from an analysis of the user's comprehension of anatomical information which was assessed using a post-test involving anatomical views, joint locations, and muscle contractions. We finished the study by asking questions to the participants about their experiences they had during the study.

Post-Study Interview Questions
1. Is this your first time using VR? If so, how did you like it? If not, how did it compare to the other times you have used VR?
2. How did you learn the anatomy information today? Was it different from your past experiences with anything biology or science related?
3. Do you remember the representation of muscles in VR? What do you remember about them?
4. Do you think that the representation of muscles was more beneficial or detrimental to your learning? Why do you think that?
5. How did you learn about movements of the skeleton in VR today? How did you like it? Do you have any suggestions?
6. How did you learn about different anatomical views in VR today? How did you like it? Do you have any suggestions?
7. Do you think walking around the model is more effective than having the model rotate? Why is that?
8. Would you be willing to learn some of the subjects that you currently are studying in a VR environment like this and what was your favorite part of this experience?

4 Results

4.1 Learning Experience

Overall, we saw varying results from each VR condition that are worth noting. The non-interactive scenes had better scores than the interactive scenes, and the realistic versions scored better than the symbolic versions for both levels of interactivity. We can observe that (see Table 1) symbolic interactive did alarmingly worse than all the other conditions. Even though the sample size was not large enough but the results are still credible. The realistic muscle conditions should be more efficient at helping with identification, and the interactivity ended up distracting the participants from learning.

Table 1. Post-study score graph

	Post-Study Anatomy Test Score Averages			
	VR Application Conditions			
Average Scores		Realistic Interactive	Realistic Non-Interactive	Symbolic Interactive	Symbolic Non-Interactive
	High Spatial Visualization	80	93.33	41.67	88.33

We also noticed in a few studies that the participants preferred walking around the model in virtual reality over rotating the model, but others preferred rotation. The interactivity of the application had some influences here. Non-interactive conditions required students to walk around the model in order to review anatomical views. The non-interactive system proved to be less distracting based on test scores, but also from the qualitative information gathered during the post-study interview. Users could focus more on learning the anatomy information because there was nothing else presented in the application to draw attention away from the user.

4.2 Study Conditions

The interactivity of the system defined the rest of the VR conditions, being either interactive or non-interactive. The interactive condition had 5 buttons that controlled the thoracic limb's walk cycle animation speed and rotation on the y (vertical) axis. The non-interactive version had no interactive elements. The participants were read slightly different scripts during the application to account for this change.

The average score for the non-interactive version is more than double the average from the interactive version. Looking at why the non-interactive versions did so much better in this section of the test, we see that several participants who mixed up their anatomical views from the first 4 questions of the test also did on this section for the same reason. In each section of our anatomy test, non-interactive learning had the best memory retention.

5 Discussion

The realistic non-interactive scene scored best while the realistic interactive version scored slightly lower because participants struggled to understand bicep/triceps contractions as effectively. The shocking, seemingly coincidental result is the symbolic interactive version with the lowest score. Aside from the outlier in the symbolic non-interactive scene, all the worst scores on the test happen to emerge from this VR condition. Analyzing each test individually, we see participants primarily chose opposite anatomical views, but determining muscle contraction also caused problems, and sometimes both were switched. Based on previous research and some of our hypotheses, the results show what is to be expected, but the way in which they have come to be is quite questionable. A larger scale study would be beneficial in determining more accurate numbers, and definitively proving the results we found from this study. Additionally, we noticed in a few sessions that the participants preferred walking around the model in VR rather than rotating the model, but others preferred rotation. The interactivity of the application had some influence here because non-interactive conditions required students to walk around the model to review anatomical views and see muscle contractions from different angles if they were inclined to.

5.1 Conclusion and Future Plan

This experiment utilizes virtual reality technology to assess varying teaching methods of canine anatomy using dynamic visualizations. Spatial visualization, muscle representations, and levels of interactivity were tested as independent variables in our user studies to determine which conditions would promote the most effective form of memory retention. We observed through 24 user studies that low spatial visualization users gained an advantage through dynamic visualization learning to almost perform as well as their high spatial visualization counterparts. Realistic muscles assisted participants with identifying anatomical views more efficiently, and therefore had a significantly better average compared to the symbolic representation. Despite the symbolic muscle representation's simplistic contractions, first time anatomy learners still performed better in the realistic version. The non-interactive system proved to be less distracting based on test scores, but also from the qualitative information gathered during the post-study interview. Users could focus more on learning the anatomy information because there was nothing else presented in the application to draw attention away from the user. Because of the small sample size, additional user studies should be done with this experiment for more accurate results, but the conclusion should be expected to show similar findings.

References

Albanese, M.: The gross anatomy laboratory: a prototype for simulation-based medical education. Med. Educ. **44**(1), 7–9 (2010)

Argelaguet, F., Hoyet, L., Trico, M., Lecuyer, A.: The role of interaction in virtual embodiment: effects of the virtual hand representation. In: 2016 IEEE Virtual Reality (VR), Greenville, SC, pp. 3–10 (2016)

Berney, S., Betrancourt, M., Molinari, G., Hoyek, N.: How spatial abilities and dynamic visualizations interplay when learning functional anatomy with 3D anatomical models. Anat. Sci. Educ. **8**(5), 452–462 (2015)

Nguyen, N., Mulla, A., Nelson, A.J., Wilson, T.D.: Visuospatial anatomy comprehension: the role of spatial visualization ability and problem-solving strategies. Nguyen Anatomical Sciences Education - Wiley Online Library (2013)

Seo, J., Storey, J., Chavez, J., Reyna, D., Suh, J., Pine, M.: ARnatomy: tangible AR app for learning gross anatomy. In: ACM SIGGRAPH. ACM, New York (2014). Article 25

Juanes, J., Ruisoto, P., Briz-Ponce, L.: Immersive visualization anatomical environment using virtual reality devices. In: Proceedings of the Fourth International Conference on Technological Ecosystems for Enhancing Multiculturality, pp. 473–477 (2016)

Lu, W., et al.: Virtual interactive human anatomy. In: Proceedings of the 2017 CHI Conference Extended Abstracts on Human Factors in Computing Systems, pp. 429–432 (2017)

Yoon, S.Y.: Psychometric Properties of the Revised Purdue Spatial Visualization Tests: Visualization of Rotations (The Revised PSVT-R). ProQuest LLC (2011)

Roussou, M., Oliver, M., Slater, M.: Virtual reality **10**, 227 (2006). https://doi.org/10.1007/s10055-0060035-5

Designing a History Tool for a 3D Virtual Environment System

Min Gyeong Kim[1], Joong-Jae Lee[2], and Jung-Min Park[1(✉)]

[1] Center for Intelligent and Interactive Robotics, Robotics and Media Institute,
Korea Institute of Science and Technology, Seoul 02792, Republic of Korea
mg.kim.918@gmail.com, pjm@kist.re.kr
[2] Center for Human-Centered Interaction for Coexistence,
Seoul 02792, Republic of Korea
arbitlee@gmail.com

Abstract. The aim of this paper is to design a history tool for a 3D virtual environment system using hand interaction. This system would require a new history tool because it creates a different user experience from existing 2D applications. We discuss two challenges for designing the history tool: user needs and interfaces. First, we explore the user needs for a history tool, assuming that the characters' intent to return to the past in time-travel films is analogous to the reasons for changing previous commands using a history tool in a 3D environment system. We analyze time-travel films and then define three design concepts of a history tool. Second, we ideate possible interfaces for a history tool considering hand-based object manipulation. We present the interface types using hands, other body parts, and an additional device. We also discuss the opportunities and constraints of each type. Combining these two discussions, we propose ten design ideas for a history tool in a 3D virtual environment system that provides hand-based interaction. The results of the pilot survey suggest that the history tool design concepts derived from time-travel films would be relevant to the history tool in 3D virtual environment systems.

Keywords: History tool · History interaction · 3D virtual environment system

1 Introduction

This paper aims to design a history tool for a 3D virtual environment system interacting hands. While impossible in the real world, history interaction—to access and change past actions—is feasible in the virtual world with a computer-aided history tool. The history tool has a positive influence on system usability [1], task performance [1], and learning [2].

In this paper, a 3D virtual environment system refers to a system with the following features. (See Fig. 1) First, it imitates the physics of the real world. Thus, various real-world tasks can be simulated in the system. Second, it provides a hand-based interface that replicates the movement and posture of the user's hands in those of the virtual

© Springer Nature Switzerland AG 2019
C. Stephanidis (Ed.): HCII 2019, CCIS 1033, pp. 398–405, 2019.
https://doi.org/10.1007/978-3-030-23528-4_54

hands in the system. Just as the user manipulates objects with his bare hands in the real world, the user can naturally hold, translate, and rotate virtual objects in the system [3].

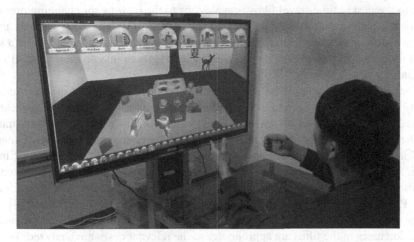

Fig. 1. A 3D virtual environment system with the hand-based user interface

This system would require a new history tool because it creates a different user experience from existing 2D applications, which are usually based on a mouse and a keyboard. Most of the current 3D applications, however, borrow the history tools of 2D applications, which are Undo, Redo, and History List [4, 5]. Moreover, there is a lack of research on history tools with 3D interfaces.

In this paper, (1) we discuss user needs of history interaction based on the analysis of time-travel films, (2) we discuss possible interfaces for a history tool with the consideration of the hand-based interaction of the system, (3) we propose design ideas for a history tool in the 3D environment system, and (4) we conduct a pilot study to validate the design ideas.

2 Design Idea Generation

Designing a history tool for a 3D environment system using interaction by hands requires a discussion on two challenges: user needs and interfaces.

2.1 User Needs of History Interaction

We study history interaction by analogy with the characters' time-travels in films and then define design concepts of the history tool.

Some papers on 3D environment systems mentioned experimental participants or researchers' opinion on the needs for an undo facility for error recovery [6–8], and performance retrace [9]. However, those papers did not discuss through what user experience journey a user would go when utilizing a history tool, or in what contexts a history tool would be useful.

Everyone has a desire to go back to the past and modify their previous actions to obtain better results. We assume the universality of this underlying need despite its varying expressions depending on the domain. On this assumption, characters' intent to return to the past in time-travel films is analogous to the reasons for changing previous commands using a history tool in the 3D environment system. This enables us to explore history interaction from films; time-travels to the past in films, which are a kind of history interaction cases, can inspire new history tools as imagination in sci-fi films has done for new technology [10].

First, four main factors of history interaction are identified based on the causality model [11]. (See Fig. 2) Second, it is stipulated which history interaction cases can be reflected in the history tool design. A relevant case is one in which a character moves into the past not into the future; the character changes the past instead of merely reviewing it; and the character can manipulate the main factors of the history inter-action. Third, the time-travel films are analyzed to identify the characters' intent to return to the past and their journeys based on the four main factors. The four films— Harry Potter and the Prisoner of Azkaban [12], Deja Vu [13], About Time [14], and Doctor Strange [15]—are studied, for they include relevant cases. Not all history interaction cases in the films are appropriate, so the relevant cases are analyzed. Fourth, the primary purposes for history tools in the 3D environment system are extracted from the film characters' intentions in returning to the past. Among several possible pur-poses, three that are expected to have a positive impact on user experience are selected. Finally, design concepts develop according to the three primary purposes of history tools, concretizing each of their user journeys. Table 1 lists the identified details for each of the main factors of the film characters' journeys. The combination of these produces sixty possible history interactions. Suitable options for each concept develop as the user journey.

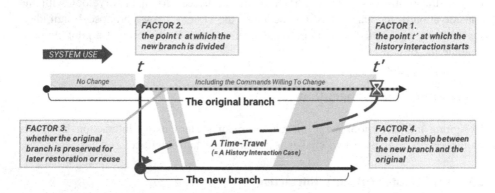

Fig. 2. The four main factors of history interaction

The three design concepts developed in this process are as follows. Concept I is the solving of the current problem by modifying the specific past commands (the cause of the problem); Concept II is the creation of a completely different version from the

Table 1. The details for each of the main factors of the film characters' journeys

The four main factors	The details of the journeys
(1) The point t' at which the history interaction starts	(1–1) The point when the user wants to go to the past
	(1–2) The point when certain conditions are met (Automatically triggered)
(2) The point t at which the new branch is divided	(2–1) Decide the point t through result of the past actions from the current point of view
	(2–2) Decide the point t by moving forward or backward one by one unit
	(2–3) Decide the point t in advance, when the original action performed
	(2–4) Decide the point t through exact coordinate values
	(2–5) Decide the point t by moving continuously forward or backward one by one command
(3) Whether the original branch is preserved for later restoration or reuse	(3–1) Delete the original branch immediately so that the user is not able to retrieve it
	(3–2) Preserve the original branch so that the user can re-access it
(4) The relationship between the new branch and the original	(4–1) Not relevant at all (although the user can memorize it)
	(4–2) Copying all the complete elements of the whole/part of the original branch

previous one; and Concept III is the repetition of a specific frequently failed process to achieve the goal.

2.2 Interfaces for the History Tool

We ideate interfaces for a history tool considering their opportunities and constraints attributed to the hand-based interaction of the system. Determining the most appropriate solution requires a discussion of the following issues.

The interface of a history tool should support communications to manipulate the main factors of history interaction. The concrete user journeys of the design concepts suggest that the history tools entail three types of input commands. One is choosing either 0 or 1, which is to trigger the desired function or to turn on/off the history interaction mode. Another type is to linearly move forward or backward when a user decides the point where the new branch is divided; it can be discrete or continuous. The other is to choose one among several alternatives.

Moreover, the interface of a history tool should be applicable in the context of performing other interactions in the system, for a user will use history tools for the sake of accomplishing a specific task. In this paper, the 3D environment system provides hand-based object manipulation; the interface of a history tool should be compatible with it.

The history tool can utilize the hand-based interface, too. The uni-modality of the hand motion does not demand a critical changeover between object manipulation and use of the history tool. However, errors in which the system misrecognizes the intention of the user's hand motion and trigger a wrong function can occur. One of the available hand-based interfaces for the history tool is a virtual controller inside the 3D environment. The user can use the history tool by manipulating the virtual controller in a similar way as he manipulates virtual objects with his hands. The virtual controller's mimicry of a real-world physical controller, such as a button and a dial, or time-metaphoric objects, such as an hourglass and a clock, would lead to its intuitiveness [16]. Another possible interface is hand gestures, where each hand posture or movement is assigned to a certain function. The system can make use of countless hand gestures, but postures or movement that are closely similar to those of object manipulation would cause trouble in implementing the desired commands.

The history tool can utilize the hands-free interfaces using other body parts, such as eyes, voice, head pose, etc. This type of interface would be less likely to cause misrecognition errors between object manipulation and use of the history tools due to their different modalities. However, this type entails a big shift to switch between object manipulation and use of the history tool, leading to limited user engagement [17, 18].

Despite the non-instrument technique of object manipulation of the system, the history tool can utilize additional input devices, like a foot pedal or a wearable wristband. The user would usually focus on the 3D environment when manipulating virtual objects. If the user must move his attention toward the additional device to use the history tool, it will bring about a significant switch between object manipulation and use of the history tool, and user engagement will be hindered [17, 18].

2.3   Design Ideas for the History Tool

Based on these two discussions, we generate ten design ideas for the history tool for a 3D environment system that provides hand-based interaction with virtual objects. (See Table 2) Through combining the interface option with the function and the user journey of the design concepts, a user experience scenario for each of the design ideas develops. We represent each of the user experience scenarios in a storyboard consisting of five to eight images. (See Fig. 3 for an example).

Table 2. The design ideas for the history tool for a 3D environment system with hand-based object manipulation

The Design Concepts	The Design Ideas		
	No.	Idea title	Interface
Design Concept I: solving the current problem by modifying a specific command in the past	1.	It's All in There	A virtual dial controller in the 3D environment
	2.	Can You Hear Me?	A voice-based user interface
	3.	Wrist to Wrist	A wearable wristband input device

(*continued*)

Table 2. (*continued*)

The Design Concepts	No.	Idea title	Interface
The Design Ideas			
Design Concept II: creating a different work from the previous one	4.	User of Virtual World: The Sand of Time	A virtual sandglass controller in the 3D environment and pre-defined hand gestures
	5.	Rubbing the Table	Pre-defined patterns drawn by dragging fingers on the table/desk
	6.	When Putting Your Hand on the Corner	Pre-defined hand gestures based on the Window-Icon-Menu-Pointer interface
Design Concept III: repeating a frequently failed process	7.	Left Foot and Right Foot	A foot pedal input device
	8.	Rhythm Is Essential to Claps	Pre-defined hand gestures
	9.	The Menu Bar Is Hiding on Top	Pre-defined hand gestures based on the Window-Icon-Menu-Pointer interface
	10.	Watch Controller	A wristwatch input device

IDEA #05) Rubbing the table

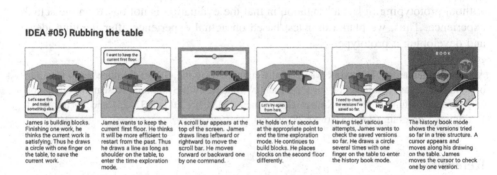

James is building blocks. Finishing one work, he thinks the current work is satisfying. Thus he draws a circle with one finger on the table, to save the current work.

James wants to keep the current first floor. He thinks it will be more efficient to restart from the past. Thus he draws a line as long as shoulder on the table, to enter the time exploration mode.

A scroll bar appears at the top of the screen. James draws lines leftward or rightward to move the scroll bar. He moves forward or backward one by one command.

He holds on for seconds at the appropriate point to end the time exploration mode. He continues to build blocks. He places blocks on the second floor differently.

Having tried various attempts, James wants to check the saved versions so far. He draws a circle several times with one finger on the table to enter the history book mode.

The history book mode shows the versions tried so far in a tree structure. A cursor appears and moves along his drawing on the table. James moves the cursor to check one by one version.

Fig. 3. An example of the storyboards: design idea No. 5 "Rubbing the Table"

3 Pilot User Survey

A pilot study was conducted to evaluate the design ideas for the history tool. A user survey based on the Speed Dating technique [19] utilizes the storyboards to describe the design ideas. This method, which is a quick and dirty evaluation without prototyping, enabled a reduction in time and cost. Reviewing the design idea descriptions, each participant answered a questionnaire regarding his or her overall impression and preference. We recruited a total of 6 participants (age 26–53; three of them were female) who have tried 3D virtual environment applications.

The result of the pilot user survey suggests that users of the 3D environment system would identify with the needs of the three design concepts defined by the analysis of time-travel films. None of the participants had negative opinions about all the design concepts, and some of the participants commented on the needs of the history tool.

- The P2's comment Concept I: "[The relevant problems] most often occur. Because it does not erase the rest of the history parts when modifying a part, I think that this concept is most necessary."
- The P5's comment about Concept II: "It seems to be useful when a user tries various attempts or collaboration."
- The P4's comment about Concept III: "I do like the ability to repeat actions until I am successful."

4 Conclusion and Future Work

In this paper, we studied the history tool design of a 3D virtual environment system that interacts through hands. The design challenges, user needs and interfaces, were discussed, and the ten design ideas for the history tool developed within the three design concepts. The result of the pilot user survey suggests that the design concepts would be relevant in the 3D environment systems.

We conducted a pilot user survey using storyboards to evaluate the design ideas of the history tool. Even though this enabled us to conduct a quick and dirty evaluation without prototyping, it has a limitation in that the evaluation is not based on the actual experience. Thus, we plan a user test based on actual experience after iterating ideas and developing a prototype.

Acknowledgements. This work was partially supported by the Global Frontier R&D Program on "Human-centered Interaction for Coexistence" funded by the National Research Foundation of Korea grant funded by the Korean Government (MSIP) (2011-0031425) and by the KIST Institutional Program (Project No. 2E28250).

References

1. Sayers, H.M.: Desktop virtual environments: a study of navigation and age. Interact. Comput. **16**(5), 939–956 (2004)
2. Mostafa, A.E., Ryu, W.H.A., Takashima, K., Chan, S., Sousa M.C., Sharlin, E.: ReflectiveSpineVR: an immersive spine surgery simulation with interaction history capabilities. In: Proceedings of the 5th Symposium on Spatial User Interaction, pp. 20–29. ACM, New York (2017)
3. Kim, J.S, Park, J.M.: Direct and realistic handover of a virtual object. In: 2016 IEEE/RSJ International Conference on Intelligent Robots and Systems (IROS), pp. 994–999. IEEE, New York (2016)
4. SketchUp. https://www.sketchup.com/. Accessed 19 Feb 2019
5. Blender. https://www.blender.org/. Accessed 19 Feb 2019

6. Dudley, J.J., Schuff, H., Kristensson, P.O.: Bare-handed 3D drawing in augmented reality. In: Proceedings of the 2018 Designing Interactive Systems Conference, pp. 241–252. ACM, New York (2018)
7. Jensen, S.Q., Fender, A., Müller, J.: Inpher: inferring physical properties of virtual objects from mid-air interaction. In: Proceedings of the 2018 CHI Conference on Human Factors in Computing Systems, paper no. 530. ACM, New York (2018)
8. Khamis, M., Oechsner, C., Alt, F., Bulling, A.: VRpursuits: interaction in virtual reality using smooth pursuit eye movements. In: Proceedings of the 2018 International Conference on Advanced Visual Interfaces, article no. 18. ACM, New York (2018)
9. McNeill, M.D.J., Sayers, H.M., Wilson, S., Mc Kevitt, P.: A spoken dialogue system for navigation in non-immersive virtual environments. Comput. Graph. Forum **21**(4), 713–722 (2002)
10. Magazine Staff, Shedroff, N., Noess, C.: Make it so: five lessons in interaction design from star trek. https://uxmag.com/articles/make-it-so-five-lessons-in-interaction-design-from-star-trek. Accessed 20 Feb 2019
11. Nancel, M., Cockburn, A.: Causality: a conceptual model of interaction history. In: Proceedings of the SIGCHI Conference on Human Factors in Computing Systems, pp. 1777–1786. ACM, New York (2014)
12. Cuarón, A.: Harry Potter and the Prisoner of Azkaban. Warner Bros. Pictures, Heyday Films, 1492 Pictures, United Kingdom, United States (2004)
13. Scott, T.: Deja Vu. Touchstone Pictures, Jerry Bruckheimer Films, Scott Free Productions, United States, United Kingdom (2004)
14. Curtis, R.: About Time. Translux, Working Title Films, United Kingdom (2013)
15. Derrickson, S.: Doctor Strange. Marvel Studios, Walt Disney Pictures, United States (2016)
16. Interaction Design Foundation: Skeuomorphism. https://www.interaction-design.org/literature/topics/skeuomorphism. Accessed 19 Feb 2019
17. Hand, C.: A survey of 3D interaction techniques. Comput. Graph. Forum **16**(5), 269–281 (1997)
18. Jankowski, J., Hachet, M.: Advances in interaction with 3D environments. Comput. Graph. Forum **34**(1), 152–190 (2015)
19. Davidoff, S., Lee, M.K., Dey, Anind K., Zimmerman, J.: Rapidly exploring application design through speed dating. In: Krumm, J., Abowd, Gregory D., Seneviratne, A., Strang, T. (eds.) UbiComp 2007. LNCS, vol. 4717, pp. 429–446. Springer, Heidelberg (2007). https://doi.org/10.1007/978-3-540-74853-3_25

Evaluation of the Impact of Mobile VR Interaction Methods on Performance, Preference, and Enjoyment

Summer Lindsey[✉], Meredith Carroll, and Deborah Carstens

Florida Institute of Technology, Melbourne, FL 32901, USA
slindsey2013@my.fit.edu

Abstract. Virtual Reality (VR) has expanded from the training and high-end entertainment world into the homes of everyday users through mobile head mounted displays (HMDs). Currently, several different interaction methods for mobile VR HMDs exist, including remotes, external controllers, motion controllers, touch, and free form hand tracking. The goal of this study was to evaluate the impact that these interaction methods have on specifically mobile VR HMD user experience, including performance, user preference, and enjoyment. It was hypothesized that interaction methods would vary significantly in enjoyment, preference, and performance as many factors such as ease of use and familiarity can influence these factors. To evaluate the interaction methods, participants performed trials of a matching task utilizing menus in a VR environment in which the participants selected the features of an object (e.g., shape, color, pattern) from a menu to the right of the object. The Leap Motion had usability issues that impacted it's performance and enjoyment scores resulting in it being the poorest performer of the group. Overall the gamepad was most preferred and performed the best due to its ease of use and familiarity, but the touchpad and leap motion offered immersive aspects. These results highlight the importance of ease of use in interaction methods and the impact it has on overall user experience. This paper will discuss these results and implications for design of interaction methods and associated VR HMD controllers.

Keywords: Virtual Reality · Interaction methods · User experience

1 Introduction

Virtual Reality (VR) is quickly becoming a leading tech industry. Between the years of 2018 and 2021, VR is expected to grow from a 4.5 billion-dollar industry to a 19 billion-dollar industry (Superdata 2018). Furthermore, over 50 million VR headsets are projected to be sold by 2020 (Scottsdale 2016). VEs utilize state-of-the-art technology to provide environments that are usually costly to implement or impossible to enact in real life. In the past, VR for entertainment purposes was few and far between due to the high cost of VR setups (Bowman and McMahan 2007). However, with the development of recent low-cost technology, VR is now accessible to the everyday user by mounting a smartphone into a headset. This can be accomplished with a simple piece of cardboard or by using prebuilt head mounted devices (HMD) with added functionality

C. Stephanidis (Ed.): HCII 2019, CCIS 1033, pp. 406–413, 2019.
https://doi.org/10.1007/978-3-030-23528-4_55

and comfort for as low as $100. However, "The VR equivalent of the mouse-has yet to be developed" (Perry 2015, p. 57) even though the technology and processing power is updating and releasing at an alarming rate. This study aims to evaluate existing VR controllers to develop recommendations for mobile based VR headsets moving forward. The goal of the recommendations is to aid in developing a universal user-friendly controller for VR purposes.

Due to the growth of the VR market, interface development is highly important to differentiate from competitors. A high level of user satisfaction can be attributed to the experience with the user interface (Sanchez 2011). For virtual environments (VE) in particular, a high level of presence, or feeling of being within the environment, is a large contributor to the VR user experience (Shafer, Carbonara, and Popova 2011). Research shows that controllers that naturally map or match the real-world task, in terms of motions or gestures, are shown to increase feelings of presence (Held and Durlach 1992). Non-intuitive interfaces that may require additional cognitive resources can reduce enjoyment or in some cases, cause anxiety (Johnson and Wiles 2010). In fact, even if a naturally mapped control performs worse, users will still prefer it over a non-naturally mapped controller (McEwan, Johnson, Wyeth, and Blackler 2012). These studies show the importance of developing a naturally mapped controller and their effects on presence and enjoyment.

Past research examining VR controllers has evaluated prototype, or high end input methods. Bowman and Wingrave (2001) discovered that users had a desire for their hands themselves to be input devices; however, arm strain is a concern when using handheld objects as controllers or when a prolonged period or reach is needed. Contrary to user's desire for gestural based inputs and the rapid growth of consumer VR, little research has been done on consumer grade input methods for VR. The Leap Motion serves as a hand tracking device that allows users to utilize their hands as the controller itself. Studies of the first-generation release model have found that the Leap Motion had more errors than a traditional mouse for computer interaction and that users were much more accustomed to using a mouse for a computer and preferred this method input (Bachmann, Weichert, and Rinkenauer 2015). Other studies have explored using head position as an interaction method and found it more immersive and quicker (Tregillus, Zayer, and Folmer 2017). This study assessed the performance, preference, and enjoyment for existing controllers available to the consumer at an affordable cost. The VR market is shifting to a more low-cost consumer centered market. Although previous research has focused on expensive top-of-the-line technology, or validated a prototype that has not been released to market, this study utilized existing low budget interaction technology with the target consumer and evaluated the controllers from a usability perspective.

2   Methods

Participants were recruited via an email distribution at a south eastern university contacting existing students and faculty who have subscribed. The total number of participants consisted of 17 males and 6 females. Ten participants had experienced at least one head mounted VR headset prior to this study. The VR setup utilized a

Samsung Galaxy S7 was used for the display along with a 2017 model Samsung Gear VR. To evaluate these hypotheses, an experiment was conducted in which three different mobile VR HMD interaction methods were evaluated, including: (1) unfamiliar and incomplete interaction (i.e., not directly mapped with the real world task) which was operationalized using head position and a touchpad on the side of the HMD, (2) familiar but incomplete interaction (i.e., one users have prior experience with but not directly mapped with the real world task) operationalized using a gamepad, and (3) kinesic naturally mapped interaction (i.e., one that uses the body and naturally maps to the real world) operationalized using the Leap Motion - a motion tracking device that renders the users hands in the virtual world real time. The gamepad consisted of using joysticks and the A button to make selections. The touchpad consisted of fixing one's gaze on a button and tapping the touchpad on the side of the HMD. The Leap Motion rendered the user'shands in VR and allowed participants to reach out in front of them and "touch" a button.

Performance measures included number of errors and time to complete trial. The beginning of each trial was auto-recorded by the game software's output log with a timestamp. Each input (correct or incorrect) was recorded in the software output log with a timestamp. Using the output log, average trial times and the number of incorrect inputs were calculated. Preference was measured by asking participants to rank the controllers from favorite to least favorite and filling out a table of their most and least favorite aspects of each controller. To measure enjoyment a question from Kendzierski and DeCarlo's (1991) physical activity enjoyment scale. Participants rated how they felt about the activity in the moment on a scale of 1 to 10 from "I enjoy it" to "I hate it." In addition, presence scores were collected, and the results of each controller presence ratings are reported in Lindsey, Carstens, and Carroll (2017).

2.1 Experimental Design and Matching Task

This study aimed to evaluate different controllers for a mobile based VR application from a usability perspective. In alignment with previous controller interaction studies for VEs (Bowman and Wingrave 2001; Gebhardt, Pick, Leithold, Hentschel, and Kuhlen 2013), this study utilized a matching task to evaluate the three different controllers. The experimental method used to compare the controllers effectively was a one-way repeated measures within-subjects design. This allowed every participant to have exposure to each controller, as well as allow the evaluation of multiple outcome variables for each controller condition. The independent variable is the controller type. Controller order was counterbalanced across participants to account for order effects by using a Latin square rotation method.

The participants wore the Samsung Gear VR headset and viewed a virtual mockup of a room with gray walls and a gray floor. A shape rendered on the left field of view. The shape spawned with a combination of possibilities. The possible shape options were: cube, sphere, or cylinder. The possible color options were: red, blue, or green. The possible texture options were: stripes, dots, or checkered (See Fig. 1).

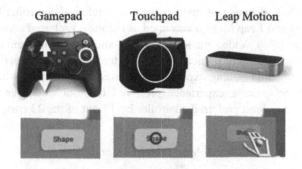

Fig. 1. Matching task and selection methods

On the right field of view, a menu fixed in the 3D space was displayed. The participants used the menu to match the properties of the shape shown on the screen. If the participant attempted to select an incorrect button, including selecting the color submenu before the shape submenu, the button appeared red during press-down and did nothing. A correct button pressed resulted in the next menu popping up. Once all three parameters were selected, a continue button appeared. Once the continue button was pressed, it was recorded as one trial. The participants had 10 matching trials for each controller. The enjoyment question was administered after each controller. Once all three conditions were completed, the preference rating was administered where participants ranked the controllers from most favorite to least favorite. Participants also filled out a table identifying what they liked most and least for each controller. A repeated measures MANOVA was run to analyze the performance and enjoyment metrics.

3 Results

Before data analysis began, 9 outliers were removed as these were due to the virtual environment recording one button press multiple times rapidly in succession. In addition, learning curves were analyzed to identify where performance seemed to plateau as the goal was to look at interaction effects on performance void of any learning and familiarity effects. Learning curves of time appeared to plateau between trials 5 and 6 and learning curves of errors appeared to plateau to some degree between trials 6 and 7, thus trials 7 through 10 were used for calculations of both time and errors. A repeated measures MANOVA showed a significant multivariate effect ($p < .001$) with significant univariate effects for time ($p < .001$) and enjoyment ($p = .001$). Errors approached significance with p = .061. Post hoc analyses are discussed below along with participant preference ratings and comments.

3.1 Preference

For preference, participants ranked the controllers in order from their most preferred to least preferred. Gamepad was rated as the most preferred controller by 13 out of 23 participants (56%). Touchpad was rated as the most preferred controller by 8 out of 23 participants (35%) and Leap Motion was rated as the most preferred controller by 2 out of 23 participants (9%). Video game experience showed an influence on preferred controller. Fifty five percent of participants with extensive gaming experience and 70% of participants with some gaming experience preferred the gamepad, whereas 100% of participants with no gaming experience preferred the touchpad (See Fig. 2). Leap Motion was ranked as least preferred controller by 17 out of the 23 participants (74%).

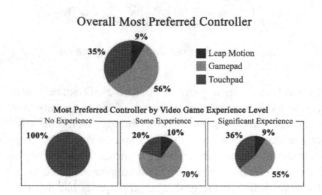

Fig. 2. Overall preference and preference based on gaming experience

3.2   Performance and Enjoyment

The Leap Motion was found to have significantly longer trial times compared to gamepad ($p < .001$) and touchpad ($p < .001$) taking on average 6 s longer per trial. Errors were not significant, however it was seen that the leap motion experienced more errors than the gamepad and touchpad. Leap Motion was found to have significantly lower enjoyment ratings compared to gamepad ($p = .006$) and touchpad ($p = .001$). Gamepad and touchpad were not significantly different (See Table 1).

Table 1. Averages per Controller. Errors and trial times are per trial for trials 7 to 10. Trial time is in seconds.

Measure	Leap Motion	Gamepad	Touchpad
Average # of errors	.21	.09	.05
Average trial time	15	8.81	9.39
Average enjoyment score	6.83	7.96	8.09

4   Discussion

The gamepad was the most preferred controller with 12 participants noting it as easy and 5 noting it as familiar. However, 6 participants mentioned that it offered no immersion and 4 mentioned was too easy and made the task boring. For the touchpad,

13 participants noted it as easy and 2 as immersive. Negative comments included ergonomic issues as 6 participants noted issues finding the touchpad on the headset, 4 disliked moving their head, and 4 did not enjoying holding up their hand for the duration of the trials. For the Leap Motion, 7 participants noted it as immersive and 4 as fun. However, the Leap Motion was the least preferred controller as many users experienced several issues during its use with 8 participants noting accuracy issues, 7 finding it difficult, and 3 finding it tiring to hold up their hands. One main issue occurred as a result of rapid head movement during task performance. Rapid head movement resulted in users experiencing visual "drift" and a need to rotate their chair during the experiment in order to keep the shape and menu in center view. Some users also experienced issues reaching the menu buttons due to the menu distance being too great for the real-life length of their arms. Most users attempted to lean forward instead of reaching forward to select a button. As the Samsung Gear VR only has rotational tracking and does not have positional tracking, leaning forward does not bring the user closer to the menu and resulted in user frustration. Many users needed a full arm extension in order to reach the buttons. With the arm at full extension, it became difficult for the Leap Motion to determine the positioning of the finger and would often curve the virtual fingers. As a result, this makes it difficult to press the button as the fingertips are the trigger for a button press to occur. Users noted "As events passed, the room appeared to reset in orientation, requiring me to rotate my chair in order to keep a persistent field of view that I desired. Hand recognition was not 100% what I intended to do (bending fingers)." However, those that did not experience drift or reach issues noted the Leap Motion as a positive experience: "The Leap Motion was really impressive & the hands in VR were really accurate," "Felt almost real. Being more involved." Some users found that using one finger, using a jabbing motion, or flicking their fingers worked best for them. These issues made the Leap Motion difficult for most users and resulted in the other controllers being rated higher as participants' most preferred controller. As Wickens, Lee, Liu and Becker (2004) states, users will often try out or require references to tutorials when first performing a task until errors decrease. Users then can focus on then experience a reduction in errors and then can perform the task more efficiently and can reduce task time. From there, the cognitive and attention demands of the task decrease and users can experience a more automatic state. Participants may have still been within this learning development phase for the Leap Motion and thus did not produce comparable performance to the other two controllers. Nevertheless, these decrements in performance may have contributed the participant's preference and enjoyment results.

4.1 Recommendations and Future Research

Based on the results of this study, the Leap Motion is not at a performance level which is ready for VR headsets. However, considering that the menu in the VE was a large distance away, these performance issues may be mediated by altering the depth and size of the menu in VEs. The Leap Motion "Blocks" demo featured a menu style that was presented along the fingertips. This would allow users minimal reach distance and less arm fatigue as users could hold their hands lower and simply look down. This menu style was not available to developers from Leap Motion at the time of this study while reach based menus had just been released as a Unity asset. However, past research with the TULIP menu styles show that this can be non-intuitive for first time users (Bowman and Wingrave 2001) and this should be evaluated again as the coming generations may be more tech savvy than when the study was conducted. Users who have gaming experience show a pre-disposition towards a gamepad controller. If a universal controller is developed for VR, support for gamepad controllers should continue. The touchpad resulted in high presence scores and low performance issues. Nevertheless, users noted that holding a hand by the side of the head was tiring and tapping the side of the headset made them more aware of the headset itself. A hands free timed-gaze selection should be considered as many users enjoyed the gaze cursor. Considering that the two participants without gaming experience preferred the touchpad, future studies should evaluate these measures and controllers with a non-gaming demographic as they may produce different results. This study consisted of mainly gamers as 21 of 23 of participants had at least some gaming experience and may not be generalizable to all consumer VR users. Additionally, the Leap Motion performed poorly with the menu presented in this study. Different menu types, shapes, and depths should be evaluated to create design guidelines for virtual hand-based menus. The Leap Motion did not flourish in this use case yet, it may in other novel environments. VR controllers should continue to be compared and analyzed in training, video game, and task based environments to determine the optimal controller for each use case. The pros and cons of each controller were presented in addition to recommendations to improve them. This study was not a comprehensive analysis of all types of VR controllers on the market today. Regardless, it sets the framework for user experience research to continue as a means to improve the quality of the VR experience for consumers of VR headsets for entertainment purposes.

References

Superdata: State of the XR Market. SuperData Research Holdings Inc. (2018)

Scottsdale, A.: ABI research anticipates more than 50 million mobile VR devices to ship by 2020 as virtual reality takes step forward at the 2016 GSMA mobile world congress. ABI Research (2016)

Bowman, D., McMahan, R.: Virtual reality: how much immersion is enough? Computer **40**(7), 36–43 (2007)

Sanchez, J.: Playability: analyzing user experience in video games. Behav. Inf. Technol. **31**, 1033–1054 (2011)

Held, R., Durlach, N.: Telepresence. Presence: Teleoperators Virtual Environ. **1**(1), 109–112 (1992)

Johnson, D., Wiles, J.: Effective affective user interface design in games. Ergonomics **46**(13–14), 1332–1345 (2010). https://doi.org/10.1080/00140130310001610865

McEwan, M., Johnson, D., Wyeth, P., Blackler, A.: Videogame control device impact on the play experience. In: IE 2012 Proceedings of the 8th Australian Conference on Interactive Entertainment: Playing the System (2012). https://doi.org/10.1145/2336727.2336745

Lindsey, S., Carstens, D., Carroll, M.: Presence level of low cost controllers for mobile based virtual reality headsets. J. Manag. Eng. Integr. **10**(1), 59–63 (2017)

Bowman, D., Wingrave, C.: Design and evaluation of menu systems for immersive virtual environments. In: Proceedings of the Virtual Reality 2001 Conference, pp. 149–156 (2001)

Bachmann, D., Weichert, F., Rinkenauer, G.: Evaluation of the leap motion controller as a new contact-free pointing device. Sensors **15**, 214–233 (2015). https://doi.org/10.3390/s150100214

Tregillus, S., Zayer, M., Folmer, E.: Handsfree omnidirectional VR navigation using head tilt. In: Proceedings of the 2017 CHI Conference on Human Factors in Computing Systems, pp. 4063–4068 (2017)

Gerbhardt, S., Pick, S., Leithold, F., Hentschel, B., Kuhlen, T.: Extended pie menus for immersive virtual environments. IEEE Trans. Vis. Comput. Graph. **19**(4), 644–651 (2013)

Perry, T.: Virtual reality goes social. IEEE Spectr. **53**(1), 56–57 (2015). https://doi.org/10.1109/MSPEC.2016.7367470

Shafer, D., Carbonara, C., Popova, L.: Spatial presence and perceived reality as predictors of motion-based video game enjoyment. Presence **20**(6), 591–619 (2011)

Wickens, C., Lee, J., Liu, Y., Becker, S.: An Introduction to Human Factors Engineering. Pearson Education Inc., Upper Saddle River (2004)

Kendzierski, D., DeCarlo, K.: Physical activity enjoyment scale: two validation studies. J. Sport Exerc. Psychol. **13**, 50–64 (1991)

The Potential of Spatial Computing to Augment Memory: Investigating Recall in Virtual Memory Palaces

Tara O'Grady[⊠] and Caglar Yildirim

State University of New York at Oswego, Oswego, NY 13126, USA
{togrady, caglar.yildirim}@oswego.edu

Abstract. The Method of Loci (MoL) is an ancient mnemonic technique rooted in the encoding of spatial context into episodic memory through the use of memory palaces. The increasing availability of consumer-grade virtual reality (VR) headsets has ushered in a new era of research into whether VR technology could be used to support and enhance the construction and navigation of memory palaces, and hence, augment human memory. The current study investigated recall in a traditional mental memory palace, compared to a virtual memory palace with prepopulated objects navigated on a VR headset. Participants were randomly assigned into one of two conditions: building a memory palace using a traditional, imaginative technique or being introduced to a pre-existing and pre-populated virtual memory palace. In each condition, participants were asked to memorize lists of various objects. Results revealed that the use of MoL to memorize the lists improved recall of objects compared to baseline performance, which involved unstructured recall with no mnemonic technique. That said, recall performances were comparable in the VR-based MoL and traditional MoL conditions, indicating that virtual memory palaces are as effective as traditional, imaginative technique, but not more effective. Of note, participants in the VR-based MoL condition reported greater confidence in the effectiveness of the MoL technique, when compared to the traditional MoL condition. For naive users, this increased level of confidence in utilizing the MoL could be a factor when introducing the technique. A virtual memory palace could serve as a structured memory augmentation environment using the MoL, affording a greater ability and motivation to apply the technique mentally in the future. The study highlights the potential of VR-based spatial computing to augment human memory.

Keywords: Method of Loci · Memory palace · Episodic memory · Spatial computing · Virtual Reality

1 Introduction

1.1 Virtual Reality

Virtual Reality (VR) allows users to view and interact within a simulated environment, generally through physical movements and head-based image rendering from a first-person perspective. As VR has become more accessible, research into its applications

© Springer Nature Switzerland AG 2019
C. Stephanidis (Ed.): HCII 2019, CCIS 1033, pp. 414–422, 2019.
https://doi.org/10.1007/978-3-030-23528-4_56

has become more prolific. Frequently utilized in training applications, virtual environments (VEs) can mirror that of reality, however, for other implementations, the environments must be carried out creatively with consideration of supporting specific cognitive processes.

One of the distinct features of a VE is its use of 3-dimensional space. When experiencing a virtual environment, a user can explore large spaces relative to themselves using a head-mounted display (HMD). Research into how VEs may facilitate learning has revealed that spatial organization within an environment supports spatial indexing [1]. Taking advantage of 3D environments to create spatial mappings in a VE can allow users to utilize spatial strategies, such as the Method of Loci, to learn and recall information.

1.2   Method of Loci

Originating in ancient Greece, the Method of Loci (MOL), also known as the memory palace technique, is a spatial mnemonic born out of tragedy. Around 500 BC, the Greek poet Simonides was attending the banquet of Scopas. He left for a short amount of time, during which the banquet hall collapsed, killing everyone inside. The collapse had so dismembered the bodies that families were unable to identify their loved ones. Simonides was able to recall where each attendee had been seated during the banquet and was, therefore, able to identify each body successfully, founding the object and place memory system known as the Ars Memoria, or the Method of Loci [2].

The MOL was understood in the Classical Period to be a type of artificial memory, as it extended natural memory ability by employing mnemonic techniques. A memory palace was defined by having two features, place - locus, and things - images. The locus anchors a memory into a specific structure or location, while the images serve as representations of memory [2].

The techniques success relies on spatial associative memory to assist recall [3]. To use the MOL, a person creates a visual mental symbol associated with the concept they want to remember. The symbol is then mentally placed in a familiar scene or location. To recall the concept, a person imagines navigating this scene to 'view' the placed items [4].

While this initially may seem to complicate recall, it is actually intuitive. Spatial context is a crucial feature of episodic memory; all events that occur within an individual's lifetime occur at some location. It has been demonstrated that events that occur with spatial context are recalled more vividly and can be described in a higher level of detail [5]. Neurological research has shown that both spatial navigation and recall both activate the same region of the brain, the hippocampus. Studies on individuals who employ the MOL at a high level, such as those who participate in memory competitions, have demonstrated activity in brain regions associated with spatial awareness, such as the medial parietal cortex, the retrosplenial cortex, and the right posterior hippocampus [4].

2 Related Works

Early studies in VR demonstrated that recalling information with spatial context acti-vated the same neural regions of the brain as episodic memory, including the hip-pocampus [6]. Researchers in the fields of computer science and psychology theorized that the MOL, memory encoded with spatial context, could be enhanced through hypermedia [7].

One of the challenges of implementing the MOL effectively in a virtual space is that the method is specific to the individual using it. Traditionally, someone employing the mnemonic technique is advised to use a familiar environment from reality when cre-ating a mental map. The objects are encouraged to be strange, eccentric, and even obscene to increased memorability [8]. Additionally, the training phase of using the MOL technique is mentally tiring, ranging from hours to days [9].

Fassbender and Heiden [10] created a virtual memory environment to investigate whether this would reduce the cognitive demand of an individual tasked with creating a mental environment. Participants were able to self-select objects, which were animated and with sound, and place them within the environment. Using this structure, they found that the virtual MOL improved long term memory.

Legge et al. [9] further investigated whether a briefly presented virtual environment could be used as a basis for the MOL. The study compared word list recall of par-ticipants in three different conditions; use of a mental environment for MOL, use of a virtual environment as a basis for MOL on a 2-dimensional desktop, and a control group that was given no MOL instruction. Those in the virtual MOL condition were given a brief period to explore the 2D environment and were then asked to place the word list items mentally within the virtual space. Results indicated that participants using the MOL technique recalled words significantly better than the control group; however, there was no significant difference between the two MOL conditions. It was extrapolated that the spatial context of the environment does not play a significant factor regarding the recall of objects placed in it.

More recently, Krokos and Varshney [11] investigated whether virtual memory palaces employed with high levels of immersion using a HMD result in better recall when compared to 2D desktop environments. Participants in this study were exposed to celebrity faces so that they would be familiar with the objects prepopulated in the virtual environment. After a training period with either a 2D desktop VE or a 3D VE using a HMD, they were shown an environment with the faces distributed around them. Following this, participants were asked to recall the locations of each of the faces. Results showed there was increased recall with fewer errors in the HMD condition compared to the desktop condition.

3 Current Research

Research on the MOL is challenging as it relies heavily on individualistic processes [9]; traveling through the environment is an autobiographic journey specific to the user's perceptions. It is traditionally a full mental exercise, subject to much ambiguity. A person is tasked with creating a mental environment and then populating it with objects. Joshua Foer, a "memory champion," advises to use familiar environments, and recommends using strange, obscene, and eccentric objects as they are more memorable [8]. Aside from generating these mental spaces using traditional methods, extensive training is required which can be mentally tiring.

Several studies have focused on the comparison of the traditional MOL technique using mental environments to 2D, and 3D virtual environments as a basis for MOL, without the use of prepopulated objects or with objects participants were familiarized with during a training period. The purpose of this study is to investigate whether a virtual memory palace experienced in a HMD increases recall, confidence in recall, and perceived effectiveness in use of the MOL technique when compared to the traditional, mental MOL technique when both the environment and objects are predefined, with objects unfamiliar to the participant, for naive users. The aim is to contribute to design guidelines for virtual memory palaces.

3.1 Design

To investigate whether the use of an immersive VE with predefined objects for persons previously naive to the MOL improves recall compared to the traditional technique, participants were randomly assigned into one of two conditions: building a memory palace using a traditional, imaginative technique or being introduced to a pre-existing and pre-populated memory palace. Objects populated into the virtual environment were explicitly chosen as concrete nouns to avoid the ambiguous interpretation. They were labeled with text in line with dual coding theory, that recall is improved when lexical and pictorial stimuli are used simultaneously [12].

The dependent variables measured in this experiment were the number of correct words recalled during free recall tasks, the participants confidence in their responses, as well as how effectively they felt they used the MOL to complete the tasks as a measure of compliance. The experiment was a mixed design, between subjects (vMOL, tMOL) and within subjects (before and after utilizing MOL).

3.2 Participants

Thirty-three graduate and undergraduate students attending SUNY Oswego participated in the experiment in exchange for a chance to win a raffle for a ten-dollar gift card. Three participants were excluded from the experiment due to their previous knowledge and frequent practice of the Method of Loci. Two additional participants were excluded as they were unable to complete the experiment secondary to cyber-sickness in the VR condition. In total, twenty-eight participants produced data that was analyzed. Among the twenty-eight participants, there were 14 female and 14 male all with normal or corrected vision, with a mean age of 23. At the beginning of each experimental session, consent was obtained from each participant. This study was reviewed and approved by the local Institutional Review Board prior to the experiment taking place.

3.3 Procedure

Participants were randomly assigned to one of two conditions: a traditional MOL technique, or a vMOL with a pre-constructed memory palace pre-populated with objects. The vMOL condition was run using the Oculus Rift; navigation was mapped to an Xbox One controller. The virtual environment was developed using Unity. Assets within the environment not constructed by the author were imported from Google Poly. The environment was made up of three rooms: a classroom, an apartment, and a restaurant. Participants could navigate using the controller, as well as turn their heads and bodies to change orientation within the VE. Those in the vMOL condition were given the opportunity to familiarize themselves with the VE and the controls prior to learning about the MOL. During this learning period, there were no objects present in the environment.

The experiment was divided into two main sections. First, participants in both conditions were presented with three subsequent, randomized lists for two minutes at a time. A distraction task followed to avoid recall from short term memory. After the two minutes, the participants were given 60 s to recall each list. Participants completed this task through free recall, typing their responses into a textbox. Participants then completed a survey detailing their confidence in the accuracy of their responses. After this initial recall task, those who were assigned the vMOL condition were given time in the VE to familiarize themselves with the controls for navigating the environment. During this period, participants in the vMOL were encouraged to familiarize themselves with the layout of each room, given that the MOL is often more successful using familiar locations.

Both conditions were then given a written description of the Method of Loci and were encouraged to ask for clarification of the text if needed. Participants were then instructed to use the MOL for the next task. Those in the tMOL were asked to choose three locations that would be used prior to moving onto the recall task to avoid them having to create one and place objects within in simultaneously. In the tMOL condition, three lists of 12 words were shown in random order, and participants were given two minutes to memorize each list. Participants in the vMOL were given two minutes in each of the three rooms to memorize the objects placed within them; the order of the rooms was randomized.

Participants in both conditions were then presented with the task of recalling state capitals, again to prevent recalling from short term memory. Participants were then given 60 s for each list to recall the items, entered as free recall into a textbox. Afterward, participants were again asked to rate their confidence in their responses. They were also asked to rate how effectively they used the MOL in the second recall task, as a measure of compliance. Lastly, participants were surveyed to determine if they had previously known and or used the MOL as a memory technique.

4 Results

4.1 Recall

The primary purpose of this study was to investigate the recall between the tMOL and vMOL conditions. Using a repeated measures ANOVA statistical test it was found that overall, there was a significant difference between the control recall task and the two MOL conditions $F(1,26) = 22.304$, $p < .001$. However, there was no significant difference between the tM-OL and vMOL conditions ($p = 0.111$) (Table 1).

Table 1. Overall recall accuracy within subjects for control and MOL conditions, between subjects for tMOL (condition 1) and vMOL (condition 2).

Within subjects effects

	Sum of squares	df	Mean square	F	p
Method	1075.149	1	1075.149	22.304	< .001
Method * Condition	146.702	1	146.720	3.044	0.093
Residual	125.333	26	48.205		

Note: Type III Sum of Squares

Between subjects effects

	Sum of squares	df	Mean square	F	p
Condition	176.095	1	176.095	2.716	0.111
Residual	1685.958	26	64.845		

Note: Type III Sum of Squares

4.2 Confidence

Participants were asked to rate their confidence in their answers after each recall task. Using a repeated measures ANOVA statistical test it was found that overall, there was a significant difference between the confidence of answers given in the control recall task and the two MOL conditions $F(1,26) = 31.431$, $p < .001$. However, there was no significant difference between the tMOL and vMOL conditions ($p = 0.408$) (Table 2)

Table 2. Overall confidence in accurate recall within subjects for control and MOL conditions, between subjects for tMOL (condition 1) and vMOL (condition 2).

Within Subjects Effects

	Sum of Squares	df	Mean Square	F	p
Method	375.513	1	375.513	31.431	< .001
Method * Condition	20.371	1	20.371	1.714	0.202
Residual	308.969	26	11.883		

Note: Type III Sum of Squares

Between Subjects Effects

	Sum of Squares	df	Mean Square	F	p
Condition	12.871	1	12.871	0.707	0.408
Residual	473.469	26	18.210		

Note: Type III Sum of Squares

4.3   Effectiveness

Participants were asked to rate how effectively they felt they employed the MOL technique after each recall task in the tMOL and vMOL conditions. Results indicate that participants in the vMOL condition felt that they had utilized the MOL more effectively than participants in the tMOL condition, $F(1,26) = 6.279$, $p = 0.019$ (Table 3).

Table 3. Overall perceived effectiveness in use of MOL conditions, between subjects for tMOL (condition 1) and vMOL (condition 2).

Between subjects effects					
	Sum of squares	df	Mean square	F	p
Condition	40.741	1	40.741	6.269	0.019
Residual	168.688	26	6.488		

Note: Type III Sum of Squares

5   Discussion

The results of this study reaffirmed findings of several other studies demonstrating that the MOL improves recall for using both mental and virtual environments when compared to unstructured recall with no mnemonic technique, such as Legge et al. [9], with the exception that the objects were predefined and prepopulated into the virtual memory palaces and participants were given no MOL training. This structure demonstrates that individuals naive to the MOL could use such an environment as successfully as a mental virtual memorypalace.

Of note, participants in the vMOL conditions felt that they utilized the MOL technique more effectively than the tMOL condition. For naive users, this increased level of confidence in utilizing the MOL could be a factor when introducing the technique. A virtual memory palace could serve as a structured learning environment using the MOL, allowing a greater ability and motivation to apply the technique mentally in the future.

6   Limitations and Future Research

This demonstrated that the use of prepopulated objects, specifically concrete nouns, could be used effectively within a virtual memory palace. Concrete nouns were chosen to avoid ambiguity in understanding but limited the complexity of data stored within the environment. Further investigations could focus on the ambiguity of prepopulated objects in a virtual environment which could be useful when designing virtual memory palaces to be used as learning environments for more complex data.

Notably, this research demonstrated that participants in the VR-based MOL condition reported greater perceived effectiveness of the MOL technique when compared to the traditional MOL condition. Given that past and present research demonstrates improved recall when using the MOL, the use of a virtual environment to learn the technique itself would be beneficial and could motivate individuals to apply the technique mentally in future tasks. Further investigations could focus on long term use and implementation of the MOL technique for naïve users first exposed in a virtual environment.

7 Conclusion

This study has demonstrated that virtual memory palaces can be used as effectively to aid recall as traditional memory palaces. Predefined objects can be prepopulated into virtual memory palaces with no difference in recall compared to objects populated in mental memory palaces. Future research into design differences between virtual memory palaces and ambiguity of objects placed in the virtual environments could lead to more successful implementations of virtual memory palaces. This study also demonstrated that participants in the VR-based MOL condition had greater perceived effectiveness in their use of the technique. This finding indicates that the use of a VE could be beneficial to naïve users who are learning the MOL technique itself and motivate them to apply the technique to recall tasks in the future.

References

1. Ragan, E.D., Bowman, D.A., Huber, K.J., Author, F.: Supporting cognitive processing with spatial information presentations in virtual environments. Virtual Reality 16(4), 301–314 (2012)
2. Wilson, S.: Building a memory palace through video installation. Int. J. Pract. Humanit. 2(1), 1–15 (2016)
3. Irie, K., Al Sada, M., Yamada, Y., Gushima, K., Nakajima, T.: Pervasive HoloMoL: a mobile pervasive game with mixed reality enhanced method of loci. In: Proceedings of the 15th International Conference on Advances in Mobile Computing & Multimedia, pp. 141–145. ACM (2017)
4. Rosello, O., Exposito, M., Maes, P.: NeverMind: using augmented reality for memorization. In: Proceedings of the 29th Annual Symposium on User Interface Software and Technology, pp. 215–216. ACM (2016)
5. Robin, J., Wynn, J., Moscovitch, M.: The spatial scaffold: the effects of spatial context on memory for events. J. Exp. Psychol.: Learn. Mem. Cogn. 42(2), 308 (2016)
6. Burgess, N., Maguire, E.A., Spiers, H.J., O'Keefe, J.: A temporoparietal and prefrontal network for retrieving the spatial context of lifelike events. Neuroimage 14(2), 439–453 (2001)
7. Storkerson, P.: Hypertext and the art of memory. Vis. Lang. 31(2), 126 (1997)
8. Foer, J.: Moonwalking with Einstein: the art and science of remembering everything. Penguin (2012)
9. Legge, E.L., Madan, C.R., Ng, E.T., Caplan, J.B.: Building a memory palace in minutes: equivalent memory performance using virtual versus conventional environments with the method of loci. Actapsychologica 141(3), 380–390 (2012)

10. Fassbender, E., Heiden, W.: The virtual memory palace. J. Comput. Inf. Syst. **2**(1), 457–464 (2006)
11. Krokos, E., Plaisant, C., Varshney, A.: Virtual memory palaces: immersion aids recall. Virtual Reality **23**, 1–15 (2018)
12. Huttner, J.P., Pfeiffer, D., Robra-Bissantz, S.: Imaginary versus virtual loci: evaluating the memorization accuracy in a virtual memory palace. In: Proceedings of the 51st Hawaii International Conference on System Sciences (2018)

Understanding Avatar Identification Through Visual Similarity for Richer Story Creation

Hannah Park[1], Sarah Brown[2(✉)], and Sharon Lynn Chu[2]

[1] Texas A&M University, College Station, USA
[2] Embodied Learning & Experience Lab, University of Florida, Gainesville, USA
sarah.brown@ufl.edu

Abstract. This paper explores avatar identification in creative storytelling applications where users create their own story and environment. We present a study that investigated the effects of avatar facial similarity to the user on the quality of the story product they create. The children told a story using a digital puppet-based storytelling system by interacting with a physical puppet box that was augmented with a real-time video feed of the puppet enactment. We used a facial morphing technique to manipulate avatar facial similarity to the user. The resulting morphed image was applied to each participant's puppet character, thus creating a custom avatar for each child to use in story creation. We hypothesized that the more familiar avatars appeared to participants, the stronger the sense of character identification would be, resulting in higher story quality. The proposed rationale is that visual familiarity may lead participants to draw richer story details from their past real-life experiences. Qualitative analysis of the stories supported our hypothesis. Our results contribute to avatar design in children's creative storytelling applications.

Keywords: Avatar identification · Children's storytelling · Puppet play

1 Introduction

Much research has explored how to design effective user avatars for different types of virtual environments. Previous research, however, does not fully explore the effects of avatar identification with respect to at least two dimensions. First, studies investigating avatar identification has addressed more performance-based activities, such as video games and digital exercise applications. In these cases, the goal of the application is for the user to perform a generally pre-defined task, rather than produce some creative output. And second, studies of avatar identification has focused on investigating the effects of customizing one's avatar, as opposed to existing physical similarity between the user and avatar itself. This

C. Stephanidis (Ed.): HCII 2019, CCIS 1033, pp. 423–431, 2019.
https://doi.org/10.1007/978-3-030-23528-4_57

leaves room to explore the benefits of avatar physical similarity within creative applications.

Hence, the goal of our study was to investigate facial similarity between the user and their respective avatar in a creative story application and its effect on story quality and storytelling self-efficacy. Specifically, we use a puppet-based storytelling system that allowed children to produce open-ended stories given a prompt. We posited that through increased avatar identification achieved via the facial morphing of a cartoon avatar with the participant's own face, participants would draw from personal experiences to come up with stories that are inherently richer. If our hypothesis correct, increasing avatar identification through differing levels of facial similarity should then result in better quality of written stories, if the children were asked to write down their stories.

2   Background

Prior research has established the facial appearance of an avatar has an effect on how we perceive the avatar's personality traits [W01]. Similarly, the fidelity of an avatar, for example its level of realism, can also have an effect on aspects such as psychological co-presence [K01]. When it comes to research investigating specifically avatar identification, the ability to connect with one's avatar, investigations have focused on allowing the user to customize their given avatar in some manner [B01, NL01].

2.1   Related Work

Fox and Bailenson found that providing facial similarity between user and avatar in a digital application that guided the user through exercise activities actually had a behavioral effect on participants in their study [FB01]. While the task supported by their system was not creative in nature, this shows promise that avatar facial similarity can impact the outcome of a digital application, perhaps even if the outcome were some sort of creative product. Suh et al introduced another study directly exploring the effects of avatar similarity to a user [S01]. They investigated both facial and body similarity as two dimensions of their experimental design, with low and high conditions for each. In their research, higher avatar similarity resulted in participants reporting increased positive attitudes and higher levels of avatar identification.

2.2   Theoretical Framework

Our hypothesis that avatars of greater visual similarity would lead children to produce more creative stories is grounded in Gee's tripartite model of identities in virtual environments [G02, G01]. Any process of story creation is intrinsically grounded in one's previous life experiences [V01]. The brain "combines and creatively reworks elements of this past experience and uses them to generate new

propositions and new behavior" [V01]. In a virtual storytelling environment however, this real-world identity that provides the underlying mental structures for
story creation interplays with the virtual identity that the user forms from her
avatar. This is represented in Fig. 1.

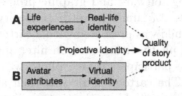

Fig. 1. Theoretical framework

The virtual identity may also constrain the user's creative process in a storytelling task (Box B). According to Gee [G01], what the user projects from
her real-world identity onto the virtual identity, and vice-versa, becomes her
projective identity. We posit that the degree to which the projective identity
emphasizes the real-world identity (that we manipulated in our study through
avatar facial similarity to one's real-life self) determines one's likelihood, and
perhaps even ability, to recall and draw from one's real-life experiences in story
creation.

3   Research Questions

The questions we sought to answer in this study were as follows:

RQ1a: Does increasing the level of an avatar's facial similarity to its user
affect the user's sense of character identification?
RQ1b: Does increasing an avatar's facial similarity to its user increase the
user's sense of immersion in the story creation experience?
RQ2: Does the level of an avatar's facial similarity to its user affect the
quality of the stories created by the user?
RQ3: Does the level of an avatar's facial similarity to its user affect the user's
sense of creative self-efficacy?

Our specific hypotheses for the study were as follows:

(1) The greater the avatar facial similarity, the greater the user's sense of character identification.
(2) The greater the avatar facial similarity, the greater the user's immersion in
the story creation experience.
(3) There is a significant difference in the quality of stories resulting from the
use of avatars of varying levels of facial similarity.
(4) There is a significant difference in the user's sense of creative self-efficacy
from the use of avatars of varying levels of facial similarity.

We did not provide any hypothesis for RQ2b since that research question
was more exploratory.

4 Study

4.1 Study Materials

Avatars: To produce avatars with varying levels of facial similarity to the user, we used a facial morphing software and graphic processing software to create three similarity conditions: 0% similarity; 60% similarity; and 100% similarity.

In 0% similarity, the child was presented with a cartoon puppet avatar whose face was a stranger's face photo with a cartoon filter applied.

In 60% similarity, the participant's face photo was morphed at 60% with a stranger's face photo. The cartoon filter was then applied to the resultant morphed face photo and integrated into the cartoon puppet avatar. In this case, the avatar would produce somewhat of a sense of familiarity - i.e., the participant might not recognize the puppet avatar as themselves, but might feel that the avatar looks familiar.

In 100% similarity, the child was presented with a cartoon puppet avatar whose face was exactly his or her face photo with a cartoon filter applied. In the study, participants were always given avatars of the same gender as them.

Story Starters: Four story starters with different contexts were created to allow for a child's participation in all of the study conditions. The story starters differed in terms of environment (grandparents' house, beach, national park or ranch) and in terms of focus objects (a strange necklace, a spatial seashell, a mysterious mushroom, or a magic rock). All the story starters, however, were made as comparable as possible with the same structure: "a boy/girl went to the [context] with family. He/she found [focus object]. Create a short story about what happens next."

Puppet-Based Storytelling System: A puppet theater was made with white foam board (14 × 8.5 × 11 in.) with backgrounds depicting different scenes printed on large sheets of paper. The puppet theater was placed on the table in front of a camera connected to a large TV screen (Fig. 2). In the study, the child participant was asked to create a story by enacting using avatar puppets. When the child enacted a story with the avatar puppets, the camera recorded the child's puppet story enactment and projected the play on the TV screen in real-time so the child could see his/her play. The system produced a video file of the enacted puppet story at the end of the child's enactment.

4.2 Study Design

The study used a within-subjects design. The independent variable was 'level of facial similarity' with three levels: 0%, 60% and 100%. A participant also engaged in a baseline condition whereby he/she was asked to write a story without any intervention. One story starter was given for each level of facial similarity and the baseline, such that a child only did a story starter once. The order in which the

Fig. 2. From left to right: 60% morphed puppet above 100% morphed puppet; puppet box photo; diagram of study set up

story starters were assigned was counterbalanced across the participant sample. The order of the study conditions in general was also counterbalanced across the sample.

4.3 Study Description

We conducted the study with 14 children aged 7 to 14 years old (3 boys and 11 girls) recruited through university e-mail listservs. All children participated individually, and the study consisted of two sessions spread over two days. The duration for each session was approximately 1.5 h.

Day 1 (Session 1): At the beginning of session 1, the child completed a questionnaire capturing baseline data. The child then engaged in the baseline condition. He/she was provided with the first story starter, and asked to write the story on paper. No time limit was given. Afterwards, the child engaged in the 0% similarity condition. The child was given the 'stranger' avatar puppet and given a different story starter. To make sure that the child paid attention to the avatar's face, the researcher casually asked the child participant before he/she was allowed to start story creation: "Please look closely at the avatar's face. What can you explain about your character?". Each child was given enough time to brainstorm the story ideas and allowed to create paper-based story props if so desired. When the child was ready to enact a story, he/she moved to the story enactment station. After story enactment, the child was asked to write the story that he/she just enacted on paper. No time limit was imposed. The child was allowed to review at will the video of his/her story enactment during story writing. At the end of the session, the child was asked to complete a post-questionnaire, and the investigator conducted a short interview with him/her. The child's parent was also asked permission for the investigator to take a photo of the child. No information or indication was given to the child and parents that the photo would be used for avatar creation.

Day 2 (Session 2): In-between day 1 and day 2, we created the child's avatar puppets for the 60% and 100% similarity conditions by using the child's photo taken at the end of session 1. The procedures for session 2 were essentially the same as session 1, except that the child engaged in the 60% and 100% similarity conditions (order differed depending on counterbalancing). At the end of session 2, the child was given the opportunity to ask any questions, debriefed, and given a toy gift before he/she was released from the study. We provided a copy of the children's stories to them if they so requested.

4.4   Measures

The dependent variables for this study included the following:

- *manipulation check.* We included two single items to measure how effective our morphing was in providing varying levels of avatar similarity, as perceived by the participant: "The looks of my paper puppet is similar to me", and "My looks resemble my paper puppet".
- *sense of character identification.* This was measured after each condition using the appropriate sub-scales from a scale created for measuring identification in MMOGs [VL01];
- *sense of immersion in the storytelling experience.* This was measured using the General Engagement Questionnaire [BF01] after each condition;
- *quality of written stories.* This was assessed by coding the stories in terms of number of adjectives, adverbs, nouns, and descriptive verbs (e.g., whisper, chat, mutter are descriptive verbs, but talk is not);
- *sense of creative self-efficacy.* This was measured at baseline and after each condition using the creative self-efficacy scale proposed by Tierney and Farmer [TF01]. The scale consists of 3 items: "I am good at coming up with new ideas"; "I have a lot of good ideas", and "I have a good imagination".

5   Data Analysis and Results

We present the results of the study below by research question:

5.1   Manipulation Check

Our manipulation involved varying the extent to which the avatar puppet's face resembled the child participant using a facial morphing technique together with cartoon filter applied. Average scores were calculated for the two items that were included in the post-questionnaire for the manipulation check. A repeated measures ANOVA was ran on the scores. There was a statistically significant effect of facial similarity on the perceived resemblance scores, $F(2, 26) = 12.25$, $p = .000$. Pairwise comparisons showed that the 100% similarity condition (M = 3.64) was significantly different from both the 0% (M = 2.99) and 60% (M = 2.55) conditions.

5.2   RQ1a: Facial Similarity and Character Identification

A repeated measures ANOVA was ran on character identification scores. Since the assumption of sphericity was violated for this test, greenhouse-geisser adjustments were applied. There was a statistically significant effect of facial similarity on character identification, $F(2, 26) = 12.00$, $p = .001$. Pairwise comparisons showed that the 100% similarity condition ($M = 4.00$) was significantly different from both the 0% ($M = 2.61$) and 60% ($M = 2.86$) conditions.

5.3   RQ1b: Facial Similarity and Experience Immersion

A repeated measures ANOVA was ran on immersion scores. No significant differences were found, although the means were higher the greater the facial similarity (0% $M = 2.71$; 60% $M = 2.84$; 100% $M = 2.98$).

5.4   RQ2: Facial Similarity and Story Quality

The first seven participants were selected from our dataset, and their stories were analyzed for this paper. To analyze the quality of the stories, each story was first broken down into an 'idea digest' [RH01]. The idea digest deconstructs a story into individual units of thought or essence of meaning. This deconstruction could even occur within sentences. For example, a story sentence reading "She ate it and felt really special and found out she could fly!" would be broken down into two ideas: "She ate it and felt really special", "and found out she could fly!". After an idea digest had been extracted for each story (including the baseline stories), it was coded for *details*, that we operationalized as the 5Ws+1H (Who/What/When/Where/Why/How's), *conjunctions* (e.g., because, then, so), and *richness descriptors*, operationalized as adjectives, nouns used as adjectives, adverbs, and descriptive verbs. Repeated measures ANOVAs with were ran on the number of details, conjunctions and richness descriptors with baseline story quality values as covariate. We standardized the value of the story quality scores in two ways, by word count, and by number of ideas. This way, even if a story was significantly shorter than another, and naturally possessed fewer descriptors, we could still gauge a sense of its richness.

There was a statistically significant effect of facial similarity on richness descriptors scores standardized by story word count, $F(2, 10) = 4.81$, $p = .034$. The mean values were .08, .09 and .05 for the 0%, 60% and 100% similarity conditions respectively. The effect on richness descriptors scores standardized by number of story ideas was marginally significant ($p = .06$) and showed the same trend. Details digest: There was also a marginal effect of facial similarity on details scores standardized by number of story ideas ($p = .06$). Mean values for this were .62, .64 and .47 for the 0%, 60% and 100% similarity conditions respectively. No significant effects were found for conjunctions scores.

5.5   RQ3: Facial Similarity and Creative Self-efficacy

A repeated measures ANOVA was ran on creative self-efficacy scores. No statistically significant differences were found.

6 Discussion

Our manipulation check showed that the 60% morph condition did not result in the children being able perceive any distinct resemblance to themselves, but they were able to do so for the 100% condition. This means that while morphing did provide facial similarity for the avatar, it did not manage to create a familiarity effect that we expected in the 60% morph condition. We posit that the effect may have been washed out by the filter we applied to the avatars.

As for character identification, it was only significantly different between the 0% and 100% similarity conditions, and the 60% & 100% conditions. This seems to imply that character identification occurs primarily when participants can fully recognize themselves.

The difference in terms of sense of immersion was not statistically significant, but it appears to have an upwards trend increasing with facial similarity. This could perhaps be due to the participants paying more attention to the kind of story they create, or engaging more with the storytelling experience when the avatar puppet resembles them.

For story quality, facial similarity impacted the number of richness descriptors used as well as the level of details in the stories. The story quality was better for the 60% similarity condition. We encountered an interesting recurring phenomenon in the participants' stories where after using the puppet storytelling system, their written stories became more like scripts than actual short story essays. This made comparison to the baseline difficult, as this effect was not found among the baseline stories.

Sense of self efficacy was flat across all conditions, which makes sense when considering this was a brief intervention and self efficacy typically takes longer to impact.

7 Conclusion

We investigated primarily two things: the effects of avatar similarity through facial morphing on avatar identification, and the effects of avatar identification on the output of a task that is both digital and creative. Through the use of a puppet storytelling system intended for children, we invited children participants to create stories with puppets of varying facial similarity, measuring character identification, immersion, and creative self-efficacy after each use of our system.

There are a few key limitations with this study thus far. Our sample size was small (N = 14), leaving ample room to conduct our study with more participants in the future. A more thorough analysis involving the rest of the participants' stories could also provide more clarity as to the final impact of character identification on the creative output. There is also the possibility of looking at the enacted story recordings as the creative output instead of written re-tellings from the participants use of the system. Lastly, it could be the case that a fully digital storytelling system would have differing results. While the puppet storytelling set-up we implemented made use of digital feedback, it largely existed in a physical context.

References

[B01] Birk, M., Atkins, C., Bowey, J.T., Mandryk, R.: Fostering intrinsic motivation through avatar identification in digital games, pp. 2982–2995 (2016). https://doi.org/10.1145/2858036.2858062

[BF01] Brockmyer, J., Fox, C.M., Curtiss, K.A., McBroom, E., Burkhart, K.M., Pidruzny, J.N.: The development of the game engagement questionnaire: a measure of engagement in video game-playing. J. Exp. Soc. Psychol. **45**(4), 624–634 (2009)

[FB01] Fox, J., Bailenson, J.: Virtual self-modeling: the effects of vicarious reinforcement and identification on exercise behaviors. Media Psychol. **12**(1), 1–25 (2009)

[G01] Gee, J.P.: Pleasure, learning, video games, and life: the projective stance. E-Learn. Digit. Media **2**(3), 211–223 (2005)

[G02] Gee, J.P.: What video games have to teach us about learning and literacy. Comput. Entertain. (CIE) **1**(1), 20–20 (2003)

[K01] Kang, S.-H., Watt, J.H.: The impact of avatar realism and anonymity on effective communication via mobile devices. Comput. Hum. Behav. **29**, 1169–1181 (2013)

[S01] Suh, K.-S., Kim, H., Suh, E.K.: What if your avatar looks like you? Dual-congruity perspectives for Avatar use. MIS Q. **35**(3), 711-A4 (2011)

[NL01] Ng. R., Lindgren, R.: Examining the effects of avatar customization and narrative on engagement and learning in video games. In: Proceedings of CGAMES 2013 USA, 2013 18th International Conference On Computer Games: AI, Animation, Mobile, Interactive Multimedia, Educational & Serious Games (CGAMES), p. 87 (2013)

[W01] Wang, Y.: Reading personality: avatar vs. human faces. In: 2013 Humaine Association Conference on Humaine Association Conference on Affective Computing and Intelligent Interaction, Affective Computing and Intelligent Interaction (ACII), ACII, p. 479 (2013)

[V01] Vygotsky, L.S.: Imagination and creativity in childhood. J. Russ. East Eur. Psychol. **42**(1), 7–97 (2004)

[VL01] Van Looy, J., Courtois, C., De Vocht, M., De Marez, L.: Player identification in online games: validation of a scale for measuring identification in MMOGs. Media Psychol. **15**(2), 197–221 (2012)

[TF01] Tierney, P., Farmer, S.M.: Creative self-efficacy: its potential antecedents and relationship to creative performance. Acad. Manag. J. **45**(6), 1137–1148 (2002)

[RH01] Register, L.M., Henley, T.B.: The phenomenology of intimacy. J. Soc. Pers. Relat. **9**(4), 467–481 (1992)

HandyTool: Object Manipulation Through Metaphorical Hand/Fingers-to-Tool Mapping

Eunbi Seol and Gerard J. Kim(⊠)

Digital Experience Laboratory, Korea University, Seoul, Korea
{agoremember, gjkim}@korea.ac.kr

Abstract. In this paper, we introduce "HandyTool" a method (and an interface) for virtual object manipulation based on a metaphorical/structural mapping of various everyday tools to our hands and fingers. The basic idea is to virtually transform the hand/fingers into a proper tool (e.g. a fist becoming a hammer head) and gesturally apply it (e.g. hammer in to insert) to and manipulate the target object (e.g. a nail) directly. The main intended objective of HandyTool is to enhance the tool usage experience by one (or one's body part) becoming the tool itself and thereby also possibly improving the task performance. A usability experiment was carried out to assess the projected merits, comparing HandyTool to the case of the as-is emulation of the tool usage (i.e. the tracked hand/finger controlling the tool to apply it to the target object) and to the case of using the controller. Our experiment was not able to show the clear and full potential of HandyTool because of the current performance limitation of the hand/fingers tracking sensor and due to the simplicity in the structural mapping between the tool and hand/fingers. The structural metaphor itself was still shown to be helpful when the controller was used (i.e. stable sensing).

Keywords: Virtual reality · Mixed/augmented reality ·
Interactive learning environments

1 Introduction

Effective object manipulation, one of the basic interaction tasks in any virtual space, is important for the fluent usability, and as such, many interaction techniques and tools have been suggested for it [1, 2, 7]. However, most of them can be categorized as the "magic" techniques. That is, the "tools" are not reality-inspired, but purposely "designed" to achieve the task as effectively as possible. It is only natural to take advantage of the virtuality to free oneself from the bounds of the physical reality. After all, tools may be useful in the physical world but not necessarily in the virtual.

On the other hand, virtual reality (VR) also aims to provide a difficult-to-get "experiences", if not in its entirety but at least the core. Take an example of providing the fun experience of carpentering and assembling a wooden desk using an assortment of hand tools without having to gather all the materials and set up a shop. Surely, one component of such a VR experience would be to employ an interaction method that is based on reality, e.g. sensing the hand/fingers movement as to pick up and apply the needed tool.

© Springer Nature Switzerland AG 2019
C. Stephanidis (Ed.): HCII 2019, CCIS 1033, pp. 432–439, 2019.
https://doi.org/10.1007/978-3-030-23528-4_58

Instead, in this paper, we introduce "HandyTool" a method (and an interface) for virtual object manipulation based on a metaphorical/structural mapping of various everyday tools to our hands and fingers. The basic idea is to transform the hand/fingers into a proper tool (e.g. a fist becoming a hammer head) and gesturally apply it to and manipulate the target object (e.g. inserting a nail) directly. The intended objective of HandyTool is to enhance the experience of usage of the tool by one (or one's body part) becoming the tool itself and thereby also improving the task performance. While the mapping is already intuitive and easily understood, it can be guided using a visual interface overlaying the control skeleton over the target tool (see Fig. 1). Once the mapping is established, the user can gesturally enact (and not indirectly control) the tool using one's hand and fingers as if the tool was the one's hand (applying fisted hand as if it was the hammer head to insert a nail).

This paper is organized as follows. We first shortly review related research. Then we present the detailed design of HandyTool and the usability experiment carried out to assess the projected merits. We also show the results of applying the method to partially controlling an avatar or virtual puppets as an educational tool for young children to train their hand skills, called HandyMan. Finally, we summarize and discuss our findings and conclude the paper.

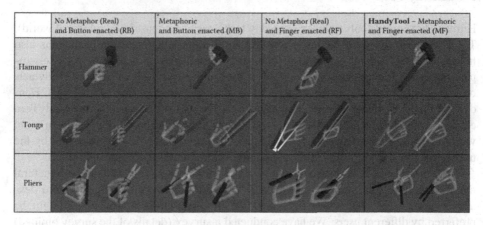

Fig. 1. The concept of HandyTool (or using both the structural metaphor and finger tracking, right-most) and other tool-object manipulation methods (from the left, RB, MB, RF).

2   Related Work

Various 3D interaction techniques, including those for object selection and manipulation, have been developed over the years for use in the virtual space [1, 2, 7]. Among many, we review those that are hand-based (or equally hand gesture based). The most prevalent form of object selection and manipulation is the "Direct Hand" method [2, 11]. Usually a tracker/button device attached to the user hand tracks and maps the hand into the virtual space to select an object by simple touch (i.e. collision with the object). Once selected, the target object is attached to the hand, and follows the moves of the hand (translate/rotate) to be manipulated. The button device or simple gestures can be used to simplify more complicated moves (e.g. twisting motion) or make logical commands (e.g. change color). Interaction controllers are a popular commercial realization of the tracker/button device today [4, 10, 14].

Secondary tools, especially those that are reality inspired, are rarely used in VR. For instance, to insert a nail, the direct hand itself can be used to accomplish the task either by physical movement (and simulation), gesture or button command. To truly emulate the usage of a tool, the user would have to somehow select/grab the handle portion of the tool, move it to "control" the tool and apply it to the target object. In this regard, such an approach requires more exact tracking of finger movements. Gloves [12, 13] and more recent advanced sensors (e.g. Microsoft Kinect [9], Leap Motion [6] can be used for this purpose, but more so for just 1:1 mapped animation or making logical gestural commands [8].

3   HandyTool

Humans have used tools to make everyday tasks easier (at least in the physical world). Tools are more efficient for the given task by design. But interestingly humans also make appearance hand gestures of tools to communicate as well (e.g. rock-scissor-paper play). A tool is grossly composed of the handle and the part which directly acts on the target object – called the "actor" (e.g. hammer head acting on the nail). HandyTool maps the hand structure to that of the actor part of the tool. Thus, HandyTool eliminates the indirectness of having to use the handle and possibly provides a more vivid/interesting experience and even improved performance of using the tool by the user becoming "actor" itself. The mapping is both structural and metaphorical.

One immediate issue in the design of HandyTool is how to establish the structural mapping between the tool and the hand. The hand/fingers are usually the more dexterous with higher degrees of freedom than the tool. Different mappings might be preferred by different users. We have conducted a survey (details of the survey omitted) asking users to designate the most preferred, intuitive and natural mapping for various tools (see Table 1 for few examples). Most tools we surveyed came up with one or two prevalent mapping forms. Note that in the actual usage, the user simply has to follow the visually guided mapping which is expected to be easily understood and accepted (see Fig. 1).

Table 1. Examples of survey for intuitive mapping

Tool		Preferred Metaphor	
Hammer			Not shown
		90.9%	
Tongs			
		63.6%	27.3%
Pliers			
		63.6%	18.2%

4 Usability Experiment

A usability experiment was carried out to assess the projected merits, comparing HandyTool by two factors: (1) the use of metaphor and (2) the type of interaction device used for hand-based tool activation (the hand itself was tracked using a 3D tracker for all treatments). The experiment was therefore designed as a 2 factors × 2 levels within subject repeated measure. The four treatments are as follows (see Fig. 1):

- RB: No metaphor (Real) + Button (Hand/fingers movement enacts the tool by a button press, and virtual hand/fingers is visually overlaid as if grabbing the handle).
- MB: Metaphoric + Button (Hand/fingers movement enacts the tool by a button press, but virtual hand/fingers is visually overlaid and shown according to the structural metaphor).
- RF: No metaphor (Real) + Finger tracking sensor (Hand/fingers movement enacts the tool by moving the handle grabbed by the hand/fingers).
- MF: Metaphoric + Finger tracking sensor (Hand/fingers movement enacts the tool according to the structural metaphor, i.e. **HandyTool**).

The experimental task involved the subject to take the tool and carry out an associated task. Three tools/tasks were selected to be tested and evaluated: (1) hammer/striking in nails (2) tongs/picking and placings object, (3) pliers/rotating screws in (see Fig. 2). The quantitative dependent variables included the task completion time and accuracy (defined differently for different tasks). We also administered a subjective survey assessing general usability (NASA-TLX [3]), simulation sickness (SSQ, [5]), enjoyment/preference and presence/immersion level (modified and reduced PQ, [15]).

Fig. 2. The three experimental tasks: hammer: strike nails, plier: pick and rotate/place cubes, plier: twisting in screws.

The testing platform was implemented with Unity3D and run on a desktop PC with the HTC VIVE head set. For MF and RF, finger movement was tracked by the Leap Motion sensor and likewise for the hand position. The virtual hand/fingers were visualized according to the motion data (scaled properly depending on the size of the hand and tool). As for MB and RB, the HTC VIVE controller was used for hand tracking and button press (no finger movement tracking). When the controller was used, a default hand/fingers pose (appropriate for the given tool) was visualized over the target tool (see Fig. 1). Further experiment procedural details are omitted due to space restriction.

5 Results and Discussion

A total of 17 subjects participated in the experiment (11 females and 6 males, average age of 23.4), who were given the 4 treatments in a balanced order. Our basic expected outcomes were that both quantitative and subjective performance will be significantly better with the use of HandyTool (MF). ANOVA/Tukey (or Kruskal-Wallis/Mann-Whitney) was applied with the Bonferroni's adjustment to analyze the experimental data.

It was found that, overall, the task completion time and accuracy were significantly better with use of the button (MB-RB over MF/RF) when enacting the tool. However, the use of the metaphor was not helpful especially when finger tracking sensors was used. The similar trend was found for the subjective ratings, i.e. better usability, higher immersion/presence and enjoyment/presence were found with the use of the controller button, and the structural metaphor was found to be helpful, but not significantly (See Fig. 3).

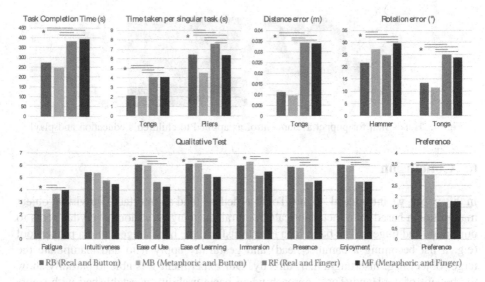

Fig. 3. Experimental results – Quantitative (above) and subjective ratings (below)- ∗ indicate $p < 0.05$.

In summary, contrary to our conviction, the use of the metaphor did not bring about the projected merits. It was apparent that the instability of the finger tracking sensor much affected the general usability and other subject evaluation criteria. The only solace was that the use of metaphor was somewhat a factor when the stable button device was used (namely, MB > RB for the tongs and pliers, but not for the hammer), partially confirming our hypothesis that the direct tool enactment improved task performance. Given the interaction is stable, the subjective indicators were generally very high when the metaphor was used (MB). Perhaps, the effect of the metaphor could be different for different tools and tasks as well. In addition, subjects reported the clear preference for the use of controller (button device) through which the user is able to get tangible feedback of the tool (vs. the use of Leap motion sensor to track finger movement in the mid-air).

One observation was that it seemed that metaphoric control was not all that different from the real (no metaphor case): e.g. fist posture over the hammer head vs. grabbing the handle, or tweezing over the blade vs. over handle (too simplistic). The evaluation was also somewhat oriented toward task efficiency rather than in the experience itself. Considering this, we have applied the idea of HandyTool to controlling virtual puppets (e.g. mapping fingers to body joins) and deployed it for children's education (e.g. dexterity development) and play (see Fig. 4).

Fig. 4. HandyMan for puppet avatar/control as applied to children's education and play.

6   Conclusion

In this paper, we introduced "HandyTool" a method (and an interface) for virtual object manipulation based on a metaphorical/structural mapping of various everyday tools to our hands and fingers. The basic idea is to transform the hand/fingers into a proper tool (e.g. a fist becoming a hammer head) and gesturally apply it to and manipulate the target object (e.g. inserting a nail) directly. Our experiment was able to partially show the benefit of the HandyTool approach when basic usability is established with stable tracking. Therefore, in the future, we would like to test the use of gloves as a more stable finger tracking device. Metaphors may also be useful depending on how much the metaphor reduces the complexity and the therefore the type of tool being used.

Acknowledgments. This work was partially supported by the Global Frontier R&D Program on <Human-centered Interaction for Coexistence> funded by the National Research Foundation of Korea grant funded by the Korean Government (MEST) (NRF-2015M3A6A3076490), and by the National Research Foundation of Korea (NRF) grant funded by the Korea government (MSIT) (NRF-2017M3C1B6070980).

References

1. Argelaguet, F., Andujar, C.: A survey of 3D object selection techniques for virtual environments. Comput. Graph. **37**(3), 121–136 (2013)
2. Bowman, D., Kruijff, E., LaViola Jr., J.J., Poupyrev, I.P.: 3D User Interfaces: Theory and Practice, CourseSmart eTextbook. Addison-Wesley, Boston (2004)
3. Hart, S.G., Staveland, L.E.: Development of NASA-TLX (Task Load Index): results of empirical and theoretical research. In: Advances in Psychology, North-Holland, vol. 52, pp. 139–183 (1988)
4. HTC VIVE. https://www.vive.com/us/product/vive-virtual-reality-system/
5. Kennedy, R.S., Lane, N.E., Berbaum, K.S., Lilienthal, M.G.: Simulator sickness questionnaire: an enhanced method for quantifying simulator sickness. Int. J. Aviat. Psychol. **3**(3), 203–220 (1993)
6. LeapMotion. https://www.leapmotion.com/
7. Mendes, D., Caputo, F. M., Giachetti, A., Ferreira, A., Jorge, J.: A survey on 3D virtual object manipulation: from the desktop to immersive virtual environments. In: Computer Graphics Forum. Wiley Online Library (2018)
8. Mendes, D., Fonseca, F., Araujo, B., Ferreira, A., Jorge, J.: Mid-air interactions above stereoscopic interactive tables. In: 3D User Interfaces (3DUI), pp. 3–10 (2014)

9. Microsoft. Kinect Sensor. https://msdn.microsoft.com/ko-kr/library/hh438998.aspx
10. Oculus. Oculus Rift. https://www.oculus.com/rift/oui-csl-rift-games=mages-tale
11. Poupyrev, I., Billinghurst, M., Weghorst, S., Ichikawa, T.: The go-go interaction technique: non-linear mapping for direct manipulation in VR. In: Proceedings of the 9th Annual ACM Symposium on User Interface Software and Technology, pp. 79–80 (1996)
12. Quam, D.L.: Gesture recognition with a dataglove. In: Aerospace and Electronics Conference, pp. 755–760 (1990)
13. Rekimoto, J.: Gesturewrist and gesturepad: unobtrusive wearable interaction devices. In: Proceedings of Fifth International Symposium on Wearable Computers, pp. 21–27 (2001)
14. Sony. PlayStation VR. https://www.vive.com/us/product/vive-virtual-reality-system/
15. Witmer, B.G., Singer, M.J.: Measuring presence in virtual environments: a presence questionnaire. Presence **7**(3), 225–240 (1998)

Making Multi-platform VR Development More Accessible: A Platform Agnostic VR Framework

Cameron Tynes[✉] and Jinsil Hwaryoung Seo[✉]

Department of Visualization, Texas A&M University, College Station, TX, USA
{Camtynes,Hwaryoung}@tamu.edu

Abstract. Virtual Reality offers developers an immersive and engaging new medium to create simulation applications, training tools, and educational games. One of the first decisions a VR developer will face is which platform to target. In 2014 consumer choice was limited to Google Cardboard. By 2016 this had expanded to six devices, including popular platforms such as Oculus Rift, HTC Vive, and PSVR. Today there are not only more platforms, but even more variation in platform hardware, input devices, and interaction methods. This overwhelming amount of variance can be daunting for developers who want to create a VR application where the goal is to develop and deliver for multiple platforms, typically to reach the largest audience. With applications in so many fields like medical, educational, and cyber security, it is becoming more important that VR experiences can run on multiple platforms in different environments. Therefore, we present and apply our approach to unify these differences with a platform agnostic framework for the Unity game engine that allows developers to focus on creating their vision, without worrying about individual SDKs and the intricacies of each platform.

Unity does a great job natively supporting the popular SDKs such as SteamVR and OculusVR, but these SDKs only apply to their own family of hardware, leaving the developer to re-write or even duplicate and alter code just so they can deploy their experience on multiple platforms. As project scope grows, this becomes more and more complex and can be a time-consuming task.

Keywords: VR · Virtual Reality · Platform agnostic · Unity · Abstraction · Multi-platform

1 Introduction

With the boom of current generation VR development in the last decade, many new headsets and VR technologies have become available to consumers. In 2017 alone, approximately 13.7 million units were shipped with growth expected to surpass 81 million by 2021 [6]. Virtual Reality as an educational and training tool is becoming ever more popular for its relatively low cost of entry and wide array of applications in fields like education [1], medical [2], data analysis [3], and national security [4]. With so many applications in such a wide array of fields, Schlueter et al. argue that VR applications, "…should not be limited by the accessibility and compatibility of the

© Springer Nature Switzerland AG 2019
C. Stephanidis (Ed.): HCII 2019, CCIS 1033, pp. 440–445, 2019.
https://doi.org/10.1007/978-3-030-23528-4_59

hardware, instead the applications should be made to support multiple hardware platforms" [5].

In the last few years several popular headsets have emerged: HTC Vive and Oculus Rift (PC VR), Cardboard, Gear VR, and Daydream (Mobile VR), and Oculus Go (Standalone VR). With each of these platforms comes a different set of hardware requirements, inputs, and interaction methods. For user inputs, PC-tethered HMDs use a pair of 6-DOF tracked motion controllers, containing a mix of analog sticks, touchpads, triggers and grip buttons. Mobile VR platforms are significantly cheaper and thus either come with no controller like Google's Cardboard - relying on gaze-based interactions - or use a single simplified controller with a trackpad and trigger, better suited for point-and-click interactions, such as the Oculus Go and Daydream.

By 2018, developers had 5 major SDKs to choose from when developing their applications [7]. Without a platform agnostic approach, developers need to write code specific to their target platform's SDK and repeat this process for every SDK they wish to deliver on. Each individual SDK only applies to their own specific hardware, e.g. SteamVR for HTC Vive, OVR for Oculus products, Google VR for Google products etc. This process of re-writing code to support each SDK can be a time-consuming process that only makes an application's codebase more complex. The platform agnostic approach presented in this paper seeks to abstract and generalize all the similarities between platforms and treat them as one, thereby allowing a developer to create content only once, irrespective of target platform, and deliver on multiple devices with little to no overhead.

2   Framework Goals

For our platform-agnostic framework we used the Unity game engine, version 2017.1.2. Unity is one of the most widely used publicly available game engines and works closely with VR software developers to keep up to date with the ever-changing VR landscape. Furthermore, Unity offers multi-platform support 'out-of-the-box', including native support for many popular VR SDKs (native meaning SDKs are already included with the software). In this section we'll discuss some of the goals that define our platform-agnostic framework.

2.1   Abstract as Much as Possible

Our first goal is to create an abstraction layer between the individual SDKs and game logic, whereby the abstraction layer creates a single point of entry for all SDKs, separating them from developers' game logic while creating generic events and actions that developers can use in their scripts. The abstraction layer generalizes key components of the SDKs such as inputs, haptics, hardware tracking, and platform specific settings, split among a small number of individually managed core classes. This abstraction is important because different SDKs handle all of these things using their own methods. For example, SteamVR (Vive's SDK) allows direct control over haptic effects given a force and duration, while Oculus's OVR SDK (Rift) generates an audio waveform to create a haptic effect. Similarly, the X/Y coordinate system on the Vive controllers' trackpads is not the same as the Gear VR controller's trackpad. Thus, we began by identifying common denominators like these between platforms, and then focused on creating generic actions that can be called by developers. Figure 1 demonstrates how we abstract inputs between different SDKs, returning generic events that can be used by the developer.

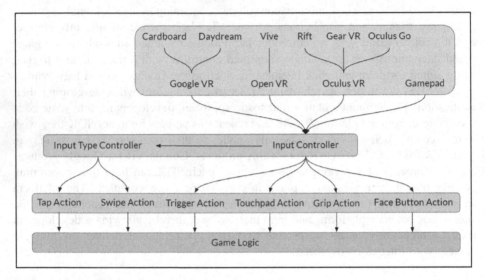

Fig. 1. SDK Input abstraction handled by two core classes. SDKs in orange, our abstraction layer in green, game logic in blue. (Color figure online)

2.2   Few Core Classes, Many Components

Building off Unity's Entity-Component system, whereby objects are treated as empty containers and are given functionality by adding components, our second goal was to create as few core classes as possible with many smaller attachable components. The core classes are broken up based on the main shared functionalities between platforms such as hardware tracking, inputs, haptics, and platform specific hardware management such as foveated rendering, refresh rate, and render scale. The core classes abstract these individual differences of SDKs into more generalized functionality. Additionally, these core classes provide a reference point for attachable components that can be used by the developer to give objects multi-platform functionality. Core classes are clearly separated from components and use a different naming convention.

While core classes abstract the SDKs and treat them as one generic environment, components function as smaller independent modules to give a game object functionality, like turning on a light when the player enters a room. These components refer to the core classes to automatically decide how they should function on a per-platform basis. Within our framework, attachable components consist of heavily repeated actions in VR applications such as grabbing/picking-up objects, haptics, object physics, and triggered events.

Our approach to reduce and generalize the number of core classes and keep them separate from attachable components presents an advantage over working with individual SDKs. For instance, when working with SteamVR, attachable components and core classes are all mixed together; there is no clear naming convention or separation between what the developer should use and what they shouldn't. Furthermore, core classes and attachable components from one SDK will not work when trying to develop for another, immediately limiting the number of platforms a developer can develop for. If you tried to attach a SteamVR "grabbable" component to an object when developing for the Oculus platform, it simply would not work.

2.3   Easy to Understand Workflow

The final goal for our framework is to make it as easy to use as possible for the widest range of developers possible, whether they're an artist or a programmer, student or professional. Unity is more code-heavy than the Unreal game engine which uses a node based visual programming system. In a classroom study, students reported that while Unity was easier to learn overall, programming in Unity was difficult [1]. Therefore, we have created our framework around the premise that developers should be able to easily create a VR application with little prior Unity knowledge, programming or otherwise. We do this in four ways. (1) By offering the framework as a unitypackage, users can directly install it into their already existing Unity projects. (2) The framework is organized into clearly named folders following common game development organizational practices. These folders keep core classes and commonly used attachable components separated. (3) We include a library of pre-made components that can be drag and dropped onto game objects to instantly give them functionality on any platform. (4) The framework is fully documented with images and videos, breakdowns of every class and component including all variables and methods, and how to set the project up using source control software like Github or Sourcetree.

3   Application

Working with Pacific Northwest National Laboratory (PNNL), we developed a chemical lab security and safety training application to train lab workers how to identify potential safety and security hazards in a lab environment. Our VR Framework was used to develop this application as seen in Fig. 2. The goal for this application was that it needed to be portable for conferences and demonstrations, but also include a high-end standalone version for sponsors visiting PNNL. With a team of one developer, the application took four weeks to make, including all art and gameplay logic. The application was deployed on Oculus Rift, HTC Vive, Cardboard, and Gear VR with no additional overhead to make modifications for specific platforms. Oculus Go and Daydream were not added to the framework yet.

Fig. 2. Chemical lab security and safety app on gear VR

4 Conclusion

An easy to use solution to multi-platform VR development was presented in this paper. The need to develop for multiple platforms is growing as new VR hardware continues to enter the market. Mobile VR platforms make up most users, but the business sector relies heavily on 6-DOF VR headsets to showcase high-end products. Being able to develop applications for both types of platforms at the same time greatly increases the reachable audience.

In the future we plan to implement our framework at a STEM summer camp for high school students to investigate how the platform agnostic VR development impacts on students' creativity, overall quality of outcomes, and engagement.

References

1. Dickson, P., Block, J., Echevarria, G., Keenan, K.: An experience-based comparison of unity and unreal for a stand-alone 3d game development course. In: 2017 ACM Conference on Innovation and Technology in Computer Science Education, Bologna, Italy, pp. 70–75 (2017)
2. Christou, C.G., Michael-Grigoriou, D., Sokratous, D.: Virtual buzzwire: assessment of a prototype VR game for stroke rehabilitation. In: 2018 IEEE Conference on Virtual Reality and 3D User Interfaces (VR), Reutlingen, Germany, pp. 531–532 (2018)
3. Ardulov, V., Pariser, O.: Immersive data interaction for planetary and earth sciences. In: 2017 IEEE Virtual Reality (VR), Los Angeles, CA (2017)
4. Sharma, S., Otunba, S.: Virtual reality as a theme-based game tool for homeland security applications. In: 2011 Military Modeling & Simulation Symposium, Boston, MA, pp. 61–65 (2011)

5. Schlueter, J., Baiotto, H., Hoover, M., Kalivarapu, V., Evans, G., Winer, E.: Best practices for cross-platform virtual reality development. In: Degraded Environments: Sensing, Processing, and Display 2017, SPIE 10197, Anaheim, CA, p. 1019709 (2017)
6. Forbes.com: Lamkin,'VR and AR Headsets to hit 80 million by 2021'. https://www.forbes.com/sites/paullamkin/2017/09/29/vr-and-ar-headsets-to-hit-80-million-by-2021/#6a4cc53824bc. Accessed 05 Jan 2019
7. ThinkMobiles.com, 'Best virtual reality SDKs to build VR apps in 2018'. https://thinkmobiles.com/blog/best-vr-sdk/. Accessed 06 Jan 2019

Study of Eye Gaze and Presence Effect
in Virtual Reality

Yoon Seok Ju[1(✉)], Joon Sun Hwang[1(✉)], S. J. Kim[2(✉)],
and Hae Jung Suk[1(✉)]

[1] Ajou University, #206 Worldcupp-ro, Youngtong, Suwon, Korea
dbdip@ajou.ac.kr
[2] University of Nevada Las Vegas, Las Vegas, NV 89052, USA
sj.kim@unlv.edu

Abstract. This study explores the characteristics of eye gaze in an immersive virtual environment. The study investigated the eye gaze data of users by using VR stimuli and analyzing users' concentration. The goal of the study was to investigate how eye movements are affected by the story of an animation. In the study, users' level of concentration as well as presence effect were measured with 53 participants by analyzing their eye gaze movements and gaze fixations.

Keywords: VR · Eye tracking · Gaze · Presence

1 Introduction

Virtual Reality (VR) allows users to experience the contents of a software program as if it was a real physical space through human senses such as sight and hearing [1]. The psychological responses and state that occur in the virtual space are called Presence. Marvin Minsky [2] uses the term "telepresence" to define the user experience as a phenomenon wherein he feels physically present in an imaginary space through feedback he receives from the machine using teleoperation technology. Steuer argues that Presence leads to a natural perception of the environment [3]. Slater and Usoh define Presence as a degree of confidence that one is in a place other than where one is, i.e. that the user has left the real world and is in a virtual environment [4]. Witmer and Singer define it as a subjective experience in which the user feels he or she is physically in another place or environment [5]. Lombard defined Presence as psychological state and the subjective perception state [6]. Kim and Yoon identified the subjective structure of an audience using 3D media through Q methodology [7]. In the Q methodology, subjectivity is determined by an individual's 'internal frame of reference' in a way that allows people to relate to the social phenomena through behavioral studies.

This study investigates the eye gaze in a VR story and measures their concentration when animation changes.

C. Stephanidis (Ed.): HCII 2019, CCIS 1033, pp. 446–449, 2019.
https://doi.org/10.1007/978-3-030-23528-4_60

2 Methodology

The FOVE HMD was used to receive users' orientation and position information. The gaze data includes information from both the left and right eyes. Tare Orientation and Tare Position match the position of different users' focus and Calibrate allows users with physically different characteristics to optimize their eyeball. The user is more likely to use the same content after optimization with the device. Interaction with FOVE was implemented as 'Unity'. Unity is an integrated creative tool for creating interactive content such as 3D video games, architectural visualizations, and real-time 3D animation, which an editor can run on Windows and Mac OS. The editor also contains an asset store for downloading needed assets directly. 'R' is a statistical analysis program specializing in data analysis, visualization, machine learning, etc. We let the user experience the virtual environment created with Unity through the FOVE HMD and analyze the user's gaze tracking data using 'R'. The mean and standard deviation of this data are determined, and the objects being viewed by the user are analyzed and visualized. For the analysis, users' x, y, z-axis time data are collected, and the average is calculated for each frame. By calculating the standard deviation using these averages it is possible to grasp how many users' eyes are scattered in each frame shown in Table 1. When visualizing the frames, researchers can specify which frames have the most eye movements and identify the objects of focus on the screen. The animation was created as typical story develop line. It is a FPS (First person shooting) game style, so the user will find he or she has a gun in front. The camera-view shows where the user sees, and the gun aims along the gaze. The BGM (Back ground music) is very heavy and dark so the user can become tense. The animation was made with the assets provided by Unity Asset store.

Table 1. User screen by frame

Intro	Frame 0: Experiment text appears on the front and no objects are visible.
	Frame 300: The phrase disappears and the screen appears.
	Frame 300: A soldier corresponding to the back label runs from behind in the same frame.
	Frames 300~1150: The soldier who ran from behind and a meteor that falls from the sky simultaneously appear on the front screen.
Rising Action	Frame 1150: The soldier stops at the front of the screen.
	Frame 2000: Two soldiers run from behind the building on the left.
Climax	Frame 2300: Aliens appear behind the building on the left. A soldier shoots an alien.
	Frame 3000: Aliens turn from the front of the screen and begin to walk in the user's direction, while soldiers flee from every direction.
Ending	Frame 3400: The alien stops at the front of the screen.
	Frame 3700: The ending phrase appears and the content ends.

3 Results and Discussions

53 people (male 27, female 26) participating first listened to an explanation of the experiment. A pre-survey was conducted to analyze the types of users before they experience the VR content. After sitting in a designated chair and putting on the FOVE HMD, the position and angle of the user could be adjusted with the Tare Orient and Tare Position functions. After adjustment, the device calibrates and optimizes the subject's gaze and eye tracking. After optimization, all participants could enjoy the experimental content. Following this, users removed the FOVE HMD and answered a simple post-survey.

Figure 1 is the SD-graphs of Presence as an extended personal enjoyment of the various experiences provided by the VR (PAEPP) (left) and Presence as sensory organ enlargement (PASE) (right). The result shows that the concentration of PAEPP is relatively low as expected from the previous study. The SD value even when the eyes are all focused is high, and the time to hold each object is also short. They react to certain events that attract attention in all sections, but they soon turn off interest and the gaze spread to various parts. The users in PASE, they not afraid of immersion. This group's data is stable with less rapid eye movement and is characterized by an ability to react to all factors vying to have their attention yet keeping a good level of concentration. See the section of 1150–2300 frame (Rising Action) in both graphs. The concentration level between PAEPP and PASE are clearly different. In the section of 2300–3400 frame (Climax), the tension of story capture PAEPP's eyes for short time, but their attention doesn't remain long as much as PASE's.

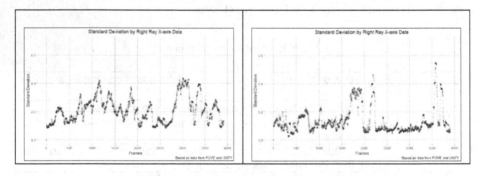

Fig. 1. Standard deviations of PAEPP & PASE

Figure 2 shows the concentration of gaze difference between men and women can be seen at a glance.

The focus intense of the experiment is initially similar for all users, but there is a clear distinction beginning near the middle frame. In the male experimental group, the concentration of section of 2300–3400 frame, which is the climax of the story, is significantly lower than the intensity of section 1150–2300 frame. Even within 'Rising Action' part, the concentration on the gaze of men is relatively low and distracted, while the gaze of women is stable and concentrated. The female users' concentration

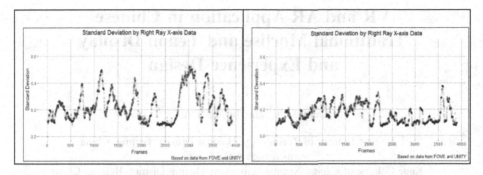

Fig. 2. Standard deviations of PAEPP & PASE in two genders.

on the section of 'Climax' is high and the gaze was collected on 'Tripod', which is the alien coming out from the front according to the data that detect from the collided objects in Unity editor.

In the story, section 'Rising Action' which is the development of the story, the number of collision event detected from the eye gaze hitting the objects were 27 times per object with the PAEPP 31 times per object with the PASE. In the section of 'Climax', the numbers were 45 times per object with PAEPP, 61 times per object with PASE. As a result, more than twice as much as the appearance of an object. The result show that the frequency of eye movements increases in the climax of the story in both groups.

4 Conclusions

This study examined the presence effect through eye gaze movements in a VR storytelling. Users' presence level in a VR storytelling is not much different from a conventional storytelling. The concentration between the two groups is related to the time length that the gaze of each type of group remains on objects in the animation. Particularly, 24% (12 out of 51) has the same gaze pattern in the climax of the VR story.

References

1. Collins Cobuild Advanced Learner's English Dictionary
2. Minsky, M.: Telepresence. Omni, pp. 45–51, June 1980
3. Steuer, J.: Defining virtual reality: dimensions determining telepresence. J. Commun. **42**(4), 73–93 (1992)
4. Slater, M., Usoh, M.: Representation systems, perceptual position, and presence in immersive virtual environments. Presence: Teleoperators Virtual Environ. **2**(3), 221–233 (1993)
5. Witmer, B.G., Singer, M.J.: Measuring presence in virtual environments: a presence questionnaire. Presence: Teleoperators Virtual Environ. **7**(3), 225–240 (1998)
6. Lombard, M., Reich., R.D., Grabe, M.E., Bracken, C.C., Ditton, T.B.: Presence and television: the role of screen size. Hum. Commun. Res. **26**(1), 75–98 (2000)
7. Kim, H.K., Yoon, Y.P.: A study on the subjective typology of stereoscopic presence. Korean J. Broadcast. Telecommun. Res. **71**, 164–204 (2010)

VR and AR Application in Chinese Traditional Mortise and Tenon Display and Experience Design

Dehua Yu[1] and Jiping Yue[2(✉)]

[1] Beijing Institute of Technology, Haidian District, Beijing, China
yudehuabit@163.com
[2] Kede College of Capital Normal University, Daxing District, Beijing, China
40664675@qq.com

Abstract. Chinese traditional mortise and tenon is one important part of Chinese traditional furniture. Traditional display methods of Chinese traditional mortise and tenon is just physical models and photos. Using the technology of VR and AR, we can not only display the 3D models on the screen, but also interact with 3D models, which adds to interaction and interest. VR and AR display demanding of Chinese Traditional Mortise and Tenon is real three-dimensional display, interaction and interest. VR display can show inside of Chinese traditional mortise and tenon, which can also control the movement and change of mortise and tenon with certain operation and gesture. AR display can set up virtual Chinese traditional mortise and tenon in the real environment, for example, the education environment and the museum environment. VR display can provide more chances to show the secrets of Chinese traditional mortise and tenon, using interaction and game settings.

Keywords: Chinese traditional furniture · Mortise and tenon · VR and AR

1 Display of Chinese Traditional Mortise and Tenon

1.1 Chinese Traditional Mortise and Tenon

Chinese traditional mortise and tenon is the connection construction of Chinese traditional furniture, which is the essence of Chinese traditional culture. Mortise and tenon comes only from the wood itself, which is carved to the concave and convex. Chinese traditional furniture uses mortise and tenon to connect the different parts of furniture, without iron nails or chemical glue. Physical glue is also used sometimes to assist the connection of mortise and tenon, which is made from pigskin and fishskin. Mortise and tenon comes from the wood itself, which is the basic parts of wood furniture. Because of the physical properties of wood are the same, and the physical deformation of heat expansion and cold contraction is the same, which can keep the furniture for a longer time. Because of the strong structure of mortise and tenon, Chinese traditional furniture can be used and saved for even several hundred years, which is one of the most important advantage of Chinese traditional furniture.

© Springer Nature Switzerland AG 2019
C. Stephanidis (Ed.): HCII 2019, CCIS 1033, pp. 450–455, 2019.
https://doi.org/10.1007/978-3-030-23528-4_61

Different parts of Chinese traditional furniture use different mortise and tenon, and the same part of Chinese traditional furniture also might use different mortise and tenon. Only after we take apart the parts of Chinese traditional furniture, can we learn and study the accurate mortise and tenon. But most of the time, we can not take apart them, the display and virtual display seems important.

1.2 Present Situation of Display and Experience Design of Chinese Traditional Mortise and Tenon

In the past years, the general display of Chinese traditional mortise and tenon are just pictures and words. The earliest people to draw the earliest surveying and mapping of Mortise and Tenon is Yang who is a famous scholar to study Chinese traditional furniture in 1948 [1].

In these years, some physical and 3D models of mortise and tenon are made to help display the secrets of mortise and tenon. Physical models of mortise and tenon are basic methods, which is used widely in all kinds of areas, for example the classes of universities and museums. However, physical models of Mortise and Tenon has its own limitation, as it paid much, there should be specific places to save, and only a limited number of people can join to touch and study the knowledge of mortise and tenon at the same time. 3D models of Mortise and Tenon can be displayed on any electronic equipment, for example computer, pad, and mobile phone, which is more flexible than physical models. You can interact with the 3D models on the screen.

However, 3D models on this electronic equipment can only be displayed on the screen, and you can not interact with 3D models freely and all the interaction is limited by modeling itself. In all, physical and 3D models are not enough to display how mortise and tenon works inside the furniture.

2 VR and AR Display Demanding of Chinese Traditional Mortise and Tenon

With the development of modern science and technology, VR and AR technology has developed rapidly, which can be used to display Chinese traditional Mortise and Tenon.

Chinese traditional Mortise and Tenon are three-dimensional objects, which has different structural information from different viewpoints. How to display the real and comprehensive details of mortise and tenon in front of people, and how to set up the interaction between people and Chinese traditional mortise and tenon, this is a good research direction.

Based on the characteristics of mortise and tenon, the display demanding of Chinese traditional mortise and tenon with VR and AR technology is as follows:

2.1 Real Three-Dimensional Display

Chinese traditional Mortise and Tenon are three-dimensional parts inside the furniture, which can not be seen outside but simple structural lines. Only by the virtual three-dimensional display, can we see the real structure through the wood. Therefore, three-dimensional display is a good way to study and interact with Chinese traditional Mortise and Tenon.

In order to get real three-dimensional models of Chinese traditional furniture, Mortise and Tenon, accurate measurement and modeling is vital. The size, scale, structure, and even the wood should be recorded accurately (see Fig. 1).

Fig. 1. A Chinese traditional folding chair and its mortise and tenon is in the process of modeling.

2.2   Interaction

The greatest advantage is the interaction of VR and AR technology. With the help of VR and AR technology, Chinese traditional mortise and tenon can be displayed in the virtual or real environment to interact with people.

In reality, the two basic condition of mortise and tenon is just fixed and unfixed. But in VR or AR environment, all different conditions of mortise and tenon can be displayed or even participated in. Here in this paper, three important scenes which are useful to display mortise and tenon are as follows:

Different Perspectives of the Process of Fix and Unfix. The process of fix and unfix can be displayed from different perspectives, which can help us catch the key and different perspective. Furthermore, all the process of fix and unfix can be played repeatedly, and you can interact in the process.

Translucent Perspective. The internal structure inside the furniture can be watched from a translucent perspective, which is impossible in reality. From the translucent perspective, we can get the connection of different parts of Chinese traditional furniture directly.

Active Feedback and Guide. In the process of fix and unfixed, some active feedback and guide can be added to help people to follow the right process and correct possible mistakes.

2.3   Interest

In the process of display of Chinese traditional mortise and tenon, Interest is one of the most important factors.

All the process of display of Chinese traditional mortise and tenon would be more attracting and effective if interest is added to. Interaction is one of the methods to add to interest. Other methods include designed environment, attractive storyline, proper game settings.

3   VR and AR Display Methods of Chinese Traditional Mortise and Tenon

Using AR and VR technology, we aim to set up an imaginary simulated environments, which is even more creative than real world. Furthermore, the combination of virtual environment and real world to set up a more exciting environment seems more attracting.

3.1   VR Display

VR Display means interacting with a virtual and immersive environment, in which the ancient life scenario and all the interior of the ancient life scenario would be shown. Chinese traditional furniture would be put on the proper position, and even ancient people or modern people live inside to perform a virtual costume play. In a particular scenario, one Chinese traditional furniture would be taken apart. Mortise and tenon inside would be shown, and we can also control the movement and change of tenon and mortise with certain operation and gesture.

For example, in a program, an ancient painting "Kazakhstan pays tribute horses to the imperial" [2] has been restored into a 3D model (see Fig. 2). Emperor Qianlong sat in a chair with a screen and a square table behind him. The furniture has be transformed into real 3D models to be shown in the virtual and immersive painting. When we walk near, certain gestures can control the furniture to move, rotate, zoom in or out, even watch the explosive view to fix and unfix the mortise and tenon inside the furniture.

To achieve this, we need certain head-mounter display device for virtual reality, for example, HTC Vive Pro and so on.

VR Display of Chinese traditional mortise and tenon can achieve a virtual environment for people to immerse inside to study the secrets of Chinese traditional mortise and tenon. The virtual environment might be historical scene, living houses, which is difficult to restore, but easy in VR Display. However, VR Display depends on the quality of modeling, simulating visual, auditory and tactile senses, and does not have any relationship with the real world.

Fig. 2. An ancient painting "Kazakhstan pays tribute horses to the imperial" has been restored into a 3D model

3.2 AR Display

AR Display applies information to the real world through computer technology. The real environment and virtual objects are superimposed in the same environment or space in the same time. AR Display imposes virtual objects into the real world, which helps display virtual Chinese traditional mortise and tenon in the real environment, for example, the education environment [3] and the museum environment [4].

The advantage of AR Display is that we can study Chinese traditional mortise and tenon in the real world without making the real mortise and tenon. With the development of modern AR and MR technology, we can use certain gestures and actions to control the virtual mortise and tenon, and also we can share the display scene with the team, to join together into the fix and unfix process. This is more real and vivid than the VR Display.

For example, in education environment, Chinese traditional mortise and tenon would be shown in front of the all the students and teacher. The teacher would explain and demonstrate the structure of Chinese traditional mortise and tenon. After the demonstration, all the students can join in the fix and unfix process on their desks. They can finish the process themselves and study further the connection. In the same time, they can communicate with other students and talk about the details of one part of mortise and tenon. It seems that there were real models of Chinese traditional mortise and tenon in front of the desks. And students can also practice and study the process in any places, which gives them more chances to study further (see Fig. 3).

In museum environment, any visitor can experience the structure of Chinese traditional mortise and tenon with the help of related devices, which saves the costs of making real models and more vivid and flexible than physical models. Some game settings can also be added to increase interest and attraction.

To achieve the AR Display, we can have the aid of hardware facilities, for example, MicrosoftHoloLens 2 [5].

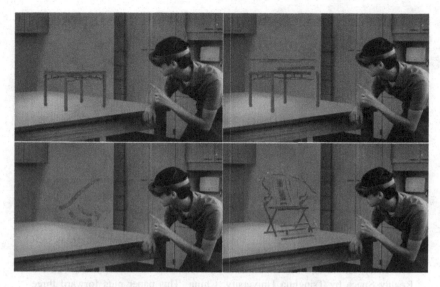

Fig. 3. The AR display of Chinese traditional mortise and tenon

4 Conclusion

Chinese traditional mortise and tenon is the particular structure of Chinese traditional furniture, which help the furniture to maintain for several hundred years to be strong. And the study and display of Chinese traditional mortise and tenon are necessary and essential.

With the help of VR and AR technology, we can display the inner structure which is invisible in real models. VR Display provides an absolute virtual and immerse scene, and we can set up a historical scene or ancient living environment to display the structure. VR Display connects the virtual objects and the real world, and we can display the virtual mortise and tenon in real world. Further research and application continues now.

References

1. Yang, Y.: Research on Ming-Style Furniture, 2nd edn. Beijing Construction Industry Publishing, Beijing (1984)
2. The painting "Kazakhstan pays tribute horses to the imperial" is collected in Musée Guimet
3. Di Serio, Á., Ibáñez, M.B., Kloos, C.D.: Impact of an augmented reality system on students motivation for a visual art course. Comput. Educ. **68**, 586–596 (2013)
4. Madsen, C.B., Madsen, J.B., Morrison, A.: Aspects of what makes or breaks a museum AR experience. In: IEEE International Symposium on Mixed & Augmented Reality. IEEE (2013)
5. Hockett, P., Ingleby, T.: Augmented reality with Hololens: experiential architectures embedded in the real world (2016)

Interactive Design for Real-World Mapping of Virtual Reality

Fengjie Zhang$^{(\boxtimes)}$ and Qiong Wu

Academy of Arts and Design, Tsinghua University, Beijing, China
zhangfj17@mails.tsinghua.edu.cn

Abstract. Immersive virtual reality brings many new challenges for interactive design because of technical limitations and virtual reality features. This paper conducts semantic analysis on case studies from 2015 to 2018 including Virtual Reality Museum design and the archaeology virtual reality game design 'Archaeological Journey to Staffa' that were participated by the author, as well as the Virtual Reality-based Earthquake Simulation System by Henan Normal University, China and the experiment Reorientation in Uncontinuous Virtual Reality Space by Tsinghua University, China. This paper puts forward three problems brought by real-world mapping of virtual reality from three perspectives and also proposes the interactive design solutions to these problems as results.

Keywords: Immersive virtual reality · Interaction design · Three-dimensional space · User experience

1 Introduction

The advantages of immersive virtual reality have been frequently mentioned by researchers in recent years: In addition to providing users with excellent immersion experience in the simulation of real activities, it is also capable of making interaction more familiar for users. The kind of virtual reality discussed in this paper is Immersive virtual reality, which offers users with immersive experience through VR googles and controllers, etc. and has been widely used.

Nevertheless, compared with traditional mobile phone and PC games, immersive virtual reality brings not only opportunities but also challenges in design, including current technical limitations such as motion sickness, lack of tactile feedback, heavy head display, etc. The way of interaction changes from finger movement to body movement; User interface becomes 3D instead of 2D [1]. These changes lead to some differences between UI design in VR and traditional 2D interface design. In addition, there are also differences between the immersive VR space and the real space, while the cognitive differences may also have an impact on user experience to some extent. Based on characteristics of immersive virtual reality, this paper discusses the real-world mapping of immersive virtual reality from the perspective of interactive design and how to solve technical problems with UX design as effective as possible, to create better user experience.

C. Stephanidis (Ed.): HCII 2019, CCIS 1033, pp. 456–460, 2019.
https://doi.org/10.1007/978-3-030-23528-4_62

2   The Significance of the Real-World Mapping of Virtual Reality

One of the application directions of virtual reality is to simulate the real world, which allows users to get more experience that can't be easily achieved in reality because of geographical and time constraints. Things or spaces that exist in the real world yet cannot be perceived by human beings can be seen and touched in VR, such as VR outer space travel and VR Pompeii.

3   Problems Caused by the Real-World Mapping of Virtual Reality and Corresponding Solutions

How to improve the user experience of real-world mapping has been discussed for a long time. A series of research has been carried out by various universities and institutions for users' cognition and interaction in VR in recent years. Problems will be discussed from the following three perspectives as follows:

(1) The better interactive behavior in the real world is imitated to virtual reality does not always lead to the better user's experience in VR.

Despite that VR can't fully simulate the real world now, many people in recent years are devoting themselves to exploring the technical solutions to improve the simulation effect of VR in the aspects of environment construction, 3D modelling, which makes it seem that the simulation degree has become one of the criteria for evaluating the application of virtual reality.

As one of the characteristics of virtual reality, discontinuous space can let users directly enter from one space to another through scene switching without corridors, stairs or other connecting spaces in real world. Experiment "Reorientation in Uncontinuous Virtual Reality Space" [2] compared the difference of human's reorientation ability in real world continuous space and virtual reality discontinuous space in 2016, which is carried out by the Department of Psychology, Tsinghua University. It has proved that the discontinuous space in VR can be rapidly adapted to by human beings, which implies that it is not necessary to completely imitate the real-world space in the design of VR application space. In actual design case, VR museum travel reflects that discontinuous space of virtual reality can make visit more efficient than real space of the real world. As one of the most renowned museums in the world, the Louvre covers an area of about 198 hectares and assumes an extreme complex exhibition area, which makes it common for tourists to get lost. Considering the characteristics of virtual reality, the two choices of "switching scenes" and "roaming exhibition hall" are provided to users, which not only greatly reduces visiting time but also enables users travel more easily by directly switching from one exhibition hall to another.

In another design case named "Archaeological Journey to Staffa", users are allowed to simulate archaeological excavation in VR game which the author participates in interaction design. After interviewing archaeologists and prototype test, we found that real excavation usually needs hours of squatting labor and real archaeological sites are often in a really large space. Lots of users put forward that "I felt pain in my knees in the middle of the excavation." and "Squatting and standing up in VR game is much more vertiginous than it is in reality." We assumed that it is not appropriate for users to experience the real excavation process in immersive virtual reality (Fig. 1).

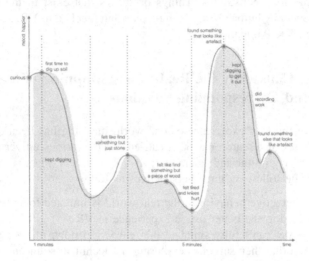

Fig. 1. User mood map in first archaeology excavation

In order to achieve the improvement of the user experience, the design strategy is to shorten the excavation time and divide the whole game into several short segments. We designed simple experiment to verify the effectiveness of the solution. The subjects consisted of five men and five women aged between 20 and 25 who were healthy and had no major diseases. In the same 2.2 * 2.2 m space, participants played the excavation game prototype with the same Oculus Rift CV1 googles and touch handle. With the shovel simulated by the handle, participants were required to swing the handle to dig the designated area and feedback their feelings through thinking aloud. Recording the user's feedback from the beginning to the completion of the task with videos, the experiment concluded that excavation immersive virtual reality for less than 2 min was considered to be a better experience by users.

(2) Existing technology shortcomings which effect user experience

Due to the lack of tactile feedback, users fail to feel tension in VR seismic simulation system in that they cannot actually be hurt by the object falling off and the crowd colliding [3]. In this design case, the designer can use game task to compensate for the tactile feedback: When the player collides with the object falling due to the earthquake, the life value of the player displayed on the interface will be reduced accordingly. This design solution successfully makes seismic simulation more real and tensive. To make up technology shortcomings, designers need to achieve a comprehensive understanding of VR technology and set a clear design goal before planning.

(3) The differences between the interface in the 3D world and that in the 2D screen
Firstly, compared with 2D interface, one of the characteristics of 3D interface is depth, while the tiny angle deviation of the handle in the 3D space may result in long distance from the target area. In addition, when users operate with interactive devices such as handles, there is usually no external objects such as desk to lean to maintain the stability of wrists and arms, which brings about the reduction of click accuracy. In order to solve this problem, it is suggested that designers to build larger 3d hot zones in three-dimensional space for keys and other operable areas and increase the distance between keys.

Secondly, users are allowed to freely look up, down or around without restriction of the screen in immersive virtual reality. At present, the operation interface and information presentation of immersive virtual reality mainly include three modes. The first one is absolutely fixation, which is more suitable for the interface closely related to the environment. While its disadvantage is that the deviation of user's visual field may cause the user to lose the target object and thus certain guidance might be required when the user's visual field deviates. The second one is complete following, a long period of which may cause users' discomfort in spite of ensuring the user's attention. It is more suitable for modal dialog boxes and other operating interfaces that have to be responded before proceeding with other operations; The third one is partial following, in which the relative position of the interface and environment is kept unchanged yet interface's angles are changed with the movement of the user's head. It makes users can see word or 2D pictures from any perspectives. These three presentation modes are expected to be integrated by designers in the actual design of immersive virtual reality interfaces.

Thirdly, despite that the immersive virtual reality interface no longer has to adapt to different sized screen, various user experience can be brought about due to different heights, pupil distance and visual acuity of users. There are two major situations for designers to judge whether to adopt self-adaptation in interface design: The first one is that the size and location of interface elements as well as the size of environment elements should be adjusted adaptively in accordance with different users' heights to provide more individualized experience for different users such as VR home decoration; The other is that if the design goal is to provide the same experience for different users, the relative size and location of interface elements are required to be consistent.

(4) The cognitive dilemma brought by VR from the perspective of social development and moral ethics
In spite of our limited power, designers should be aware of existing problems and minimize the adverse consequences of cognitive dilemmas by adopting design strategies. Three feasible solutions are put forward here: Firstly, designers can set time limitation to prevent excessive indulgence; Secondly, violent, bloody, pornographic content and behavior should be prohibited in virtual reality application interaction design; Thirdly, VR interface and environment should remind users that they are in virtual space by displaying prompt information.

4   Conclusion

In the interactive design for real-world mapping of VR, attention should be paid to using design solutions to make up for good user experience and taking into account users' cognitive difference in the real world and virtual space from the perspective of user experience and social ethics. As the design cases shown above, Designers are able to make up for technical shortcomings with design solutions by analyzing each activity involved in the UX design, which can show interactive design's value in VR. However, we still need greater exploration and reflection in the future.

Acknowledgments. This research was supported by 2016 Culture and Arts Research Project, Ministry of Culture, P.R. China, the number is 16DG56; and 2015 Tsinghua Research Fund project "Research on Interaction Design in Smart Information Service" (2015Z21083).

References

1. Zhao, Y., Wang, F.: Primary research on nature-oriented virtual reality interaction design. Art Technol. **30**(01), 111 (2017)
2. Zhou, X., Wan, X., Du, D.: Reorientation in uncontinuous virtual reality space. Acta Psychologica Sinica **48**(08), 924–932 (2016)
3. Lv, Z., Wang, T., Zhang, F.: Design of earthquake escape game based on VR technology. Comput. Knowl. Technol. **11**(11), 208–209 (2015)
4. Rua, H., Alvito, P.: Living the past: 3D models, virtual reality and game engines as tools for supporting archaeology and the reconstruction of cultural heritage. J. Archaeol. Sci. **38**(12), 3296–3308 (2011)
5. Loiseau, M., Lavoué, E., Marty, J.-C., George, S.: Raising awareness on archaeology: a multiplayer game-based approach with mixed reality. In: 7th European Conference on Games Based Learning (ECGBL 2013), October 2013, Porto, Portugal, pp. 336–343 (2013)

Investigating the Interaction Experience with Augmented Reality Based Writing Tools

Wei Zheng[✉], Xin Yi, and Yuanchun Shi

Pervasive Human-Computer Interaction Group, Department of Computer
Science and Technology, Tsinghua University, Beijing 100084, China
18530991509@qq.com

Abstract. The contents of this paper include the design methodology of perceptual computing products, the innovative design of the AR writing and its technical feasibility, the writing interactive experience test of different hardware platforms, etc. It has certain reference value for the research work of paperless writing.

Keywords: AR (Augmented Reality) · Writing interaction · Design methods · Paperless writing · Intelligent pen

1 Introduction

With the development of micro-element technology, portable hardware with various sensing and computing functions is gradually reduced in volume, and paperless writing tool is an important portable device. However, most of the writing work is still carried out on the traditional paper, which not only causes a negative impact on the environment, but also has a certain degree of obstacles to work sharing, collaborative work and so on. With the rapid development of scientific and technological products, there are our theoretical research on writing interactive tools and the exploration of product forms are still insufficient to some extent.

2 Related Works

At present, the writing instruments are characterized by their different performance in the writing process and they vary considerably in their portability and the sharing and collaborating of manuscripts. There is no product which can not only possess many properties consisting of the good writing performance, good portability, datamation of manuscripts and the sharing and collaborating of manuscripts, but also possess the characteristics of the paperless concept aimed to protect environment and the preservation of eyesight.

The thesis is aimed to explore the new plan of writing instruments, come up with the reliability argument and the new design plan based on the experimental data of users in order to deal with the problems of traditional writing instruments and the current intelligent writing instruments, provide the design thoughts and demonstrative

© Springer Nature Switzerland AG 2019
C. Stephanidis (Ed.): HCII 2019, CCIS 1033, pp. 461–466, 2019.
https://doi.org/10.1007/978-3-030-23528-4_63

results for the paperless process and popularity of new writing instruments and office, further optimize the design of paperless writing instruments, improve the users' interactive experience of writing, drawing, learning and working.

3 Writing Tools

3.1 Design Methods and Results

For a new type of product with perceptual and computing functions, previous products can not provide a clear new use requirements, and it is difficult for us to speculate on the function settings of new products. As for the current pain point, how to deduce the functional requirement of new intelligent product, design its function combination form and interactive scheme, this process is difficult to conduct without the combination of design method. Therefore, this paper puts forward the design methodology for perceptual computing product, and then to guide the design process of perceptual computing products (Fig. 1).

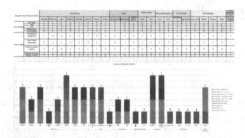

Fig. 1. Context/situation interactive map

Context/situation interactive map is an interactive design plan which is characterized by broader adaptability and wider application situations. The content consists of two dimensions, such as the users' application situation and their interactive action. The design thoughts can be divided into two parts:

(1) Firstly, it achieves the integrating design aimed at the feedback of writing and eyesight and complies with the principal standards in the field of interactive design. –'direct interaction'
(2) As for the nib and body, it is very important to pay more attention to the material choice and the pressure sensitivity of nibs (Fig. 2).

3.2 Explore Technical Details

This paper focus on the exploration and compare of technical details of portable writing tools with augmented reality, so as to obtain the technical scheme of AR (Augmented Reality) writing tools, and then to verify the technical feasibility of the first step design

Fig. 2. The Pen body and interaction design

scheme and revise the design scheme by cyclic verification and finally realize the unity of feasibility and availability.

Content can be displayed on the desktop when the writing instruments are active by using the technology of Pico-Projector. The virtual content can be displayed on the plane in the real world. Users can work by holding the pen in the area and complying with the writing method of direct interaction. The technology of the light module is divided into three types, such as the process of processing light, the light source technology and the technology of ray path projection (Fig. 3).

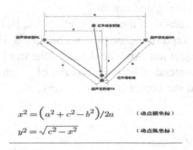

$$x^2 = \left(a^2 + c^2 - b^2\right)/2a \qquad (\text{动点横坐标})$$
$$y^2 = \sqrt{c^2 - x^2} \qquad (\text{动点纵坐标})$$

Fig. 3. Technical details

3.3 User Experiment and Comparative Analysis

Based on situational simulation AR writing, to carry out the user experience, which can be divided into two aspects: one is the influence of different setting of writing interface on writing experience; the other is the influence of different environment on writing experience. Based on the experience test data of AR writing condition, to conduct the horizontal contrast test and statistical analysis. There are two main contrast objects: one is the traditional paper writing data; the other is the writing data based on touch screen. On the basis of the statistical results, to discuss the correlation between the writing data under projection and the other two kinds of data, so as to obtain the quantitative report of writing experience under augmented reality (Fig. 4).

The writing instruments with touch screens: With its touch and digital screen, the AIO named Wacom embodies the feature of writing. The size of its screen is larger than the standard size A4, one volume of the indicative data of experiments.

Fig. 4. Simulated writing environment

Paper and writing instruments: few sheets of A4 printing paper (210 mm * 297 mm, 70 g/m^2), M&G ARP50701the pen with black ink 0.5 mm, a Deli 9226 splint, one volume of the indicative data of experiments.

The tool for collection and observation: WPSONDS-1660Wscanner, subjective questionnaire, the tool for analyzing the handwriting.

Among them, the details of Chinese can be divided into three parts, such as the paragraph (the excerpt from Brief History of Humankind), special words (力, 需, 厦, 永, 教, 六, 毡) and handwriting and poems

The details of English consist of the special letters (A, B, C, E, H, J, K, M, O, R, S, X, Z the letter case), paragraph (the excerpt from Shelley's The worship the heart lifts above, And the heavens reject not, And the desire of the moth for the star, Of the night for the morrow); Arabic numerals (0–9); the content of graphic plotting consists of the basic geometric figure and the copies of patterns (Fig. 5).

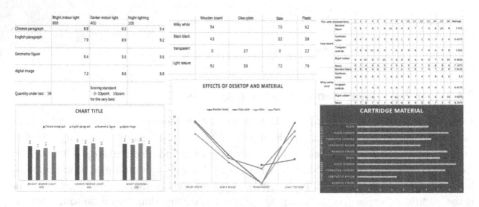

Fig. 5. Test data

According to the comparative analysis of the writing environment and instrument factors of the writing instruments of augmented reality based on the desktop projection, the results can be summarized as follows:

1. The nib uses the hard rubber material.
2. Desktop color priority ranking: white > light color > dark color > transparent
   Material priority ranking: wood > plastic > stone > glass
3. The illumination priority ranking in the writing environment (100–400 lx) > under
   50 lx > above 500 lx (Fig. 6).

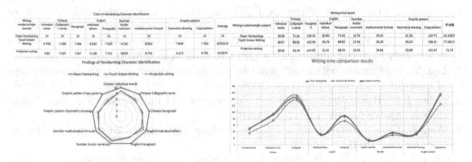

Fig. 6. Test data

According the analysis of identifying the writing time, the results are attained as follows.

1. Taking the paper writing as the criteria, the writing time of digital products can add 7–9% for the same sample.
2. The writing time spent in touch screen is as same as the time in AR writing.

All in all, the new writing instruments apply the method of handwriting identification different from touch screen, the short-focus projection method which is rare in the desktop writing, transform the ordinary desktop into the interactive area in writing by the method of AR, and verify the availability of the writing experience and efficiency through experiment tests.

References

1. Leng, Q.: Research on high precision ultrasonic ranging method and device, pp. 21–37. School of Control and Computer Engineering (2015)
2. Weining, N., Zuyang, Z., Wei, Z., Sanguo, L., Sheng, L.: High-precision ultrasonic measurement system for micro-distance. Instrum Tech. Sens. **1**, 1–2 (2014)
3. Hu, Z.: An intelligent Chinese handwriting tool with stroke error detection. University of Science and Technology of China (2010)
4. Jongmans, M.J., Linthorst-Bakker, E., Westenberg, Y., Smits-Engelsman, B.C.M.: Use of a task-oriented self-instruction method to support children in primary school with poor handwriting quality and speed. Hum. Mov. Sci. **22**, 549–566 (2003)
5. Zhuge, J.: Precise ultrasonic method based on self-adaptive wavelet denoising. J. Jilin Univ. (Eng. Technol. Ed.) **2017**(4), 1302–1303 (2017)

6. Ghali, B., Mamun, K.A., Chau, T.: Long term consistency of handwriting grip kinetics in adults. J. Biomech. Eng. **136**(4), 221–224 (2014)
7. Chen, X.: Empirical research on the characteristics of common handwritten written in four standing positions, pp. 12–13. East China University of Political Science and Law (2016)
8. Huang, F., Gao, N., Qiu, H., Li, Y.: The correlation experiment between neatness of touch screen writing and paper writing. Instr. Teach. Prof. Dev. **2015**, 122–124 (2015)
9. Song, H., Benko, H., Guimbretiere, F., Izadi, S., Cao, X., Hinckley, K.: Grips and gestures on a multi-touch pen. In: CHI (2009)
10. Fuquan, L., Zhao Yan, W., Zhenjin, C.E., Tailiang, G.: Research on photoelectric test of the typical catadioptric ultrashort throw radio projection system. Opt. Tech. **1**, 57–58 (2018)
11. Chen, H., Gao, Y., Cheng, D., Huang, Y., Wang, Y.: Optical description and design method of annularly piecewise surface. ACTA OPTICA SINICA (5) (2018)
12. Lou, Y.: The foundational research about the pick-up and identification of pressure character of handwriting. Zhejiang University (2006)
13. Feder, K.P.: Handwriting development, competency and intervention. Soc. Res. Hydrocephalus Spinabifida **49**(51), 312–317 (2007)
14. Wen, J., Chen, J.: Multi-templates pen tip tracking algorithm based on particle filtering. Comput. Eng. **2011**(21), 48 (2011)
15. Qian, L., Zhu, X., Cui, H., Wang, Y.: Design of optical path for miniature projection systems. Laser Technol. (3) (2018)
16. An, X.: The design and implementation of intelligent writing system. Shanxi University (2016)
17. Li, Y., Hinckley, K., Guan, Z., Landay, J.A.: Experimental analysis of mode switching techniques in pen-based user interfaces. In: Proceedings of CHI, pp. 461–470 (2005)
18. Liu, P.: Several optical engineer key techniques in the LCoS Pico-project. Zhejiang University (2017)
19. Preece, J., Rogers, Y., Sharp, H.: Interaction design—Beyond Human-Computer Interaction (2003)

Intelligent Interactive Environments

Designing and Developing Architectures to Tangible User Interfaces: A "Softwareless" Approach

Lucas Barreiro Agostini[✉] and Tatiana Aires Tavares

Pós Graduação em Ciências da Computação, Universidade Federal de Pelotas
(UFPel) e Instituto Federal Sul-rio-grandense (IFSul), Pelotas, RS, Brazil
{lbagostini,tatianatavares}@inf.ufpel.edu.br
http://www.ufpel.edu.br

Abstract. This paper main goal is to explore the architectures of TUIs, discussing an integrated approach of developing this kind of interface as a generic architecture model. To do so, research in the state of art was made, using search engines and considering the RSL methodology. In the end, a new architecture will be proposed, without the use of a software layer, therefore a "softwareless" approach.

Keywords: Tangible User Interface · Hardware Design · System on Chip

1 Introduction

Human-Computer Interaction (HCI) is a multidisciplinary area that is concerned with providing design guidelines to developers who create applications to users needs and expectations. In this process, the HCI includes the **project**, the **implementation**, and **evaluation** of the interaction between users and the computer systems [14].

The difference for the applications based on **Tangible User Interfaces (TUI)** is the presence of physical objects as elements of interaction. In a scenario of tangible interactions, there is the object and a set of movements or actions that the user can perform with this physical element that recognizes this interaction and reacts visually or about the object itself or the environment [10].

Hence, if in a TUI the physical element is the input and output device of the interface, it can be assumed that the interaction process is more intuitive and natural for the user with a real-world analogy [7].

Interacting in a TUI application is different from a GUI, it is suggested that the evaluation methods currently used regularly for common graphical interfaces may not fit fully into the evaluation of a tangible application.

The objective of this paper is to compare some of the research that is being done in this area, and after that propose a new type of architecture using concepts of hardware design. Starting from results of a Systematic Review of Literature (SRL), in which other studies published were found in the last five years that

© Springer Nature Switzerland AG 2019
C. Stephanidis (Ed.): HCII 2019, CCIS 1033, pp. 469–475, 2019.
https://doi.org/10.1007/978-3-030-23528-4_64

developed TUI applications, analyzing the architectures, hardware and software used to perform them, considering their particularities.

Next section presents a theoretical background about Tangible Interaction and Hardware Design; Sect. 3 presents and discuss the results of the Systematic Review of Literature (SRL) about Architectures used in building TUIs; Sect. 4 presents a brief description of our new architectural model and Sect. 5 discusses the results and main contribution of this paper which is to show the potential of developing specific hardware to TUIs.

2   Background

2.1   Tangible Interaction

The development of TUI applications is a new process and recent research is emerging that discusses a way to evaluate this type of interface. Usually, the methods that are being applied for the development of TUIs are the same methods for UI already used in daily life. Therefore, it is probably that there are specific evaluation criteria for tangible interfaces, since this is an unconventional approach to human-computer communication.

Tangible Interaction is a term suggested by Hornecker and Buur to present a comprehensive field than TUI, considering social interaction through tangible applications, thus including the issue of interaction with the environment and body gesticulation [5].

[11] brought the term Reality-Based Interaction to conceptualize new user interaction styles for user skills. This context suggests that interaction with digital information is closer to interaction with the real world.

Reality-Based Interaction has four concepts:

- **Intuitive Physics:** the user's perception of the real world;
- **Body consciousness:** the user's notion of his body and the ability to coordinate his gestures;
- **Environmental awareness:** the user's perception of the environment around him and his ability to interact with it;
- **Social understanding:** the perception that the user has with other users in the same environment, the communication between them and the ability to perform tasks together to achieve the same goal.

2.2   Hardware Design

The development of specific hardware is known to have several advantages [18] when comparing its usage with general-purpose hardware, among these advantages are:

- **Reduced energy** consumption;
- **Reduced power** dissipation;
- **Lower price**, when producing in large scale;

In specific hardware, these advantages exist due to the fact that the embedded system will only contain the exact hardware needed for a specific application. This means that the number of transistors will be the minimum amount for the project, the frequency of operation will have the lowest value possible and the technology will not necessarily be the newest.

If the cost of producing a single unity of a System on Chip (SoC) is taken into consideration, the price of developing specific hardware would be higher than simply buying a general-purpose processor, but if we scale this production, the prices will go down to a point when the developed hardware will be cheaper than a similar general-purpose hardware [4].

2.3 Methodology

The systematization of this SRL used the software StArt (State of the Art through Systematic Review) as a tool[1] [3], which allows the creation, execution, selection, and extraction of data, within an information management software that can be shared by a group of researchers.

Two research questions were answered in the papers raised:

- (a) What approaches are used in TUIs evaluation?
- (b) What tools/instruments are used to measure the proposed goal in these TUIs evaluation?

The SRL protocol also demands to specify the search string generated based on a set of keywords defined from the most recurring ones found in the papers preliminary listed in the search:

("TUI" *or* "tangible user interface" *or* "tangible interface") **AND** ("hardware design" *or* "specific hardware" *or* "vhdl").

This search string was applied to scientific indexers who returned the collection of papers. In this mapping the following Academic Search Engines (ASEs) were adopted:

- *ACM Digital Library*[2];
- *IEEE Xplore Digital Library*[3];
- *Science Direct*[4];
- *Springer*[5].

These ASEs were selected because they aggregate a considerable amount of work within the research area considered.

In order to restrict the amount of work retrieved in this stage of selection, for subsequent extraction of the data, some criteria were used for the exclusion/inclusion of papers.

---

[1] Tool to support the planning and execution of systematic reviews. Available at: http://lapes.dc.ufscar.br/tools/.

[2] http://dl.acm.org.

[3] http://ieeexplore.ieee.org.

[4] http://www.sciencedirect.com.

[5] http://link.springer.com/.

Criteria for inclusion of papers:

- Full papers;
- Published as of 2013;
- Presents some TUI application with specific hardware.

3   Results and Discuss

The SRL was performed on the ASEs and as a result, **51 references were returned**, retrieved and stored in the StArt tool. The total set of papers resulting from this initial phase, classified according to the search engine used, is presented in Table 1.

Table 1. Distribution of papers found in each ASE

Search engine	Result	Selected
ACM Digital Library	7	1
IEEE Xplore Digital	5	5
Science Direct	18	3
Springer	21	4
Total	**51**	**13**

The first filter the group of researchers carried out a screening by analyzing: title, keywords and abstract. In order to make this selection, we used the inclusion criteria of papers, established on SRL protocol, resulting in a subset of **13 papers**. Then, the final filtering cycle involved the three researchers with a complete reading of the papers to identify the answers to the research questions. Thus the final set listed in this SRL comprises the total of **6 papers** that are listed below:

[1, 6, 12, 13, 20].

About the research questions listed above, the answers give some information to discuss:

(a) In which way is the architecture (of systems that have TUIs) built?
The SRL was able to show that all of the systems researched use the same generic structure, shown in Fig. 1(a).

Some systems have other peculiarities, but in general, can fit this basic model represented in the Figure mentioned below.

If we take [2] as an example, the architecture is built as shown in Fig. 1(b), and can be simplified to our generic architectural example in Fig. 1(a). To do so, we consider the computer, kinect and projector as our processing unit, the GUI is also used by an intermediate who controls the usage and the sandbox is our TUI.

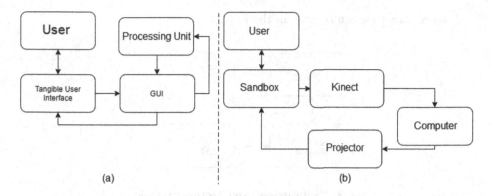

Fig. 1. (a) Basic architecture example; (b) Darley's approach to ARSandbox;

(b) Are there any solutions that do not make use of any software layer?

As far as we could search, there is not a single system that does not make use of a software layer, this comes in a lot of different ways, for instance, using an Arduino with its code written in any programming language, or even using a desktop computer or a smartphone.

4   A "Softwareless" Approach

The main challenge of a "softwareless" approach is to find an alternative architecture to the ones used nowadays. Trying to discuss this question is necessary to point out some reasons, amongst them:

- Being able to have a device that uses less energy. This is important if the goal is to develop a mobile system with TUIs;
- Develop systems that dissipate less power;
- Walk a step closer to a **"Genuine" TUI**;
- Simplification of the hardware needed;

In [8,9], the author talks about the future of TUIs, with characteristics that seem hard to reach using traditional systems. At one point, the author states that systems that use TUI usually are not multi-purpose, they can be reconfigurable but will not be generic. This fact goes in the same direction of hardware development since when hardware development is implemented, specific hardware will be used instead of a general-purpose one.

The approach came from the idea of "cutting" parts in the systems so software was not needed anymore. This can be obtained in a different number of ways like using FPGAs, describing hardware in VHDL [15,16] or even drawing each transistor [19]. Each way has its own advantages, like faster time-to-market [17], or being more energy efficient. Which way of hardware development will be used by the system builder is up to the developer, but by cutting the software you can achieve an easier usage of TUIs, like the ones in [2] and [6].

A basic structure can be seen in the Fig. 2:

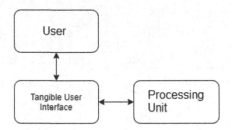

Fig. 2. "Softwareless" architecture example;

5   Conclusion and Future Works

Applications that make use of Tangible User Interfaces are something new and incorporate various forms of interaction, and just as common interfaces are evaluated the TUIs should also be.

The forms of interaction of the TUIs are diverse, the possibility of the user interacting with their body to manipulate the interaction element and the responding application in the same object stimulates the feeling of immersion.

This work evidenced the possibility to develop an appropriate architecture for TUIs without the usage of software. According to the results of the SRL developed in this work, architectures are being used in a generic way for TUIs, complicating the possibility to improve the applications.

From this study, as future works, it is intended to apply the idea proposed in a case study, which will be conducted by using a TUI system with a layer of software and developing the same TUI system without the utilization of any software. The expected outcome is that there will be no effect on the user, but will bring improvement for the system in general.

References

1. Darley, N., Tavares, T., Collares, G., Costa, V.: Interfaces tangíveis: Uma análise da experiência de usuário utilizando o projeto ar sandbox. In: Proceedings of the XVI Brazilian Symposium on Human Factors in Computing Systems, p. 16. SBC (2017)
2. Darley, N.T., Tavares, T.A., Costa, V., Collares, G., Terra, V.: Tangible interfaces: an analysis of user experience using the AR sandbox project. In: XVI Brazilian Symposium on Human Factors in Computing Systems IHC 2017, October 2017
3. Fabbri, S., Silva, C., Hernandes, E., Octaviano, F., Di Thommazo, A., Belgamo, A.: Improvements in the start tool to better support the systematic review process. In: Proceedings of the 20th International Conference on Evaluation and Assessment in Software Engineering, EASE 2016, pp. 21:1–21:5. ACM, New York (2016). https://doi.org/10.1145/2915970.2916013

4. Flamm, K.: Has moore's law been repealed? An economist's perspective. Comput. Sci. Eng. **19**(2), 29 (2017)
5. Hornecker, E., Buur, J.: Getting a grip on tangible interaction: a framework on physical space and social interaction. Proceedings of the SIGCHI Conference on Human Factors in Computing Systems, pp. 437–446 (2006). https://doi.org/10.1145/1124772.1124838
6. Hossain, M.S., Hardy, S., Alamri, A., Alelaiwi, A., Hardy, V., Wilhelm, C.: AR-based serious game framework for post-stroke rehabilitation. Multimedia Syst. **22**(6), 659–674 (2016)
7. Ishii, H.: Tangible bits: beyond pixels. In: Proceedings of the 2nd International Conference on Tangible and Embedded Interaction, pp. xv–xxv. ACM (2008)
8. Ishii, H.: The tangible user interface and its evolution. Commun. ACM **51**(6), 32–36 (2008)
9. Ishii, H., Lakatos, D., Bonanni, L., Labrune, J.B.: Radical atoms: beyond tangible bits, toward transformable materials. Interactions **19**(1), 38–51 (2012)
10. Ishii, H., Ullmer, B.: Tangible bits: towards seamless interfaces between people, bits and atoms. In: Proceedings of the ACM SIGCHI Conference on Human Factors in Computing Systems, pp. 234–241. ACM (1997)
11. Jacob, R.J., et al.: Reality-based interaction: a framework for post-wimp interfaces. In: Proceedings of the SIGCHI Conference on Human Factors in Computing Systems, pp. 201–210. ACM (2008)
12. Kubitza, T.: Apps for environments: running interoperable apps in smart environments with the meSchup IoT platform. In: Podnar Žarko, I., Broering, A., Soursos, S., Serrano, M. (eds.) InterOSS-IoT 2016. LNCS, vol. 10218, pp. 158–172. Springer, Cham (2017). https://doi.org/10.1007/978-3-319-56877-5_10
13. Liu, X., London, K.: Tai: a tangible AI interface to enhance human-artificial intelligence (AI) communication beyond the screen. In: Proceedings of the 2016 ACM Conference on Designing Interactive Systems, pp. 281–285. ACM (2016)
14. Marsh, S.: Human computer interaction: an operational definition. SIGCHI Bull. **22**(1), 16–22 (1990). https://doi.org/10.1145/101288.101291
15. Navabi, Z.: VHDL: Analysis and Modeling of Digital Systems. McGraw-Hill Inc., New York (1997)
16. Perry, D.L.: VHDL: Programming by Example, vol. 4. McGraw-Hill, New York (2002)
17. Sangiovanni-Vincentelli, A., Martin, G.: Platform-based design and software design methodology for embedded systems. IEEE Des. Test Comput. **18**(6), 23–33 (2001)
18. Stitt, G., Vahid, F., Nematbakhsh, S.: Energy savings and speedups from partitioning critical software loops to hardware in embedded systems. ACM Trans. Embed. Comput. Syst. (TECS) **3**(1), 218–232 (2004)
19. Stoica, A.: Toward evolvable hardware chips: experiments with a programmable transistor array. In: Proceedings of the Seventh International Conference on Microelectronics for Neural, Fuzzy and Bio-Inspired Systems, pp. 156–162. IEEE (1999)
20. Yeo, K.P., Nanayakkara, S., Ransiri, S.: StickEar: making everyday objects respond to sound. In: Proceedings of the 26th Annual ACM Symposium on User Interface Software and Technology, pp. 221–226. ACM (2013)

Perception of Smart Home Devices and Privacy by Chinese Users

Kathy Huang and Zhanwei Wu[✉]

Shanghai Jiaotong University, Shanghai, China
{kathyhuang16, zhanwei_wu}@sjtu.edu.cn

Abstract. Smart home products have become more and more popular in China, especially from local brands. Being connected devices, they facilitate the collection and sharing of data gathered from inside the home. However, there is little understanding how Chinese users feel about privacy in the context of the smart home. In this study, we interview nine users about smart home products and potential privacy concerns. We found three major themes: users expect products to be smarter, different aspects of privacy matter in different contexts, and protection from harm as the most important factor. These findings have design implications for both Chinese and foreign smart home companies.

Keywords: Smart home · Privacy · China

1 Introduction

Smart home devices are steadily making their way into homes around the world. In the United States, the market has seen a 31% compound annual growth rate over the last few years, with one in four Americans owning a smart home device in 2017 [1]. The smart home presents a unique set of challenges for IoT devices, in terms of set up, maintenance, and privacy. In particular, the issue of privacy is of growing interest as new regulations and privacy breaches unfold.

The concept of privacy in the smart home context for Chinese users is not well understood. While smart home penetration is higher in Western countries, China's market is growing [2]. As more Chinese users purchase smart home products and more such products are produced in China, the attitude of Chinese users towards smart home products and privacy holds relevancy.

While a number of studies have been done on the topic of privacy in the smart home [3–5], these have all been conducted in Western countries. The concept of privacy in China differs greatly from that in Western countries, with origins in the term 阴私 meaning a shameful secret [6]. Although the concept of privacy is evolving and expanding in China, one cannot assume the conclusions from studies done in Western cultures would hold true.

This study takes some first steps towards understanding the attitudes of Chinese users towards smart home products and privacy. Qualitative information is collected through semi-structured interviews with nine participants. The resulting information is then organized into a set of themes and implications are discussed.

C. Stephanidis (Ed.): HCII 2019, CCIS 1033, pp. 476–481, 2019.
https://doi.org/10.1007/978-3-030-23528-4_65

2 Related Work

The bulk of existing studies on issues of privacy in the context of smart home devices were conducted with Western users. In particular, studies have considered how individuals respond to being surveilled in the home. Oulasvirta et al. studied the longterm effects of placing recording devices in households [3]. Choe et al. determined through survey which activities individuals would be most concerned about being recorded [4].

Other studies looked at specific types of smart home products and the privacy concerns of users. As an example, Burrows et al. [7] studied the use of health-related smart home products and Ur et al. [8] studied the perception of teenagers and parents with regards to home-entryway surveillance. In a more general study, Zheng et al. interviewed smart home users to understand their thoughts and concerns regarding privacy [5].

In China, there have been studies regarding privacy in the context of social networking [9]. Wang et al. studied acceptance of IOT devices by Chinese consumers and found that perceived privacy (among other factors) would impact intention to use such products [10]. However, the perceptions of current smart home device users with regards to privacy has not been explored.

3 Research Method and Participants

To better understand Chinese users' concerns and perceptions about privacy with respect to smart home products, semi-structured interviews were conducted with nine participants over a period of four months in 2018. Due to the exploratory nature of this study, qualitative research methods were the most appropriate [11]. The user interview is a common research method in user experience, especially among design practitioners.

3.1 Participants

Participants were recruited by posting notices about the study on social media. From the responses, nine participants were chosen based on their interest and familiarity with smart home devices. The participants' ages were between 20 and 40, and there were four male and five female participants. All of the individuals except one were residing in Shanghai, China.

3.2 Interviews

The interviews were conducted over a period of four months, and done in person in Shanghai with the exception of one interviewee. Audio recordings were made for the purpose of later analysis and transcription, with the permission of the participants. Before the interview, participants were given a questionnaire to collect basic demographic information, including age, location, and profession. In addition, questions were included regarding the participants' attitudes towards privacy and their familiarity with smart home products. The smart home products the participants have used is listed in Table 1.

Table 1. Smart home products used by interviewees.

Product name	Chinese name	Description
Tmall genie	天猫精灵	Smart speaker with voice assistant
Xiaodu smart speaker	小杜智能音箱	Smart speaker with voice assistant
Xiaomi MiJia 360° smart home PTZ camera	小米小白摄像头	Smart security camera with voice assistant and app
Xiaomi air purifier	小米空气净化器	Air purifier used with Xiaomi home app
Midea air purifier	美的净化器H32	Smart air purifier
Ecovacs Deebot	科沃斯地宝扫地机器人	Robot vacuum that can be operated through mobile app
PICOOC smart body fat scale	PICOOC有品智能体脂秤	Smart scale with health app

Each interview lasted 20–30 min, starting with the devices the interviewees had used before, and then speaking about smart home devices in general. Some of the questions asked were:

- How do you use and interact with the product?
- Where was the product placed in the home?
- Who else in the household used the product?
- Did you have any privacy concerns when using the product?

Participants were also shown images of existing smart products of four types: smart speakers, smart displays, robot vacuum cleaners, and smart security cameras. The interviewer provided a brief description of the functionality and data collection of the aforementioned devices. Participants were then asked about their privacy concerns with the products, especially in the following three scenarios:

- Use of the products within a household where all members have access to the device data
- Using smart cameras, displays, and speakers for surveillance of young children or the elderly
- Visiting others' homes where such devices are installed

These questions formed the framework of the interview, but follow-up questions were asked based on the responses and specific situations of the interview participants.

3.3 Analysis

The collected interview data was processed using a simplified form of thematic analysis. Thematic analysis is commonly used with data collected from qualitative research methods such as focus groups and interviews. Only the first three steps of the standard process was used as the themes at this level of granularity is most useful for design [12]. The three steps are as follows. First, the audio recordings of the interviews were transcribed in the original language, Chinese. Then, sections of the text were coded with English phrases that captured their essence and meaning. Finally, these codes were reviewed and organized into a set of themes.

4 Findings

In general, we found that privacy was not a major concern when using smart home products, in part because they felt their devices were not capturing large amounts of sensitive data. They did have some concerns about interpersonal privacy, but by and large safety was the most important aspect.

4.1 "Smart" Home Not Smart Enough

Almost all of the participants commented on the limited 'smartness' they perceived from their interaction with smart home products. They felt that the functionality of their products was not sophisticated enough to be considered 'smart'. In particular, several participants commented on the limited ability of voice assistants to understand their speech, which led to less desire to use voice interaction. Similarly, for other products, users stopped using the associated mobile apps or other connectivity functions. Smart features were considered a novelty that users eventually grew tired of and stopped using frequently.

As such, users felt their interaction with their smart devices limited the amount and type of information exposed to the devices. One participant made a comparison between truly smart products and his smart air purifier, saying "there are smart refrigerators that can predict and buy [products], remind you of the expiration dates of the things inside. Many products similar to the air purifier app, their functionality is still relatively surface-level." This participant felt that the data collected by their products was "very simple", such as music preferences and air quality metrics, and so did not pose the threat more sophisticated smart devices might.

4.2 Privacy in Different Contexts

Within the Household. Generally, individuals considered their privacy to be protected if information stayed within household members. This finding is in keeping with the traditional Chinese view that there is little privacy within the family [6]. Since it is very common to live in a household with the nuclear or extended family, this was the living arrangement discussed in the interview.

When considering sharing access to smart home devices between family members, most individuals accepted the idea. In particular, common rooms within a house were considered acceptable places for audio or video recording devices. A couple interviewees rejected any devices since they considered the entire home a private space.

Among Friends. The relationship among friends lead most individuals to accept smart home devices in other's homes. They would trust their friends not to misuse data collected. In addition, they felt that a friend's home was not so much a private space as their own home, although this effect was heightened by the presence of recording devices. As a result, they felt they would already pay more attention to their image.

In Public. Generally, individuals felt there was little privacy in public given the amount of security cameras everywhere. At the same time, they felt there was little sensitive information they felt they needed to keep private. One interviewee said, "I think what I talk about is universal. Everybody has these problems so it's not a big deal, so I already accept - I know that anything we say might be monitored." The prevalence of surveillance in public areas desensitized participants to further data capture in the home. Participants felt that with the amount of personal information they already provide through other online services, the additional data collected by smart home devices was very commonplace and uninteresting.

4.3 Protection from Harm

Privacy was valued when its loss lead to possible harm. They were concerned about exposing information such as account numbers, passwords, and phone numbers in the presence of recording devices, primarily in the context of someone else's home. Some participants also expressed concern of being caught in states of undress if recording devices were placed in the bathroom or bedroom.

On the other hand, it was also acceptable to sacrifice some privacy for the sake of safety. All participants approved of the use of security cameras for monitoring young children and elderly relatives, and also for monitoring the home for burglars. Some did mention it was necessary to solicit the opinion the elderly first because there was some compromise to their privacy. Others were wary of parents using cameras as a surveillance tool with their children, especially older children, reflecting the generation gap in privacy concerns as noted by Dong [13].

5   Discussion and Conclusions

One of the strongest themes from the interviews was the insufficient "smartness" of their smart home products. One issue may be the lack of integration between devices. Only one of the individuals interviewed used their smart speaker as a hub to control other devices. The end effect is that people end up with a few "smart" devices rather than an integrated system, making smart features seem like a gimmick. Companies may want to spend more effort on integrating their different products, especially with their hub devices and centralized apps.

Users concern for privacy is also different in China as compared to Western countries. Overall, users seem to have lower privacy concern as compared to American users [5]. Furthermore, individuals were mostly concerned with interpersonal privacy rather than misuse of their information by the government or third party companies. These differences hold implications for foreign and Chinese smart home companies. In particular, Chinese companies wishing to expand to the global market may need to consider redesigning some functionality to suit foreign users' privacy expectations.

As an exploratory study, a small number of individuals were interviewed. These individuals were younger and mostly lived in Shanghai. Further research is needed with larger sample sizes to determine if the themes identified here hold true in the wider population. We hope this preliminary study shows the potential in further studies and the complexity of the topic of privacy and smart home technology in China.

Acknowledgements. This study is funded by the Ministry of Education Humanities and Social Sciences Fund (教育部人文社会科学基金资助) [14YJC860029]; the China Social Sciences Fund (中国社会科学基金资助) [16BGL191].

References

1. PWC: Smart home, seamless life: unlocking a culture of convenience. Consum. Intell. Ser. (2017). https://doi.org/10.1016/S0266-4356(98)90742-2
2. China Smart Home Market, Number, Household Penetration & Key Company Profiles. iGATE Research (2019)
3. Oulasvirta, A., et al.: Long-term effects of ubiquitous surveillance in the home (2012). https://doi.org/10.1145/2370216.2370224
4. Choe, E.K., Consolvo, S., Jung, J., Harrison, B., Kientz, J.A.: Living in a glass house: a survey of private moments in the home. In: Proceedings of the 13th International conference on Ubiquitous Computing (2011)
5. Zheng, S., Chetty, M., Feamster, N.: User Perceptions of Privacy in Smart Homes. In: Proceedings of ACM Hum.-Comput. Interact. (2018). https://doi.org/10.1145/327
6. Yao-Huai, L.: Privacy and data privacy issues in contemporary China. Ethics Inf. Technol. (2005). https://doi.org/10.1007/s10676-005-0456-y
7. Burrows, A., Coyle, D., Gooberman-Hill, R.: Privacy, boundaries and smart homes for health: an ethnographic study. Heal. Place (2018). https://doi.org/10.1016/j.healthplace.2018.01.006
8. Ur, B., Jung, J., Schechter, S.: Intruders versus intrusiveness: teens' and parents' perspectives on home-entryway surveillance. In: Proceedings of 2014 ACM International Joint Conference on Pervasive Ubiquitous Computing, UbiComp 2014 Adjunct (2014). https://doi.org/10.1145/2632048.2632107
9. Yang, H.C.: Young Chinese consumers' social media use, online privacy concerns, and behavioral intents of privacy protection. Int. J. China Mark. (2013)
10. Wang, H., Yan, Y., Hu, Z., Zhang, Y.: Consumer Acceptance of IOT Technologies in China: An Exploratory Study (2011). https://doi.org/10.1061/41184(419)401
11. Adams, A., Lunt, P., Cairns, P.: A qualitative approach to HCI research. In: Research Methods for Human–Computer Interaction, pp. 138–157. Cambridge University Press, Cambridge (2016). https://doi.org/10.1017/cbo9780511814570.008
12. Brown, N., Stockman, T.: Examining the use of thematic analysis as a tool for informing design of new family communication technologies. In: 27th International BCS Human Computer Interaction Conference (2013)
13. Dong, X.-P.: On the generation gap of view of privacy in family. Youth Study **6**, 8–14 (2004)

Phenomenology of Experience
in Ambient Intelligence

Sofia Kaloterakis[✉]

Utrecht University, Utrecht, The Netherlands
Sofia.kaloterakis@gmail.com

Abstract. In the last 20 years, the concept of ambient intelligence has been at the centre of technological research and philosophical dialectic around the human experience of technology. Part of this dialectic includes gaining a phenomenological understanding of the interaction of the human body with its environment, in order to adjust the environments to its needs (i.e., the being-in-the-world of Heidegger). Into this perspective of technology's convergence with the philosophical phenomenological line, this paper proposes to explore the notion of worldly experience in its different theoretical connotations, and focus on Mark Hansen's concept of worldly sensibility, that reconstructs human sensory experiences as not only determined by the subject/user, but heterogeneous and multi-scalar. The paper will raise explicitly the issue of how the understanding of worldly experience under the lens of Hansen's worldly sensibility could inform and propose models of thinking of ambient-human coevolution and entanglement. The paper will reflect into why this shift on theorization of the sensory experience is useful for ambient intelligence environments, focusing on the advances that ambient intelligence can achieve.

Keywords: Ambient intelligence · Sensory experience · Worldly sensibility · Smart environments

1 Introduction

We are in the middle of massive and significant changes of the form and application of technology, in almost all domains of human experience. This process includes the emergence of experiencing modalities of technology that have the potential to modify our biological functions (i.e. cyborgs), our perception of, and relation with, the physical world (e.g. Augmented Reality), as well as our knowledge production (e.g. VR for learning). Indeed, the numerous specializations of technology render it quite difficult or even impossible to grasp technology at its whole into the human experience, while the question remains open to possible interpretations: how do we relate to the new technological potential and co-evolve with it? This discourse has created controversies, dystopian and utopian scenarios and a sense of mystery and obscurity around technology.

Mark Hansen in 2015 has contributed along with other theorists into this discourse in his book Feed Forward: on the future of 21st century media [1]. In the first chapter, entitled *Prehensity*, Hansen analyses what he calls 21st century media, with the

© Springer Nature Switzerland AG 2019
C. Stephanidis (Ed.): HCII 2019, CCIS 1033, pp. 482–489, 2019.
https://doi.org/10.1007/978-3-030-23528-4_66

intention to understand how such media relate to humans not only as perceiving minds, but also as sensory bodies and worldly consciousness.

This paper addresses the issue of how the sensory experience is reshaped and extended by ambient intelligence applications, and how this modification leads to re-theorize sensory experience based on Hansen's insights. The idea is to connect philosophy informed theories of the environment to design the modalities of artificial environments in order to produce positive affect in the body-mind of humans.

2 Worldly Sensibility

Hansen elaborates his analysis maintaining a phenomenological understanding of experience and enriching it with an analysis of the operationality between 21st century media and human experience. To do so, he focuses on how media interrelate with humans at a level that involves not only conscious perception, but more extensively the sensory experience, which gains new meaning by the affordances of 21st century media.

Because they primarily and directly address the vibratory continuum that composes the world, twenty-first-century media must be said to impact experience through embodied and environmental sensory processes that are peripheral to consciousness and sense perception ([1], p. 38).

21st century media interact with us not only by their input to our direct conscious experience, but also through the input of all the indirect elements (non-human and environmental) that constitute part of the human experience. Our sensory experience is affected, and affects our conscious perception and memory as well. Hansen marks this revolution of the sensory experience in the light of advanced technologies, such as micro-sensors, that are able to access and visualize data that constitute what he calls worldly sensibility:

One of the crucial claims I shall advance in this book concerns the displacement of perception in favor of sensation—or rather of what I shall call "worldly sensibility"— that results as a necessary experiential correlate of twenty-first-century media ([1], p. 46).

Indeed, Hansen reconstructs a post-phenomenology of experience as worldly sensibility in continuity with Whitehead's concept of causal efficacy [2], in order to move beyond the phenomenology of human experience as intrinsically subjective or merely human. He sees 21st century media affordances as the possibility to expand our direct sensory experience and our meaning of it by entering in the domains of larger environmental networks of sensibility. Experience has to be reconnected to the environmental elements that constitute the basis of the primordiality left out of human consciousness and language. Hansen mentions as an example ubiquitous computing, which challenges to act upon these microlevels of sub-perceptual and subconscious interaction and coevolution of the human and the environment.

For, as I have already suggested, today's ubiquitous computational environments and bionic bodily supplementations operate more by fundamentally reconfiguring the very sensory field within which our experience occurs than by offering new contents for our consciousness to process or new sensory affordances for us to enframe through our embodiment ([1], p. 45).

Hansen emphasizes the direction towards which ubiquitous computing moves, which is peripheral to the human in the form of sensation as experience of the environment, enriching this experience with the use of data that already play a peripheral role in its formation. This process creates a feed-forward loop which enhances the causal efficacy of the environmental components of the experience that are not processed through our consciousness. This implies an important transformation not only of our perception, but affecting also the micro and macro functions of our bodies. All this discourse is specifically around technologies of micro-sensors, interactive ubiquitous environments and the data that constitute the body of knowledge of how we function as organisms within our bodies in continuous communication with our surroundings.

These devices meet the challenge posed by the combination of massive and multi-scalar informational complexity and fine-grained temporal acuity: because of their capacity for gathering data from bodily processes in their operational presencing, as they are actually occurring, these devices are able to overcome the opacity of consciousness, and thus to supplement consciousness with insight—"digital insight"—in which it can never directly participate but in virtue of which it can, subsequently, act ([1], p. 60).

The sphere where ubiquitous computing and other technology enact is not part of the conscious process of the world, but constitute the sensation. By gathering data related to it, such technologies can modify it and extend sensation. The components of this sensory reconstruction are to be found in brainwave, eye movements, emotional frequencies and biological data tracked from the human experience. These data can be analysed with respect to what they mean for our understanding of the world, allowing to design networks of system that interact optimally with these data of sensory experience. A moral imperative is also posed by Hansen himself regarding the distribution of the data in the feed-forward loop:

the potential offered by twenty-first-century media for data collection, analysis, and prediction—and especially for the feeding-forward of data into ongoing experience—is a potential that is, and must be made to remain, fundamentally common to all, publicly accessible, and open to multiple uses ([1], p. 74).

To exemplify the above mentioned concepts, the next section discusses ambient intelligence as an example of how sensation is enhanced and potentially extended, and analyses the dynamics of this environmental forming of human experience.

3   Ambient Intelligence and Theories of Perception

Ubiquity is the state of being everywhere, and ubiquitous computing is a form of technology that works as an invisible part of the surroundings. The term has been coined by Marc Wieser in 1999 is his seminal article *The computer for the 21st century* [3]. Ubiquitous computing turns around the idea of creating computers that serves silently and invisibly as information providers, producing calmness and a sense of unity with our human capabilities forming the background of our experience.

Wieser's idea was later re-elaborated using the term ambient intelligence, meaning the design of environments where people are surrounded by intelligent intuitive interfaces that are embedded in all kinds of objects and an environment that is capable of recognising and responding to the presence of different individuals in a seamless, unobtrusive and often invisible way [4].

The term was proposed as a vision of the future, and has attracted considerable scientific and research interest. Indeed, many computer scientists have worked around this idea during the last 20 years. Ambient intelligence is characterised by embeddedness, context awareness, personalisation, adaptiveness, anticipation.

To create the above mentioned affordances, ambient intelligence designers often use theoretical constructions of perceptive mechanisms mainly from neurosciences and psychology. Phenomenology plays a role of meta-analysis of the interaction in the technological experience or in some cases of an a priori value for design. For example, the theory of enaction in perception of Noe [5], as discussed by Morse [6], provides means for the understanding of sensorimotor perception in intelligent environments.

That is to say while sensorimotor perception is focused on the effect of bodily action on the environment, enaction is focused on the effect of environment on body. By combining the two together we can focus on the effect of actions on the environment and their bodily consequences ([6], p. 240).

Enaction in perception theoretically roots the act of perception itself in continuous interaction with the environment. In this perspective, the environmental element is indeed an intrinsic part of perception itself, in a similar way to worldly sensibility, in the sense that our bodies enact into the shaping process of perception together with environmental elements. However, the concept of enaction leaves uncovered the gap of how the environment acts a priori into this shaping. The body's own sensorimotor functions shape perception, but how the environment determines the sensorimotor functions as being intrinsic part of their shaping? This gap could be filled by theorizing the sensing functions not only as part of the body which senses the environment, but also as part of the environmental networks that create the sensory experience. The ability of technology to enact into our senses is indeed an instantiation of how the environment enacts on them. The post-phenomenological claim upon the living experience is that of a semantic order of the factors that generate a conscious experience perceptible by the senses. The environmental qualities that form the fruition of consciousness can be enhanced through mediated sensations that extend the human experience of the world through networks that reconstruct the elements of the experience. To give a macro perspective, the human experience is reconstructed by the very environment that situates the mediated micro-elements that are part of the non-conscious process of the world, but have an effect on the conscious process.

Figure 1 depicts the complementarity between enaction and wordly sensibility with respect to the environment and human perception.

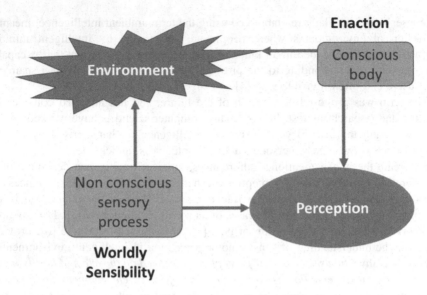

Fig. 1. Enaction vs. wordly sensibility

4 Affective and Aesthetic Qualities of Ubiquity

Technological environments are, just like living physical environment, intrinsic in the creation of the human experience and generate its affective and aesthetic qualities. Many theorists have relied upon this mediated affect to describe it as created *situationality* and *aesthetic presence*. An example of mediated sensory experience in the artistic process is Rafael Lozano's *Pulse Room*[1]. Pulse Room is an interactive installation featuring one to three hundred clear incandescent light bulbs, 300 W each and hung from a cable at a height of three meters. The bulbs are uniformly distributed over the exhibition room, filling it completely. An interface placed on a side of the room has a sensor that detects the heart rate of participants. When someone holds the interface, a computer detects his or her pulse and immediately sets off the closest bulb to flash at the exact rhythm of his or her heart. The moment the interface is released, all the lights turn off briefly and the flashing sequence advances by one position down the queue, to the next bulb in the grid. Each time someone touches the interface, a heart pattern is recorded and this is sent to the first bulb in the grid, pushing ahead all the existing recordings. At any given time, the installation shows the recordings from the most recent participants. A brilliant analysis of the aesthetic dimension of this mediation is given by Mitchell Whitelaw [7], emphasizing the materiality and the computation as elementary characteristics of media art. Whitelaw calls Presence –Aesthetics the capacity of media through their interaction with materiality to affect it by creating a situation of being-in-the-world.

---

[1] http://www.lozano-hemmer.com/pulse_room.php.

The room is full of human pulses, all characteristic double beats, faster and slower, brighter and duller, but palpably reembodied in glass and glowing wire. Pulse Room is one example of what I argue a significant turn within recent media arts emphasizing the materiality of media and computation: a materiality that we are directly implicates in, as this work show ([7], p. 181).

This process of *trans-materiality* is the dynamic creation of a situation where immaterial computing elements are fused into material presence. At the same time, this process is at the essence of the purpose of ubiquitous computing as well. The affordance of trans-material ubiquity that creates a situation of presence is relevant to Hansen's concern on all the data that process our experience while staying out of our conscious perception. In a similar way, the data that are implemented in the material presence form the user's experiences. In this context, one of the biggest challenges is how to create affective and aesthetic experiences into the interaction design process of such technological environments. How does ubiquity affect the aesthetic process of being in the world?

Coming to context awareness, the generated affect/situation can be bodily or sensible through one of the five senses, but the dimension of affective recognition is indeed difficult to entail as a user's signal. Some of the ways used are through facial expression recognition, eye tracking, motion tracking, speech tracking, but there is much more to decode towards the creation of affective computing, leading to the basic debate of whether an algorithm will ever be capable of detecting human emotions and fundamentally interact with them in a human-human like way.

5 Future Perspectives

Worldly sensibility constitutes a lens to enlarge the understanding of phenomenology of experience by linking it to the wider context where experience happens. Indeed, this connection is reflected in ubiquitous computing and ambient intelligence systems. There have been many applications of smart environments with the aim of creating affective responses to the user and/or of creating an aesthetic quality. As it is difficult to technologically create human affective mechanisms, the affective quality may cause controversy and even fear. As for the aesthetic quality, ubiquitous materiality is embedded into media art, thus potentially creating a mode-of-being (a situation of experience) and aesthetic presence.

What does worldly sensibility mean then for ambient intelligence and how can post-phenomenology inform system design? One possible answer is by returning to Hansen's feed-forward loop, involving the data that our senses give to the system, whose output in turn can enhance our senses: touch, vision, smell, sound but also frequencies and aspects that we cannot sense. The objective is to create an extra-sensory augmented experience, or to even create environments that enhance harmony into the situation where we are immersed. In the book *See yourself sensing* by Schwartzman [11], there are plenty of case studies of connecting technology with the body as a form of artistic exploration of human capabilities. Examples are LED eyelashes and goggles that allow their user to communicate with an electric fish, and solar-powered contact lenses that augment reality.

While all these stand as examples of extended consciousness and sensory experience through mediation which modify the way-of-being, more attention should also be paid to smart environments that interact with humans through creating a sensory experience which is aesthetically present and which form the process of environmental consciousness. Much research has also been conducted on sensory augmentation [8], meaning the translation of non-human sensor data to signals that are compatible with the human senses and can therefore augment our abilities to make sense of the world, as well as sensory substitution, meaning the translation from one sensing modality to another one, and implanted human–machine technologies [9]. While we gain more understanding of the co-evolution of the human body with the environment, we can create these environmental elements to regulate this interaction. By this means, we can create the worldly sensibility that we experience by using the micro-elements that make it happen.

Human experience, in a post-phenomenological perspective, is a derivative of environmental micro-elements that can be tracked by technology and implemented into forming new senses, and by doing so new body and aesthetic experiences. This process of becoming would eventually operate the same way Hansen describes worldly sensibility, as a process that is not generated by conscious elaboration but by simply being into the space with the body. This theoretical framework of environmental becoming can be enhanced by ambient intelligence design. In this way, the design would inform the interaction of, for example, our body situation with the atmospheric elements or the surrounding frequency, and the result would be an environment which forms the small invisible details of our being in the world. In a similar way, this operation can include other variables such as brain-wave activity and sound. At a philosophical level, this provides a perspective of the scope and the scale of future evolution for such technologies. This is to reform the body experience through new senses that can be of artistic nature, of biotechnological, of medical technology or of mixed combinations. By intelligently connecting the above with the affordances of ambient intelligence design, we can explore and create grounds that are fruitful for all the domains of philosophy of consciousness, phenomenology, HCI, and design research, among others, and hold straight the bond where these disciplines meet and exchange knowledge. In this trajectory, we have to insert more speculative design before the practical and technical part, as well as a more humanistic and moral imprint into technological logic. An example of such moral evaluation is the concept of material morality introduced by Verbeek [10], which aims to the construction of a priori values intrinsic in the design process.

Every future vision of technological development or use of already existing technology should include a priori a moral evaluation of its role into humanity. While technological design can take the form of artistic involvement and participation of the senses, it can also be merely function oriented. This is the reason why technological design is intrinsically responsible towards people as humans and not as consumers. The functionality needs to be directed by the intention that the mediation is creating and needs to be anticipated before the mediation system is in use. Peter Paul Verbeek [10] describes engineering design as material morality, and argues that the mediated connections purpose should be the freedom of the experience:

The material situatedness of human existence creates specific forms of freedom, rather than impeding them. Freedom consists in the possibilities that are opened up for human beings to have a relation to the environment in which they live and to which they are bound." ([10], p. 275)

Valuing morality in technological design would mean rebuilding the human experience of the situated environment for the freedom of the possibility to relate to it through the mediation of sensory perception and consequently to reform the human body as part of this environment. The future view of design and philosophy integrating in order to build meaningful ways of constructing possible mediations is because they play an essential role in the knowledge production and the human evolution. Not few are the opposite voices that perceive technology's potential as dangerous and destructive, but the key issue lies in how to design intelligent environments which exploit human data in a way that improves and does not hinder human-human and human-technology communication.

References

1. Hansen, M.B.N.: Feed-Forward: On the Future of Twenty-First Century Media, p. 320. University of Chicago Press, Chicago (2015)
2. Whitehead, A.N.: Process and Reality. Free Press, New York (1929/1978)
3. Weiser, M.: The computer for the 21st century. SIGMOBILE Mob. Comput. Commun. Rev. 3(3), 3–11 (1999)
4. Information Society Technologies Advisory Group: Ambient Intelligence: from Vision to Reality (2003). ftp://ftp.cordis.lu/pub/ist/docs/istag-ist2003_consolidated_report.pdf
5. Noë, A.: Action in Perception. MIT Press, Cambridge (2005)
6. Morse, A.F.: Snapshots of sensorimotor perception. In: Muller, V. (ed.) Philosophy and Theory of Artificial Intelligence. Studies in Applied Philosophy, Epistemology and Rational Ethics, pp. 237–250. Springer, Berlin (2013)
7. Whitelaw, M.: Transmateriality: presence aesthetics and the media arts. In: Arns, I., Auner, J. (eds.) Throughout: Art and Culture Emerging with Ubiquitous Computing. The MIT Press, Cambridge (2013)
8. de Rooij, A., et al.: Sensory augmentation: toward a dialogue between the arts and sciences. In: Brooks, A.L., Brooks, E., Vidakis, N. (eds.) ArtsIT/DLI -2017. LNICST, vol. 229, pp. 213–223. Springer, Cham (2018). https://doi.org/10.1007/978-3-319-76908-0_21
9. Bach-y-Rita, P., Kercel, S.W.: Sensory substitution and the human-machine interface. Trends Cogn. Sci. 7(12), 541–546 (2003)
10. Verbeek, P.P.: Moralizing technology: on the morality of technological artifacts and their design. In: Readings in the Philosophy of Technology. Rowman and Littlefield Publishers (2009)
11. Schwartzman, M.: See Yourself Sensing: Redefining Human Perception. Black Dog Publishing, London (2011)

Effective User Interface of IoT System at Nursing Homes

Jérémy Lenoir(✉)

Z-Works, Inc., 4-21-19 Shimo Ochiai, Shinjuku-ku, Tokyo 161-0033, Japan
jeremy@z-works.co.jp

Abstract. Aging population is a serious social problem in many countries. Currently, the elderly in Japan often spend the last 10 years of their life in bed in poor quality of life, whether it is at home or in a facility. By 2020, 3 out of 10 people will be over 65 years old, thus increasing drastically the demand of caretakers.

Z-Works has developed a new IoT system that uses of a combination of non-wearable sensors deployed in senior's room that is easy to install and adapted for the elderly care environment. Each of these sensors can detect a large variety of information from motion to heartbeat information without disturbing the senior's daily life. From the sensors, the information is transmitted to a centralized server from which it analyzes and detects patterns indicating an abnormality. The centralized server then proceeds in sending visual alert notifications to indicate that a caregiver should visit the senior's room.

This notification approach is a crucial element of our system. While controlling the amount and frequency of information to provide, it transforms raw data in a way untrained caretaker can absorb without difficulty. Current similar systems simply transmit raw information that are visually inadequate for most. Therefore, our visual alert as well as an integration into existing nurse call system can convey the information more effectively than others.

Z-Works has shipped more than 4,000 devices to over 150 facilities all over Japan. The Z-Works system provides three key values to elderly care facilities: improved operational efficiency as staff can sort in what is more and less important based on the notifications; improved care as staff get more aware of when emergences happen; and reduced staff retention as staff feel more peace of mind with the right supportive tools to handle a heavy responsibility.

Keywords: Elderly care · IoT · Quality of life

1 Introduction

1.1 Current Situation

Modern day elderly care does not use recent advanced technology in large scale. This lack of adoption from the market indicates that the existing solutions are not meeting the desired results for the care givers.

Most elderly care facilities are still heavily relying on simple call system. This system is in many cases not enough to provide useful information to the care givers. To

C. Stephanidis (Ed.): HCII 2019, CCIS 1033, pp. 490–498, 2019.
https://doi.org/10.1007/978-3-030-23528-4_67

improve the workflow and the efficiency of the care, new systems are required. Those systems will need to be driven by the need of the care givers, to adapt to the specific environment of a facility and to provide new type of information that will help knowing the situation in the room without disturbing the senior [1].

1.2   Problem

Due to the specific environment in elderly facility, where senior suffer from wild range of health problem and mental condition, technology company has often failed to modernize the market. Several problems are observable:

Showing data, such as temperature, humidity, luminosity or presence, without any purpose is one of the main issues that the industry needs to overcome. Displaying data without any meaning is a complains from carers we interviewed. They do not understand or do not know what to do with the information. Rather than simply showing data, like typical IoT system for home use [2], the system must translate it into a human readable information so that it will be easily interpreted by the care givers.

Systems are not made to improve the workflow, and thus, the added value of such solution are not understood by the care givers. By improving the workflow of the work done, the system proves that it is useful. As an example, knowing if the senior is awake or not can allow care givers to avoid checking in the room if everything is alright.

Learning phase is critical in the adoption of new systems. Care givers has limited time to adapt to a new system and do not have high medical degree that would help them to link data together and make a diagnosis.

2   Objectives

Our objective is to create an effective user interface with a rich ecosystem of connected devices and based on a solution using analytics that provide needed information to the end user.

We will look at solutions from Z-Works and some competitors that are trying or tried to combine similar elements either partially or fully and analyse components that fails or succeed to answer the problems.

3   Method

Several solutions were studied to achieve a product that satisfy the end user. We've made an evaluation between solutions from Konica Minolta, Paramount Bed, Carecom, Medicustek and Z-Works solution in terms of system usage, privacy concerns and carers' needs.

3.1 Konica Minolta

Konica Minolta has created a care support solution primary focus on improving the work efficiency of carers by using a detection sensor and visualize the information via smartphones. The solution can be used for elderly healthcare facility or in-home care.

The solution is simple to install and provide basic information regarding the condition of the senior when being under the device. The device needs to be placed on the ceiling and pointing toward the bed for optimal results (Fig. 1).

Fig. 1. Activity recognition algorithm of Konica Minolta's solution [3]

3.2 Paramount Bed

Paramount Bed has created a sensor called "Nemuri SCAN", it can monitor the senior's sleep-wake activities in the bed in real-time. The objective is to provide the information in real-time to carers via a simple interface and adapt the colour of the tile whenever there is a change in activity.

The solution is relying solely on this sensor for the entire solution and does not require a server to work. The main interface displays the current situation in the bed in a simple to understand way (Fig. 2).

3.3 Carecom

Carecom is using a solution based on a matt sensor placed alongside the bed. It is connected via a cable to the nurse call system and can provide immediate alert when someone is touching it. This alert is then displayed on a call board in the nurse station or via a phone (PHS type) to the carers (Fig. 3).

3.4 Medicustek

Medicustek's solution relies on a sensor pad and mattress placed on the bed which provide the information to their system. They are providing several methods to

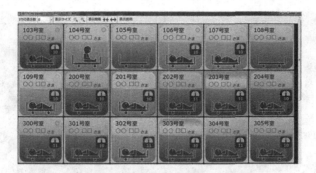

Fig. 2. Real-time monitor [4]

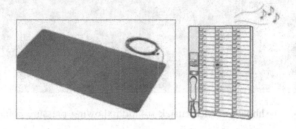

Fig. 3. Mat sensor placed next to the bed and the call board in the nurse station [5]

interface with the user, such as a mobile application and a dashboard to monitor from nursing station or on the go (Fig. 4).

3.5 Z-Works

Z-Works solution relies on using hardware developed with our partners, a centralized server, local or cloud-based, and a front end. The server receives data from the hardware which will then be analysed, the output being provided to the front end when necessary (Fig. 5).

The key element is to provide only analysed information to the user. While being available, most carers do not see all the data that our system has received. This is intentional, the system is filtering the information for the user so that only useful and meaningful data is visible (Fig. 6).

Our analytics processing unit and detect an abnormality in a situation and provide the information as an alert (Fig. 7):

4 Results

Z-Works solution has moved from demo setup to production in last 2 years, and it continues to evolve based on feedbacks from carers and seniors. Consequently, this study is still in progress and feedbacks are still being received and analysed.

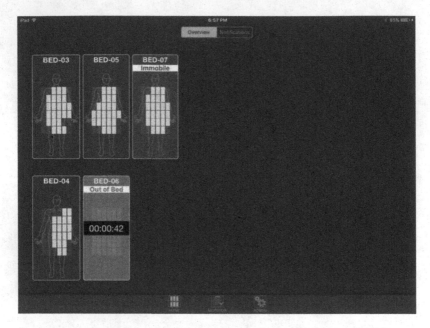

Fig. 4. Dashboard of Medicustek solution showing pressure point [6]

Fig. 5. Z-Works solution overview and Main user interface (Live Connect Facility)

Konica Minolta, while answering some needs of carers, is intrusive due to the use of a camera on top of the bed.

Paramount Bed is limited to bed activity and not the entire room, carers cannot tell if the senior is in toilet or if a fall occurred.

Carecom mat sensor is wildly used sensor in facility in Japan, however this sensor is very sensitive and has a large amount of false alert. A simple sound alert is displayed on the call board and increase the stress of carers through the false alert. It is not a reliable system in the eye of carers.

Medicustek provide a comprehensible interface but limited in term of functionality, no vital signs information is available to provide in-depth analysis.

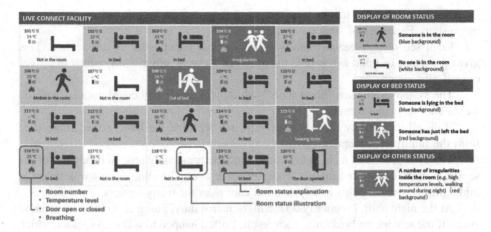

Fig. 6. Explanation of each element of the User Interface

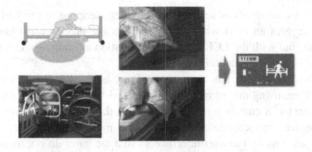

Fig. 7. Alert of possible leaving/falling from bed

Z-Works solution is viewed as to answer the concerns of carers in terms of usability and comprehension, while the other listed previously are regarded as limited in the usage due to concern with the technology used (Fig. 8).

Fig. 8. Installation of Live Connect Facility in a Japanese elderly care facility

The user experience has been positive and provided useful information to improve the system. Examples of such comments:

"I can see status of each room while processing paper work at care station. This gives me peace of mind and enable me to better focus on other work, which improves overall efficiency".

"The system eliminates "blind spots", which you previously could not verify if you weren't in the actual room".

"With all the activity records been kept, we feel that we have gained more trust from the family of seniors".

"The system enables us to better understand the previously unseen behaviour of the senior at night time. For example, going to toilet every 30 min, always waking up at midnight, etc. which helps to improve the care plan for many seniors."

"At the night shift, I regularly do the night patrol duty, going from room to room to check if the seniors are breathing. As a result, I often happen to wake up seniors, which leads unnecessary troubles. With LCF I can do this remotely with collected vital data, which significantly reduces the burdens for the staff at night and improve the experience for seniors".

"We have many incidents of seniors falling when stepping out of bed at night. Mat sensor (which triggers an alert when steps on it in the proper way) has not been of much help for us, but with the LCF we get a notification as soon as someone is about to leave the bed which is very useful".

Additionally, the system has been recognized as a compliance tool for facility management. When using one of our most advanced sensors, the "Piezola" sensor, we were able to detect if a care is provided as expected. In the case shown in the figure below, the care was missed around 01:00 in the morning, such case can trigger a warning and an alert using our user interface so that the carer do not miss an important care (Fig. 9).

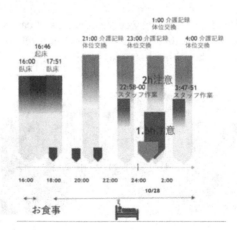

Fig. 9. Result of Piezola sensor from a facility showing a warning (Yellow) and an alert (red) (Color figure online)

5 Conclusion

From the feedbacks and the response from the early adapter, Z-Works solution has started to change the market by providing a comprehensive and intuitive solution to the care givers. They can visualize the situation of each room effectively where before they had blind spot using the set of non-wearable sensor, thus improving the workflow. The data visualization is now translated into an alert system that is provided via the analytics processing unit and remove any burden on reading complex data for the care givers.

5.1 Limitations

The solution has limitations that might affect the user, but some limitations are in place in order to have a high level of accuracy.

On the sensor side, due to privacy concern, cameras cannot be used everywhere and sometimes requires written agreement. Sensor accuracy has a limitation such as delay in reading information or providing results. Elderly care has limitation in term of cost, large scale modification of room is not a practical solution and would be limiting the market of a solution.

The main target of these systems is often focused on facility and not in-home care; thus, such systems are not directly applicable to such market. Adapting these systems would requires a consequent amount of customization and therefore, being not practical at this point.

5.2 Improvements

Clear improvements are necessary for the system, such as improving the alerting system to provide more diverse information to the end user or increase the frequency of data reception.

Providing long term trend and predictive information by using the data over a long period is an improvement that is likely to be the next essential element to be included. This improvement will require to re-think the user interface to provide a potential risk for the future.

All improvements will need to be tested and analysed to verify that they are used and effective for the carers.

References

1. The Journal of mHealth. https://thejournalofmhealth.com/could-carer-technology-help-battle-elderly-loneliness/. Accessed 26 Mar 2019
2. Mort, M., Milligan, C., Roberts, C.: Ageing. Technology and Home Care. Presses des Mines, Paris (2008)
3. Konica Minolta. https://www.konicaminolta.com/uk-en/future/care_support/index.html. Accessed 26 Mar 2019

4. Paramount Bed. https://www.paramount.co.jp/english/product/detail/index/20/96. Accessed 26 Mar 2019
5. Carecom. https://www.carecom.jp/global/solutions/option/#mat. Accessed 26 Mar 2019
6. MedicusTek. https://www.medicustekusa.com. Accessed 26 Mar 2019

Designing Value-Centric AmI: Building a Vision for a Caring AI Using Ambient Intelligent Systems

Scott Penman[✉], Sara Colombo, Milica Pavlovic, Yihyun Lim, and Federico Casalegno

MIT Design Lab, Cambridge, MA, USA
sdpenman@mit.edu

Abstract. The proliferation of Artificially Intelligent agents and embedded, publicly-available sensing systems has placed great importance on the field of study known as Ambient Intelligence (AmI). AmI systems point to a future where urban areas are at least partially aware of (and responsive to) their inhabitants.

AmI systems present significant technical hurdles for implementation; less studied, however, is their potential impact in terms of user experience. This research reviews the process of creating a design vision for such a system, where user values act as the driver for design. Specifically, the process of designing a vision for a future personal lighting AmI, in collaboration with a leading light provider, is used as a case study to describe a framework for the generation of a caring AmI system.

In order to keep the idea of a caring AmI system at the center of the design vision, a value-centric design approach is utilized. Furthermore, scenario-based design is used to construct a series of storytelling videos that describe various possible interactions of users with the system and communicate the user values.

As an additional contribution, the scenarios were then dissected using a graphic scene-by-scene analysis. This technique provides an armature for hosting the complex discussions needed to review both the technological features and user values inherent to any future AmI system.

Keywords: Ambient Intelligence · User experience · User values · Design vision

1 Introduction

The proliferation of Artificially Intelligent agents and embedded, publicly-available sensing systems has placed great importance on the growing field of study known as Ambient Intelligence (AmI). AmI systems point to a future where increasingly dense urban areas are aware of, and responsive to, their inhabitants. Such a category of connected, intelligent systems extends beyond the private environs of the home and instead exists in the contexts that define our workplaces, our transit routes, and our everyday interactions in the public sector.

© Springer Nature Switzerland AG 2019
C. Stephanidis (Ed.): HCII 2019, CCIS 1033, pp. 499–506, 2019.
https://doi.org/10.1007/978-3-030-23528-4_68

The technical and infrastructural hurdles facing the successful construction and deployment of AmI are high, and include research on everything from context awareness and interfacing inputs to behavioral studies and privacy concerns. Less studied, however, is the potential impact of AmI in terms of user experience. While the fields of user experience design and, more recently, value-sensitive design have made great strides in bringing these topics to the forefront of HCI discussions, significant effort is needed to ensure they remain central to discussions of AmI. In this research, we review a process of designing a vision for a future AmI system that keeps user experience - specifically, user values - at the center of the design.

The design process in question is the result of a year-long collaboration with a leading lighting provider. Thus, the vision for the AmI system in question is modeled as a personal lighting AmI agent. The central challenge was to envision an AmI agent that utilized connected lighting to create a more caring city. The proposed design vision takes advantage of near-future technological advances, both in terms of artificial intelligence and interface design. As a future-looking vision, this proposal acknowledges that possible technological advancements have the potential to raise unforeseen questions during the design process. Consequently, the broader challenge of designing an AmI agent is to allow for such unknowns without shifting the focus away from human-centered design.

2 Background

2.1 Ambient Intelligence

Ambient Intelligence is defined as a specific class of information communication technology (ICT) applications enabling physical environments to become sensitive, adaptive, and responsive to human activities (Mukherjee et al. 2009). AmI systems define a new landscape for human-computer interaction, since interactions cease to be directly human-to-machine. Streitz (Streitz 2007) goes so far as to argue in favor of a transition from Human–Computer Interaction to Human–Environment Interaction, which in turn leads to responsive environments (Alves Lino et al. 2010). Cook et al. (2009) explain that AmI systems are sensitive, responsive, adaptive, transparent, ubiquitous, and intelligent.

Beyond the integration of ICT devices into the physical environment, the AmI paradigm promotes the creation of new, enhanced user experiences (Aarts and Encarnaçao 2006). AmI systems can involve AI agents (O'Grady et al. 2013; Burr et al. 2018) and perform as autonomous systems (Gams et al. 2019). Furthermore, because AmI systems must be sensitive, adaptive, and responsive to people, they must be aware of their preferences, intentions, and needs (Plötz et al. 2008).

2.2 Scenario-Based Design and Value-Centric Design

Value-Sensitive Design is a design approach that incorporates considerations of shared human values into the design of technological systems, where values refer broadly to what people find important in life (Friedman et al. 2006). Similarly, Goguen (2005) uses the term Value-Centered Design to argue for the design of complex technological systems that consider the values of user communities. This approach becomes essential to the development of socially sensitive design as increasingly complex technological systems expand their impact on users and communities. Furthermore, human values are becoming increasingly central to discussions of HCI. One method for studying these interactions is Scenario-Based Design, where the use of a system is held central to the design process through narrative descriptions of possible usage scenarios (Rosson and Carroll 2003). Nathan et al. (2008) propose a new type of Scenario-Based Design, the Value Scenario, to consider the effects of a designed system not only in the present time and on direct stakeholders, but also in the near future and on indirect stakeholders. In doing this, they consider common and shared human values as guides to evaluate and imagine potential negative effects of the developed solution on society. However, Value Scenarios do not provide a way to design value-based technological systems, but only suggest a framework for their evaluation. Additionally, as argued by Le Dantec et al. (2009), Value-Sensitive Design focuses on abstract human values, instead of considering specific user values connected to lived experiences. Le Dantec et al. (2009) therefore propose a method to identify specific user values within a given context. Our approach extends the above methods to develop scenarios for near-future complex systems based on specific user values, using fully-developed video prototypes as representations of such scenarios. Furthermore, we propose an additional analysis step, in which the scenarios are dissected into a framework that describes both technical features and human values, useful to assess both the feasibility of the proposed design and its adherence to specific user values.

3   Designing Value-Centric AmI

3.1   Defining Values from Primary Research

Our approach seeks to support the design of future visions for complex and ubiquitous systems based on emerging and future technologies. Rather than focus on specific users, our intent is to design for user values that will remain valid in the future. The concept of the caring city was created during an earlier phase of this project, and yielded a clear initial direction for the value-centric design process: How can the city care for its inhabitants? Following the secondary research phase, primary research was conducted (in the form of interviews) to analyze what specific experiences the users associated with the larger value of caring in order to refine the term further.

Values. Perhaps the most critical component of the primary research involved the clarification of the word caring. Rather than extract this from secondary sources, we asked our interviewees directly what it meant to be cared for. From their responses, we defined six distinct values related to the idea of caring: Protected, Assisted, Acknowledged, Invited, Accompanied, and Accepted. One of these values is illustrated in Fig. 1, mapped along with various associated terms and quotes.

Personas. Only after we had defined these values did we embody them in a set of constructed personas. As our lighting agent was designed to serve a broad range of

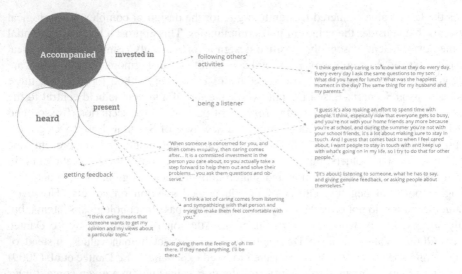

Fig. 1. The caring values were mapped and defined based on the primary research.

urban dwellers, our primary research spanned individuals from age 18 to 89. The four personas we developed followed suit, and represent four roughly-defined generations: Gen Z, Millennials, Baby Boomers, and the Silver Generation. The personas were designed to represent our interviewees' thoughts, daily activities, considerations, and needs. Specifically, each persona embodied a specific notion of what it means to feel cared for, complete with identified values and relevant issues. In this way, values could be shared amongst personas, and while each value had its own definition, how that value became expressed could change based on each persona's characteristics and context.

3.2   Storytelling as a Form of Vision Prototyping

Scenario Development. During the design phase of the project, scenario-based design was used to define the features of the system. Each of the four personas was placed into three different scenarios. By designing for particular experiences based on the values that we had defined, we were able to focus on specific interactions with the AmI agent. These twelve scenarios capture a broad range of activities, including particular details that were identified during our primary research, such as issues related to living in the city, dealing with technology, and interacting with light. This iterative process of scenario development enabled us to identify and consider many different aspects of the design vision and how various features might impact the core values expressed in each story. The scenarios were iteratively storyboarded (Fig. 2).

Video Development. Having finalized the scenarios, the next step involved realizing them in a compelling format. Eight of the scenarios were selected to be filmed - two for each persona. These videos visualized possible interactions of users with our proposed personal lighting AmI agent. By using this storytelling approach as a form of vision

Fig. 2. Scenario storyboards were iteratively produced in order to study the features of the personal lighting AmI agent and how those might impact the core values.

prototyping, we were able to communicate both our overall value-centric approach and specific technical features in a single medium (Fig. 3).

Fig. 3. Videos were created to convey possible user interactions with the personal lighting AmI agent, including both technical features and conveyed values.

3.3   From Scenarios to Scenes

Having completed the storytelling videos, our next step involved dissecting each scenario into moment-by-moment scenes. Since each scenario was comprised of several interactions with the lighting agent, this process enabled us to study individual interactions in greater detail and further determine what technical features would be required at each moment.

To perform this step, we constructed scene analysis cards. Each card represents a single interaction between the persona and the AmI agent. At the top of each card is an outline of the user experience. The scenario, persona, and relevant values are listed at the top right, alongside additional information about how light is used by the personal AmI agent in the scene at the top left. In the center of the card, a video still depicts what is happening, and overlay graphics illustrate particular details of the interaction. At the bottom of the card, the technical features are listed, including the context, the required data and sensing input, and the user input, if any (Fig. 4).

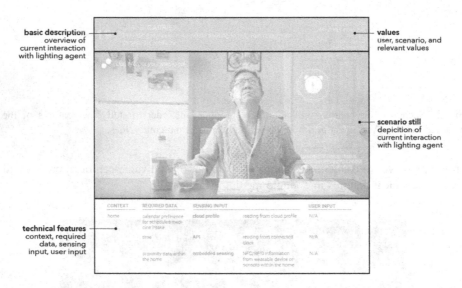

Fig. 4. Scene analysis cards depict individual scenes and relevant information from each scenario.

4   Results and Discussion

Each of the eight video scenarios was broken down into several scenes, for a total of 24 scene analysis cards. Example scene analysis cards can be seen in Fig. 5.

The technological complexity required of AmI will bring a host of technical issues into focus. Additionally, as AmI systems mature and develop, their roles and responsibilities will shift from human-prescribed actions to real-time, unsupervised behavior. As with other technologically complex systems, the design of AmI runs the risk of becoming overly focused on issues of technical implementation and losing sight of considerations of human experience.

Through our storytelling design process and subsequent scene analysis, we have demonstrated how human values and experience can remain at the center of the AmI design process. Value-centric design visions for future AmI systems ground the design direction on longer-lasting principles and allow technical features to be discussed in relation to human experience. Moreover, scene analysis cards provide a way to analyze technical features of such visions and their impact on human values at the same time. These cards enable structured, critical discussions with both stakeholders and potential

Fig. 5. Twenty four scene analysis cards were created, enabling a more in-depth study of technical features and user experience.

users on the feasibility, impact, and acceptability of future AmI systems. As a next step, we will use the cards to discuss these issues with our stakeholder as we work to create a roadmap for the gradual implementation of the design vision.

Acknowledgments. This research was part of a year-long collaboration between the MIT Design Lab and Signify. Doctoral research of the author Milica Pavlovic has been funded by TIM S.p.A., Services Innovation Department, Joint Open Lab Digital Life, Milan, Italy.

References

Aarts, E., Encarnacao, J.: True visions: tales on the realization of ambient intelligence. Into Ambient Intelligence (2006)

Alves Lino, J., Salem, B., Rauterberg, M.: Responsive environments: user experiences for ambient intelligence. J. Ambient Intell. Smart Environ. **2**, 347–367 (2010)

Burr, C., Cristianini, N., Ladyman, J.: An analysis of the interaction between intelligent software agents and human users. Mind. Mach. **28**, 735–774 (2018). https://doi.org/10.1007/s11023-018-9479-0

Cook, D.J., Augusto, J.C., Jakkula, V.R.: Ambient intelligence: technologies, applications, and opportunities. Pervasive Mob. Comput. **5**, 277–298 (2009). https://doi.org/10.1016/j.pmcj.2009.04.001

Friedman, B., Kahn, P.H., Borning, A.: Value sensitive design and information systems. In: Zhang, P., Galletta, D. (eds.) Human-Computer Interaction in Management Information Systems: Foundations, pp. 348–372. M.E. Sharpe, New York (2006)

Gams, M., Gu, I.Y.-H., Härmä, A., et al.: Artificial intelligence and ambient intelligence. J. Ambient Intell. Smart Environ. **11**, 71–86 (2019). https://doi.org/10.3233/AIS-180508

Goguen, J.A.: Semiotics, compassion and value-centered design. In: Liu, K. (ed.) Virtual, Distributed and Flexible Organisations: Studies in Organisational Semiotics, pp. 3–14. Springer, Dordrecht (2005). https://doi.org/10.1007/1-4020-2162-3_1

Le Dantec, C.A., Poole, E.S., Wyche, S.P.: Values as lived experience: evolving value sensitive design in support of value discovery. In: Proceedings of the 27th International Conference on Human factors in Computing Systems - CHI 2009, p. 1141. ACM Press, Boston (2009)

Mukherjee, S., Aarts, E., Doyle, T.: Special issue on ambient intelligence. Inf. Syst. Front. **11**, 1–5 (2009). https://doi.org/10.1007/s10796-008-9146-8

Nathan, L.P., Friedman, B., Klasnja, P., et al.: Envisioning systemic effects on persons and society throughout interactive system design. In: Proceedings of the 7th ACM Conference on Designing Interactive Systems - DIS 2008, pp. 1–10. ACM Press, Cape Town (2008)

O'Grady, M.J., O'Hare, G.M.P., Poslad, S.: Smart environment interaction: a user assessment of embedded agents. J. Ambient Intell. Smart Environ. **5**, 331–346 (2013)

Plötz, T., Kleine-Cosack, C., Fink, G.A.: Towards human centered ambient intelligence. In: Aarts, E., Crowley, J.L., de Ruyter, B., et al. (eds.) Ambient Intelligence. LNCS, vol. 5355, pp. 26–43. Springer, Heidelberg (2008). https://doi.org/10.1007/978-3-540-89617-3_3

Rosson, M.B., Carroll, J.M.: Scenario-Based Design. In: Jacko, J.A., Sears, A. (eds.) The Human-Computer Interaction Handbook: Fundamentals, Evolving Technologies, and Emerging Applications, pp. 1032–1050. Lawrence Erlbaum Associates, Mahwah (2003)

Streitz, N.A.: From human-computer interaction to human-environment interaction: ambient intelligence and the disappearing computer. In: Stephanidis, C., Pieper, M. (eds.) Universal Access in Ambient Intelligence Environments, vol. 4397, pp. 3–13. Springer, Heidelberg (2007). https://doi.org/10.1007/978-3-540-71025-7_1

An Application to Generate Air Quality Recommendations and Alerts on a Smart Campus

Pablo Leon Rodrigues[✉], Roberto dos Santos Rabello[✉],
and Cristiano Roberto Cervi[✉]

University of Passo Fundo - ICEG, Passo Fundo, Rio Grande do Sul, Brazil
{65375,rabello,cervi}@upf.br

Abstract. Due to the need to monitor the emission of harmful gases for human health and generate recommendations in real time, we sought to create an affordable solution to be deployed in any city. This process happens through the use of a LoRaWan network and sensors distributed within a university campus, space that reproduces a city in smaller dimensions. In this research it is proposed the development of an application to analyze the collected data and generate recommendations and alerts for the academic community and the administration of the campus in order to improve the quality of life of the people.

Keywords: Smart campus · Smart cities · Recommendation systems · Alerts · LoRaWan · Machine learning · Air quality · Air pollution

1 Introduction

The population growth in urban areas demands an increase in the basic services of cities such as energy consumption and traffic problems. As a consequence, the energy consumption through non-renewable sources such as fossil fuels also increases, contributing to the atmospheric pollution. The World Health Organization estimates that 4.2 million deaths per year are due to exposure to polluting gases in the environment and that 91% of the world population lives in areas where air pollution exceeds acceptable limits.

Monitoring Informations of air quality in Brazil are provided each ten years by the Brazilian Institute of Geography and Statistics for the next census to be held in 2020, estimated cost is approximately three billion Reais. Given these facts, the need arises to monitor the environment in which we live constantly. Through the use of a network of low cost for collecting data obtained from outdoor air quality monitoring at one university, the work presented proposes the development of a mobile application aimed at academic community, presenting information, recommendations and warnings about the quality of the air on campus to minimize exposure in environments where the air pollution become harmful to human health.

© Springer Nature Switzerland AG 2019
C. Stephanidis (Ed.): HCII 2019, CCIS 1033, pp. 507–514, 2019.
https://doi.org/10.1007/978-3-030-23528-4_69

2   Referential

2.1   Effects of Air Pollution on Human Health

The exposure to pollutant gases is associated with an increase in mortality and admissions in hospitals due to respiratory and cardiovascular diseases [1]. The presence of these gases in places with high population concentrations and other environmental factors such as low air humidity can result in diseases in the population exposed to long-term and short-term effects such as rhino conjunctivitis, irritation of the mucous membranes of the nose and eyes, irritation in the throat and respiratory problems in the short term [2–4], and in the long term, quality of life, development of cardiopathies and respiratory tract diseases such as bronchitis, emphysema and asthma [5,6].

The emission of polluting gases into the environment occurs daily and its sources are divided into three main categories - fixed, mobile and natural processes. Fixed sources are industries, landfills, generators and electric term. Mobile sources originate from means of transport in general through the burning of fossil fuels in motorcycles and motors. Natural sources originate from agriculture, burning, deforestation, volcanic and sandstorms [7,8].

2.2   Regulation

Programs such as the National Air Quality Control Program (PRONAR) and Pro-automotive pollution control (PROCONVE), were created with the objective of to control and improve air quality in the country. Information on the emission of gases is obtained during the census carried out by the Brazilian Institute of Geography and Statistics (IBGE), a high cost process that demands time and manpower, being estimated a cost of three billions Reals for the realization in 2020, due to this high price the process only takes place every ten years by IBGE [9]. Within a university campus, a number of daily at the most different times. It is possible that the emission of some gases tends to exceed acceptable levels of safety and have harmful effects on health.

Regarding the Brazilian National Environmental Policy, Law No. 6.938 from 1981 and Resolution CONAMA Nº 03/1990 (National Council of the Environment) [14], atmospheric pollution is defined as any activity that throws in the atmosphere matter or energy outside of environmental standards and render it unfit for human health, flora or fauna [13].

According to Boubel [7], pollutants can be classified as primary and secondary, the primary products being the sources of pollution, while the secondary ones are generated from the chemical reactions between the primary pollutants and gases present in the atmosphere.

CONAMA Resolution Nº 03/1990 [14] establishes air quality standards, where the primary standard is the maximum level at which a given pollutant can be found in the atmosphere before having effects on human health or the environment, and secondary standard is the concentration at which pollutants can

Table 1. Limits established by Resolution CONAMA N⁰ 03/1990 [14].

Pollutant	Time to sampling	Primary pattern	Secondary pattern
Total particles in suspension	24 h *	240 (μg/m^3)	150 (μg/m^3)
	MGA	80 (μg/m^3)	60 (μg/m^3)
Particles inhalables	24 h *	150 (μg/m^3)	150 (μg/m^3)
	MAA	50 (μg/m^3)	50 (μg/m^3)
Ozone (O3)	1 h *	160 (μg/m^3)	160 (μg/m^3)
Carbon Monoxide (CO)	1 h *	35 ppm	35 ppm
	8 h *	9 ppm	9 ppm
Dioxide of Nitrogen (NO2)	1 h	320 (μg/m^3)	190 (μg/m^3)
	MAA	100 (μg/m^3)	100 (μg/m^3)
Dioxide of Sulfur (SO2)	24 h *	365 (μg/m^3)	100 (μg/m^3)
	MAA	80 (μg/m^3)	40 (μg/m^3)

* Must not exceed more than once a year.
MAA: Annual Arithmetic Average
MGA: Annual Geometric Average
ppm: Parts per million
(μg/m^3): Microgram per cubic meter

be found in the atmosphere without causing harmful effects. Table 1 exemplifies the limits established by CONAMA Resolution N⁰ 03/1990.

In the state of Rio Grande do Sul, the Air Quality Index (IQAr) is established by the State Foundation for Environmental Protection (FEPAM) [16] based on the definition proposed by the United States Environmental Protection Agency (EPA)) [17], establishing levels of attention, alert and emergency regarding air quality. The purpose of this index is to inform the population about local air quality levels in relation to air pollutants sampled at monitoring stations, in compliance with the standards established by CONAMA Resolution No. 03/1990. Table 2 exemplifies the air quality index according to FEPAM.

2.3 Smart Campus and Smart Cities

Thinking about the city in a broad context is possible to identify transit routes, sanitation, industries, commerce and residences, and most importantly, its population. A university campus can be used as a structure that replicates a micro-territory providing the complete structure of a city, which facilitates experimentation, somehow transforming the scope of a smart city into a smart campus. Within the concept of smart campus are suggested distinct areas of intelligence such as: infrastructure, education, management, health and services [10,11]. The area that competes for health, to monitor and improve aspects related to the quality of life and health of the users of the campus, associated with ecological initiatives to maintain a healthy environment.

Table 2. Air quality index FEPAM [16].

Quality	Good	Regular	Inadequate	Bad	Very bad	Critical
Index	0–50	51–100	101–199	200–299	300–399	>= 400
Health levels	Secure	Tolerable	Unhealthy	Very unhealthy (attention)	Dangerous	Dangerous (emergency)
PTS ($\mu g/m^3$)	0–80	81–240	241–374	375–624	625–874	⩾875
PI10 ($\mu g/m^3$)	0–50	51–150	151–249	250–419	420–499	⩾500
SO$_2$ ($\mu g/m^3$)	0–100	101–365	366–799	800–1599	1600–2099	⩾2100
NO$_2$ ($\mu g/m^3$)	0–190	191–320	321–1129	1130–2259	2260–2999	⩾3000
CO (ppm)	0–4,5	4,6–9,0	9,1–14,9	15,0–29,9	30,0–39,9	⩾40
O$_3$ ($\mu g/m^3$)	0–80	81–160	161–399	400–799	800–999	⩾1000

PTS: Total suspended particles
PI10: Inhalation particles

For Berst [18], the factors that make a city smart are: instrumentation and control, connectivity, interoperability, security and privacy, data management, computational resources and analysis.

Instrumentation and control how the city monitors and controls factors related to the city, such as energy, gas, air quality, closed circuit video, TV and traffic meters, fire alarms and other sensors that provide information sensitive to the functioning of the city.

Connectivity is about communicating all the instrumentation that the city has and how these devices communicate and interact with the control of the city, such as WiFi networks, LoRaWan networks or cellular networks.

Interoperability ensures that products from multiple manufacturers work seamlessly together and can share information with each other or with a data center. It is essential to ensure that the city is not tied to a single supplier.

Security and privacy encompasses technologies, policies and practices to keep the data and devices that are resources for the city safe, among the measures there are clear rules on the privacy of data managed by the city, it is necessary to build a trust between the city and its without this, the city may find it difficult to implement new technologies and practices.

Data management is the process of storing, protecting and processing data ensuring accuracy, accessibility and integrity while maintaining the value of the data for the city and its population.

Computational resources are any and all equipment or device that manages or interprets important data for the city, softwares or servers or data.

Analysis generates value from collected data, meteorological forecasts, pollution control, identification of traffic patterns, and produces information about the consume of energy to generate forecasts in the most diverse areas.

The Smart Campus concept originates in the smart city, and can be interpreted as a city on a smaller scale, facing the various problems and challenges that a city faces daily. Issues such as safety, transportation, quality of life, conscious use of energy and natural resources are addressed within the Smart Campus. Ferreira and Araujo [10] define the Smart Campus as: "a collaborative ecosystem, enriched with technology, capable of responding to the demands of the interested parties, aiming to increase the quality of life in the Campus, the delivery of value and the balance of interests (p. 13)." Even though it is related to the use of information and communication technologies, the implementation of the smart campus must be in line with the management of the campus and with all the involved areas, through planning, meeting the needs of each area of interest and encouraging new campus solutions.

With intense and increasing movement of vehicles entering and exiting a university campus, concentrations of polluting gases tend to exceed acceptable limits, producing health risks for the academic community and the environment. In order to improve the quality of life on campus, there is a need to monitor the emission levels of gases harmful to human health, generating a base for application on a larger scale as in a city.

2.4 LoRaWan

LoRaWan is the abbreviation for Long Range Wide Area Network, a type of Low Power Wide Area Network (LPWAN), a low-power, long-range network with bi-directional, mobile, and localization service, usually implemented using star topology. Data communication is performed through the use of radio frequency bands and defined data rate, so different devices can send data at different frequencies. LoRaWan uses a gateway for communication between the devices and the network server.

With an open standard defined and certified by LoRa [19], which allows the use for the development of modules such as sensors or devices, it also defines the frequency bands to be used in each continent, so as not to interfere with critical device communication. In Brazil the National Telecommunication Agency (ANATEL) is responsible for the registration of restricted frequency bands.

LoRa Alliance categorizes devices into different classes to address different needs:

- Class A: This is the default class that must be supported by all LoRaWan devices, maintaining asynchronous, bidirectional communication, it can send network control commands if necessary. The device can go into a low-power state by scheduling wake-up commands without requiring a network to do so making this class of devices the one with the lowest power consumption.
- Class B: In addition to the characteristics of class A, class B can receive synchronized messages from time to time, indicating the time the device will

be listening, increasing the power consumption slightly compared to the class A.

- Class C: It has the same characteristics as class A, but has the ability to receive messages at any time, being the class that consumes the most energy.

In his work Manchini [12] on the use of LPWan network for smart cities, sensors were installed at certain points of the campus for constant monitoring of health and environmental harmful gases such as: nitrogen dioxide (NO2), sulfur dioxide (SO2) and carbon monoxide (CO). The data obtained by the sensors at certain time intervals are collected through a LoRaWan network and received through a gateway, then sent through TCP/IP and then stored. Parallel to this, Mazutti [15] has developed a study on the importance of air monitoring in the construction of a smart and learning campus. By monitoring the polluting gases it is possible to make decisions to improve the quality of life of the users of the campus, indicating for example places where permanence should be avoided and advising the administration of the campus about possible anomalies and risk factors.

2.5   Recommendation Systems

Recommendation systems can be defined as a strategy for making decisions for the user according to a large amount of information [21]. The recommendation systems used in e-commerce, for example, benefit both the buyer and the seller, several times helping the buyer to choose the option that pleases or complements a purchase and allowing a greater view of the products offered by the seller [20,22]. To generate a recommendation it is necessary to know the user or the products in which the user has an interest by creating a profile for the user.

Content-Based Filtering. Content-based filtering uses similarity across products to generate a recommendation. When the user consumes a product the system stores the characteristics of that product, then compare with other products and identify similarities, using the definition that if a user liked a particular product he tends to like a similar product.

Collaborative Filtering. In the collaborative filtering, the profile of two or more users are compared and from the similarities found a recommendation is generated. This concept is used to generate recommendations for movies, music, events.

2.6   Collected Data

Since July 2018, two bus stations with intense traffic were chosen inside the university to monitor the quality of the air in real time. Through the use of LoRaWan network and sensors to obtain data concerning quantity gases emitted into the environment. An example of the collected data is shown in Table 3.

By analyzing these data it is possible to generate recommendations and graphs for both the academic community and the campus administration.

Table 3. Data sample

Time	NO2	SO2	CO	Relative humidity	Temperature C°
2018-12-11T03:32:44.349227873Z	19	44	0,179	41	28,1
2018-12-11T03:34:13.768119711Z	21	29	0,178	41,5	28,1
2018-12-11T03:35:43.189340263Z	15	34	0,179	41,5	28,1
2018-12-11T03:37:12.608671123Z	23	18	0,177	41,5	28
2018-12-11T03:38:42.031406048Z	15	18	0,174	41,5	28
2018-12-11T03:40:11.459127214Z	19	26	0,171	41,5	28
2018-12-11T03:41:40.87642159Z	17	18	0,172	41,5	28
2018-12-11T03:43:10.289251289Z	24	31	0,175	41,5	28
2018-12-11T03:44:39.715815956Z	17	34	0,169	41,5	27,9
2018-12-11T03:46:09.1295776Z	9	29	0,176	42	28

3   Considerations

Increasingly the high concentration of harmful gases has been damaging the health of the population, through the use of an application to monitor air quality it is possible to obtain recommendations and information to improve the quality of life of the population.

The project is being developed by students of the PPGCA (Post-Graduate Program in Applied Computing) together with students of the PPGENG (Post-Graduate Program in Civil and Environmental Engineering) of the University of Passo Fundo and is expected to launch in August. 2019.

Through the use of the application, it is expected that the recommendations and warnings generated, help both the population and those responsible for the management of these territories, to have a greater control over the emission of the pollutants.

References

1. Brunekreef, B., Holgate, S.T.: Air pollution and health. The Lancet **360**, 1233–1242 (2002)
2. Butland, B.K., et al.: Ambient air pollution and the prevalence of rhinoconjunctivitisin adolescents: a worldwide ecological analysis. Air Qual. Atmos. Health **11**, 755–764 (2018). ISSN 1873-9318
3. Machin, A.B., Nascimento, L.F.C.: Efeitos da exposição a poluentes do ar na saúde das crianças de Cuiabá, Mato Grosso Brasil. Cadernos de saúde Pública **34**, 1–9 (2018). ISSN 1678-4464
4. Ashikin, N., et al.: Human health and wellbeing: human health effect of air pollution. Soc. Behav. Sci. **153**, 221–229 (2014). ISSN1877-0428
5. Gouveia, N., et al.: Air pollution and hospitalizations in the largest Brazilian metropolis. Rev. Saúde Pública (2017). ISSN 1518-8787
6. Katsouyanni, K., et al.: Short term effects of air pollution on health: a European approach using epidemiologic time series data: the APHEA protocol. J. Epidemiol. Commun. Health **50**, 12–18 (1996)

7. Stern, A., Boubel, R., Turner, C.B.: Fundamentals of Air Pollution, 4th edn. Academic Press, Cambridge (2008)
8. Programa Nacional de Controle de Qualidade do Ar. http://www.brasil.gov.br/noticias/meio-ambiente/2012/04/programa-nacional-de-controle-de-qualidade-do-ar-estabelece-metas-para-area
9. Amorim, D.: IBGE precisa de R$ 3 bi para Censo 2020. http://economia.estadao.com.br/noticias/seu-dinheiro,ibge-confirma-concurso-para-censo-2020,70002024324
10. Ferreira, F.H.C., Araujo, R.M.: Campus Inteligentes: Conceitos, aplicações, tecnologias e desafios, UNIRIO (2018)
11. Muhamad, W., et al.: Smart campus features, technologies, and applications: a systematic literature review. In: International Conference on Information Technology Systems and Innovation (ICITSI) (2017)
12. de Souza, F.V.M.: Uma arquitetura lpwan acessível para smart cities. Dissertação (Mestrado) – Universidade de Passo Fundo (2018)
13. Lei nº 6.938, de 31 de agosto de 1981. Politica Nacional do Meio Ambiente. http://www.planalto.gov.br/Ccivil_03/leis/L6938.htm
14. Resolução CONAMA nº 3, de 28 de junho de 1990. http://www.mma.gov.br/port/conama/legiabre.cfm?codlegi=100
15. Mazutti, J.: A aplicação do monitoramento da qualidade do ar na construção de um smart elearning campus. UPF (2018)
16. FEPAM: Índice de Qualidade do Ar IQAr. http://www.fepam.rs.gov.br/qualidade/iqar.asp
17. EPA: Criteria Air Pollutants. https://www.epa.gov/criteria-air-pollutants
18. Berst, J.: Smart cities readiness guide, Smart Cities Council. http://www.estudislocals.cat/wp-content/uploads/2016/11/SmartCitiesReadinessGuide.pdf
19. LoRa Alliance. https://lora-alliance.org
20. Bhasker, B., Srikumar, K.: Recommender Systems in E-Commerce. Tata McGraw Hill Education (2010)
21. Rashid, A.M., et al.: Getting to know you. In: Proceedings of the 7th International Conference on Intelligent User Interfaces. http://portal.acm.org/citation.cfm?doid=502716.502737
22. Sivaplan, S., Sadeghian, A.: Recommender Systems in E-Commerce Recommender Systems in E-Commerce (2015). ISSN 1384-5810

The Integration of BIM and IoT for Air Quality Monitoring and Visualization

Yang Ting Shen[1], Chia En Yang[1(✉)], and Pei Wen Lu[2]

[1] School of Architecture, Feng Chia University, Taichung, Taiwan
bowbowshen@gmail.com, Gaeunt@gmail.com
[2] Department of Geography, National Changhua University of Education,
Changhua City, Taiwan
b88208035@gmail.com

Abstract. This research developed an BIM-based system to monitor and visualize the real-time building information. Focusing on building in-use stages, advantages in tracking the micro-climate should be derived through the availability of real-time information. In this way, as-delivered physical assets (monitored and visualized in real-time) could be established to explore how BIM and IOT could improve a data-driven management. The integrated system called SyncBIM is developed based on 5 characteristics: (1) BIM environment to support decision making, (2) Object-oriented design for services embedded, (3) Dynamic DB based on real-time monitoring, (4) Mapping data-driven visualized results, and (5) Context awareness and system operation. In this research we use air quality (PM 2.5) to be an example parameter to demonstrate our SyncBIM system.

Keywords: BIM · FM · IoT · Building performance · Information visualization

1 Introduction

The BIM (Building Information Modelling) adoption in the Architecture, Construction, and Engineering (ACE) industries is currently accelerating rapidly. With BIM technology, an accurate virtual model of a building is digitally constructed. This model, known as a building information model, can be used for design, construction, and operation in the building life cycle [2]. The BIM maturity model (Fig. 1), also known as the iBIM modelor the BIM Wedge, was developed by Mark Bew and Mervyn Richards in 2008. The BIM maturity model describes 4 levels of maturity with regards to the ability of the construction supply chain to operate and exchange information based on BIM.

BIM level 0: the building practice concentrates on 2D drawings.

BIM level 1: developments in BIM incorporate standards, managed Computer-Aided Design (CAD), collaboration, etc.

BIM level 2: data from various disciplines get compiled though BIM execution plans, BIM data requirements and projects' specific standards.

© Springer Nature Switzerland AG 2019
C. Stephanidis (Ed.): HCII 2019, CCIS 1033, pp. 515–520, 2019.
https://doi.org/10.1007/978-3-030-23528-4_70

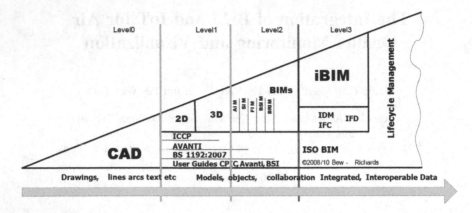

Fig. 1. UK maturity model (Mark Bew and Mervyn Richards 2008)

BIM level 3: more collaboration is expected. While level 2 is limited to 3D, level 3 incorporates 4D (construction sequencing), 5D (cost) and 6D (project life cycle information). It is the integration of these aspects which makes level 3 more encompassing although it is not yet clear how these aspects will be integrated.

So far the application of BIM may locate in the level 2. Lots of construction projects use BIM as the integration and collaboration tool to solve the problems occurring in the design and construction stages. However, the potential trend and benefits will shift to the operation stage (level 3: life cycle management) due to the strong needs of building lifecycle management [5]. In this paper, we will describe how we develop the building operation system with BIM for the building performance management.

2   BIM for FM

In the stage of building operation, how BIM can interfere and function is the hot topic of smart building. Currently, enormous researches focus on the FM (Facility Management) based on BIM [1, 5]. The British Standards Institute (BSi) defines FM as "the integration of processes within an organization to maintain and develop the agreed services that support and improve the effectiveness of its primary activities" [2]. FM is a complex issue encompassing multi-disciplines to ensure the functionality of built environment by integrating people, place, process and technology [7]. With the successful integration, BIM can be a powerful tool for FM to improve buildings' performance and manage operations more efficiently throughout the life-cycle of buildings. Some key benefits are: [1]

- Accurate geometrical representation of the spatial relationship of the building,
- Faster and more effective information sharing for the building operation,
- More predictable environmental performance and life cycle costing,

However, there is still lack of clear evidence on whether and how BIM could benefit decision-making in FM. Most of FM applications stay on the asset management which only focuses on the static facility sheets. That is to say, despite acting as a data pool, BIM for FM just function as a database, not a platform for building operation. Therefore, four key challenges must be overcome for BIM intervening building operation: (1) identification of critical information required to inform operational decisions, (2) the high level of effort to create new or modify existing BIM models for the building, (3) the management of information transfer between real-time operations and monitoring systems and the BIM model, and (4) the handling of uncertainty based on incomplete building documentation [10, 5].

3 The Integration of BIM and IOT

3.1 The Framework of SyncBIM

This research proposes a structure to integrate BIM and IOT to create the context awareness building for the building operation service. We develop an integrated system called SyncBIM to monitor and visualize the critical information based on BIM to support the decision making during the building operation. The digitally enabled framework by which it has been possible to analyze how information collected during operations could inform end-users about the context of building's environment is delivered in this paper. Focusing on building in-use stages, advantages in tracking the micro-climate and in satisfying the needs of users should be derived through the availability of real-time information. In this way, as-delivered physical assets (monitored and visualized in real-time) could be established to explore how BIM practices and IOT technologies could improve a data-driven management, by enriching building information in operation. The results should allow pointing out how monitored data and visualized information gathered along building life cycle could provide services to users.

Our SyncBIM system takes building and its related components as operational objects to monitor and visualize the building's real-time performance. The SyncBIM interface has 5 characteristics (Fig. 2) including (1) BIM environment to support decision making, (2) Object-oriented design for services embedded, (3) Dynamic DB based on real-time monitoring, (4) Mapping data-driven visualized results, and (5) Context awareness and system operation.

1. BIM environment to support decision making:
   The 3D model interface based on BIM provides end-users the clear idea about the spatial relationship between buildings and their related information.
2. Object-oriented design for services embedded:
   Here the term "object" means building masses, not the components in the programming language. The building performance information such as EUI (Energy Use Intensity) or air quality is embedded in the object for further services.
3. Dynamic DB based on real-time monitoring
   The building performance information is monitored by several sensors and updated to the databased in real time.

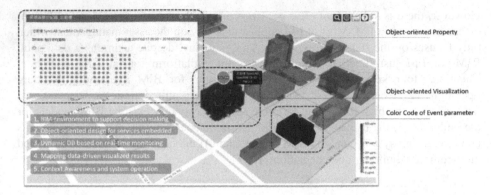

Fig. 2. SyncBIM system and operation interface

4. Mapping data-driven visualized results

   The color code method is used to visualize the real-time building performance information. The color scale is linked to the performance degree in the databased and visualized via building mass.

5. Context awareness and system operation

   The BIM-based interface provides the navigation function to view the context and operate spatial information.

3.2 The Practice of SyncBIM

The SyncBIM system is developed and implemented in the Feng-Chia university for the pilot study. In this research we use air quality (PM 2.5) to be an example parameter to demonstrate our SyncBIM system. We install PM2.5 sensors in several buildings to detect the PM2.5 level. The real-time data are uploaded to the SyncBIM cloud through wireless sensor network. The PM2.5 records are deployed and assigned to corresponding virtual building masses according to the color code method. The building masses change their colors according to the real-time PM 2.5 level to visualize the air quality of entire building context. In addition, the building masses are designed as object-oriented buttons to trigger detail property sheets such as PM 2.5 history records or real-time data (Fig. 3). Users can right click the building mass to pop up the menu and select the target property.

The object-oriented building masses also function as the alarm of building performance.

Through the historical records, the dynamic and instant average of PM 2.5 level can be calculated. The SyncBIM system keeps comparing the real-time and average data of PM2.5. Once the result is above the average, the alarm tag will pop up on the building mass to warm users the odd building performance.

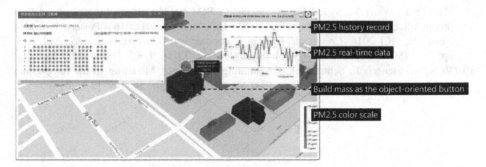

Fig. 3. The building mass as the object-oriented button to call the detail property function.

4 Conclusion

The SyncBIM system provides the novel interface to monitor and visualize the building operation information. It presents a more intuitive method for users to negative the building context and inspect the individual building performance. Compared with traditional paper-based building operation, the SyncBIM system provides not only the BIM-based operation, but also the visualized building performance. In the future, the development of BAS (Build Automation System) based on parameters will be the potential issue of next generation SyncBIM.

References

1. Arayici, Y., Onyenobi, T., Egbu, C.: Building information modelling (BIM) for facilities management (FM): the MediaCity case study approach. Int. J. 3-D Inf. Model. (IJ3DIM) **1** (1), 55–73 (2012)
2. Azhar, S.: Building information modeling (BIM): trends, benefits, risks, and challenges for the AEC industry. Leadersh. Manag. Eng. **11**(3), 241–252 (2011)
3. Becerik-Gerber, B., Jazizadeh, F., Li, N., Calis, G.: Application areas and data requirements for BIM-enabled facilities management. J. Constr. Eng. Manag. **138**(3), 431–442 (2011)
4. British Standards Institute: Facility Management - Part 1: Terms and Definitions: BS EN 15221-1:2006, vol. 44, 19 p. BSI Standards Publication, London (2007)
5. McArthur, J.J.: A building information management (BIM) framework and supporting case study for existing building operations, maintenance and sustainability. Proc. Eng. **118**, 1104–1111 (2015)
6. Motamedi, A., Hammad, A.: Lifecycle management of facilities components using radio frequency identification and building information model. J. Inf. Technol. Constr. (ITCON) **14**(18), 238–262 (2009)
7. Roper, K., Payant, R.: The Facility Management Handbook. Amacom, New York (2014)
8. Shen, Y.T., Lu, P.W.: Development of Kinetic facade units with BIM-Based active control system for the adaptive building energy performance service (2016)

9. Shen, Y.T., Wu, T.Y.: Sync-BIM: the interactive BIM-Based platform for controlling data-driven kinetic façade. In: Stephanidis, C. (ed.) HCI International 2016 – Posters' Extended Abstracts, HCI 2016. Communications in Computer and Information Science, vol. 618, pp. 445–450. Springer, Cham (2016). https://doi.org/10.1007/978-3-319-40542-1_72
10. Volk, R., Stengel, J., Schultmann, F.: Building Information Modeling (BIM) for existing buildings—Literature review and future needs. Autom. Constr. **38**, 109–127 (2014)

Identification of Living Human Objects from Collapsed Architecture Debris to Improve the Disaster Rescue Operations Using IoT and Augmented Reality

Shiva Subhedar[1]([X]), Naveen Kumar Gupta[2], and Abhishek Jain[3]

[1] Cognizant Technology Solutions, Pune, India
shivasubhedar05@gmail.com
[2] Mastercard, Pune, India
naveenguptal489@gmail.com
[3] KPIT Technologies Ltd., Pune, India
abhishek.jain520@gmail.com

Abstract. With the fast urbanization cities are getting dense, demand of finding place to live is increasing tremendously. To fulfill the demand of availing the houses quickly the construction team and builders are putting pressure in construction work. Resulting high probability of errors in construction, which leads to accidents like architecture collapse. Bad construction quality, age of building, overload, fire, lack of maintenance, bad engineering are key man made error reasons for buildings getting collapsed. Apart from them, seismic forces like earthquake also affect the stability of buildings and collapse them if they are not designed for the earthquake magnitude of accelerations occurring. Collapsed building is a critical and complex maze for disaster rescue team, from the debris of building their key responsibility is to save the people. The rescue operation of a collapsed building area can get executed in a day to several days and this increases the chances of trapped people losing their lives. The key problem in performing the rescue starts with search and analysis of field and identification of trapped people location. In this paper we are presenting an innovative and futuristic way to perform the rescue of human survivors using Internet of things, drones and augmented reality. IOT based network like fitness bands will be equipped with disaster mode, drones will be equipped with BLE based transmitter/receiver. With the help of Drones and IOT bands, human tracking system can plot the 3D rendering of collapsed building area virtual map and highlight the trapped human survivors' location in an Augmented Reality view. This method of rescue will bring the technical advancement and increase efficiency of rescue operations, results in saving human lives.

Keywords: Disaster management · IOT · Wearable · Rescue ·
Augmented Reality · Productivity

© Springer Nature Switzerland AG 2019
C. Stephanidis (Ed.): HCII 2019, CCIS 1033, pp. 521–527, 2019.
https://doi.org/10.1007/978-3-030-23528-4_71

1 Introduction

A disaster is an abrupt, cataclysmic event that truly upsets the working of a network or society and causes human, material, and financial or ecological misfortunes that surpass the network's or society's capacity to adapt utilizing its very own assets. Disasters can take many different forms, and the duration can range from an hourly disruption to days or weeks of ongoing destruction. Disaster can be both natural (earthquakes, hurricanes and tropical storm, thunderstorm & lightning etc.) and man-made (explosion, power service disruption & blackout etc.) Specific kinds of cataclysmic events are bound to happen specifically parts of the world. In any case, practically every spot you could live is inclined to one kind of cataclysmic event or another. No spot is completely sheltered from cataclysmic event. Also, obviously it's a given, that no spot is protected from the risk of psychological oppression and other man-made debacle occasions. Breakdown of synthetic structures, for example, structures and scaffolds, happen with fluctuating recurrence over the world. Normal reason for such falls includes over-burden because of defective development, broken plan, fire, gas blasts, psychological oppressor acts, yet the absolute most normal and obliterating reason for breakdown of man-made structures is earthquake. [1] Over time, the threat of earthquakes will increase in parallel with the growing demand for global urbanization and millions of people will be vulnerable to earthquakes. [2] Ranjbar, Ardalan, Dehghani, Serajeyan, Alidousti has talked about how building conditions whether destroyed or not, as well as the building damage level, can be precisely prepared using high spatial resolution satellite image to facilitate response phase of disaster management. [3] Porter, Jaiswal, Wald, Earle, Hearne has talked about how to calculate the amount of damage to buildings and to estimate the number of casualties. [4] Ranjbar, Dehghani, Ardalan and Saradjian has proposed a framework to loss estimation method is proposed by combining data from remote sensing technology and geographic information system (GIS). [5] Joshi, Poudel, Bhandari has talked about how robotic system can help in detecting alive human body detection and rescue operation using PIR, IR & temperature sensors. [6] Krishnakumar, Dinakar and Reddy has talked about detection and monitoring of victims trapped under collapsed buildings using piezoelectric plate and GPS. The rescue and inspection operation during cataclysmic event requires identification of the affected areas, estimation of loss of life, allocation of personnel and adequate medical supplies, search for survivors under the ruins, prevention of the spread of communicable diseases in the region in turmoil, psychological assistance to survivors and the reconstruction of areas hit by the earthquake [7].

Information about the location of buried person and other details regarding the condition of the human subject, would be of great value for the rescue personnel. This would help in reducing the time of operation and thereby, help to save more lives by providing them adequate medical care. Time is thereby a critical factor, efforts spent in shoring and breaching operations in the wrong area will waste valuable time and resources and unnecessarily fatigue the rescuers. In order to increase the probability of saving lives of the victim, the rescue operation needs to be faster. But, sometimes, it is difficult for rescue personnel to enter into some parts/areas of the Warfield or earthquake affected areas.

In this research we are presenting framework using Internet of things, drones and augmented reality. IOT based network like fitness bands will be equipped with disaster mode, drones will be equipped with BLE (Bluetooth Low Energy) based transmitter/receiver. With the assistance of drones and IOT bands, human tracking system can plot the 3D rendering of collapsed building area virtual map and highlight the trapped human survivors' location in an Augmented Reality view. This technique will significantly decrease time spent on finding exploited people with the goal that unfortunate casualties can identified early, and we can spare their lives by giving early prescription.

2 Reimagining the Rescue Operations Using AR and IOT

2.1 Prerequisites and Assumptions

In this IOT & AR based framework to reimagine the rescue operations we have identified some prerequisites and assumptions like, people are using wearable devices like Fitness trackers, IOT & AR based technological integration, AR headsets or AR mobile app with rescue team, BLE mounted transceiver drone, wireless communication, digital platform (web application), 3D mapping using drone coordinates, conversion of 3D rendered map to Augmented reality information

2.2 Overview

Wearable devices are becoming popular and people have started using different wearable devices like Fitness band, smart jewelry, smart clothing, smart watch, implantable, head mounted devices etc. These devices serve some specific services and use cases like Fitness band tracks the physical activities and records the data, communicates with smartphone using wireless communication to sync data, monitors the individual person biometric profiles etc. The framework starts with the IOT wearable band (e.g. Fitness band) and integrating the Disaster Emergency mode in that. Disaster Emergency mode in wearable device should get activated in can of earthquake or other disaster conditions arises like collapse of a building etc. Once the Disaster Emergency mode gets activated in wearable device, it will start emitting the RF signals (specially tuned to a specified frequency for emergency cases).

Disaster rescue team would be equipped with BLE receivers (frequency tuned to emergency cases), this receiver can be mounted on Drones which can be handled by rescue team. A digital platform would keep track of drone path and map on a 3D map. BLE receiver on Drones receive the signals getting emitted by wearable device and when the signal strength becomes high, digital platform (Web application) will mark that spot as living object prospect spot on 3D map. Drones can cover complete collapsed building debris and help digital platform to mark the spots of living object prospects.

3D map with living object prospects spot can be converted in to live data which can be augmented on real footage of collapsed debris in form of augmentation. With the help of Augmented Reality glasses or mobile app rescue team can view highlighted spots on real collapsed debris (Fig. 1).

Fig. 1. Sample depiction of identification of trapped living objects in a building collapsed through Augmented reality mobile app

2.3 Methodological Framework

The overall technical framework of proposed solution can be divided in to three stages, detection & transmission, processing & conversion and augmentation. In first stage of detection & transmission, BLE transceiver mounted drones receive signals from wearable devices from trapped objects under collapsed architectural debris and transmit it to centralized processing unit. BLE is a form of wireless communication designed especially for short-range communication. BLE is very similar to Wi-Fi in the sense that it allows devices to communicate with each other. However, BLE is meant for situations where battery life is preferred over high data transfer speeds [8]. Along with signals from wearable devices, it would also transmit its latitude and longitude, object profile. At second stage of processing & conversion, centralized processing unit would analyze the data received from BLE receivers and map it on 3D plane. Also, it would analyze the signal strength and mark the highest peak of signal strength as prospected spots. At third stage, the centralized processing unit would create the augmentation of 3D plane and mark prospected spot on augmented view, which rescue team can view from a mobile app or augmented reality-based glasses (Fig. 2).

2.4 Rescue Strategy Planning – Defining Priorities

Moving ahead from identification of living trapped objects and locating prospects spot to planning rescue strategies. The proposed solution also brings insights to rescue team on prioritizing rescue operations in an effective way so that more human lives can be saved in time. With the help of people profile received from wearables, core platform can perform certain analysis and guide rescue team on preparing the strategy. Priorities will be decided based on following parameters.

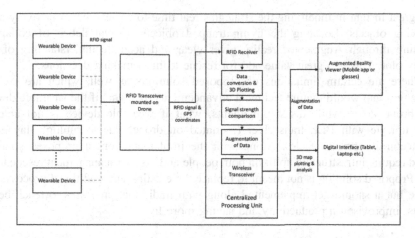

Fig. 2. Technical Architecture of IOT & NFC based Rescue operations framework

1. Demographic of trapped person (Age and Gender)
2. Health condition based on health record of the person
3. Heart rate of the person
4. Identification of current situation of trapped object.

An intelligent algorithm will decide the priorities based on these parameters. Information will be augmented on rescuers mobile or AR glasses to navigate. Medical and other facilities can be rearranged based on pre collected data.

3 Discussions

In case of any disaster like earth quake, Fire, building collapse any unwanted tragedy where a lot of human casualties happen. Current rescue methods are executed on the basis of trial and error. This is because rescue team does not have accurate information about the site and people. Like how many people are inside. How old are they. What is the current location of them? What is their health status? What is their current status? These are some questions which rescue team faces while rescuing. If we are able to answer these questions, then it will be great for the rescue team. This will allow them for fast, reliable and under control rescue. Our solution focuses not only answering these questions but provides a great way to represent answers to rescuer team, so that they can perform rescue operations efficiently and save more lives without any delay.

This framework is not only beneficial to detect and locate the living objects in disaster conditions but also can be a value add in giving valuable insights in planning rescue strategies. Along with location details of trapped objects, personalized profiles can also be achieved which can communicate key information like Age, Gender and any specific medical information (with the consent from user while configuring wearable device for use). This information is very crucial for rescue team and helpful to them for defining priorities. Also, real time information can be gathered on periodic basis to get biometric information of trapped object like heath beat etc. which can also be a great insight in modifying the strategies real time to achieve better recovery ratio of living objects. Locating the living trapped objects on real debris of collapsed structure through Augmented reality gives clear and accurate understanding of the survey plot. This is a great value add for rescue team in making decisions.

There are certain limitations of proposed solutions as well, which are current challenges and would require technical advancements like what if the wearable device gets broke down while disaster incidents, what if wearable device is not able to communicate with BLE transceiver (mounted on drone) due to multiple layers of architectural debris obstacles. Along with the implementation of proposed solution would require infrastructure uplift on both people and disaster management rescue team side. Proposed solution is not meant to replace the existing and traditional processes of rescue but it should get implemented along with traditional processes to reach better results, improvise on productivity and saving more lives.

4   Conclusion

The most critical stage of the relief and rescue operation after mishap is to estimate the amount of destruction and number of causalities. This estimation helps managers in allocating resources and deploying rescue workers. Locating the exact position of buried victims is a challenge as efforts spent on in wrong area will not only waste valuable time but also reduces the probability of saving victim life. The proposed arrangement not just aides in identifying the location of buried victims but also provide data related like their pulse rate, heart beat etc. which will help workers to take better and quicker informed decision. We will keep on progressing in the direction of upgrading this framework.

References

1. Voigt, S., Kemper, T., Riedlinger, T., Kiefl, R., Scholte, K., Mehl, H.: Satellite image analysis for disaster and crisis-management support. IEEE Trans. Geosci. Remote **45**, 1520–1528 (2007)
2. Ranjbar, H.R., Ardalan, A.R.A., Dehghani, H., Serajeyan, M.R., Alidousti, A.: Facilittating response phase of disaster management by automatic extraction of building based on texture analysis using high resolution satellite images. J. Emerg. Manag. **3**, 5–19 (2014)
3. Porter, K., Jaiswal, K., Wald, D., Earle, P., Hearne, M.: Fatality models for the US geological survey's prompt assessment of global earthquake for response (PAGER) system. In: Proceedings of the 14th World Conference of Earthquake Engineering, 12–17 October 2008, Beijing (CN). International Association for Earthquake Engineering (IAEE) (2008)
4. Ranjbar, H.R., Dehghani, H., Ardalan, A.R.A., Saradjian, M.R.: A GIS-based approach for earthquake loss estimation based on the immediate extraction of damaged buildings. Geomatics Nat. Hazards Risk **8**(2), 772–791 (2017). https://doi.org/10.1080/19475705.2016.1265013
5. Joshi, R., Poudel, P.C., Bhandari, P.: An Embedded Autonomous Robotic System for Alive Human Body Detection and Rescue Operation (2014)

6. Bethanney Janney, J., Krishnakumar, S., Dinakar, J.V., Reddy, S.D.K.: Detection and monitoring of victims trapped under collapsed buildings using wireless communication (2016)
7. Zhang, L., et al.: Emergency medical rescue efforts after a major earthquake: lessons from the 2008 Wenchuan earthquake. Lancet **379**, 853–861 (2012)
8. En.wikipedia.org. Bluetooth Low Energy (2019). https://en.wikipedia.org/wiki/Bluetooth_Low_Energy

Running Tour Generation
for Unknown Environments

Jutta Willamowski$^{(\boxtimes)}$, Stephane Clinchant, Christophe Legras,
Sofia Michel, and Shreepriya Shreepriya

Naver Labs Europe, 38240 Meylan, France
{jutta.willamowski,Stephane.clinchant,
christophe.legras,sofia.michel,
shreepriya.shreepriya}@naverlabs.com

Abstract. In this paper, we present an approach to generate pleasant running tours for unknown environments. We start from a first version, able to generate basic pleasant tours, but without explicitly catering for elevation. Based on observations on how runners appreciate elevation gain and steepness and on interviews with local runners, we identified corresponding additional needs. Indeed, runners usually have specific implicit or explicit objectives or limits with respect to the elevation gain they want to target or to avoid with a tour. In consequence, we extend our first approach. We expose the algorithm we have defined to address elevation constraints during tour generation and the under-lying intuitions. An important differentiator with prior art is that we address elevation constraints *during the tour generation phase* and not *a posteriori*. This means that our approach is able to *efficiently generate new* tours that match the user's constraints, while prior art rather finds matching tours by searching *a posteriori* among a set of available tours, and only finds matching ones if they are already present.

Keywords: Running · Tour generation · Optimization

1 Introduction

Our aim is to develop a tool that is able to propose personalized and pleasant round-trip tours to runners visiting an unknown location similar to [5, 7]. Given a starting point, a target distance (or duration) and a set of preferences, the tool should produce a path (or a variety of paths) of the requested length, that starts and ends at the given point and that corresponds to the user's preferences.

To propose personalized pleasant tours to a user we first have to formalize what such a pleasant tour is. The quality or pleasantness of a tour should indicate to which extent it matches the user's preferences. It is based on two aspects: (i) the quality of the arcs (or path segments) that compose the tour and (ii) its form or geometry. The quality of the path depends on various data (e.g. path type, environment, close POIs) and needs to be translated into a numerical value to be used as input for the optimization algorithm. Given the routing graph that represents the network and the scores on each arc,

© Springer Nature Switzerland AG 2019
C. Stephanidis (Ed.): HCII 2019, CCIS 1033, pp. 528–535, 2019.
https://doi.org/10.1007/978-3-030-23528-4_72

the goal is to find a tour of the requested length that maximizes the score on the visited arcs.

Intuitively, the optimization problem can be seen as a combination between two NP-hard combinatorial problems: (i) a knapsack problem where the goal is to select on a map the best locations for the user within a constraint budget (in distance/duration); and (ii) a traveling salesman problem where the goal is to find the shortest route that visits those locations. We model this problem as an arc orienteering problem [4] and use a greedy randomized adaptive search procedure to solve it heuristically. We started by implementing a first version considering essentially the path type (i.e. whether the path is a pedestrian path or, whether it allows for traffic and what type of traffic) and the environment surrounding it (i.e. parks, forest ...) to compute the path score. We prevent the algorithm from taking the same segments multiple times to avoid going back and forth on the same segments to accumulate score on one hand, and to achieve a more pleasant geometry on the other hand. Figure 1 illustrates a tour generated with this algorithm.

Fig. 1. Sample 10 km tour generated for a selected location with the initial algorithm.

2   User Requirements

To improve our initial algorithm, and to better understand what runners would expect and want from a tour generation service and building on existing work such as [5, 6], we carried out interviews with seven local runners, five male and two female with different ages and backgrounds. While two were occasional runners with basic health and fitness objectives, three mainly wanted to disconnect from their day-to-day routine and to explore the environment, whereas the last group had more specific performance objectives, in one case even training for particular races and following more specific training plans. A first objective of our study was to understand the different runners' evaluation criteria for tours, and to see whether different runners generally agree on the importance of various criteria. Another objective was to understand whether individual runner's preferences were always the same or whether they varied according to the actual context and situation.

During our interviews, we therefore proposed a list of criteria for evaluating tours and a list of impact factors to the interviewees that may change the runners' preferences. We let then interviewees rate them on a Likert scale with possible free text explanations. We considered the following evaluation criteria, also inspired by prior art such as [5]: environment (nature, viewpoints, …), elevation gain and steepness, surface of the path, traffic, possible interruptions (traffic lights, crossings, crowds, …), simplicity (i.e. being easy to remember and navigate), geometry (loop versus back -and-forth), and safety. We furthermore asked the interviewees whether their preferences were modified by the following factors: time of the day (e.g. through lightning conditions), temperature, training objectives, current mood, company they run with. For both, evaluation criteria and factors, we let the interviewees also add new personal ones, in case they were not listed already.

While all interviewees generally agreed on the importance of some critical characteristics of the tour (e.g. avoiding traffic or preferring running in a green environment), the importance of other criteria differed from one individual to another, e.g. the desire to avoid running on asphalt surfaces was rated as crucial by three individuals and negligible for the others. Another criterion that was considered as crucial especially by the female runners was safety, i.e. the necessity to avoid any dangerous encounters while running. Some criteria were only considered important by some individuals under certain conditions (e.g. access to water being important only when the temperature is high). Finally, elevation gain and steepness was considered as important by *all* interviewees. This prominence of elevation gain is probably also due to the fact that our local area, in which the interviewees usually run, is hilly and close to the mountains. Still, elevation gain is definitely an important criterion to consider everywhere: proposing even a slightly hilly tour to an occasional runner will not be acceptable.

On one hand, our user study revealed evidence that we should extend our initial version of the algorithm (where we essentially tried to aggregate a set of consensual criteria only) to include also more individual criteria like safety or surface of the path. On the other hand, our study also revealed the importance of elevation gain and steepness. We decided to address elevation gain and steepness first for several reasons. First, gathering data about elevation gain and steepness is more easily accessible than data about the surface of a path and its safety; second, elevation gain and steepness were considered crucial by *all* our interviewees; and, even if elevation gain and steepness are tackled in some existing work, their solution has important limits. Indeed, as discussed below, they do not take into account elevation constraints during tour generation but rather in an *a posteriori* filtering step.

3   Taking Elevation into Account for Pedestrian Tour Generation

Elevation gain and steepness make running tours substantially more or less difficult. The expressed desires with respect to the difficulty of the tour we observed depended on one hand on the runner's profile and on the other on his actual objectives. Some runners mainly aim at covering a rough target distance or time but want to avoid any difficulty and thus search for a flat tour, others aim at exercising more intensely and search for significant elevation gain. Trail runners preparing particular races have even more specific training objectives and search, depending on their training plan, for tours that reach corresponding elevation gain targets. Our objective is to generate suitable tours for the variety of all these runners. Therefore, we want to enable the users to specify the elevation gain and steepness they either target or want to avoid in advance and generate a corresponding tour in consequence.

Prior Art

Although there are several tour generation applications on the market, we did not find any that is able to build a new personalized tour for a user that matches the his or her elevation gain preferences without relying on previously collected tours. Currently, in commercial tools, the only proposed way to provide a user with a tour matching particular elevation preferences is to search and filter out among existing tours those that match the elevation preferences. However, such tours may not exist as such a priori, especially when the user has further constraints such as a specific starting point, a target distance, including particular types of attractions such as nature or cultural attractions etc. Also in existing literature we did not find any approach using elevation preferences during tour construction. In the literature, similar to what we observe with existing commercial tools, user-specific criteria are also taken into account *a posteriori*, i.e. to rank independently generated tours and filter out, among those found during tour generation, those that match the users constraints. Therefore, they cannot guarantee that a tour matching the elevation preferences is constructed during the generation phase. Especially in cases when the user has very specific objectives, they will find such a tour only if it is generated "by chance" in the first place.

Our approach, in contrast, is to generate a *new* tour for a user and to take the user's elevation constraints into account in the tour generation phase. To do this, we will extend our initial algorithm. This initial algorithm works as follows: Given a starting point, a target distance (or duration) and a set of preferences, the method produces a path of the desired length, that starts and ends at the given point and that is pleasant for the user with respect to his preferences. The method relies on a scored routing graph where the vertices represent the crossings, the arcs represent the road segments between the crossings, and the score on each arc reflects how pleasant the segment is for the user. The algorithm has then a first preprocessing step that consists of computing the shortest paths between all the vertices that are within a certain Euclidian distance of each other (below a co-called cutoff parameter). Starting from an initial basic tour (linking the starting point to an adjacent vertice), the algorithm iteratively augments the current tour by replacing shortest paths segments by an insertion of an arc, linked to the rest of the tour by shortest paths. Therefore, the final tour is composed of a number of chosen arcs linked by shortest paths.

3.1 Appreciating Elevation Gain and Steepness

Elevation has two aspects: elevation gain and steepness. Both have an important impact on the difficulty of a tour. With respect to elevation gain it is the total cumulative elevation gain of the tour, i.e. the sum of elevation gains of all successive segments, that is generally taken as the measure for the difficulty of a tour, whereas with respect to steepness the difficulty is rather measured on the steepest parts of the tour. We have studied online communities to better grasp this impact and to best cater for the impact of elevation gain and steepness. We first discuss our findings from these communities and then explain how we translated them into an implementation for our algorithm.

In walking (or hiking), a famous rule defines the impact of elevation in walking (uphill), the Naismith's rule [1]: "Allow one hour for every 3 miles (5 km) forward, plus an additional hour for every 2,000 feet (600 m) of ascent." In the trail running community, the additional effort brought by elevation gain is usually converted into adding extra distance to the itinerary. A rule of thumb is to consider that, in terms of time and effort, 100 m of height difference (D+) is equivalent to running 1 km horizontal [2]. For example, running 10 km with 300 m of D+ is equivalent to running 13 km. This community also thinks about elevation in terms of its impact on speed: "every percent gradient of incline (going uphill) will slow you by 7–9 s/km, and every percent gradient of decline (going downhill) will aid you by 5 s/km." [3].

We observe that steepness also plays an important role in the way runs are described within the community. Depending on the climbing experience, the ground surface and the fitness of the athlete, we observe a threshold after which runners tend to walk. This threshold may vary from a 5% to 20% slope.

In general, elevation gain and steepness translate thus to greater effort compared to flat tours, i.e. to cover the same distance, a runner will have to spend much more energy if the elevation gain and steepness are high compared to a flat tour. However, if a user wants to cover a certain distance in trail running s/he expects at the same time to cover a corresponding amount of elevation gain. An occasional runner, in contrast, will rather expect and desire to cover the same distance without elevation gain. We thus have to cater for these different cases, and the typical difficulty levels that these different types of users will expect.

3.2 Elevation Profiles

According to our observations we predefined three basic profiles corresponding to three successive classes or difficulty levels: flat, hilly and alpine. Each of them corresponds to and implements a different acceptable range of cumulated elevation gain and steepness for tours. Table 1 shows the ranges we adopted as reasonable in our current method.

Table 1. Elevation profiles with their cumulated elevation gain and steepness thresholds.

Profile	Cumulated elevation gain	Steepness
Flat	Less than 1% of the distance, e.g. <100 m for 10 km	Avoid above 5%
Hilly	1% to 3% of the distance, e.g. [100, 300] m for 10 km	Avoid above 10%
Alpine	More than 3% of the distance, e.g. >300 m for 10 km	Avoid above 15%

With respect to elevation gain, some users may even have very specific needs and target a specific interval. As we will show below we can tackle such requirements with our solution. Indeed, on top of the chosen profile, the user may enter any elevation gain interval s/he desires and the algorithm will produce a corresponding tour (if one exists in the neighborhood).

For steepness we do not define an overall target steepness to match, but rather steepness values to (try to) avoid. Indeed, with steepness the objective is not to produce a tour that has always the same acceptable steepness, but rather one that contains flat but also steeper segments preferably only up to a certain degree. While the elevation gain objective applies to the whole tour (it is constituted by the sum of the elevation gain of each segment), the steepness constraint rather applies to most segments of the tour, but not necessarily all. Indeed, the user may sometimes prefer and accept to include a very short steep segment in a tour if that segment enables to reach a very pleasant area or path within the tour. As we will show below, we thus do not strictly forbid to go over the preferred steepness threshold and rather penalize too steep segments. One possible extension could be to restrict the cumulated length of subsequent segments that are above the steepness threshold to avoid including too many difficult segments in the tour.

In any case, the elevation gain already provides a natural limit for steepness in the sense that with a flat profile for a given total distance, the total elevation gain is already limited, and thus the resulting tour may either only include in a small proportion or cumulated distance with high steepness or a higher proportion or cumulated distance with lower steepness.

3.3   Algorithm

As explained above, our approach supports three predefined profiles for runners that search for tours of a prototypical difficulty level, namely flat, hilly or alpine. Each profile includes two aspects, and elevation gain range to reach and a steepness threshold to avoid. To take these into account, we extended the original algorithm as follows: To limit steepness, we penalize the segments that are steeper than the profile threshold in the computation of the shortest paths. We do not exclude them from the tour completely which translates the following underlying idea: to avoid taking a steep direct path to reach a given destination, people will accept making detours, i.e. covering more distance but using less steep segments. The weighted shortest paths that include this penalty will represent exactly this preference.

To reach the target elevation gain, we propose two solutions, hierarchical optimization and selecting an intermediate point located at an appropriate level of elevation. The first solution applies hierarchical optimization: here the algorithm considers elevation gain as the first objective and the pleasantness score only as secondary objective until the current solution has the right elevation. At that point, the algorithm will switch back to maximizing the pleasantness keeping the elevation range as a constraint. However, this solution is limited by the cutoff parameter: it is able to find matching tours only if the regions with the required elevation gain are close enough.

Therefore, we propose to introduce an additional first step, choosing an intermediate point located at an appropriate level of elevation, and then start the tour generation from there (for the remaining distance). Indeed, a natural way to reach an objective for humans is rather to go for the objective relatively directly and without much detour, except if a detour makes sense, e.g. to avoid too much steepness. With respect to elevation, this means that if a user has an elevation target, s/he will rather start by going in the direction where the elevation is going to be reached without deviating too much, e.g. without going in the opposite direction or going first further down and later up again. To mimic this behavior and also to better direct the algorithm towards meaningful solutions we therefore included an initial step that consists of selecting an intermediate point that is at an appropriate minimum elevation level and computing the weighted shortest path to reach that point from the starting point, still penalizing too steep segments, and then we run the algorithm from that intermediate point to create a tour. This means that we relaxed the constraint of not taking the same arcs several times. Indeed, the tour now starts and ends with the same access path between the start (and end) point(s) and the intermediate point. For the rest it stays a round tour. Figure 2 shows a tour generated with this second solution.

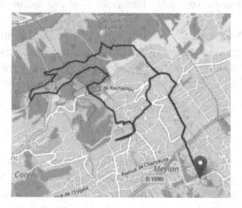

Fig. 2. Sample 10 km tour generated for a selected location selecting first an intermediate point at appropriate elevation and generating a tour from there for the remaining distance.

4   Conclusion

In this paper, we discussed user needs with respect to running tours in unknown environments. Based on existing work and our own user study we identified elevation gain and steepness as crucial parameters to take into account when proposing running tours to users. Existing solutions address elevation constraints always *a posteriori*, i.e. by filtering already existing or pre-computed tours and searching for tours that match these constraints. However, such tours may not be readily available. Our solution, instead, takes the runner's personal elevation targets and constraints into account when *generating a novel tour*. Our solution includes two options to achieve this, hierarchical optimization and selecting an appropriate intermediate point as additional first step. In the future, we want to address the other pain points raised by the users, such as proposing safe tours. We may think about either taking into account related data about path segments such as lightning conditions as explored also by [5], or, in a larger perspective, about ways to facilitate running together and thus increasing safety through company.

References

1. https://en.wikipedia.org/wiki/Naismith%27s_rule
2. https://www.blog-course-a-pied.com/ajouter-1-kilometre-100-metres-denivele-positif/
3. https://runnersconnect.net/hill-running-training/
4. Gunawan, A., Lau, H.C., Vansteenwegen, P.: Orienteering problem: a survey of recent variants, solution approaches and applications. Eur. J. Oper. Res. **255**(2), 315–332 (2016)
5. Loepp, B., Ziegler, J.: Recommending running routes: framework and demonstrator. In: ComplexRec 2018 Second Workshop on Recommendation in Complex Scenarios (2018)
6. McGookin, D.K., Brewster, S.A.: Investigating and supporting undirected navigation for runners. In: CHI 2013 Extended Abstracts (CHI EA 2013), pp. 1395–1400. ACM, New York (2013)
7. Mercier, D., Schaus, P., Saint-Guillain, M., Deville, Y.: PleasantTourFinder: an application to find the most pleasant tour from a given location. Master thesis, Catholic University of Louvain (2016)

Research on System Design of "Shared" Smart Kitchen in Youth Apartment in the Era of Internet

Zhidiankui Xu[1,2,3], Yenan Dong[1(✉)], and Shangshang Zhu[1,2,3]

[1] School of Design, Zhejiang University of Technology, Hangzhou, China
dongyenann@163.com
[2] Co-innovation Center of Creative Design and Manufacturing,
The China Academy of Art, Hangzhou, China
[3] Zhejiang Provincial Key Laboratory of Integration of Healthy Smart Kitchen
System, Hangzhou, China

Abstract. A challenge for kitchen designers, manufacturers and installers is to think in terms of kitchens that are more flexible and adaptable to people's changing needs. This study develops this work by reviewing current problems and offering recommendations that others could follow without necessarily redesigning the whole kitchen. The participatory design method is adopted to study the "shared" smart kitchen system. Young people in the youth apartment in the era of Internet are studied for an investigation into the status of their lives, work and entertainment, by means of interviews and observations, so that their eating habits and social needs can be further understood. By finding out the balance point of young people between high-quality diet activities and fast-pace life style, a new social platform is designed based on kitchen activities, and a design scheme for the "shared" smart kitchen system is proposed for the youth apartment in the era of Internet.

Keywords: Smart kitchen system · Participatory design · Young people · Youth apartment · Share

1 Introduction

Kitchen is an indispensable part in daily life, and the further kitchen will not only be a place to cook delicious food, but also a place for people to exchange feelings, to have fun and to share life [1]. The public demand for kitchen is also sublimated to the emotional level, and users have paid more and more attention to the human-computer interaction and emotional exchanges between each other when they use the kitchen, while experiencing the life in the tiny area [2]. However, the current kitchen products and appliances have met the needs of users to the highest extent, and kitchen design has attached greater importance to spatial distribution, structure and other functions, but there is a lack of interactive design of mental function in terms of emotional interaction [3, 4].

In view of the situation, this study adopts participatory design [5] to study the design of the "shared" smart kitchen system for the youth apartment in the era of

© Springer Nature Switzerland AG 2019
C. Stephanidis (Ed.): HCII 2019, CCIS 1033, pp. 536–545, 2019.
https://doi.org/10.1007/978-3-030-23528-4_73

Internet [1, 6]. Participatory design can be used in various stages of design, playing different roles. Users are introduced in the initial stage of design to view the product from the perspective of the master, while playing an active role in the selection and determination of the design direction. In the process of design, users can personally provide a design scheme and ideas through in-depth participation, so that they will not only fill in questionnaires and have interviews passively, but will also give play to their own initiative and become the changers and creators of products. It is a common method to introduce user participation in the stage of design evaluation in the traditional approaches of design and development, while users find out the deficiencies of products by trying products, which also enable designers to understand the wide gap between products and user cognition, so as to take more effective measures to improve the products [7–11].

With the increasing focus on human-centric approaches, the scope of Participatory Design has engulfed a wider spectrum of design and developmental processes [5, 7]. The goal of our research project is to understand the interactions happening in the home, in particular in the kitchen. The kitchen is one of the most important places in the family home and a place where a large variety and number of interactions take place every day. We want to understand what shapes the interactions and how the interactions connect with the everyday life and activities of the users [12–14]. While most of the existing work focuses on special user groups, such as the elderly (e.g.,) [15], people with disabilities [16] and technology-savvy customers [17], we focus on the young users, which usually represent the majority of users.

Therefore, the participatory design method is adopted to design the smart kitchen system.

2 Design Process of Smart Kitchen System Based on Participatory Design

2.1 Relation Analysis of Participatory Design in the Smart Kitchen

We analyze the relations between the user, the designer and the kitchen in the process of users participating in the design of the smart kitchen in accordance with PD (participatory design) and EPUI design (exploration, participation, understanding and integration) [12]. The user communicates with the designer concerning the experience in use in real time, and then chooses the model for building based on their own needs. Users participate in the scenario of constructing the kitchen and describe how they feel after using it. As for the relations between the designer and the kitchen, the designer constructs the model of the kitchen scenario and analyses the user's behavior and psychology through user participation. The relations between the three are shown in Fig. 1.

2.2 EPUI Design Model Targeted at Smart Kitchen Design

Based on the EPUI design method proposed by Researcher Damjan and Emilija [12], we discussed the EPUI model of the smart kitchen based on the characteristics of the

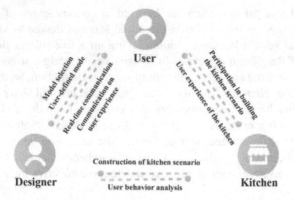

Fig. 1. Relations diagram of participatory design in the smart kitchen

smart kitchen, and put forward our own ideas, including the ways in the user exploration stage. User exploration is the foundation for the implementation of the entire project and the most important stage. The core work of this stage is to tap the existing kitchen-related activities and experience of target users, to analyze user needs and to develop creative concepts through user research. In the 2D concept development and design stage, we will build a 2D model for specific users, so that users can participate in the conceptual design, and users and kitchen appliances will work together to find out some problems in design and use. The development and design of 3D concepts are the deepening of 2D concept development and design. Next, we will build a 3D model, aiming to solve the problems found in the process of 2D concept development and design and build the immersive design. System integration and collaborative design is to conduct more refined interaction, operation and system design based on the development and design of 3D concepts, as shown in Fig. 2.

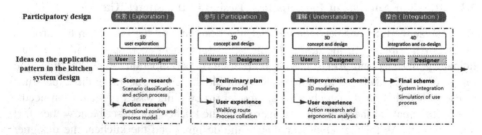

Fig. 2. Participatory design model of the smart kitchen

Based on the model of participatory design of the smart kitchen in Fig. 2, we analyzed both the roles of designers and users, and the detailed design tools in each stage, as shown in Fig. 3.

To be specific, in the user exploration stage, we first conduct a series of studies on scenario interaction on target users, and then build a 2D model on these users, enabling

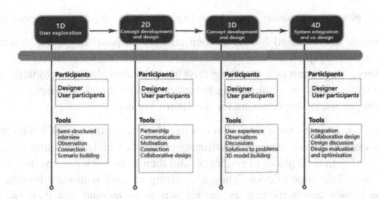

Fig. 3. Tools in various stages of participatory design

users and kitchen appliances to interact with each other to find out some problems in design and use. Next, we build a 3D model, aiming to solve the problems found in the construction of the 2D model and build the immersive design. Finally, the system integration is carried out to complete the design of the whole kitchen system.

3 Participatory Design of "Shared" Smart Kitchen System Targeted at Youth Apartments in the Era of Internet

In the context of youth apartments, this project mainly studies young people. It reorganizes the role of kitchen in life, and attempts to build a new social platform around kitchen activities, in order to find out the balance point of young people between high-quality diet activities and fast-pace life style, and to attract more young people to increase their exchanges and interaction with others while enjoying themselves in cooking. Its purpose is to improve the quality of life of young people, increase their communication and interaction, and explore a more interesting, comfortable and harmonious diet and lifestyle.

3.1 User Exploration

In today's fast-paced life, dietary activities, which are extremely important for human beings, are a suitable opportunity to increase the communications and interactions with each other. With the improvement of living standard and the change of thinking mode, young people have regarded the kitchen as a integrated and multi-functional place from a basic place for cooking, changing from adequate food to a dual enjoyment of body and mind.

We use interviews, observations, contacts and scenario building. Firstly, through in-depth interviews, typical young users are investigated. We interviewed 8 young singles, including 4 male users and 4 female users. They are all aged between 22 and 30 years old, and live in single youth apartments. They are mainly young white collars, postgraduates living alone and designers in cities.

User exploration is mainly carried out from the following three perspectives:

1. to describe user demand for the kitchen and the purpose they want to achieve in using the kitchen;
2. to observe the process of users using the kitchen, and explore the problems existing in the current kitchen by observing the users' behavior and emotions;
3. to know the users' expectations for the future kitchen.

Through interviews, we learned that our target users are the post-90s who have just started to work and lived in single apartments on their own. These young people have led to instability in their places of residence, and their busy work has resulted in the fact that they have little time to cook. They are willing to cook with their friends, hoping that more friends can participate in the kitchen activities and that there will be an interesting and interactive "shared" smart kitchen.

As for the expectations and pain points of design of the users as summarized above, it becomes particularly important to design a social "shared" smart kitchen for young people to communicate and interact with each other.

3.2 Conception of "Shared" Smart Kitchen System Targeted at Youth Apartments in the Era of Internet

Users are invited to participate in building the 2D model of the kitchen. In this stage, we establish a good partnership with our users, and communicate with, contact and motivate them in a timely manner, and then propose a 2D design concept.

The product is positioned to design a "shared" kitchen system for single apartments of young people. Through the construction of mobile APP, users can order the kitchen and materials, the youth apartment is equipped with a public space and a mobile "shared" kitchen. Merchants distribute the materials ordered by tenants, and the kitchen is recovered, cleaned and maintained by a special person, so as to maximize the use of resources. And the public kitchen is suitable for many people to cook together. When friends or tenants prepare meals here, the public kitchen becomes a very important communication platform, which provides a suitable social space and opportunity for young people to not only enjoy the fun of cooking, but also to enhance their affections.

Construction of the Mode of Saving Preparation Time Before Meals and Cleaning Time After Meals. The "shared" kitchen prepares materials in advance. As long as the user orders the recipe and the number of people on the APP, the APP can automatically convey the data to suppliers and distributors. The supplier provides the original materials for the shared kitchen and the distributor preliminarily processes the materials, such as washing and cutting, and then delivers the processed materials and the product to the public space offered in the apartment. The public space is equipped with food storage cabinets to keep the materials fresh and store them for a short time. Users can open the corresponding cabinet by using their mobile phones, which will greatly save the time for users to purchase and process the materials.

Construction of Interesting and Interactive Kitchen Experience. Through the interviews with users in Sect. 3.1, it can be seen that many young people hope to enjoy interesting and interactive kitchen experience with friends. We design a mobile app, in which users can order the shared kitchen and materials, and contact the distributor. It is also equipped with an online platform and a mobile client. The APP is like a virtual community, where users can share the experience of public kitchens in shared apartments, make friends with users in the same community to share the cooking experience with each other, while inviting their friends and neighbors to cook and have meals together.

Construction of a Complete Smart Kitchen System. Many young people love cooking, but they have no time to think about what to cook, so they are eager to be able to have some smart recipes and enjoy different user experience in conjunction with the complete smart kitchen system. Mobile shared kitchen is designed as a complete smart kitchen system, while there are complete functions, which can be used separately. The folding storage method is adopted to compress the space to the greatest extent so as to provide a variety of functions. The cooking utensils can meet various functions of steaming, boiling, frying, stir-frying and roasting. When ordering different dishes, users can be provided with corresponding appliances.

3.3   Concept Development and Design Stage

Next, we carry out conceptual development and detailed design to show the characteristics of the concept, participants, usage environment and other data information as comprehensively as possible. In the design scheme, we divide the "shared" kitchen system targeted at the youth apartments in the era of Internet into two parts of hardware facilities and software interface. The design shows the whole process from analysis, to process to preliminary design, and finally to in-depth design.

The usage process consists of various parts from the user's order of the number of people, recipe, taste, time and location, to the merchant's confirmation of the order and distribution, and then to the user's cooking based on the utensils, finally to the merchant's recovery and maintenance of the kitchen, which will maximize the convenience of the users in the process and provide the best experience. Figure 4 shows the usage process.

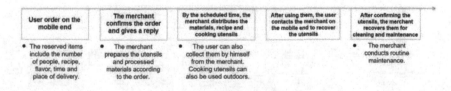

Fig. 4. Usage process

System design involves stakeholders in all aspects, including major stakeholders and minor stakeholders. Starting from the user's order, material suppliers provide the original materials, and kitchen ware suppliers provide the kitchen ware, and the distributor is set up in the community to be responsible for processing the original materials and allocating proper kitchen ware. And then the materials and kitchen ware

are distributed to the user. The product will be recycled and cleaned after users use it. The conception of system design is shown in Fig. 5.

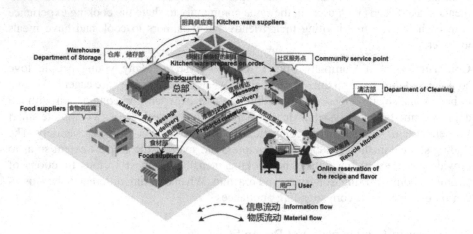

Fig. 5. Conception of system design

3.4 System Integration and Collaborative Design

Finally, users are invited to participate in the stage of system integration and collaborative design to help researchers in perfecting the design, so as to further enhance the value of the concept and rationality of operation. Through the integration of software and hardware system, we can complete the design of the mobile "shared" kitchen app.

Figure 6 shows the design process of the software app, which fully shows our design process and ideas on the app end, ranging from the design of login process, the process of kitchen reservation, as well as the content of personal records and the friend mode.

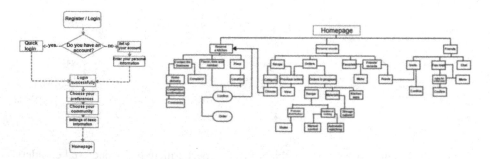

Fig. 6. App design process

Figure 7 shows the product scenario, and Fig. 8 shows the product usage scenario, including a cooking area, a preparation area and a storage area to maximize the use of inner space, and drawers are set to hold condiments, dishes and so on. It is simple and attractive in shape, easy to clean.

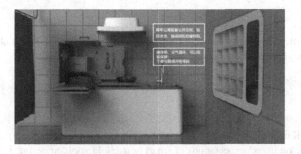

Fig. 7. Product scenario

Fig. 8. Product usage scenario

It is conducive to the sustainable development of the "shared" kitchen in youth apartments.

4 Conclusion and Future Work

In this paper, the method of participatory design is adopted to design the "shared" smart kitchen system targeted at youth apartments. Young people in the youth apartment in the era of Internet are studied in this paper for an investigation into the status of their lives, work and entertainment by means of interviews and observations, so that their eating habits and social needs can be further understood, and a design scheme for the "shared" smart kitchen system is proposed for the youth apartments in the era of Internet.

The mobile "shared" kitchen simplifies the mode of kitchen usage. Youth apartments are equipped with public space, and a mobile "shared" kitchen is provided, where the reserved materials of the tenants are distributed and a special person cleans and maintains the kitchen after it is recovered, so as to maximize the use of resources.

In this study, we mainly explore the youth apartments in the developed areas of Eastern China. In the follow-up study, we will further study the behavioral habits and psychology of young people in the application of kitchens in other regions, and seek for more possibilities of the "shared" smart kitchen system for the youth apartments in the era of Internet.

Acknowledgement. This paper is supported by Zhejiang Provincial Key Laboratory of integration of healthy smart kitchen system.

References

1. Coskun, A., Kaner, G., Bostan, I.: Is smart home a necessity or a fantasy for the mainstream user? A study on users' expectations of smart household appliances. Int. J. Des. **12**(1), 7–20 (2017)
2. Chen, J., Chang, K., Chi, P., Chu, H.: A smart kitchen to promote healthy cooking. Hum. Factors (2006)
3. Johansson, K., Lundberg, S., Borrell, L.: "The cognitive kitchen"–Key principles and suggestions for design that includes older adults with cognitive impairments as kitchen users. Technol. Disabil. **23**(1), 29–40 (2011)
4. Maguire, M., Peace, S., Marshall, R., Nicolle, C., Percival, J., Sims, R.: The Easier Kitchen: Making it Happen, Transitions in Kitchen Living Project, New Dynamics of Ageing Programme. The Open University, Milton Keynes (2012)
5. Hirom, U., Shyama, V.S., Doke, P., Lobo, S., Devkar, S., Pandey, N.: A critique on participatory design in developmental context: a case study. In: Rau, P.-L.P. (ed.) CCD 2017. LNCS, vol. 10281, pp. 647–658. Springer, Cham (2017). https://doi.org/10.1007/978-3-319-57931-3_52
6. BBC. 'Smart' kitchen appliances connect to web (2011). http://news.bbc.co.uk/1/hi/programmes/click_online/9362154.stm. Accessed August 2013
7. Spinuzzi, C.: The methodology of participatory design. Tech. Commun. **52**, 163–174 (2005)
8. Argyris, C., Schön, D.A.: Participatory action research and action science compared: a commentary. Am. Behav. Sci. **32**(5), 612–623 (1989)
9. Bilandzic, M., Venable, J.: Towards participatory action design research: adapting action research and design science research methods for urban informatics. J. Community Inform. Spec. Issue: Res. Action: Linking Communities Univ. **7**(3) (2011)
10. Bødker, S.: Creating conditions for participation: conflicts and resources in systems design. Hum. Comput. Interact. **11**(3), 215–236 (1996)
11. Grudin, J., Pruitt, J.: Personas, participatory design and product development: an infrastructure for engagement. In: Proceedings of PDC, pp. 144–161 (2002)
12. Damjan, O., Emilija, S.: Experience to understand: a methodology for integrating users into the design for kitchen interactions. Multimedia Tools Appl. **71**(1), 97–117 (2014)
13. Kerr, S.J., Tan, O., Chua, J.C.: Cooking personas: goal-directed design requirements in the kitchen. Int. J. Hum.-Comput. Stud. **72**, 255–274 (2014)
14. Maguire, M.: Kitchen living in later life: exploring ergonomic problems, coping strategies and design solutions. Int. J. Des. **8**(1), 73–91 (2014)

15. Pogorelc, B., Bosnić, Z., Gams, M.: Automatic recognition of gait-related health problems in the elderly using machine learning. Multimedia Tools Appl. **58**, 333–354 (2011)

16. Holzinger, A.: User-centered interface design for disabled and elderly people: first experiences with designing a patient communication system (PACOSY). In: Miesenberger, K., Klaus, J., Zagler, W. (eds.) ICCHP 2002. LNCS, vol. 2398, pp. 33–40. Springer, Heidelberg (2002). https://doi.org/10.1007/3-540-45491-8_8

17. Warren, J.Y.: Tech-Savvy users' perceptions of consumer health portals. Health Care Inform. Rev. Online **12**(3), 2–5 (2008)

Author Index

Printed in the United States
By Bookmasters